Edward Walford, Thomas Percy

**Reliques of Ancient English Poetry**

Consisting of Old Heroic Ballads and Songs

Edward Walford, Thomas Percy

**Reliques of Ancient English Poetry**
*Consisting of Old Heroic Ballads and Songs*

ISBN/EAN: 9783744774628

Printed in Europe, USA, Canada, Australia, Japan

Cover: Foto ©Thomas Meinert / pixelio.de

More available books at **www.hansebooks.com**

# RELIQUES

OF

# ANCIENT ENGLISH POETRY.

"Though some make slight of libels, yet you may see by them how the wind sits; as, take a straw and throw it up into the air, you may see by that which way the wind is, which you shall not do by casting up a stone. More solid things do not show the complexion of the times so well as ballads and libels."—SELDEN's *Table-Talk*.

"An ordinary song or ballad, that is the delight of the common people, cannot fail to please all such readers as are not unqualified for the entertainment by their affectation or their ignorance; and the reason is plain, because the same paintings of Nature which recommend it to the most ordinary reader will appear beautiful to the most refined."—ADDISON in *Spectator*, No. 70.

*THE CHANDOS CLASSICS.*

# RELIQUES

OF

# ANCIENT ENGLISH POETRY,

CONSISTING OF

*OLD HEROIC BALLADS, SONGS, ETC.*

BY

THOMAS PERCY.

A New Edition.

EDITED BY

EDWARD WALFORD, M.A.

*WITH A GLOSSARY AND LIFE*

LONDON AND NEW YORK:
FREDERICK WARNE AND CO.
1887

# PREFACE BY THE EDITOR.

THE Reliques of Bishop Percy have for a century been favourites with all lovers of ancient poetry and of English literature ; and as they were among the chief friends of my boyhood, it has been a great pleasure to me, in advanced manhood, to help in giving to the world a popular edition of them. I have added a few brief foot-notes, where the Author's meaning, or a passing allusion, seemed obscure ; and the Glossaries to each of the three original volumes have been drafted into one in this edition. Those of the " Reliques " which are to be found also in Percy's " Folio Manuscript " have been duly noted ; and I have prefixed to the volume a new biography of the venerable author himself.

E. WALFORD.

HAMPSTEAD, N.W.
    *Sept.* 1880.

# CONTENTS.

| | PAGE |
|---|---|
| DEDICATION, | 9 |
| ADVERTISEMENT TO THE FOURTH EDITION, | 9 |
| THE AUTHOR'S PREFACE, | 11 |
| LIFE OF BISHOP PERCY, | 15 |
| BALLADS, | 18 |
| PREFACE TO THE PRESENT EDITION, | 21 |
| AN ESSAY ON THE ANCIENT MINSTRELS IN ENGLAND, | 22 |

## SERIES THE FIRST.

BOOK I.—

| | PAGE |
|---|---|
| 1. The Ancient Ballad of Chevy-Chase, | 39 |
| 2. The Battle of Otterbourne, | 45 |
| 3. The Jew's Daughter. A Scottish Ballad, | 50 |
| 4. Sir Cauline, | 52 |
| 5. Edward, Edward. A Scottish Ballad, | 57 |
| 6. King Estmere, | 58 |
| 7. Sir Patrick Spence. A Scottish Ballad, | 63 |
| 8. Robin Hood and Guy of Gisborne, | 64 |
| 9. An Elegy on Henry, Fourth Earl of Northumberland, by Skelton, | 68 |
| 10. The Tower of Doctrine, by Stephen Hawes, | 73 |
| 11. The Child of Elle, | 75 |
| 12. Edom of Gordon. A Scottish Ballad, | 73 |

BOOK II. BALLADS THAT ILLUSTRATE SHAKESPEARE—

| | PAGE |
|---|---|
| On the Origin of the English Stage, | 81 |
| 1. Adam Bell, Clym of the Clough, and Will'am of Clouderly | 95 |
| 2. The Aged Lover renounceth Love, | 105 |
| 3. Jephthah, Judge of Israel, | 106 |
| 4. A Robyn Jolly Robyn, | 107 |
| 5. A Song to the Lute in Musicke, | 107 |
| 6. King Cophetua and the Beggar Maid, | 108 |
| 7. Take thy Old Cloak about thee, | 110 |
| 8. Willow, Willow, Willow, | 111 |
| 9. Sir Lancelot Du Lake, | 113 |
| 10. Corydon's Farewell to Phillis, | 115 |
| 11. Gernutus, the Jew of Venice, | 115 |
| 12. The Passionate Shepherd to his Love, by Marlow, | 118 |
| The Nymph's Reply, by Sir W. Raleigh, | 119 |
| 13. Titus Andronicus's Complaint, | 119 |
| 14. Take those Lips away, | 122 |
| 15. King Leir and his Three Daughters, | 122 |
| 16. Youth and Age, by Shakespeare, | 125 |
| 17. The Frolicksome Duke, or the Tinker's Good Fortune, | 125 |
| 18. The Friar of Orders Gray, | 127 |

BOOK III.—

| | PAGE |
|---|---|
| 1. The more Modern Ballad of Chevy-Chase, | 130 |
| 2. Death's Final Conquest, | 135 |
| 3. The Rising in the North, | 135 |
| 4. Northumberland betrayed by Douglas, | 138 |
| 5. My Mind to me a Kingdom is, | 142 |
| 6. The Patient Countess, by W. Warner, | 143 |
| 7. Dowsabell, by Drayton, | 145 |

|  | PAGE |
|---|---|
| 8. The Farewell to Love, from Beaumont and Fletcher, | 147 |
| 9. Ulysses and the Syren, by S. Daniel, | 147 |
| 10. Cupid's Pastime, by Davidson, | 149 |
| 11. The Character of a Happy Life, by Sir H. Wotton, | 150 |
| 12. Gilderoy. A Scottish Ballad, | 150 |
| 13. Winifreda, | 151 |
| 14. The Witch of Wokey, | 152 |
| 15. Bryan and Pereene. A West Indian Ballad, by Dr. Grainger, | 153 |
| 16. Gentle River, Gentle River. Translated from the Spanish, | 154 |
| 17. Alcanzor and Zayda, a Moorish Tale, | 155 |

### SERIES THE SECOND.

BOOK I.—

| | |
|---|---|
| 1. Richard of Almaigne, | 157 |
| 2. On the Death of King Edward the First, | 158 |
| 3. An Original Ballad by Chaucer, | 160 |
| 4. The Turnament of Tottenham, | 161 |
| 5. For the Victory at Agincourt, | 165 |
| 6. The Not-browne Mayd, | 166 |
| 7. A Ballad by the Earl Rivers, | 171 |
| 8. Cupid's Assault, by Lord Vaux, | 171 |
| 9. Sir Aldingar, | 172 |
| 10. The Gaberlunzie Man, a Scottish Song, by King James V., | 176 |
| 11. On Thomas, Lord Cromwell, | 177 |
| 12. Harpalus. An ancient English Pastoral, | 179 |
| 13. Robin and Makyne. An ancient Scottish Pastoral, | 181 |
| 14. Gentle Herdsman, tell to me, | 183 |
| 15. King Edward IV. and the Tanner of Tamworth, | 184 |
| 16. As ye came from the Holy Land, | 187 |
| 17. Hardyknute. A Scottish Fragment, | 188 |

BOOK II.—

| | |
|---|---|
| 1. A Ballad of Luther, the Pope, a Cardinal, and a Husbandman, | 194 |
| 2. John Anderson my Jo. A Scottish Song, | 196 |
| 3. Little John Nobody, | 196 |

|  | PAGE |
|---|---|
| 4. Queen Elizabeth's Verses while Prisoner at Woodstock, | 198 |
| 5. The Heir of Linne, | 199 |
| 6. Gascoigne's Praise of the Fair Bridges, afterwards Lady Sandes, | 202 |
| 7. Fair Rosamond. By Thomas Delone, | 203 |
| 8. Queen Eleanor's Confession, | 207 |
| 9. The Sturdy Rock, | 209 |
| 10. The Beggar's Daughter of Bednall Green, | 210 |
| 11. Fancy and Desire, by the Earl of Oxford, | 215 |
| 12. Sir Andrew Barton, | 217 |
| 13. Lady Anne Bothwell's Lament. A Scottish Song, | 223 |
| 14. The Murder of the King of Scots, | 224 |
| 15. A Sonnet by Queen Elizabeth, | 225 |
| 16. The King of Scots and Andrew Browne, by W. Elderton, | 226 |
| 17. The Bonny Earl of Murray. A Scottish Song, | 228 |
| 18. Young Waters. A Scottish Song, | 228 |
| 19. Mary Ambree, | 229 |
| 20. Brave Lord Willoughby, | 232 |
| 21. Victorious men of Earth, by James Shirley, | 233 |
| 22. The Winning of Cales, | 234 |
| 23. The Spanish Lady's Love, | 236 |
| 24. Argentile and Curan, by W. Warner, | 238 |
| 25. Corin's Fate, | 242 |
| 26. Jane Shore, | 243 |
| 27. Corydon's Doleful Knell, | 246 |

BOOK III.—

| | |
|---|---|
| 1. The Complaint of Conscience, | 247 |
| 2. Plain Truth and Blind Ignorance, | 250 |
| 3. The Wandering Jew, | 252 |
| 4. The Lye, by Sir Walter Raleigh, | 254 |
| 5. Verses by King James I., | 256 |
| 6. King John and the Abbot of Canterbury, | 257 |
| 7. You Meaner Beauties, by Sir H. Wotton, | 259 |
| 8. The Old and Young Courtier, | 260 |
| 9. Sir John Suckling's Campaign, | 262 |
| 10. To Althea from Prison, by Col. Lovelace, | 263 |
| 11. The Downfall of Charing Cross, | 263 |

|     |                                                    | PAGE |
| --- | -------------------------------------------------- | ---- |
| 12. | Loyalty Confined, by Sir Roger L'Estrange,         | 264  |
| 13. | Verses by King Charles I.,                         | 266  |
| 14. | The Sale of Rebellious Household Stuff,            | 267  |
| 15. | The Baffled Knight, or Lady's Policy,              | 269  |
| 16. | Why so Pale? by Sir John Suckling,                 | 271  |
| 17. | Old Tom of Bedlam. Mad Song the First,             | 272  |
| 18. | The Distracted Puritan. Mad Song the Second,       | 273  |
| 19. | The Lunatic Lover. Mad Song the Third,             | 274  |
| 20. | The Lady distracted with Love. Mad Song the Fourth,| 275  |
| 21. | The Distracted Lover. Mad Song the Fifth,          | 276  |
| 22. | The Frantic Lady. Mad Song the Sixth,              | 277  |
| 23. | Lilli Burlero, by Lord Wharton,                    | 277  |
| 24. | The Braes of Yarrow. In imitation of the ancient Scottish manner, by W. Hamilton, | 279 |
| 25. | Admiral Hosier's Ghost, by Mr. Glover,             | 281  |
| 26. | Jemmy Dawson, by Mr. Shenstone,                    | 283  |

### SERIES THE THIRD.

BOOK I. POEMS ON KING ARTHUR—

|     | On the Ancient Metrical Romances, | 285 |
| --- | --------------------------------- | --- |
| 1.  | The Boy and the Mantle,           | 296 |
| 2.  | The Marriage of Sir Gawaine,      | 299 |
| 3.  | King Ryence's Challenge,          | 304 |
| 4.  | King Arthur's Death. A Fragment,  | 305 |
| 5.  | The Legend of King Arthur,        | 308 |
| 6.  | A Dyttie to Hey Downe,            | 310 |
| 7.  | Glasgerion,                       | 310 |
| 8.  | Old Robin of Portingale,          | 312 |
| 9.  | Child Waters,                     | 314 |
| 10. | Phillida and Corydon, by Nic. Breton, | 317 |
| 11. | Little Musgrave and Lady Barnard, | 317 |
| 12. | The Ew-Bughts, Marion. A Scottish Song, | 319 |

|     |                                                  | PAGE |
| --- | ------------------------------------------------ | ---- |
| 13. | The Knight and Shepherd's Daughter,              | 320  |
| 14. | The Shepherd's Address to his Muse, by N. Breton,| 321  |
| 15. | Lord Thomas and Fair Ellinor,                    | 322  |
| 16. | Cupid and Campaspe, by John Lilye,               | 323  |
| 17. | The Lady turned Serving-Man,                     | 323  |
| 18. | Gil Morrice. A Scottish Ballad,                  | 326  |

BOOK II.—

| 1.  | The Legend of Sir Guy,                        | 329 |
| --- | --------------------------------------------- | --- |
| 2.  | Guy and Amarant, by Sam. Rowlands,            | 331 |
| 3.  | The Auld Good-Man. A Scottish Song,           | 335 |
| 4.  | Fair Margaret and Sweet William,              | 336 |
| 5.  | Barbara Allen's Cruelty,                      | 338 |
| 6.  | Sweet William's Ghost. A Scottish Ballad,     | 339 |
| 7.  | Sir John Grehme and Barbara Allan,            | 340 |
| 8.  | The Bailiff's Daughter of Islington,          | 341 |
| 9.  | The Willow Tree. A Pastoral Dialogue,         | 342 |
| 10. | The Lady's Fall,                              | 342 |
| 11. | Waly, Waly, Love be Bonny. A Scottish Song,   | 344 |
| 12. | The Bride's Burial,                           | 345 |
| 13. | Dulcina,                                      | 347 |
| 14. | The Lady Isabella's Tragedy,                  | 348 |
| 15. | A Hue and Cry after Cupid, by Ben Jonson,     | 349 |
| 16. | The King of France's Daughter,                | 350 |
| 17. | The Sweet Neglect, by Ben Jonson,             | 353 |
| 18. | The Children in the Wood,                     | 353 |
| 19. | A Lover of Late,                              | 356 |
| 20. | The King and the Miller of Mansfield,         | 356 |
| 21. | The Shepherd's Resolution, by Geo. Wither,    | 362 |
| 22. | Queen Dido, or the Wandering Prince of Troy,  | 363 |
| 23. | The Witches' Song, by Ben Jonson,             | 365 |
| 24. | Robin Good-Fellow,                            | 366 |
| 25. | The Fairy Queen,                              | 368 |
| 26. | The Fairies Farewell, by Dr. Corbet,          | 369 |

## CONTENTS.

BOOK III.—

| | PAGE |
|---|---|
| 1. The Birth of St. George, | 370 |
| 2. St. George and the Dragon, | 373 |
| 3. Love will find out the Way, | 377 |
| 4. Lord Thomas and Fair Annet. A Scottish Ballad, | 377 |
| 5. Unfading Beauty, by Thomas Carew, | 379 |
| 6. George Barnwell, | 380 |
| 7. The Stedfast Shepherd, by Geo. Wither, | 385 |
| 8. The Spanish Virgin, or the Effects of Jealousy, | 386 |
| 9. Jealousy, Tyrant of the Mind, by Dryden, | 388 |
| 10. Constant Penelope | 389 |
| 11. To Lucasta, on going to the Wars, by Colonel Lovelace, | 390 |
| 12. Valentine and Ursine, | 390 |
| 13. The Dragon of Wantley, | 396 |
| 14. St. George for England. The First Part, | 399 |
| 15. St. George for England. The Second Part, by J. Grubb, | 402 |
| 16. Margaret's Ghost, by David Mallet, | 407 |
| 17. Lucy and Colin, by Tho. Tickell, | 409 |
| 18. The Boy and the Mantle, revised, etc., | 410 |
| 19. The Ancient Fragment of the Marriage of Sir Gawaine, | 413 |
| GLOSSARY, | 419 |

# RELIQUES OF ANCIENT ENGLISH POETRY:

### CONSISTING OF

## OLD HEROIC BALLADS, SONGS, AND OTHER PIECES OF OUR EARLIER POETS;

#### TOGETHER WITH SOME FEW OF LATER DATE.

---

### DEDICATION.

#### TO

## ELIZABETH,

#### LATE DUCHESS AND COUNTESS OF NORTHUMBERLAND,

##### IN HER OWN RIGHT BARONESS PERCY,

###### ETC. ETC. ETC.,

Who, being sole heiress to many great families of our ancient nobility, employed the princely fortune, and sustained the illustrious honours, which she derived from them, through her whole life with the greatest dignity, generosity, and spirit, and who for her many public and private virtues will ever be remembered as one of the first characters of her time, this little work was originally dedicated; and, as it sometimes afforded her amusement, and was highly distinguished by her indulgent approbation, it is now, with the utmost regard, respect, and gratitude, consecrated to her beloved and honoured memory.

T. P.

---

### ADVERTISEMENT TO THE FOURTH EDITION.

TWENTY years have near elapsed since the last edition of this work appeared. But although it was sufficiently a favourite with the public, and had long been out of print, the original Editor had no desire to revive it. More important pursuits had, as might be expected, engaged his attention; and the present edition would have remained unpublished, had he not yielded to the importunity of his friends, and accepted the humble offer of an Editor in a nephew, to whom, it is feared, he will be found too partial.

These volumes are now restored to the public with such corrections and improvements as have occurred since the former impression; and the text in particular hath been emended in many passages by recurring to the old copies. The instances being frequently trivial, are not always noted in the margin; but the alteration hath never been made without good reason: and especially in such pieces as were extracted from the folio Manuscript so often mentioned in the following pages, where any variation occurs from the former impression, it will be understood to have been given on the authority of that MS.

The appeal publicly made to Dr. Johnson in the first page of the following Preface, so long since as in the year 1765, and never once contradicted by him during so large a portion of his life, ought to have precluded every doubt concerning the existence of the MS. in question. But such, it seems, having been suggested, it may now be mentioned that while this edition passed through his press, the MS. itself was left for near a year with Mr. Nichols, in whose house, or in that of its possessor, it was examined with more or less attention by many gentlemen of eminence in literature. At the first publication of these volumes, it had been in the hands of all, or most of, his friends; but, as it could hardly be expected that he should continue to think of nothing else but these amusements of his youth, it was afterwards laid aside at his residence in the country. Of the many gentlemen above mentioned, who offered to give their testimony to the public, it will be sufficient to name the Honourable Daines Barrington, the Reverend Clayton Mordaunt Cracherode, and those eminent critics on Shakespeare, the Reverend Dr. Farmer, George Steevens, Esq., Edmund Malone, Esq., and Isaac Reed, Esq., to whom I beg leave to appeal for the truth of the following representation.

The MS. is a long narrow folio volume,* containing 195 sonnets, ballads, historical songs, and metrical romances, either in the whole or in part, for many of them are extremely mutilated and imperfect. The first and last leaves are wanting; and of fifty-four pages near the beginning, half of every leaf hath been torn away, and several others are injured towards the end; besides that through a great part of the volume the top or bottom line, and sometimes both, have been cut off in the binding.

In this state is the MS. itself: and even where the leaves have suffered no injury, the transcripts, which seem to have been all made by one person (they are at least all in the same kind of hand), are sometimes extremely incorrect and faulty, being in such instances probably made from defective copies, or the imperfect recitation of illiterate singers; so that a considerable portion of the song or narrative is sometimes omitted; and miserable trash or nonsense not unfrequently introduced into pieces of considerable merit. And often the copyist grew so weary of his labour as to write on without the least attention to the sense or meaning; so that the word which should form the rhyme is found misplaced in the middle of the line; and we have such blunders as these, *want and will* for *wanton will*,† even *pan and wale* for *wan and pale*,‡ etc.

Hence the public may judge how much they are indebted to the composer of this

---

\* It is now in the British Museum (E. W.).
† Page 130, ver. 117. This must have been copied from a reciter.
‡ Page 139, ver. 164, viz. "His visage waxed pan and wale."

collection, who, at an early period of life, with such materials and such subjects, formed a work which hath been admitted into the most elegant libraries; and with which the judicious antiquary hath just reason to be satisfied, while refined entertainment hath been provided for every reader of taste and genius.

THOMAS PERCY,<br>Fellow of St. John's College, Oxford.

## THE AUTHOR'S PREFACE.

THE reader is here presented with select remains of our ancient English Bards and Minstrels, an order of men, who were once greatly respected by our ancestors, and contributed to soften the roughness of a martial and unlettered people by their songs and music.

The greater part of them are extracted from an ancient folio Manuscript, in the Editor's possession, which contains near 200 poems, songs, and metrical romances. This MS. was written about the middle of the last century, but contains compositions of all times and dates, from the ages prior to Chaucer, to the conclusion of the reign of Charles I.*

This Manuscript was shown to several learned and ingenious friends, who thought the contents too curious to be consigned to oblivion, and importuned the possessor to select some of them, and give them to the press. As most of them are of great simplicity, and seem to have been merely written for the people, he was long in doubt whether, in the present state of improved literature, they could be deemed worthy the attention of the public. At length the importunity of his friends prevailed, and he could refuse nothing to such judges as the author of the *Rambler* and the late Mr. Shenstone.

Accordingly such specimens of ancient poetry have been selected, as either show the gradation of our language, exhibit the progress of popular opinions, display the peculiar manners and customs of former ages, or throw light on our earlier classical poets.

They are here distributed into three independent series of poems, arranged chiefly according to the order of time, and showing the gradual improvements of the English language and poetry from the earliest ages down to the present. Each series is divided into three books, to afford so many pauses, or resting-places to the reader, and to assist him in distinguishing between the productions of the earlier, the middle, and the latter times.

In a polished age like the present, I am sensible that many of these reliques of antiquity will require great allowances to be made for them. Yet have they, for the most part, a pleasing simplicity, and many artless graces, which in the opinion of no mean critics† have been thought to compensate for the want of higher beauties, and, if they do not dazzle the imagination, are frequently found to interest the heart.

---

\* Chaucer quotes the old romance of *Libius Disconius*, and some others, which are found in this MS. (See the essay prefixed to vol. iii. p. 15 et seq.) It also contains several songs relating to the Civil War in the last century, but not one that alludes to the Restoration.

† Addison, Dryden, the witty Lord Dorset, etc. See the *Spectator*, No. 70. The learned Selden appears also to have been fond of collecting these old things.

To atone for the rudeness of the more obsolete poems, each volume concludes with a few modern attempts in the same kind of writing : and, to take off from the tediousness of the longer narratives, they are everywhere intermingled with little elegant pieces of the lyric kind. Select ballads in the old Scottish dialect, most of them of the first-rate merit, are also interspersed among those of our ancient English minstrels ; and the artless productions of these old rhapsodists are occasionally confronted with specimens of the composition of contemporary poets of a higher class ; of those who had all the advantages of learning in the times in which they lived, and who wrote for fame and for posterity. Yet perhaps the palm will be frequently due to the old strolling minstrels, who composed their rhymes to be sung to their harps, and who looked no farther than for present applause and present subsistence.

The reader will find this class of men occasionally described in the following volume, and some particulars relating to their history in an Essay subjoined to this Preface.

It will be proper here to give a short account of the other collections that were consulted, and to make my acknowledgments to those gentlemen who were so kind as to impart extracts from them ; for while this selection was making, a great number of ingenious friends took a share in the work, and explored many large repositories in its favour. The first of these that deserved notice was the Pepysian Library at Magdalen College, Cambridge. Its founder, Sam. Pepys, Esq., Secretary of the Admiralty in the reigns of Charles II. and James II., had made a large collection of ancient English ballads, near 2000 in number, which he has left pasted in five volumes in folio ; besides *Garlands* and other smaller miscellanies. This collection, he tells us, was "begun by Mr. Selden ; improved by the addition of many pieces elder thereto in time ; and the whole continued down to the year 1700 ; when the form peculiar till then thereto, viz. of the black letter with pictures, seems (for cheapness' sake) wholly laid aside for that of the white letter without pictures."

In the Ashmolean Library at Oxford is a small collection of ballads made by Anthony Wood in 1676, containing somewhat more than 200. Many ancient popular poems are also preserved in the Bodleian Library.

The archives of the Antiquarian Society at London contain a multitude of curious political poems in large folio volumes, digested under the several reigns of Henry VIII., Edward VI., Mary, Elizabeth, James I., etc.

In the British Museum is preserved a large treasure of ancient English poems in MS., besides one folio volume of printed ballads.

From all these some of the best pieces were selected ; and from many private collections, as well printed as manuscript, particularly from one large folio volume which was lent by a lady.

Amid such a fund of materials, the Editor is afraid he has been sometimes led to make too great a parade of his authorities. The desire of being accurate has perhaps seduced him into too minute and trifling an exactness ; and in pursuit of information he may have been drawn into many a petty and frivolous research. It was however necessary to give some account of the old copies ; though often, for the sake of brevity, one or two of these only are mentioned, where yet assistance was received from several. Where anything was altered that deserved particular notice, the passage is generally distinguished by two inverted " commas." And the Editor has endeavoured to be as faithful as the imperfect state of his materials would admit. For, these old popular rhymes being many of them copied only from illiterate transcripts, or the imperfect recitation of itinerant ballad-singers, have, as might be expected, been handed down to us with less care than any other writings in the world. And the old copies, whether MS. or printed, were often so defective or corrupted, that a scrupulous adherence to their wretched readings would only have exhibited unintelligible nonsense, or such poor meagre stuff as neither came from the bard nor was worthy the press; when, by a few slight corrections or additions, a most beautiful or interesting sense hath started forth, and this so naturally and easily, that the Editor could seldom prevail on himself to indulge the vanity of making a formal claim to the improvement; but must plead guilty to the charge of concealing his own share in the amendments under some such general title as a "Modern Copy," or the like. Yet it has been his design to give sufficient intimation where any considerable liberties * were taken with the old copies, and to have retained either in the text or margin any word or phrase which was antique, obsolete, unusual, or peculiar, so that these might be safely quoted as of genuine and undoubted antiquity. His object was to please both the judicious antiquary and the reader of taste; and he hath endeavoured to gratify both without offending either.

The plan of the work was settled in concert with the late elegant Mr. Shenstone, who was to have borne a joint share in it had not death unhappily prevented him.† Most of the modern pieces were of his selection and arrangement, and the Editor hopes to be pardoned if he has retained some things out of partiality to the judgment of his friend. The old folio MS. above mentioned was a present from Humphrey Pitt, Esq. of Prior's-Lee, in Shropshire,‡ to whom this public acknowledgment is due for that and many other obliging favours. To Sir David Dalrymple, Bart., of Hales, near Edinburgh, the Editor is indebted for most of the beautiful Scottish poems with which this little miscellany is enriched, and for many curious and elegant remarks with which they are illustrated. Some obliging communications of the same kind were received from John Macgowan, Esq., of Edinburgh; and many curious explanations of Scottish words in the glossaries from John Davidson, Esq., of Edinburgh, and from the Rev. Mr. Hutchinson, of Kimbolton. Mr. Warton, who has twice done so much honour to the Poetry Professor's chair at Oxford, and Mr. Hest of Worcester College, contributed some curious pieces from the Oxford Libraries. Two ingenious and learned friends at Cambridge deserve the Editor's warmest acknowledgments:

---

* Such liberties have been taken with all those pieces which have three asterisks subjoined, thus *⁎*.

† That the Editor hath not here underrated the assistance he received from his friend, will appear from Mr. Shenstone's own letter to the Rev. Mr. Graves, dated March 1, 1761. See his *Works*, vol. iii. Letter ciii. It is doubtless a great loss to this work that Mr. Shenstone never saw more than about an eighth part of it, as prepared for the press.

‡ Who informed the Editor that this MS. had been purchased in a library of old books, which was thought to have belonged to Thomas Blount, author of the *Jocular Tenures*, 1679, 4to, and of many other publications enumerated in Wood's *Athenæ*, ii. 73, the earliest of which is *The Art of Making Devises*, 1646, 4to, wherein he is described to be "of the Inner Temple." If the collection was made by this lawyer (who also published the *Law Dictionary*, 1671, folio), it should seem, from the errors and defects with which the MS. abounds, that he had employed his clerk in writing the transcripts.

to Mr. Blakeway, late fellow of Magdalen College, he owes all the assistance received from the Pepysian Library: and Mr. Farmer, fellow of Emanuel, often exerted, in favour of this little work, that extensive knowledge of ancient English literature for which he is so distinguished. *

Many extracts from ancient MSS. in the British Museum and other respositories, were owing to the kind services of Thomas Astle, Esq., to whom the public is indebted for the curious preface and index annexed to the *Harleian Catalogue*.† The worthy Librarian of the Society of Antiquaries, Mr. Norris, deserved acknowledgment for the obliging manner in which he gave the Editor access to the volumes under his care. In Mr. Garrack's curious collection of old plays are many scarce pieces of ancient poetry, with the free use of which he indulged the Editor in the politest manner. To the Rev. Dr. Birch he is indebted for the use of several ancient and valuable tracts. To the friendship of Dr. Samuel Johnson he owes many valuable hints for the conduct of the work. And, if the Glossary is more exact and curious than might be expected in so slight a publication, it is to be ascribed to the supervisal of a friend, who stands at this time the first in the world for northern literature, and whose learning is even better known and respected in foreign nations than in his own country. It is perhaps needless to name the Rev. Mr. Lye, editor of *Junius's Etymologicum*, and of the *Gothic Gospels*.

The names of so many men of learning and character the Editor hopes will serve as an amulet, to guard him from every unfavourable censure for having bestowed any attention on a parcel of Old Ballads. It was at the request of many of these gentlemen, and of others eminent for their genius and taste, that this little work was undertaken. To prepare it for the press has been the amusement of now and then a vacant hour amid the leisure and retirement of rural life, and hath only served as a relaxation

---

* To the same learned and ingenious friend, since Master of Emanuel College, the Editor is obliged for many corrections and improvements in his second and subsequent editions; as also to the Rev. Mr. Bowle, of Idmistone, near Salisbury, editor of the curious edition of *Don Quixote*, with annotations in Spanish, in six vols. 4to; to the Rev. Mr. Cole, formerly of Bletchley, near Fenny-Stratford, Bucks; to the Rev. Mr. Lambe, of Norham, in Northumberland (author of a learned *History of Chess*, 1764, 8vo, and editor of a curious poem on the *Battle of Flodden Field*, with learned notes, 1774, 8vo); and to G. Paton, Esq., of Edinburgh. He is particularly indebted to two friends, to whom the public, as well as himself, are under the greatest obligations; to the Honourable Daines Barrington, for his very learned and curious *Observations on the Statutes*, 4to; and to Thomas Tyrwhitt, Esq., whose most correct and elegant edition of Chaucer's *Canterbury Tales*, five vols. 8vo, is a standard book, and shows how an ancient English classic should be published. The Editor was also favoured with many valuable remarks and corrections from the Rev. Geo. Ashby, late Fellow of St. John's College, in Cambridge, which are not particularly pointed out, because they occur so often. He was no less obliged to Thomas Butler, Esq., F.A.S., agent to the Duke of Northumberland, and clerk of the peace for the county of Middlesex, whose extensive knowledge of ancient writings, records, and history, has been of great use to the Editor in his attempts to illustrate the literature or manners of our ancestors. Some valuable remarks were procured by Samuel Pegge, Esq., author of that curious work the *Curialia*, 4to; but this impression was too far advanced to profit by them all; which hath also been the case with a series of learned and ingenious annotations inserted in the *Gentleman's Magazine* for August 1793, April, June, July, and October 1794.

† Since Keeper of the Records in the Tower.

from graver studies. It has been taken up at different times, and often thrown aside for many months, during an interval of four or five years. This has occasioned some inconsistencies and repetitions, which the candid reader will pardon. As great care has been taken to admit nothing immoral and indecent, the Editor hopes he need not be ashamed of having bestowed some of his idle hours in the ancient literature of our own country, or in rescuing from oblivion some pieces (though but the amusements of our ancestors) which tend to place in a striking light their taste, genius, sentiments, or manners.

Except in one paragraph, and in the notes subjoined, this Preface is given with little variation from the first edition in MDCCLXV.

## LIFE OF BISHOP PERCY.

### BY THE PRESENT EDITOR.

Dr. Thomas Percy, Bishop of Dromore, and the author of *Reliques of Ancient Poetry*, was, according to his own account, of an old Worcestershire family, a branch of the noble house of Percy. He was born in April 1729, in an old-fashioned timber house, in a street called the Cartway in Bridgenorth, Shropshire, where his father, Mr. Arthur Lowe Percy, was in business as a grocer. He received his early education at the Grammar School of his native town, and, having obtained an exhibition, went in due course to Christ Church, Oxford, where he was entered as a commoner. His name appears in the books as "Thomas Piercy," and the same orthography occurs in the list of Oxford graduates, from which it appears that he took his Bachelor's degree in May 1750, and proceeded Master of Arts in July 1753. It is uncertain by what bishop he was ordained, or what curacy he served; but in the same year in which he put on his Master's gown at Oxford, he was presented by Christ Church with the small living of Easton Maundit, near Northampton. In the register of this parish he writes his name Percy, probably for the first time—the result, doubtless, of those poetical and antiquarian studies to which he had already devoted himself from childhood, like his greater and far more celebrated disciple, Sir Walter Scott. In the little vicarage of this rural village he lived for more than a quarter of a century; there he married his wife, Nancy Gutteridge, and there all his children were born. The squire of his parish was the Earl of Sussex, whilst Castle Ashby, the seat of successive Earls of Northampton, was only a mile and a half distant. In these great houses Percy met with society through whom he was kept better acquainted than most country parsons of his time with what was passing in the world of letters and of fashion in London. Here in the summer of 1764, Dr. Johnson spent several months as his guest, when doubtless the parlour and little library were the scenes of literary discussions at which more than one of the Muses would have wished to have been present unseen. A terrace in the vicarage garden is still traditionally called Dr. Johnson's Walk.

Whilst living at Easton Maundit, namely, in 1761, Percy published in four volumes a Chinese novel, translated from the Portuguese, and dedicated to the Countess of Sussex; this he followed up by *Miscellaneous Pieces from the Chinese*, dedicated to Lady Longueville, as also a *Translation of the Song of Solomon from the*

Hebrew, *with a Commentary and Notes*, and his *Key to the New Testament*. He also undertook to re-edit the *Works of the Duke of Buckingham*, and the *Spectator*, the *Guardian*, and the *Tatler*, with notes and a key to the names of the writers ; but the project fell through, on account of Percy's nomination, through the influence and introduction of Lord Sussex, as chaplain and secretary to the Duke of Northumberland, which took him to London. In this capacity he occupied apartments in Northumberland House, in the Strand, to which he brought a portion, at least, of his books ; but these were destroyed by a fire along with his rooms in March 1780. Here he was visited by many literary friends, amongst others by Dr. Johnson and Oliver Goldsmith.

In 1763, his patron, the Duke of Northumberland, was appointed Lord-Lieutenant of Ireland, and Percy went over to Dublin along with him as his chaplain. He had already in 1778 been appointed Dean of Carlisle ; and in 1782, on the Duke's recommendation, he was nominated and consecrated as Bishop of Dromore, the see which had once been held by Jeremy Taylor. On this occasion he resigned his Northamptonshire living, in which he was succeeded by another man of letters, Dr. Nares.

He now divided his attention between his duties to his flock, and his attendance in the Irish Parliament at Dublin, and his literary studies. The latter he carried on continuously until visited by partial blindness in 1805. He lost his beloved "Nancy" in 1807, and lived on till September 1811, when he quietly and calmly passed away, leaving behind the memory of a blameless life. He was buried at Dromore. His only son died long before him, in fact only a year after his appointment as Bishop. His two surviving daughters married respectively the Honourable and Venerable Pierce Meade, Archdeacon of Dromore, fourth son of the first Lord Clanwilliam, and Ambrose Isted, Esq. of Ecton, Northamptonshire.

It is perhaps worthy of note that the bishop's wife in early life had been employed as nurse to the young Prince Edward, afterwards Duke of Kent, and the father of our most gracious Queen. It was to her that he addressed those tender and touching lines,

"Oh ! Nancy, wilt thou go with me ?"

which will be found in this collection.

The *Reliques* themselves were first published in 1765, twelve years after his appointment to Easton Maundit ; they were the result of long and patient labour employed in collecting and gleaning old ballads from literary friends, such as Garrick, Goldsmith, Gray, and especially Shenstone, who first suggested to him the idea of such a publication, and who had at one time intended to be associated with him in his work, though prevented by the stroke of death. No doubt, as the book appeared in the very year after Dr. Johnson's visit to Easton Maundit, its compilation was the subject of much animated discussion in the vicarage library, between the enthusiastic gleaner and the burly doctor, whose appreciation of the simple ballad style, we happen to know, was not very high.

But still, though Dr. Percy "touched up," and in fact tampered with the text of the ballads extensively—for which he was criticised pretty severely by a rival gleaner in the same field, Ritson—yet there can be little doubt that his *Reliques* have proved, if not a well of pure Saxon undefiled, at all events a cover to such a well. And with all their faults, they will always be popular with the multitude in their present shape, though the learned student and scholar will prefer to read them in their original form as they stand in the folio Manuscript. And it may be added, in proof of the high estimation in which the name of Dr. Percy is held even by such scholars, that in the edition of the said folio Manuscript, issued by Messrs. Hales and Furnivall, under the auspices of the Early English Text Society, the *Reliques* are styled "a book destined not only to raise him (the author) to eminence in his profession, but to render his name a 'household word' wherever the English language is spoken."

Sir Walter Scott tells us that as soon as he became in his boyhood acquainted with Percy's *Reliques,* "the first time he could scrape a few shillings together, he bought himself a copy of these beloved volumes; nor (he adds) do I believe that I ever read a book half so frequently or with half the enthusiasm." It was probably at a later period of life that he made himself acquainted with the three volumes of *Old English Ballads* which had been given to the learned world in 1723-25. Sir Henry Ellis, too, expresses his mature opinion that "the *Reliques* are the most agreeable selection perhaps which exists in any language."

A Percy Society was established in 1840, in honour of the Bishop, by Mr. William Chappell, F.S.A., and some other enthusiasts in the cause; but it was not adequately supported by the British public, and it died out in 1851, having given to the world nearly a hundred publications.

Percy's folio Manuscript is styled by Mr. F. J. Furnivall "the foundation document of English balladry, the basis of that structure which Percy raised." Mr. Furnivall writes: "By his emendations and by his taste, public attention was first drawn to the ballad literature of our country; and so far am I from condemning him, that I hold him to have been a benefactor to literature." It was printed and published by Messrs. J. W. Hales and F. J. Furnivall, 1867-68, uniform with, though not actually as part of, the publications of the Early English Text Society.

It adds a very great many ballads to the stock already known, for not above a sixth or seventh part\* of its bulk was selected by Percy for publication in his *Reliques;* and its editors boast, without wishing to depreciate the Bishop's memory, that now for the first time many of the most important ballads "can be read without Percy's tawdry touches."

Percy found the Manuscript lying about on the floor at the house of a friend named Pitt, at Shifnall, where the maid-servants had begun to use it for lighting the fire. He rescued it, and after some time had it bound, in order to preserve it, or rather such part of it as remained; ultimately it found its way into the library of Mr. Isted, at Ecton, Northamptonshire, who had married one of Percy's daughters. It was purchased from the family in 1868, by the Trustees of the British Museum, where it is now to be seen. The date of the writing is probably that of Charles I., and it is said to be in the handwriting of Thomas Blount, the well-known author of *Jocular Tenures,* etc.

There can be little doubt that the change of his name from Piercy to Percy was a piece of affectation, which was probably smiled at and good-humouredly pardoned by the Duke of Northumberland, who, though Percy by favour of the Herald's College,

---

\* The first edition of the *Reliques* contained 176 pieces, and Percy says that "the greater part of them are extracted from a folio Manuscript in his possession," but of these only 45 are derived from that source.

and by royal licence, and the owner of Sion House and of the proud Castle of Alnwick, was himself not a Percy but a "Smithson" by birth. In the same spirit Dr. Percy, when he erected a monument to his wife at Dromore, designates her maiden name as Goodriche in lieu of Gutteridge. It is true also that he placed the lion rampant, the Percy cognizance, over his family monument in Dromore Cathedral. But this, if it proves anything, proves too much; for if he was a genuine Percy by legitimate descent, at all events the ancient earldom, and probably the dukedom also, of Northumberland would not have become extinct, but would have come to him by right, instead of being re-granted to the Smithsons, one of whom had married the female heir of that ancient and noble house.

## BALLADS.

He was a wise man, that friend of Fletcher of Saltoun, who said that if a man were allowed to make the ballads of a people, he cared not who made its laws. For there can be no doubt that the ballads of an infant nation are a great factor in the formation of the national character, and help to mould the minds of its future citizens. But if he had been a little more far-sighted, he would have seen that in truth it would be utterly impossible to "make" the ballads of any people whatever, for the simple reason that they are the natural outcome and product of its infancy.

The word ballad is akin to ballet, both being derived from the Greek βάλλειν, to cast, throw, or move forcibly; the former coming from the French *balade*, as the latter comes from the Italian *ballata*, which means a song accompanied by or accompanying a dance.

A ballad poetry more or less rude has been in almost all countries the earliest memorial of public events; and where the infancy of a tribe is savage and warlike, it has always been applied, consciously or unconsciously, to the work of fostering a martial spirit. Tacitus tells us in his *Annals*[*] that long after his death, Arminius was remembered in the rude songs of his country; and that ballads were the chief, if not the only annals amongst the ancient German tribes. "They have a tradition," he adds, "that Hercules once visited those parts, and when they rush to battle, they sing his praises above those of other heroes."[†] A mediæval author, referring to the northern writers of a subsequent date, tells us that they drew the materials of their history from Runic songs. The Scandinavian tribes, as we know, had their "Scalds," whose office and duty it was to compose ballads, in which they also celebrated the warlike exploits of their forefathers.

It is equally certain that in our own islands there existed at an early date a race of bards whose work was substantially the same; and it is on record in our history, that when Edward I. set himself seriously to the task of subduing the Welsh to his sway, one of the first measures which he adopted was to destroy their bards—with no other object, we must believe, except that of getting rid of those ballads which fostered their nationality. In spite of the king's arms, however, their poetry survived; and a writer of the age of Elizabeth,[‡] in his description of North Wales, tells us that "upon the Sunday and holy days the multitude of all sort of men, women, and children of every parish do meet in sundry places, either on some hill

---

[*] Tacitus, *Ann.* ii. 88.      [†] *Germania*, ii. sect. 3.
[‡] Ellis, *Original Letters of English History*, Second Series, vol. iii. p. 49

or on the side of some mountain, where their harpers and crowthers sing them songs of the doings of their ancestors." Nor is this ballad style of poetry confined to our side of the Atlantic; for even the North American savages, when first discovered by our people, had their rude and warlike songs, in which they sung the praises of those who had died on the battle-field. And from another independent source we learn that a like system of national ballads prevailed among the original inhabitants of Peru.

Doubtless what was true in one country was true more or less in every other ; as the manners of each people became more refined, their ballads came to embrace a wider range of subjects. The songs were no longer confined to the rehearsal of deeds of valour, but began to include all sorts of tales of adventure, wild and marvellous, and occasionally became the vehicle of sentiment and passion; and "no festivity was esteemed complete among our ancestors in the eleventh, twelfth, and thirteenth centuries which was not set off with the exercise of the minstrel's talents, who usually sang his ballad to his own or some other harp, and was everywhere received with respect."*

As a higher intellectual taste began to prevail, however, these rude performances gradually lost their attraction with the upper ranks of society, and the bard's office fell into desuetude and comparative neglect. "When," writes Dr. Aikin,† " language became more refined, and poetical taste elevated by an acquaintance with the Greek and Latin authors, the subjects of the Epic Muse were no longer dressed in the homely garb of the popular ballad, but assumed the borrowed ornament and stately air of heroic poetry, and every poetical attempt in the sublime and beautiful Cas' was an imitation of the classic models. The native poetry of the country was reserved merely for the humorous and burlesque, and the term ballad was brought by custom to signify a comic story told in low familiar language, and accompanied by a droll trivial tune. It was much used by the wits of the time as a vehicle for laughable ridicule and mirthful satire, and a great variety of the most pleasing specimens of this kind of writing is to be found in the witty era of English genius, which I take to be between the beginning of Charles the Second's reign and the times of Swift and Prior. Since that period, the genius of the age has chiefly been characterized by the correct, elegant, and tender ; and a real or affected taste for beautiful simplicity has almost universally prevailed."

As time went on, these compositions, being quite out of date and fashion, came naturally to be regarded as objects of curiosity, chiefly on account of the insight which they afforded as to the manners, customs, and habits of thought which prevailed in the times to which they related ; while the strokes of nature with which they abounded, and the artless simplicity and force of their language, excited the admiration of such critics as were not utterly prejudiced in favour of the classical as contrasted with the romantic school. When therefore they had ceased to be current in song or recitation, they came to be carefully sought after and treasured by learned antiquaries, and illustrated by historical notes ; and thus a secondary importance was attached to them scarcely inferior to that which they possessed when chanted to the harp of the minstrel. If Sir Walter Scott in his day did good service in rescuing from oblivion the "minstrelsy of the Scottish Border," it should always

---

* *Penny Cyclopædia*, vol. iii. p. 329.　　*Essays on Song-Writing*, 1770.

be remembered that it was Bishop Percy from whom he first learned to appreciate such rhymes.

No doubt by far the greatest portion of the ballads once current and familiar in this country have perished irrevocably, for very few specimens exist of an earlier date than the reign of our first Stuart king. Being printed on single sheets, they would naturally fall chiefly into the hands of the lower orders, who would paste them not into scrap-books, but on the walls of their cottages. A few of them, however, were gleaned and stored away in little penny collections known as *Garlands*, several specimens of which are to be seen in the Pepys Library at Cambridge.

The earliest ballad now remaining in the English language, if we may accept the statement of the writer in the *Penny Cyclopædia* already quoted, is believed to be a "Cuckow Song" of the latter part of the reign of Henry III. It runs thus:

> "Sumer is icumen in,
> Lhudè sing cuccu;
> Groweth sed and bloweth med,
> And spingeth the wdè nu.
> Sing cuccu.
> Awe beteth after lamb,
> Llouth after calvè cu,
> Bulluc sterteth,
> Buckè verteth,
> Murie sing cuccu.
> Cuccu, cuccu,
> Wel singes thou, cuccu,
> Ne swik thou never nu.

This is simple and pastoral enough; it means—

> "Summer is come in,
> Loud sings the cuckoo,
> Now the seed grows and the mead blows,
> And the wood springs anew.
> The ewe bleats after the lamb,
> The cow loweth after the calf,
> The bullock starts, the buck verts,
> Merrily sing cuckoo.
> Well singest thou, cuckoo!
> Mayest thou never cease now."

The earliest specimen of Scottish song, after the Scotch adopted the English tongue, is preserved in the *Rhyming Chronicle* of Andrew Wyntown, Prior of Lochleven, written, as is generally supposed, about the year 1420, in which he relates the song made on King Alexander III., who was killed by a fall from his horse in 1286.

The earliest English song, separately printed on a single sheet, is believed to be one on the downfall of Thomas, Lord Cromwell, A.D. 1540.

The effects of ballad poetry in rousing the warlike passions of the people have been felt even in the modern prosaic times. The Irish song of "Lillyburlero," mentioned by Macaulay in his *History of England;* the "Marseillaise Song or Hymn;" and Burns's song, "Scots wha hae wi' Wallace bled," are sufficient proofs of the truth of this assertion.

The Scotch have got the credit for many of our best ballads, simply because they were called northern. But by the north country was denoted not only Scotland, or Northumberland, but all the land north of the Humber. The real fact is, that they were far more generally English than Scotch; and for this plain reason. Whilst Puritanism and Calvinism reigned or rather tyrannized over Scotland, it was not likely that that land, though in many ways a "meet nurse of a poetic child," would have produced many ballads; for we read in Chambers's *Domestic Annals of Scotland* (vol. i. p. 394), that under the Regent Morton death was the penalty for printing a ballad, and that two "poets" were actually hanged in 1579 for making ballads. Indeed, at one time no licence for a marriage could be issued north of the Tweed, unless the parties deposited £10 as a pledge that they would not have minstrels to play at it.

## PREFACE TO THE PRESENT EDITION.

THE object of the present Edition has been to simplify the *Reliques* for general reading. It professes to be nothing but a popular edition, popularly arranged, with notes that simplify and explain without entering into abstruse speculations, which, instead of enlightening, only increase the difficulties of the ordinary reader, who desires to read the ballads as a matter of amusement, and of information as to the old metrical romances, with as little effort as may be.

In order to assist without confusing, a Glossary of the very difficult words has been made. The words to be found in the Glossary are all printed in italics.

A German told me that when he first came to England, he could read Chaucer easily long before he could manage modern English, on account of many of the old words assimilating so closely to the German.

It seems to me, in looking at many of the footnotes to doubtful words, that this element is not sufficiently considered; and therefore in the Glossary I have occasionally suggested extra meanings founded on the German.

For instance, *sheene*, used as an adjective, I find *shining*, and I suggest *fine* as agreeing with the German *schön*, the pronunciation of which through the modified vowel comes not far off the English *sheene*. For *stiffe* and *stark* (the meaning of the latter word in some glossaries being given as stiff), I should suggest *cruel* and *strong*, from the German *stief*, cruel; *stark*, strong; and I find that *stark is* given in Percy's folio as *strong*. *Renisht*, for which glittering or shining is given, may, I think, come from the same root as *renigen*, to clean: it would be easy to get *renidged* or *renisht* from this; and *purified, cleansed, made all clean and presentable*, appears to be the sense in which the word *renisht* stands.

In the "Sturdy Rock," a madrigal set to music, we find the word *sline*, now used as a slang term, meaning "let it pass." It is found in Shakespeare also, and it is curious that the word which in this sense appears to have been lost to the language, was revived as a slang term by the Americans—I think the Bostonians, who pride themselves on the correctness of their English.

There are other words that differ in orthography, but which differ so slightly that it has not been thought well to burden the Glossary with them. Instead of this, a few remarks are offered.

Many words beginning with *z* must have the *z* turned into *y*, as *zour*, *ze*, your, ye. *Z* also sometimes stands for *gh*, in such words as *dozter*, daughter; *fyzt*, fight; *ryzt*, right; *doz-trough*, dough-trough. *D* and *t* are almost synonymous; also *f* and *v*. Indeed, one can perceive in many of the old words the German *v*, which is equal to our English *f—fele*, many, German *viel, viele*. *D* sometimes answers to *th*, as *Bednall*, Bethnall: *v* and *u* are also used synonymously, *giue*, give; *loue*, love.

With these remarks in view, it will be easy to understand those words that have not been considered of sufficient difficulty to add to the Glossary.

The word *Editor*, in reference to the poems, stands for Bishop Percy himself, the notes being partially abridged from his notes to the *Reliques*. Some original notes and remarks have been added.

A long disquisition on the word *Termagaunt* or *Termagant* appears in the *Reliques* in conjunction with *Mahmoud*; which latter word appears in one or two of the ballads, and Bishop Percy in his remarks says: "Termagaunt is the name given to the god of the Saracens, in which he is constantly linked with Mahmoud or Mahomet." He goes on to say that the word is derived by the editor of Junius from the Anglo-Saxon *Typ*, very, and *mazan*, mighty. But Bishop Percy suggests that the derivation seems too sublime for the Saracenic deity; he says: "Perhaps Typ-mazan, or Termagant, has been a name originally given to some Saxon idol before our ancestors were converted to Christianity, or had been the peculiar attribute of one of their false deities; and therefore the first Christian missionaries rejected it as profane and improper to be applied to the true God."

In answer to this, we would further suggest that probably Termagant alludes to the Teutonic Mars. *Tyr, Tiw, Zio;* why should not the derivation be *Tyr*, Mars; *Mazan*, Magan, mighty, the mighty Mars?

Grimm says of *Tyr Zio*: "Represented in the *Edda* as Odin's son, he may seem inferior to him in power and moment; but the two really fall into one, inasmuch as both are directors of war and battle, and the fame of victory proceeds from each of them alike."\*

The old Norse name for Tuesday was *Tysdagr*, from the god Tyr (gen. Tys), the Anglo-Saxon *Tiwesdæg*. The French *Mardi* brings us to *Dies Martis*, and we see in each the god of war as the patron of the day; therefore as Termagant or Termagaunte is always spoken of in connection with battles, may not the derivation be *Tyr mazan*, the mighty Tyr, the Mars of the northern nations, the equal in that sense to the god Wuotan or Odin?

E. W.

## AN ESSAY ON THE ANCIENT MINSTRELS IN ENGLAND.

I. The Minstrels were an order of men in the Middle Ages, who subsisted by the arts of poetry and music, and sang to the harp verses composed by themselves or others.† They also accompanied their songs with mimicry and action; and

---

\* Grimm's *Teutonic Mythology*, translated by James Steven Stallybrass, p. 196.

† Wedded to no hypothesis, the author hath readily corrected any mistakes which have been *proved* to be in this essay; and considering the novelty of the subject, and the time and place when and where he first took it up, many such had been excusable. The term "minstrel" was not confined, as some contend, to a mere musician in this country, any more than on the Continent.

practised such various means of diverting as were much admired in those rude times, and supplied the want of more refined entertainment. These arts rendered them extremely popular and acceptable in this and all the neighbouring countries; where no high scene of festivity was esteemed complete that was not set off with the exercise of their talents; and where, so long as the spirit of chivalry subsisted, they were protected and caressed, because their songs tended to do honour to the ruling passion of the times, and to encourage and foment a martial spirit.

The Minstrels seem to have been the genuine successors of the ancient Bards, who under different names were admired and revered, from the earliest ages, among the people of Gaul, Britain, Ireland, and the North; and indeed by almost all the first inhabitants of Europe, whether of Celtic or Gothic race; but by none more than by our own Teutonic ancestors, particularly by all the Danish tribes. Among these they were distinguished by the name of Scalds, a word which denotes "smoothers and polishers of language." The origin of their art was attributed to Odin or Woden, the father of their gods; and the professors of it were held in the highest estimation. Their skill was considered as something divine; their persons were deemed sacred; their attendance was solicited by kings; and they were everywhere loaded with honours and rewards. In short, poets and their art were held among them in that rude admiration which is ever shown by an ignorant people to such as excel them in intellectual accomplishments.

As these honours were paid to Poetry and Song from the earliest times in those countries which our Anglo-Saxon ancestors inhabited before their removal into Britain, we may reasonably conclude that they would not lay aside all their regard for men of this sort on quitting their German forests. At least so long as they retained their ancient manners and opinions, they would still hold them in high estimation. But as the Saxons, soon after their establishment in this island, were converted to Christianity; in proportion as literature prevailed among them, this rude admiration would begin to abate, and poetry would be no longer a peculiar profession. Thus the Poet and the Minstrel early with us became two persons. Poetry was cultivated by men of letters indiscriminately, and many of the most popular rhymes were composed amidst the leisure and retirement of monasteries. But the Minstrels continued a distinct order of men for many ages after the Norman Conquest, and got their livelihood by singing verses to the harp at the houses of the great. There they were still hospitably and respectfully received, and retained many of the honours shown to their predecessors the Bards and Scalds. And though, as their art declined, many of them only recited the compositions of others, some of them still composed songs themselves, and all of them could probably invent a few stanzas on occasion. I have no doubt but most of the old heroic ballads in this collection were composed by this order of men. For although some of the larger metrical romances might come from the pen of the monks or others, yet the smaller narratives were probably composed by the Minstrels who sang them. From the amazing variations which occur in different copies of the old pieces, it is evident they made no scruple to alter each other's productions; and the reciter added or omitted whole stanzas according to his own fancy or convenience.

In the early ages, as hinted above, the profession of oral itinerant poet was held in the utmost reverence among all the Danish tribes; and therefore we might have concluded that it was not unknown or unrespected among their Saxon brethren in Britain, even if history had been altogether silent on this subject. The original country of our Anglo-Saxon ancestors is well known to have lain chiefly in the tracts of land since distinguished by the name of Jutland, Angelen, and Holstein. The Jutes and Angles in particular, who composed two-thirds of the conquerors of Britain, were a Danish people, and their country at this day belongs to the crown of Denmark; so that when the Danes again invested England, three or four hundred years after, they made war on the descendants of their own ancestors. From this near affinity we might expect to discover a strong resemblance between both nations in their customs, manners, and even language; and, in fact, we find them to differ no more than would naturally happen between a parent country and its own colonies, that had been severed in a rude uncivilised state, and had dropt all intercourse for three or four centuries: especially if we reflect that the colony here settled had adopted a new religion, extremely opposite in all respects to the ancient Paganism of the mother country; and that even at first, along with the original Angli, had been incorporated a large mixture of Saxons from the neighbouring parts of Germany; and afterwards, among the Danish invaders, had come vast multitudes of adventurers from the more northern parts of Scandinavia. But all these were only different tribes of the same common Teutonic stock, and spoke only different dialects of the same Gothic language.

From this sameness of original and similarity of manners, we might justly have wondered if a character so dignified and distinguished among the ancient Danes as the Scald or Bard had been totally unknown or unregarded in his sister nation. And indeed this argument is so strong, and at the same time the early annals of the Anglo-Saxons are so scanty and defective, that no objections from their silence could be sufficient to overthrow it. For if these popular bards were confessedly revered and admired in those very countries which the Anglo-Saxons inhabited before their removal into Britain, and if they were afterwards common and numerous among the other descendants of the same Teutonic ancestors, can we do otherwise than conclude that men of this order accompanied such tribes as migrated hither; that they afterwards subsisted here, though perhaps with less splendour than in the North; and that there never was wanting a succession of them to hand down the art, though some particular conjunctures may have rendered it more respectable at one time than another? And this was evidently the case. For though much greater honours seem to have been heaped upon the northern Scalds, in whom the characters of historian, genealogist, poet, and musician were all united, than appear to have been paid to the Minstrels and Harpers of the Anglo-Saxons, whose talents were chiefly calculated to entertain and divert; while the Scalds professed to inform and instruct, and were at once the moralists and theologues of their Pagan countrymen; yet the Anglo-Saxon Minstrels continued to possess no small portion of public favour; and the arts they professed were so extremely acceptable to our ancestors, that the word Glee, which peculiarly denoted their art, continues still in our own language to be of all others the most expressive of that popular mirth and jollity, that strong sensation of delight, which is felt by unpolished and simple minds.

II. Having premised these general considerations, I shall now proceed to collect from history such particular incidents as occur on this subject; and, whether the facts themselves are true or not, they are related by authors who lived too near the Saxon times, and had before them too many recent monuments of the Anglo-Saxon nation, not to know what was conformable to the genius and manners of that people; and therefore we may presume that their relations prove at least the existence of the customs and habits they attribute to our forefathers before the Conquest, whatever becomes of the particular incidents and events themselves. If this be admitted, we shall not want sufficient proofs to show that Minstrelsy and Song were not extinct among the Anglo-Saxons; and that the professor of them here, if not quite so respected a personage as the Danish Scald, was yet highly favoured and protected, and continued still to enjoy considerable privileges.

Even so early as the first invasion of Britain by the Saxons, an incident is recorded which, if true, shows that the Minstrel or Bard was not unknown among this people; and that their princes themselves could, upon occasion, assume that character. Colgrin, son of that Ella who was elected king or leader of the Saxons in the room of Hengist, was shut up in York, and closely besieged by Arthur and his Britons. Baldulph, brother of Colgrin, wanted to gain access to him, and to apprise him of a reinforcement which was coming from Germany. He had no other way to accomplish his design, but to assume the character of a Minstrel. He therefore shaved his head and beard, and, dressing himself in the habit of that profession, took his harp in his hand. In this disguise he walked up and down the trenches without suspicion, playing all the while upon his instrument as a Harper. By little and little he advanced near to the walls of the city, and, making himself known to the sentinels, was in the night drawn up by a rope.

Although the above fact comes only from the suspicious pen of Geoffry of Monmouth, the judicious reader will not too hastily reject it; because, if such a fact really happened, it could only be known to us through the medium of the British writers; for the first Saxons, a martial but unlettered people, had no historians of their own; and Geoffry, with all his fables, is allowed to have recorded many true events that have escaped other annalists.

We do not, however, want instances of a less fabulous era and more indubitable authority; for later History affords us two remarkable facts which I think clearly show that the same arts of poetry and song, which were so much admired among the Danes, were by no means unknown or neglected in this sister nation; and that the privileges and honours which were so lavishly bestowed upon the northern Scalds, were not wholly withheld from the Anglo-Saxon Minstrels.

Our great King Alfred, who is expressly said to have excelled in music, being desirous to learn the true situation of the Danish army, which had invaded his realm, assumed the dress and character of a Minstrel, when, taking his harp and one of the most trusty of his friends disguised as a servant (for in the early times it was not unusual for a Minstrel to have a servant to carry his harp), he went with the utmost security into the Danish camp; and, though he could not but be known to be a Saxon by his dialect, the character he had assumed procured him a hospitable reception. He was admitted to entertain the king at table, and stayed among them long enough to contrive that assault which afterwards destroyed them. This was in the year 878.

About sixty years after, a Danish king made use of the same disguise to explore the camp of our king Athelstan. With his harp in his hand, and dressed like a

Minstrel, Anlaff, or rather Aulaff, king of the Danes, went among the Saxon tents, and, taking his stand near the king's pavilion, began to play, and was immediately admitted. There he entertained Athelstan and his lords with his singing and his music, and was at length dismissed with an honourable reward, though his songs must have discovered him to have been a Dane. Athelstan was saved from the consequences of this stratagem by a soldier, who had observed Aulaff bury the money which had been given him, either from some scruple of honour or motive of superstition. This occasioned a discovery.

Now if the Saxons had not been accustomed to have Minstrels of their own, Alfred's assuming so new and unusual a character would have excited suspicions among the Danes. On the other hand, if it had not been customary with the Saxons to show favour and respect to the Danish Scalds, Aulaff would not have ventured himself among them, especially on the eve of a battle. From the uniform procedure then of both these kings, we may fairly conclude that the same mode of entertainment prevailed among both people, and that the Minstrel was a privileged character with each.

But, if these facts had never existed, it can be proved from undoubted records, that the Minstrel was a regular and stated officer in the court of our Anglo-Saxon kings: for in Domesday Book, *Joculator Regis*, the king's Minstrel, is expressly mentioned in Gloucestershire; in which county it should seem that he had lands assigned him for his maintenance.

III. We have now brought the inquiry down to the Norman Conquest; and as the Normans had been a late colony from Norway and Denmark, where the Scalds had arrived at the highest pitch of credit before Rollo's expedition into France, we cannot doubt but this adventurer, like the other northern princes, had many of these men in his train, who settled with him in his new Duchy of Normandy, and left behind them successors in their art; so that when his descendant, William the Conqueror, invaded this kingdom in the following century, that mode of entertainment could not but be still familiar with the Normans. And that this is not mere conjecture will appear from a remarkable fact, which shows that the arts of Poetry and Song were still as reputable among the Normans in France as they had been among their ancestors in the North; and that the profession of Minstrel, like that of Scald, was still aspired to by the most gallant soldiers. In William's army was a valiant warrior named Taillefer, who was distinguished no less for the minstrel arts than for his courage and intrepidity. This man asked leave of his commander to begin the onset, and obtained it. He accordingly advanced before the army, and with a loud voice animated his countrymen with songs in praise of Charlemagne and Roland, and other heroes of France; then rushing among the thickest of the English, and valiantly fighting, lost his life.

Indeed, the Normans were so early distinguished for their minstrel talents, that Le Grand, the author of the *History of the Troubadours*, refers to them the origin of all modern poetry, and shows that they were celebrated for their songs near a century before the Troubadours of Provence, who are supposed to have led the way to the Poets of Italy, France, and Spain.

We see then that the Norman Conquest was rather likely to favour the establishment of the Minstrel profession in this kingdom than to suppress it; and although the favour of the Norman conquerors would be probably confined to such of their own countrymen as excelled in the Minstrel arts, and in the first ages after the Conquest no other songs would be listened to by the great nobility but such as were composed in their own Norman-French, yet as the great mass of the original inhabitants were not extirpated, these could only understand their own native Gleemen or Minstrels, who must still be allowed to exist, unless it can be proved that they were all proscribed and massacred, as it is said the Welsh Bards were afterwards by the severe policy of King Edward I. But this we know was not the case; and even the cruel attempts of that monarch, as we shall see below, proved ineffectual.

The honours shown to the Norman or French Minstrels, by our princes and great barons, would naturally have been imitated by their English vassals and tenants, even if no favour or distinction had ever been shown here to the same order of men in the Anglo-Saxon and Danish reigns. So that we cannot doubt but the English Harper and Songster would, at least in a subordinate degree, enjoy the same kind of honours, and be received with similar respect among the inferior English gentry and populace. I must be allowed therefore to consider them as belonging to the same community, as subordinate members at least of the same College; and therefore, in gleaning the scanty materials for this slight history, I shall collect whatever incidents I can find relating to Minstrels and their art, and arrange them, as they occur in our own annals, without distinction; as it will not always be easy to ascertain, from the slight mention of them by our regular historians, whether the artists were Norman or English. For it need not be remarked that subjects of this trivial nature are but incidentally mentioned by our ancient annalists, and were fastidiously rejected by other grave and serious writers; so that, unless they were accidentally connected with such events as became recorded in history, they would pass unnoticed through the lapse of ages, and be as unknown to posterity as other topics relating to the private life and amusements of the greatest nations.

On this account it can hardly be expected that we should be able to produce regular and unbroken annals of the Minstrel art and its professors, or have sufficient information whether every Minstrel or Harper composed himself, or only repeated, the songs he chanted. Some probably did the one, and some the other; and it would have been wonderful indeed, if men whose peculiar profession it was, and who devoted their time and talents to entertain their hearers with poetical compositions, were peculiarly deprived of all poetical genius themselves, and had been under a physical incapacity of composing those common popular rhymes which were the usual subjects of their recitation. Whoever examines any considerable quantity of these, finds them in style and colouring as different from the elaborate production of the sedentary composer at his desk or in his cell, as the rambling Harper or Minstrel was remote in his modes of life and habits of thinking from the retired scholar or the solitary monk.

It is well known that on the Continent, whence our Norman nobles came, the Bard who composed, the Harper who played and sang, and even the Dancer and the Mimic, were all considered as of one community, and were even all included under the common name of Minstrels. I must therefore be allowed the same application of the term here, without being expected to prove that every singer composed, or every composer chanted, his own song; much less that every one excelled in all the arts which were occasionally exercised by some or other of this fraternity.

IV. After the Norman Conquest, the first occurrence which I have met with relating to this order of men is the founding of a priory and hospital by one of them—*scil.* the Priory and Hospital of St. Bartholomew, in Smithfield, London, by Royer or Raherus, the king's Minstrel, in the third year of Henry I., A.D. 1102. He was the first Prior of his own establishment, and presided over it to the time of his death.

In the reign of Henry II., we have upon record the name of Galfrid or Jeffrey, a Harper, who in 1180 received an annuity from the Abbey of Hyde, near Winchester; and, as in the early times every Harper was expected to sing, we cannot doubt but this reward was given to him for his music and his songs; which, if they were for the solace of the monks there, we may conclude would be in the English language.

Under his romantic son, Richard I., the Minstrel profession seems to have acquired additional splendour. Richard, who was the great hero of chivalry, was also the distinguished patron of Poets and Minstrels. He was himself of their number, and some of his poems are still extant.* They were no less patronized by his favourites and chief officers. His Chancellor, William, Bishop of Ely, is expressly mentioned to have invited Singers and Minstrels from France, whom he loaded with rewards; and they in return celebrated him as the most accomplished person in the world. This high distinction and regard, although confined perhaps in the first instance to Poets and Songsters of the French nation, must have had a tendency to do honour to Poetry and Song among all his subjects, and to encourage the cultivation of these arts among the natives; as the indulgent favour shown by the monarch or his great courtiers to the Provençal *Troubadour*, or Norman *Rymour*, would naturally be imitated by their inferior vassals to the English Gleeman or Minstrel. At more than a century after the Conquest, the national distinctions must have begun to decline, and both the Norman and English languages would be heard in the houses of the great; so that probably about this era, or soon after, we are to date that remarkable intercommunity and exchange of each other's compositions, which we discover to have taken place at some early period between the French and English Minstrels; the same set of phrases, the same species of characters, incidents, and adventures, and often the same identical stories, being found in the old metrical romances of both nations.

The distinguished service which Richard received from one of his own Minstrels, in, rescuing him from his cruel and tedious captivity, is a remarkable fact, which ought to be recorded for the honour of Poets and their art. This fact I shall relate in the following words of an ancient writer,† Mons. Favine:—

"The Englishmen were more than a whole yeare without hearing any tydings of their king, or in what place he was kept prisoner. He had trained up in his court a Rimer or Minstrill, called Blondell de Nesle: who (so saith the Manuscript of old Poesies,‡ and an auncient Manuscript French Chronicle) being so long without the sight of his lord, his life seemed wearisome to him, and he became confounded with melancholly. Knowne it was, that he came backe from the Holy Land; but none could tell in what countrey he arrived. Whereupon this Blondel, resolving to make

---

* See a pathetic song of his in Mr. Walpole's *Catalogue of Royal Authors*, vol. i. p. 5. The reader will find a translation of it into modern French in *Hist. Littéraire des Troubadours*, 1774, 3 tom. 12mo. See vol. i. p. 58, where some more of Richard's poetry is translated. In Dr. Burney's *History of Music*, vol. ii. p. 238, is a poetical version of it in English.

†*Theatre of Honour and Knighthood*, translated from the French, London 1623. An elegant relation of the same event (from the French of President Fauchet's *Recueil*, etc.) may be seen in *Miscellanies in Prose and Verse*, by Anna Williams, London 1766, 4to.

‡ This the author calls in another place, "An ancient MS. of old Poesies, written about those very times."

search for him in many countries, but he would heare some newes of him; after expence of divers dayes in travaile, he came to a towne (by good hap) neere to the castell where his maister King Richard was kept. Of his host he demanded to whom the castell appertained, and the host told him that it belonged to the Duke of Austria. Then he enquired whether there were any prisoners therein detained or no: for alwayes he made such secret questionings wheresoever he came. And the hoste gave answer, there was one onely prisoner, but he knew not what he was, and yet he had bin detained there more then the space of a yeare. When Blondel heard this, he wrought such meanes, that he became acquainted with them of the castell, as Minstrels doe easily win acquaintance anywhere: but see the king he could not, neither understand that it was he. One day he sat directly before a window of the castell, where King Richard was kept prisoner, and began to sing a song in French, which King Richard and Blondel had some time composed together. When King Richard heard the song, he knew it was Blondel that sung it: and when Blondel paused at halfe of the song, the king 'began the other half and completed it.' Thus Blondel won knowledge of the king his maister, and returning home into England, made the barons of the countrie acquainted where the king was." This happened about the year 1193.

The following old Provençal lines are given as the very original song, which I shall accompany with an imitation offered by Dr. Burney:—

BLONDEL.

| | |
|---|---|
| Domna vostra beutas | Your beauty, lady fair, |
| Elas bellas faissos | None views without delight; |
| Els bels oils amoros | But still so cold an air |
| Els gens cors ben taillats | No passion can excite; |
| Don sieu empresenats | Yet this I patient see |
| De vostra amor que mi lia. | While all are shunn'd like me. |

RICHARD.

| | |
|---|---|
| Si bel trop affansia | No nymph my heart can wound |
| Ja de vos non portrai | If favour she divide, |
| Que major honorai | And smiles on all around |
| Sol en votre deman | Unwilling to decide: |
| Que sautra des beisan | I'd rather hatred bear |
| Tot can de vos volria. | Than love with others share. |

The access which Blondel so readily obtained in the privileged character of a Minstrel, is not the only instance upon record of the same nature. In this very reign of King Richard I. the young heiress of D'Evreux, Earl of Salisbury, had been carried abroad and secreted by her French relations in Normandy. To discover the place of her concealment, a knight of the Talbot family spent two years in exploring that province, at first under the disguise of a Pilgrim; till having found where she was confined, in order to gain admittance he assumed the dress and character of a Harper, and being a jocose person exceedingly skilled in "the Gesta of the ancients;" so they called the romances and stories, which were the delight of that age; he was gladly received into the family. Whence he took an opportunity to carry off the young lady, whom he presented to the king; and he bestowed her on his natural brother **William Longespee** (son of fair **Rosamond**), who became in her right Earl of **Salisbury.**

The next memorable event which I find in history reflects credit on the English Minstrels; and this was their contributing to the rescue of one of the great Earls of Chester, when besieged by the Welsh. This happened in the reign of King John, and is related to this effect:—

"Hugh, the first Earl of Chester, in his charter of foundation of St. Werburg's Abbey in that city, had granted such a privilege to those who should come to Chester fair, that they should not be then apprehended for theft or any other misdemeanour, except the crime were committed during the fair. This special protection occasioning a multitude of loose people to resort to that fair, was afterwards of signal benefit to one of his successors. For Ranulph, the last Earl of Chester, marching into Wales with a slender attendance, was constrained to retire to his Castle of Rothelan (or Rhuydland), to which the Welsh forthwith laid siege. In this distress he sent for help to the Lord De Lacy, Constable of Chester, 'who, making use of the Minstrels of all sorts, then met at Chester fair; by the allurement of their music, got together a vast number of such loose people as, by reason of the before-specified privilege, were then in that city; whom he forthwith sent under the conduct of Dutton (his steward),' a gallant youth, who was also his son-in-law. The Welsh, alarmed at the approach of this rabble, supposing them to be a regular body of armed and disciplined veterans, instantly raised the siege and retired."

For this good service, Ranulph is said to have granted to De Lacy, by charter, the patronage and authority over the Minstrels and the loose and inferior people, who, retaining to himself that of the lower artificers, conferred on Dutton the jurisdiction of the Minstrels; and under the descendants of this family the Minstrels enjoyed certain privileges, and protection for many ages. For even so late as the reign of Elizabeth, when this profession had fallen into such discredit that it was considered in law as a nuisance, the Minstrels under the jurisdiction of the family of Dutton are expressly excepted out of all Acts of Parliament made for their suppression, and continued to be so excepted down to the reign of George III.

The ceremonies attending the exercise of this jurisdiction are thus described by Dugdale, as handed down to his time, viz.: "That at Midsummer fair there, all the Minstrels of that countrey resorting to Chester do attend the heir of Dutton, from his lodging to St. John's Church (he being then accompanied by many gentlemen of the countrey), one of 'the Minstrels' walking before him in a surcoat of his arms depicted on taffata; the rest of his fellows proceeding (two and two) and playing on their several sorts of musical instruments. And after Divine service ended, give the like attendance on him back to his lodging; where a court being kept by his [Mr. Dutton's] steward, and all the Minstrels formally called, certain orders and laws are usually made for the better government of that society, with penalties on those who transgress." In the same reign of John we have a remarkable instance of a Minstrel, who to his other talents superadded the character of Soothsayer, and by his skill in drugs and medicated potions was able to rescue a knight from imprisonment. This occurs in Leland's *Narrative of the Gesta of Guarine* (or *Warren*) *and his Sons*, which he "excerptid owte of an old Englisch boke yn ryme," and is as follows:—

Whitington Castle in Shropshire, which, together with the co-heiress of the original proprietor, had been won in a solemn tournament by the ancestor of the Guarines, had in the reign of John been seized by the Prince of Wales, and was afterwards possessed by Morice, a retainer of that prince, to whom the king, out of hatred to the true heir Fulco Guarine (with whom he had formerly had a quarrel at chess), not only confirmed the possession, but also made him governor of the marches, of which Fulco himself had the custody in the time of King Richard. The Guarines demanded justice of the king, but obtaining no gracious answer, renounced their allegiance and fled into Bretagne. Returning into England, after various conflicts, "Fulco resortid to one John of Raumpayne, a Soothsayer and Jocular and Minstrelle, and made hym his spy to Morice at Whitington." The privileges of this character we have already seen, and John so well availed himself of them, that in consequence of the intelligence which he doubtless procured, "Fulco and his brethrene laide waite for Morice, as he went toward Salesbyri, and Fulco ther woundid hym, and Bracy," a knight, who was their friend and assistant, "cut off Morice['s] hedde." This Sir Bracy being in a subsequent rencounter sore wounded, was taken and brought to King John, from whose vengeance he was however rescued by this notable Minstrel; for "John Rampayne founde the meanes to cast them that kepte Bracy into a deadely slepe, and so he and Bracy cam to Fulco to Whitington," which on the death of Morice had been restored to him by the Prince of Wales. As no further mention occurs of the Minstrel, I might here conclude this narrative, but I shall just add, that Fulco was obliged to flee into France, where, assuming the name of Sir Amice, he distinguished himself in jousts and tournaments ; and, after various romantic adventures by sea and land, having in the true style of chivalry rescued "certayne ladies owt of prison," he finally obtained the king's pardon, and the quiet possession of Whitington Castle.

In the reign of Henry III., we have mention of Master Richard the king's Harper, to whom in his 36th year (1252) that monarch gave not only forty shillings and a pipe of wine, but also a pipe of wine to Beatrice his wife. The title of *Magister*, or Master, given to this Minstrel, deserves notice, and shows his respectable situation.

V. The Harper, or Minstrel, was so necessary an attendant on a royal personage, that Prince Edward (afterwards Edward I.) in his Crusade to the Holy Land, in 1271, was not without his Harper, who must have been officially very near his person ; as we are told by a contemporary historian, that, in the attempt to assassinate that heroic prince, when he had wrested the poisoned knife out of the Saracen's hand, and killed him with his own weapon, the attendants, who had stood apart while he was whispering to their master, hearing the struggle, ran to his assistance, and one of them, to wit his Harper, seizing a tripod or trestle, struck the assassin on the head and beat out his brains. And though the prince blamed him for striking the man after he was dead, yet his near access shows the respectable situation of this officer, and his affectionate zeal should have induced Edward to entreat his brethren the Welsh Bards afterwards with more lenity.

Whatever was the extent of this great monarch's severity towards the professors of Music and of Song in Wales ; whether the executing by martial law such of them as fell into his hands was only during the heat of conflict, or was continued afterwards with more systematic rigour ; yet in his own court the Minstrels appear to have been highly favoured : for when, in 1306, he conferred the order of knighthood on his son and many others of the young nobility, a multitude of Minstrels were introduced to invite and induce the new knights to make some military vow.

Under Edward II., such extensive privileges were claimed by these men, and by dissolute persons assuming their character, that it became a matter of public grievance, and was reformed by an express regulation in A.D. 1315. Notwithstanding which, an incident is recorded in the ensuing year, which shows that Minstrels still retained the liberty of entering at will into the royal presence, and had something peculiarly splendid in their dress. It is thus related by Stow:—

"In the year 1316, Edward II. did solemnize his feast of Pentecost at Westminster, in the great hall: where sitting royally at the table with his peers about him, there entered a woman adorned like a Minstrel, sitting on a great horse trapped, as Minstrels then used; who rode round about the tables, showing pastime; and at length came up to the king's table, and laid before him a letter, and forthwith turning her horse saluted every one and departed." The subject of this letter was a remonstrance to the king on the favours heaped by him on his minions, to the neglect of his knights and faithful servants.

The privileged character of a Minstrel was employed on this occasion, as sure of gaining an easy admittance; and a female the rather deputed to assume it, that, in case of detection, her sex might disarm the king's resentment. This is offered on a supposition that she was not a real Minstrel; for there should seem to have been women of this profession, as well as of the other sex; and no accomplishment is so constantly attributed to females, by our ancient Bards, as their singing to, and playing on, the harp.

In the fourth year of Richard II., John of Gaunt erected at Tutbury in Staffordshire, a Court of Minstrels, similar to that annually kept at Chester, and which, like a Court-Leet or Court Baron, had a legal jurisdiction, with full power to receive suit and service from the men of this profession within five neighbouring counties, to enact laws, and determine their controversies; and to apprehend and arrest such of them as should refuse to appear at the said court annually held on the 16th of August. For this they had a charter, by which they were empowered to appoint a king of the Minstrels with four officers to preside over them. These were every year elected with great ceremony; the whole form of which, as observed in 1680, is described by Dr. Plot in his *History of Staffordshire:* in whose time, however, they appear to have lost their singing talents, and to have confined all their skill to "wind and string music."

The Minstrels seem to have been in many respects upon the same footing as the Heralds: and the king of the Minstrels, like the King-at-Arms, was both here and on the Continent an usual officer in the courts of princes. Thus we have in the reign of King Edward I., mention of a King Robert, and others. And in 16 Edward II., is a grant to William de Morlee, "the king's Minstrel, styled *Roy de North,*" of houses which had belonged to another king, John le Boteler. Rymer hath also printed a licence granted by Richard II., in 1387, to John Caumz, the king of his Minstrels, to pass the seas, recommending him to the protection and kind treatment of all his subjects and allies.

In the subsequent reign Henry IV., we meet with no particulars relating to the Minstrels in England, but we find in the statute book a severe law passed against their brethren the Welsh Bards, whom our ancestors could not distinguish from their own *Rimours Ministralx;* for by these names they describe them. This Act plainly shows, that far from being extirpated by the rigorous policy of Edward I., this order of men were still able to alarm the English Government, which attributed to them "many diseases and mischiefs in Wales," and prohibited their meetings and contributions.

When his heroic son Henry V. was preparing his great voyage for France, in 1415, an express order was given for his Minstrels, fifteen in number, to attend him: and eighteen are afterwards mentioned, to each of whom he allowed 12d. a day, when that sum must have been of more than ten times the value it is at present. Yet when he entered London in triumph after the battle of Agincourt, he, from a principle of humility, slighted the pageants and verses which were prepared to hail his return; and as we are told by Holingshed, would not suffer "any Dities to be made and song by Minstrels, of his glorious victorie; for that he would whollie have the praise and thankes altogether given to God." But this did not proceed from any disregard for the professors of Music or of Song; for at the feast of Pentecost, which he celebrated in 1416, having the Emperor and the Duke of Holland for his guests, he ordered rich gowns for sixteen of his Minstrels, of which the particulars are preserved by Rymer. And having before his death orally granted an annuity of 100 shillings to each of his Minstrels, the grant was confirmed by his son Henry VI., in A.D. 1423, and payment ordered out of the Exchequer.*

The unfortunate reign of Henry VI. affords no occurrences respecting our subject; but in his thirty-fourth year, A.D. 1456, we have in Rymer a commission for impressing boys or youths, to supply vacancies by death among the king's Minstrels: in which it is expressly directed that they shall be elegant in their limbs, as well as instructed in the Minstrel art, wherever they can be found, for the solace of his Majesty.

In the ninth year of Edward IV. (1469), upon a complaint that certain rude husbandmen and artificers of various trades had assumed the title and livery of the king's Minstrels, and under that colour and pretence had collected money in divers parts of the kingdom, and committed other disorders, the king grants to Walter Haliday, marshal, and to seven others his own Minstrels whom he names, a charter, by which he creates, or rather restores, a fraternity or perpetual gild (such as, he understands, the brothers and sisters of the fraternity of Minstrels had in times past), to be governed by a marshal appointed for life, and by two wardens to be chosen annually; who are empowered to admit brothers and sisters into the said gild, and are authorized to examine the pretensions of all such as affected to exercise the Minstrel profession; and to regulate, govern, and punish them throughout the realm (those of Chester excepted). This seems to have some resemblance to the Earl Marshal's Court among the Heralds, and is another proof of the great affinity and resemblance which the Minstrels bore to the members of the College of Arms.

It is remarkable that Walter Haliday, whose name occurs as marshal in the foregoing charter, had been retained in the service of the two preceding monarchs, Henry V. and VI. Nor is this the first time he is mentioned as marshal of the king's Minstrels, for in the third year of this reign, 1464, he had a grant from Edward of 10 marks per annum during life, directed to him with that title.

But besides their marshal we have also in this reign mention of a serjeant of the Minstrels, who upon a particular occasion was able to do his royal master a singular service, wherein his confidential situation and ready access to the king at all hours is very apparent: for "as he [Edward IV.] was in the north contray in the monneth of Septembre, as he lay in his bedde, one namid Alexander Carlile, that was sariaunt of the Mynstrellis, cam to him in grete hast, and badde hym aryse for he hadde enemyes

---

* *Rymer*, tom. x. 287. They are ............. by name, being ten in number one of them was named Thomas Chatterton.

C

cummyng for to take him, the which were within vi. or vii. mylis, of the which tydinges the king gretely marveylid," etc. This happened in the same year, 1469, wherein the king granted or confirmed the charter for the fraternity or gild above mentioned; yet this Alexander Carlile is not one of the eight Minstrels to whom that charter is directed.

The same charter was renewed by Henry VIII., in 1520, to John Gilman, his then marshal, and to seven others his Minstrels: and on the death of Gilman, he granted in 1529 this office of marshal of his Minstrels to Hugh Wodehouse, whom I take to have borne the office of his serjeant over them.

VI. In all the establishments of royal and noble households, we find an ample provision made for the Minstrels; and their situation to have been both honourable and lucrative. In proof of this it is sufficient to refer to the household book of the Earl of Northumberland, A.D. 1512. And the rewards they received so frequently recur in ancient writers, that it is unnecessary to crowd the page with them here.

The name of Minstrel seems, however, to have been gradually appropriated to the musician only, especially in the fifteenth and sixteenth centuries; yet we occasionally meet with applications of the term in its more enlarged meaning, as including the singer, if not the composer, of heroic or popular rhymes.

In the time of Henry VIII. we find it to have been a common entertainment to hear verses recited, or moral speeches learned for that purpose, by a set of men who got their livelihood by repeating them, and who intruded without ceremony into all companies, not only in taverns, but in the houses of the nobility themselves. This we learn from Erasmus, whose argument led him only to describe a species of these men who did not sing their compositions; but the others that did, enjoyed, without doubt, the same privileges.

For even long after, in the reign of Queen Elizabeth, it was usual "in places of assembly" for the company to be "desirous to heare of old adventures and valiaunces of noble knights in times past, as those of King Arthur and his knights of the round table, Sir Bevys of Southampton, Guy of Warwicke and others like," in "short and long meters, and by breaches or divisions [*sc.* Fits or Fyttes], to be more commodiously sung to the harpe," as the reader may be informed, by a courtly writer, in 1589. Who himself had "written for pleasure a little brief romance or historical ditty . . . of the isle of Great Britaine" in order to contribute to such entertainment. And he subjoins this caution: "Such as have not premonition hereof" (viz. that his poem was written in short metre, etc., to be sung to the harpe in such places of assembly) "and consideration of the causes alledged, would peradventure reprove and disgrace every romance, or short historicall ditty, for that they be not written in long meeters or verses Alexandrins," which constituted the prevailing versification among the Poets of that age, and which no one now can endure to read.

And that the recital of such romances sung to the harp was at that time the delight of the common people, we are told by the same writer, who mentions that "common Rimers" were fond of using rhymes at short distances, "in small and popular Musickes song by these Cantabanqui" [the said common Rimers] "upon benches and barrels' heads," etc., "or else by blind Harpers or such like taverne Minstrels that give a Fit of mirth for a groat; and their matter being for the most part stories of old time, as the tale of Sir Topas, the reportes of Bevis of Southampton, Guy of Warwicke, Adam Bell, and Clymme of the Clough, and such other old romances, or historicall rimes," etc., "also they be used in carols and rounds, and such light or lascivious poemes, which are commonly more commodiously uttered by these buffons, or vices in playes, than by any other person. Such were the rimes of Skelton (usurping the name of a Poet Laureat), being in deede but a rude railing rimer, and all his doings ridiculous."

But although we find here that the Minstrels had lost much of their dignity, and were sinking into contempt and neglect : yet that they still sustained a character far superior to anything we can conceive at present of the singers of old ballads, I think, may be inferred from the following representation.

When Queen Elizabeth was entertained at Kenilworth * Castle by the Earl of Leicester in 1575, among the many devices and pageants which were contrived for her entertainment, one of the personages introduced was to have been that of an ancient Minstrel ; whose appearance and dress are so minutely described by a writer there present, and gives us so distinct an idea of the character, that I shall quote the passage at large :—

"A person very meet seemed he for the purpose, of a xlv. years old, apparelled partly as he would himself. His cap off, his head seemly rounded Tonsterwise, fair kembed, that with a sponge daintily dipt in a little capon's greace was finely smoothed, to make it shine like a mallard's wing. His beard smugly shaven, and yet his shirt after the new trink, with ruffs fair starched, sleeked and glistering like a pair of new shoes, marshalled in good order with a setting stick, and strut, that every ruff stood up like a wafer. A side [*i.e.* long] gown of Kendal green, after the freshness of the year now, gathered at the neck with a narrow gorget, fastened afore with a white clasp and a keeper close up to the chin, but easily, for heat to undo when he list. Seemly begirt in a red caddis girdle, from that a pair of capped Sheffield knives hanging a' two sides. Out of his bosom drawn forth a lappet of his napkin, edged with a blue lace, and marked with a true love, a heart, and a D for Damian, for he was but a batchelor yet.

"His gown had side [*i.e.* long] sleeves down to mid-leg, slit from the shoulder to the hand, and lined with white cotton. His doublet-sleeves of black worsted, upon them a pair of poynets of tawny chamlet laced along the wrist with blue threaden points, a wealt towards the hand of fustian-a-napes. A pair of red neather stocks. A pair of pumps on his feet, with a cross cut at the toes for corns : not new indeed, yet cleanly blackt with soot, and shining as a shoing horn.

"About his neck a red ribband suitable to his girdle. His harp in good grace dependent before him. His wrest tyed to a green lace and hanging by. Under the gorget of his gown a fair flaggon chain (pewter, for) silver, as a Squire Minstrel of Middlesex, that travelled the country this summer season, unto fairs and worshipful men's houses. From his chain hung a scutcheon, with metal and colour, resplendant upon his breast, of the ancient arms of Islington."

This Minstrel is described as belonging to that village. I suppose such as were retained by noble families wore the arms of their patrons hanging down by a silver chain as a kind of badge.† From the expression of Squire Minstrel above, we may conclude there were other inferior orders, as Yeomen Minstrels, or the like.

---

\* See a curious "Letter," printed in Nichols's *Collection of Queen Elizabeth's Progresses*, etc., in 2 vols. 4to.

† As the house of Northumberland had anciently three minstrels attending on them in their castles in Yorkshire, so they still retain three in their service in Northumberland, who wear the

This Minstrel, the author tells us a little below, "after three lowly curtsies, cleared his voice with a hem ... and ... wiped his lips with the hollow of his hand for 'filing his napkin, tempered a string or two with his Wrest, and after a little warbling on his Harp for a prelude, came forth with a solemn song, warranted for story out of *King Arthur's Acts*, etc." This song the reader will find printed in this work.

Towards the end of the sixteenth century this class of men had lost all credit, and were sunk so low in the public opinion, that in the thirty-ninth year of Elizabeth, a statute was passed by which "Minstrels, wandering abroad," were included among "rogues, vagabonds, and sturdy beggars," and were adjudged to be punished as such. This Act seems to have put an end to the profession.

VII. I cannot conclude this account of the ancient English Minstrels, without remarking that they are most of them represented to have been of the north of England. There is scarce an old historical song or ballad wherein a Minstrel or Harper appears, but he is characterized by way of eminence to have been "of the North Countrye;" and indeed the prevalence of the northern dialect in such compositions, shows that this representation is real. On the other hand, the scene of the finest Scottish ballads is laid in the south of Scotland, which should seem to have been peculiarly the nursery of Scottish Minstrels. In the old song of Maggy Lawder, a Piper is asked, by way of distinction, "Come ze frae the Border?" The martial spirit constantly kept up and exercised near the frontier of the two kingdoms, as it furnished continual subjects for their songs, so it inspired the inhabitants of the adjacent counties on both sides with the powers of poetry. Besides, as the southern metropolis must have been ever the scene of novelty and refinement, the northern countries, as being most distant, would preserve their ancient manners longest, and of course the old poetry, in which those manners are peculiarly described.

The reader will observe in the more ancient ballads of this collection, a cast of style and measure very different from that of contemporary poets of a higher class; many phrases and idioms, which the Minstrels seem to have appropriated to themselves, and a very remarkable licence of varying the accent of words at pleasure, in order to humour the flow of the verse, particularly in the rhymes; as

| *Countrìe* | *harpèr* | *battèl* | *mornìng* |
|---|---|---|---|
| *Ladìe* | *singèr* | *damsèl* | *lovìng* |

instead of *coúntry, láddy, hárper, sínger,* etc. This liberty is but sparingly assumed by the classical poets of the same age, or even by the later composers of heroical ballads; I mean, by such as professedly wrote for the press. For it is to be observed, that so long as the Minstrels subsisted, they seem never to have designed their rhymes for literary publication, and probably never committed them to

---

badge of the family (a silver crescent on the right arm), and are thus distributed, viz. one for the barony of Prudhoe, and two for the barony of Rothbury. These attend the court leets and fairs held for the lord, and pay their annual suit and service at Alnwick Castle; their instrument being the ancient Northumberland bagpipe (very different in form and execution from that of the Scots, being smaller, and blown, not with the breath, but with a small pair of bellows). This, with many other venerable customs of the ancient Lords Percy, was revived by their illustrious representatives, the late Duke and Duchess of Northumberland.

writing themselves: what copies are preserved of them were doubtless taken down from their mouths. But as the old Minstrels gradually wore out, a new race of Ballad-writers succeeded, an inferior sort of minor poets, who wrote narrative songs merely for the press. Instances of both may be found in the reign of Elizabeth. The two latest pieces in the genuine strain of the old Minstrelsy that I can discover, are Nos. III. and IV. of Book III. in this volume. Lower than these I cannot trace the old mode of writing.

The old Minstrel ballads are in the northern dialect, abound with antique words and phrases, are extremely incorrect, and run into the utmost licence of metre; they have also a romantic wildness, and are in the true spirit of chivalry. The other sort are written in exacter measure, have a low or subordinate correctness, sometimes bordering on the insipid, yet often well adapted to the pathetic; these are generally in the southern dialect, exhibit a more modern phraseology, and are commonly descriptive of more modern manners. To be sensible of the difference between them, let the reader compare in this volume No. III. of Book III. with No. XI. of Book II.

Towards the end of Queen Elizabeth's reign (as is mentioned above), the genuine old Minstrelsy seems to have become extinct, and thenceforth the Ballads that were produced were wholly of the latter kind, and these came forth in such abundance, that in the reign of James I. they began to be collected into little miscellanies, under the name of Garlands, and at length to be written purposely for such collections.

# RELIQUES OF ANCIENT POETRY, ETC.

## SERIES THE FIRST.—BOOK I.

"I never heard the old song of *Percie and Douglas*, that I found not my heart moved more than with a trumpet: and yet 'it' is sung but by some blinde crowder, with no rougher voice, than rude style; which beeing so evill apparelled in the dust and cobweb of that uncivill age, what would it work, trimmed in the gorgeous eloquence of Pindare!"

Sir Philip Sidney's *Defence of Poetry*.

### I.—THE ANCIENT BALLAD OF CHEVY-CHASE.

The fine heroic song of *Chevy-Chase* has ever been admired by competent judges. Those genuine strokes of nature and artless passion which have endeared it to the most simple readers have recommended it to the most refined, and it has equally been the amusement of our childhood, and the favourite of our riper years.

Addison has given an excellent critique* on this ballad, but is mistaken with regard to the antiquity of the common-received copy; for this, if one may judge from the style, cannot be older than the time of Elizabeth, and was probably written after the eulogium of Sir Philip Sidney; perhaps in consequence of it. I flatter myself i have here recovered the genuine antique poem; the true original song, which appeared rude even in the time of Sir Philip, and caused him to lament that it was so evil-apparelled in the rugged garb of antiquity.

This curiosity is printed from an old MS. at the end of Hearne's *Gul. Newbrigiensis Hist.* 1719, 8vo, vol. i. To the MS. copy is subjoined the name of the author Rychard Sheale; whom Hearne supposed to be the same with a R. Sheale, who was living in 1588. But whoever examines the gradation of language and idiom in this volume, will be convinced that this is the production of an earlier poet. It is indeed expressly mentioned among some very ancient songs in an old book, *The Complaint of Scotland,*† under the title of the *Huntis of Chevet*, where the two following lines are also quoted:

"The Perssee and the Mongumrye mette,‡<br>
That day, that day, that gentil day,"§

which, though not quite the same as they stand in the ballad, yet differ not more

---

\* *Spectator*, Nos. 70, 74.
   † One of the earliest productions of the Scottish press. It is supposed to have been printed in 1540.
‡ See Fit ii. v. 25.          § See Fit i. v. 99.

than might be owing to the author's quoting from memory. Indeed, whoever considers the style and orthography of this old poem, will not be inclined to place it lower than the time of Henry VI.; as, on the other hand, the mention of James the Scottish king,* with one or two anachronisms, forbids us to assign it an earlier date. James I., who was a prisoner in this kingdom at the death of his father,† did not wear the crown of Scotland till the second year of our Henry VI.,‡ but before the end of that long reign a third James had mounted the throne. A succession of two or three Jameses, and the long detention of one of them in England, would render the name familiar to the English, and dispose a poet in those rude times to give it to any Scottish king he happened to mention.

So much for the date of this old ballad; with regard to its subject, although it has no countenance from history, there is room to think it had originally some foundation in fact. It was one of the laws of the marches, frequently renewed between the two nations, that neither party should hunt in the other's borders, without leave from the proprietors or their deputies. There had long been a rivalship between the two martial families of Percy and Douglas, which, heightened by the national quarrel, must have produced frequent challenges and struggles for superiority, petty invasions of their respective domains, and sharp contests for the point of honour, which would not always be recorded in history. Something of this kind, we may suppose, gave ..se to the ancient ballad of the *Hunting a' the Cheviat*.§ Percy, Earl of Northumberland, had vowed to hunt for three days in the Scottish border without condescending to ask leave from Earl Douglas, who was either lord of the soil, or lord warden of the marches. Douglas would not fail to resent the insult, and endeavour to repel the intruders by force; this would naturally produce a sharp conflict between the two parties; something of which, it is probable, did really happen, though not attended with the tragical circumstances recorded in the ballad; for these are evidently borrowed from the Battle of Otterbourn (see the next ballad),—a very different event, but which aftertimes would easily confound with it. That battle might be owing to some such previous affront as this of Chevy-Chase, though it has escaped the notice of historians. Our poet has evidently jumbled the two subjects together; if indeed the lines‖ in which this mistake is made are not rather spurious, and the after-insertion of some person, who did not distinguish between the two stories.

Hearne has printed this ballad without any division of stanzas, in long lines, as he found it in the old written copy.

---

\* Fitt ii. v. 36, 140. † Who died Aug. 5, 1406, in the seventh year of our Henry IV.
‡ James I. was crowned 1424, murdered Feb. 1436-37.
§ This was the original title. See the ballad, Fitt i. v. 101; Fitt ii. v. 165.
‖ *Viae* Fitt ii. v. 167.

# THE ANCIENT BALLAD OF CHEVY-CHASE.

## THE FIRST FIT.*

The Persè owt of Northombarlande,
   And a vowe to God mayd he,
That he wolde hunte in the mountayns
   Off Chyviat within dayes thre,
In the *mauger* of doughtè Doglas,
   And all that ever with him be.

The fattiste hartes in all Cheviat
   He sayd he wold kill, and carry them
     away:
Be my *feth*, sayd the dougheti Doglas
   agayn,
I wyll *let* that hontyng yf that I may.

Then the Persè owt of Bamborowe cam,
   With him a myghtye meany;
With fifteen hundrith archares bold;
   The wear chosen out of *shyars* thre.†

This begane on a Monday at morn
   In Cheviat the hillys so *he;*
The chyld may rue that ys unborn,
   It was the mor pittè.

The dryvars thorowe the woodès went
   For to *reas* the dear;
Bomen *bickarte* uppone the *bent*
   With ther browd *aras* cleare.

Then the *wyld* thorowe the woodès went
   On every sydè *shear;*
Grea-hondes thorowe the *greves glent*
   For to kyll *thear* the dear.

*The* begane in Chyviat the hyls above
   *Yerly* on a Monynday;
*Be* that it drewe to the *oware* off *none*
   A hondrith fat hartes ded ther lay.

---

\* *Fit, fyt, fytte,* a part of a poem or a song.

† Three districts in Northumberland, which still go by the name of *shires,* and are all in the neighbourhood of *Cheviot.* These are—*Islandshire,* so named from Holy Island; *Norhamshire,* so called from the town and castle of Norham; and *Bamboroughshire,* the ward or hundred belonging to Bamborough Castle.

---

*The* blewe a *mort* uppone the bent,
   The *semblyd* on *sydis shear;*
To the *quyrry* then the Persè went
   To se the *bryttlynge* off the deare.

He sayd, It was the Duglas promys
   This day to meet me hear;
But I wyste he wold faylle *verament:*
   A gret *oth* the Persè swear.

At the laste a squyar of Northombelonde
   Lokyde at his hand full ny,
He was *war* ath the doughetie Doglas
   comynge:
With him a mightè meany,
Both with spear, "*byll,*" and brande:
   Yt was a myghti sight to se.
Hardyar men both off hart nar hande
   Wear dot in Christiantè.

The wear twenty hondrith spearmen good
   Withouten any fayle;
The wear borne along be the watter a
   Twyde,
I'th bowndes of Tividale.

Leave off the *brytlyng* of the dear, he
   sayde,
And to your bowys look ye tayk good
   heed;
For never sithe ye wear on your mothars
   borne
Had ye never so *mickle* need.

The dougheti Dogglas on a stede
   He rode att his men beforne;
His armor glytteryde as dyd a *glede;*
   A bolder *barne* was never born.

Tell me "what" men ye are, he says,
   O whos men that ye be:
Who gave youe leave to hunt in this
   Chyviat chays in the spyt of me:

The first mane that ever him an answear
   mayd,
   Yt was the good lord Persè:

We wyll not tell the what men we ar, he
 sayd,
Nor whos men that we be;
But we wyll *hount* hear in this chays
In the spyte of thyne, and of the.

The fattiste hartes in all Chyviat
We have kyld, and cast to carry them
 a-way.
Be my troth, sayd the doughtè Dogglas
 agayn,
Ther-for the *ton* of us shall *de* this day.

Then sayd the doughtè Doglas
Unto the lord Persè:
To kyll all thes giltless men,
A-las! it wear great pittè.

But, Persè, thowe art a lord of lande,
I am a *yerle* callyd within my contre;
Let all our men uppone a parti stande;
And do the battell off the and of me.

Nowe *Cristes cors* on his crowne, sayd the
 lord Persè,
Who-soever ther-to says nay.
Be my troth, doughtè Doglas, he says,
Thow shalt never se that day;

Nethar in Ynglonde, Skottlonde nar
 France,
Nor for no man of a woman born,
But and fortune be my chance,
I dar met him on man for on.\*

Then bespayke a squyar off Northombar-
 londe,
Ric. Wytharynton † was his nam;
It shall never be told in Sothe-Ynglonde,
 he says,
To kyng Herry the fourth for sham.

I *wat* youe byn great lordes *twaw*,
I am a poor squyar of lande;
I wyll never se my captayne fyght on a
 fylde,
And stande my-selffe, and looke on,
But whyll I may my weppone *welde*,
I wyll not "fayl" both harte and hande.

That day, that day, that dredfull day:
The first *fit* here I fynde.
And youe wyll here any mor *athe hountyng
 athe Chyviat*,
Yet *ys* ther mor behynde.

### THE SECOND FIT.

The Yngglishe men hade ther bowys
 yebent,
Ther hartes were good yenoughe;
The first of arros that the shote off,
Seven skore spear-men the sloughe.

Yet bydys the yerle Doglas uppon the bent,
A captayne good yenoughe,
And that was sene *verament*,
For he wrought hom both woo and
 wouche.

The Dogglas *pertyd* his *ost* in thre,
Lyk a cheffe cheften off pryde,
With *suar* speares off myghttè tre
The cum in on every syde.

Thrughe our Yngglishe archery
Gave many a wounde full wyde;
Many a *doughete* the *garde* to dy,
Which ganyde them no pryde.

The Yngglyshe men let thear bowys be,
And pulde owt brandes that wer bright;
It was a hevy syght to se
Bryght swordes on *basnites* lyght.

Thorowe ryche *male, and myne-ye-ple*
Many sterne\* the stroke downe streght:

---

\* Man to man.
† This is probably corrupted in the MS. for *Rog. Widdrington*, who was at the head of the family in the reign of King Edward III. There were several successively of the names of *Roger* and *Ralph*, but none of the name of *Richard*, as appears from the genealogies in the Heralds' Office.

\* Why should not *sterne* (star) be heroes or shining men of valour, even as *Degen*, sword or blade, stands in German for champion or hero? Blucher in the song is called the *alte Degen*, aged champion.

Many a freyke, that was full free,
  Ther undar foot dyd lyght.

At last the Duglas and the Persè met,
  Lyk to captayns of myght and mayne;
The *swapte togethar* tyll the both swat ·
  With swordes, that wear of *fyn myllan.*

Thes worthè *freckys* for to fyght
  Ther-*to the* wear full fayne,
Tyll the bloode owte off thear basnetes
    *sprente,*
  As ever dyd *heal* or *rayne.*

Holde the, Persè, sayd the Doglas,
  And *i'feth* I shall the brynge
Wher thowe shalte have a *yerls* wagis
  Of Jamy our Scottish kynge.

Thoue shalte have thy ransom fre,
  I *hight* the hear this thinge,
For the manfullyste man yet art thowe,
  That ever I conqueryd in filde fightyng.

Nay "then," sayd the lord Persè,
  I tolde it the beforne,
That I wolde never *yeldyde* be
  To no man of a woman born.

With that ther cam an arrowe hastely
  Forthe off a mightie wane,*
Hit hathe strekene the yerle Duglas
  In at the brest bane.

Thoroue *lyvar* and *longs* bathe
  The sharp arrowe ys gane,
That never after in all his lyffe days,
  He spayke mo wordes but ane,
That was, Fyghte ye, my merry men,
    whyllys ye may,
  For my lyff days ben *gan*.

The Persè leanyde on his brande,
  And sawe the Duglas de;
He tooke the dede man be the hande,
  And sayd, Wo ys me for the!

To have savyde thy lyffe I wold have
    pertyd with
  My landes for years thre,
For a better man of hart, nare of hande,
  Was not in all the north countrè,

Off all that se a Skottishe knyght,
  Was callyd Sir Hewe the Mongon-
    byrry,
He sawe the Duglas to the deth was
    dyght;
  He *spendyd* a spear a trusti tre:

He rod uppon a *corsiare*
  Throughe a *hondrith* archery;
He never *styntyde*, nar never *blane,*
  Tyll he cam to the good lord Persè.

He set uppone the lord Persè
  A *dynte,* that was full soare;
With a *suar* spear of a myghtè tre
  Clean thorow the body he the Persè
    bore,

*Athe tothar* syde, that a man myght se,
  A large cloth yard and mare:
*Towe* bettar captayns wear nat in
    Christiantè,
  Then that day slain wear ther.

An archar off Northomberlonde
  *Say slean* was the lord Persè,
He bar a bende-bow in his hande,
  Was made off trusti tre:

An arow, that a cloth yarde was lang,
  To th' hard stele *halyde* he;
A *dynt,* that was both sad and soar,
  He sat on Sir Hewe the Mongon-byrry.

The dynt yt was both sad and sar,
  That he of Mongon-byrry sete;
The swane-fethars, that his arrowe bar,
  With his hart blood the wear wete.†

---

* *Wane, i.e. ane,* one, sc. man: an arrow came from a mighty one, from a mighty man.

† This incident is taken from the Battle of Otterbourne, in which Sir Hugh Montgomery, knight (son of John, Lord Montgomery), was slain with an arrow. See Crawford's *Peerage.*

Ther was never a *freake wone* foot wolde
   fle,
But still in *stour* dyd stand,
Heawyng on *yche* othar, whyll the myght
   dre,
With many a bal-ful brande.

This battell begane in Chyviat
   An *owar* befor the none,
And when even-song bell was rang
   The battell was nat half done.

The tooke " on " on ethar hand
   Be the lyght off the mone ;
Many hade no strenght for to stande,
   In Chyviat the *hyllys* aboun.

Of fifteen hondrith archars of Ynglonde
   Went away but fifti and thre ;
Of twenty hondrith spear-men of Skot-
   londe,
   But even five and fifti :

But all wear slayne Cheviat within :
   The hade no strengthe to stand on *hie* ;
The *chylde* may rue that ys un-borne,
   It was the mor pittè.

Thear was slayne with the lord Persè
   Sir John of Agerstone,\*
Sir Roge the *hinde* Hartly,
   Sir Wyllyam the bolde Hearone.†

Sir *Jorg* the worthè Lovelè‡
   A knyght of great renowen,
Sir *Raff* the ryche Rugbè §
   With dyntes wear beaten dowene.

---

\* Haggerston of Haggerston, near Berwick. The name is also spelt Agerstone in Leland's *Itinerary*.
† *Hearone* or *Heron*, a family of great antiquity in Northumberland.
‡ De Lavale or de Lovel, probably of the ancient family of Delaval, of Seaton Delaval, Northumberland.
§ Probably Rokeby, Ralph being a common name in the Rokeby family. Another suggestion is, Ralph Neville of Raby Castle, Durham.

For Wetharryngton\* my harte was wo,
   That ever he slayne shulde be ;
For when both his leggis wear hewyne in
   to,
   Yet he knyled and fought on hys kne.

Ther was slayne with the dougheti
   Douglas
Sir Hewe the Mongon-byrry,
Sir Davye Lwdale,† that worthè was,
   His sistars son was he :

Sir Charles a Murrè,‡ in that place,
   That never a foot wolde fle ;
Sir Hewe Maxwell, a lorde he was,
   With the Duglas dyd he dey.

So on the morrowe the mayde them
   *byears*
Off byrch, and *hasell* so "gray" ;
Many *wedous* with wepyng tears
   Cam to fach ther makys a-way.

Tivydale may *carpe* off care,
Northombarlond may mayk grat mone,
For towe such captayns, as slayne wear
   thear,
   On the march perti shall never be none.

Word ys commen to Edden-burrowe,§
   To Jamy the Skottishe kyng,
That dougheti Duglas, lyff-tenant of the
   Merches,‖
   He lay slean Chyviot with-in.

His handdes dyd he weal and wryng,
   He sayd, Alas, and woe ys me !
Such another captayn Skotland within,
   He sayd, y-feth shuld never be.

Worde ys commyn to lovly Londone
   Till the fourth Harry our kyng,

---

\* Wydrington or Witherington.
† Liddell ; lords of Liddell Castle and of the barony of Buff.
‡ Sir Charles Murray of Cockpoole, ancestor of the Murrays, Earls of Annandale.
§ Edinburgh.
‖ Life-tenant of the Marches.

That lord Persè, leyff-tennante of the
  Merchis,
He lay slayne Chyviat within.

God have merci on his soll, sayd kyng
  Harry,
Good lord, yf thy will it be!
I have a hondrith captayns in Ynglonde,
  he sayd,
As good as ever was hee :
But Persè, and I *brook* my lyffe,
  Thy deth well *quyte* shall be.

As our noble kyng made his a-vowe,
  Lyke a noble prince of renowen,
For the deth of the lord Persè,
  He dyd the battel of Hombyll-down :\*

Wher syx and thritte Skottish knyghtes
  On a day wear beaten down :
Glendale glytteryde on ther armor bryght,
  Over castill, towar, and town.

This was the hontynge off the Cheviat ;
  That *tear* begane this *spurn:*
Old men that knowen the grownde well
  yenoughe,
  Call it the Battell of Otterburn.

\* Humbledon.

At Otterburn began this spurne
  Uppon a *monnyn* day :
Ther was the dougghtè Doglas slean,
  The Persè never went away.

Ther was never a tym on the march partes
  Sen the Doglas and the Persè met,
But yt was marvele, and the redde blude
  ronne not,
As the *reane* doys in the stret.

Jhesue Christ our *balys bete*,
  And to the *blys* us brynge !
Thus was the hountynge of the Chevyat,
  God send us all good ending !

The Battle of Hombyll-down, or Humbledon, was fought Sept. 14, 1402 (anno 3 Henry IV.), wherein the English, under the command of the Earl of Northumberland, and his son Hotspur, gained a complete victory over the Scots. The village of Humbledon is one mile northwest from Wooler, in Northumberland. The battle was fought in a field below the village, near the present turnpike road, in a spot called *Battle-Riggs* or *Red-Riggs*. Humbledon is in Glendale Ward, a district so named in this county, and mentioned above in ver. 163.

## II.—THE BATTLE OF OTTERBOURNE.

The only battle wherein an Earl of Douglas was slain fighting with a Percy was that of Otterbourne, which is the subject of this ballad. It is here related with the allowable partiality of an English poet, and much as it is recorded in the *English Chronicles*. The Scottish writers have, with a partiality at least as excusable, related it no less in their own favour. Luckily, we have a very circumstantial narrative of the whole affair from Froissart, a French historian, who appears to be unbiassed, and his account carries with it a great appearance of truth. He gives the victory to the Scots, but does justice to the courage of both parties ; and represents their mutual generosity in such a light that the present age might edify by the example.

The Battle of Otterbourne was fought on the 9th or 15th of August, in the twelfth year of Richard II., 1388. The Scots, taking advantage of the confusion into which England had fallen, ravaged the country about Carlisle, and carried off 300 prisoners. Afterwards they invaded Northumberland, wasted part of Durham, and advanced to the gates of Newcastle, capturing a pennon belonging to Henry, Lord Percy. On their return home they attacked a castle near Otterbourne, were surprised by Henry, Lord Percy, son of the Earl of Northumberland, and thence ensued one of the best fought actions of the age, both armies showing the greatest bravery. The Earl of Douglas was slain on the spot, the Earl of Murray mortally wounded, and Henry Percy and his brother Ralph were taken prisoners. Froissart maintains that the Scotch remained masters of the field, whilst English writers give the victory to the English.

The ballad in the present edition is given from an old MS. in the Cotton Library (Cleopatra, c. iv.).

Yt felle *abowght* the Lamasse tyde,\*
Whan husbonds wynn ther haye,†
The dowghtye Dowglasse bowynd him to ryde,
In Ynglond to take a *praye:*

The *yerlle* of Fyffe,‡ *withowghten stryffe,*
He *bowynd* hym over Sulway : §
The grete wolde ever together ryde ;
That race they may rue for aye.

Over "Ottercap" *hyll* they ‖ came in,
And so dowyn by Rodelyffecragge.

\* Lammas-tide.—August 1st, Lammas-day. In Midlothian there were curious customs observed at Lammas-tide, which gave rise to the building of the Lammas towers. These were built by the herdsmen, who made mock raids on each other, and tried to raze the opponents' tower to the ground. Thus we see that in their sports a martial spirit was engendered, which fitted the southern counties of Scotland for more serious encounters.

† "Winn their heaye." Harl. MS. This is the Northumberland phrase to this day, by which they always express "getting in their hay."

‡ Robert Stuart, second son of King Robert II.

§ *i.e.* "Over Solway frith." This evidently refers to the other division of the Scottish army, which came in by way of Carlisle.

‖ The Earl of Douglas and his party. Well-known places in Northumberland. Ottercap Hill is in the parish of Kirk-Whelpington, in Tynedale Ward. Rodeliffe (or, as it is more usually pronounced, Rodeley) Cragge is a noted cliff near Rodeley, a small village in the parish of Hartburn, in Morpeth Ward. Green Leyton is another small village in the same parish of Hartburn, south-east of Rodeley.

Upon Grene "Leyton" they lyghted dowyn,
*Styrande* many a stagge ;

And boldely *brente* Northomberlonde,
And *haryed* many a towyn ;
They dyd owr Ynglyssh men grete wrange,
To battell that were not *bowyn*.

Than spake a *berne* upon the *bent,*
Of comforte that was not colde,
And sayd, We have brent Northomberlond,
We have all welth in holde.

Now we have haryed all Bamboroweshyre,
All the welth in the worlde have wee ;
I rede we ryde to Newe Castell,\*
So *styll* and *stalwurthlye.*

Uppon the morowe, when it was daye,
The standards schone fulle bryght ;
To the Newe Castelle the toke the waye,
And thether they cam fulle ryght.

Sir Henry Percy laye at the Newe Castelle,
I telle yow withowtten drede ;
He had *byn* a march-man † all hys dayes,
And kepte Barwyke upon Twede.‡

To the Newe Castell when they cam,
The *Skottes* they *cryde on hyght,*
Syr Harye Percy, and thow *byste* within,
Com to the fylde, and fyght :

---

\* Newcastle.
† Marche-man, *i.e.* a scowrer of the marches.
‡ Berwick-on-Tweed.

For we have brente Northomberlonde,
  Thy eritage good and ryght ;
And syne * my *logeyng* I have take,
  With my *brande* dubbyd many a knyght.

Sir Harry Percy cam to the walles,
  The Skottyssh *oste* for to se ;
"And thow hast brent Northomberlond,
  Full sore it *rewyth* me.

"Yf thou hast haryed all Bambarowe
    shyre,†
  Thow hast done me grete envye ;
For the trespasse thow hast me done,
  The tone of us schall dye."

Where schall I *byde* the ? sayd the
    Dowglas,
  Or where wylte thow come to me ?
"At Otterborne in the hygh way,‡
  Ther maist thow well logeed be.

"The roo full *rekeles* ther sche *rinnes*,
  To make the game and glee :
The *fawkon* and the *fesaunt* both,
  Amonge on the *holtes* on 'hee.'

"Ther maist thow have thy welth at wyll,
  Well looged ther maist be.
Yt schall not be long, or I com *the tyll*,"
  Sayd Syr Harry Percye.

Ther schall I byde the, sayd the Dowglas,
  By the fayth of my bodye.
Thether schall I com, sayd Syr Harry
    Percy ;
  My trowth I plyght to the.

A pype of wyne he gave them over the
    walles,
  For soth, as I yow saye :

---

\* *Syne* seems here to mean since.
† Bamboroughshire, so called from the town and castle of Bamborough, formerly the residence of the Northumbrian kings.
‡ Otterbourn is near the old Watling Street Road, in the parish of Elsdon. The Scots were encamped in a grassy plain near the river Read. The place where the Scotch and English fought is still called Battle Riggs.

Ther he mayd the Douglas drynke,
  And all hys oste that daye.

The Dowglas turnyd him homewarde
    agayne,
  For soth withowghten naye,
He tooke his *logeyng* at Otterborne
  Uppon a Wedyns-day :

And ther he *pyght* hys standerd downn,
  Hys gettyng more and lesse,
And *syne* he warned hys men to goo
  To chose ther geldyngs *grosse*.

A Skottysshe knyght hoved upon the *bent*,
  A wache I dare well saye :
So was he ware on the noble Percy
  In the dawnynge of the daye.

He prycked to his *pavyleon dore*,
  As faste as he myght *ronne*,
Awaken, Dowglas, cryed the knyght,
  For hys love that syttes yn trone.\*

Awaken, Dowglas, cryed the knyght,
  For thow *maiste* waken wyth *wynne* :
Yender have I spyed the prowde Percy,
  And seven standardes wyth hym.

Nay by my trowth, the Douglas sayed,
  It ys but a *fayned taylle* :
He durste not loke on my *bred* banner,
  For all Ynglonde so haylle.†

Was I not yesterdaye at the Newe Castell,
  That stonds so fayre on Tyne ?
For all the men the Percy hade,
  He cowde not *garre* me ones to dyne.

He stepped owt at hys pavelyon dore,
  To loke and it were *lesse ;*
Araye yow, lordyngs, one and all,
  For here bygynnes no *peysse*.

The yerle of Mentaye,‡ thow arte my *eme*,
  The *forwarde* I gyve to the :

---

\* Sits upon the throne.
† To gain.
‡ The Earl of Menteith.

The yerlle of Huntlay, *cawte* and kene,
   He schall wyth the be.

The lorde of Bowghan * in armure bryght
   On the other hand he schall be ;
Lorde Jhonstone, and lorde Maxwell,†
   They to schall be with me.

Swynton ‡ fayre fylde upon your pryde
   To batell make yow *bowen :*
Syr Davy Scotte,§ Syr Walter Stewarde,
   Syr Jhon of Agurstone.
        A FYTTE.

The Perssy came byfore hys oste,
   Wych was ever a gentyll knyght,
Upon the Dowglas lowde can he crye,
   I wyll holde that I have *hyght :*

For thow haste brente Northumberlonde,
   And done me grete envye ;
For thys trespasse thou hast me done,
   The tone of us schall dye.

The Dowglas answerde hym agayne
   With grete wurds up on "hee,"
And sayd, I have twenty agaynst "thy" one,
   Byholde and thow maiste see.

Wyth that the Percye was *grevyd* sore,
   For soothe as I yow saye :
‖[He lyghted dowyn upon his fote,
   And *schoote* his horsse clene away.

Every man sawe that he dyd soo,
   That ryall was ever in *rowght ;*

---

\* The Lord Buchan.
† The families of Johnstone and Maxwell were always powerful on the borders.
‡ Swinton is a small village within the Scotch border. The family of Swinton still exists, and is very ancient.
§ Sir David Scott, one of the ancestors of the Dukes of Buccleuch.
‖ All that follows included in brackets was not in the first edition.

Every man schoote hys horsse him froo,
   And lyght hym *rowynde* abowght.

Thus Syr Hary Percye toke the fylde,
   For soth, as I yow saye :
Jesu Cryste in hevyn on hyght
   Dyd helpe hym well that daye.

But *nyne* thowzand, ther was no moo ;
   The *cronykle* wyll not *layne :*
Forty thowsande Skottes and fowre
   That day fowght them agayne.

But when the batell byganne to joyne,
   In hast ther came a knyght,
"Then" letters fayre furth hath he tayne,
   And thus he sayd full ryght :

My lorde, your father he gretes yow well,
   Wyth many a noble knyght ;
And he desyres yow to byde
   That he may see thys fyght.

The Baron of Grastoke ys com owt of the west,
   Wyth hym a noble companye ;
All they loge at your fathers thys nyght,
   And the Battel fayne wold they see.

For Jesu's love, sayd Syr Harye Percy,
   That dyed for yow and me,
*Wende* to my lorde my Father agayne,
   And saye thow saw me not with yee :

My trowth ys plyght to yonne Skottysh knyght,
   It needes me not to layne,
That I schulde byde hym upon thys bent,
   And I have hys trowth agayne :

And if that I *wende* off thys grownde
   For soth unfoughten awaye,
He wolde me call but a kowarde knyght
   In hys londe another daye.

Yet had I *lever* to be *rynde* and rente,
   By Mary that mykel maye ;
Then ever my manhod schulde be reprovyd
   Wyth a Skotte another daye.

# THE BATTLE OF OTTERBOURNE.

Wherfore *schote*, archars, for my sake,
   And let scharpe arowes flee :
Mynstrells, playe up for your *waryson*,
   And well quyt it schall be.

Every man thynke on hys trewe love,
   And marke hym to the Trenite :
For to God I make myne avowe
   Thys day wyll I not fle.

The blodye Harte in the Dowglas armes,
   Hys standerde stode on hye ;
That every man myght full well knowe :
   By syde stode Starres thre :

The whyte Lyon on the Ynglysh parte,
   Forsoth as I yow sayne ;
The Lucetts and the Cressawnts both :
   The Skotts faught them agayne.]*

Upponsent Andrewe lowde cane they crye,
   And thrysse they schowte on hyght,
And syne marked them one owr Ynglysshe men,
   As I have tolde yow ryght.

Sent George the bryght owr ladyes knyght,
   To name they were full fayne,
Owr Ynglysshe men they cryde on hyght,
   And thrysse the schowtte agayne.

Wyth that scharpe arowes bygan to flee,
   I tell yow in sertayne ;
Men of armes byganne to joyne ;
   Many a dowghty man was ther slayne.

The Percy and the Dowglas mette,
   That ether of other was fayne ;

---

\* The ancient arms of Douglas are pretty accurately emblazoned in the former stanza, and if the readings were, "The crowned harte," and "Above stode starres thre," it would be minutely exact at this day. As for the Percy family, one of their ancient badges or cognizances was *a white lyon statant*, and the *silver crescent* continues to be used by them to this day ; they also give *three luces argent* for one of their quarters.

They schapped together, whyll that the swette,
   With swords of fyne Collayne ; *

Tyll the bloode from ther *bassonetts* ranne,
   As the roke doth in the rayne.
Yelde the to me, sayd the Dowglàs,
   Or ells thow schalt be slayne :

For I see, by thy bryght bassonet,
   Thow arte sum man of myght ;
And so I do by thy burnysshed *brande*,
   Thow art an yerle, or ells a knyght.

By my good faythe, sayd the noble Percy,
   Now haste thou rede full ryght,
Yet wyll I never yelde me to the,
   Whyll I may stonde and fyght.

They swapped together, whyll that they swette,
   Wyth swordes scharpe and long ;
Ych on other so faste they beette,
   Tyll ther helmes cam in peyses dowyn.

The Percy was a man of strenghth,
   I tell yow in thys *stounde*,
He smote the Dowglas at the swordes length,
   That he felle to the growynde.

The sworde was scharpe and sore can byte,
   I tell yow in sertayne ;
To the harte, he cowde hym smyte,
   Thus was the Dowglas slayne.

The stonderds stode styll on eke syde,
   With many a grevous grone ;
Ther they fowght the day, and all the nyght,
   And many a dowghty man was "slone."

Ther was no *freke*, that ther wolde flye,
   But styffly in *stowre* can stond,
Ychone hewyng on other whyll they myght drye,
   Wyth many a bayllefull *bronde*.

---

\* Cologne steel.

Ther was slayne upon the Skottes syde,
  For soth and sertenly,
Syr James a Dowglas ther was slayne,
  That daye that he cowde dye.

The yerlle Mentaye of he was slayne,
  Grysely groned uppon the growynd;
Syr Davy Scotte, Syr Walter Steward,*
  Syr "John" of Augurstonne.

Syr Charlles Morrey in that place,
  That never a fote wold flye;
Sir Hughe Maxwell, a lorde he was,
  With the Dowglas dyd he dye.

Ther was slayne upon the Skottes syde,
  For soth as I yow saye,
Of fowre and forty thowsande Scotts
  Went but cyghtene awaye.

Ther was slayne upon the Ynglysshe syde,
  For soth and sertenlye,
A gentell knyght, Sir John Fitz-hughe,†
  Yt was the more petye.

Syr James Harebotell ther was slayne,
  For hym ther hartes were sore,
The gentyll "Lovelle" ther was slayne,
  That the Perceyes standerd bore.

---

\* Stewart, Lord of Dalswinton.
† *Fitz-hughe* and *Harebotell* are Northumbrian families. Harbottle is a village upon the river Coquet, and gives its name to the family.

Ther was slayne uppon the Ynglyssl perte,
  For soth as I yow saye;
Of nyne thowsand Ynglyssh men
  Fyve hondert cam awaye:

The other were slayne in the fylde,
  Cryste kepe their sowles from wo,
Seyng ther was so fewe fryndes
  Agaynst so many a foo.

Then one the morne they mayd them beeres
  Of byrch, and *haysell* graye;
Many a wydowe with wepyng teyres
  Ther makes they fette awaye.

Thys fraye bygan at Otterborne,
  Bytwene the nyghte and the day:
Ther the Dowglas lost his lyfe,
  And the Percy was lede awaye.*

Then was ther a Scottyshe prisoner tayne,
  Syr Hughe Mongomery was hys name,
For soth as I yow saye,
  He borowed the Percy home agayne.†

Now let us all for the Percy praye
  To Jesu most of myght,
To bryng hys sowle to the blysse of heven,
  For he was a gentyll knyght.

---

\* Sc. captive.
† "Syr Hewe Mongomery takyn prizonar, was delyvered for the restorynge of Perssy."—See Cotton MS.

## III.—THE JEW'S DAUGHTER,*

### A SCOTTISH BALLAD,

Is founded upon the supposed practice of the Jews in crucifying or otherwise murthering Christian children, out of hatred to the religion of their parents: a practice which hath been always alleged in excuse for the cruelties exercised upon that wretched people, but which probably never happened in a single instance.

  The following ballad is probably built upon some Italian legend, and bears a great resemblance to the *Prioresse's Tale* in Chaucer. The poet seems also to have had

---

\* Printed from a MS. copy sent from Scotland.

an eye to the known story of *Hugh of Lincoln*, a child said to have been there murthered by the Jews in the reign of Henry III.

Bishop Percy says that *Mirry-land toune* is a corruption of Milan, and *Pa* stands for Po. Another commentator suggests, and it would seem with better reason, that "Lincoln is meant—Merry Lincoln corrupted into Merry Lin-town."

Everything seems to point to this. Doubtless the legend of Hugh of Lincoln's murder gave rise to the ballad, the name of the child being *Hew*. There is at Lincoln "the Jew's house," a curious piece of architecture, said to have been originally possessed by Belassel de Wallingford, a Jewess who was hanged for clipping in the reign of Edward I., and of whom doubtless many stories, true and false, were handed down to posterity. The *Pa* may be an abbreviation of palace,—John of Gaunt's palace, or the Bishop's palace of those days.

Ball-play in ancient days in England was a famous game, partaken of by all classes, and less likely to be played in Italy on account of the exertion required.

THE rain rins doun through Mirry-land toune,
Sae dois it doune the Pa :
Sae dois the lads of Mirry-land toune,
Quhan they play at the ba'.

Than out and cam the Jewis *dochtèr*,
Said, Will ye cum in and dine ?
'I winnae cum in, I cannae cum in,
Without my *play-feres* nine."

*Scho powd* an apple reid and white
To intice the zong thing in :
Scho powd an apple white and reid,
And that the sweit bairne did win.

And scho has taine out a little pen-knife,
And low down by her *gair*,
Scho has twin'd the zong thing and his life ;
A word he nevir spak mair.

And out and cam the thick thick bluid,
And out and cam the thin ;
And out and cam the bonny herts bluid :
Thair was nae life left in.

Scho laid him on a dressing borde,
And drest him like a swine,
And laughing said, Gae nou and pley
With zour sweit play-feres nine.

Scho *rowd* him in a cake of lead,
Bade him lie stil and sleip.

Scho cast him in a deip draw-well,
Was fifty fadom deip.

*Quhan* bells wer rung, and mass was sung,
And every lady went hame :
Than *ilka* lady had her zong sonne,
Bot lady Helen had nane.

Scho rowd hir mantil hir about,
And sair sair gan she weip :
And she ran into the Jewis castèl,
Quhan they wer all asleip.

My bonny sir Hew, my pretty sir Hew,
I pray thee to me speik.
"O lady, rinn to the deip draw-well,
Gin ze zour sonne wad seik."

Lady Helen ran to the deip draw-well,
And knelt upon her kne :
My bonny sir Hew, an ze be heire,
I pray thee speik to me.

"The lead is wondrous heavy, mither,
The well is wondrous deip,
A keen pen-knife sticks in my hert,
A word I dounae speik.

"Gae hame, gae hame, my mither deir,
Fetch me my windeing sheet,
And at the back o' Mirry-land toun
Its thair we twa sall meet."

. . . . . .

## IV.—SIR CAULINE.

It may be proper to inform the reader, before he comes to Pt. II., v. 110, 111, that the round table was not peculiar to the reign of King Arthur, but was common in all the ages of chivalry. The proclaiming a great tournament (probably with some peculiar solemnities) was called "holding a round table."

This ballad is given in its original form in the folio edition, together with Bishop Percy's own version, which is the one here printed. There are two opening verses of the original not given here, then the original is quoted up to verse 140, with a few interpolations by the bishop, after which he proceeds with the ending of the story in his own fashion. In the original fragment the ending is less tragical. Sir Cauline not only conquers the pagan giant, but, unarmed, he kills a lion by thrusting his mantle down its throat. He then marries the king's daughter, who bears him fifteen sons.

Sir Cauline may possibly have been founded on the legend of Charlemagne's daughter and the Secretary Eginhardt. There are many points of resemblance in the story, with the exception of the one winning by deeds of valour what the other gained through learning and scholarship.

As to what will be observed in this ballad of the art of healing being practised by a young princess, it is no more than what is usual in all the old romances, and was conformable to real manners; it being a practice derived from the earliest times among all the Gothic and Celtic nations, for women, even of the highest rank, to exercise the art of surgery.

### THE FIRST PART.

In Ireland, ferr over the sea,
  There dwelleth a bonnye kinge;
And with him a yong and comlye knighte,
  Men call him syr Cauline.

The kinge had a ladye to his daughter,
  In fashyon she hath no peere;
And princely wightes that ladye wooed
  To be theyr wedded *feere*.

Syr Cauline loveth her best of all,
  But nothing durst he saye;
Ne *descreeve* his counsayl to no man,
  But deerlye he lovde this *may*.

Till on a daye it so beffell,
  Great *dill* to him was dight;
The maydens love removde his mynd,
  To care-bed went the knighte.

One while he spred his armes him fro,
  One while he spred them nye:
And aye! but I winne that ladyes love,
  For *dole* now I mun dye.

And whan our parish-masse was done,
  Our kinge was bowne to dyne:
He sayes, Where is syr Cauline,
  That is wont to serve the wyne?

Then aunswerde him a courteous knighte,
  And fast his handes gan wringe:
Sir Cauline is sicke, and like to dye
  Without a good *leechinge*.

Fetche me downe my daughter deere,
  She is a *leeche* fulle fine:
Goe take him doughe, and the baken bread,
And serve him with the wyne soe red;
  Lothe I were him to *tine*.

Fair Christabelle to his chaumber goes,
  Her maydens followyng nye:

O well, she sayth, how doth my lord?
  O sicke, thou fayr ladyè.

Nowe ryse up *wightlye*, man, for shame,
  Never lye soe cowardlee;
For it is told in my fathers halle,
  You dye for love of mee.

Fayre ladye, it is for your love
  That all this dill I *drye:*
For if you wold comfort me with a kisse,
  Then were I brought from *bale* to blisse,
  No lenger wold I lye.

Sir knighte, my father is a kinge,
  I am his onlye heire;
Alas! and well you knowe, syr knighte,
  I never can be youre *fere.*

O ladye, thou art a kinges daughtèr,
  And I am not thy peere,
But let me doe some deedes of armes
  To be your *bacheleere.*

Some deedes of armes if thou wilt doe,
  My bacheleere to bee,
But ever and aye my heart wold rue,
  Giff harm shold happe to thee,)

Upon Eldridge hill there groweth a thorne,
  Upon the *mores brodinge;*
And dare ye, syr knighte, wake there all nighte
  Untill the fayre morninge?

For the Eldridge knighte, so *mickle* of mighte,
  Will examine you beforne:
And never man bare life awaye,
  But he did him *scath* and scorne.

That knighte he is a foul paynim,
  And large of limb and bone;
And but if heaven may be thy speede,
  Thy life it is but gone.

Nowe on the Eldridge hilles Ile walke,[*]
  For thy sake, fair ladie;

---
[*] Perhaps *wake*, as in ver. 61.

And Ile either bring you a ready tokèn,
  Or Ile never more you see.

The lady is gone to her own chaumbère,
  Her maydens following bright:
Syr Cauline *lope* from care-bed soone,
And to the Eldridge hills is gone,
  For to wake there all night.

Unto midnight, that the moone did rise,
  He walked up and downe;
Then a lightsome bugle heard he blowe
  Over the *bents* soe browne;
Quoth hee, If *cryance* come till my heart,
  I am ffar from any good towne.

And soone he spyde on the mores so broad,
  A furyous wight and fell;
A ladye bright his brydle led,
  Clad in a fayre kyrtèll:

And soe fast he called on syr Cauline,
  O man, I *rede* thee flye,
For "but" if cryance comes till my heart,
  I weene but thou mun dye.

He sayth, "No" *cryance* comes till my heart,
  Nor, in faith, I wyll not flee;
For, cause thou *minged* not Christ before,
  The less me dreadeth thee.

The Eldridge knighte, he pricked his steed;
  Syr Cauline bold abode:
Then either shooke his trustye speare,
And the timber these two children [*] bare
  Soe soone *in sunder slode.*

Then tooke they out theyr two good swordes,
  And layden on full faste,
Till helme and hawberke, mail and sheelde,
  They all were well-nye *brast.*

The Eldridge knight was mickle of might,
  And stiffe in *stower* did stande,

---
[*] *i.e.* knights.

But syr Cauline with a "backward" stroke
   He smote off his right hand ;
That soone he with paine and lacke of bloud
   Fell downe on that *lay-land*.

Then up syr Cauline lift his *brande*
   All over his head so hye :
And here I sweare by the holy *roode*,
   Nowe, caytiffe, thou shalt dye.

Then up and came that ladye brighte,
   Fast wringing of her hande :
For the maydens love, that most you love,
   Withold that deadlye brande :

For the maydens love, that most you love,
   Now smyte no more I praye ;
And aye whatever thou wilt, my lord,
   He shall thy hests obaye.

Now sweare to mee, thou Eldridge knighte,
   And here on this lay-land,
That thou wilt believe on Christ his *laye*,
   And therto plight thy hand :

And that thou never on Eldridge come
   To sporte, gamon, or playe :
And that thou here give up thy armes
   Until thy dying daye.

The Eldridge knighte gave up his armes
   With many a sorrowfulle sighe ;
And sware to obey syr Caulines hest,
   Till the tyme that he shold dye.

And he then up and the Eldridge knighte
   Sett him in his saddle anone,
And the Eldridge knighte and his ladye
   To theyr castle are they gone.

Then he tooke up the bloudy hand,
   That was so large of bone,
And on it he founde five ringes of gold
   Of knightes that had be *slone*.

Then he tooke up the Eldridge sworde,
   As hard as any flint :
And he tooke off those ringes five,
   As bright as fyre and *brent*.

Home then pricked syr Cauline
   As light as leafe on tree :
I-wys he neither *stint ne blanne*,
   Till he his ladye see.

Then downe he knelt upon his knee
   Before that lady gay :
O ladye, I have bin on the Eldridge hills :
   These tokens I bring away.

Now welcome, welcome, syr Cauline,
   Thrice welcome unto mee,
For now I perceive thou art a true knighte,
   Of valour bolde and free.

O ladye, I am thy own true knighte,
   Thy hests for to obaye :
And mought I hope to winne thy love !—
   Ne more his tonge colde say.

The ladye blushed scarlette redde,
   And *fette* a gentill sighe :
Alas ! syr knight, how may this bee,
   For my degree's soe highe ?

But *sith* thou hast *hight*, thou comely youth,
   To be my batchilere,
Ile promise if thee I may not wedde
   I will have none other fere.

Then shee held forthe her lilly-white hand
   Towards that knighte so free ;
He give to it one gentill kisse,
His heart was brought from bale to blisse,
   The teares *sterte* from his ee.

But keep my counsayl, syr Cauline,
   Ne let no man it knowe ;
For and ever my father sholde it ken,
   I wot he wolde us *sloe*.

From that daye forthe that ladye fayre
   *Lovde* syr Cauline the knighte :
From that daye forthe he only joyde
   Whan shee was in his sight.

Yea and oftentimes they mette
   Within a fayre arboure,
Where they in love and sweet daliaunce
   Past manye a pleasaunt houre.

## PART THE SECOND.

Everye white will have its blacke,
   And everye sweete its sowre:
This founde the ladye Christabelle
   In an untimely howre.

For so it befelle, as syr Cauline
   Was with that ladye faire,
The kinge her father walked forthe
   To take the evenyng aire:

And into the arboure as he went
   To rest his wearye feet,
He found his daughter and syr Caulіne
   There sette in daliaunce sweet.

The kinge hee sterted forthe, i-wys,
   And an angrye man was hee:
Nowe, traytoure, thou shalt hange or drawe,
   And *rewe* shall thy ladie.

Then forthe syr Cauline he was ledde,
   And throwne in dungeon deepe:
And the ladye into a towre so hye,
   There left to wayle and weepe.

The queene she was syr Caulines friend,
   And to the kinge sayd shee:
I praye you save syr Caulines life,
   And let him banisht bee.

Now, dame, that traitor shall be sent
   Across the salt sea fome:
But here I will make thee a band,
   If ever he come within this land,
A foule deathe is his doome.

All woe-begone was that gentil knight
   To parte from his ladyè;
And many a time he sighed sore,
   And cast a wistfulle eye:
Faire Christabelle, from thee to parte,
   Farre *lever* had I dye.

Faire Christabelle, that ladye bright,
   Was had forthe of the towre;

But ever shee droopeth in her minde,
   As nipt by an ungentle winde
Doth some faire lillye flowre.

And ever shee doth lament and weepe
   To *tint* her lover soe:
Syr Cauline, thou little think'st on mee,
   But I will still be true.

Manye a kinge, and manye a duke,
   And lorde of high degree,
Did sue to that fayre ladye of love;
   But never shee wolde them nee.

When manye a daye was past and gone,
   Ne comforte she colde finde,
The kynge proclaimed a tourneament,
   To cheere his daughters mind:

And there came lords, and there came knights,
   Fro manye a farre countryè,
To break a spere for theyr ladyes love
   Before that faire ladyè.

And many a ladye there was sette
   In *purple and in palle:*
But faire Christabelle soe woe-begone
   Was the fayrest of them all.

Then manye a knighte was mickle of might
   Before his ladye gaye;
But a stranger wight, whom no man knewe,
   He wan the prize eche daye.

His acton it was all of blacke,
   His hewberke, and his sheelde,
Ne noe man *wist* whence he did come,
Ne noe man knewe where he did gone,
   When they came from the feelde.

And now three days were *prestlye* past
   In feates of chivalrye,
When lo upon the fourth morninge
   A sorrowfulle sight they see.

A hugye giaunt *stiffe* and *starke*,
  All foule of limbe and *lere*;
Two goggling eyen like fire farden,
  A mouthe from eare to eare.

Before him came a dwarffe full lowe,
  That waited on his knee,
And at his backe five heads he bare,
  All wan and pale of *blee*.

Sir, quoth the dwarffe, and louted lowe,
  Behold that hend Soldàin!
Behold these heads I beare with me!
  They are kings which he hath slain.

The Eldridge knight is his own cousine,
  Whom a knight of thine hath *shent:*
And hee is come to avenge his wrong,
And to thee, all thy knightes among,
  Defiance here hath sent.

But yette he will appease his wrath
  Thy daughters love to winne:
And but thou yeelde him that fayre mayd,
  Thy halls and towers must *brenne*.

Thy head, syr king, must goe with mee;
  Or else thy daughter deere;
Or else within these lists soe broad
  Thou must finde him a peere.

The king he turned him round aboute,
  And in his heart was woe:
Is there never a knighte of my round tablè,
  This matter will undergoe?

Is there never a knighte amongst yee all
  Will fight for my daughter and mee?
Whoever will fight yon grimme *soldàn*,
  Right fair his *meede* shall bee.

For hee shall have my broad *lay-lands*,
  And of my crowne be heyre;
And he shall winne fayre Christabelle
  To be his wedded *fere*.

But every knighte of his round tablè
  Did stand both still and pale;

For whenever they lookt on the grim soldàn,
  It made their hearts to quail.

All woe-begone was that fayre ladyè,
  When she sawe no helpe was nye:
She cast her thought on her owne true-love,
  And the teares gusht from her eye.

Up then *sterte* the stranger knighte,
  Sayd, Ladye, be not affrayd:
Ile fight for thee with this grimme soldàn,
  Thoughe he be *unmacklye* made.

And if thou wilt lend me the Eldridge sworde,
  That lyeth within thy bowre,
I truste in Christe for to slay this fiende
  Thoughe he be stiff in stowre.

Goe fetch him downe the Eldridge sworde,
  The kinge he cryde, with speede:
Nowe heaven assist thee, courteous knighte;
  My daughter is thy meede.

The gyaunt he stepped into the lists,
  And sayd, Awaye, awaye:
I sweare, as I am the hend soldàn,
  Thou lettest me here all daye.

Then forthe the stranger knight he came
  In his blacke armoure dight:
The ladye sighed a gentle sighe,
  "That this were my true knighte!"

And nowe the gyaunt and knighte be mett
  Within the lists soe broad;
And now with swordes soe sharpe of steele,
  They gan to lay on load.

The soldan strucke the knighte a stroke,
  That made him reele asyde;
Then woe-begone was that fayre ladyè,
  And thrice she deeply sighde.

The soldan strucke a second stroke,
  And made the bloude to flowe:
All pale and wan was that ladye fayre,
  And thrice she wept for woe.

The soldan strucke a third fell stroke,
  Which brought the knighte on his knee:
Sad sorrow pierced that ladyes heart,
  And she shriekt loud shriekings three.

The knighte he leapt upon his feete,
  All recklesse of the pain:
Quoth hee, But heaven be now my speede,
  Or else I shall be slaine.

He grasped his sworde with mayne and mighte,
  And spying a secrette part,
He drave it into the soldan's syde,
  And pierced him to the heart.

Then all the people gave a shoute,
  Whan they sawe the soldan falle:
The ladye wept, and thanked Christ,
  That had reskewed her from thrall.

And nowe the kinge with all his barons
  Rose uppe from offe his seate,
And downe he stepped into the listes,
  That curteous knighte to greete.

But he for payne and lacke of bloude
  Was fallen into a swounde,
And there all walteringe in his gore,
  Lay lifelesse on the grounde.

Come downe, come downe, my daughter deare,
  Thou art a leeche of skille;

Farre lever had I lose halfe my landes,
  Than this good knighte sholde *spille*.

Downe then steppeth that fayre ladyè,
  To helpe him if she maye;
But when she did his beavere raise,
It is my life, my lord, she sayes,
  And shriekte and swound awaye.

Sir Cauline just lifte up his eyes
  When he heard his ladye crye,
O ladye, I am thine owne true love;
  For thee I wisht to dye.

Then giving her one partinge looke,
  He closed his eyes in death,
Ere Christabelle, that ladye milde,
  Begane to drawe her breathe.

But when she found her comelye knigète
  Indeed was dead and gone,
She layde her pale cold cheeke to his,
  And thus she made her moane:

O staye, my deare and onlye lord,
  For mee thy faithfulle feere;
'Tis meet that I shold followe thee,
  Who hast bought my love soe deare.

Then fayntinge in a deadlye swoune,
  And with a deepe-feete sighe,
That burst her gentle hearte in twayne,
  Fayre Christabelle did dye.

## V.—EDWARD, EDWARD.

### A SCOTTISH BALLAD.

*From a MS. copy transmitted from Scotland.*

Quhy dois *zour* brand sae drop wi' bluid,
  Edward, Edward?
Quhy dois zour brand sae drop wi' bluid?
  And quhy sae sad gang zee, O?
O, I hae killed my *hauke* sae guid,
  Mither, mither:
O, I hae killed my hauke sae guid:
  And I had nae mair bot hee, O.

Zour haukis *bluid* was nevir sae reid,
  Edward, Edward.
Zour haukis bluid was nevir sae reid,
  My deir son I tell thee, O.
O, I hae killed my reid-roan *steid*,
  Mither, mither:
O, I hae killed my reid-roan steid,
  That *erst* was sae fair and free, O.

Zour steid was auld, and ze hae gat mair,
  Edward, Edward:
Zour steid was auld, and ze hae gat mair,
  Sum other *dule ze drie*, O.
O, I hae killed my fadir deir,
  Mither, mither:
O, I hae killed my fadir deir,
  Alas! and wae is mee, O!

And *quhatten* penance wul ze drie for that,
  Edward, Edward?
And quhatten penance will ze drie for that?
  My deir son, now tell me, O.
He set my feit in zonder boat,
  Mither, mither:
He set my feit in zonder boat,
  And He fare ovir the sea, O.

And *quhat* wul ze doe wi' zour *towirs* and zour *ha'*,
  Edward, Edward?
And quhat wul ze doe wi' zour towirs and zour ha',
  That were sae fair to see, O?
He let *thame* stand til they doun fa',
  Mither, mither:
He let thame stand till they doun fa',
  For here nevir mair maun I bee, O.

And quhat wul ze leive to zour bairns and zour wife,
  Edward, Edward?
And quhat wul ze leive to zour bairns and zour wife,
  *Quhan* ze gang ovir the sea, O?
The warldis room, let thame beg throw life,
  Mither, mither:
The warldis room, let thame beg throw life,
  For thame nevir mair wul I see, O.

And quhat wul ze leive to zour ain mither deir,
  Edward, Edward?
And quhat wul ze leive to zour ain mither deir?
  My deir son, now tell me, O.
The curse of hell frae me sall ze beir,
  Mither, mither:
The curse of hell frae me sall ze beir,
  Sic counseils ze gave to me, O.

---

This curious song was transmitted to the Editor by Sir David Dalrymple, Bart., late Lord Hailes.

## VI.—KING ESTMERE.

THIS old romantic legend (partly from two copies) bears marks of considerable antiquity, and perhaps ought to have taken place of any in this volume. It appears to have been written while part of Spain was in the hands of the Saracens or Moors; whose empire there was not fully extinguished before the year 1491. The Mahometans are spoken of in ver. 49, etc., just in the same terms as in all other old romances.

I cannot help observing that the reader will see, in this ballad, the character of the old minstrels (those successors of the bards) placed in a very respectable light. The further we carry our inquiries back, the greater respect we find paid to the professors of poetry and music among all the Celtic and Gothic nations. Their character was deemed so sacred, that under its sanction our famous King Alfred (as we have already seen) made no scruple to enter the Danish camp, and was at once admitted to the king's headquarters. Our poet has suggested the same expedient to the heroes of this ballad. Even so late as the time of Froissart we find minstrels and heralds mentioned together as those who might securely go into an enemy's country.

As to Estmere's riding into the hall while the kings were at table, this was usual in the ages of chivalry; and even to this day we see a relic of this custom still kept up in the champion's riding into Westminster hall during the coronation dinner.

Some liberties have been taken with this tale by the editor, but none without notice to the reader in that part which relates to the subject of the harper and his attendant.

HEARKEN to me, gentlemen,
  Come and you shall heare;
Ile tell you of two of the boldest brethren
  That ever borne y-were.

The tone of them was Adler younge,
  The tother was kyng Estmere;
The were as bolde men in their deeds,
  As any were farr and neare.

As they were drinking ale and wine
  Within kyng Estmeres halle:
When will ye marry a wyfe, brother,
  A wyfe to glad us all?

Then bespake him kyng Estmere,
  And answered him hastilee:
I know not that ladye in any land
  That's able to marrye with mee.

Kyng Adland hath a daughter, brother,
  Men call her bright and *sheene;*
If I were kyng here in your stead,
  That ladye shold be my queene.

Saies, Reade me, reade me, deare brother,
  Throughout merry Englànd,
Where we might find a messenger
  Betwixt us towe to sende.

Saies, You shal ryde yourselfe, brother,
  Ile beare you companye;
Many throughe fals messengers are deceived,
  And I feare lest soe shold wee.

Thus the *renisht* them to ryde
  Of twoe good renisht steeds,
And when the came to king Adlands halle,
  Of redd gold shone their weeds.

And when the came to kyng Adlands hall
  Before the goodlye gate,

There they found good kyng Adlànd
  Rearing himselfe theratt.

Now Christ thee save, good kyng Adlànd;
  Now Christ you save and see.
Sayd, You be welcome, king Estmere,
  Right hartilye to mee.

You have a daughter, said Adler younge,
  Men call her bright and *sheene,*
My brother wold marrye her to his wiffe,
  Of Englande to be queene.

Yesterday was att my deere daughtèr
  Syr Bremor the kyng of Spayne;
And then she *nicked* him of naye,
  And I doubt sheele do you tne same.

The kyng of Spayne is a foule paynim,
  And 'leeveth on *Mahound;*
And pitye it were that fayre ladyè
  Shold marrye a heathen hound.

But grant to me, sayes kyng Estmere,
  For my love I you praye;
That I may see your daughter deere
  Before I goe hence awaye.

Although itt is seven yeers and more
  Since my daughter was in halle,
She shall come once downe for your sake
  To glad my guestès alle.

Downe then came that mayden fayre,
  With ladyes laced in *pall,*
And halfe a hundred of bold knightes,
  To bring her from bowre to hall;
And as many gentle squiers,
  To tend upon them all.

The *talents* of golde were on her head sette,
  Hanged low downe to her knee;

And everye ring on her small fingèr
  Shone of the chrystall free.

Saies, God you save, my deere madàm;
  Saies, God you save and see.
Said, You be welcome, kyng Estmere,
  Right welcome unto mee.

And if you love me, as you saye,
  Soe well and hartilèe,
All that ever you are comen about
  Soone sped now itt shal bee.

Then bespake her father deare:
  My daughter, I saye naye;
Remember well the kyng of Spayne,
  What he sayd yesterdaye.

He wold pull downe my halles and castles,
  And reave me of my lyfe.
I cannot blame him if he doe,
  If I *reave* him of his wyfe.

Your castles and your towres, father,
  Are stronglye built aboute;
And therefore of the king of Spaine
  Wee neede not stande in doubt.

Plight me your troth, nowe, kyng Estmère,
  By heaven and your righte hand,
That you will marrye me to your wyfe,
  And make me queene of your land.

Then kyng Estmere he plight his troth
  By heaven and his righte hand,
That he wolde marrye her to his wyfe,
  And make her queene of his land.

And he tooke leave of that ladye fayre,
  To goe to his owne countree,
To fetche him dukes and lordes and knightes,
  That marryed the might bee.

They had not ridden scant a myle,
  A myle forthe of the towne,
But in did come the kyng of Spayne,
  With *kempès* many one.

But in did come the kyng of Spayne,
  With manye a bold baròne,
*Tone* day to marrye kyng Adlands daughter,
  Tother daye to carrye her home.

Shee sent one after kyng Estmère
  In all the spede might bee,
That he must either turne againe and fighte,
  Or goe home and loose his ladyè.

One whyle then the page he went,
  Another while he ranne;
Till he had oretaken king Estmere,
  I wis, he never blanne.

Tydings, tydings, kyng Estmere!
  What tydinges nowe, my boye?
O tydinges I can tell to you,
  That will you sore annoye.

You had not ridden scant a mile,
  A mile out of the towne,
But in did come the kyng of Spayne
  With kempès many a one:

But in did come the kyng of Spayne
  With manye a bold baròne,
Tone daye to marrye king Adlands daughter,
  Tother daye to carry her home.

My ladye fayre she greetes you well,
  And ever-more well by mee:
You must either turne againe and fighte,
  Or goe home and loose your ladyè.

Saies, *Reade* me, reade me, deere brothèr,
  My reade shall ryde* at thee,
Whether it is better to turne and fighte,
  Or goe home and loose my ladye.

Now hearken to me, sayes Adler yonge,
  And your reade must rise at me,
I quicklye will devise a waye
  To sette thy ladye free.

---

* *Sic* MS. It should probably be *ryse*, *i.e.* my counsel shall arise from thee. See v. 140.

My mother was a westerne woman,
  And learned in gramaryè,*
And when I learned at the schole,
  Something shee taught itt mee.

There growes an hearbe within this field,
  And iff it were but knowne,
His color, which is whyte and redd,
  It will make blacke and browne:

His color, which is browne and blacke,
  Itt will make redd and whyte;
That sworde is not all Englande,
  Upon his coate will byte.

And you shal be a harper, brother,
  Out of the north countrye;
And Ile be your boy, soe *faine* of fighte,
  And beare your harpe by your knee.

And you shal be the best harpèr,
  That ever tooke harpe in hand;
And I wil be the best singèr,
  That ever sung in this lande.

Itt shal be written in our forheads
  All and in gramaryè,
That we towe are the boldest men,
  That are in all Christentyè.

And thus they renisht them to ryde,
  On tow good renish steedes;
And when they came to king Adlands hall,
  Of redd gold shone their weedes.

And whan the came to kyng Adlands hall,
  *Untill* the fayre hall *yate*,
There they found a proud portèr
  Rearing himselfe thereatt.

Sayes, Christ thee save, thou proud portèr;
  Sayes, Christ thee save and see.
Nowe you be welcome, sayd the portèr,
  Of what land soever ye bee.

---

\* A knowledge of certain spells and enchantments, mixing of potions, philtres, etc., to which noble ladies of mediæval times were much given: a refined sort of witchcraft.

Wee beene harpers, sayd Adler younge,
  Come out of the northe countrye;
Wee beene come hither untill this place,
  This proud weddinge for to see.

Sayd, And your color were white and redd,
  As it is blacke and browne,
I wold saye king Estmere and his brother
  Were comen untill this towne.

Then they pulled out a ryng of gold,
  Layd itt on the porters arme;
And ever we will thee, proud portèr,
  Thow wilt saye us no harme.

Sore he looked on kyng Estmère,
  And sore he handled the ryng,
Then opened to them the fayre hal yates,
  He *lett* for no kind of thyng.

Kyng Estmere he stabled his steede
  Soe fayre att the hall bord;
The froth, that came from his brydle bitte,
  Light in kyng Bremors beard.

Saies, Stable thy steed, thou proud harpèr,
  Saies, Stable him in the stalle;
It doth not beseeme a proud harpèr
  To stable "him" in a kyngs halle.

My ladde he is so *lither*, he said,
  He will doe nought that's meete;
And is there any man in this hall
  Were able him to beate?

Thou speakst proud words, sayes the king of Spaine,
  Thou harper, here to mee:
There is a man within this halle
  Will beate thy ladd and thee.

O let that man come downe, he said,
  A sight of him wold I see;
And when hee hath beaten well my ladd,
  Then he shall beate of mee.

Downe then came the *kemperye man*,
  And looked him in the eare;
For all the gold, that was under heaven,
  He durst not *neigh him neare*.

And how nowe, kempe, said the kyng of
    Spaine,
And how what aileth thee?
He saies, It is writt in his forhead
    All and in gramaryè,
That for all the gold that is under heaven
    I dare not neigh him nye.

Then kyng Estmere pulld forth his harpe,
    And plaid a pretty thinge:
The ladye upstart from the borde,
    And wold have gone from the king.

Stay thy harpe, thou proud harpèr,
    For Gods love I pray thee,
For and thou playes as thou beginns,
    Thou'lt *till* * my bryde from mee.

He stroake upon his harpe againe,
    And playd a pretty thinge;
The ladye lough a loud laughter,
    As shee sate by the king.

Saies, Sell me thy harpe, thou proud
    harper,
    And thy stringès all,
For as many gold nobles "thou shalt have"
    As heere bee ringes in the hall.

What wold ye doe with my harpe, "he
    sayd,"
    If I did sell itt yee?
"To playe my wiffe and me a fitt,†
    When abed together wee bee."

Now sell me, quoth hee, thy bryde soe gay,
    As shee sitts by thy knee,
And as many gold nobles I will give,
    As leaves been on a tree.

And what wold ye doe with my bryde soe
    gay,
    Iff I did sell her thee?
More seemelye it is for her fayre bodye
    To lye by mee then thee.

Hee played agayne both loud and shrille,*
    And Adler he did syng,
"O ladye, this is thy owne true love;
    Noe harper, but a kyng.

"O ladye, this is thy owne true love,
    As playnlye thou mayest see;
And Ile rid thee of that foule paynim,
    Who partes thy love and thee."

The ladye looked, the ladye blushte,
    And blushte and lookt agayne,
While Adler he hath drawne his brande,
    And hath the *Sowdan* slayne.

Up then rose the kemperye men,
    And loud they gan to crye:
Ah! traytors, yee have slayne our kyng,
    And therefore yee shall dye.

Kyng Estmere threwe the harpe asyde
    And *swith* he drew his brand;
And Estmere he, and Adler yonge
    Right stiffe in stour can stand.

And aye their swordes soe sore can byte,
    Throughe help of Gramaryè,
That soone they have slayne the kempery
    men,
Or forst them forth to flee.

Kyng Estmere tooke that fayre ladyè,
    And marryed her to his wiffe,
And brought her home to merry Englànd
    With her to leade his life.

---

\* *i.e.* entice.
† A part of a song. Here a strain of music

\* Some liberties have been taken in the following stanzas, but wherever this edition differs from the preceding, it hath been brought nearer to the folio MS.

## VII.—SIR PATRICK SPENCE,

### A SCOTTISH BALLAD,

Is given from two MS. copies transmitted from Scotland. In what age the hero of this ballad lived, or when this fatal expedition happened that proved so destructive to the Scots nobles, I have not been able to discover; yet am of opinion that their catastrophe is not altogether without foundation in history, though it has escaped my own researches. In the infancy of navigation, such as used the northern seas were very liable to shipwreck in the wintry months; hence a law was enacted in the reign of James III. (a law which was frequently repeated afterwards), "That there be na schip frauched out of the realm with any staple gudes, fra the feast of Simons day and Jude, unto the feast of the purification of our Lady, called Candelmess." Jam. III. Parlt. 2, ch. 15.

THE king sits in Dumferling toune,
   Drinking the blude-reid wine:
O *quhar* will I get guid sailor,
   To sail this schip of mine?

Up and spak an eldern knicht,
   Sat at the kings richt kne:
Sir Patrick Spence is the best sailòr,
   That sails upon the se.

The king has written a braid letter,*
   And signd it wi' his hand;
And sent it to Sir Patrick Spence,
   Was walking on the sand.

The first line that Sir Patrick red,
   A loud lauch lauched he:
The next line that Sir Patrick red,
   The teir blinded his ee.

O *quha* is this has don this deid,
   This ill deid don to me;
To send me out this time o' the *zeir*,
   To sail upon the se?

Mak hast, mak haste, my mirry men all,
   Our guid schip sails the morne.

O say na sae, my master deir,
   For I feir a deadlie storme.

Late late yestreen I saw the new moone
   Wi' the auld moone in hir arme;
And I feir, I feir, my deir mastèr,
   That we will com to harme.

O our Scots nobles wer richt *laith*
   To weet their cork-heild *schoone;*
Bot lang owre a' the play wer playd,
   Thair hats they swam aboone.

O lang, lang, may thair ladies sit
   Wi' thair fans into their hand,
Or eir they se Sir Patrick Spence
   Cum sailing to the land.

O lang, lang, may the ladies stand
   Wi' thair gold kems in their hair,
Waiting for thair ain deir lords,
   For they'll se thame na mair.

Have owre, have owre to Aberdour,*
   It's fiftie fadom deip:
And thair lies guid Sir Patrick Spence,
   Wi' the Scots lords at his feit.

---

\* *A braid letter, i.e.* open or patent, in opposition to close rolls.

\* A village lying upon the river Forth, the entrance to which is sometimes denominated *De mortuo mari.*

## VIII.—ROBIN HOOD AND GUY OF GISBORNE.

WE have here a ballad of Robin Hood (from the Editor's folio MS.) which was never before printed, and carries marks of much greater antiquity than any of the common popular songs on this subject.

Among all those, none was ever more famous than the hero of this ballad, whose chief residence was in Sherwood Forest, in Nottinghamshire; and the heads of whose story, as collected by Stow, are briefly these :

"In this time [about the year 1190, in the reign of Richard I.] were many robbers and outlawes, among the which Robin Hood and Little John, renowned theeves, continued in woods, despoyling and robbing the goods of the rich. They killed none but such as would invade them, or by resistance for their own defence.

"The saide Robert entertained an hundred tall men and good archers with such spoiles and thefts as he got, upon whom four hundred (were they ever so strong) durst not give the onset. He suffered no woman to be oppressed, violated, or otherwise molested : poore mens goods he spared, abundantlie relieving them with that which by theft he got from abbeys and the houses of rich carles : whom Maior (the historian) blameth for his rapine and theft, but of all theeves he affirmeth him to be the prince, and the most gentle theefe." *Annals*, p. 159.

The personal courage of this celebrated outlaw, his skill in archery, his humanity, and especially his levelling principle of taking from the rich and giving to the poor, have in all ages rendered him the favourite of the common people, who, not content to celebrate his memory by innumerable songs and stories, have erected him into the dignity of an earl. Indeed, it is not impossible but our hero, to gain the more respect from his followers, or they to derive the more credit to their profession, may have given rise to such a report themselves ; for we find it recorded in an epitaph, which, if genuine, must have been inscribed on his tombstone near the convent of Kirklees in Yorkshire, where (as the story goes) he was bled to death by a treacherous nun to whom he applied for phlebotomy :

> Hear underneab bis laitl stean
> laiȝ robert earl of huntingtun
> nea arcir ber aȝ hie sae geub
> an pipl kauld him Robin Heub
> sick utlawȝ as hi an is men
> bil England nibir si agen.
> obiit 24 kal. dekembris, 1247.

This epitaph appears to me suspicious. However, a late antiquary has given a pedigree of Robin Hood, which, if genuine, shows that he had real pretensions to the earldom of Huntington, and that his true name was Robert Fitz-ooth or Fitzotho.

Some liberties were, by the Editor, taken with this ballad, which in this edition hath been brought nearer to the folio MS.

WHEN *shawes* beene *sheene*, and shradds
    full fayre,
And leaves both large and longe,
Itt is merrye walking in the fayre forrèst
    To heare the small birdes songe.

The *woodweele* sang, and wold not cease,
    Sitting upon the spraye,
Soe lowde, he wakened Robin Hood,
    In the greenwood where he lay.

Now by my faye, sayd jollye Robin,
    A *sweaven* I had this night ;
I dreamt me of tow *wighty* yemen,
    That fast with me can fight.

Methought they did mee beate and binde,
    And tooke my bow mee froe ;
If I be Robin alive in this lande,
    Ile be *wroken* on them towe.

*Sweavens* are swift, Master, quoth John,
    As the wind that blowes ore a hill ;
For if itt be never so loude this night,
    To-morrow itt may be still.

*Buske* yee, *bowne* yee, my merry men all,
    And John shall goe with mee,
For Ile goe seeke yond wight yeomen,
    In greenwood where the bee.

Then the cast on their gownes of grene,
    And tooke theyr bowes each one ;
And they away to the greene forrèst
    A shooting forth are gone ;

Until they came to the merry greenwood,
    Where they had gladdest bee,
There were the ware of a wight yeomàn,
    His body leaned to a tree.

A sword and a dagger he wore by his side,
    Of manye a man the bane ;
And he was clad in his *capull hyde*
    Topp and tayll and mayne.

Stand you still, master, quoth Little John,
    Under this tree so grene,
And I will go to yond wight yeoman
    To know what he doth meane.

Ah ! John, by me thou settest noe store,
    And that I *farley* finde :
How offt send I my men beffore,
    And tarry my selfe behinde ?

It is no cunning a knave to ken,
    And a man but heare him speake ;
And itt were not for bursting of my bowe,
    John, I thy head wold breake,

As often wordes they *breeden bale*,
    So they parted Robin and John ;
And John is gone to Barnesdale :
    The *gates* \* he knoweth eche one.

But when he came to Barnesdale,
    Great heavinesse there hee hadd,
For he found tow of his owne fellòwes
    Were slaine both in a slade.

And Scarlette he was flyinge a-foote
    Fast over stocke and stone,
For the Sheriffe with seven score men
    Fast after him is gone.

One shoote now I will shoote, quoth John,
    With Christ his might and mayne ;
Ile make yond fellow that flyes soe fast,
    To stopp he shall be fayne.

Then John bent up his long *bende*-bowe,
    And *fetteled* him to shoote :
The bow was made of a tender boughe,
    And fell downe to his foote.

Woe worth, woe worth thee, wicked wood,
    That ere thou grew on a tree ;
For now this day thou arte my *bale*,
    My *boote* when thou shold bee.

His shoote it was but loosely shott,
    Yet flewe not the arrowe in vaine,
For itt mett one of the sherriffes men,
    Good William a Trent was slaine.

It had bene better of William a Trent
    To have bene abed with sorrowe,

---

\* *i.e.* ways, passes, paths, ridings. *Gate* is a common word in the north for *way*.

Than to be that day in the green wood slade
To meet with Little Johns arrowe.

But as it is said, when men be mett
Fyve can doe more than three,
The sheriffe hath taken Little John,
And bound him fast to a tree.

Thou shalt be drawen by dale and downe,
And hanged hye on a hill.
But thou mayst fayle of thy purpose, quoth John,
If itt be Christ his will.

Let us leave talking of Little John,
And thinke of Robin Hood,
How he is gone to the wight yeoman,
Where under the leaves he stood.

Good morrowe, good fellowe, sayd Robin so fayre,
"Good morrowe, good fellowe," quoth he:
Methinks by this bowe thou beares in thy hande
A good archere thou sholdst bee.

I am wilfull of my waye, quo' the yeman,
And of my morning tyde.
He lead thee through the wood, sayd Robin;
Good fellow, Ile be thy guide.

I seeke an outlàwe, the straunger sayd,
Men call him Robin Hood;
Rather Ild meet with that proud outlàwe
Than fortye pound soe good.

Now come with me, thou wighty yeman,
And Robin thou soone shalt see:
But first let us some pastime find
Under the greenwood tree.

First let us some *masterye* make
Among the woods so even,
Wee may chance to meet with Robin Hood
Here att some *unsett steven*.

They cutt them downe two summer *shroggs*,
That grew both under a *breere*,
And sett them threescore rood in twaine
To shoot the *prickes y-fere*.

Leade on, good fellowe, quoth Robin Hood,
Leade on, I doe bidd thee.
Nay by my faith, good fellowe, hee sayd,
My leader thou shalt bee.

The first time Robin shot at the pricke,
He mist but an inch it froe:
The yeoman he was an archer good,
But he cold never shoote soe.

The second shoote had the wightye yeman,
He shote within the *garlànde*:
But Robin he shott far better than hee,
For he clave the good pricke wande.

A blessing upon thy heart, he sayd;
Good fellowe, thy shooting is goode;
For an thy hart be as good as thy hand,
Thou wert better then Robin Hoode.

Now tell me thy name, good fellowe, sayd he,
Under the leaves of *lyne*.
Nay by my faith, quoth bolde Robin,
Till thou have told me thine.

I dwell by dale and downe, quoth hee,
And Robin to take Ime sworne;
And when I am called by my right name
I am Guye of good Gisborne.

My dwelling is in this wood, sayes Robin,
By thee I set right nought:
I am Robin Hood of Barnèsdale,
Whom thou so long hast sought.

He that had neither beene kithe nor kin,
Might have seene a full fayre sight,
To see how together these yeomen went
With blades both browne * and bright.

---

* The common epithet for a sword or other offensive weapon in the old metrical romances is *brown*; as, "brown brand," or "brown sword, brown bill," etc., and sometimes even "bright brown sword."

To see how these yeomen together they
    fought
  Two howres of a summers day :
Yett neither Robin Hood nor Sir Guy
  Them fettled to flye away.

Robin was *reachles* on a roote,
  And stumbled at that tyde ;
And Guy was quicke and nimble with-all,
  And hitt him ore the left side.

Ah deere Lady, sayd Robin Hood, "thou
  That art both mother and may,"
I think it was never mans destinye
  To dye before his day.

Robin thought on our ladye deere,
  And soone leapt up againe,
And strait he came with a "backward"
  stroke,
And he sir Guy hath slayne.

He took sir Guys head by the hayre,
  And sticked itt on his bowes end :
Thou hast beene a traytor all thy liffe,
  Which thing must have an ende.

Robin pulled forth an Irish kniffe,
  And *nicked* sir Guy in the face,
That he was never on woman born,
  Cold tell whose head it was.

Saies, Lye there, lye there, now sir Guye,
  And with me be not wrothe ;
If thou have had the worse strokes at my
  hand,
Thou shalt have the better clothe.

Robin did off his gowne of greene,
  And on sir Guy did it throwe,
And hee put on that *capull hyde*,
  That cladd him topp to toe.

The bowe, the arrowes, and litle horne,
  Now with me I will beare ;
For I will away to Barnesdale,
  To see how my men doe fare.

Robin Hood sett Guyes horne to his mouth,
  And a loud blast in it did blow,
That beheard the sheriffe of Nottingham,
  As he leaned under a *lowe.*

Hearken, hearken, sayd the sheriffe,
  I heare nowe tydings good,
For yonder I heare sir Guyes horne blowe,
  And he hath slaine Robin Hoode.

Yonder I heare sir Guyes horne blowe,
  Itt blowes soe well in tyde,
And yonder comes that wightye yeoman,
  Cladd in his capull hyde.

Come hyther, come hyther, thou good sir
  Guy,
Aske what thou wilt of mee.
O I will none of thy gold, sayd Robin,
  Nor I will none of thy fee :

But now I have slaine the master, he sayes,
  Let me goe strike the knave ;
This is all the rewarde I aske ;
  Nor noe other will I have.

Thou art a madman, said the sheriffe,
  Thou sholdest have had a knights fee :
But seeing thy asking hath beene soe bad,
  Well granted it shale be.

When Litle John heard his master speake,
  Well knewe he it was his *steven :*
Now shall I be looset, quoth Litle John,
  With Christ his might in heaven.

Fast Robin hee hyed him to Little John,
  He thought to loose him *belive ;*
The sheriffe and all his companye
  Fast after him did drive.

Stand abacke, stand abacke, sayd Robin ;
  Why draw you mee soe neere ?
Itt was never the use in our countryè,
  Ones shrift another shold heere.

But Robin pulled forth an Irysh kniffe,
  And losed John hand and foote,
And gave him sir Guyes bow into his hand,
  And bade it be his *boote.*

Then John he took Guyes bow in his hand,
   His boltes and arrowes eche one:
When the sheriffe saw Little John bend
   his bow,
He fettled him to be gone.

Towards his house in Nottingham towne
   He fled full fast away;
And soe did all his companye;
   Not one behind wold stay.

But he cold neither runne soe fast,
   Nor away soe fast cold ryde,
But Litle John with an arrowe soe broad
He shott him into the "backe"-syde.

*₊* The title of "Sir" was not formerly peculiar to knights; it was given to priests, and sometimes to very inferior personages.

## IX.—AN ELEGY ON HENRY, FOURTH EARL OF NORTHUMBERLAND.

THE subject of this poem, which was written by Skelton, is the death of Henry Percy, Fourth Earl of Northumberland, who fell a victim to the avarice of Henry VII. In 1489 the Parliament had granted the king a subsidy for carrying on the war in Bretagne. This tax was found so heavy in the north, that the whole country was in a flame. The Earl of Northumberland, then lord lieutenant of Yorkshire, wrote to the king praying an abatement. But the king wrote back that not a penny should be abated. This message being delivered by the earl with too little caution, the populace rose, and supposing him to be the promoter of their calamity, broke into his house and murdered him. This melancholy event happened at the earl's seat at Cocklodge, near Thirske, in Yorkshire, April 28, 1489. See Lord Bacon, etc.

John Skelton, who commonly styled himself Poet Laureat, died June 21, 1529. The following poem, which appears to have been written soon after the event, is printed from an ancient MS. copy preserved in the British Museum, being much more correct than that printed among Skelton's Poems, in bl. let. 12mo, 1568.—It is addressed to Henry Percy, Fifth Earl of Northumberland, and is prefaced, etc. in the following manner:—

*Poeta Skelton Laureatus libellum suum metrice alloquitur.*

   Ad dominum properato meum, mea pagina, Percy,
     Qui Northumbrorum jura paterna gerit,
   Ad nutum celebris tu prona repone leonis,
     Quæque suo patri tristia justa cano.
   Ast ubi perlegit, dubiam sub mente volutet
     Fortunam, cuncta quæ male fida rotat.
   Qui leo sit felix, et Nestoris occupet annos;
     Ad libitum cujus ipse paratus ero.

SKELTON LAUREAT UPON THE DOLORUS DETHE AND MUCH LAMENTABLE CHAUNCE OF THE MOOST HONORABLE ERLE OF NORTHUMBERLANDE.

I WAYLE, I wepe, I sobbe, I sigh ful sore
  The dedely fate, the dolefulle destenny
Of him that is gone, alas! withoute restore,
  Of the blode\* royall descendinge nobelly;
Whos lordshepe doutles was slayne lamentably
Thorow treson agen hym compassyd and wrought;
Trew to his prince, in worde, in deede, and thought.

Of hevenly poems, O Clyo calde by name
  In the college of musis goddess *hystoriall*,
Adres the to me, whiche am both halt and lame
  In elect uteraunce to make memoryall:
To the four soccour, to the for helpe I call
Myne homely rudnes and drighness to expelle.
With the freshe waters of Elyconys† welle.

Of noble actes auncyently enrolde,
  Of famous princis and lordes of astate,
By thy report ar wonte to be extold,
  Regestringe trewly every formare date;
Of thy bountie after the usuall rate,
Kyndle in me suche plenty of thy *noblès*,
Thes sorrowfulle dities that I may shew expres.

In sesons past who hathe harde or sene
  Of formar writinge by any presidente
That vilane hastarddis in ther furious tene,
  Fulfyled with malice of froward entente,
*Confeterd* togeder of commoun concente
Falsly to slo ther moste singular goode lorde?
It may be registerde of shamefull recorde.

So noble a man, so valiaunt lorde and knight,
  Fulfilled with honor, as all the worlde dothe ken;
At his commaundement, whiche had both day and night
  Knyghtis and squyers, at every season when
He calde upon them, as menyall household men:
Were no thes commones uncurteis *Karlis of Kynde*
To slo ther owne lorde? God was not in their minde.

And were not they to blame, I say also,
  That wereaboute hym, his owne servants of trust,
To suffre hym slayn of his mortall fo?
  Fled away from hym, let hym ly in the dust:
They bode not till the reckning wer discust.
What shuld I flatter? what shuld I *glose* or paynt?
Fy, fy for shame, their harts wer to faint.

In Englande and Fraunce, which gretly was redouted;
  Of whom both Flaunders and Scotland stode in drede;

---

\* The mother of Henry, First Earl of Northumberland, was Mary, daughter to Henry, Earl of Lancaster, whose father Edmond was second son of King Henry III. The mother and the wife of the Second Earl of Northumberland were both lineal descendants of King Edward III.

† Helicon.

To whome grete astates obeyde and *lowttede;*
  A mayny of rude villayns made him for to blede:
Unkindly they slew hym, that holp them oft at nede:
He was their bulwark, their *paves,* and their wall,
Yet shamfully they slew hym; that shame mot them befal,

I say, ye commoners, why wer ye so stark mad?
What frantyk frensy fyll in youre brayne?
Wher was your wit and reson, ye shuld have had?
What willfull foly made yow to ryse agayne
Your naturall lord? alas! I can not fayne.
Ye armed you with will, and left your wit behynd;
Well may you be called comones most unkynd.

He was your chyfteyne, your shelde, your chef defence,
  Redy to assyst you in every tyme of nede:
Your worship depended of his excellence:
Alas! ye mad men, to far ye did excede:
Your hap was unhappy, to ill was your spede:
What movyd you agayn hym to war or to fight?
What aylde you to sle your lord agyn all right?

The grounde of his quarel was for his sovereyn lord,
  The welle concernyng of all the hole lande,
Demaundyng soche dutyes as nedis most acord
  To the right of his prince which shold not be withstand;
For whos cause ye slew hym with your awne hande:
But had his nobill mendone wel that day,
Ye had not been hable to have saide him nay.

But ther was fals packinge, or els I am begylde:
  How-be-it the matter was evident and playne,
For yf they had occupied ther spere and ther shelde,
  This noble man doutles had not be slayne.
Bot men say they wer lynked with a double chayn,
And held with the commouns under a cloke,
Whiche kindeled the wyld fyre that made all the smoke.

The commouns *renyed* ther taxes to pay
  Of them demaunded and asked by the kinge;
With one voice importune, they playnly said nay:
They *buskt* them on a *bushment* themself in *baile* to bringe:
Agayne the kings plesure to wrastle or to wringe,
Bluntly as bestis withe boste and with cry
They saide, they *forsede* not, nor carede not to dy.

The noblenes of the northe this valiant lorde and knyght,
  As man that was innocent of trechery or trayne,
Presed forthe boldly to witstand the myght,
  And, lyke marciall Hector, he fauht them agayne,
Vigorously upon them with myght and mayne,
Trustinge in noble men that wer with hym there:
Bot all they fled from hym for falshode or fere.

Barons, knights, squyers, one and alle,
  Togeder with servaunts of his famuly,

Turnd their backis, and let ther master fall,
Of whos [life] they counted not a flye;
Take up whose wolde for them, they let hym ly.
Alas! his golde, his fee, his annuall rente
Upon suche a sort was ille bestowde and spent.

He was envyronde aboute on every syde
Withe his enemys, that were stark mad and *wode;*
Yet whils he stode he gave them woundes wyde:
Alas for *routhe!* what touche his mynde were goode,
His corage manly, yet ther he shed his bloode!
All left alone, alas! he fawte in vayne;
For cruelly amonge them ther he was slayne.

Alas for pite! that Percy thus was *spylt,*
The famous erle of Northumberlande:
Of knightly prowès the sworde pomel and hylt,
The myghty lyoun * doutted by se and lande!
O dolorous chaunce of fortuns fruward hande!
What man remembring how shamfully he was slayne,
From bitter weepinge hymself kan restrayne?

O cruell Mars, thou dedly god of war!
O dolorous teusday, dedicate to thy name,
When thou shoke thy sworde so noble a man to mar!
O grounde ungracious, unhappy be thy fame,
Whiche wert endyed with rede blode of the same!

---

\* Alluding to his crest and supporters. *Doutted* is abridged for *redoubted.*

Moste noble erle! O fowle *mysuryd* grounde
Whereon he gat his fynal dedely wounde!

O Atropos, of the fatall systers thre,
Goddes mooste cruell unto the lyf of man,
All merciles, in the ys no pitè!
O homycide, whiche sleest all that thou kan,
So forcibly upon this erle thow ran,
That with thy sworde *enharpid* of mortall drede,
Thou kit asonder his *perfight* vitall thredel!

My wordis unpullysht be nakide and playne,
Of *aureat* poems they want ellumynynge;
Bot by them to knoulege ye may attayne
Of this lordis dethe and of his murdrynge.
Which whils he lyvyd had *fuyson* of every thing,
Of knights, of squyers, chef lord of toure and toune,
Tyl fykkill fortune began on hym to frowne.

*Paregall* to dukis, with kings he myght compare,
Surmountinge in honor all erls he did excede,
To all cuntreis aboute hym reporte me I dare.
Lyke to Eneas benygne in worde and dede,
Valiaunt as Hector in every marciall nede,
Provydent, discrete, circumspect, and wyse,
Tyll the chaunce ran agyne him of fortunes duble dyse.

What nedethe me for to extoll his fame
With my rude pen enkankerd all with rust?
Whos noble actis shew worsheply his name,

Transcendyng far myne homely muse,
  that must
Yet sumwhat wright supprisid with
  *hartly lust,*
Truly reportinge his right noble astate,
Immortally whiche is immaculate.

His noble blode never disteynyd was,
  Trew to his prince for to defende his right,
Doublenes hatinge, fals maters to compas,
  Treytory and treson he bannesht out of
    syght,
  With trowth to medle was all his hole
    delyght,
As all his kuntrey kan testefy the same:
To *slo* suche a lord, alas, it was grete shame.

If the hole quere of the musis nyne
  In me all onely wer sett and comprisyde,
Embrethed with the blast of influence
    dyvyne,
  As perfightly as could be thought or
    devysyd;
To me also allthouche it were promysyde
Of laureat Phebus holy the eloquence,
All were to litill for his magnyficence.

O yonge lyon, bot tender yet of age,
  Grow and encrease, remembre thyn
    astate,
God the assyst unto thyn herytage,
  And geve the grace to be more fortunate,
  Agayne rebellyouns arme to make debate.
And, as the lyoune, whiche is of bestis
    kinge,
Unto thy subjectis be kurteis and benyngne.

I pray God sende the prosperous lyf and
    long,
  Stabille thy mynde constant to be and
    fast,
Right to mayntein, and to resist all wronge:
  All flattringe faytors abhor and from the
    east,
  Of foule detraction God kepe the from
    the blast:
Let double delinge in the have no place,
And be not light of credence in no case.

Wythe hevy chere, with dolorous hart and
    mynd,
  Eche man may sorow in his inward
    thought,
Thys lords death, whose pere is hard to
    fynd
  *Allgyf* Englond and Fraunce were
    thorow saught.
Al kings, all princes, all dukes, well they
    ought
Bothe temporall and spirituall for to com-
    playne
This noble man, that crewelly was slayne.

More specially barons, and those knygtes
    bold,
  And all other gentilmen with hym enter-
    teynd,
In fee, as meny all men of his housold,
  Whom he as lord worsheply manteynd:
  To sorowfull weping they ought to be
    constreynd,
As oft as thei call to ther remembraunce,
Of ther good lord the fate and dedely
    chaunce.

O perlese prince of heveyn emperyalle,
  That with one worde formed al thing of
    noughte;
Hevyn, hell, and erth obey unto thi kall;
  Which to thy resemblance wondersly
    hast wrought
  All mankynd, whom thou full dere hast
    boght,
With thy blode precious our *finaunce* thou
    dyd pay,
And us redemed, from the *fendys pray:*

To the pray we, as prince incomperable,
  As thou art of mercy and pite the well,
Thou bringe unto thy joye etermynable
  The sowle of this lorde from all daunger
    of hell,
  In endles blis with the to byde and dwell
In thy palace above the orient,
Where thou art lorde, and God omnipotent.

O quene of mercy, O lady full of grace,
    Maiden moste pure, and goddis moder dere,
To sorowfull harts chef comfort and solace,
    Of all women O floure withouten pere,
    Pray to thy son above the starris clere,
He to vouchesaf by thy mediatioun
    To pardon thy servant, and bringe to salvacion.

In joy triumphant the hevenly yerarchy,
    With all the hole sorte of that glorious place,
His soule mot receyve into ther company
    Thorowe bounte of hym that formed all solace:
Well of pite, of mercy, and of grace,
    The father, the son, and the holy goste
In Trinitate one God of myghts moste.

## X.—THE TOWER OF DOCTRINE.

THE reader has here a specimen of the descriptive powers of Stephen Hawes, a celebrated poet in the reign of Henry VII., though now little known. It is extracted from an allegorical poem (written in 1505), entitled, *The Hist. of Graunde Amoure & La Belle Pucel, called the Palace of Pleasure*, etc., 4to, 1555.

The following stanzas are taken from chaps. iii. and iv., "How Fame departed from Graunde Amour and left him with Governaunce and Grace, and howe he went to the Tower of Doctrine," etc.

I LOOKED about and saw a craggy roche,
    Farre in the west neare to the element,
And as I dyd then unto it approche,
    Upon the tope I sawe refulgent
    The royal tower of Morall Document,
Made of fine copper with turrettes fayre and hye,
Which against Phebus shone soe marveylously,

That for the very perfect bryghtenes
    What of the tower, and of the cleare sunne,
I could nothyng behold the goodlines
    Of that palaice, whereas Doctrine did *wonne:*
    Tyll at the last, with mysty wyndes donne,
The radiant brightnes of golden Phebus
Auster * gan cover with clowde tenebrus.

    * A pernicious wind from the south brought dark or shady clouds to cover the sun. The wind Auster was said to bring rain and to blight the flowers.

Then to the tower I drewe, nere and nere,
    And often mused of the great hyghnes
Of the craggy rocke, which *quadrant* did appeare:
    But the fayre tower (so much of ryches
    Was all about), sexangled doubtles:
*Gargeyld* with grayhoundes, and with many lyons,
Made of fyne golde; with divers sundry dragons.*

The little turrets with ymages of golde
    About was set, whiche with the wynde aye moved
With propre vices, that I did well beholde
    About the tower, in sundry wyse they hoved
    With goodly pypes, in their mouthes ituned,
That with the wynd they pyped a daunce
*Iclipped Amour de la hault pleasaunce.*

    * Greyhounds, lions, dragons, were at that time the royal supporters.

The toure was great of marveylous wydnes,
  To whyche ther was no way to passe
    but one,
Into the toure for to have an *intres:*
  A grece there was *ychesyld* all of stone
  Out of the rocke, on whyche men dyd
    gone
Up to the toure, and in lykewyse dyd I
Wyth bothe the Grayhoundes in my com-
    pany :

Tyll that I came unto a ryall gate,
  Where I sawe stondynge the goodly
    Portres,
Whyche axed me from whence I came a-
    late ;
  To whome I gan in every thynge ex-
    presse
All myne adventure, chaunce, and busy-
    nesse,
And *eke* my name ; I tolde her every *dell :*
Whan she herde this she lyked me right
    well.

Her name, she sayd, was called Counten-
    aunce ;
  Into the "base" courte she dyd me then
    lede,
Where was a fountayne *depured* of ples-
    aunce,
  A noble sprynge, a ryall conduyte-hede,
  Made of fyne golde enameled with reed ;
And on the toppe four dragons blewe
    and stoute
Thys dulcet water in four partes dyd
    spoute,
Of whyche there flowed foure ryvers ryght
    clere,

Sweter than Nylus * or Ganges was ther
    odoure ;
Tygrys or Eufrates unto them no pere :
  I dyd than taste the aromatyke ly-
    coure,
Fragraunt of fume, and swete as any
    floure ;
And in my mouthe it had a marveylous
    scent
Of divers spyces, I knewe not what it ment.

And after thys further forth me brought
  Dame Countenaunce into a goodly Hall,
Of jasper stones it was wonderly wrought :
  The wyndowes cleare *depured* all of
    crystall,
  And in the roufe on hye over all
Of golde was made a ryght crafty vyne ;
Instede of grapes the rubies there did
    shyne.

The flore was paved with berall clarified,
  With pillers made of stones precious,
Like a place of pleasure so gayely glorified,
  It myght be called a palaice glorious,
  So muche delectable and solacious ;
The hall was hanged hye and circuler
With cloth of arras in the rychest maner,

That treated well of a ful noble story,
  Of the doubty waye to the Tower
    Perillous ; †
Howe a noble knyght should wynne the
    victory
Of many a serpente foule and odious.

·    ·    ·    ·    ·    ·    ·

---

\* Nile.     † The story of the poem.

## XI.—THE CHILD OF ELLE.

This poem is given from a fragment in the Editor's folio MS., "which, though extremely defective and mutilated, appeared to have so much merit that it excited a strong desire to attempt a completion of the story;" so says Bishop Percy, but the fragment alluded to consists of but thirty lines. Of these in the ballad before us, Percy has omitted some. Those retained are printed in italics, and these are not given *verbatim*. The reader will therefore see upon how slender a foundation the present poem of two hundred lines has been built.

On yonder hill a castle standes
   With walles and towres bedight,
And yonder lives the Child of Elle,
   A younge and comely knighte.

The Child of Elle to his garden went,
   And stood at his garden pale,
Whan, lo! he beheld fair Emmelines page
   Come trippinge downe the dale.

The Child of Elle he hyed him thence,
   *Y-wis* he stoode not stille,
And soone he mette faire Emmelines page
   Come climbing up the hille.

Nowe Christe thee save, thou little foot-page,
   Now Christe thee save and see!
Oh telle me how does thy ladye gaye,
   And what may thy tydinges bee?

My lady shee is all woe-begone,
   And the teares they fall from her eyne;
And aye she laments the deadlye feude
   Betweene her house and thine.

And here shee sends thee a silken scarfe
   Bedewde with many a teare,
And biddes thee sometimes thinke on her,
   Who loved thee so deare.

And here shee sends thee a ring of golde,
   The last boone thou mayst have,
And biddes thee weare it for her sake,
   Whan she is layde in grave.

For, ah! her gentle heart is broke,
   And in grave soone must shee bee,

*Sith* her father hath chose her a new new love,
   And forbidde her to think of thee.

Her father hath brought her a *carlish* knight,
   Sir John of the north countràye,
And within three dayes shee must him wedde,
   Or he vowes he will her slaye.

Nowe hye thee backe, thou little foot-page,
   And greet thy ladye from mee,
And telle her that I her owne true love
   Will dye, or sette her free.

Nowe hye thee backe, thou little foot-page,
   And let thy fair ladye know
This night will I bee at her bowre-windowe,
   Betide me weale or woe.

The boye he tripped, the boye he ranne,
   He neither stint ne stayd
Untill he came to fair Emmelines bowre,
   Whan kneeling downe he sayd,

O ladye, I've been with thy own true love,
   And he greets thee well by mee;
This night will he bee at thy bowre-windowe,
   And dye or sette thee free.

Nowe daye was gone, and night was come,
   And all were fast asleepe,
All save the ladye Emmeline,
   Who sate in her bowre to weepe:

And soone shee heard her true loves voice
  Lowe whispering at the walle,
Awake, awake, my deare ladyè,
  Tis I thy true love call.

Awake, awake, my ladye deare,
  Come, mount this faire palfràye:
This ladder of ropes will lette thee downe,
  He carrye thee hence awaye.

Nowe nay, nowe nay, thou gentle knight
  Nowe nay, this may not bee;
For aye shold I *tint* my maiden fame,
  If alone I should wend with thee.

O ladye, thou with a knighte so true
  Mayst safelye wend alone,
To my ladye mother I will thee bringe,
  Where marriage shall make us one.

"My father he is a baron bolde,
  Of lynage proude and hye;
And what would he saye if his daughtèr
  Awaye with a knight should fly?

"Ah! well I wot, he never would rest,
  Nor his meate should doe him no goode,
Until he had slayne thee, Child of Elle,
  And seene thy deare hearts bloode."

*O ladye, wert thou in thy saddle sette,*
  *And a little space him fro,*
*I would not care for thy cruel fathèr,*
  *Nor the worst that he could doe.*

O ladye, wert thou in thy saddle sette,
  And once without this walle,
I would not care for thy cruel fathèr,
  Nor the worst that might befalle.

Faire Emmeline sighed, fair Emmeline wept,
  And aye her heart was woe:
At length he seized her lilly-white hand,
  And downe the ladder he drewe:

And thrice he clasped her to his breste,
  *And kist her tenderlìe:*
*The teares that fell from her fair eyes*
  **Ranne like the fountayne free.**

Hee mounted himselfe on his steede so talle,
  And her on a fair palfràye,
And slung his bugle about his necke,
  And roundlye they rode awaye.

All this beheard her owne damsèlle,
  In her bed whereas shee ley,
Quoth shee, My lord shall knowe of this,
  Soe I shall have golde and fee.

Awake, awake, thou baron bolde!
  Awake, my noble dame!
Your daughter is fledde with the Child of Elle
  To doe the deede of shame.

The baron he woke, the baron he rose,
  And called his merrye men all:
"And come thou forth, Sir John the knighte,
  Thy ladye is carried to thrall."

Faire Emmeline scant had ridden a mile,
  A mile forth of the towne,
When she was aware of her fathers men
  Come galloping ove: the downe:

And foremost came the carlish knight,
  Sir John of the north countràye:
"Nowe stop, nowe stop, thou false traitòure,
  Nor carry that ladye awaye.

For she is come of hye lineàge,
  And was of a ladye borne,
And ill it beseems thee a false churl's sonne
  To carry her hence to scorne."

Nowe loud thou lyest, Sir John the knight,
  Nowe thou doest lye of mee;
A knight mee gott, and a ladye me bore,
  Soe never did none by thee.

But light nowe downe, my ladye faire,
  Light downe, and hold my steed,
While I and this discourteous knighte
  **Doe try this arduous deede.**

*But light nowe downe, my deare ladyè,*
*Light downe, and hold my horse;*
*While I and this discourteous knighte*
*Doe try our valour's force.*

Fair Emmeline sighed, fair Emmeline
 wept,
And aye her heart was woe,
While twixt her love and the carlish knight
Past many a baleful blowe.

The Child of Elle hee fought soe well,
As his weapon he waved amaine,
That soone he had slaine the carlish
 knight,
And layd him upon the plaine.

And nowe the baron and all his men
Full fast approached nye :
Ah ! what may ladye Emmeline doe?
Twere nowe no boote to flye.

Her lover he put his horne to his mouth,
And blew both loud and shrill,
And soone he saw his owne merry men
Come ryding over the hill.

"Nowe hold thy hand, thou bold baròn,
I pray thee hold thy hand,
Nor ruthless rend two gentle hearts
Fast knit in true love's band.

Thy daughter I have dearly loved
Full long and many a day ;
But with such love as holy kirke
Hath freelye sayd wee may.

O give consent, shee may be mine,
And blesse a faithfull paire ;
My lands and livings are not small,
My house and lineage faire :

My mother she was an earl's daughtèr,
And a noble knyght my sire "—

The baron he frowned, and turn'd away
With *mickle dole* and ire.

Fair Emmeline sighed, faire Emmeline
 wept,
And did all tremblinge stand :
At lengthe she sprang upon her knee,
And held his lifted hand.

Pardon, my lorde and father deare,
This faire yong knyght and mee :
Trust me, but for the carlish knyght,
I never had fled from thee.

Oft have you called your Emmeline
Your darling and your joye ;
O let not then your harsh resolves
Your Emmeline destroye.

The baron he stroakt his dark-browz
 cheeke,
And turned his heade asyde
To whipe away the starting teare
He proudly strave to hyde.

In deepe revolving thought he stoode,
And mused a little space ;
Then raised faire Emmeline from the
 grounde,
With many a fond embrace.

Here take her, Child of Elle, he sayd,
And gave her lillye white hand ;
Here take my deare and only child,
And with her half my land :

Thy father once mine honour wrongde
In dayes of youthful pride ;
Do thou the injurye repayre
In fondnesse for thy bride.

And as thou love her, and hold her deare,
Heaven prosper thee and thine :
And nowe my blessing wend wi' thee,
My lovelye Emmeline.

## XII.—EDOM OF GORDON.\*

This Scottish ballad was printed at Glasgow, by Robert and Andrew Foulis, MDCCLV., 8vo, 12 pages. We are indebted for its publication to Sir David Dalrymple, Bart., who gave it as it was preserved in the memory of a lady now dead.

The reader will here find it improved and enlarged with several fine stanzas, recovered from a fragment of the same ballad, in the Editor's folio MS. The fragment is there given under the title of *Captain Carre*, and the Castle of the Rodes is called Brittons-borrow. The fragment consists of eighty-five lines. It is supposed that the minstrels who recited this and other ballads were accustomed to change the names of their heroes according to the company they were in, and hence the confusion of Edom of Gordon (Adam Gordon) and Captain Adam Carre. But the note at the end of the poem seems to fix the inhuman deed upon Adam Gordon, brother of the Earl of Huntley.

It fell about the Martinmas,
   *Quhen* the wind blew shril and cauld,
Said Edom of Gordon to his men,
   We maun draw *till* a *hauld*.

And *quhat* a hauld sall we draw till,
   My mirry men and me?
We wul gae to the house o' the Rodes,
   To see that fair ladie.

The lady stude on hir castle wa',
   Beheld baith dale and down :
There she was ware of a host of men
   Cum ryding towards the toun.

O see ze nat, my mirry men a'?
   O see ze nat quhat I see?
Methinks I see a host of men :
   I marveil quha they be.

She *weend* it had been hir luvely lord,
   As he cam ryding hame ;
It was the traitor Edom o' Gordon,
   Quha *reekt* nae sin nor shame.

She had nae sooner *buskit* hirsel,
   And putten on hir goun,
But Edom o' Gordon and his men
   Were round about the toun.

They had nae sooner supper sett,
   Nae sooner said the grace,
But Edom o' Gordon and his men
   Were light about the place.

The lady ran up to hir towir head,
   So fast as she could hie,
To see if by hir fair speeches
   She could wi' him agree.

But quhan he see this lady saif,
   And hir *yates* all locked fast,
He fell into a rage of wrath,
   And his look was all aghast.

Cum doun to me, ze lady gay,
   Cum doun, cum doun to me :
This night sall ye *lig* within mine armes,
   To-morrow my bride sall be.

I winnae cum doun, ze fals Gordon,
   I winnae cum doun to thee ;
I winnae forsake my ain dear lord,
   That is sae far frae me.

Give owre *zour* house, ze lady fair,
   Give owre zour house to me,
Or I sall *breun* yoursel therein,
   Bot and zour babies three.

---

\* Given in folio as *Captain Carre.*

# EDOM OF GORDON.

I winnae give owre, ze false Gordòn,
   To nae *sik* traitor as zee;
And if ze brenn my ain dear babes,
   My lord sall make ze *drie*.

But reach my pistoll, Glaud, my man,
   And charge ze weil my gun:
For, but an I pierce that bluidy butcher,
   My babes we been undone.

She stude upon hir castle wa',
   And let twa bullets flee:
She mist that bluidy butchers hart,
   And only raz'd his knee.

Set fire to the house, quo' fals Gordòn,
   All *wood* wi' *dule* and ire:
Fals lady, ze sall rue this deid,
   As ze bren in the fire.

*Wae worth*, wae worth ze, Jock, my man,
   I paid ze weil zour fee;
*Quhy* pu' ze out the ground-wa' stane,
   Lets in the reek to me?

And *ein* wae worth ze, Jock, my man,
   I paid ze weil zour hire;
Quhy pu' ze out the ground-wa' stane,
   To me lets in the fire?

Ze paid me weil my hire, lady;
   Ze paid me weil my fee:
But now I'm Edom o' Gordons man,
   Maun either doe or die:

O than bespaik hir little son,
   Sate on the nurses knee:
Sayes, Mither deare, gi' owre this house,
   For the *reek* it smithers me.

I wad gie a' my gowd, my childe,
   Sae wald I a' my fee,
For ane blast o' the western wind
   To blaw the reek frae thee.

O then bespaik hir dochter dear,
   She was baith *jimp* and sma:
O *row* me in a pair o' sheits,
   And tow me ower the wa.

They rowd hir in a pair o' sheits,
   And *towd* hir ower the wa:
But on the point o' Gordons spear
   She gat a deadly fa.

O bonnie bonnie was hir mouth,
   And cherry were her cheiks,
And clear clear was hir zellow hair,
   Whereon the reid bluid dreips.

Then wi' his spear he turnd hir owre,
   O gin hir face was wan!
He sayd, Ze are the first that eir
   I wisht alive again.

He turnd hir owre and owre againe,
   O gin hir skin was whyte!
I might ha spared that bonnie face
   To hae been sum mans delyte.

*Busk* and *boun*, my merry men a',
   For ill dooms I doe guess;
I cannae luik in that bonnie face,
   As it lyes on the grass.

Thame, *luiks to freits*, my master deir,
   Then freits wil follow thame:
Let it neir be said brave Edom o' Gordon
   Was daunted by a dame.

But quhen the ladye see the fire
   Cum flaming owre hir head,
She wept, and kist her children twain,
   Sayd, Bairns, we been but dead.

The Gordon then his *bougill* blew,
   And said, Awa', awa';
This house o' the Rodes is a' in flame,
   I hauld it time to ga'.

O then bespyed hir ain dear lord,
   As hee cam owr the lee;
He sied his castle all in blaze
   Sa far as he could see.

Then sair, O sair his mind misgave,
   And all his hart was wae;
Put on, put on, my wighty men,
   So fast as ze can gae.

Put on, put on, my wighty men,
  Sa fast as ze can drie;
For he that is hindmost of the thrang
  Sall neir get guid o' me.

*Than* sum they rade, and sum they rin,
  Fou fast out owr the bent;
But eir the foremost could get up,
  Baith lady and babes were *brent*.

He wrang his hands, he rent his hair,
  And wept in *teenefu'* muid:
O traitors, for this cruel deid
  Ze sall weep teirs o' bluid.

And after the Gordon he is gane,
  Sa fast as he might drie;
And soon i' the Gordon's foul hartis bluid
  He's *wroken* his dear ladie.

\*\*\* Since the foregoing ballad was first printed, the subject of it has been found recorded in Archbishop Spottiswood's *History of the Church of Scotland*, p. 259, who informs us that—

"Anno 1571. In the north parts of Scotland, Adam Gordon (who was deputy for his brother the Earl of Huntley) did keep a great stir; and under colour of the queen's authority, committed divers oppressions, especially upon the Forbes's . . . Having killed Arthur Forbes, brother to the Lord Forbes . . . Not long after he sent to summon the house of Tavoy pertaining to Alexander Forbes. The lady refusing to yield without direction from her husband, he put fire unto it, and burnt her therein, with children and servants, being twenty-seven persons in all.

"This inhuman and barbarous cruelty made his name odious, and stained all his former doings; otherwise he was held very active and fortunate in his enterprises."

**THE END OF THE FIRST BOOK.**

## SERIES THE FIRST.—BOOK II.

### I.—BALLADS THAT ILLUSTRATE SHAKESPEARE.

Our great dramatic poet having occasionally quoted many ancient ballads, and even taken the plot of one, if not more, of his plays from among them, it was judged proper to preserve as many of these as could be recovered, and, that they might be the more easily found, to exhibit them in one collective view. This second book is therefore set apart for the reception of such ballads as are quoted by Shakespeare, or contribute in any degree to illustrate his writings; this being the principal point in view, the candid reader will pardon the admission of some pieces that have no other kind of merit.

The design of this book being of a dramatic tendency, it may not be improperly introduced with a few observations on the origin of the English stage, and on the conduct of our first dramatic poets—a subject which, though not unsuccessfully handled by several good writers already,* will yet perhaps admit of some further illustration.

### ON THE ORIGIN OF THE ENGLISH STAGE, ETC.

It is well known that dramatic poetry in this and most other nations of Europe owes its origin, or at least its revival, to those religious shows which in the Middle Ages were usually exhibited on the more solemn festivals. At those times they were wont to represent in the churches the lives and miracles of the saints, or some of the more important stories of Scripture. And as the most mysterious subjects were frequently chosen, such as the Incarnation, Passion, and Resurrection of Christ, etc., these exhibitions acquired the general name of Mysteries. At first they were probably a kind of dumb shows, intermingled, it may be, with a few short speeches; at length they grew into a regular series of connected dialogues, formally divided into acts and scenes. Specimens of these in their most improved state (being at best but poor artless compositions) may be seen among Dodsley's *Old Plays*, and in Osborne's *Harleian Miscel.* How they were exhibited in their most simple form, we may learn from an ancient novel, often quoted by our old dramatic poets,† entitled, . . . 𝕬 𝖒𝖊𝖗𝖞𝖊 𝕵𝖊𝖘𝖙 𝖔𝖋 𝖆 𝖒𝖆𝖓 𝖙𝖍𝖆𝖙 𝖜𝖆𝖘 𝖈𝖆𝖑𝖑𝖊𝖉 𝕳𝖔𝖜𝖑𝖊𝖌𝖑𝖆𝖘,‡ etc., being a translation from the Dutch language, in which he is named *Ulenspiegle*. Howleglass, whose waggish tricks are the subject of this book, after many adventures comes to live with a priest, who makes him his parish clerk. This priest is described as keeping a leman or concubine, who had but one eye, to whom Howleglass owed a grudge for revealing his rogueries to his master. The story thus proceeds : . . . "And than in the meane season, while Howleglas was parysh clarke at Easter they should play the Resurrection

---

\* Bishop Warburton's *Shakespeare*; preface to Dodsley's *Old Plays*; Riccoboni's *Acct. of Theat. of Europe*, etc. These were all the Author had seen when he first drew up this essay.
† See Ben Jonson's *Poetaster*, Act iii. Sc. iv., and his masque of *The Fortunate Isles*.
‡ Howleglass is said in the preface to have died in 1450; at the end of the book, in 1350

of our Lorde: and for because than the men wer not learned, nor could not read, the priest toke his leman, and put her in the grave for an aungell: and this seing Howleglas, toke to hym iij of the symplest persons that were in the towne, that played the iij Maries; and the person [*i.e.* parson or rector] played Christe, with a baner in his hand. Than saide Howleglas to the symple persons, Whan the aungel asketh you whome you seke, you may saye, The parsons leman with one iye. Than it fortuned that the tyme was come that they must playe, and the aungel asked them whom they sought, and than sayd they, as Howleglas had shewed and lerned them afore, and than answered they, We seke the priests leman with one iye. And than the prieste might heare that he was mocked. And whan the priestes leman herd that, she arose out of the grave, and would have smyten with her fist Howleglas upon the cheke, but she missed him and smote one of the simple persons that played one of the thre Maries; and he gave her another; and than toke she him by the heare [hair]; and that seing his wyfe, came running hastely to smite the priestes leaman; and than the priest seeing this, caste down hys baner and went to helpe his woman, so that the one gave the other sore strokes, and made great noyse in the churche. And than Howleglas seyng them lynge together by the eares in the bodi of the churche, went his way out of the village, and came no more there." \*

As the old Mysteries frequently required the representation of some allegorical personage, such as Death, Sin, Charity, Faith, and the like, by degrees the rude poets of those unlettered ages began to form complete dramatic pieces consisting entirely of such personifications. These they entitled Moral Plays or Moralities. The Mysteries were very inartificial, representing the Scripture stories simply according to the letter. But the Moralities are not devoid of invention; they exhibit outlines of the dramatic art: they contain something of a fable or plot, and even attempt to delineate characters and manners. I have now before me two that were printed early in the reign of Henry VIII.; in which I think one may plainly discover the seeds of tragedy and comedy; for which reason I shall give a short analysis of them both.

One of them is entitled 𝔈𝔟𝔢𝔯𝔶 𝔐𝔞𝔫.† The subject of this piece is the summoning of man out of the world by death; and its moral, that nothing will then avail him but a well-spent life and the comforts of religion. This subject and moral are opened in a monologue spoken by the Messenger (for that was the name generally given by our ancestors to the Prologue on their rude stage): then God‡ is represented; who, after some general complaints on the degeneracy of mankind, calls for Death, and orders him to bring before his tribunal Every Man, for so is called the personage who represents the human race. Every Man appears, and receives the summons with all the marks of confusion and terror. When Death is withdrawn, Every Man applies for relief in this distress to Fellowship, Kindred, Goods, or Riches, but they successively renounce and forsake him. In this disconsolate state he betakes himself to Good Dedes, who, after upbraiding him with his long neglect of her,§ introduces him to her sister Knowledge, and she leads him to

---

\* Imprynted . . . by Wyllyam Copland: without date, in 4to bl. let. among Mr. Garrick's *Old Plays*, K. vol. x.

† This play has been reprinted by Mr. Hawkins in his three vols. of old plays, entitled, *The Origin of the English Drama*, 12mo. Oxford, 1773. See vol. i. p. 27.

‡ The Second Person of the Trinity seems to be meant.

§ The before-mentioned are male characters.

the "holy man Confession," who appoints him penance: this he inflicts upon himself on the stage, and then withdraws to receive the sacraments of the priest. On his return he begins to wax faint, and after Strength, Beauty, Descretion, and Five Wits[*] have all taken their final leave of him, gradually expires on the stage; Good Dedes still accompanying him to the last. Then an Aungell descends to sing his *Requiem;* and the Epilogue is spoken by a person, called Doctour, who recapitulates the whole, and delivers the moral:—

> "This memoriall men may have in mynde,
> Ye herers, take it of worth old and yonge,
> And forsake Pryde, for he disceyveth you in thende,
> And remembre Beauté, Five Witts, Strength, and Discretion,
> They all at last do Every Man forsake;
> Save his Good Dedes there dothe he take;
> But beware, for and they be small,
> Before God he hath no helpe at all," etc.

From this short analysis it may be observed, that **Every Man** is a grave solemn piece, not without some rude attempts to excite terror and pity, and therefore may not improperly be referred to the class of tragedy. It is remarkable that in this old simple drama the fable is conducted upon the strictest model of the Greek tragedy. The action is simply one, the time of action is that of the performance, the scene is never changed, nor the stage ever empty. Every Man, the hero of the piece, after his first appearance never withdraws, except when he goes out to receive the sacraments, which could not well be exhibited in public; and during his absence, Knowledge descants on the excellence and power of the priesthood, somewhat after the manner of the Greek chorus. And, indeed, except in the circumstance of Every Man's expiring on the stage, the *Sampson Agonistes* of Milton is hardly formed on a severer plan.[†]

The other play is entitled **Hick Scorner**,[‡] and bears no distant resemblance to Comedy: its chief aim seems to be to exhibit characters and manners, its plot being much less regular than the foregoing. The Prologue is spoken by Pity, represented under the character of an aged pilgrim; he is joined by Contemplacyon and Perseverance, two holy men, who, after lamenting the degeneracy of the age, declare their resolution of stemming the torrent. Pity then is left upon the stage, and presently found by Frewyll, representing a lewd debauchee, who, with his dissolute companion Imaginacion, relate their manner of life, and not without humour describe the stews and other places of base resort. They are presently joined by Hick Scorner, who is drawn as a libertine returned from travel, and, agreeably to his name, scoffs at religion. These three are described as extremely vicious, who glory in every act of wickedness: at length two of them quarrel, and Pity endeavours to part the fray; on this they fall upon him, put him in the stocks, and there leave him. Pity, thus imprisoned, descants in a kind of lyric measure on the profligacy of the age, and in this situation

---

[*] *i.e.* the five senses. These are frequently exhibited as five distinct personages upon the Spanish stage (see Riccoboni, p. 98); but our moralist has represented them all by one character.

[†] See more of *Every Man* in vol. ii. Preface to B. ii. note.

[‡] Imprynted by me Wynkyn de Worde, no date; in 4to bl. let. This play has also been reprinted by M*r*. Hawkins in his *Origin of the English Drama*, vol. i. p. 69.

is found by Perseverance and Contemplacion, who set him at liberty, and advise him to go in search of the delinquents. As soon as he is gone, Frewill appears again; and after relating in a very comic manner some of his rogueries and escapes from justice, is rebuked by the two holy men, who, after a long altercation, at length convert him and his libertine companion Imaginacioun from their vicious course of life: and then the play ends with a few verses from Perseverance by way of Epilogue. This and every morality I have seen conclude with a solemn prayer. They are all of them in rhyme; in a kind of loose stanza, intermixed with distichs.

It would be needless to point out the absurdities in the plan and conduct of the foregoing play: they are evidently great. It is sufficient to observe, that, bating the moral and religious reflection of pity, etc., the piece is of a comic cast, and contains a humorous display of some of the vices of the age. Indeed, the author has generally been so little attentive to the allegory, that we need only substitute other names to his personages, and we have real characters and living manners.

We see then that the writers of these moralities were upon the very threshold of real tragedy and comedy: and therefore we are not to wonder that tragedies and comedies in form soon after took place, especially as the revival of learning about this time brought them acquainted with the Roman and Grecian models.

II. At what period of time the moralities had their rise here, it is difficult to discover. But plays of miracles appear to have been exhibited in England soon after the Conquest. Matthew Paris tells us that Geoffrey, afterwards Abbot of St. Albans, a Norman, who had been sent for over by Abbot Richard to take upon him the direction of the school of that monastery, coming too late, went to Dunstable, and taught in the abbey there; where he caused to be acted (probably by his scholars) a miracle play of St. Catherine, composed by himself. This was long before the year 1119, and probably within the eleventh century. The above play of St. Catherine was, for aught that appears, the first spectacle of this sort that was exhibited in these kingdoms: and an eminent French writer thinks it was even the first attempt towards the revival of dramatic entertainments in all Europe; being long before the representations ot mysteries in France, for these did not begin till about the year 1398.\*

But whether they derived their origin from the above exhibition or not, it is certain that holy plays, representing the miracles and sufferings of the saints, were become common in the reign of Henry II.; and a lighter sort of interludes appear not to have been then unknown.† In the subsequent age of Chaucer, "Plays of Miracles" in Lent were the common resort of idle gossips.‡

They do not appear to have been so prevalent on the Continent, for the learned

---

\* See *Abrégé Chron. de l'Hist. de France* by M. Henault, 1179.

† See Fitzstephen's description of London, preserved by Stow (and reprinted with notes, etc., by the Rev. Mr. Pegge, in 1774, 4to), *Londonia pro spectaculis theatralibus, pro ludis scenicis, ludos habet sanctiores, representationes miraculorum*, etc. He is thought to have written in the reign of Henry II., and to have died in that of Richard I. It is true, at the end of this book we find mentioned *Henricum regem tertium*; but this is doubtless Henry the Second's son, who was crowned during the life of his father, in 1170, and is generally distinguished as *Rex juvenis, Rex filius*, and sometimes they were jointly named *Reges Angliæ*. From a passage in his chapter *De Religione*, it should seem that the body of St. Thomas Becket was just then a new acquisition to the Church of Canterbury.

‡ See Chaucer, Prologue to *Wife of Bath's Tale*.

historian of the Council of Constance, M. l'Enfant, ascribes to the English the introduction of plays into Germany. He tells us that the emperor, having been absent from the council for some time, was at his return received with great rejoicings, and that the English fathers in particular did, upon that occasion, cause a sacred comedy to be acted before him on Sunday, Jan. 31, 1417, the subjects of which were: The Nativity of our Saviour; the Arrival of the Eastern Magi; and the Massacre by Herod. Thence it appears, says this writer, that the Germans are obliged to the English for the invention of this sort of spectacles, unknown to them before that period.

The fondness of our ancestors for dramatic exhibitions of this kind, and some curious particulars relating to this subject, will appear from the Household Book of the Fifth Earl of Northumberland, A.D. 1512;[*] whence I shall select a few extracts, which show that the exhibiting Scripture dramas on the great festivals entered into the regular establishment, and formed part of the domestic regulations of our ancient nobility; and, what is more remarkable, that it was as much the business of the chaplain in those days to compose plays for the family, as it is now for him to make sermons:—

"My lordes chapleyns in household vj. viz. the almonar, and if he be a maker of interludys, than he to have a servaunt to the intent for writynge of the parts; and clls to have non. The maister of gramer," etc.—Sect. v. p. 44.

"Item, my lorde usith and accustomyth to gyf yerely if is lordship kepe a chapell and be at home, them of his lordschipes chapell, if they doo play the play of the *Nativite* uppon Cristynmes day in the mornnynge in my lords chapell befor his lordship—xxs."—Sect. xliv. p. 343.

"Item, . . . to them of his lordship chappell and other his lordshipis servaunts that doith play the play befor his lordship uppon Shrof-Tewsday at night, yerely in reward—xs."—Ibid. p. 345.

"Item, . . . to them . . . that playth the play of *Resurrection* upon Estur day in the mornnynge in my lordis 'chapell' befor his lordshipe—xxs."—Ibid.

"Item, my lorde useth and accustomyth yerly to gyf hym which is ordynede to be the master of the revells yerly in my lordis hous in Cristmas for the overseyinge and orderinge of his lordschips playes, interludes, and dresinge, that is plaid befor his lordship in his hous in the xijth dayes of Cristenmas, and they to have in rewarde for that caus yerly—xxs."—Ibid. p. 346.

"Item, my lorde useth and accustomyth to gyf every of the iiij parsones that his lordschip admyted as his players to com to his lordship yerly at Cristynmes ande at all other such tymes as his lordship shall comande them for playing cf playe and interludes affor his lordship in his lordshipis hous for every of their fees for an hole yere" . . .—Ibid. p. 351.

"Item, to be payd . . . for rewards to players for playes playd at Christynmas by stranegeres in my house after xxd.[†] every play, by estimacion somme—xxxiijs. iiij."[‡] —Sect. i. p. 22.

---

[*] *The Regulations and Establishments of the Household of Hen. Alg. Percy, Fifth Earl of Northumb.*, Lond. 1770, 8vo. A small impression was printed by order of the then Duke of Northumberland, to bestow in presents to his friends.

[†] This was not so small a sum then as it may now appear; for in another part of this MS. the price ordered to be given for a fat ox is but 13s. 4d. and for a lean one 8s.

[‡] At this rate the number of plays acted must have been twenty.

"Item, my lorde usith, and accustometh to gif yerely when his lordshipp is at home, to every erlis players that comes to his lordshipe betwixt Cristynmas ande Candelmas, if he be his special lorde and frende and kynsman—xxs."—Sect. xliiii. p. 340.

"Item, my lorde usith and accustomyth to gyf yerely, when his lordship is at home to every lordis players, that comyth to his lordshipe betwixt Crystynmas and Candilmas—xs."—Ibid.

The reader will observe the great difference in the rewards here given to such players as were retainers of noble personages, and such as are styled strangers, or, as we may suppose, only strollers.

The profession of a common player was about this time held by some in low estimation. In an old satire, entitled Jock Lorrels Bote,* the author, enumerating the most common trades or callings, as "carpenters, coopers, joyners," etc., mentions

"Players, purse-cutters, money-batterers,
Golde-washers, tomblers, jogelers,
Pardoners," etc.—Sign. B, vj.

III. It hath been observed already, that plays of miracles, or Mysteries, as they were called, led to the introduction of moral plays, or Moralities, which prevailed so early, and became so common, that towards the latter end of King Henry the Seventh's reign, John Rastel, brother-in-law to Sir Thomas More, conceived a design of making them the vehicle of science and natural philosophy. With this view he published ¶ A new interlude and a mery of the nature of the iiij elements declarynge many proper points of philosophy naturall, and of dyvers straynge landys,† etc. It is observable that the poet speaks of the discovery of America as then recent:

"Within this xx yere
Westwarde be founde new landes
That we never harde tell of before this," etc.

The West Indies were discovered by Columbus in 1492, which fixes the writing of this play to about 1510 (two years before the date of the above Household Book). The play of Hick Scorner was probably somewhat more ancient, as he still more imperfectly alludes to the American discoveries, under the name of "the Newe founde Ilonde."—Sign. A. vij.

It is observable that in the older Moralities, as in that last mentioned, *Every Man*, etc., is printed no kind of stage direction for the exits and entrances of the person-

---

* Printed at the Sun in Fleet Street by W. de Worde, no date, b. l. 4to.

† Mr. Garrick has an imperfect copy (*Old Plays*, i. vol. iii.). The *dramatis personæ* are—"The Messenger [or Prologue]. Nature naturate. Humanyte. Studyous Desire. Sensuall Appetyte. The Taverner. Experyence. Ygnoraunce. (Also yf ye lyste ye may brynge in a dysgysynge.)" Afterwards follows a table of the matters handled in the interlude; among which are,—"Of certeyn conclusions prouvynge the yerthe must nedes be rounde, and that yt is in circumference above xxi M. myle."—"Of certeyne points of cosmographye—and of dyvers straunge regyons,—and of the new founde landys and the maner of the people." This part is extremely curious, as it shows what notions were entertained of the new American discoveries by our own countrymen.

ages, no division of acts and scenes. But in the moral interlude of 𝔏𝔲𝔰𝔱𝔶 𝔍𝔲𝔟𝔢𝔫𝔱𝔲𝔰,\* written under Edward VI., the exits and entrances begin to be noted in the margin : † at length in Queen Elizabeth's reign Moralities appeared formally divided into acts and scenes, with a regular Prologue, etc. One of these is reprinted by Dodsley.

Before we quit this subject of the very early printed plays, it may just be observed, that, although so few are now extant, it should seem many were printed before the time of Elizabeth, as at the beginning of her reign, her injunctions in 1559 are particularly directed to the suppressing of "many pamphlets, playes, and ballads; that no manner of person shall enterprize to print any such," etc., but under certain restrictions. *Vid.* sect. v.

In the time of Henry VIII., one or two dramatic pieces had been published under the classical names of Comedy and Tragedy,‡ but they appear not to have been intended for popular use: it was not till the religious ferments had subsided that the public had leisure to attend to dramatic poetry. In the reign of Elizabeth, tragedies and comedies began to appear in form, and could the poets have persevered, the first models were good. 𝔊𝔬𝔯𝔟𝔬𝔡𝔲𝔠, a regular tragedy, was acted in 1561; § and Gascoigne, in 1566, exhibited 𝔍𝔬𝔠𝔞𝔰𝔱𝔞, a translation from Euripides, as also 𝔗𝔥𝔢 𝔍𝔲𝔭𝔭𝔬𝔰𝔢𝔯𝔰, a regular comedy from Ariosto: near thirty years before any of Shakespeare's were printed.

The people, however, still retained a relish for their old Mysteries and Moralities,∥ and the popular dramatic poets seem to have made them their models. From the graver sort of Moralities our modern Tragedy appears to have derived its origin, as our Comedy evidently took its rise from the lighter interludes of that kind. And as most of these pieces contain an absurd mixture of religion and buffoonery, an eminent critic ¶ has well deduced from thence the origin of our unnatural Tragi-comedies. Even after the people had been accustomed to Tragedies and Comedies, Moralities still kept their ground: one of them, entitled 𝔗𝔥𝔢 𝔑𝔢𝔴 𝔒𝔲𝔰𝔱𝔬𝔪,\*\* was printed so late as 1573 : at length they assumed the name of Masques,†† and, with some classical improvements, became in the two following reigns the favourite entertainments of the court.

---

\* Described in vol. ii. Preface to Book ii. The *dramatis personæ* of this piece are,— "Messenger, Lusty Juventus, Good Counsail, Knowledge, Sathan the Devyll, Hypocrisie, Fellowship, Abominable Lyving [an Harlot], God's Merciful Promises."

† I have also discovered some few "Exeats" and "Intrats" in the very old interlude of the *Four Elements*.

‡ Bishop Bale had applied the name of Tragedy to his Mystery of *God's Promises*, in 1538. In 1540, John Palsgrave, B.D., had republished a Latin comedy called *Acolastus*, with an English version. Holingshed tells us (vol. iii. p. 850), that so early as 1520 the king had "a good comedie of Plautus plaied" before him at Greenwich; but this was in Latin, as Mr. Farmer informs us in his curious *Essay on the Learning of Shakespeare*, 8vo, p. 31.

§ See *Ames*, p. 316. This play appears to have been first printed under the name of *Gorboduc*, then under the name of *Ferrex and Porrex* in 1569, and again under *Gorboduc*, 1590. Ames calls the first edition, quarto; Langbaine, octavo; and Tanner, 12mo.

∥ The general reception which the old Moralities had upon the stage, will account for the fondness of all our first poets for allegory. Subjects of this kind were familiar with every one.

¶ Bishop Warburton, *Shakespeare*, vol. v.

\*\* Reprinted among Dodsley's *Old Plays*, vol. i.

†† In some of these appeared characters full as extraordinary as in any of the old Moralities. In Ben Jonson's masque of *Christmas*, 1616, one of the personages is Minced Pye.

IV. The old Mysteries, which ceased to be acted after the Reformation, appear to have given birth to a third species of stage exhibition, which, though now confounded with tragedy and comedy, were by our first dramatic writers considered as quite distinct from them both : these were historical plays, or Histories, a species of dramatic writing which resembled the old Mysteries in representing a series of historical events simply in the order of time in which they happened, without any regard to the three great unities. These pieces seem to differ from tragedies, just as much as historical poems do from epic : as *Lucanes Pharsalia* does from the *Æneid* of Virgil.

What might contribute to make dramatic poetry take this form was, that soon after the Mysteries ceased to be exhibited, was published a large collection of poetical narratives, called 𝕿𝖍𝖊 𝕸𝖎𝖗𝖗𝖔𝖚𝖗 𝖋𝖔𝖗 𝕸𝖆𝖌𝖎𝖘𝖙𝖗𝖆𝖙𝖊𝖘,* wherein a great number of the most eminent characters in English history are drawn relating their own misfortunes. This book was popular, and of a dramatic cast ; and therefore, as an elegant writer† has well observed, might have its influence in producing historical plays. These narratives probably furnished the subjects, and the ancient Mysteries suggested the plan.

There appears, indeed, to have been one instance of an attempt at an historical play itself, which was perhaps as early as any Mystery on a religious subject ; for such, I think, we may pronounce the representation of a memorable event in English history, that was expressed in actions and rhymes. This was the old Coventry play of 𝕳𝖔𝖈𝖐 𝕿𝖚𝖊𝖘𝖉𝖆𝖞,‡ founded on the story of the massacre of the Danes, as it happened on St. Brice's night, November 13, 1002.§ The play in question was performed by certain men of Coventry, among the other shows and entertainments at Kenilworth Castle, in July 1575, prepared for Queen Elizabeth, and this the rather "because the matter mentioneth how valiantly our English women, for the love of their country, behaved themselves."

The writer, whose words are here quoted,‖ hath given a short description of the performance, which seems on that occasion to have been without recitation or rhymes, and reduced to mere dumb-show : consisting of violent skirmishes and encounters, first between Danish and English "lance knights on horseback," armed with spear and shield ; and afterwards between "hosts" of footmen : which at length ended in the Danes being "beaten down, overcome, and many led captive by our English women."

---

\* The first part of which was printed in 1559.
† *Catalogue of Royal and Noble Authors*, vol. i. pp. 166, 167.
‡ This must not be confounded with the Mysteries acted on Corpus Christi day by the Franciscans at Coventry, which were also called Coventry plays, and of which an account is given from T. Warton's *History of English Poetry*, etc., in Malone's *Shakespeare*, vol. ii. Part ii. pp. 13, 14.
§ Not 1012, as printed in Laneham's Letter, mentioned below.
‖ Ro. Laneham, whose Letter, containing a full description of the shows, etc., is reprinted at large in Nichols' *Progresses of Queen Elizabeth*, etc., vol. i. 4to, 1788. That writer's orthography, being peculiar and affected, is not here followed. Laneham describes this play of *Hock Tuesday*, which was "presented in an historical cue by certain good-hearted men of Coventry" (p. 32), and which was "wont to be play'd in their citie yearly" (p. 33), as if it were peculiar to them, terming it "their old storial show" (p. 32). And so it might be as represented and expressed by them "after their manner" (p. 33); although we are also told by Bevil Higgons, that St. Brice's Eve was still celebrated by the Northern English in commemoration of this massacre of the Danes, the women beating brass instruments, and singing old rhymes, in praise of their cruel ancestors. See his *Short View of English History*, 8vo, p. 17. (The Preface is dated 1734.)

This play, it seems, which was wont to be exhibited in their city yearly, and which had been of great antiquity and long continuance there, had of late been suppressed, at the instance of some well-meaning but precise preachers, of whose "sourness" herein the townsmen complain; urging that their play was "without example of ill-manners, papistry, or any superstition;" which shows it to have been entirely distinct from a religious Mystery. But having been discontinued, and, as appears from the narrative, taken up of a sudden after the sports were begun, the players apparently had not been able to recover the old rhymes, or to procure new ones, to accompany the action; which, if it originally represented "the outrage and importable insolency of the Danes, the grievous complaint of Huna, King Ethelred's chieftain in wars;" his counselling and contriving the plot to despatch them; concluding with the conflicts above mentioned, and their final suppression—"expressed in actions and rhymes after their manner," one can hardly conceive a more regular model of a complete drama; and, if taken up soon after the event, it must have been the earliest of the kind in Europe.[*]

Whatever this old play or "storial show" was at the time it was exhibited to Queen Elizabeth, it had probably for a spectator our young Shakespeare, who was then in his twelfth year, and doubtless attended with all the inhabitants of the surrounding country at these "princely pleasures of Kenilworth" when Stratford is only a few miles distant. And as the Queen was much diverted with the Coventry play, "whereat Her Majesty laught well," and rewarded the performers with 2 bucks, and 5 marks in money: who, "what rejoicing upon their ample reward, and what triumphing upon the good acceptance, vaunted their play was never so dignified, nor ever any players before so beatified:" but especially if our young bard afterwards gained admittance into the castle to see a play, which the same evening, after supper, was there "presented of a very good theme, but so set forth by the actors' well-handling, that pleasure and mirth made it seem very short, though it lasted two good hours and more," we may imagine what an impression was made on his infant mind. Indeed, the dramatic cast of many parts of that superb entertainment, which continued nineteen days, and was the most splendid of the kind ever attempted in this kingdom; the addresses to the Queen in the personated characters of a Sybille, a savage man, and Sylvanus, as she approached or departed from the castle; and, on the water, by Arion, a Triton, or the Lady of the Lake, must have had a very great effect on a young imagination, whose dramatic powers were hereafter to astonish the world.

But that the historical play was considered by our old writers, and by Shakespeare himself, as distinct from tragedy and comedy, will sufficiently appear from various passages in their works. "Of late days," says Stow, "in place of those stage playes[†] hath been used comedies, tragedies, enterludes, and histories both true and fayned."[‡] Beaumont and Fletcher, in the Prologue to The Captain, say,

"This is nor Comedy, nor Tragedy,
Nor History."

---

[*] The rhymes, etc., prove this play to have been in English, whereas Mr. Thomas Warton thinks the Mysteries composed before 1328 were in Latin. Malone's *Shakespeare*, vol. ii. Part ii. p. 9.

[†] *The Creation of the World*, acted at Skinners Well in 1409.

[‡] *Survey of London*, 1603, 4to. See also Warton's *Observations on Spenser*, vol. ii. p. 109.

Polonius in 𝔥𝔞𝔪𝔩𝔢𝔱 commends the actors as the best in the world, "either for tragedie, comedie, historic, pastorall," etc. And Shakespeare's friends, Heminge and Condell, in the first folio edition of his plays, in 1623,* have not only entitled their book *Mr. William Shakespeare's Comedies, Histories, and Tragedies:* but in their table of contents have arranged them under those three several heads ; placing in the class of histories, " King John, Richard II., Henry IV., two parts Henry V., Henry VI., three parts Richard III., and Henry VIII ;" to which they might have added such of his other plays as have their subjects taken from the old Chronicles, or Plutarch's *Lives*.

Although Shakespeare is found not to have been the first who invented this species of drama,† yet he cultivated it with such superior success, and threw upon this simple inartificial tissue of scenes such a blaze of genius, that his histories maintain their ground in defiance of Aristotle and all the critics of the classic school, and will ever continue to interest and instruct an English audience.

Before Shakespeare wrote, historical plays do not appear to have attained this distinction, being not mentioned in Queen Elizabeth's licence in 1574‡ to James Burbage and others, who are only empowered "to use, exercyse, and occupie the arte and facultye of playenge Comedies, Tragedies, Enterludes, Stage Playes, and such other like." But when Shakespeare's histories had become the ornaments of the stage, they were considered by the public, and by himself, as a formal and necessary species, and are thenceforth so distinguished in public instruments. They are particularly inserted in the licence granted by King James I., in 1603,§ to William Shakespeare himself, and the players his fellows ; who are authorized "to use and exercise the arte and faculty of playing Comedies, Tragedies, Histories, Interludes, Morals, Pastorals, Stage Plaies, and such like." The same merited distinction they continued to maintain after his death, till the theatre itself was extinguished ; for they are expressly mentioned in a warrant in 1622, for licensing certain "late comedians of Queen Anne deceased, to bring up children in the qualitie and exercise of playing Comedies, Histories, Interludes, Morals, Pastorals, Stage Plaies, and such like."‖ The same appears in an admonition issued in 1637¶ by Philip, Earl of Pembroke and Montgomery, then Lord Chamberlain, to the master and wardens of the company of printers and stationers ; wherein is set forth the complaint of His Majesty's servants the players, that "diverse of their books of comedyes and tragedyes, chronicle historyes, and the like," had been printed and published to their prejudice, etc.

This distinction, we see, prevailed for near half a century ; but after the Restoration, when the stage revived for the entertainment of a new race of auditors, many of whom had been exiled in France, and formed their taste from the French theatre, Shakespeare's histories appear to have been no longer relished ; at least, the distinction respecting them is dropt in the patents that were immediately granted after the king's return.

---

\* The same distinction is continued in the 2d and 3d folios, etc.
† See Malone's *Shakespeare*, vol. i. Part ii. p. 31
‡ Ibid. p. 37. § Ibid. p. 40.
‖ Ibid. p. 49. Here histories, or historical plays, are found totally to have excluded the mention of tragedies—a proof of their superior popularity. In an order for the king's comedians to attend King Charles I. in his summer's progress, 1636 (ibid. p. 144), histories are not particularly mentioned ; but so neither are tragedies ; they being briefly directed to "act Playes, Comedyes, and Interludes, without any lett," etc. ¶ Ibid. p. 139.

This appears not only from the allowance to Mr. William Beestone in June 1660, to use the house in Salisbury Court "for a play-house, wherein Comedies, Tragedies, Tragi-Comedies, Pastoralls, and Interludes may be acted;" but also from the fuller grant (dated August 21, 1660) to Thomas Killigrew, Esq., and Sir William Davenant, knight, by which they have authority to erect two companies of players, and to fit up two theatres "for the representation of Tragydies, Comedyes, Playes, Operas, and all other entertainments of that nature."

But while Shakespeare was the favourite dramatic poet, his histories had such superior merit, that he might well claim to be the chief, if not the only historic dramatist that kept possession of the English stage; which gives a strong support to the tradition mentioned by Gildon,* that, in a conversation with Ben Jonson, our bard vindicated his historical plays, by urging that, as he had found "the nation in general very ignorant of history, he wrote them in order to instruct the people in this particular." This is assigning not only a good motive, but a very probable reason for his preference of this species of composition; since we cannot doubt but his illiterate countrymen would not only want such instruction when he first began to write, notwithstanding the obscure dramatic chroniclers who preceded him; but also that they would highly profit by his admirable lectures on English history so long as he continued to deliver them to his audience. And, as it implies no claim to his being the *first* who introduced our chronicles on the stage, I see not why the tradition should be rejected.

Upon the whole, we have had abundant proof that both Shakespeare and his contemporaries considered his histories, or historical plays, as of a legitimate distinct species, sufficiently separate from tragedy and comedy—a distinction which deserves the particular attention of his critics and commentators, who, by not adverting to it, deprive him of his proper defence and best vindication for his neglect of the unities, and departure from the classical dramatic forms. For, if it be the first canon of sound criticism to examine any work by whatever rule the author prescribed for his own observance, then we ought not to try Shakespeare's histories by the general laws of tragedy or comedy. Whether the rule itself be vicious or not, is another inquiry; but certainly we ought to examine a work only by those principles according to which it was composed. This would save a deal of impertinent criticism.

V. We have now brought the inquiry as low as was intended, but cannot quit it, without entering into a short description of what may be called the economy of the ancient English stage.

Such was the fondness of our forefathers for dramatic entertainments, that not fewer than nineteen play-houses had been opened before the year 1633, when Prynne published his *Histriomastix*.† From this writer it should seem that "tobacco,

---

* See Malone's *Shakespeare*, vol. vi. p. 427.

† He speaks in p. 492 of the play-houses in Bishopsgate Street, and on Ludgate Hill, which are not among the seventeen enumerated in the Preface to Dodsley's *Old Plays*. Nay, it appears from Rymer's MSS. that twenty-three play-houses had been at different periods open in London; and even six of them at one time. See Malone's *Shakespeare*, vol. i. Part ii. p. 48.

wine, and beer," * were in those days the usual accommodations in the theatre, as within our memory at Sadler's Wells.

With regard to the players themselves, the several companies were (as hath been already shown†) retainers, or menial servants to particular noblemen,‡ who protected them in the exercise of their profession : and many of them were occasionally strollers, that travelled from one gentleman's house to another. Yet so much were they encouraged, that, notwithstanding their multitude, some of them acquired large fortunes. Edward Allen, master of the play-house called the Globe, who founded Dulwich College, is a known instance. And an old writer speaks of the very inferior actors, whom he calls the hirelings, as living in a degree of splendour which was thought enormous in that frugal age.§

---

\* So, I think, we may infer from the following passage, viz.: "How many are there who, according to their several qualities, spend 2d., 3d., 4d., 6d., 12d., 18d., 2s., and sometimes 4s. or 5s. at a play-house day by day, if coach-hire, boat-hire, tobacco, wine, beere, and such like vaine expences, which playes do usually occasion, be cast into the reckoning?" Prynne's *Histriom.* p. 322.

But that tobacco was smoked in the play-houses, appears from Taylor the Water poet, in his *Proclamation for Tobacco's Propagation:* "Let play-houses, drinking schools, taverns, etc., be continually haunted with the contaminous vapours of it ; nay (if it be possible), bring it into the churches, and there choak up their preachers." (*Works*, p. 253.) And this was really the case at Cambridge : James I. sent a letter in 1607, against "taking tobacco" in St. Mary's. So I learn from my friend Dr. Farmer.

A gentleman has informed me, that once going into a church in Holland, he saw the male part of the audience sitting with their hats on, smoking tobacco, while the preacher was holding forth in his morning-gown.

† See the extracts above, in pp. 85 and 86, from the Earl of Northumberland's Household Book.

‡ See the Preface to Dodsley's *Old Plays.* The author of an old invective against the stage, called *A Third Blast of Retrait from Plaies*, etc., 1580, 12mo, says : "Alas! that private affection should so raigne in the nobilitie, that to pleasure their servants, and to upholde them in their vanitye, they should restraine the magistrates from executing their office ! . . . They [the nobility] are thought to be covetous by permitting their servants . . . to live at the devotion or almes of other men, passing from countrie to countrie, from one gentleman's house to another, offering their service, which is a kind of beggerie. Who indeede, to speake more trulie, are become beggars for their servants. For comonlie the good-wil men beare to their lordes, makes them draw the stringes of their purses to extend their liberalitie." *Vide* pp. 75, 76, etc.

§ Stephen Gosson, in his *Schoole of Abuse*, 1579, 12mo, fo. 23, says thus of what he terms in his margin Players-men :—"Over lashing in apparel is so common a fault, that the very hyerlings of some of our players, which stand at revirsion of vi s. by the weck, jet under gentlemens noses in sutis of silke, exercising themselves to prating on the stage, and common scoffing when they come abrode, where they look askance over the shoulder at every man, of whom the Sunday before they begged an almes. I speake not this, as though everye one that professeth the qualitie so abused himselfe, for it is well-knowen, that some of them are sober, discrecte, properly learned, honest housholders and citizens, well-thought on among their neighbours at home" (he seems to mean Edward Allen above mentioned), "though the pryde of their shadowes (I meane those hangbyes whom they succour with stipend) cause them to be somewhat il-talked of abroad."

In a subsequent period we have the following satirical fling at the showy exterior and supposed profits of the actors of that time (*vide* Greene's *Groatsworth of Wit*, 1625, 4to) :— "What is your profession?" "Truly, sir, . . . I am a player." "A player? . . . I took you rather for a gentleman of great living ; for, if by outward habit men should be censured, I

## ON THE ORIGIN OF THE ENGLISH STAGE.

At the same time the ancient prices of admission were often very low. Some houses had penny benches.* The "two-penny gallery" is mentioned in the Prologue to Beaumont and Fletcher's *Woman-hater*.† And seats of threepence and a groat seem to be intended in the passage of Prynne above referred to. Yet different houses varied in their prices; that play-house called the Hope had seats of five several rates from sixpence to half-a-crown.‡ But a shilling seems to have been the usual price § of what is now called the Pit, which probably had its name from one of the playhouses having been a cock-pit.‖

The day originally set apart for theatrical exhibition appears to have been Sunday; probably because the first dramatic pieces were of a religious cast. During a great part of Queen Elizabeth's reign, the play-houses were licensed to be opened only on that day; ¶ but before the end of her reign, or soon after, this abuse was probably removed.

---

tell you, you would be taken for a substantial man." "So I am where I dwell . . . What, though the world once went hard with me, when I was fayne to carry my playing-fardle a footbacke: *Tempora mutantur* . . . for my very share in playing apparrell will not be sold for two hundred pounds. . . . Nay more, I can serve to make a pretty speech, for I was a country author, passing at a moral," etc. See Roberto's tale, sign. D. 3. b.

\* So a MS. of Oldys, from Tom Nash, an old pamphlet-writer. And this is confirmed by Taylor the Water poet in his *Praise of Beggerie*, p. 99:—

"Yet have I seen a beggar with his many [*sc.* vermin]
Come at a play-house, all in for one penny."

† So in the *Belman's Night-Walks* by Decker, 1616, 4to, "Pay thy twopence to a player, in this gallery thou mayest sit by a harlot."

‡ Induct. to Ben Jonson's *Bartholomew Fair*. An ancient satirical piece called *The Blacke Book*, Lond. 1604, 4to, talks of "The Six-Penny Roomes in Play-houses;" and leaves a legacy to one whom he calls "Arch-tobacco-taker of England, in ordinaries, upon stages both common and private."

§ Shakespeare, Prologue to *Henry VIII.*; Beaumont and Fletcher, Prologue to the *Captain*, and to the *Mad Lover*.

‖ This etymology hath been objected to by a very ingenious writer (see Malone's *Shakespeare*, vol. i. Part ii. p. 59), who thinks it questionable because, in St. Mary's Church at Cambridge, the area that is under the pulpit, and surrounded by the galleries, is (*now*) called the pit, which, he says, no one can suspect to have been a *cock-pit*, or that a play-house phrase could be applied to a church. But whoever is acquainted with the licentiousness of boys, will not think it impossible that they should thus apply a name so peculiarly expressive of its situation; which from frequent use might at length prevail among the senior members of the University, especially when those young men became seniors themselves. The name of pit, so applied at Cambridge, must be deemed to have been a cant phrase, until it can be shown that the area in other churches was usually so called.

¶ So Stephen Gosson, in his *Schoole of Abuse*, 1579, 12mo, speaking of the players, says: "These, because they are allowed to play every Sunday, make iiii or v Sundayes at least every week," fol. 24. So the author of *A Second and Third Blast of Retrait from Plaies*, 1580, 12mo: "Let the magistrate but repel them from the libertie of plaeing on the Sabboth-daie. . . . To plaie on the Sabboth is but a priviledge of sufferance, and might with ease be repelled, were it thoroughly followed," pp. 61, 62. So again: "Is not the Sabboth of al other daies the most abused? . . . Wherefore abuse not so the Sabbath day, my brethren; leave not the temple of the Lord." . . . "Those unsaverie morsels of unseemelie sentences passing out of the mouth of a ruffenlie plaier, doth more content the hungrie humors of the rude multitude, and carrieth better rellish in their mouthes, than the bread of the worde," etc. *Vide* pp. 63, 65, 69, etc. I do

The usual time of acting was early in the afternoon,* plays being generally performed by day-light.† All female parts were performed by men, no English actress being ever seen on the public stage ‡ before the civil wars.

Lastly, with regard to the play-house furniture and ornaments, a writer of King Charles the Second's time,§ who well remembered the preceding age, assures us, that in general "they had no other scenes nor decorations of the stage, but only old tapestry, and the stage strewed with rushes, with habits accordingly." ‖

Yet Coryate thought our theatrical exhibitions, etc., splendid, when compared with what he saw abroad. Speaking of the theatre for comedies at Venice, he says: "The house is very beggarly and base in comparison of our stately play-houses in England: neyther can their actors compare with ours for apparrell, shewes, and musicke. Here I observed certaine things that I never saw before: for I saw women act, a thing that I never saw before, though I have heard that it hath been sometimes used in London: and they performed it with as good a grace, action, gesture, and whatsoever convenient for a player, as ever I saw any masculine actor."¶

It ought, however, to be observed, that, amid such a multitude of play-houses as subsisted in the metropolis before the civil wars, there must have been a great difference between their several accommodations, ornaments, and prices; and that some would be much more showy than others, though probably all were much inferior in splendour to the two great theatres after the Restoration.

---

not recollect that exclamations of this kind occur in Prynne, whence I conclude that this enormity no longer subsisted in his time. It should also seem, from the author of the *Third Blast* above quoted, that the churches still continued to be used occasionally for theatres. Thus, in p. 77, he says that the players (who, as hath been observed, were servants of the nobility), "under the title of their maisters, or as reteiners, are priviledged to roave abroad, and permitted to publish their mametree in everie temple of God, and that throughout England, unto the horrible contempt of praier."

* "He entertaines us" (says Overbury in his character of an actor) "in the best leasure of our life, that is, betweene meales; the most unfit time either for study or bodily exercise." Even so late as in the reign of Charles II., plays generally began at three in the afternoon.

† See *Biogr. Brit.* i. 117, n. D.

‡ I say "no English actress—on the public stage," because Prynne speaks of it as an unusual enormity, that "they had French women actors in a play not long since personated in Blackfriars Play-house." This was in 1629. And though female parts were performed by men or boys on the public stage, yet in masques at court, the queen and her ladies made no scruple to perform the principal parts, especially in the reigns of James I. and Charles I. Sir William Davenant, after the Restoration, introduced women, scenery, and higher prices. See Cibber's *Apology for his own Life*.

§ See a short discourse on the English stage, subjoined to Flecknor's *Love's Kingdom*, 1674, 12mo.

‖ It appears from an epigram of Taylor the Water poet, that one of the principal theatres in his time, viz. The Globe on the Bankside, Southwark (which Ben Jonson calls the Glory of the Bank, and Fort of the whole parish), had been covered with thatch till it was burnt down in 1613. (See Taylor's *Sculler*, Epig. 22, p. 31. Jonson's *Execration on Vulcan*.) Puttenham tells us they used vizards in his time, "partly to supply the want of players, when there were more parts than there were persons, or that it was not thought meet to trouble ... princes chambers with too many folkes." [*Art of English Poesy*, 1589, p. 26.] From the last clause, it should seem that they were chiefly used in the masques at court.

¶ Coryate's *Crudities*, 4to, 1611, p. 247.

Since it was first published, the *History of the English Stage* hath been copiously handled by Mr. Thos. Warton in his *History of English Poetry*, 1774, etc., 3 vols. 4to (wherein is inserted whatever in these volumes fell in with his subject); and by Edmond Malone, Esq., who, in his "Historical Account of the English Stage" (*Shakesp.* vol. i. Pt. ii. 1790), hath added greatly to our knowledge of the economy and usages of our ancient theatres. To those names should be added that of the veteran Shakespearian scholar and accomplished editor, Mr. J. P. Collier.

## I.—ADAM BELL, CLYM OF THE CLOUGH, AND WILLIAM OF CLOUDESLY,

WERE three noted outlaws, whose skill in archery rendered them formerly as famous in the north of England as Robin Hood and his fellows were in the Midland counties. Their place of residence was in the forest of Englewood, not far from Carlisle (called corruptly in the ballad, Englishwood; whereas Engle or Ingle wood signifies wood for firing).

Our northern archers were not unknown to their southern countrymen: their excellence at the long-bow is often alluded to by our ancient poets. Shakespeare, in his *Much ado about Nothing*, Act i., makes Benedicke confirm his resolves of not yielding to love, by this protestation: "If I do, hang me in a bottle like a cat,\* and shoot at me, and he that hits me, let him be clapt on the shoulder, and called Adam:" meaning Adam Bell, as Theobald rightly observes, who refers to one or two other passages in our old poets wherein he is mentioned. The Oxford editor has also well conjectured, that "Abraham Cupid" in *Romeo and Juliet*, Act ii. Sc. i., should be "Adam Cupid," in allusion to our archer. Ben Jonson has mentioned Clym of the Clough in his *Alchemist*, Act i. Sc. ii. And Sir William Davenant, in a mock poem called *The Long Vacation in London*, describes the attorneys and proctors as making matches to meet in Finsbury Fields.

> "With loynes in canvas bow-case tyde,
> Where arrowes stick with mickle pride; . . .
> Like ghosts of Adam Bell and Clymme.
> Sol sets for fear they'l shoot at him."
> *Works*, 1673, fol. p. 291.

### PART THE FIRST.

MERY it was in the grene forest
　Amonge the levès grene,
Whereas men hunt east and west
　Wyth bowes and arrowes kene;

To raise the dere out of theyr denne;
　Suche sightes hath ofte bene sene;
As by thre yemen of the north countrèy,
　By them it is I meane.

---

\* Bottles formerly were of leather, though perhaps a wooden bottle might be here meant. It is a diversion in Scotland to hang up a cat in a small cask or firkin half filled with soot; and then a parcel of clowns on horseback try to beat out the ends of it, in order to show their dexterity in escaping before the contents fall upon them.

The one them hight Adam Bel,
  The other Clym of the Clough,*
The thyrd was William of Cloudesly,
  An archer good ynough.

They were outlawed for venyson,
  These yemen everychone;
They swore them brethren upon a day,
  To Englyshe wood for to gone.

Now lith and lysten, gentylmen,
  That of myrthes loveth to here:
Two of them were single men,
  The third had a wedded fere.

Wyllyam was the wedded man,
  Muche more then was hys care:
He sayde to hys brethren upon a day,
  To Carleile he would fare,

For to speke with fayre Alyce his wife,
  And with hys chyldren thre.
By my trouth, sayde Adam Bel,
  Not by the counsell of me:

For if ye go to Carlile, brother,
  And from thys wylde wode *wende*,
If that the justice may you take,
  Your lyfe were at an ende.

If that I come not to-morrowe, brother,
  By *pryme* to you agayne,
Truste you then that I am "taken,"
  Or else that I am slayne.

He toke hys leave of hys brethren two,
  And to Carlile he is gon:
There he knocked at his owne windowe
  Shortlye and anone.

Wher be you, fayre Alyce, he sayd,
  My wife and chyldren three?
Lyghtly let in thyne owne husbande,
  Wyllyam of Cloudeslee.

Alas! then sayd fayre Alyce,
  And syghed wonderous sore,

---

\* Clym of the Clough means Clem. (Clement)
of the Cliff; for that is what Clough signifies
in the north.

Thys place hath ben *besette* for you
  Thys halfe a yere and more.

Now am I here, sayde Cloudeslee,
  I would that in I were.
Now fetche us meate and drynke ynoughe,
  And let us make good chere.

She fetched hym meate and drynke plentye,
  Lyke a true wedded wyfe;
And pleased hym with that she had,
  Whome she loved as her lyfe.

There lay an old wyfe in that place,
  A lytle besyde the fyre,
Whych Wyllyam had found of charytyè
  More than seven yere.

Up she rose, and forth shee goes,
  Evill mote shee speede therfore;
For shee had sett no foote on ground
  In seven yere before.

She went unto the justice hall,
  As fast as she could hye:
Thys night, shee sayd, is come to town
  Wyllyam of Cloudeslyè.

Thereof the justice was full *fayne*,
  And so was the shirife also:
Thou shalt not *trauaile* hither, dame, for
  nought,
Thy meed thou shalt have ere thou go.

They gave to her a ryght good goune,
  Of scarlate, "and of *graine*:"
She toke the gyft, and home she wente,
  And couched her doune agayne.

They raysed the towne of mery Carleile
  In all the haste they can;
And came thronging to Wyllyames house,
  As fast as they might gone.

There they besette that good yemàn
  Round about on every syde:
Wyllyam hearde great noyse of folkes,
  That thither-ward fast hyed.

Alyce opened a backe wyndòwe,
　And loked all aboute,
She was ware of the justice and shirife bothe,
　Wyth a full great route.

Alas! treason, cryed Alyce,
　Ever wo may thou be!
Goe into my chamber, my husband, she sayd,
　Swete Wyllyam of Cloudeslee.

He toke hys sweard and hys bucler,
　Hys bow and hys chyldren thre,
And wente into hys strongest chamber,
　Where he thought surest to be.

Fayre Alyce, like a lover true,
　Took a pollaxe in her hande:
Said, He shall dye that cometh in
　Thys dore, whyle I may stand.

Cloudeslee bente a right good bowe,
　That was of a trusty tre,
He smot the justise on the brest,
　That hys arowe burst in three.

"A" curse on his harte, saide William,
　Thys day thy *cote* dyd on!
If it had ben no better then myne,
　It had gone nere thy bone.

Yelde the Cloudeslè, sayd the justise,
　And thy bowe and thy arrowes the fro.
"A" curse on hys hart, sayd fair Alyce,
　That my husband councelleth so.

Set fyre on the house, saide the sherife,
　*Syth* it wyll no better be,
And *brenne* we therin William, he saide,
　Hys wyfe and chyldren thre.

They fyred the house in many a place,
　The fyre flew up on hye:
Alas! then cryed fayre Alice,
　I se we here shall dye.

William openyd a backe wyndòw,
　That was in hys chamber hie,
And there with sheetes he did let downe
　His wyfe and children three.

Have you here my treasure, sayde William,
　My wyfe and my chyldren thre:
For Christès love do them no harme,
　But wreke you all on me.

Wyllyam shot so wonderous well,
　Tyll hys arrowes were all agoe,
And the fyre so fast upon hym fell,
　That hys bowstryng brent in two.

The sparkles brent and fell upon
　Good Wyllyam of Cloudeslè:
Than was he a wofull man, and sayde,
　Thys is a cowardes death to me.

Leever had I, sayde Wyllyam,
　With my sworde in the route to renne,
Then here among myne enemyes *wode*
　Thus cruelly to bren.

He toke hys sweard and hys buckler,
　And among them all he ran,
Where the people were most in *prece*,
　He smot downe many a man.

There myght no man abyde hys stroakes,
　So *fersly* on them he ran:
Then they threw wyndowes and dores on him,
　And so toke that good yemàn.

There they hym bounde both hand and fote,
　And in a deepe dungeon him cast
Now, Cloudesle, sayd the justice,
　Thou shalt be hanged in hast.

"A payre of new gallowes," sayd the sherife,
　"Now shal I for thee make;"
And the gates of Carleil shal be shutte:
　No man shal come in therat.

Then shall not helpe Clym of the Cloughe,
　Nor yet shall Adam Bell,
Though they came with a thousand mo,
　Nor all the devels in hell.

Early in the mornynge, the justice uprose,
　To the gates first can he gone,

And commaunded to be shut full close
  Lightilè everychone.

Then went he to the markett place,
  As fast as he coulde hye;
There a payre of new gallowes he set up
  Besyde the pyllorye.

A lytle boy "among them asked,"
  What meaned that gallow-tre?
They sayde to hange a good yemàn,
  Called Wyllyam of Cloudeslè.

That lytle boye was the towne swyne-
  heard,
  And kept fayre Alyces swyne;
Oft he had seene William in the wodde,
  And *geuen* hym there to dyne.

He went out att a crevis of the wall,
  And lightly to the woode dyd gone;
There met he with these wightye yemen
  Shortly and anone.

Alas! then sayde the lytle boye,
  Ye tary here all too longe;
Cloudeslee is taken, and *dampned* to death,
  And readye for to honge.

Alas! then sayd good Adam Bell,
  That ever we saw thys daye!
He had better have tarryed with us,
  So ofte as we dyd him praye.

He myght have dwelt in grene forèste,
  Under the shadowes greene,
And have kepte both hym and us att reste,
  Out of all trouble and *teene*.

Adam bent a ryght good bow,
  A great hart sone hee had slayne:
Take that, chylde, he sayde, to thy dynner,
  And bryng me myne arrowe agayne.

Now go we hence, sayed these wightye
  yeomen,
  Tarry we no longer here;
We shall hym *borowe* by God his grace,
  Though we buy itt full dere.

To Caerleil wente these bold yemen,
  All in a mornyng of maye.
Here is a *fyt* of Cloudeslye,
  And another is for to saye.

### PART THE SECOND.

And when they came to mery Carleile,
  All in "the" mornyng tyde,
They founde the gates shut them untyll
  About on every syde.

Alas! then sayd good Adam Bell,
  That ever we were made men!
These gates be shut so wonderous fast,
  We may not come therein.

Then bespake him Clym of the Clough,
  Wyth a wyle we wyl us in bryng;
Let us saye we be messengers,
  Streyght come nowe from our king.

Adam said, I have a letter written,
  Now let us wysely werke,
We wyl saye we have the kynges seale;
  I holde the porter no clerke.

Then Adam Bell bete on the gates
  With strokes great and stronge:
The porter marveiled, who was therat,
  And to the gates he thronge.

Who is there now, sayde the porter,
  That maketh all thys knockinge?
We be tow messengers, quoth Clim of
  the Clough,
  Be come ryght from our kyng.

We have a letter, sayd Adam Bel,
  To the justice we must itt bryng;
Let us in our messnge to do,
  That we were agayne to the kyng.

Here commeth none in, sayd the porter
  By hym that dyed on a tre,
Tyll a false thefe be hanged,
  Called Wyllyam of Cloudeslè.

Then spake the good yeman Clym of the
 Clough,
And swore by Mary fre,
And if that we stande long wythout,
 Lyke a thefe hanged shalt thou be.

Lo! here we have the kynges seale:
 What, *Lurden*,* art thou *wode?*
The porter went it had ben so,
 And lyghtly dyd off hys hode.

Welcome is my lordes seale, he saide;
 For that ye shall come in.
He opened the gate full shortlye:
 An euyl openyng for him.

Now are we in, sayde Adam Bell,
 Wherof we are full faine;
But Christ he knowes, that *harowed hell*,
 How we shall com out agayne.

Had we the keys, said Clim of the Clough,
 Ryght wel then shoulde we spede,
Then might we come out wel ynough
 When we se tyme and nede.

They called the porter to counsell,
 And wrang his necke in two,
And caste hym in a depe dungeon,
 And toke hys keys hym fro.

Now am I porter, sayd Adam Bel,
 Se brother the keys are here,
The worst porter to merry Carleile
 That "the" had thys hundred yere.

And now wyll we our bowes bend,
 Into the towne wyll we go,
For to delyuer our dere brother,
 That lyeth in care and wo.

Then they bent theyr good ewe bowes,
 And loked theyr stringes were round,†
The markett place in mery Carleile
 They beset that *stound*.

---
* Ver. 38.
† So Ascham in his *Toxophilus* gives a precept, "The stringe must be rounde" (p. 149, ed. 1761), otherwise, we may conclude from mechanical principles, the arrow will not fly true.

And, as they loked them besyde,
 A paire of new galowes "they" see,
And the justice with a *quest* of squyers,
 That judged William hanged to be.

And Cloudeslè lay redy there in a cart,
 Fast bound both fote and hand;
And a stronge rop about hys necke,
 All readye for to hange.

The justice called to him a ladde,
 Cloudeslees clothes hee shold have,
To take the measure of that yemàn,
 Therafter to make hys grave.

I have sene as great marveile, said
 Cloudesle,
As betweyne thys and *pryme*,
He that maketh a grave for mee,
 Hymselfe may lye therin.

Thou speakest proudlye, said the justice,
 I will thee hange with my hande.
Full wel herd this his brethren two,
 There styll as they dyd stande.

Then Cloudeslè cast his eyen asyde,
 And saw hys "brethren twaine"
At a corner of the market place,
 Redy the justice for to slaine.

I se comfort, sayd Cloudeslè,
 Yet hope I well to fare,
If I might have my handes at wyll
 Ryght lytle wolde I care.

Then spake good Adam Bell
 To Clym of the Clough so free,
Brother, se you marke the justyce wel;
 Lo! yonder you may him se:

And at the shyrife shote I wyll
 Strongly wyth an arrowe kene;
A better shote in mery Carleile
 Thys seven yere was not sene.

They loosed their arrowes both at once,
 Of no man had they dread;

The one hyt the justice, the other the
   sheryfe,
That both theyr sides gan blede.

All men *voyded*, that them stode nye,
   When the justice fell to the grounde,
And the sherife nye hym by;
   Eyther had his deathes wounde.

All the citezens fast gan flye,
   They durst no longer abyde:
There lyghtly they losed Cloudeslee,
   Where he with ropes lay tyde.

Wyllyam *start* to an officer of the towne,
   Hys axe "from" hys hand he wronge,
On eche syde he smote them downe,
   Hee thought he taryed to long.

Wyllyam sayde to hys brethren two,
   Thys daye let us lyve and die,
If ever you have nede, as I have now,
   The same shall you finde by me.

They shot so well in that tyde,
   Theyr stringes were of silke ful sure,
That they kept the stretes on every side;
   That batayle did long endure.

They fought together as brethren true,
   Lyke hardy men and bolde,
Many a man to the ground they threw,
   And many a herte made colde.

But when their arrowes were all gon,
   Men preced to them full fast,
They drew theyr swordès then anone,
   And theyr bowes from them cast.

They went lyghtlye on theyr way,
   Wyth swordes and buclers round;
By that it was mydd of the day,
   They made many a wound.

There was an *out-horne*\* in Carleil blowen,
   And the belles backwàrd dyd ryng,

---

\* Outhorne is an old term signifying the calling forth of subjects to arms by the sound of a horn.

Many a woman sayde, Alas!
   And many theyr handes dyd wryng.

The mayre of Carleile forth com was,
   Wyth hym a ful great route:
These yemen dred hym full sore,
   Of theyr lyves they stode in great doute.

The mayre came armed a full great pace,
   Wyth a pollaxe in hys hande;
Many a strong man wyth hym was,
   There in that *stowre* to stande.

The mayre smot at Cloudeslee with his
   bil,
Hys bucler he *brast* in two,
Full many a yeman with great evyll,
   Alas! Treason they cryed for wo.
Kepe well the gates fast, they bad,
   That these traytours therout not go.

But al for nought was that they wrought,
   For so fast they downe were layde,
Tyll they all thre, that so manfulli fought,
   Were gotten without, abraide.

Have here your keys, sayd Adam Bel,
   Myne office I here forsake,
And yf you do by my counsell
   A new porter do ye make.

He threw theyr keys at theyr heads,
   And bad them well to thryve,\*
And all that *letteth* any good yeman
   To come and comfort his wyfe.

Thus be these good yeman gon to the
   wod,
As lyghtly as *lefe* on *lynde;*
*The lough* and be mery in theyr mode,
   Theyr enemyes were ferr behynd.

When they came to Englyshe wode,
   Under the trusty tre,
There they found bowes full good,
   And arrowes full great plentye.

---

\* This is spoken ironically.

So God me help, sayd Adam Bell,
   And Clym of the Clough so fre,
I would we were in mery Carleile,
   Before that fayre meynye.

They set them downe, and made good chere,
   And eate and dranke full well.
A second *fyt* of the wightye yeomen:
   Another I wyll you tell.

### PART THE THIRD.

As they sat in Englyshe wood,
   Under the green-wode tre,
They thought they herd a woman wepe,
   But her they mought not se.

Sore then syghed the fayre Alyce:
   "That ever I sawe thys day!"
For nowe is my dere husband slayne,
   Alas! and wel-a-way!

Myght I have spoken wyth hys dere brethren,
   Or with eyther of them twayne,
To show them what him befell,
   My hart were out of payne.

Cloudeslè walked a lytle beside,
   He looked under the grene wood lynde,
He was ware of his wife, and chyldren three,
   Full wo in harte and mynde.

Welcome, wyfe, then sayde Wyllyam,
   Under "this" trusti tre:
I had *wende* yesterday, by swete saynt John,
   Thou sholdest me never "have" se.

"Now well is me that ye be here,
   My harte is out of wo."
Dame, he sayde, be mery and glad,
   And thanke my brethren two.

Herof to speake, said Adam Bell,
   I-wis it is no *bote:*
The meate, that we must supp withall,
   It runneth yet fast on fote.

Then went they downe into a launde,
   These noble archares all thre;
Eche of them slew a hart of *greece*,
   The best that they cold se.

Have here the best, Alyce, my wyfe,
   Sayde Wyllyam of Cloudeslye;
By cause ye so bouldly stode by me
   When I was slayne full nye.

Then went they to suppère
   Wyth suche meate as they had
And thanked God of ther fortune
   They were both mery and glad.

And when they had supped well,
   Certayne withouten lease,
Cloudeslè sayd, We wyll to our kyng,
   To get us a charter of peace.

Alyce shal be at our sojournyng
   In a nunnery here besyde;
My tow sonnes shall wyth her go,
   And there they shall abyde.

Myne eldest son shall go wyth me;
   For hym have "you" no care:
And he shall bring you worde agayn,
   How that we do fare.

Thus be these yemen to London gone,
   As fast as they myght "he,"
Tyll they came to the kynges pallàce,
   Where they woulde nedes be.

And whan they came to the kynges courte,
   Unto the pallace gate,
Of no man wold they aske no leave,
   But boldly went in therat.

They *preced prestly* into the hall,
   Of no man had they dreade:
The porter came after, and dyd them call,
   And with them began to chyde.

The usher sayde, Yemen, what wold ye have?
   I pray you tell to me:
You myght thus make offycers *shent:*
   Good syrs, of whence be ye?

Syr, we be out-lawes of the forest
   Certayne withouten lease;
And hether we be come to the kyng,
   To get us a charter of peace.

And whan they came before the kyng,
   As it was the lawe of the lande,
The kneled downe without lettyng,
   And eche held up his hand.

The sayed, Lord, we beseche the here,
   That ye wyll graunt us grace;
For we have slayne your fat falow dere
   In many a sondry place.

What be your nams, then said our king,
   Anone that you tell me?
They sayd, Adam Bell, Clim of the Clough,
   And Wyllyam of Cloudeslè.

Be ye those theves, then sayd our kyng,
   That men have tolde of to me?
Here to God I make an avowe,
   Ye shal be hanged al thre.

Ye shal be dead without mercy,
   As I am kynge of this lande.
He commanded his officers *everichone*,
   Fast on them to lay hande.

There they toke these good yemen,
   And arested them al thre:
So may I thryve, sayd Adam Bell,
   Thys game lyketh not me.

But, good lorde, we beseche you now,
   That yee graunt us grace,
Insomuche as "frely" we be to you come,
   "As frely" we may fro you passe,

With such weapons, as we have here,
   Tyll we be out of your place;
And yf we lyve this hundreth yere,
   We wyll aske you no grace.

Ye speake proudly, sayd the kynge;
   Ye shal be hanged all thre.
That were great pityc, then sayd the quene,
   If any grace myght be.

My lorde, when I came fyrst into this lande
   To be your wedded wyfe,
The fyrst boone that I wold aske,
   Ye would graunt it me *belyfe:*

And I asked you never none tyll now;
   Therefore, good lorde, graunt it me.
Now aske it, madam, sayd the kynge,
   And graunted it shal be.

Then, good my lord, I you beseche,
   These yemen graunt ye me.
Madame, ye myght have asked a boone,
   That shuld have been worth them all thre.

Ye myght have asked towres, and townes,
   Parkes and forestes plentè.
None soe pleasant to my *pay*, shee sayd;
   Nor none so *lefe* to me.

Madame, sith it is your desyre,
   Your askyng graunted shal be;
But I had *lever* have given you
   Good market townes thre.

The quene was a glad woman,
   And sayde, Lord, gramarcy;
I dare undertake for them,
   That true men shal they be.

But, good my lord, speke som mery word,
   That comfort they may se.
I graunt you grace, then sayd our king;
   Washe, felos, and to meate go ye.

They had not setten but a whyle
   Certayne without *lesynge*,
There came messengers out of the north
   With letters to our kyng.

And whan the came before the kynge,
   They knelt downe on theyr kne;
And sayd, Lord, your officers grete you well,
   Of Carleile in the north cuntrè.

How fareth my justice, sayd the kyng,
   And my sherife also?

Syr, they be slayne without leasynge,
  And many an officer mo.

Who hath them slayne? sayd the kyng;
  Anone that thou tell me.
"Adam Bell, and Clime of the Clough,
  And Wyllyam of Cloudeslè."

Alas for *rewth!* then sayd our kynge:
  My hart is wonderous sore;
I had *lever* than a thousande pounde,
  I had knowne of thys before;

For I have graunted them grace,
  And that forthynketh me:
But had I knowne all thys before,
  They had been hanged all thre.

The kyng hee opened the letter anone,
  Himselfe he red it thro,
And founde how these outlawes had slain
  Thre hundred men and mo:

Fyrst the justice, and the sheryfe,
  And the mayre of Carleile towne;
Of all the constables and catchipolles
  Alyve were "scant" left one:

The baylyes, and the bedyls both,
  And the sergeauntes of the law,
And forty *fosters of the fe,*
  These outlawes had *yslaw:*

And broke his parks, and slayne his dere;
  Of all they chose the best;
So perelous out-lawes, as they were,
  Walked not by easte nor west.

When the kynge this letter had red,
  In hys harte he syghed sore:
Take up the tables anone he bad,
  For I may eat no more.

The kyng called hys best archars
  To the buttes wyth hym to go:
I wyll se these felowes shote, he sayd,
  In the north have wrought this wo.

The kynges bowmen buske them *blyve,*
  And the quenes archers also;

So dyd these thre wyghyte yemen;
  With them they thought to go.

There twyse, or thryse they shote about
  For to assay theyr hande;
There was no shote these yemen shot,
  That any *prycke* myght stand.

Then spake Wyllyam of Cloudeslè;
  By him that for me dyed,
I hold hym never no good archar,
  That shoteth at buttes so wyde.

"At what a butte now wold ye shote?"
  I pray thee tell to me.
At suche a but, syr, he sayd,
  As men use in my countree.

Wyllyam wente into a fyeld,
  And "with him" his two brethren:
There they set up two hasell roddes
  Twenty score paces betwene.

I hold him an archar, said Cloudeslè,
  That yonder wande cleveth in two.
Here is none suche, sayd the kyng,
  Nor no man can so do.

I shall assaye, syr, sayd Cloudeslè,
  Or that I farther go.
Cloudesly with a *bearyng arowe*
  Clave the wand in two.

Thou art the best archer, then sayd the king,
  Forsothe that ever I se.
And yet for your love, sayd Wyllyam,
  I wyll do more maystery.

I have a sonne is seven yere olde,
  He is to me full deare;
I wyll hym tye to a stake;
  All shall se, that be here;

And lay an apple upon hys head,
  And go syxe score paces hym fro,
And I my selfe with a brode arow
  Shall cleve the apple in two.

Now haste the, then sayd the kyng,
  By hym that dyed on a tre,
But yf thou do not, as thou hest sayde,
  Hanged shalt thou be.

And thou touche his head or gowne,
  In syght that men may se,
By all the sayntes that be in heaven,
  I shall hange you all thre.

That I have promised, said William,
  That I wyll never forsake.
And ther even before the kynge
  In the earth he drove a stake:

And bound thereto his eldest sonne,
  And bad hym stand styll thereat;
And turned the childes face him fro,
  Because he should not start.

An apple upon his head he set,
  And then his bowe he bent:
Syxe score paces they were *meaten*,
  And thether Cloudeslè went.

There he drew out a fayr brode arrowe,
  Hys bowe was great and longe,
He set that arrowe in his bowe,
  That was both styffe and stronge.

He prayed the people, that wer there,
  That they "all still wold" stand,
For he that shoteth for such a wager
  Behoveth a stedfast hand.

Muche people prayed for Cloudeslè,
  That his lyfe saved myght be,
And whan he made hym redy to shote,
  There was many weeping ee.

"But" Cloudeslè clefte the apple in two,
  "His sonne he did not nee."
Over Gods forbode, sayd the kinge,
  That thou shold shote at me.

I geve thee eightene pence a day,
  And my bowe shalt thou bere,
And over all the north countrè
  I make the chyfe rydère.

And I thyrtene pence a day, said the quene,
  By God, and by my fay;
Come feche thy payment when thou wylt,
  No man shall say the nay.

Wyllyam, I make the a gentleman
  Of clothying, and of *fe:*
And thy two brethren, yemen of my chambre,
  For they are so semely to se.

Your sonne, for he is tendre of age,
  Of my wyne-seller he shall be;
And when he commeth to mans estate,
  Better avaunced shall he be.

And, Wyllyam, bring me your wife, said the quene,
  Me longeth her sore to se:
She shall be my chefe gentlewoman,
  To governe my nurserye.

The yemen thanked them all curteously,
  To some byshop wyl we wend,
Of all the synnes, that we have done,
  To be *assoyld* at his hand.

So forth be gone these good yemen,
  As fast as they might "he;"
And after came and dwelled with the kynge,
  And dyed good men all thre.

Thus endeth the lives of these good yemen,
  God send them eternall blysse;
And all, that with a hand-bowe shoteth:
  That of heven may never mysse.
  Amen.

## II.—THE AGED LOVER RENOUNCETH LOVE.

THE Gravedigger's song in *Hamlet*, Act v., is taken from three stanzas of the following poem, though greatly altered and disguised, as the same were corrupted by the ballad-singers of Shakespeare's time; or perhaps so designed by the poet himself, the better to suit the character of an illiterate clown. The original is preserved among *Surrey's Poems*, and is attributed to Lord Vaux by George Gascoigne. It is also ascribed to Lord Vaux in a manuscript copy preserved in the British Museum.

I LOTH that I did love,
  In youth that I thought swete,
As time requires: for my behove
  Me thinkes they are not mete.

My lustes they do me leave,
  My fansies all are fled;
And tract of time begins to weave
  Gray heares upon my hed.

For Age with steling steps
  Hath clawde me with his crowch,
And lusty "Youthe" awaye he leapes,
  As there had bene none such.

My muse doth not delight
  Me, as she did before:
My hand and pen are not in plight,
  As they have bene of yore.

For Reason me denies,
  "All" youthly idle rime;
And day by day to me she cries,
  Leave off these toyes in tyme.

The wrinkles in my brow,
  The furrowes in my face
Say, Limping age will "lodge" him now,
  Where youth must geve him place.

The harbenger of death,
  To me I se him ride,
The cough, the cold, the gasping breath
  Doth bid me to provide

A pikeax and a spade,
  And eke a shrowding shete,

A house of clay for to be made
  For such a guest most mete.

Me thinkes I heare the clarke,
  That knoles the carefull knell;
And bids me leave my "wearye" warke,
  Ere nature me compell.

My kepers * knit the knot,
  That youth doth laugh to scorne,
Of me that "shall bee cleane" forgot,
  As I had "ne'er" bene borne.

Thus must I youth geve up,
  Whose badge I long did weare:
To them I yeld the wanton cup,
  That better may it beare.

Lo here the bared skull;
  By whose balde signe I know,
That stouping age away shall pull
  "What" youthful yeres did sow.

For Beautie with her band,
  These croked cares had wrought,
And shipped me into the land,
  From whence I first was brought.

And ye that bide behinde,
  Have ye none other trust:
As ye of claye were cast by kinde,
  So shall ye "turne" to dust.

---

* Alluding perhaps to Eccles. xii. 3.

### III.—JEPHTHAH, JUDGE OF ISRAEL.

In Shakespeare's *Hamlet*, Act ii., the hero of the play takes occasion to banter Polonius with some scraps of an old ballad, which has never appeared yet in any collection: for which reason, as it is but short, it will not perhaps be unacceptable to the reader, who will also be diverted with the pleasant absurdities of the composition.

The banter of *Hamlet* is as follows:—

*Hamlet.* "O Jepta, Judge of Israel," what a treasure hadst thou!
*Polonius.* What a treasure had he, my lord?
*Ham.* Why, "One faire daughter, and no more,
The which he loved passing well."
*Polon.* Still on my daughter.
*Ham.* Am not I i' th' right, old Jeptha?
*Polon.* If you call me Jeptha, my lord, I have a daughter, that I love passing well.
*Ham.* Nay, that follows not.
*Polon.* What follows then, my lord?
*Ham.* Why, "As by lot, God wot:" and then you know, "It came to passe, As most like it was." The first row of the pious chanson will shew you more.

Edit. 1793, vol. xv. p. 133.

Have you not heard these many years ago,
 Jeptha was judge of Israel?
He had one only daughter and no mo,
 The which he loved passing well:
  And, as by lott,
  God wot,
 It so came to pass,
 As Gods will was,
That great wars there should be,
And none should be chosen chief but he.

And when he was appointed judge,
 And chieftain of the company,
A solemn vow to God he made;
 If he returned with victory,
  At his return
  To burn
 The first live thing,
 . . . . . .
That should meet with him then,
Off his house, when he should return agen.

It came to pass, the wars was oer,
And he returned with victory;

His dear and only daughter first of all
 Came to meet her father foremostly:
  And all the way,
  She did play
 On tabret and pipe,
 Full many a stripe,
With note so high,
For joy that her father is come so nigh.

But when he saw his daughter dear
 Coming on most foremostly,
He wrung his hands, and tore his hair,
 And cryed out most piteously;
  Oh! it's thou, said he,
  That have brought me
  Low,
 And troubled me so,
That I know not what to do.

For I have made a vow, he sed,
 The which must be replenished:
 . . . . . .
  "What thou hast spoke
  Do not revoke:

What thou hast said,
 Be not afraid;
Altho' it be I;
 Keep promises to God on high.

"But, dear father, grant me one request,
 That I may go to the wilderness,
Three months there with my friends to stay;
 There to bewail my virginity;

And let there be,
 Said she,
Some two or three
 Young maids with me."
So he sent her away,
 For to mourn, for to mourn, till her
  dying day.

## IV.—A ROBYN JOLLY ROBYN.

In his *Twelfth Night*, Shakespeare introduces the Clown singing part of the two first stanzas of the following song; which song is here printed from what appears the most ancient of Dr. Harrington's poetical MSS., and which seems to have been written in the reign of King Henry VIII.

A ROBYN,
 Jolly Robyn,
Tell me how thy *leman* doeth,
 And thou shalt knowe of myn.

"My lady is unkynde perde."
 Alack! why is she so?
"She loveth an other better than me;
 And yet she will say no."

I fynde no such doublenes:
 I fynde women true.
My lady loveth me dowtles,
 And will change for no newe.

"Thou art happy while that doeth last;
 But I say, as I fynde,
That women's love is but a blast,
 And torneth with the wynde."

Suche folkes can take no harme by love,
 That can abide their torn:
"But I alas can no way prove
 In love but lake and morn."

But if thou wilt avoyde thy harme,
 Lerne this lessen of me,
At others fieres thy selfe to warme,
 And let them warme with the.

## V.—A SONG TO THE LUTE IN MUSICKE.

This sonnet (which is ascribed to Richard Edwards, in the *Paradise of Daintie Devises*, fo. 31, b.) is by Shakespeare made the subject of some pleasant ridicule in his *Romeo and Juliet*, Act iv. Sc. v., where he introduces Peter putting this question to the musicians:

*Peter.* . . . why "Silver Sound"? why "Musicke with her silver sound"? what say you, Simon Catling?

1 *Mus.* Marry, sir, because silver hath a sweet sound.

*Pet.* Pretty! what say you, Hugh Rebecke?

2 *Mus.* I say, silver sound, because musicians sound for silver.

*Pet.* Pretty too! what say you, James Sound-post?

3 *Mus.* Faith, I know not what to say.

*Pet.* . . . I will say it for you: It is "Musicke with her silver sound," because musicians have no gold for sounding.

WHERE gripinge grefes the hart would
    wounde,
And dolefulle *dumps* the mynde
    oppresse,
There musicke with her silver sound
    With spede is wont to send redresse :
Of trobled mynds, in every sore,
Swete musicke hathe a salve in store.

In joye yt maks our mirthe abounde,
    In woe yt cheres our hevy sprites ;
*Be-strawghted* heads relyef hath founde,
    By musickes pleasaunt swete delightes :
Our senses all, what shall I say more?
Are subjecte unto musicks lore.

The Gods by musicke have theire prayse ;
    The lyfe, the soul therein doth joye :
For, as the Romayne poet sayes,
    In seas, whom pyrats would destroy,
A dolphin saved from death most sharpe
Arion playing on his harpe.

O heavenly gyft, that rules the mynd,
    Even as the sterne dothe rule the shippe !
O musicke, whom the Gods *assinde*
    To comforte manne, whom cares would
    nippe !
Since thow both man and beste doest
    move,
What beste ys he, wyll the disprove?

## VI.—KING COPHETUA AND THE BEGGAR MAID

Is a story often alluded to by our old dramatic writers. Shakespeare, in his *Romeo and Juliet*, Act ii. Sc. i., makes Mercutio say :

> "Her (Venus') purblind son and heir,
> Young Adam Cupid, he that shot so true,
> When King Cophetua loved the beggar maid."

In the second part of *Henry IV.*, Act v. Sc. iii., Falstaff is introduced affectedly saying to Pistoll :

> "O base Assyrian knight, what is thy news?
> Let King Cophetua know the truth thereof."

Shakespeare also alludes to the ballad in *Love's Labour Lost*, Act iv. Sc. i. And there is an allusion to the story in *King Richard II.*, Act v. Sc. iii.

I READ that once in Affrica
    A princely wight did raine,
Who had to name Cophetua,
    As poets they did faine :
From natures lawes he did decline,
For sure he was not of my mind,
He cared not for women-kinde,
    But did them all disdaine.
But, marke, what hapned on a day,
As he out of his window lay,
He saw a beggar all in gray,
    The which did cause his paine.

The blinded boy, that shootes so trim,
    From heaven downe did hie ;
He drew a dart and shot at him,
    In place where he did lye :

Which soone did pierse him to the quicke,
And when he felt the arrow pricke,
Which in his tender heart did sticke,
    He looketh as he would dye.
What sudden chance is this, quoth he,
That I to love must subject be,
Which never thereto would agree,
    But still did it defie?

Then from the window he did come,
    And laid him on his bed,
A thousand heapes of care did runne
    Within his troubled head :
For now he meanes to crave her love,
And now he seekes which way to proove
How he his fancie might remoove,
    And not this beggar wed.

## KING COPHETUA AND THE BEGGAR MAID.

But Cupid had him so in snare,
That this poor begger must prepare
A salve to cure him of his care,
    Or els he would be dead.

And, as he musing thus did lye,
    He thought for to devise
How he might have her companye,
    That so did 'maze his eyes.
In thee, quoth he, doth rest my life;
For surely thou shalt be my wife,
Or else this hand with bloody knife
    The Gods shall sure suffice.
Then from his bed he soon arose,
And to his pallace gate he goes;
Full little then this begger knowes
    When she the king espies.

The Gods preserve your majesty,
    The beggers all gan cry:
Vouchsafe to give your charity
    Our childrens food to buy.
The king to them his pursse did cast,
And they to part it made great haste;
This silly woman was the last
    That after them did hye.
The king he cal'd her back againe,
And unto her he gave his chaine;
And said, With us you shal remaine
    Till such time as we dye:

For thou, quoth he, shalt be my wife,
    And honoured for my queene;
With thee I meane to lead my life,
    As shortly shall be seene:
Our wedding shall appointed be,
And every thing in its degree:
Come on, quoth he, and follow me,
    Thou shalt go shift thee cleane.
What is thy name, faire maid? quoth he.
Penelophon, O king, quoth she:
With that she made a lowe courtsèy,
    A trim one as I weene.

Thus hand in hand along they walke
    Unto the king's pallàce:
The king with courteous comly talke
    This begger doth imbrace:

The begger blusheth scarlet red,
And straight againe as pale as lead,
But not a word at all she said,
    She was in such amaze.
At last she spake with trembling voyce,
And said, O king, I doe rejoyce
That you wil take me for your choyce,
    And my degree's so base.

And when the wedding day was come,
    The king commanded strait
The noblemen both all and some
    Upon the queene to wait.
And she behaved herself that day,
As if she had never walkt the way;
She had forgot her gowne of gray,
    Which she did weare of late.
The proverbe old is come to passe,
The priest, when he begins his masse,
Forgets that ever clerke he was;
    He knowth not his estate.

Here you may read, Cophetua,
    Though long time fancie-fed,
Compelled by the blinded boy
    The begger for to wed:
He that did lovers lookes disdaine,
To do the same was glad and faine,
Or else he would himselfe have slaine,
    In storie, as we read.
Disdaine no whit, O lady deere,
But pitty now thy servant heere,
Least that it hap to thee this yeare,
    As to that king it did.

And thus they led a quiet life
    During their princely raigne;
And in a tombe were buried both,
    As writers sheweth plaine.
The lords they tooke it grievously,
The ladies tooke it heavily,
The commons cryed pitiously,
    Their death to them was paine,
Their fame did sound so passingly,
That it did pierce the starry sky,
And throughout all the world did flye
    To every prince's realme.

## VII.—TAKE THY OLD CLOAK ABOUT THEE.

Given in the folio under the title of *Bell my Wiffe*. This piece is more than a controversy between man and wife. It notes the tendency of the age, the struggle between social revolution and social conservatism. The man is anxious to do as his neighbours, and to do away with distinctions and rise to a higher level. The wife thinks old things are best, and wishes not to meddle with new. Shakespeare quotes the 7th stanza in Act ii. of *Othello*.

This winters weather itt waxeth cold,
  And frost doth freese on every hill,
And Boreas blowes his blasts soe bold,
  That all our cattell are like to *spill*;
Bell my wiffe, who loves noe strife,
  She sayd unto me quietlye,
Rise up, and save cow Crumbockes liffe,
  Man, put thine old cloake about thee.

### HE.

O Bell, why dost thou *flyte* "and scorne?"
  Thou kenst my cloak is very thin:
Itt is soe bare and overworne
  A *cricke* he theron cannot renn:
Then Ile noe longer borrowe nor lend,
  "For once Ile new appareld bee,
To-morrow Ile to towne and spend,"
  For Ile have a new cloake about mee.

### SHE.

Cow Crumbocke is a very good cowe,
  Shee ha beene alwayes true to the payle,
Shee has helpt us to butter and cheese, I trow,
  And other things shee will not fayle;
I wold be loth to see her pine,
  Good husband, councell take of mee,
It is not for us to go soe fine,
  Man, take thine old cloake about thee.

### HE.

My cloake it was a verry good cloake,
  Itt hath been alwayes true to the weare,
But now it is not worth a groat;
  I have had it four and forty yeere:
Sometime itt was of cloth in *graine*,
  'Tis now but a *sigh clout* as you may see,
It will neither hold out winde nor raine;
  And Ile have a new cloake about mee.

### SHE.

It is four and fortye yeeres agoe
  Since the one of us the other did ken,
And we have had betwixt us towe
  Of children either nine or ten;
Wee have brought them up to women and men;
  In the feare of God I trow they bee;
And why wilt thou thyselfe *misken*?
  Man, take thine old cloake about thee.

### HE.

O Bell my wiffe, why dost thou "floute!"
  Now is nowe, and then was then:
Seeke now all the world throughout,
  Thou kenst not clownes from gentlemen.
They are cladd in blacke, greene, yellowe, or "gray,"
  Soe far above their owne degree:
Once in my life Ile "doe as they,"
  For Ile have a new cloake about mee.

### SHE.

King Stephen was a worthy peere,
  His breeches cost him but a crowne,
He held them sixpence all too deere;
  Therefore he calld the taylor *Lowne*.
He was a wight of high renowne,
  And thouse but of a low degree:
Itt's pride that putts this countrye downe,
  Man, take thine old cloake about thee.

### HE.

"Bell my wife she loves not strife,
  Yet she will lead me if she can;
And oft, to live a quiet life,
  I am forced to yield, though Ime goodman;"
Itt's not for a man with a woman to *threape*,
  Unlesse he first gave oer the plea;
As wee began wee now will leave,
  And Ile take mine old cloake about mee.

## VIII.—WILLOW, WILLOW, WILLOW.

It is from the following stanzas that Shakespeare has taken his song of the Willow, in his *Othello*, Act iv. Sc. iii., though somewhat varied and applied by him to a female character. He makes Desdemona introduce it in this pathetic and affecting manner:

> "My mother had a maid called Barbara:
> She was in love; and he she lov'd prov'd mad,
> And did forsake her. She had a song of—Willow.
> An old thing 'twas, but it expressed her fortune,
> And she died singing it."—Ed. 1793, vol. xv. p. 613.

A poore soule sat sighing under a sicamore tree;
   O willow, willow, willow!
With his hand on his bosom, his head on his knee:
   O willow, willow, willow!
   O willow, willow, willow!
Sing, O the greene willow shall be my garlànd.

He sigh'd in his singing, and after each grone,
   Come willow, etc.
I am dead to all pleasure, my true-love is gone;
   O willow, etc.
Sing, O the greene willow shall be my garlànd.

My love she is turned; untrue she doth prove:
   O willow, etc.
She renders me nothing but hate for my love.
   O willow, etc.
Sing, O the greene willow, etc.

O pitty me (cried he) ye lovers, each one;
   O willow, etc.
Her heart's hard as marble; she rues not my mone.
   O willow, etc.
Sing, O the greene willow, etc.

The cold streams ran by him, his eyes wept apace;
   O willow, etc.

The salt tears fell from him, which drowned his face:
   O willow, etc.
Sing, O the green willow, etc.

The mute birds sate by him, made tame by his mones;
   O willow, etc.
The salt tears fell from him, which softened the stones.
   O willow, etc.
Sing, O the greene willow shall be my garlànd!

Let nobody blame me, her scornes I do prove;
   O willow, etc.
She was borne to be faire; I, to die for her love.
   O willow, etc.
Sing, O the greene willow shall be my garlànd.

O that beauty should harbour a heart that's so hard!
   Sing willow, etc.
My true love rejecting without all regard.
   O willow, etc.
Sing, O the greene willow, etc.

Let love no more boast him in palace, or bower;
   O willow, etc.
For women are trothles, and flote in an houre.
   O willow, etc.
Sing, O the greene willow, etc.

But what helps complaining? In vaine I
    complaine:
  O willow, etc.
I must patiently suffer her scorne and dis-
    daine.
  O willow, etc.
Sing, O the greene willow, etc.

Come, all you forsaken, and sit down by
    me,
  O willow, etc.
He that 'plaines of his false love, mine's
    falser than she.
  O willow, etc.
Sing, O the greene willow, etc.

The willow wreath weare I, since my love
    did fleet;
  O willow, etc.
A Garland for lovers forsaken most meete.
  O willow, etc.
Sing, O the greene willow shall be my
    garlànd!

### PART THE SECOND.

Lowe lay'd by my sorrow, begot by dis-
    daine;
  O willow, willow, willow!
Against her too cruell, still still I com-
    plaine,
  O willow, willow, willow!
  O willow, willow, willow!
Sing, O the greene willow shall be my
    garlànd!

O love too injurious, to wound my poore
    heart?
  O willow, etc.
To suffer the triumph, and joy in my
    smart:
  O willow, etc.
Sing, O the greene willow, etc.

O willow, willow, willow! the willow
    garlànd,
  O willow, etc.

A sign of her falsenesse before me doth
    stand:
  O willow, etc.
Sing, O the greene willow, etc.

As here it doth bid to despair and to
    dye,
  O willow, etc.
So hang it, friends, ore me in grave where
    I lye:
  O willow, etc.
Sing, O the greene willow shall be my
    garlànd.

In grave where I rest mee, hang this to
    the view,
  O willow, etc.
Of all that doe knowe her, to blaze her
    untrue.
  O willow, etc.
Sing, O the greene willow, etc.

With these words engraven, as epitaph
    meet,
  O willow, etc.
"Here lyes one, drank poyson for potion
    most sweet."
  O willow, etc.
Sing, O the greene willow, etc.

Though she thus unkindly hath scorned
    my love,
  O willow, etc.
And carelesly smiles at the sorrowes I
    prove;
  O willow, etc.
Sing, O the greene willow, etc.

I cannot against her unkindly exclaim,
  O willow, etc.
Cause once well I loved her, and honoured
    her name:
  O willow, etc.
Sing, O the greene willow, etc.

The name of her sounded so sweete in
    mine eare,
  O willow, etc.

It rays'd my heart lightly, the name of my
    deare ;
        O willow, etc.
Sing, O the greene willow shall be my
    garlànd.

As then 'twas my comfort, it now is my
    griefe ;
        O willow, etc.
It now brings me anguish ; then brought
    me reliefe.
        O willow, etc.

Sing, O the greene willow shall be my
    garlànd.
Farewell, faire false hearted : plaints end
    with my breath !
        O willow, willow, willow !
Thou dost loath me, I love thee, though
    cause of my death.
        O willow, willow, willow !
        O willow, willow, willow !
Sing, O the greene willow shall be my
    garlànd.

## IX.—SIR LANCELOT DU LAKE.

THIS ballad is quoted in Shakespeare's second part of *Henry IV.* Act ii. The subject of it is taken from the ancient romance of King Arthur (commonly called *Morte Arthur*), being a poetical translation of chaps. cvii., cix., cx. in Part i., as they stand in ed. 1634, 4to. In the older editions the chapters are differently numbered. This song is given from a printed copy, corrected in part by a fragment in the Editor's folio MS.

WHEN Arthur first in court began,
    And was approved king,
By force of armes great victorys wanne,
    And conquest home did bring,

Then into England straight he came
    With fifty good and able
Knights, that resorted unto him,
    And were of his round table :

And he had justs and turnaments,
    Wherto were many prest,
Wherin some knights did far excell
    And *eke* surmount the rest.

But one Sir Lancelot du Lake,
    Who was approved well,
He for his deeds and feats of armes
    All others did excell.

When he had rested him a while,
    In play, and game, and sportt,
He said he wold goe prove himselfe
    In some adventurous sort.

He armed rode in a forrest wide,
    And met a damsell faire,
Who told him of adventures great,
    Whereto he gave great eare.

Suche wold I find, quoth Lancelott :
    For that cause came I hither.
Thou seemst, quoth shee, a knight full
    good,
    And I will bring thee thither.

Wheras * a mighty knight doth dwell,
    That now is of great fame :
Therfore tell me what wight thou art,
    And what may be thy name.

"My name is Lancelot du Lake."
    Quoth she, it likes me than :
Here dwelles a knight who never was
    Yet matcht with any man :

Who has in prison threescore knights
    And four, that he did wound ;
Knights of king Arthurs court they be,
    And of his table round.

She brought him to a river side,
    And also to a tree,
Whereon a copper bason hung,
    And many shields to see.

---

* V. 29. *Where* is often used by our old writers for *whereas;* here it is just the contrary.

He struck soe hard, the bason broke;
  And Tarquin soon he spyed:
Who drove a horse before him fast,
  Whereon a knight lay tyed.

Sir knight, then sayd Sir Lancelòtt,
  Bring me that horse-load hither,
And lay him downe, and let him rest;
  Weel try our force together:

For, as I understand, thou hast,
  Soe far as thou art able,
Done great despite and shame unto
  The knights of the Round Table.

If thou be of the Table Round,
  Quoth Tarquin speedilye,
Both thee and all thy fellowship
  I utterly defye.

That's over much, quoth Lancelott tho,
  Defend thee by and by.
They sett their speares unto their steeds,
  And eache att other flie.

They coucht theire speares (their horses ran,
  As though there had been thunder),
And strucke them each immidst their shields,
  Wherewith they broke in sunder.

Their horsses backes brake under them,
  The knights were both *astound:*
To *avoyd* their horsses they made haste
  And light upon the ground.

They tooke them to their shields full fast,
  Their swords they drew out *than,*
With mighty strokes most eagerlye
  Each at the other ran.

They wounded were, and bled full sore,
  They both for breath did stand,
And leaning on their swords awhile,
  Quoth Tarquine, Hold thy hand,

And tell to me what I shall aske.
  Say on, quoth Lancelot tho.

Thou art, quoth Tarquine, the best knight
  That ever I did know;

And like a knight, that I did hate:
  Soe that thou be not hee,
I will deliver all the rest,
  And eke accord with thee.

That is well said, quoth Lancelott;
  But sith it must be soe,
What knight is that thou hatest thus?
  I pray thee to me show.

His name is Lancelot du Lake,
  He slew my brother deere;
Him I suspect of all the rest:
  I would I had him here.

Thy wish thou hast, but yet unknowne,
  I am Lancelot du Lake,
Now knight of Arthurs Table Round;
  King Hauds son of Schuwake;

And I desire thee do thy worst.
  Ho, ho, quoth Tarquin tho,
One of us two shall end our lives
  Before that we do go.

If thou be Lancelot du Lake,
  Then welcome shalt thou bee:
Wherfore see thou thyself defend,
  For now defye I thee.

They buckled then together so,
  Like unto wild boares *rashing;**
And with their swords and shields they ran
  At one another slashing:

The ground besprinkled was with blood:
  Tarquin began to yield;
For he gave backe for wearinesse,
  And lowe did beare his shield.

---

\* *Rashing* seems to be the old hunting term to express the stroke made by the wild boar with his fangs.

This soone Sir Lancelot espyde,
  He leapt upon him then,
He pull'd him downe upon his knee,
  And rushing off his helm,

Forthwith he strucke his necke in two,
  And, when he had soe done,
From prison threescore knights and four
  Delivered everye one.

## X.—CORYDON'S FAREWELL TO PHILLIS

Is an attempt to paint a lover's irresolution, but so poorly executed, that it would not have been admitted into this collection, if it had not been quoted in Shakspeare's *Twelfth Night*, Act ii. Sc. iii.

FAREWELL, dear love; since thou wilt
    needs be gone,
Mine eyes do shew, my life is almost done.
  Nay I will never die, so long as I can
    spie
  There be many mo, though that she doe
    goe,
  There be many mo, I fear not:
  Why then let her goe, I care not.

Farewell, farewell; since this I find is true,
I will not spend more time in wooing you:
  But I will seek elsewhere, if I may find
    love there:
  Shall I bid her goe? what and if I doe?
  Shall I bid her goe and spare not?
  O no, no, no, I dare not.

Ten thousand times farewell;—yet stay a
    while:—
Sweet, kiss me once; sweet kisses time
    beguile:

I have no power to move. How now am
    I in love?
Wilt thou needs be gone? Go then, all
    is one.
  Wilt thou needs be gone? Oh, hie
    thee!
  Nay stay, and do no more deny me.

Once more adieu, I see loath to depart
Bids oft adieu to her, that holds my heart.
  But seeing I must lose thy love, which
    I did choose,
  Goe thy way for me, since that may not be.
  Goe thy ways for me. But whither?
  Goe, oh, but where I may come thither.

What shall I doe? my love is now departed.
She is as fair, as she is cruel-hearted.
  She would not be intreated, with prayers
    oft repeated,
  If she come no more, shall I die therefore?
  If she come no more, what care I?
  Faith, let her goe, or come, or tarry.

## XI.—GERNUTUS, THE JEW OF VENICE.

THIS ballad, Mr. Warton thinks, gave rise to Shakspeare's *Merchant of Venice*, though other critics have based it upon a direct Italian source. Doubtless the Italian story, wherein, however, the Christian played the part of Shakspeare's Jew, was known both to the dramatist and to the author of the present ballad.

### THE FIRST PART.

IN Venice towne not long agoe
  A cruel Jew did dwell,
Which lived all on usurie,
  As Italian writers tell.

Gernutus called was the Jew,
  Which never thought to dye,
Nor ever yet did any good
  To them in streets that lie.

His life was like a barrow hogge,
  That liveth many a day,
Yet never once doth any good,
  Until men will him slay.

Or like a filthy heap of dung,
  That lyeth in a *whoard;*
Which never can do any good,
  Till it be spread abroad.

So fares it with the usurer,
  He cannot sleep in rest,
For feare the thiefe will him pursue
  To plucke him from his nest.

His heart doth thinke on many a wile,
  How to deceive the poore;
His mouth is almost ful of mucke,
  Yet still he gapes for more.

His wife must lend a shilling,
  For every weeke a penny,
Yet bring a pledge, that is double worth,
  If that you will have any.

And see, likewise, you keepe your day,
  Or else you loose it all :
This was the living of the wife,
  Her cow * she did it call.

Within that citie dwelt that time
  A marchant of great fame,
Which being distressed in his need,
  Unto Gernutus came :

Desiring him to stand his friend
  For twelve month and a day,
To lend to him an hundred crownes :
  And he for it would pay

Whatsoever he would demand of him,
  And pledges he should have.

---

\* Ver. 32. Her *cow*, etc., seems to have suggested to Shakespeare Shylock's argument for usury taken from Jacob's management of Laban's sheep, Act i., to which Antonio replies: " Was this inserted to make interest good? Or are your gold and silver *ewes* and rams? *Shylock*. I cannot tell, I make it *breed as fast.*"

No (quoth the Jew with *fleering* lookes),
  Sir, aske what you will have.

No penny for the loane of it
  For one year you shall pay ;
You may doe me as good a turne,
  Before my dying day.

But we will have a merry jeast,
  For to be talked long :
You shall make me a bond, quoth he,
  That shall be large and strong :

And this shall be the forfeyture ;
  Of your owne fleshe a pound.
If you agree, make you the bond,
  And here is a hundred crownes.

With right good will! the marchant says :
  And so the bond was made.
When twelve month and a day drew on
  That backe it should be payd,

The marchants ships were all at sea,
  And money came not in ;
Which way to take, or what to doe
  To thinke he doth begin :

And to Gernutus strait he comes
  With cap and bended knee,
And sayde to him, Of curtesie
  I pray you beare with mee.

My day is come, and I have not
  The money for to pay :
And little good the forfeyture
  Will doe you, I dare say.

With all my heart, Gernutus sayd,
  Commaund it to your minde :
In thinges of bigger waight then this
  You shall me ready finde.

He goes his way ; the day once past
  Gernutus doth not slacke
To get a sergiant presently ;
  And clapt him on the backe :

And layd him into prison strong,
  And sued his bond withall ;
And when the judgement day was come,
  For judgement he did call.

The marchants friends came thither fast,
　With many a weeping eye,
For other means they could not find,
　But he that day must dye.

### THE SECOND PART.

"Of the Jews crueltie; setting foorth the mercifulnesse of the Judge towards the Marchant. To the tune of Blacke and Yellow."

Some offered for his hundred crownes
　Five hundred for to pay;
And some a thousand, two or three,
　Yet still he did denay.

And at the last ten thousand crownes
　They offered, him to save.
Gernutus sayd, I will no gold:
　My forfeite I will have.

A pound of fleshe is my demand,
　And that shall be my hire.
Then sayd the judge, Yet, good my friend,
　Let me of you desire

To take the flesh from such a place,
　As yet you let him live:
Do so, and lo! an hundred crownes
　To thee here will I give.

No: no: quoth he; no: judgement here:
　For this it shall be tride,
For I will have my pound of fleshe
　From under his right side.

It grieved all the companie
　His crueltie to see,
For neither friend nor foe could helpe
　But he must spoyled bee.

The bloudie Jew now ready is
　With whetted blade in hand,*

---

\* The passage in Shakespeare bears so strong a resemblance to this, as to render it probable that the one suggested the other. See Act iv. Sc. ii. :

"*Bass.* Why doest thou whet thy knife so earnestly?" etc.

To spoyle the bloud of innocent,
　By forfeit of his bond.

And as he was about to strike
　In him the deadly blow:
Stay (quoth the judge) thy crueltie;
　I charge thee to do so.

Sith needs thou wilt thy forfeit have,
　Which is of flesh a pound:
See that thou shed no drop of bloud,
　Nor yet the man confound.

For if thou doe, like murderer,
　Thou here shalt hanged be:
Likewise of flesh see that thou cut
　No more than longes to thee:

For if thou take either more or lesse
　To the value of a mite,
Thou shalt be hanged presently,
　As is both law and right.

Gernutus now waxt franticke mad,
　And wote not what to say;
Quoth he at last, Ten thousand crownes
　I will that he shall pay;

And so I graunt to set him free.
　The judge doth answere make;
You shall not have a penny given;
　Your forfeyture now take.

At the last he doth demaund
　But for to have his owne.
No, quoth the judge, doe as you list,
　Thy judgement shall be showne.

Either take your pound of flesh, quoth he,
　Or cancell me your bond.
O cruell judge, then quoth the Jew,
　That doth against me stand!

And so with griping* grieved mind
　He biddeth them fare-well.
"Then" all the people prays'd the Lord,
　That ever this heard tell.

---

\* Ver. 61. *Griped*, Ashmol. copy.

Good people, that doe heare this song,
  For trueth I dare well say,
That many a wretch as ill as hee
  Doth live now at this day;

That seeketh nothing but the spoyle
  Of many a wealthey man,
And for to trap the innocent
  Deviseth what they can.

From whome the Lord deliver me,
  And every Christian too,
And send to them like sentence eke
  That meaneth so to do.

\*\*\* Since the first edition of this book was printed, the editor hath had reason to believe that both Shakespeare and the author of this ballad are indebted for their story of the Jew (however they came by it) to an Italian novel, which was first printed at Milan in the year 1554, in a book entitled, *Il Pecorone, nel quale si contengono Cinquanta Novelle antiche*, etc., republished at Florence about the year 1748 or 1749. The author was Ser. Giovanni Fiorentino, who wrote in 1378, thirty years after the time in which the scene of Boccace's *Decameron* is laid. (*Vid. Manni Istoria del Decamerone di Giov. Boccac.* 4to, Fior. 1744.)

That Shakespeare had his plot from the novel itself, is evident from his having some incidents from it, which are not found in the ballad: and I think it will also be found that he borrowed from the ballad some hints that were not suggested by the novel. (See above, Part ii. ver. 25, etc., where, instead of that spirited description of *the whetted blade*, etc., the prose narrative coldly says, "The Jew had prepared a razor," etc. See also some other passages in the same piece.) This, however, is spoken with diffidence, as I have at present before me only the abridgment of the novel which Mr. Johnson has given us at the end of his commentary on Shakespeare's play. The translation of the Italian story at large is not easy to be met with, having I believe never been published, though it was printed some years ago with this title:—"The Novel, from which the *Merchant of Venice* written by Shakespeare is taken, translated from the Italian. To which is added a translation of a novel from the *Decamerone* of Boccacio. London, printed for M. Cooper, 1755, 8vo."

## XII.—THE PASSIONATE SHEPHERD TO HIS LOVE.

This beautiful sonnet is quoted in the *Merry Wives of Windsor*, Act iii. Sc. i., and has often been ascribed (together with the reply) to Shakespeare himself.

There is, however, abundant reason to believe that it was written by Christopher Marlow. Isaac Walton in his *Compleat Angler*, first printed in the year 1658, but probably written some time before, speaks of it as "that smooth song, which was made by Kit Marlow, now fifty years ago: and . . . an answer to it which was made by Sir Walter Raleigh in his younger days."

There are also other proofs of the author of the one being Christopher Marlow; of the other, Sir Walter Raleigh.

Come live with me and be my love,
  And we wil all the pleasures prove
That hils and vallies, dale and field,
  And all the craggy mountains yield.

There will we sit upon the rocks,
  And see the shepherds feed their flocks,
By shallow rivers, to whose falls
  Melodious birds sing madrigals.

There will I make thee beds of roses
With a thousand fragrant posies,
A cap of flowers, and a kirtle
Imbrodered all with leaves of mirtle;

A gown made of the finest wool,
Which from our pretty lambs we pull;
Slippers lin'd choicely for the cold;
With buckles of the purest gold;

A belt of straw, and ivie buds,
With coral clasps, and amber studs:
And if these pleasures may thee move,
Then live with me and be my love.

The shepherd swains shall dance and sing
For thy delight each May morning:
If these delights thy mind may move,
Then live with me, and be my love.

### THE NYMPH'S REPLY.

If that the World and Love were young,
And truth in every shepherd's toung,
These pretty pleasures might me move
To live with thee, and be thy love.

But time drives flocks from field to fold,
When rivers rage, and rocks grow cold,
And Philomel becometh dumb,
And all complain of cares to come.

The flowers do fade, and wanton fields
To wayward winter reckoning yield:
A honey tongue, a hart of gall,
Is fancies spring, but sorrows fall.

Thy gowns, thy shoes, thy beds of roses,
Thy cap, thy kirtle, and thy posies,
Soon break, soon wither, soon forgotten,
In folly ripe, in reason rotten.

Thy belt of straw, and ivie buds,
Thy coral clasps, and amber studs;
All these in me no means can move
To come to thee, and be thy love.

But could youth last, and love still breed,
Had joyes no date, nor age no need;
Then those delights my mind might move
To live with thee, and be thy love.

## XIII.—TITUS ANDRONICUS'S COMPLAINT.

THE same question arises with this ballad as with that of *Gernutus*, as to whether Shakespeare took his play from the ballad, or whether the ballad was written from the play. In both cases there are marked differences. But there is good reason to believe that Shakespeare did not write, but simply improved the play of *Titus Andronicus*, which is much inferior to any of his other works.

You noble minds, and famous martiall wights,
That in defence of native country fights,
Give eare to me, that ten yeeres fought for Rome,
Yet reapt disgrace at my returning home.

In Rome I lived in fame fulle threescore yeeres,
My name beloved was of all my peeres;
Full five and twenty valiant sonnes I had,
Whose forwarde vertues made their father glad.

For when Romes foes their warlike forces bent,
Against them stille my sonnes and I were sent;
Against the Goths full ten yeeres weary warre
We spent, receiving many a bloudy scarre.

Just two and twenty of my sonnes were slaine
Before we did returne to Rome againe:
Of five and twenty sonnes, I brought but three
Alive, the stately towers of Rome to see.

When wars were done, I conquest home did bring,
And did present my prisoners to the king,
The queene of Goths, her sons, and eke a moore,
Which did such murders, like was nere before.

The emperour did make this queene his wife,
Which bred in Rome debate and deadlie strife;
The moore, with her two sonnes did growe soe proud,
That none like them in Rome might bee allowd.

The moore soe pleas'd this new-made empress' eie,
That she consented to him secretlye
For to abuse her husband's marriage bed,
And soe in time a blackamore she bred.

Then she, whose thoughts to murder were inclinde,
Consented with the moore of bloody minde
Against myselfe, my kin, and all my friendes,
In cruell sort to bring them to their endes.

Soe when in age I thought to live in peace,
Both care and griefe began then to increase:
Amongst my sonnes I had one daughter brighte,
Which joy'd, and pleased best my aged sight;

My deere Lavinia was betrothed than
To Cesars sonne, a young and noble man:
Who in a hunting by the emperours wife,
And her two sonnes, bereaved was of life.

He being slaine, was cast in cruel wise,
Into a darksome den from light of skies:
The cruell Moore did come that way as then
With my three sonnes, who fell into the den.

The moore then fetcht the emperour with speed,
For to accuse them of that murderous deed;
And when my sonnes within the den were found,
In wrongfull prison thy were cast and bound.

But nowe, behold! what wounded most my mind,
The empresses two sonnes of savage kind
My daughter ravished without remorse,
And took away her honour, quite perforce.

When they had tasted of soe swete a flowre,
Fearing this swete should shortly turne to sowre,
They cutt her tongue, whereby she could not tell
How that dishonoure unto her befell.

Then both her hands they basely cutt off quite,
Whereby their wickednesse she could not write;
Nor with her needle on her sampler sowe
The bloudye workers of her direfull woe.

My brother Marcus found her in the wood,
Staining the grassie ground with purple bloud,
That trickled from her stumpes, and bloudlesse armes:
Noe tongue at all she had to tell her harmes.

But when I sawe her in that woefull case,
With teares of bloud I wet mine aged face:
For my Lavinia I lamented more
Then for my two and twenty sonnes before.

When as I sawe she could not write nor speake,
With grief mine aged heart began to breake;
We spred an heape of sand upon the ground,
Whereby those bloudy tyrants out we found.

For with a staffe, without the helpe of hand,
She writt these wordes upon the plat of
      sand :
"The lustfull sonnes of the proud em-
      perèsse
Are doers of this hateful wickednèsse."

I tore the milk-white hairs from off mine
      head,
I curst the houre, wherein I first was
      bred,
I wisht this hand, that fought for countrie's
      fame,
In cradle rockt, had first been stroken lame.

The moore delighting still in villainy
Did say, to sett my sonnes from prison free
I should unto the king my right hand give,
And then my three imprisoned sonnes
      should live.

The moore I caus'd to strike it off with
      speede,
Whereat I grieved not to see it bleed,
But for my sonnes would willingly impart,
And for their ransome send my bleeding
      heart.

But as my life did linger thus in paine,
They sent to me my bootlesse hand againe,
And therewithal the heades of my three
      sonnes,
Which filld my dying heart with fresher
      moanes.

Then past reliefe I upp and downe did goe,
And with my tears writ in the dust my woe :
I shot my arrowes towards heaven hie,
And for revenge to hell did often crye.

The empresse then, thinking that I was
      mad,
Like Furies she and both her sonnes were
      clad

(She nam'd Revenge, and Rape and
      Murder they),
To undermine and heare what I would say.

I fed their foolish veines * a certaine space,
Until my friendes did find a secret place,
Where both her sonnes unto a post were
      bound,
And just revenge in cruell sort was found.

I cut their throates, my daughter held the
      pan
Betwixt her stumpes, wherein the bloud it
      ran :
And then I ground their bones to powder
      small,
And made a paste for pyes streight there-
      withall.

Then with their fleshe I made two mighty
      pyes,
And at a banquet served in stately wise :
Before the empresse set this loathsome
      meat ;
So of her sonnes own flesh she well did eat.

Myselfe bereav'd my daughter then of life,
The empresse then I slewe with bloudy
      knife,
And stabb'd the emperour immediatelie,
And then myself : even soe did Titus die.

Then this revenge against the moore was
      found,
Alive they sett him halfe into the ground,
Whereas he stood untill such time he
      starv'd.
And soe God send all murderers may be
      serv'd.

---

* *i.e.* encouraged them in their foolish
**humours or fancies.**

## XIV.—TAKE THOSE LIPS AWAY.

THE first stanza of this little sonnet is found in Shakespeare's *Measure for Measure*, Act iv. Sc. i. Both the stanzas are preserved in Beaum. and Fletcher's *Bloody Brother*, Act v. Sc. ii. It is not found in Jaggard's old edition of Shakespeare's *Passionate Pilgrim*, and there is some doubt as to the authorship of it.

TAKE, oh take those lips away,
  That so sweetlye were forsworne;
And those eyes, the breake of day,
  Lights, that do misleade the morne:
But my kisses bring againe,
Scales of love, but seal'd in vaine.

Hide, oh hide those hills of snowe,
  Which thy frozen bosom beares,
On whose tops the pinkes that growe
  Are of those that April wears:
But first set my poor heart free,
Bound in those icy chains by thee.

## XV.—KING LEIR AND HIS THREE DAUGHTERS.

THE reader has here an ancient ballad on the subject of King Lear, which (as a sensible female critic has well observed) bears so exact an analogy to the argument of Shakespeare's play, that his having copied it could not be doubted, if it were certain that it was written before the tragedy. Here is found the hint of Lear's madness, which the old chronicles do not mention, as also the extravagant cruelty exercised on him by his daughters. In the death of Lear they likewise very exactly coincide. The misfortune is, that there is nothing to assist us in ascertaining the date of the ballad but what little evidence arises from within; this the reader must weigh, and judge for himself.

KING LEIR once ruled in this land
  With princely power and peace;
And had all things with hearts content,
  That might his joys increase.
Amongst those things that nature gave,
  Three daughters fair had he,
So princely seeming beautiful,
  As fairer could not be.

So on a time it pleas'd the king
  A question thus to move,
Which of his daughters to his grace
  Could shew the dearest love:
For to my age you bring content,
  Quoth he, then let me hear,
Which of you three in plighted troth
  The kindest will appear.

To whom the eldest thus began;
  Dear father, mind, quoth she,
Before your face, to do you good,
  My blood shall render'd be:
And for your sake my bleeding heart
  Shall here be cut in twain,
Ere that I see your reverend age
  The smallest grief sustain.

And so will I, the second said;
  Dear father, for your sake,
The worst of all extremities
  I'll gently undertake:
And serve your highness night and day
  With diligence and love;
That sweet content and quietness
  Discomforts may remove.

In doing so, you glad my soul,
  The aged king reply'd;
But what sayst thou, my youngest girl,
  How is thy love ally'd?
My love (quoth young Cordelia then)
  Which to your grace I owe,
Shall be the duty of a child,
  And that is all I'll show.

And wilt thou shew no more, quoth he,
  Than doth thy duty bind?
I well perceive thy love is small,
  When as no more I find.
Henceforth I banish thee my court,
  Thou art no child of mine;
Nor any part of this my realm
  By favour shall be thine.

Thy elder sisters loves are more
  Than well I can demand,
To whom I equally bestow
  My kingdome and my land,
My pompal state and all my goods,
  That lovingly I may
With those thy sisters be maintain'd
  Until my dying day.

Thus flattering speeches won renown,
  By these two sisters here;
The third had causeless banishment,
  Yet was her love more dear:
For poor Cordelia patiently
  Went wandering up and down,
Unhelp'd, unpity'd, gentle maid,
  Through many an English town:

Untill at last in famous France
  She gentler fortunes found;
Though poor and bare, yet was she deem'd
  The fairest on the ground:
Where when the king her virtues heard,
  And this fair lady seen,
With full consent of all his court
  He made his wife and queen.

Her father king Leir this while
  With his two daughters staid:
Forgetful of their promis'd loves,
  Full soon the same decay'd;

And living in queen Ragan's court,
  The eldest of the twain,
She took from him his chiefest means,
  And most of all his train.

For whereas twenty men were wont
  To wait with bended knee:
She gave allowance but to ten,
  And after scarce to three;
Nay, one she thought too much for him;
  So took she all away,
In hope that in her court, good king,
  He would no longer stay.

Am I rewarded thus, quoth he,
  In giving all I have
Unto my children, and to beg
  For what I lately gave?
I'll go unto my Gonorell:
  My second child, I know,
Will be more kind and pitiful,
  And will relieve my woe.

Full fast he hies then to her court;
  Where when she heard his moan
Return'd him answer, That she griev'd,
  That all his means were gone:
But no way could relieve his wants;
  Yet if that he would stay
Within her kitchen, he should have
  What scullions gave away.

When he had heard, with bitter tears,
  He made his answer then;
In what I did let me be made
  Example to all men.
I will return again, quoth he,
  Unto my Ragan's court;
She will not use me thus, I hope,
  But in a kinder sort.

Where when he came, she gave command
  To drive him thence away:
When he was well within her court
  (She said) he would not stay.
Then back again to Gonorell
  The woeful king did hie,
That in her kitchen he might have
  What scullion boys set by.

But there of that he was deny'd
  Which she had promis'd late :
For once refusing, he should not
  Come after to her gate.
Thus twixt his daughters, for relief
  He wandred up and down ;
Being glad to feed on beggars food,
  That lately wore a crown.

And calling to remembrance then
  His youngest daughter's words,
That said the duty of a child
  Was all that love affords :
But doubting to repair to her,
  Whom he had banish'd so,
Grew frantick mad ; for in his mind
  He bore the wounds of woe :

Which made him rend his milk-white locks,
  And tresses from his head,
And all with blood bestain his cheeks,
  With age and honour spread.
To hills and woods and watry founts
  He made his hourly moan,
Till hills and woods, and senseless things,
  Did seem to sigh and groan.

Even thus possest with discontents,
  He passed o're to France,
In hopes from fair Cordelia there,
  To find some gentler chance ;
Most virtuous dame ! which when she heard
  Of this her father's grief,
As duty bound, she quickly sent
  Him comfort and relief :

And by a train of noble peers,
  In brave and gallant sort,
She gave in charge he should be brought
  To Aganippus' court ;
Whose royal king, with noble mind
  So freely gave consent,
To muster up his knights at arms,
  To fame and courage bent.

And so to England came with speed,
  To repossesse king Leir,
And drive his daughters from their thrones
  By his Cordelia dear.
Where she, true-hearted noble queen,
  Was in the battel slain ;
Yet he good king, in his old days,
  Possest his crown again.

But when he heard Cordelia's death,
  Who died indeed for love
Of her dear father, in whose cause
  She did this battle move ;
He swooning fell upon her breast,
  From whence he never parted :
But on her bosom left his life,
  That was so truly hearted.

The lords and nobles when they saw
  The end of these events,
The other sisters unto death
  They doomed by consents ;
And being dead, their crowns they left
  Unto the next of kin :
Thus have you seen the fall of pride,
  And disobedient sin.

## XVI.—YOUTH AND AGE

Is found in the little collection of Shakespeare's sonnets, entitled the *Passionate Pilgrime*, the greatest part of which seems to relate to the amours of Venus and Adonis. The following seems intended for the mouth of Venus, weighing the comparative merits of youthful Adonis and aged Vulcan.

CRABBED Age and Youth
   Cannot live together;
Youth is full of pleasance,
   Age is full of care:
Youth like summer morn,
   Age like winter weather,
Youth like summer brave,
   Age like winter bare:
Youth is full of sport,
   Ages breath is short;
Youth is nimble, Age is lame:
Youth is hot and bold,
   Age is weak and cold;
Youth is wild, and Age is tame.
Age, I do abhor thee,
Youth, I do adore thee;
   O, my love, my love is young:
Age, I do defie thee;
Oh sweet shepheard, hie thee,
   For methinks thou stayst too long.

---

## XVII.—THE FROLICKSOME DUKE, OR THE TINKER'S GOOD FORTUNE.

THE following ballad is upon the same subject as the Introduction to Shakespeare's *Taming of the Shrew:* whether it may be thought to have suggested the hint to the dramatic poet, or is not rather of later date, the reader must determine.

The story is told of Philip the Good, Duke of Burgundy, "that when at Bruges in Flanders, he would in the evening walke disguised all about the towne. It so fortuned, as he was walking late one night, he found a countrey fellow dead drunke, snorting on a bulke; he caused his followers to bring him to his palace, and there stripping him of his old clothes, and attyring him after the court fashion, when he wakened, he and they were all ready to attend upon his excellency and persuade him that he was some great duke. The poor fellow admiring how he came there, was served in state all day long: after supper he saw them dance, heard musicke, and all the rest of those court-like pleasures; but late at night, when he was well tipled, and again fast asleepe, they put on his old robes, and so conveyed him to the place where they first found him. Now the fellow had not made them so good sport the day before, as he did now, when he returned to himself: all the jest was to see how he looked upon it. In conclusion, after some little admiration, the poore man told his friends he had seen a vision; constantly believed it; would not otherwise be persuaded, and so the jest ended."—Burton's *Anatomy of Melancholy.*

Now as fame does report a young duke keeps a court,
One that pleases his fancy with frolicksome sport:
But amongst all the rest, here is one I protest,
Which will make you to smile when you hear the true jest:
A poor tinker he found, lying drunk on the ground,
As secure in a sleep as if laid in a swound.

The duke said to his men, William, Richard, and Ben,
Take him home to my palace, we'll sport with him then.
O'er a horse he was laid, and with care soon convey'd
To the palace, altho' he was poorly arrai'd:
Then they stript off his cloaths, both his shirt, shoes and hose,
And they put him to bed for to take his repose.

Having pull'd off his shirt, which was all over durt,
They did give him clean holland, this was no great hurt:
On a bed of soft down, like a lord of renown,
They did lay him to sleep the drink out of his crown.
In the morning when day, then admiring he lay,
For to see the rich chamber both gaudy and gay.

Now he lay something late, in his rich bed of state,
Till at last knights and squires they on him did wait;
And the chamberling bare, then did likewise declare,
He desired to know what apparel he'd ware:

The poor tinker amaz'd, on the gentleman gaz'd,
And admired how he to this honour was rais'd.

Tho' he seem'd something mute, yet he chose a rich suit,
Which he straightways put on without longer dispute;
With a star on his side, which the tinker offt ey'd,
And it seem'd for to swell him "no" little with pride;
For he said to himself, Where is Joan my sweet wife?
Sure she never did see me so fine in her life.

From a convenient place, the right duke his good grace
Did observe his behaviour in every case.
To a garden of state, on the tinker they wait,
Trumpets sounding before him: thought he, this is great:
Where an hour or two, pleasant walks he did view,
With commanders and squires in scarlet and blew.

A fine dinner was drest, both for him and his guests,
He was plac'd at the table above all the rest,
In a rich chair "or bed," lin'd with fine crimson red,
With a rich golden canopy over his head:
As he sat at his meat, the musick play'd sweet,
With the choicest of singing his joys to compleat.

While the tinker did dine, he had plenty of wine,
Rich canary with sherry and tent superfine.
Like a right honest soul, faith, he took off his bowl,
Till at last he began for to tumble and rou

From his chair to the floor, where he
    sleeping did snore,
Being seven times drunker than ever
    before.

Then the duke did ordain, they should
    strip him amain,
And restore him his old leather garments
    again :
'Twas a point next the worst, yet per-
    form it they must,
And they carry'd him strait, where they
    found him at first ;
Then he slept all the night, as indeed well
    he might ;
But when he did waken, his joys took
    their flight.

For his glory "to him" so pleasant did
    seem,
That he thought it to be but a meer
    golden, dream ;
Till at length he was brought to the duke,
    where he sought
For a pardon, as fearing he had set him
    at nought ;

But his highness he said, Thou 'rt a jolly
    bold blade,
Such a frolick before I think never was plaid.

Then his highness bespoke him a new
    suit and cloak,
Which he gave for the sake of this frolick-
    some joak ;
Nay, and five-hundred pound, with ten
    acres of ground,
Thou shalt never, said he, range the
    counteries round,
Crying old brass to mend, for I'll be thy
    good friend,
Nay, and Joan thy sweet wife shall my
    duchess attend.

Then the tinker reply'd, What ! must Joan
    my sweet bride
Be a lady in chariots of pleasure to ride ?
Must we have gold and land ev'ry day at
    command ?
Then I shall be a squire I well under-
    stand :
Well I thank your good grace, and your
    love I embrace,
I was never before in so happy a case.

## XVIII.—THE FRIAR OF ORDERS GRAY.

DISPERSED through Shakespeare's plays are innumerable little fragments of ancient ballads, the entire copies of which could not be recovered. Many of these being of the most beautiful and pathetic simplicity, the editor was tempted to select some of them, and with a few supplemental stanzas to connect them together, and form them into a little tale, which is here submitted to the reader's candour.

One small fragment was taken from Beaumont and Fletcher.

IT was a friar of orders gray
    Walkt forth to tell his beades ;
And he met with a lady faire
    Clad in a pilgrime's weedes.

Now Christ thee save, thou reverend friar,
    I pray thee tell to me,
If ever at yon holy shrine
    My true love thou didst see.

And how should I know your true love
    From many another one ?

O by his cockle hat, and staff,
    And by his sandal shoone. *

But chiefly by his face and mien,
    That were so fair to view ;

---

\* These are the distinguishing marks of a pilgrim. The chief places of devotion being beyond sea, the pilgrims were wont to put cockle shells in their hats to denote the intention or performance of their devotion.—Warburton's *Shakespeare*, vol. viii. p. 224.

His flaxen locks that sweetly curl'd,
  And eyne of lovely blue.

O lady, he is dead and gone!
  Lady, he's dead and gone!
And at his head a green grass turfe,
  And at his heels a stone.

Within these holy cloysters long
  He languisht, and he dyed,
Lamenting of a ladyes love,
  And 'playning of her pride.

Here bore him barefac'd on his bier
  Six proper youths and tall,
And many a tear bedew'd his grave
  Within yon kirk-yard wall.

And art thou dead, thou gentle youth!
  And art thou dead and gone!
And didst thou dye for love of me!
  Break, cruel heart of stone!

O weep not, lady, weep not soe;
  Some ghostly comfort seek:
Let not vain sorrow rive thy heart,
  Ne teares bedew thy cheek.

O do not, do not, holy friar,
  My sorrow now reprove;
For I have lost the sweetest youth,
  That e'er wan ladyes love.

And nowe, alas! for thy sad losse,
  I'll evermore weep and sigh;
For thee I only wisht to live,
  For thee I wish to dye.

Weep no more, lady, weep no more,
  Thy sorrowe is in vaine:
For violets pluckt the sweetest showers
  Will ne'er make grow againe.

Our joys as winged dreams doe flye,
  Why then should sorrow last?
Since grief but aggravates thy losse,
  Grieve not for what is past.

O say not soe, thou holy friar;
  I pray thee, say not soe:
For since my true-love dyed for mee,
  'Tis meet my tears should flow.

And will he ne'er come again?
  Will he ne'er come again?
Ah! no, he is dead and laid in his grave,
  For ever to remain.

His cheek was redder than the rose;
  The comliest youth was he!
But he is dead and laid in his grave;
  Alas, and woe is me!

Sigh no more, lady, sigh no more,
  Men were deceivers ever:
One foot on sea and one on land,
  To one thing constant never.

Hadst thou been fond, he had been false,
  And left thee sad and heavy;
For young men ever were fickle found,
  Since summer trees were leafy.

Now say not so, thou holy friar,
  I pray thee say not soe;
My love he had the truest heart:
  O he was ever true!

And art thou dead, thou much-lov'd youth,
  And didst thou dye for mee?
Then farewell home; for ever-more
  A pilgrim I will bee.

But first upon my true-loves grave
  My weary limbs I'll lay,
And thrice I'll kiss the green-grass turf,
  That wraps his breathless clay.

Yet stay, fair lady; rest awhile
  Beneath this cloyster wall:
See through the hawthorn blows the cold wind,
  And drizzly rain doth fall.

O stay me not, thou holy friar;
  O stay me not, I pray;
No drizzly rain that falls on me,
  Can wash my fault away.

Yet stay, fair lady, turn again,
  And dry those pearly tears;
For see beneath this gown of gray
  Thy owne true-love appears.

Here forc'd by grief, and hopeless love,
  These holy weeds I sought;
And here amid these lonely walls
  To end my days I thought.

But haply for my year of grace\*
  Is not yet past away,
Might I still hope to win thy love,
  No longer would I stay.

Now farewell grief, and welcome joy
  Once more unto my heart;
For since I have found thee, lovely youth,
  We never more will part.

---

\* The year of probation or noviciate.

\*\*\* As the foregoing song has been thought to have suggested to Goldsmith the plan of his beautiful ballad of *Edwin and Emma* (first printed in his *Vicar of Wakefield*), it is but justice to his memory to declare that his poem was written first, and that if there is any imitation in the case, they will be found both to be indebted to the beautiful old ballad *Gentle Herdsman*.

## SERIES THE FIRST.—BOOK III.

### I.—THE MORE MODERN BALLAD OF CHEVY-CHASE.

At the beginning of this volume we gave the old original song of Chevy-Chase. The reader has here the more improved edition of that fine heroic ballad. It will afford an agreeable entertainment to the curious to compare them together, and to see how far the latter bard has excelled his predecessor, and where he has fallen short of him. Some few passages retain more dignity in the ancient copy; for instance, the catastrophe of the gallant Witherington is in the modern copy exprest in terms which never fail at present to excite ridicule: whereas in the original it is related with a plain and pathetic simplicity that is liable to no such unlucky effect.

"The old song of Chevy-Chase," says Addison, "is the favourite ballad of the common people of England;" and Ben Jonson used to say he had rather have been the author of it than of all his works. Sir Philip Sydney, in his *Discourse of Poetry*, speaks of it in the following words: "I never heard the old song of Piercy and Douglas that I found not my heart more stirred than with a trumpet."

"An heroic poem should be founded upon some important precept of morality adapted to the constitution of the country in which the poet writes;" and this keynote of the poem Addison tells us that we have in the first verse, where the author of the ballad desires an ending of the unnatural strife that brought about so many disasters.

Prof. Henry Morley says "that the ballad that moved Sir Philip Sydney was written in the fifteenth century, and that this version before us was not composed until after Sydney's death, and after the best of Shakespeare's plays had been written." However, Addison's criticism concerns the present ballad, and we shall append footnotes to some of the verses he particularly admires.

From a passage in the *Memoirs of Carey, Earl of Monmouth*, we learn that it was an ancient custom with the Borderers of the two kingdoms, when they were at peace, to send to the lord wardens of the opposite marches for leave to hunt within their districts. If leave was granted, then towards the end of summer they would come and hunt for several days together "with their greyhounds for deer:" but if they took this liberty unpermitted, then the lord warden of the border so invaded would not fail to interrupt their sport and chastise their boldness. He mentions a remarkable instance that happened while he was warden, when some Scotch gentlemen coming to hunt in defiance of him, there must have ensued such an action as this of Chevy-Chase, if the intruders had been proportionably numerous and well-armed: for, upon their being attacked by his men-at-arms, he tells us, "some hurt was done, tho' he had given especiall order that they should shed as little blood as possible." They were in effect overpowered and taken prisoners, and only released on their promise to abstain from such licentious sporting for the future.

The following text is given from a copy in the Editor's folio MS. compared with two or three others printed in black-letter.

God prosper long our noble king,
  Our lives and safetyes all;
A woefull hunting once there did
  In Chevy-Chace befall;

To drive the deere with hound and horne,
  Erle Percy took his way;
The child may rue* that is unborne,
  The hunting of that day.

The stout Erle of Northumberland
  A vow to God did make,
His pleasure in the Scottish woods
  Three summers days to take;

The cheefest harts in Chevy-Chace
  To kill and beare away.
These tydings to Erle Douglas came,
  In Scotland where he lay:

Who sent Erle Percy present word,
  He wold prevent his sport.
The English Erle, not fearing that,
  Did to the woods resort

With fifteen hundred bow-men bold;
  All chosen men of might,
Who knew full well in time of neede
  To ayme their shafts arright.

The gallant greyhounds swiftly ran,
  To chase the fallow deere:
On munday they began to hunt,
  Ere daylight did appeare;

And long before high noone they had
  An hundred fat buckes slaine;
Then having dined, the *drovyers* went
  To rouze the deare againe.

The bow-men mustered on the hills,
  Well able to endure;
Theire backsides all, with speciall care,
  That day were guarded sure.

---

* The way of considering the misfortune which this battle would bring upon posterity ... is wonderfully beautiful and conformable to the way of thinking among the ancient poets.—ADDISON.

The hounds ran swiftly through the woods,
  The nimble deere to take,*
That with their cryes the hills and dales
  An eccho shrill did make.

Lord Percy to the quarry went,
  To view the slaughter'd deere;
Quoth he, Erle Douglas promised
  This day to meet me heere:

But if I thought he wold not come,
  Noe longer wold I stay.
With that, a brave younge gentleman
  Thus to the Erle did say:

Loe, yonder doth Erle Douglas come,
  His men in armour bright;
Full twenty hundred Scottish speres
  All marching in our sight;

All men of pleasant Tivydale,
  Fast by the river Tweede:
O cease your sports, Erle Percy said,
  And take your bowes with speede:

And now with me, my countrymen,
  Your courage forth advance;
For there was never champion yett,
  In Scotland or in France,

That ever did on horsebacke come,
  But if my hap it were,
I durst encounter man for man,
  With him to break a spere.

Erle Douglas on his milke-white steede
  Most like a baron bold,
Rode formost of his company,
  Whose armour shone like gold.

---

* Leyland, in the reign of Henry VIII., thus describes this county: "In Northumberland, as I heare say, be no forests, except Chivet Hills; where is much brushe-wood, and some okke; grownde ovargrowne with linge, and some with mosse. I have harde say that Chivet Hills stretchethe xx miles. There is greate plenté of redde-dere, and roo bukkes."

Show me, sayd hee, whose men you bee,
  That hunt soe boldly heere,
That, without my consent, doe chase
  And kill my fallow-deere.

The first man that did answer make,
  Was noble Percy hee;
Who sayd, Wee list not to declare,
  Nor shew whose men wee bee:

Yet wee will spend our deerest blood,
  Thy cheefest harts to slay.
Then Douglas swore a solempne oathe,
  And thus in rage did say,

Ere thus I will out-braved bee,
  One of us two shall dye:
I know thee well, an erle thou art;
  Lord Percy, soe am I.

But trust me, Percy, pittye it were,
  And great offence to kill
Any of these our guiltlesse men,
  For they have done no ill.

Let thou and I the battell trye,
  And set our men aside.
Accurst bee he, Erle Percy sayd,
  By whome this is denyed.

Then stept a gallant squier forth,
  Witherington was his name,
Who said, I wold not have it told
  To Henry our king for shame,

That ere my captaine fought on foote,
  And I stood looking on.
You bee two erles, sayd Witherington,
  And I a squier alone;

He doe the best that doe I may,
  While I have power to stand:
While I have power to weeld my sword,
  Ile fight with hart and hand.

Our English archers bent their bowes,
  Their harts were good and trew;
Att the first flight of arrowes sent,
  Full four-score Scots they slew.

[Yet bides Earl Douglas on the *bent*,
  As chieftain stout and good.
As valiant captain, all unmov'd,
  The shock he firmly stood.

His host he parted had in three,
  As leader ware and try'd,
And soon his spearmen on their foes
  Bare down on every side.

To drive the deere with hound and horne,
  Douglas bade on the bent;
Two captaines moved with mickle might
  Their speres to shivers went.

Throughout the English archery
  They dealt full many a wound:
But still our valiant Englishmen
  All firmly kept their ground:

And throwing strait their bows away,
  They grasp'd their swords so bright:
And now sharp blows, a heavy shower,
  On shields and helmets light.]\*

They closed full fast on everye side,
  Noe slacknes there was found;
And many a gallant gentleman
  Lay gasping on the ground.

O Christ! it was a griefe to see,
  And likewise for to heare,
The cries of men lying in their gore,
  And scattered here and there.

At last these two stout erles did meet,
  Like captaines of great might:
Like lyons wood, they layd on lode,
  And made a cruell fight:

They fought untill they both did sweat,
  With swords of tempered steele;

---

\* The five stanzas here inclosed in brackets, which are borrowed chiefly from the ancient copy, are offered to the reader instead of the following lines, which occur in the Editor's folio MS.

Until the blood, like drops of rain,
  They trickling downe did feele.

Yeeld thee, Lord Percy, Douglas sayd;
  In faith I will thee bringe,
Where thou shalt high advanced bee
  By James our Scottish king:

Thy ransome I will freely give,
  And this report of thee,
Thou art the most couragious knight,
  That ever I did see.

Noe, Douglas, quoth Erle Percy then,
  Thy proffer I doe scorne;
I will not yeelde to any Scott,
  That ever yett was borne.

With that, there came an arrow keene
  Out of an English bow,
Which struck Erle Douglas to the heart,
  A deepe and deadlye blow:

Who never spake more words than these,
  Fight on, my merry men all;
For why, my life is at an end;
  Lord Percy sees my fall.

Then leaving liffe, Erle Percy tooke
  The dead man by the hand;*
And said, Erle Douglas, for thy life
  Wold I had lost my land.

O Christ! my verry hart doth bleed
  With sorrow for thy sake;
For sure, a more redoubted knight
  Mischance cold never take.

A knight amongst the Scots there was,
  Which saw Erle Douglas dye,
Who streight in wrath did vow revenge
  Upon the Lord Percye:

Sir Hugh Mountgomery was he call'd,
  Who, with a spere most bright,
Well-mounted on a gallant steed,
  Ran fiercely through the fight;

And past the English archers all,
  Without all dread or feare;
And through Earl Percyes body then
  He thrust his hatefull spere;

With such a vehement force and might
  He did his body gore,
The staff ran through the other side
  A large cloth-yard, and more.

So thus did both these nobles dye,
  Whose courage none could staine:
An English archer then perceiv'd
  The noble erle was slaine;

He had a bow bent in his hand,
  Made of a trusty tree;
An arrow of a cloth-yard long
  Up to the head drew hee:

Against Sir Hugh Mountgomerye,
  So right the shaft he sett,
The grey goose-winge that was thereon,
  In his harts bloode was wett.

This fight did last from breake of day,
  Till setting of the sun;
For when they rung the evening-bell,*
  The battel scarce was done.

With stout Erle Percy, there was slaine
  Sir John of Egerton,
Sir Robert Ratcliff, and Sir John,
  Sir James that bold barròn:

And with Sir George and stout Sir James,
  Both knights of good account,
Good Sir Ralph Raby there was slaine,
  Whose prowesse did surmount.

For Witherington needs must I wayle,
  As one in doleful *dumpes*;†

---

\* *Sc.* the Curfew bell, usually rung at 8 o'clock, to which the modernizer apparently alludes, instead of the " Evensong bell," a bell for vespers of the original author, before the Reformation.

† *i.e.* "I, as one in deep concern, must lament." The construction here has generally been misunderstood. The old MS. reads "wofull dumpes."

---

\* Addison praises this line as wonderfully beautiful and pathetic.

For when his leggs were smitten off,
  He fought upon his stumpes.

And with Erle Douglas, there was slaine
  Sir Hugh Mountgomerye,
Sir Charles Murray, that from the feeld
  One foote wold never flee.

Sir Charles Murray, of Ratcliff, too,
  His sisters sonne was hee;
Sir David Lamb, so well esteem'd,
  Yet saved cold not bee.

And the Lord Maxwell in like case
  Did with Erle Douglas dye:
Of twenty hundred Scottish speres,
  Scarce fifty-five did flye.

Of fifteen hundred Englishmen,
  Went home but fifty-three;
The rest were slaine in Chevy-Chase,
  Under the greene woode tree.

Next day did many widowes come,
  Their husbands to bewayle;
They washt their wounds in brinish teares,
  But all wold not prevayle.

Theyr bodyes, bathed in purple gore,
  They bare with them away:
They kist them dead a thousand times,
  Ere they were cladd in clay.*

---

\* "What can be more natural or more moving than the circumstances in which the author describes the behaviour of those women who had lost their husbands on the fatal day?"—ADDISON.

The newes was brought to Eddenborrow,
  Where Scottlands king did raigne,
That brave Erle Douglas suddenlye
  Was with an arrow slaine:

O heavy newes, King James did say,
  Scottland may witnesse bee,
I have not any captaine more
  Of such account as hee.

Like tydings to King Henry came,
  Within as short a space,
That Percy of Northumberland
  Was slaine in Chevy-Chase:

Now God be with him, said our king,
  Sith it will noe better bee;
I trust I have, within my realme,
  Five hundred as good as hee:

Yett shall not Scotts nor Scotland say,
  But I will vengeance take:
I'll be revenged on them all,
  For brave Erle Percyes sake.

This vow full well the king perform'd
  After, at Humbledowne;
In one day, fifty knights were slayne,
  With lords of great renowne:

And of the rest, of small account,
  Did many thousands dye:
Thus endeth the hunting of Chevy-Chase,
  Made by the Erle Percy.

God save our king, and bless this land
  With plentye, joy, and peace;
And grant henceforth, that foule debate
  'Twixt noblemen may cease.

## II.—DEATH'S FINAL CONQUEST.

THESE fine moral stanzas were originally intended for a solemn funeral song, in a play of James Shirley's, entitled *The Contention of Ajax and Ulysses*, no date, 8vo. Shirley flourished as a dramatic writer early in the reign of Charles I.; but he outlived the Restoration. His death happened October 29, 1666, æt. 72.

This little poem was written long after many of those that follow, but is inserted here as a kind of dirge to the foregoing piece. It is said to have been a favourite song with King Charles II.

THE glories of our birth and state
  Are shadows, not substantial things;
There is no armour against fate:
  Death lays his icy hands on kings:
    Scepter and crown
    Must tumble down,
And in the dust be equal made
With the poor crooked scythe and spade.

Some men with swords may reap the field,
  And plant fresh laurels where they kill;
But their strong nerves at last must yield;
  They tame but one another still.

Early or late
  They stoop to fate,
And must give up their murmuring breath,
When they pale captives creep to death.

The garlands wither on your brow,
  Then boast no more your mighty deeds;
Upon death's purple altar now
  See where the victor victim bleeds:
    All heads must come
    To the cold tomb,
Only the actions of the just
Smell sweet, and blossom in the dust.

## III.—THE RISING IN THE NORTH.

THE subject of this ballad is the great northern insurrection in the 12th year of Elizabeth, 1569; which proved so fatal to Thomas Percy, the Seventh Earl of Northumberland.

A secret negotiation had been entered into to bring about the marriage of Mary Queen of Scots and the Duke of Norfolk; Mary was at that time a prisoner in England. The report reaching the ears of Queen Elizabeth, made her furiously angry; the Duke of Norfolk was committed to the Tower, and the northern earls were commanded to appear at court. The Earl of Northumberland was making up his mind to obey, when on the night of 14th Nov. there was an alarm that a party of his enemies had come to seize him. He rose from his bed in haste and withdrew to the Earl of Westmoreland, at Brancepeth, where the country round fell into excitement and begged the Earls to take up arms. They accordingly set up their standards, but met with but little success; and the Earl of Sussex with Lord Hunsdon, followed by Ambrose Dudley, Earl of Warwick, and a large army, caused the insurgents to retreat towards the borders; there dismissing their followers, the leaders escaped to Scotland. The Earl of Sussex and Sir George Bowes caused vast numbers of the army to be put to death. Sixty-three constables were hanged, and Sir George Bowes boasted that for sixty miles in length and forty in breadth between Newcastle and Wetherby there was hardly a village or town where some of the inhabitants had not been executed.

LISTEN, lively lordings all,
  Lithe and listen unto mee,
And I will sing of a noble earle,
  The noblest earle in the north countrie.

Earle Percy is into his garden gone,
  And after him walkes his faire ladie :*
I heard a bird sing in mine eare,
  That I must either fight, or flee.

Now heaven forefend, my dearest lord,
  That ever such harm should hap to thee:
But goe to London to the court,
  And faire fall truth and honestle.

Now nay, now nay, my ladye gay,
  Alas! thy counsell suits not mee;
Mine enemies prevail so fast,
  That at the court I may not bee.

O goe to the court yet, good my lord,
  And take thy gallant men with thee:
If any dare to doe you wrong,
  Then your warrant they may bee.

Now nay, now nay, thou lady faire,
  The court is full of subtiltle;
And if I goe to the court, lady,
  Never more I may thee see.

Yet goe to the court, my lord, she sayes,
  And I myselfe will ryde wi' thee:
At court then for my dearest lord,
  His faithfull *borrowe* I will bee.

Now nay, now nay, my lady deare;
  Far *lever* had I lose my life,
Than leave among my cruell foes
  My love in jeopardy and strife.

But come thou hither, my little foot-page,
  Come thou hither unto mee,

To maister Norton* thou must goe
  In all the haste that ever may bee.

Commend me to that gentlemàn,
  And beare this letter here fro mee;
And say that earnestly I praye,
  He will ryde in my companie.

One while the little foot-page went,
  And another while he ran;
Untill he came to his journeys end,
  The little foot-page never *blan*.

When to that gentleman he came,
  Down he kneeled on his knee;
And tooke the letter betwixt his hands,
  And lett the gentleman it see.

And when the letter it was redd
  Affore that goodlye companye,
I wis, if you the truthe wold know,
  There was many a weeping eye.

He sayd, Come thither, Christopher Norton,
  A gallant youth thou seemst to bee;
What doest thou counsell me, my sonne,
  Now that good erle's in jeopardy?

Father, my counselle's fair and free;
  That erle he is a noble lord,
And whatsoever to him you *hight*,
  I wold not have you breake your word.

Gramercy, Christopher, my sonne,
  Thy counsell well it liketh mee;
And if we speed and scape with life,
  Well advanced shalt thou bee.

Come you hither, my nine good sonnes,
  Gallant men I *trowe* you bee:
How many of you, my children deare,
  Will stand by that good erle and mee?

---

* This lady was Anne, daughter of Henry Somerset, Earl of Worcester.

* Richard Norton of Norton Conyers, who with his sons Francis, Christopher, Marmaduke, and Thomas, specially distinguished himself. There were five other sons whose names are not given.

Eight of them did answer make,
  Eight of them spake hastilie,
O father, till the daye we dye
  We'll stand by that good erle and thee.

Gramercy now, my children deare,
  You showe yourselves right bold and brave;
And whethersoe'er I live or dye,
  A fathers blessing you shal have.

But what sayst thou, O Francis Norton,
  Thou art mine eldest sonn and heire:
Somewhat lyes brooding in thy breast;
  Whatever it bee, to mee declare.

Father, you are an aged man,
  Your head is white, your bearde is gray;
It were a shame at these your yeares
  For you to ryse in such a fray.

Now fye upon thee, coward Francis,
  Thou never learnedst this of mee:
When thou wert yong and tender of age,
  Why did I make soe much of thee?

But, father, I will wend with you,
  Unarm'd and naked will I bee;
And he that strikes against the crowne,
  Ever an ill death may he dee.

Then rose that reverend gentleman,
  And with him came a goodlye band
To join with the brave Erle Percy,
  And all the flower o' Northumberland.

With them the noble Nevill came,
  The erle of Westmorland was hee:
At Wetherbye they mustred their host,
  Thirteen thousand faire to see.

Lord Westmorland his *ancyent* raisde,
  The Dun Bull he rays'd on hye,
And three Dogs with golden collars
  Were there sett out most royallye.*

Erle Percy there his *ancyent* spred,
  The Halfe-Moone shining all so faire:*
The Nortons ancyent had the crosse,
  And the five wounds our Lord did beare.

Then Sir George Bowes he straitwaye rose,
  After them some spoyle to make:
Those noble erles turn'd backe againe,
  And aye they vowed that knight to take.

That baron he to his castle fled,
  To Barnard Castle then fled hee.
The uttermost walles were *eathe* to win,
  The earles have wonne them presentlie.

The uttermost walles were lime and bricke;
  But thoughe they won them soon anone,
Long e'er they wan the innermost walles,
  For they were cut in rocke of stone.

Then newes unto leeve London came
  In all the speede that ever might bee,
And word is brought to our royall queene
  Of the rysing in the north countrie.

Her grace she turned her round about,
  And like a royall queene shee swore,†
I will ordayne them such a breakfast,
  As never was in the north before.

Shee caus'd thirty thousand men be rays'd,
  With horse and harneis faire to see;

---

* The supporters of the Nevilles, Earls of Westmoreland, were two bulls argent, ducally collared gold, armed or, etc. But I have not discovered the device mentioned in the ballad, among the badges, etc., given by that house This, however, is certain, that among those of the Nevilles, Lords Abergavenny (who were of the same family), is a dun cow with a golden collar; and the Nevilles of Chyte in Yorkshire (of the Westmoreland branch) gave for their crest, in 1513, a greyhound's head erased.

* The silver crescent is a well-known crest or badge of the Northumberland family. It was probably brought home from some of the crusades against the Saracens.

† This is quite in character; her Majesty would sometimes swear at her nobles, as well as box their ears.

She caused thirty thousand men be raised,
  To take the earles i' th' north countrie.

Wi' them the false Erle Warwick went,
  Th' Erle Sussex and the Lord Hunsden;
Untill they to Yorke castle came
  I wiss, they never *stint ne blan*.

Now spred thy ancyent, Westmorland,
  Thy dun bull faine would we spye:
And thou, the Erle o' Northumberland,
  Now rayse thy half moone up on hye.

But the dun bulle is fled and gone,
  And the halfe moone vanished away:

The Erles, though they were brave and bold,
  Against soe many could not stay.

Thee, Norton, wi' thine eight good sonnes,
  They doom'd to dye, alas! for ruth!
Thy reverend lockes thee could not save,
  Nor them their faire and blooming youthe.

Wi' them full many a gallant wight
  They cruellye bereav'd of life:
And many a childe made fatherlesse,
  And widowed many a tender wife.

---

### IV.—NORTHUMBERLAND BETRAYED BY DOUGLAS.

THIS ballad may be considered as the sequel of the preceding. After the unfortunate Earl of Northumberland had seen himself forsaken of his followers, he endeavoured to withdraw into Scotland, but falling into the hands of the thievish Borderers, was stript and otherwise ill-treated by them. He took refuge in the house of Hector of Harlaw, who basely betrayed him to the Regent Murray, who sent him to the Castle of Loch Leven, then belonging to William Douglas.

Northumberland continued at Loch Leven until 1572, when James Douglas, Earl of Morton, being elected Regent, he was given up to Lord Hunsden at Berwick, and suffered death at York.

The witch lady alluded to in v. 133 is supposed to be Lady Jane Douglas, Lady Glamis, who was put to death for the supposed crime of witchcraft.

Hector of Harlaw, according to the folio, was a Graham and not an Armstrong, as spoken of in the ballad.

How long shall fortune faile me nowe,
  And harrowe me with fear and dread?
How long shall I in *bale* abide,
  In misery my life to lead?

To fall from my bliss, alas the while!
  It was my sore and heavye lott:
And I must leave my native land,
  And I must live a man forgot.

One gentle Armstrong I doe ken,
  A Scott he is much bound to mee:
He dwelleth on the border side,
  To him I'll goe right priville.

Thus did the noble Percy 'plaine,
  With a heavy heart and wel-away,
When he with all his gallant men
  On Bramham moor had lost the day.

But when he to the Armstrongs came,
  They dealt with him all treacherouslye;
For they did strip that noble earle:
  And ever an ill death may they dye.

False Hector to Earl Murray sent,
  To shew him where his guest did hide:
Who sent him to the Lough-levèn,
  With William Douglas to abide.

And when he to the Douglas came,
  He *halched* him right curteouslie:
Say'd, Welcome, welcome, noble earle,
  Here thou shalt safelye bide with mee.

When he had in Lough-leven been
  Many a month and many a day;
To the regent * the lord warden † sent,
  That bannisht earle for to betray.

He offered him great store of gold,
  And wrote a letter fair to see:
Saying, Good my lord, grant me my boon,
  And yield that banisht man to mee.

Earle Percy at the supper sate
  With many a goodly gentleman:
The wylie Douglas then bespake,
  And thus to *flyte* with him began:

What makes you be so sad, my lord,
  And in your mind so sorrowfullyè?
To-morrow a shootinge will bee held
  Among the lords of the north countryè.

The butts are sett, the shooting's made,
  And there will be great royaltye:
And I am sworne into my bille,
  Thither to bring my lord Percye.

I'll give thee my hand, thou gentle
    Douglas,
  And here by my true faith, quoth hee,
If thou wilt ryde to the worldes end,
  I will ryde in thy companye.

And then bespake a lady faire,
  Mary à Douglas was her name:
You shall byde here, good English lord,
  My brother is a traiterous man.

He is a traitor stout and stronge,
  As I tell you in privitie:

For he hath tane liverance of the earle,*
  Into England nowe to 'liver thee.

Now nay, now nay, thou goodly lady,
  The regent is a noble lord:
Ne for the gold in all England
  The Douglas wold not break his word.

When the regent was a banisht man,
  With me he did faire welcome find;
And whether weal or woe betide,
  I still shall find him true and kind.

Betweene England and Scotland it wold
    breake truce,
  And friends againe they wold never bee,
If they shold 'liver a banisht erle
  Was driven out of his own countrie.

Alas! alas! my lord, she sayes,
  Nowe mickle is their traitorie;
Then lett my brother ryde his wayes,
  And tell those English lords from thee,

How that you cannot with him ryde,
  Because you are in an ile of the sea,†
Then ere my brother come againe
  To Edenborow castle ‡ Ile carry thee.

To the Lord Hume I will thee bring,
  He is well knowne a true Scots lord,
And he will lose both land and life,
  Ere he with thee will break his word.

Much is my woe, Lord Percy sayd,
  When I thinke on my own countrie,
When I thinke on the heavye happe
  My friends have suffered there for mee.

Much is my woe, Lord Percy sayd,
  And sore those wars my minde distresse;
Where many a widow lost her mate,
  And many a child was fatherlesse.

---

\* James Douglas, Earl of Morton, elected regent of Scotland, November 24, 1572.
† Of one of the English marches. Lord Hunsden.

\* Of the Earl of Morton, the regent.
† *i.e.* Lake of Leven, which hath communication with the sea.
‡ At that time in the hands of the opposite faction.

And now that I a banisht man
  Shold bring such evil happe with mee,
To cause my faire and noble friends
  To be suspect of treacherie:

This rives my heart with double woe;
  And lever had I dye this day,
Than thinke a Douglas can be false,
  Or ever he will his guest betray.

If you'll give me no trust, my lord,
  Nor unto mee no credence yield;
Yet step one moment here aside,
  Ile showe you all your foes in field.

Lady, I never loved witchcraft,
  Never dealt in privy wyle;
But evermore held the high-waye
  Of truth and honour, free from guile.

If you'll not come yourselfe, my lorde,
  Yet send your chamberlaine with mee;
Let me but speak three words with him,
  And he shall come again to thee.

James Swynard with that lady went,
  She showed him through the *weme* of
    her ring
How many English lords there were
  Waiting for his master and him.

And who walkes yonder, my good lady,
  So royallyè on yonder greene?
O yonder is the lord Hunsdèn:*
  Alas! he'll doe you *drie* and *teene*.

And who beth yonder, thou gay ladye,
  That walkes so proudly him beside?
That is Sir William Drury,† shee sayd,
  A keene captàine hee is and tryde.

How many miles is itt, madàme,
  Betwixt yond English lords and mee?
Marry it is thrice fifty miles,
  To saile to them upon the sea.

---

\* The lord warden of the east marches.
† Governor of Berwick.

I never was on English ground,
  Ne never saw it with mine eye,
But as my book it sheweth mee,
  And through my ring I may descrye.

My mother shee was a witch ladye,
  And of her skille she learned mee;
She wold let me see out of Lough-leven
  What they did in London citie.

But who is yond, thou lady faire,
  That looketh with sic an *austerne* face?
Yonder is Sir John Foster,* quoth shee,
  Alas! he'll do ye sore disgrace.

He pulled his hatt down over his browe;
  He wept; in his heart he was full of woe:
And he is gone to his noble Lord,
  Those sorrowful tidings him to show.

Now nay, now nay, good James Swynàrd,
  I may not believe that witch ladie:
The Douglasses were ever true,
  And they can ne'er prove false to mee.

I have now in Lough-leven been
  The most part of these years three,
Yett have I never had noe *outrake*,
  Ne no good games that I cold see.

Therefore I'll to yond shooting *wend*,
  As to the Douglas I have light:
Betide me weale, betide me woe,
  He ne'er shall find my promise light.

He *writhe* a gold ring from his finger,
  And gave itt to that gay ladie:
Sayes, It was all that I cold save,
  In Harley woods where I cold bee.†

And wilt thou goe, thou noble lord,
  Then farewell truth and honestie;
And farewell heart and farewell hand;
  For never more I shall thee see.

The wind was faire, the boatmen call'd,
  And all the saylors were on borde;

---

\* Warden of the middle march.
† *i.e. where I was*, an ancient idiom.

Then William Douglas took to his boat,
　And with him went that noble lord.

Then he cast up a silver wand,
　Says, Gentle lady, fare thee well!
The lady fett a sigh soe deep,
　And in a dead swoone down shee fell.

Now let us goe back, Douglas, he sayd,
　A sickness hath taken yond faire ladie;
If ought befall yond lady but good,
　Then blamed for ever　shall bee.

Come on, come on, my lord, he sayes;
　Come on, come on, and let her bee:
There's ladyes enow in Lough-leven
　For to cheere that gay ladie.

If you'll not turne yourself, my lord,
　Let me goe with my chamberlaine;
We will but comfort that faire lady,
　And wee will return to you againe.

Come on, come on, my lord, he sayes,
　Come on, come on, and let her bee:
My sister is craftye, and wold beguile
　A thousand such as you and mee.

When they had sayled\* fifty myle,
　Now fifty mile upon the sea;
Hee sent his man to ask the Douglas,
　When they shold that shooting see.

Faire words, quoth he, they make fooles *faine*,
　And that by thee and thy lord is seen:
You may hap to thinke itt soone enough,
　Ere you that shooting reach, I ween.

---

\* There is no navigable stream between Loch Leven and the sea; but a ballad-maker is not obliged to understand geography.

Jamye his hatt pulled over his browe,
　He thought his lord then was betray'd;
And he is to Erle Percy againe,
　To tell him what the Douglas sayd.

Hold upp thy head, man, quoth his lord;
　Nor therefore lett thy courage fayle,
He did it but to prove thy heart,
　To see if he cold make it quail.

When they had other fifty sayld,
　Other fifty mile upon the sea,
Lord Percy called to Douglas himselfe,
　Sayd, What wilt thou nowe doe with mee?

Looke that your brydle be *wight*, my lord,
　And your horse goe swift as shipp att sea:
Looke that your spurres be bright and sharpe,
　That you may pricke her while she'll away.

What needeth this, Douglas? he sayth;
　What needest thou to *flyte* with mee?
For I was counted a horseman good
　Before that ever I mett with thee.

A false Hector hath my horse,
　Who dealt with mee so treacherouslie:
A false Armstrong hath my spurres,
　And all the geere belongs to mee.

When they had sayled other fifty mile,
　Other fifty mile upon the sea;
They landed low by Berwicke side,
　A deputed "laird" landed Lord Percye.

Then he at Yorke was doomde to dye,
　It was, alas! a sorrowful sight:
Thus they betrayed that noble earle,
　Who ever was a gallant wight.

## V.—MY MIND TO ME A KINGDOM IS.

This excellent philosophical song appears to have been famous in the sixteenth century. It is quoted by Ben Jonson in his play of *Every Man out of his Humour,* first acted in 1599, Act i. Sc. i.

My minde to me a kingdome is;
  Such perfect joy therein I finde
As farre exceeds all earthly blisse,
  That God or Nature hath assignde:
Though much I want, that most would have,
Yet still my mind forbids to crave.

Content I live, this is my stay;
  I seek no more than may suffice:
I presse to beare no haughtie sway;
  Look what I lack my mind supplies.
Loe! thus I triumph like a king,
Content with that my mind doth bring.

I see how plentie surfets oft,
  And hastie clymbers soonest fall:
I see that such as sit aloft
  Mishap doth threaten most of all:
These get with toile, and keep with feare:
Such cares my mind could never beare.

No princely pompe, nor welthie store,
  No force to winne the victorie,
No wylie wit to salve a sore,
  No shape to winne a lovers eye;
To none of these I yeeld as thrall,
For why my mind despiseth all.

Some have too much, yet still they crave,
  I little have, yet seek no more:
They are but poore, tho' much they have;
  And I am rich with little store:
They poor, I rich; they beg, I give;
They lacke, I lend; they pine, I live.

I laugh not at anothers losse,
  I grudge not at anothers gaine;
No worldly wave my mind can tosse,
  I brooke that is anothers bane:

I feare no foe, nor fawne on friend;
I loth not life, nor dread mine end.

I joy not in no earthly blisse,
  I weigh not Cresus' welth a straw;
For care, I care not what it is;
  I feare not fortunes fatall law:
My mind is such as may not move
For beautie bright or force of love.

I wish but what I have at will;
  I wander not to seeke for more;
I like the plaine, I clime no hill;
  In greatest stormes I sitte on shore,
And laugh at them that toile in vaine
To get what must be lost againe.

I kisse not where I wish to kill;
  I feigne not love where most I hate;
I breake no sleep to winne my will;
  I wayte not at the mighties gate;
I scorne no poore, I feare no rich;
I feele no want, nor have too much.

The court, ne cart, I like, ne loath;
  Extreames are counted worst of all:
The golden meane betwixt them both
  Doth surest sit, and fears no fall:
This is my choyce, for why I finde,
No wealth is like a quiet minde.

My welth is health, and perfect ease;
  My conscience clere my chiefe defence:
I never seeke by brybes to please,
  Nor by desert to give offence:
Thus do I live, thus will I die;
Would all did so as well as I!

## VI.—THE PATIENT COUNTESS.

THE subject of this tale is taken from an entertaining colloquy of Erasmus. The following stanzas are extracted from William Warner's poem, entitled *Albion's England*. Warner is said to have been a Warwickshire man, and to have been educated in Oxford at Magdalen Hall. He died in 1608-1609, at Amwell in Hertfordshire. He held a fair rank as poet in the reign of Queen Elizabeth, and was by profession an "attorney of the Common Pleas."

IMPATIENCE chaungeth smoke to flame,
  But jelousie is hell;
Some wives by patience have reduc'd
  Ill husbands to live well:
As did the ladie of an earle,
  Of whom I now shall tell.

An earle "there was" had wedded, lov'd;
  Was lov'd, and lived long
Full true to his fayre countesse; yet
  At last he did her wrong.

Once hunted he untill the chace,
  Long fasting, and the heat
Did house him in a peakish graunge
  Within a forest great.

Where knowne and welcom'd (as the place
  And persons might afforde)
Browne bread, *whig*, bacon, curds and milke
  Were set him on the borde.

A cushion made of lists, a stoole
  Halfe backed with a hoope
Were brought him, and he sitteth down
  Besides a sorry coupe.

The poore old couple wisht their bread
  Were wheat, their whig were perry,
Their bacon beefe, their milke and curds
  Were creame, to make him merry.

Mean while (in russet neatly clad,
  With linen white as swanne,
Herselfe more white, save rosie where
  The ruddy colour ranne:

Whome naked nature, not the aydes
  Of arte made to excell),
The good man's daughter sturres to see
  That all were *feat* and well;
The earle did marke her, and admire
  Such beautie there to dwell.

Yet fals he to their homely fare,
  And held him at a feast:
But as his hunger slaked, so
  An amorous heat increast.

When this repast was past, and thanks,
  And welcome too; he says
Unto his host and hostesse, in
  The hearing of the mayd:

Yee know, quoth he, that I am lord
  Of this, and many townes;
I also know that you be poore,
  And I can spare you pownes.

Soe will I, so yee will consent,
  That yonder lasse and I
May bargaine for her love; at least,
  Doe give me leave to trye.
Who needs to know it? nay who dares
  Into my doings pry?

First they mislike, yet at the length
  For lucre were misled;
And then the gamesome earle did wowe
  The damsell for his bed.

He took her in his armes, as yet
  So coyish to be kist,
As mayds that know themselves belov'd,
  And yieldingly resist.

In few, his offers were so large
  She lastly did consent ;
With whom he lodged all that night,
  And early home he went.

He tooke occasion oftentimes
  In such a sort to hunt.
Whom when his lady often mist,
  Contrary to his wont,

And lastly was informed of
  His amorous haunt elsewhere ;
It greev'd her not a little, though
  She seem'd it well to beare.

And thus she reasons with herselfe,
  Some fault perhaps in me ;
Somewhat is done, that soe he doth :
  Alas ! what may it be ?

How may I winne him to myself?
  He is a man, and men
Have imperfections ; it behooves
  Me pardon nature then.

To checke him were to make him checke,*
  Although hee now were chaste ;
A man controuled of his wife,
  To her makes lesser haste.

If duty then, or daliance may
  Prevayle to alter him ;
I will be dutifull, and make
  My selfe for daliance trim.

So was she, and so lovingly
  Did entertaine her lord,
As fairer, or more faultles none
  Could be for bed or bord.

Yet still he loves his *leman*, and
  Did still pursue that game,
Suspecting nothing less, than that
  His lady knew the same :

---

\* To check is a term in falconry, applied when a hawk stops and turns away from his proper pursuit ; to check also signifies to reprove or chide. It is in this verse used in both senses.

Wherefore to make him know she knew,
  She this devise did frame :

When long she had been wrong'd, and sought
  The foresayd meanes in vaine,
She rideth to the simple graunge
  But with a slender traine.

She lighteth, entreth, greets them well,
  And then did looke about her :
The guiltie houshold knowing her,
  Did wish themselves without her ;
Yet, for she looked merily,
  The lesse they did misdoubt her.

When she had seen the beauteous wench
  (Then blushing fairnes fairer),
Such beauty made the countesse hold
  Them both excus'd the rather.

Who would not bite at such a bait?
  Thought she ; and who (though loth)
So poore a wench, but gold might tempt?
  Sweet errors lead them both.

Scarse one in twenty that had bragg'd
  Of proffer'd gold denied,
Or of such yeelding beautie baulkt,
  But, tenne to one, had lied.

Thus thought she : and she thus declares
  Her cause of coming thether ;
My lord, oft hunting in these partes,
  Through travel, night or wether,

Hath often lodged in your house;
  I thanke you for the same ;
For why? it doth him jolly ease
  To lie so neare his game.

But, for you have not furniture
  Beseeming such a guest,
I bring his owne, and come myselfe
  To see his lodging drest.

With that two sumpters were discharg'd,
  In which were hangings brave,
Silke coverings, curtens, carpets, plate,
  And al such turn should have.

When all was handsomly dispos'd,
  She prayes them to have care
That nothing hap in their default,
  That might his health impair :

And, Damsell, quoth shee, for it seemes
  This houshold is but three,
And for thy parents age, that this
  Shall chiefely rest on thee ;

Do me that good, else would to God
  He hither come no more.
So tooke she horse, and ere she went
  Bestowed gould good store.

Full little thought the countie that
  His countesse had done so ;
Who now return'd from far affaires
  Did to his sweet-heart go.

No sooner sat he foote within
  The late deformed cote,
But that the formall change of things
  His wondring eies did note.

But when he knew those goods to be
  His proper goods ; though late,
Scarce taking leave, he home returnes
  The matter to debate.

The countesse was a-bed, and he
  With her his lodging tooke ;

Sir, welcome home (quoth shee); this night
  For you I did not looke.

Then did he question her of such
  His stuffe bestowed soe.
Forsooth, quoth she, because I did
  Your love and lodging knowe :

Your love to be a proper wench,
  Your lodging nothing lesse ;
I held it for your health, the house
  More decently to dresse.

Well wot I, notwithstanding her,
  Your lordship loveth me ;
And greater hope to hold you such
  By quiet, then brawles, you see.

Then for my duty, your delight,
  And to retaine your favour,
All done I did, and patiently
  Expect your wonted 'haviour.

Her patience, witte and answer wrought
  His gentle teares to fall :
When (kissing her a score of times)
  Amend, sweet wife, I shall :
He said, and did it ; "so each wife
  Her husband may" recall.

## VII.—DOWSABELL.

THE following stanzas were written by Michael Drayton,\* a poet of some eminence in the reigns of Queen Elizabeth, James I., and Charles I. They are inserted in one of his pastorals, and are inscribed with the author's name at length, "To the noble and valerous gentleman master Robert Dudley," etc.

FARRE in the countrey of Arden,
There won'd a knight, hight Cassemen,
  As bolde as Isenbras :
Fell was he, and eger bent,
In battell and in tournament,
  As was the good Sir Topas.

He had, as antique stories tell,
A daughter *cleaped* Dowsabel,
  A mayden fayre and free ;
And for she was her fathers heire,
Full well she was *y-cond* the *leyre*
  Of mickle curtesie.

---

\* Drayton was born in 1563, and died in 1631.

The silke well couth she twist and twine,
And make the fine *march-pine*,
  And with the needle werke:
And she couth helpe the priest to say
His mattins on a holy-day,
  And sing a psalme in kirke.

She ware a frock of frolicke greene,
Might well beseeme a mayden queene,
  Which seemly was to see;
A hood to that so neat and fine,
In colour like the colombine,
  Y-wrought full *featously*.

Her features all as fresh above,
As is the grasse that growes by Dove;
  And lyth as lasse of Kent.
Her skin as soft as Lemster wooll,
As white as snow on Peakish Hull,
  Or swanne that swims in Trent.

This mayden in a morne betime
Went forth, when May was in her prime,
  To get sweete *cetywall*,
The honey-suckle, the *harlocke*,
The lilly and the lady-smocke,
  To deck her summer hall.

Thus, as she wandred here and there,
Y-picking of the bloomed breere,
  She chanced to espie
A shepheard sitting on a bancke,
Like chanteclere he crowed *crancke*,
  And pip'd full merrilie.

He lear'd his sheepe as he him list,
When he would whistle in his fist,
  To feede about him round;
Whilst he full many a carroll sung,
Untill the fields and medowes rung,
  And all the woods did sound.

In favour this same shepheards swayne
Was like the bedlam Tamburlayne,*
  Which helde prowd kings in awe:

---

\* Alluding to *Tamburlaine the Great, or the Scythian Shepheard*, 1590, 8vo, an old ranting play ascribed to Marlowe.

But meeke he was as lamb mought be;
An innocent of ill as he
  Whom his lewd brother slaw.

The shepheard ware a sheepe-gray cloke,
Which was of the finest *loke*,
  That could be cut with sheere:
His mittens were of *bauzens* skinne,
His *cockers* were of *cordiwin*,
  His hood of *menivecre*.

His *aule* and *lingell* in a thong,
His tar-boxe on his broad belt hong,
  His breech of coyntrie blewe:
Full crispe and curled were his lockes,
His browes as white as Albion rocks:
  So like a lover true,

And pyping still he spent the day,
So merry as the *popingay;*
  Which liked Dowsabel:
That would she ought, or would she nought,
This lad would never from her thought;
  She in love-longing fell.

At length she tucked up her frocke,
White as a lilly was her smocke,
  She drew the shepheard nye;
But then the shepheard *pyp'd a good*,
That all his sheepe forsooke their foode,
  To hear his melodye.

Thy sheepe, quoth she, cannot be *leane*,
That have a jolly shepheards swayne,
  The which can pipe so well:
Yea but, sayth he, their shepheard may,
If pyping thus he pine away
  In love of Dowsabel.

Of love, fond boy, take thou no keepe,
Quoth she; looke thou unto thy sheepe,
  Lest they should hap to stray.
Quoth he, So had I done full well,
Had I not seen fayre Dowsabell
  Come forth to gather maye.

With that she gan to vaile her head,
Her cheeks were like the roses red,
  But not a word she sayd:

With that the shepheard gan to frowne,
He threw his pretie pypes adowne,
   And on the ground him layd.

Sayth she, I may not stay till night,
And leave my summer-hall undight,
   And all for long of thee.

My coate, sayth he, nor yet my foulde
Shall neither sheepe nor shepheard hould,
   Except thou favour mee.

Sayth she, Yet *lever* were I dead,
Then I should lose my mayden-head,
   And all for love of men.

Sayth he, Yet are you too unkind,
If in your heart you cannot finde
   To love us now and then.

And I to thee will be as kinde
As Colin was to Rosalinde,
   Of curtesie the flower.

Then will I be as true, quoth she,
As ever mayden yet might be
   Unto her paramour.

With that she bent her snow-white knee,
Downe by the shepheard kneeled shee,
   And him she sweetely kist:

With that the shepheard whoop'd for joy,
Quoth he, Ther's never shepheards boy
   That ever was so blist.

## VIII.—THE FAREWELL TO LOVE.

From Beaumont and Fletcher's play, entitled *The Lover's Progress*, Act iii. Sc. i.

ADIEU, fond love, farewell you wanton powers;
   I am free again.
Thou dull disease of bloud and idle hours,
   Bewitching pain,
Fly to fools, that sigh away their time:
My nobler love to heaven doth climb,
And there behold beauty still young,

That time can ne'er corrupt, nor death destroy,
Immortal sweetness by fair angels sung,
   And honoured by eternity and joy:
There lies my love, thither my hopes aspire,
Fond love declines, this heavenly love grows higher.

## IX.—ULYSSES AND THE SYREN

AFFORDS a pretty poetical contest between Pleasure and Honour. It is found at the end of *Hymen's Triumph: A Pastoral Tragicomedie*, written by Daniel, and printed among his works, 4to, 1623.—Daniel, who was a contemporary of Drayton's, and is said to have been poet laureate to Queen Elizabeth, was born in 1562, and died in 1619. Anne, Countess of Dorset, Pembroke, and Montgomery (to whom Daniel had been tutor), has inserted a small portrait of him in a full-length picture of herself, preserved at Appleby Castle, in Cumberland.

### SYREN.

COME, worthy Greeke, Ulysses come,
   Possesse these shores with me,
The windes and seas are troublesome,
   An here we may be free.

Here may we sit and view their toyle,
   That travaile in the deepe,
Enjoy the day in mirth the while,
   And spend the night in sleepe.

#### ULYSSES.

Faire nymph, if fame or honour were
   To be attain'd with ease,
Then would I come and rest with thee,
   And leave such toiles as these:
But here it dwels, and here must I
   With danger seek it forth;
To spend the time luxuriously
   Becomes not men of worth.

#### SYREN.

Ulysses, O be not deceiv'd
   With that unreall name:
This honour is a thing conceiv'd,
   And rests on others' fame,
Begotten only to molest
   Our peace, and to beguile
(The best thing of our life) our rest,
   And give us up to toyle!

#### ULYSSES.

Delicious nymph, suppose there were
   Nor honor, nor report,
Yet manlinesse would scorne to weare
   The time in idle sport:
For toyle doth give a better touch
   To make us feele our joy;
And ease findes tediousnes, as much
   As labour yeelds annoy.

#### SYREN.

Then pleasure likewise seemes the shore,
   Whereto tendes all your toyle;
Which you forego to make it more,
   And perish oft the while.
Who may disport them diversly,
   Find never tedious day;
And ease may have variety,
   As well as action may.

#### ULYSSES.

But natures of the noblest frame
   These toyles and dangers please;
And they take comfort in the same,
   As much as you in ease:
And with the thought of actions past
   Are recreated still:
When pleasure leaves a touch at last
   To shew that it was ill.

#### SYREN.

That doth opinion only cause,
   That's out of custom bred;
Which makes us many other laws
   Than ever nature did.
No widdowes waile for our delights,
   Our sports are without blood;
The world we see by warlike wights
   Receives more hurt than good.

#### ULYSSES.

But yet the state of things require
   These motions of unrest,
And these great spirits of high desire
   Seem borne to turne them best:
To purge the mischiefes, that increase
   And all good order mar:
For oft we see a wicked peace
   To be well chang'd for war.

#### SYREN.

Well, well, Ulysses, then I see
   I shall not have thee here;
And therefore I will come to thee,
   And take my fortune there.
I must be wonne that cannot win,
   Yet lost were I not woone:
For beauty hath created bin
   T' undoo or be undone.

## X.—CUPID'S PASTIME.

THIS beautiful poem, which possesses a classical elegance hardly to be expected in the age of James I., is printed from the 4th edition of Davidson's *Poems*,* etc, 1621. It is also found in a later miscellany, entitled *Le Prince d'Amour*, 1660, 8vo.— Francis Davison, editor of the poems above referred to, was son of that unfortunate secretary of state who suffered so much from the affair of Mary Queen of Scots. These poems, he tells us in his preface, were written by himself, by his brother [Walter], who was a soldier in the wars of the Low Countries, and by some dear friends "anonymoi."

IT chanc'd of late a shepherd swain,
  That went to seek his straying sheep,
Within a thicket on a plain
  Espied a dainty nymph asleep.

Her golden hair o'erspred her face ;
  Her careless arms abroad were cast ;
Her quiver had her pillows place ;
  Her breast lay bare to every blast.

The shepherd stood and gaz'd his fill ;
  Nought durst he do ; nought durst he say ;
Whilst chance, or else perhaps his will,
  Did guide the god of love that way.

The crafty boy that sees her sleep,
  Whom if she wak'd he durst not see ;
Behind her closely seeks to creep,
  Before her nap should ended bee.

There come, he steals her shafts away,
  And puts his own into their place ;
Nor dares he any longer stay,
  But, ere she wakes, hies thence apace.

Scarce was he gone, but she awakes,
  And spies the shepherd standing by :
Her bended bow in haste she takes,
  And at the simple swain lets flye.

Forth flew the shaft, and pierc'd his heart,
  That to the ground he fell with pain :
Yet up again forthwith he start,
  And to the nymph he ran amain.

Amazed to see so strange a sight,
  She shot, and shot, but all in vain ;
The more his wounds, the more his might,
  Love yielded strength amidst his pain.

Her angry eyes were great with tears,
  She blames her hand, she blames her skill ;
The bluntness of her shafts she fears,
  And try them on herself she will.

Take heed, sweet nymph, trye not thy shaft,
  Each little touch will pierce thy heart :
Alas ! thou know'st not Cupids craft ;
  Revenge is joy ; the end is smart.

Yet try she will, and pierce some bare ;
  Her hands were glov'd, but next to hand
Was that fair breast, that breast so rare,
  That made the shepherd senseless stand.

That breast she pierc'd ; and through that breast
  Love found an entry to her heart ;
At feeling of this new-come guest,
  Lord ! how this gentle nymph did start ?

She runs not now ; she shoots no more ;
  Away she throws both shaft and bow :
She seeks for what she shunn'd before,
  She thinks the shepherds haste too slow.

Though mountains meet not, lovers may :
  What other lovers do, did they :
The god of love sate on a tree,
  And laught that pleasant sight to see.

---

,* See the full title in vol. ii. Book iii. No. iv.

## XI.—THE CHARACTER OF A HAPPY LIFE.

THIS little moral poem was writ by Sir Henry Wotton, who died Provost of Eaton in 1639, æt. 72. It is printed from a little collection of his pieces, entitled *Reliquiæ Wottonianæ*, 1651, 12mo; compared with one or two other copies.

How happy is he born or taught,
  That serveth not anothers will ;
Whose armour is his honest thought,
  And simple truth his highest skill :

Whose passions not his masters are ;
  Whose soul is still prepar'd for death ;
Not ty'd unto the world with care
  Of princes ear, or vulgar breath :

Who hath his life from rumours freed ;
  Whose conscience is his strong retreat :
Whose state can neither flatterers feed,
  Nor ruine make oppressors great :

Who envies none, whom chance doth raise,
  Or vice : Who never understood
How deepest wounds are given with praise ;
  Nor rules of state, but rules of good ;

Who God doth late and early pray
  More of his grace and gifts to lend ;
And entertaines the harmless day
  With a well-chosen book or friend.

This man is freed from servile bands
  Of hope to rise, or feare to fall ;
Lord of himselfe, though not of lands ;
  And having nothing, yet hath all.

## XII.—GILDEROY.

A FAMOUS Scotch robber, who for daring acts of violence was executed at Edinburgh in 1638, with five of his followers. In Thompson's *Orpheus Caledonius* is a copy of this ballad, which though corrupt and interpolated, contains the following lines, which appear to be of genuine antiquity :—

    "The Queen of Scots possessed nought,
      That my love let me want ;
    For cow and ew to me he brought,
      And ein whan they were scant."

The version of "Gilderoy" here given to the reader is printed from a written copy.

GILDEROY was a bonnie boy,
  Had roses tull his shoone,
His stockings were of silken *soy*,
  Wi' garters hanging doune :
It was, I weene, a comelie sight,
  To see sae trim a boy ;
He was my jo and hearts delight,
  My handsome Gilderoy.

Oh ! sike twa charming een he had,
  A breath as sweet as rose,
He never ware a Highland plaid,
  But costly silken clothes ;

He gain'd the luve of ladies gay,
  Nane eir tull him was coy :
Ah ! wae is mee ! I mourn the day
  For my dear Gilderoy.

My Gilderoy and I were born,
  Baith in one toun together,
We scant were seven years beforn,
  We gan to luve each other ;
Our dadies and our mammies thay,
  Were fill'd wi mickle joy,
To think upon the bridal day,
  Twixt me and Gilderoy.

For Gilderoy that luve of mine,
  Gude faith, I freely bought
A wedding sark of holland fine,
  Wi' silken flowers wrought:
And he gied me a wedding ring,
  Which I receiv'd wi' joy,
Nae lad nor lassie eir could sing,
  Like me and Gilderoy.

Wi' mickle joy we spent our prime,
  Till we were baith sixteen,
And aft we past the langsome time,
  Among the leaves sae green;
Aft on the banks we'd sit us thair,
  And sweetly kiss and toy,
Wi' garlands gay wad deck my hair
  My handsome Gilderoy.

Oh! that he still had been content,
  Wi' me to lead his life;
But, ah! his manfu' heart was bent,
  To stir in feates of strife:
And he in many a venturous deed,
  His courage bauld would try;
And now this *gars* mine heart to bleed,
  For my dear Gilderoy.

And when of me his leave he tuik,
  The tears they wat mine ee,
I gave tull him a parting luik,
  "My *benison* gang wi' thee;
God speed thee weil, mine ain dear heart,
  For gane is all my joy;
My heart is rent sith we maun part,
  My handsome Gilderoy."

My Gilderoy baith far and near,
  Was fear'd in every toun,
And bauldly bare away the gear,
  Of many a lawland loun:

Nane eir durst meet him man to man,
  He was sae brave a boy;
At length wi' numbers he was tane,
  My winsome Gilderoy.

Wae worth the loun that made the laws,
  To hang a man for gear,
To 'reave of life for ox or ass,
  For sheep, or horse, or mare:
Had not their laws been made sae strick,
  I neir had lost my joy,
Wi' sorrow neir had wat my cheek,
  For my dear Gilderoy.

Giff Gilderoy had done amisse,
  He mought hae banisht been;
Ah! what sair cruelty is this,
  To hang sike handsome men:
To hang the flower o' Scottish land,
  Sae sweet and fair a boy;
Nae lady had sae white a hand,
  As thee, my Gilderoy.

Of Gilderoy sae fraid they were,
  They bound him mickle strong,
Tull Edenburrow they led him thair,
  And on a gallows hung:
They hung him high aboon the rest,
  He was sae trim a boy;
Thair dyed the youth whom I lued best,
  My handsome Gilderoy.

Thus having yielded up his breath,
  I bare his corpse away,
Wi' tears, that trickled for his death,
  I washt his comelye clay;
And siker in a grave sae deep,
  I laid the dear-lued boy,
And now for evir maun I weep,
  My winsome Gilderoy.

---

## XIII.—WINIFREDA.

THIS beautiful address to conjugal love, a subject too much neglected by the libertine Muses, was first printed in a volume of *Miscellaneous Poems*, by several hands, published by D. Lewis, 1726, 8vo. It is there said, how truly I know not, to be a translation "from the ancient British language."

Away; let nought to love displeasing,
  My Winifreda, move your care;
Let nought delay the heavenly blessing,
  Nor squeamish pride, nor gloomy fear.

What tho' no grants of royal donors
  With pompous titles grace our blood;
We'll shine in more substantial honors,
  And to be noble we'll be good.

Our name, while virtue thus we tender,
  Will sweetly sound where-e'er 'tis spoke:
And all the great ones, they shall wonder
  How they respect such little folk.

What though from fortune's lavish bounty
  No mighty treasures we possess;
We'll find within our pittance plenty,
  And be content without excess.

Still shall each returning season
  Sufficient for our wishes give;
For we will live a life of reason,
  And that's the only life to live.

Through youth and age in love excelling,
  We'll hand in hand together tread;
Sweet-smiling peace shall crown our dwelling,
  And babes, sweet-smiling babes, our bed.

How should I love the pretty creatures,
  While round my knees they fondly clung;
To see them look their mothers features,
  To hear them lisp their mothers tongue.

And when with envy time transported
  Shall think to rob us of our joys,
You'll in your girls again be courted,
  And I'll go a wooing in my boys.

## XIV.—THE WITCH OF WOKEY

Was published in a small collection of poems, entitled *Euthemia, or the Power of Harmony*, etc., 1756, written, in 1748, by the ingenious Dr. Harrington, of Bath, who never allowed them to be published, and withheld his name till it could no longer be concealed. The following copy was furnished by the late Mr. Shenstone, with some variations and corrections of his own, which he had taken the liberty to propose, and for which the author's indulgence was entreated.

Wokey-hole is a noted cavern near Wells, in Somersetshire, which has given birth to as many wild fanciful stories as the Sybils Cave, in Italy. It goes winding a great way underground, is crossed by a stream of very cold water, and is all horrid with broken pieces of rock: many of these are evident petrifactions; which, on account of their singular forms, have given rise to the fables alluded to in this poem.

In aunciente days tradition showes
A base and wicked elfe arose,
  The Witch of Wokey *hight:*
Oft have I heard the fearfull tale
From Sue, and Roger of the vale,
  On some long winter's night.

Deep in the dreary dismall cell,
Which seem'd and was *ycleped* hell,
  This blear-eyed hag did hide:
Nine wicked elves, as legends sayne,
She chose to form her guardian trayne,
  And kennel near her side.

Here screeching owls oft made their nest,
While wolves its craggy sides possest,
  Night-howling thro' the rock:
No wholesome herb could here be found;
She blasted every plant around,
  And blister'd every flock.

Her haggard face was foull to see;
Her mouth unmeet a mouth to bee;
  Her eyne of deadly leer,
She nought devis'd, but neighbour's ill;
She wreak'd on all her wayward will,
  And marr'd all goodly chear.

All in her prime, have poets sung,
No gaudy youth, gallant and young,
  E'er blest her longing armes;
And hence arose her spight to vex,
And blast the youth of either sex,
  By dint of hellish charms.

From Glaston came a lerned wight,
Full bent to marr her fell despight,
  And well he did, I ween:
Sich mischief never had been known,
And, since his mickle leringe shown,
  Sich mischief ne'er has been.

He chauntede out his godlie booke,
He crost the water, blest the brooke,
  Then—pater noster done,—
The ghastly hag he sprinkled o'er;
When lo! where stood a hag before,
  Now stood a ghastly stone.

Full well 'tis known adown the dale:
Tho' passing strange indeed the tale,
  And doubtfull may appear,
I'm bold to say, there's never a one,
That has not seen the witch in stone,
  With all her houschold gear.

But tho' this lernede clerke did well;
With grieved heart, alas! I tell,
  She left this curse behind:
That Wokey nymphs forsaken quite,
Tho' sense and beauty both unite,
  Should find no leman kind.

For lo! even, as the fiend did say,
The sex have found it to this day,
  That men are wondrous scant:
Here's beauty, wit, and sense combin'd,
With all that's good and virtuous join'd,
  Yet hardly one gallant.

Shall then sich maids unpitied moane?
They might as well, like her, be stone,
  As thus forsaken dwell.
Since Glaston now can boast no clerks;
Come down from Oxenford, ye sparks,
  And, oh! revoke the spell.

Yet stay—nor thus despond, ye fair;
Virtue's the gods' peculiar care;
  I hear the gracious voice:
Your sex shall soon be blest agen,
We only wait to find sich men,
  As best deserve your choice.

---

## XV.—BRYAN AND PEREENE.

### A WEST-INDIAN BALLAD,

Is founded on a real fact, that happened in the island of St. Christophers about the beginning of the reign of George III. The editor owes the following stanzas to the friendship of Dr. James Grainger, physician in that island when this tragical incident happened, and died there much honoured and lamented in 1767.

THE north-east wind did briskly blow,
  The ship was safely moor'd;
Young Bryan thought the boat's-crew slow,
  And so leapt over-board.

Pereene, the pride of Indian dames,
  His heart long held in thrall;
And whoso his impatience blames,
  I wot, ne'er lov'd at all.

A long long year, one month and day,
  He dwelt on English land,
Nor once in thought or deed would stray,
  Tho' ladies sought his hand.

For Bryan he was tall and strong,
  Right blythsome roll'd his een,
Sweet was his voice whene'er he sung,
  He scant had twenty seen.

But who the countless charms can draw,
   That grac'd his mistress true ;
Such charms the old world seldom saw,
   Nor oft I ween the new.

Her raven hair plays round her neck,
   Like tendrils of the vine ;
Her cheeks red dewy rose buds deck,
   Her eyes like diamonds shine.

Soon as his well-known ship she spied,
   She cast her weeds away,
And to the palmy shore she hied,
   All in her best array.

In sea-green silk so neatly clad,
   She there impatient stood ;
The crew with wonder saw the lad
   Repell the foaming flood,

Her hands a handkerchief display'd,
   Which he at parting gave ;
Well pleas'd the token he survey'd,
   And manlier beat the wave.

Her fair companions one and all,
   Rejoicing crowd the strand ;
For now her lover swam in call,
   And almost touch'd the land.

Then through the white surf did she haste,
   To clasp her lovely swain ;
When, ah ! a shark bit through his waste :
   His heart's blood dy'd the main !

He shriek'd ! his half sprang from the wave,
   Streaming with purple gore,
And soon it found a living grave,
   And ah ! was seen no more.

Now haste, now haste, ye maids, I pray,
   Fetch water from the spring :
She falls, she swoons, she dies away,
   And soon her knell they ring.

Now each May morning round her tomb,
   Ye fair, fresh flowerets strew,
So may your lovers scape his doom,
   Her hapless fate scape you.

## XVI.—GENTLE RIVER, GENTLE RIVER.

GENTLE river, gentle river,
   Lo, thy streams are stain'd with gore,
Many a brave and noble captain
   Floats along thy willow'd shore.

All beside thy limpid waters,
   All beside thy sands so bright,
Moorish Chiefs and Christian Warriors
   Join'd in fierce and mortal fight.

Lords, and dukes, and noble princes
   On thy fatal banks were slain :
Fatal banks that gave to slaughter
   All the pride and flower of Spain.

There the hero, brave Alonzo,
   Full of wounds and glory died :
There the fearless Urdiales
   Fell a victim by his side.

Lo ! where yonder Don Saavedra
   Thro' their squadrons slow retires ;
Proud Seville, his native city,
   Proud Seville his worth admires.

Close behind a renegado
   Loudly shouts with taunting cry ;
Yield thee, yield thee, Don Saavedra,
   Dost thou from the battle fly ?

Well I know thee, haughty Christian,
   Long I liv'd beneath thy roof ;
Oft I've in the lists of glory
   Seen thee win the prize of proof.

Well I know thy aged parents,
   Well thy blooming bride I know ;
Seven years I was thy captive,
   Seven years of pain and woe.

May our prophet grant my wishes,
  Haughty chief, thou shalt be mine:
Thou shalt drink that cup of sorrow,
  Which I drank when I was thine.

Like a lion turns the warrior,
  Back he sends an angry glare:
Whizzing came the Moorish javelin,
  Vainly whizzing thro' the air.

Back the hero full of fury
  Sent a deep and mortal wound:
Instant sunk the Renegado,
  Mute and lifeless on the ground.

With a thousand Moors surrounded,
  Brave Saavedra stands at bay:
Wearied out but never daunted,
  Cold at length the warrior lay.

Near him fighting great Alonzo
  Stout resists the Paynim bands;
From his slaughter'd steed dismounted
  Firm intrench'd behind him stands.

Furious press the hostile squadron,
  Furious he repels their rage:
Loss of blood at length enfeebles:
  Who can war with thousands wage!

Where yon rock the plain o'ershadows,
  Close beneath its foot retir'd,
Fainting sunk the bleeding hero,
  And without a groan expir'd.

## XVII.—ALCANZOR AND ZAYDA: A MOORISH TALE.
### IMITATED FROM THE SPANISH.

SOFTLY blow the evening breezes,
  Softly fall the dews of night;
Yonder walks the Moor Alcanzor,
  Shunning every glare of light.

In yon palace lives fair Zaida,
  Whom he loves with flame so pure:
Loveliest she of Moorish ladies;
  He a young and noble Moor.

Waiting for the appointed minute,
  Oft he paces to and fro;
Stopping now, now moving forwards,
  Sometimes quick, and sometimes slow.

Hope and fear alternate teize him,
  Oft he sighs with heart-felt care.—
See, fond youth, to yonder window
  Softly steps the timorous fair.

Lovely seems the moon's fair lustre
  To the lost benighted swain,
When all silvery bright she rises,
  Gilding mountain, grove, and plain.

Lovely seems the sun's full glory
  To the fainting seaman's eyes,
When some horrid storm dispersing
  O'er the wave his radiance flies.

But a thousand times more lovely
  To her longing lover's sight
Steals half-seen the beauteous maiden
  Thro' the glimmerings of the night.

Tip-toe stands the anxious lover,
  Whispering forth a gentle sigh:
Allah keep thee, lovely lady;
  Tell me, am I doom'd to die?

Is it true the dreadful story,
  Which thy damsel tells my page,
That seduc'd by sordid riches
  Thou wilt sell thy bloom to age?

An old lord from Antiquera
  Thy stern father brings along;
But canst thou, inconstant Zaida,
  Thus consent my love to wrong?

If 'tis true now plainly tell me,
  Nor thus trifle with my woes;
Hide not then from me the secret,
  Which the world so clearly knows.

Deeply sigh'd the conscious maiden,
  While the pearly tears descend:
Ah! my lord, too true the story;
  Here our tender loves must end.

Our fond friendship is discover'd,
  Well are known our mutual vows:
All my friends are full of fury;
  Storms of passion shake the house.

Threats, reproaches, fears surround me;
  My stern father breaks my heart:
Allah knows how dear it costs me,
  Generous youth, from thee to part.

Ancient wounds of hostile fury
  Long have rent our house and thine;
Why then did thy shining merit
  Win this tender heart of mine?

Well thou know'st how dear I lov'd thee
  Spite of all their hateful pride,
Tho' I fear'd my haughty father
  Ne'er would let me be thy bride.

Well thou know'st what cruel chidings
  Oft I've from my mother borne;
What I've suffer'd here to meet thee
  Still at eve and early morn.

I no longer may resist them;
  All, to force my hand combine;
And to-morrow to thy rival
  This weak frame I must resign.

Yet think not thy faithful Zaida
  Can survive so great a wrong;

Well my breaking heart assures me
  That my woes will not be long.

Farewell then, my dear Alcanzor!
  Farewell too my life with thee!
Take this scarf a parting token;
  When thou wear'st it think on me.

Soon, lov'd youth, some worthier maiden
  Shall reward thy generous truth;
Sometimes tell her how thy Zaida
  Died for thee in prime of youth.

—To him all amaz'd, confounded,
  Thus she did her woes impart:
Deep he sigh'd, then cry'd,—O Zaida!
  Do not, do not break my heart.

Canst thou think I thus will lose thee?
  Canst thou hold my love so small?
No! a thousand times I'll perish!—
  My curst rival too shall fall.

Canst thou, wilt thou yield thus to them?
  O break forth, and fly to me!
This fond heart shall bleed to save thee,
  These fond arms shall shelter thee.

'Tis in vain, in vain, Alcanzor,
  Spies surround me, bars secure:
Scarce I steal this last dear moment,
  While my damsel keeps the door.

Hark, I hear my father storming!
  Hark, I hear my mother chide!
I must go: farewell for ever!
  Gracious Allah be thy guide!


**THE END OF THE THIRD BOOK.**

# SERIES THE SECOND.—BOOK I.

## I.—RICHARD OF ALMAIGNE.

A BALLAD made by one of the adherents of Simon de Montfort, Earl of Leicester, soon after the battle of Lewes, which was fought May 14, 1264, affords a curious specimen of ancient satire, and shows that the liberty assumed by the good people of this realm, of abusing their kings and princes at pleasure, is a privilege of very long standing.

The reader to understand the libel must know that just before the battle of Lewes, which proved so fatal to the interests of Henry III., the barons had offered his brother Richard, king of the Romans, £30,000 to promise peace upon such terms as would have divested Henry of all regal power. The treaty proved abortive, the battle was the sequence, and the royal party fell into the hands of the Barons, whilst the Earl of Warren and Hugh Bigot, who had remained faithful to the king, fled to France.

The satire points at the supposed rapacity and greediness of Richard, thirty thousand pounds being in those days an exorbitant sum ; but this sum is a malevolent exaggeration of the libeller.

The ballad is said to have occasioned a law in our statute book against slanderous reports or tales to cause discord between king and people (Westm. Primer, c. 34, *anno* 3, *Edw. I.*).

The ballad is copied from a very ancient MS. in the British Museum (Harl. MSS. 2253, § 23).

SITTETH alle stille, ant herkneth to me ;
The kyng of *Alemaigne, bi mi leaute,*
Thritti thousent pound askede he
For te make the *pees* in the countre,
  Ant so he *dude* more.
 Richard, *thah* thou be ever *trichard,*
 *Tricthen* shalt thou never more.

Richard of Alemaigne, whil that he wes kying,
He spende al is tresour upon *swyvyng,*
Haveth he nout of Walingford * *oferlyng,*
Let him *habbe, ase he brew, bale* to *dryng,*
  *Maugre* Wyndesore,†
 Richard, thah thou be ever, etc.

The kyng of Alemaigne *wende* do ful wel,
He saisede the *mulne* for a castel,
With *hare* sharpe swerdes he grounde the stel,
He wende that the sayles were *mangonel*
  To helpe Wyndesore.
 Richard, thah thou be ever, etc.

The kyng of Alemaigne *gederede ys host,*
Makede him a castel of a *mulne* post,*
*Wende* with is *prude,* ant is *muchele bost,*
Brohte † from Alemayne mony sori gost
  To store Wyndesore.
 Richard, thah thou be ever, etc.

---

\* Richard, as well as the earldom of Cornwall, had the honours of Wallingford and Eyre conferred upon him.

† Windsor Castle was the chief fortress belonging to the king, and had been garrisoned by foreigners, which circumstance furnishes out the burden of each stanza.

\* Richard, after the battle was lost, took refuge in a windmill, which he defended for some time against the Barons, but was in the evening obliged to surrender.

† Richard was accused of bringing over foreigners to overrun the kingdom.

By God, that is above ous, he dude muche
    synne,
That lette passen over see the erl of
    Warynne :
He hath robbed Engelond, the mores, ant
    th fenne,
The gold, ant the selver, and *y-boren*
    *henne,*
        For love of Wyndesore.
    Richard, thah thou be ever, etc.

Sire Simond de Mountfort hath *suore bi
    ys chyn,*
*Hevede* he nou here the erl of Waryn,
Shuld he never more come to is *yn,*
Ne with sheld, ne with spere, ne with
    other *gyn,*
        To help of Wyndesore.
    Richard, thah thou be ever, etc.

Sire Simond de Montfort hath *suore bi ys
    cop,*
*Hevede* he nou here Sire Hue de Bigot :
Al he shulde grante here twelfmoneth *scot*
Shulde he never more with his sot pot
        To helpe Wyndesore.
    Richard, thah thou be ever, etc.

*Be* the *luef, be* the *loht,* sire Edward,
Thou shalt ride *sporeles* o thy *lyard*
Al the ryhte way to Dovere-*ward,*
Shalt thou never more breke foreward ;
    Ant that *reweth* sore
    Edward, thou *dudest* as a *shreward,*
        Forsoke thyn *emes lore*
    Richard, etc.

\*<sub>\*</sub>\* This ballad will rise in its importance with the reader, when he finds that it is even believed to have occasioned a law in our statute book, viz. "Against slanderous reports or tales, to cause discord betwixt king and people." (Westm. Primer, c. 34, *anno* 3, *Edw. I.*) That it had this effect, is the opinion of an eminent writer. See *Observations upon the Statutes,* etc., 4to, 2d ed. 1766, p. 71.

However, in the Harl. Collection may be found other satirical and defamatory rhymes of the same age, that might have their share in contributing to this first law against libels.

## II.—ON THE DEATH OF KING EDWARD THE FIRST.

WE have here an early attempt at elegy. Edward I. died July 7, 1307, in the 35th year of his reign and 69th of his age. The writer dwells more upon his devotion than his skill in government, and pays less attention to the martial and political abilities of this great monarch, in which he had no equal, than to some little weaknesses of superstition which he had in common with all his contemporaries. The king had in the decline of life vowed an expedition to the Holy Land ; but finding his end approach, he dedicated the sum of £32,000 to the maintenance of a large body of knights (140 say historians, 80 says our poet), who were to carry his heart with them into Palestine. This dying command of the king was never performed. Our poet, with the honest prejudices of an Englishman, attributes this failure to the advice of the king of France, whose daughter Isabel the young monarch who succeeded immediately married. But the truth is, Edward and his destructive favourite Piers Gaveston spent the money upon their pleasures.—To do the greater honour to the memory of his hero, our poet puts his eloge in the mouth of the Pope, with the same poetic licence as a more modern bard would have introduced Britannia, or the Genius of Europe, pouring forth his praises.

## ON THE DEATH OF KING EDWARD THE FIRST.

Alle, that beoth of *huerte* trewe,
    A *stounde* herkneth to my song
Of *duel*, that Deth hath *diht* us newe,
    That maketh me syke, ant sorewe among;
Of a knyht, that wes so strong,
    Of wham God hath don ys wille;
*Me-thuncheth* that deth has don us wrong,
    That he so sone shall *ligge* stille.

Al Englond *ahte* for te knowe
    Of wham that song is, that *y* synge;
Of Edward kyng, that lith so lowe,
    Zent al this world is *nome con springe:*
Trewest mon of alle thinge,
    Ant in werre *war ant wys*,
For him we *ahte* oure honden wrynge,
    Of Christendome he ber the *prys*.

Byfore that oure kyng was ded,
    He spek ase mon that wes in care,
"Clerkes, knyhtes, barons, he sayde,
    Y charge ou bȳ oure *sware*,
That ye to Engelonde be trewe.
    Y *deze*, y ne may lyven na more;
Helpeth mi sone, ant crouneth him newe,
    For he is nest to *buen y-core*.

"*Ich* biqueth myn herte arhyt,
    That hit be write at my *devys*,
Over the see that Hue * be *diht*,
    With fourscore knyhtes al of *prys*,
In werre that *buen war ant wys*,
    *Azeiu* the hethene for te fyhte,
To wynne the *croiz* that lowe lys,
    Myself ycholde *zef* that y myhte."

Kyng of Fraunce, thou *hevedest* "sinne,"
    That thou the counsail woldest *fonde*,
To *latte* the wille of "Edward kyng"
    To *wende* to the holy londe:
That oure kyng hede take on honde
    All Engelonde to *zeme* ant wysse,
To wenden in to the holy londe
    To wynnen us *heveriche* blisse.

---

\* The name of the person who was to preside over this business.

The messager to the pope com,
    And seyde that our kynge was ded:
Ys oune hond the lettre he *nom*,
    *Ywis* his herte was full gret:
The Pope him self the lettre redde,
    Ant spec a word of gret honour.
"Alas! he seid, is Edward ded?
    Of Christendome he *ber* the flour."

The Pope to is chaumbre wende,
    For *dol* ne mihte he speke na more;
Ant after cardinals he sende,
    That muche *couthen* of Cristes lore,
Bothe the *lasse*, ant *eke* the *more*,
    Bed hem bothe *rede* ant *synge:*
Gret *deol* me myhte se thore,
    Mony mon is honde wrynge.

The Pope of Peyters stod at is masse
    With ful gret solempneté,
Ther me con the soule blesse:
    "Kyng Edward honoured thou be
God love thi sone come after the,
    Bringe to ende that thou hast Ly-gonne,
The holy crois y-mad of tre,
    So fain thou woldest hit have y-wonne.

"Jerusalem, thou hast i-lore
    The flour of al chivalrie
Now kyng Edward liveth na more:
    Alas! that he *zet* shulde deye!
He wolde ha rered up ful *heyze*
    Oure banners, that bueth *broht* to grounde;
Wel! longe we mowe *clepe* and crie
    Er we a such kyng *hau y-founde*."

Nou is Edward of Carnarvan
    King of Engelond al *aplyht*,
God lete him ner be worse man
    Then his fader, ne lasse of myht,
To holden is pore men to ryht,
    And understonde good counsail,
Al Engelond for to *wysse ant dyht*;
    Of gode knyhtes *d'arh* him *nout* fail.

Thah mi tonge were mad of stel,
  Ant min herte *yzote* of bras,
The godness myht y never telle,
  That with kyng Edward was:
Kyng, as thou art *cleped* conquerour,
  In uch bataille thou hadest *prys;*

God bringe thi soule to the honour,
  That ever wes, ant ever ys.
That lasteth ay withouten ende,
  Bidde we God, ant oure Ledy to thilke blisse
Jesus us sende.   Amen.

---

### III.—AN ORIGINAL BALLAD BY CHAUCER.

THIS little sonnet, which hath escaped all the editors of Chaucer's works, is from an ancient MS. in the Pepysian Library, that contains many other poems of its venerable author. The versification is of that species which the French call Rondeau. Geoffrey Chaucer died Oct. 25, 1400, aged 72.

#### I.

YOURE two *eyn* will *sle* me sodenly,
I may the beaute of them not sustene,
So wendeth it thorowout my herte kene.

And but your words will *helen* hastely
My hertis wound, while that it is grene,
Youre two eyn will sle me sodenly.

Upon my trouth I sey yow feithfully,
That ye ben of my liffe and deth the quene;
For with my deth the trouth shal be sene.
    Youre two eyn, etc.

#### II.

So hath youre beauty fro your herte chased
Pitee, that me n' availeth not to *pleyn;*
For daunger *halt* your mercy in his cheyne.

Giltless my deth thus have ye purchased;
I sey yow *soth*, me nedeth not to fayn:
So hath your beaute fro your herte chased.

Alas, that nature hath in yow compassed
So grete beaute, that no man may atteyn
To mercy, though he sterve for the peyn.
    So hath youre beaute, etc.

#### III.

*Syn* I fro love escaped am so fat,
I nere thinke to ben in his prison lene;
Syn I am fre, I counte hym not a *bene.*

He may answere, and sey this and that,
I do no fors, I speak ryght as I mene;
Syn I fro love escaped am so fat.

Love hath my name i-strike out of his *sclat,*
And he is strike out of my bokes clene:
For ever mo "ther" is non other mene,
    Syn I fro love escaped, etc.

## IV.—THE TURNAMENT OF TOTTENHAM;

### OR, "THE WOOEING, WINNING, AND WEDDING OF TIBBE, THE REEV'S DAVGHTER THERE,"

WRITTEN, it is supposed, by Gilbert Pilkington, who is said to have been parson of the parish of Tottenham in the 15th century. It was first printed in 1631, through the assistance of the Rev. Wilhelm Bedwell, rector of Tottenham, and afterwards bishop of Kilmore, and one of the translators of the Bible.

Bedwell believed it to be the true account of a tournament that took place before the reign of Edward III., and failed to see the humour and the satire of the production. Romance and chivalry were bewitching the eyes of Europe when Chaucer wrote his *Sir Thopas* in ridicule of the former; and the poem before us is a humorous burlesque upon the latter. In it we have all the solemnities of the Tourney.

Here we have the regular challenge—the appointed day—the lady for the prize—the formal preparations—the display of armour—the scutcheons and devices—the oaths taken on entering the lists—the various accidents of the encounter—the victor leading off the prize—and the magnificent feasting—with all the other solemn fopperies that usually attended the pompous tournament. And how acutely the sharpness of the author's humour must have been felt in those days, we may learn from what we can perceive of its keenness now, when time has so much blunted the edge of his ridicule.

OF all thes kene conquerours to *carpe*
   it were kynde;
Of *fele feyztyng* folk *ferly* we fynde,
The Turnament of Totenham have we in
   mynde;
It were harme sych hardynes were holden
   byhynde,
     In story as we rede
       Of Hawkyn, of Herry,
       Of Tomkyn, of Terry,
       Of them that were *dughty*
     And stalworth in dede.

It befel in Totenham on a *dere day*,
Ther was mad a *shurtyng* be the hy-
   way:
Theder come al the men of the con-
   tray,
Of Hyssylton, of Hy-gate, and of
   Hakenay,[*]

[*] Islington, Highgate, Hackney.

And all the swete *swynkers*.
   Ther hopped Hawkyn,
   Ther daunsed Dawkyn,
   Ther trumped Tomkyn,
     And all were trewe drynkers.

Tyl the day was gon and evyn-song past,
That thay schuld reckyn ther *scot* and ther
   counts cast;
Perkyn the potter into the press past,
And sayd Randol the *refe*, a *dozter* thou
   hast,
     Tyb the dere:
       Therfor faine wyt wold I,
       Whych of all thys bachelery
       Were best worthye
         To wed hur to hys *fere*.

Upstyrt thos *gadelyngys* wyth ther lang
   staves,
And sayd, Randol the refe, lo! thys lad
   raves;

Boldely amang us thy dozter he craves;
We er rycher men than he, and mor gode haves
    Of cattell and corn;
      Then sayd Perkyn, to Tybbe I have *hyzt*
      That I schal be alway redy in my *ryzt*,
      If that it schuld be thys day *sevenyzt*,
        Or elles zet to *morn*.

Then sayd Randolfe the refe, Ever be he *waryd*,
That about thys carpyng lenger wold be taryd:
I wold not my dozter, that *scho* were miscaryd,
But at hur most worschip I wold scho were maryd;
    Therfor a Turnament schal begynne
    Thys day *sevenyzt*,—
    Wyth a flayl for to fyzt:
    And he that is most of myght
      Schal *brouke* hur wyth *wynne*.

Whoso berys hym best in the turnament,
Hym schal be granted the *gre* be the comon assent,
For to wynne my dozter wyth "dughtynesse" of *dent*,
And "coppell"\* my brode-henne "that" was brozt out of Kent:
    And my dunnyd kowe
    For no spens wyl I spare,
    For no cattell wyl I care,
    He schal have my gray mare,
    And my spottyd sowe.

Ther was many "a" bold lad ther bodyes to *bede*:
Than thay toke thayr leve, and homward they *zede*;

And all the weke afterward graythed ther *wede*,
Tyll it come to the day, that thay suld do ther dede.
    They armed *ham* in matts;
    Thay set on ther *nollys*,
    For to kepe ther *pollys*,
    Gode blake *bollys*,
      For batryng of *bats*.

Thay sowed tham in schepeskynnes, for thay schuld not brest:
*Ilk - on* toke a blak hat, insted of a crest:
"A basket or a panyer before on ther brest,"
And a flayle in ther hande; for to fyght prest,
    Furth gon thay *fare:*
    Ther was *kyd* mekyl *fors*,
    Who schuld best *fend* hys *cors:*
    He that had no gode hors,
      He gat hym a mare.

Sych another gadryng have I not sene oft,
When all the gret company com rydand to the croft:
Tyb on a gray mare was set up on loft
On a sek ful of fedyrs, for scho schuld syt soft,
    And led "till the gap."
    For cryeng of the men
    Forther wold not Tyb then,
    Tyl scho had hur brode hen
      Set in hur Lap.

A gay gyrdyl Tyb had on, borowed for the *nonys*,
And a garland on hur hed ful of rounde bonys,
And a broche on hur brest ful of "sapphyre" stonys,
Wyth the holy-rode tokenyng, was *wrotyn* for the nonys;

---

\* We still use the phrase "a copple-crowned hen."

For no "spendings" thay had spared.
When joly Gyb saw hur thare,
He *gyrd* so hys gray mare,
"That scho lete a fowkin" fare
At the rereward.

I wow to God, quoth Herry, I schal not lefe behynde,
May I mete wyth Bernard on Bayard the blynde,
Ich man kepe hym out of my wynde,
For whatsoever that he be, before me I fynde,
I wot I schall hyme greve.
Wele sayd, quoth Hawkyn,
And I wow, quoth Dawkyn,
May I mete wyth Tomkyn,
Hys flayle I schal hym *reve*.

I make a vow, quoth Hud, Tyb, son schal thou se,
Whych of all thys bachelery "granted" is the gre:
I schal *scomfet* thaym all, for the love of the;
In what place so I come thay schal have *dout* of me,
Myn armes ar so clere:
I bere a reddyl, and a rake,
*Poudred* wyth a *brenand drake*,
And three *cantells* of a cake
In *ycha* cornere.

I vow to God, quoth Hawkyn, yf "I" have the gowt,
Al that I fynde in the felde "thrustand" here aboute,
Have I twyes or thryes redyn thurgh the route,
In ycha stede ther thay me se, of me thay schal have doute,
When I begyn to play.
I make avowe that I ne schall,
But yf Tybbe wyl me call,
Or I be thryes don fall,
*Ryzt* onys com away.

Then sayd Terry, and swore be hys crede;
Saw thou never yong boy forther hys body bede,
For when thay fyzt fastest and most ar in drede,
I schall take Tyb by the hand, and hur away lede:
I am armed at the full;
In myn armys I bere wele
A *dozt rogh*, and a pele,
A sadyll wythout a panell,
Wyth a *fles* of woll.

I make a vow, quoth Dudman, and swor be the stra,
Whyls me ys left my "mare," thou gets hurr not swa;
For scho ys wele schapen, and *lizt* as the rae,
Ther is no *capul* in thys myle befor hur schal ga;
Sche wul ne *nozt begyle*:
Sche wyl me bere, I dar say,
On a lang somerys day,
Fro Hyssylton to Hakenay,
Nozt other half myle.

I make a vow, quoth Perkyn, thow speks of *cold rost*,
I schal *wyrch* "*wyselyer*" withouten any bost:
Five of the best capulys, that ar in thys ost,
I wot I schal thaym wynne, and bryng thaym to my cost,
And here I grant thaym Tybbe.
Wele boyes here ys he,
That wyl fyzt, and not fle,
For I am in my jolyte,
Wyth so forth, Gybbe.

When thay had ther vowes made, furth can thay hie,
Wyth flayles, and hornes, and trumpes *mad of tre:* \*

---

\* Probably wooden trumpets.

Ther were all the bachelerys of that
   contre ;
Thay were dyzt in aray, as thaymselfes
   wold be :
      Thayr baners were ful bryzt
      Of an old rotten *fell ;*
      The cheveron of a *plow-mell ;*
      And the schadow of a bell,
         Poudred wyth the *mone lyzt.*

I wot yt "was" no *chylder* game, whan
   thay togedyr met,
When *icha freke* in the feld on hys *feloy*
   bet,
And layd on styfly, for nothyng wold thay
   let,
And foght ferly fast, tyll ther horses swet,
   And few wordys spoken.
      Ther were flayles al to *slatred,*
      Ther were scheldys al to *flatred,*
      Bollys and dysches al to *schatred,*
         And many hedys brokyn.

Tnere was clynkyng of cart-sade-lys, and
   clatteryng of cannes ;
Of *fele frekys* in the feld brokyn were their
   *fannes ;*
Of sum were the hedys brokyn, of sum
   the brayn-pannes,
And yll were thay besene, or thay went
   thanns,
      Wyth *swyppyng* of *sweepyls :*
      Thay were so wery for-foght,
      Thay myzt not fyzt mare oloft,
      But creped about in the "croft,"
         As thay were croked *crepyls.*

Perkyn was so wery, that he began to
   *loute ;*
Help, Hud, I am ded in thys *ylk* rowte :
An hors for forty pens, a gode and a
   stoute !
That I may lyztly come of my noye oute,
   For no cost wyl I spare.
      He styrt up as a snayle,
      And *hent* a capul be the tayle,
      And "*reft*" Dawkin hys flayle,
         And wan there a mare.

Perkyn wan five, and Hud wan twa :
Glad and blythe thay ware, that they had
   don sa ;
They wold have tham to Tyb, and pre-
   sent hur with tha :
The Capulls were so wery, that thay myzt
   not ga,
   But styl gon they stond.
      Alas ! quoth Hudde, my joye I
         *lese ;*
      Mee had *lever* then a ston of
         chese,
      That dere Tyb had al these,
         And wyst it were my sond.

Perkyn turnyd hym about in that *yeh*
   thrang,
Among thos wery boyes he wrest and he
   wrang ;
He threw tham doun to the erth, and
   thrast tham amang,
When he saw Tyrry away wyth Tyb *fang,*
   And after hym ran ;
      Off his horse he hym drogh,
      And gaf hym of hys flayl *inogh :*
      *We te he!* quoth Tyb, and *lugh,*
         Ye er a dughty man.

"Thus" they tugged, and *rugged,* tyl yt
   was nere nyzt :
All the wyves of Tottenham came to se
   that syzt
Wyth wyspes, and kexis, and *ryschys* there
   lyzt,
To fetch hom ther husbandes, that were
   tham trouth plyzt ;
   And sum brozt gret harwos,
      Ther husbandes hom to fetch,
      Sum on dores, and sum on *hech,*
      Sum on hyrdyllys, and som on
         *crech,*
         And sum on whele-barows.

Thay gaderyd Perkyn about, "on"
   everych syde,
And grant hym ther "the *gre,*" the more
   was hys pryde :

Tyb and he, wyth gret "mirth," homward
 con thay ryde,
And were al nyzt togedyr, tyl the morn
 tyde;
  And thay "to church went:"
  So wele hys nedys he has sped,
  That dere Tyb he "hath" wed;
  The prayse-folk,* that hur led,
  Were of the Turnament.

To that *ylk* fest com many for the nones;
Some come *hyphalte*, and some trippand
 "thither" on the stonys:
Sum a staf in hys hand, and sum two at
 onys;
Of sum where the hedes broken, of some
 the schulder bonys;

With sorrow come thay thedyr.
 Wo was Hawkyn, wo was Herry,
 Wo was Tomkyn, wo was Terry,
 And so was all the bachelary,
 When they met togedyr.

At that fest thay wer servyd with a
 ryche aray,
Every fyve and fyve had a *cokenay;*
And so thay sat in jolyte al the lung day;
And at the last thay went to bed with ful
 gret deray:
 Mekyl myrth was them among;
 In every corner of the hous
 Was melody delycyous
 For to here precyus
 Of six menys song.

---

## V.—FOR THE VICTORY AT AGINCOURT.

THAT our plain and martial ancestors could wield their swords much better than their pens, will appear from the following homely rhymes, which were drawn up by some poet laureate of those days to celebrate the immortal victory gained at Agincourt, Oct. 25, 1415. This song or hymn is given merely as a curiosity, and is printed from a MS. copy in the Pepys Collection, vol. I. folio. It is there accompanied with the musical notes, which are copied in a small plate at the end of this volume.

*Deo gratias Anglia redde pro victoria!*

OWRE kynge went forth to Normandy,
With grace and myzt of chivalry;
The God for hym wrouzt marvelously,
Wherefore Englonde may calle, and cry
  *Deo gratias:*
*Deo gratias Anglia redde pro victoria.*

He sette a sege, the sothe for to say,
To Harflue toune with ryal aray;
That toune he wan, and made a fray,
That Fraunce shall rywe tyl domes day.
  *Deo gratias, etc.*

Then went owre kynge, with alle his
 oste,
Thorowe Fraunce for all the Frenshe
 boste;

He spared "for" drede of leste, ne most,
Tyl ne come to Agincourt coste.
  *Deo gratias, etc.*

Than for sothe that knyzt comely
In Agincourt feld he fauzt manly,
Thorow grace of God most myzty
He had bothe the felde, and the victory:
  *Deo gratias, etc.*

Ther dukys, and erlys, lorde and barone,
Were take, and slayne, and that wel sone,
And some were ledde in to Lundone
With joye, and merthe, and grete renone.
  *Deo gratias, etc.*

Now gracious God he save owre kynge,
His peple, and all his wel wyllynge,
Gef him gode lyfe, and gode endynge,
That we with merth mowe savely synge
  *Deo gratias:*
*Deo gratias Anglia redde pro victoria.*

---

* Chief men.

## VI.—THE NOT-BROWNE MAYD.

THE sentimental beauties of this ancient ballad have always recommended it to readers of taste, notwithstanding the rust of antiquity which obscures the style and expression. The text is formed from two copies found in two different editions of *Arnolde's Chronicle*, a book supposed to be first printed about 1521.

The ballad of the "Nutbrowne Mayd" was first revived in *The Muses' Mercury* for June 1707, 4to, being prefaced with a little "Essay on the old English Poets and Poetry," in which this poem is concluded to be "near 300 years old," upon reasons which, though they appear inconclusive to us now, were sufficient to determine Prior, who there first met with it. However, this opinion had the approbation of the learned Wanley, an excellent judge of ancient books. For that whatever related to the reprinting of this old piece was referred to Wanley, appears from two letters of Prior's preserved in the British Museum [Harl. MSS. No. 3777].

BE it ryght, or wrong, these men among
   On women do complayne ;
Affyrmynge this, how that it is
   A labour spent in vayne,
To love them wele ; for never a dele
   They love a man agayne :
For late a man do what he can,
   Theyr favour to attayne,
Yet, yf a newe do them persue,
   Theyr first true lover than
Laboureth for nought ; for from her thought
   He is a banyshed man.

I say nat nay, but that all day
   It is bothe writ and sayd
That womans faith is, as who sayth,
   All utterly decayd ;
But, neverthelesse, ryght good wytnèsse
   In this case might be layd,
That they love true, and continûe :
   Recorde the Not-browne Mayde :
Which, when her love came, her to prove,
   To her to make his mone,
Wolde nat depart ; for in her hart
   She loved but hym alone.

Than betwaine us late us dyscus
   What was all the *manere*
Betwayne them two : we wyll also
   Tell all the payne, and *fere*,
That she was in. Nowe I begyn,
   So that ye me answère ;
Wherfore, all ye that present be,
   I pray you, gyve an ere.
"I am the knyght ; I come by nyght,
   As secret as I can ;
Sayinge, Alas ! thus standeth the case,
   I am a banyshed man."

SHE.

And I your wyll for to fulfyll
   In this wyll nat refuse ;
Trustying to shewe, in wordès fewe,
   That men have an yll use
(To theyr own shame) women to blame,
   And causelesse them accuse ;
Therfore to you I answere nowe,
   All women to excuse,—
Myne owne hart dere, with you what chere?
   I pray you, tell anone ;
For, in my mynde, of all mankynde
   I love but you alone.

HE.

It standeth so ; a dede is do
   Wherof grete harme shall growe :
My destiny is for to dy
   A shamefull deth, I trowe ;
Or elles to fle : the one must be,
   None other way I knowe,

But to withdrawe as an outlawe,
  And take me to my bowe.
Wherfore, adue, my owne hart true!
  None other *rede* I can:
For I must to the grene wode go,
  Alone, a banyshed man.

### SHE.

O Lord, what is thys worldys blysse,
  That changeth as the mone!
My somers day in lusty may
  Is derked before the none.
I here you say, farewell: Nay, nay,
  We depart nat so sone.
Why say ye so? wheder wyll ye go?
  Alas! what have ye done?
All my welfàre to sorrowe and care
  Sholde chaunge, yf ye were gone;
For, in my mynde, of all mankynde
  I love but you alone.

### HE.

I can beleve, it shall you greve,
  And somewhat you *dystrayne;*
But, aftyrwarde, your paynes harde
  Within a day or twayne
Shall sone aslake; and ye shall take
  Comfort to you agayne.
Why sholde ye ought? for, to make
    thought,
  Your labour were in vayne.
And thus I do; and pray you to,
  As hartely, as I can;
For I must to the grene wode go,
  Alone, a banyshed man.

### SHE.

Now, syth that ye have shewed to me
  The secret of your mynde,
I shall be playne to you agayne,
  Lyke as ye shall me fynde.
Syth it is so, that ye wyll go,
  I wolle not leve behynde;
Shall never be sayd, the Not-browne
    Mayd
  Was to her love unkynde:

Make you redy, for so am I,
  Allthough it were anone;
For, in my mynde, of all mankynde
  I love but you alone.

### HE.

Yet I you rede to take good hede
  What men wyll thynke, and say:
Of yonge, and olde, it shall be tolde,
  That ye be gone away,
Your wanton wyll for to fulfill,
  In grene wode you to play;
And that ye myght from your delyght
  No lenger make delay.
Rather than ye sholde thus for me
  Be called an yll woman,
Yet wolde I to the grene wode go,
  Alone, a banyshed man.

### SHE.

Though it be songe of old and yonge,
  That I sholde be to blame,
Theyrs be the charge, that speke so large
  In hurtynge of my name:
For I wyll prove, that faythfulle love
  It is devoyd of shame;
In your dystresse, and hevynesse,
  To part with you, the same:
And sure all tho, that do not so,
  True lovers are they none;
For, in my mynde, of all mankynde
  I love but you alone.

### HE.

I counceyle you, remember howe,
  It is no maydens lawe,
Nothynge to *dout*, but to *renne* out
  To wode with an outlàwe:
For ye must there in your hand bere
  A bowe, redy to drawe;
And, as a thefe, thus must you lyve,
  Ever in drede and awe;
Wherby to you grete harme myght
    growe:
Yet had I *lever* than,
That I had to the grene wode go,
  Alone, a banyshed man.

#### SHE.

I thinke nat nay, but as ye say,
  It is no maydens lore:
But love may make me for your sake,
  As I have sayd before,
To come on fote, to hunt, and shote
  To gete us mete in store;
For so that I your company
  May have, I aske no more:
From which to part, it maketh my hart
  As colde as ony stone;
For, in my mynde, of all mankynde
  I love but you alone.

#### HE.

For an outlawe this is the lawe,
  That men hym take and bynde;
Without pytè, hanged to be,
  And waver with the wynde.
If I had nede (as God forbede !),
  What rescous coude ye fynde?
Forsoth, I trowe, ye and your bowe
  For fere wolde drawe behynde:
And no *mervayle;* for lytell avayle
  Were in your counceyle than:
Wherfore I wyll to the grene wode go,
  Alone, a banyshed man.

#### SHE.

Ryght wele knowe ye, that women be
  But feble for to fyght;
No womanhede it is indede
  To be bolde as a knyght:
Yet, in such fere yf that ye were
  With enemyes day or nyght,
I wolde withstande, with bowe in hande,
  To greve them as I myght,
And you to save; as women have
  From deth "men" many one:
For, in my mynde, of all mankynde
  I love but you alone.

#### HE.

Yet take good hede; for ever I drede
  That ye coude nat sustayne
The thornie wayes, the depe valèies,
  The snowe, the frost, the rayne,
The colde, the hete: for dry, or wete,
  We must lodge on the playne;
And, us above, none other rofe
  But a brake bush, or twayne:
Which sone sholde greve you, I beleve;
  And ye wolde gladly than
That I had to the grene wode go,
  Alone, a banyshed man.

#### SHE.

Syth I have here bene partynère
  With you of joy and blysse,
I must also parte of your wo
  Endure, as reson is:
Yet am I sure of one plesùre;
  And, shortely, it is this:
That, where ye be, me semeth, *pardè,*
  I coude nat fare amysse.
Without more speche, I you beseche
  That we were sone agone;
For, in my mynde, of all mankynde
  I love but you alone.

#### HE.

If ye go thyder, ye must consyder,
  Whan ye have *lust* to dyne,
There shall no mete be for you gete,
  Nor drinke, bere, ale, ne wyne.
No shetès clene, to lye betwene,
  Made of threde and twyne;
None other house, but leves and bowes,
  To cover your hed and myne,
O myne harte swete, this evyll dyète
  Sholde make you pale and wan;
Wherfore I wyll to the grene wode go,
  Alone, a banyshed man.

#### SHE.

Amonge the wylde dere, such an archère,
  As men say that ye be,
Ne may nat fayle of good vitayle,
  Where is so grete plentè:
And water clere of the ryvère
  Shall be full swete to me;
With which in *hele* I shall ryght wele
  Endure, as ye shall see;

And, or we go, a bedde or two
  I can provyde anone ;
For, in my mynde, of all mankynde
  I love but you alone.

**HE.**

Lo yet, before, ye must do more,
  Yf ye wyll go with me :
As cut your here up by your ere,
  Your kyrtel by the kne ;
With bowe in hande, for to withstande
  Your enemyes, yf nede be :
And this same nyght before day-lyght,
  To *wode-warde* wyll I fle.
Yf that ye wyll all this fulfill,
  Do it shortely as ye can :
Els wyll I to the grene wode go,
  Alone, a banyshed man.

**SHE.**

I shall as nowe do more for you
  Than longeth to womanhede ;
To shote my here, a bowe to bere,
  To shote in tyme of nede.
O my swete mother, before all other
  For you I have most drede :
But nowe, adue ! I must ensue,
  Where fortune doth me lede.
All this make ye : Now let us fle ;
  The day cometh fast upon ;
For, in my mynde, of all mankynde
  I love but you alone.

**HE.**

Nay, nay, nat so ; ye shall nat go,
  And I shall tell ye why,—
Your appetyght is to be lyght
  Of love, I wele espy :
For, lyke as ye have sayed to me,
  In lyke wyse hardely
Ye wolde answere whosoever it were,
  In way of company.
It is sayd of olde, Sone hote, sone colde ;
  And so is a woman.
Wherfore I to the wode wyll go,
  Alone, a banyshed man.

**SHE.**

Yf ye take hede, it is no nede
  Such wordes to say by me ;
For oft ye prayed, and longe assayed,
  Or I you loved, pardè :
And though that I of auncestry
  A barons daughter be,
Yet have you proved howe I you loved
  A squyer of lowe degrè ;
And ever shall, whatso befall ;
  To dy therfore\* anone ;
For, in my mynde, of all mankynde
  I love but you alone.

**HE.**

A barons chylde to be begylde !
  It were a cursed dede ;
To be felàwe with an outlawe !
  Almighty God forbede !
Yet beter were, the pore squyère
  Alone to forest yede,
Than ye sholde say another day,
  That, by my cursed dede,
Ye were betray'd : Wherfore, good mayd,
  The best rede that I can,
Is, that I to the grene wode go,
  Alone, a banyshed man.

**SHE.**

Whatever befall, I never shall
  Of this thyng you upbrayd :
But yf ye go, and leve me so,
  Than have ye me betrayd.
Remember you wele, how that ye dele ;
  For, yf ye, as ye sayd,
Be so unkynde, to leve behynde,
  Your love, the Not-browne Mayd,
Trust me truly, that I shall dy
  Sone after ye be gone ;
For, in my mynde, of all mankynde
  I love but you alone.

---

\* *i.e.* for this cause ; though I were to die for having loved you.

##### HE.

Yf that ye went, ye sholde repent;
  For in the forest nowe
I have purvayed me of a mayd,
  Whom I love more than you;
Another fayrère, than ever ye were,
  I dare it wele avowe;
And of you bothe eche sholde be wrothe
  With other, as I trowe:
It were myne ese, to lyve in pese;
  So wyll I, yf I can;
Wherfore I to the wode wyll go,
  Alone, a banyshed man.

##### SHE.

Though in the wode I undyrstode
  Ye had a paramour,
All this may nought remove my thought,
  But that I wyll be your:
And she shall fynde me soft, and kynde,
  And courteys every hour;
Glad to fulfyll all that she wyll
  Commaunde me to my power:
For had ye, lo, an hundred mo,
  "Of them I wolde be one;"*
For, in my mynde, of all mankynde
  I love but you alone.

##### HE.

Myne owne dere love, I se the prove
  That ye be kynde, and true;
Of mayde, and wyfe, in all my lyfe,
  The best that ever I knewe.
Be mery and glad, be no more sad,
  The case is chaunged newe;
For it were *ruthe*, that, for your truthe,
  Ye sholde have cause to *rewe*.
Be nat dismayed; whatsoever I sayd
  To you, whan I began;
I wyll nat to the grene wode go,
  I am no banyshed man.

---

\* So the Editor's MS. All the printed copies read, "Yet wold I be that one."

##### SHE.

These tydings be more gladd to me,
  Than to be made a quene,
Yf I were sure they sholde endure:
  But it is often sene,
Whan men wyll breke promyse, they speke
  The wordès on the splene.*
Ye shape some wyle me to begyle,
  And stele from me, I wene:
Than were the case worse than it was,
  And I more wo-begone:
For, in my mynde, of all mankynde
  I love but you alone.

##### HE.

Ye shall nat nede further to drede;
  I wyll nat dysparàge
You (God defend!), syth ye descend
  Of so grete a lynàge.
Nowe undyrstande; to Westmarlande,
  Which is myne herytage,
I wyll you brynge; and with a rynge,
  By way of maryage
I wyll you take, and lady make,
  As shortely as I can:
Thus have you won an erlys son,
  And not a banyshed man.

##### AUTHOR.

Here may ye se, that women be
  In love, meke, kynde, and stable
Late never man reprove them than,
  Or call them variable;
But, rather, pray God, that we may
  To them be comfortable;
Which sometyme proveth such, as he
  loveth,
  Yf they be charytable.
For syth men wolde that women sholde
  Be meke to them each one;
Moche more ought they to God obey,
  And serve but hym alone.

---

\* "On a sudden." C. Dell.

## VII.—A BALLAD BY THE EARL RIVERS.

THE amiable light in which the character of Anthony Widville, the gallant Earl Rivers, has been placed by the elegant author of the *Catalogue of Noble Writers*, interests us in whatever fell from his pen. It is presumed, therefore, that the insertion of this little sonnet will be pardoned, though it should not be found to have much poetical merit. It is the only original poem known of that nobleman's, his more voluminous works being only translations. And if we consider that it was written during his cruel confinement in Pomfret Castle, a short time before his execution in 1483, it gives us a fine picture of the composure and steadiness with which this stout earl beheld his approaching fate.

SUMWHAT musyng, And more mornyng,
   In remembring The unstydfastnes;
This world being Of such *whelyng*,
   Me contrarieng, What may I gesse?

I fere dowtles, Remediles,
   Is now to sese My wofull chaunce.
[For unkyndness, Withouten less,
   And no redress, Me doth *avaunce*,

With displesaunce, To my grevaunce,
   And no suraunce Of remedy.]

Lo in this traunce, Now in substaunce,
   Such is my dawnce, Wyllyng to dye.
Me thynkys truly, *Bowndyn* am I,
   And that grely, To be content:
Seyng playnly, Fortune doth wry
   All contrary From myn entent.

My lyff was lent Me to on intent,
   Hytt is ny spent. Welcome fortune!
But I ne went Thus to be *shent*,
   But sho hit ment; such is hur *won*.

## VIII.—CUPID'S ASSAULT: BY LORD VAUX.

IT is supposed with much reason that this poem was not written by Sir Nicholas Vaux, who died 1523, as some have believed, but by a Lord Vaux mentioned by the old writers as a poet contemporary with or rather posterior to Sir Thomas Wyatt and the Earl of Surrey, who neither of them made any figure until after the death of the first Lord Nicholas Vaux.

Thomas Lord Vaux of Harrowden in Northamptonshire was summoned to Parliament in 1531. When he died, does not appear, but he probably lived to the latter end of Queen Mary's reign, and is most likely the poet who wrote the following ballad.

WHEN Cupide scaled first the fort,
   Wherein my hart lay wounded sore;
The batry was of such a sort,
   That I must yelde or die therfore.

There sawe I Love upon the wall,
   How he his banner did display:
Alarme, alarme, he gan to call:
   And bad his souldiours kepe aray.

The armes, the which that Cupide bare,
   Were pearced hartes with teares besprent,

In silver and sable to declare
   The stedfast love, he alwayes ment.

There might you se his band all drest
   In colours like to white and blacke,
With powder and with pelletes prest
   To bring the fort to spoile and sacke.

Good-wyll, the maister of the shot,
   Stode in the rampire brave and proude,
For *spence* of pouder he spared not
   Assault! assault! to crye aloude.

There might you heare the cannons rore ;
  Eche pece discharged a lovers loke ;
Which had the power to rent, and tore
  In any place whereas they toke.

And even with the trumpettes sowne
  The scaling ladders were up set,
And Beautie walked up and downe,
  With bow in hand, and arrowes whet.

Then first Desire began to scale,
  And shrouded him under "his" *targe;*
As one the worthiest of them all,
  And aptest for to geve the charge.

Then pushed souldiers with their pikes,
  And halberdes with handy strokes ;
The *argabushe* in fleshe it lightes,
  And duns the ayre with misty smokes.

And, as it is the souldiers use
  When shot and powder gins to want,
I hanged up my flagge of truce,
  And pleaded up for my livès grant.

When Fansy thus had made her breche,
  And Beauty entred with her band,
With bagge and baggage, *sely* wretch,
  I yelded into Beauties hand.

Then Beautie bad to blow retrete,
  And every souldier to retire,
And mercy wyll'd with spede to fet
  Me captive bound as prisoner.

Madame, quoth I, sith that this day
  Hath served you at all assayes,
I yeld to you without delay
  Here of the fortresse all the kayes.

And sith that I have ben the marke,
  At whom you shot at with your eye ;
Nedes must you with your handy warke,
  Or salve my sore, or let me die.

---

## IX.—SIR ALDINGAR.

This old fabulous legend is given from the Editor's folio MS. with conjectural emendations, and the insertion of some additional stanzas to supply and complete the story.

It has been suggested that the author of this poem seems to have had in his eye the story of Gunhilda, who is sometimes called Eleanor, and who was married to the Emperor (here called King) Henry.

Sir Walter Scott regards *Sir Aldingar* as founded on the kindred ballad of *Sir Hugh le Blond*. "The incidents," he says, "are nearly the same in both ballads, excepting that in *Aldingar* an *angel* combats for the queen instead of a mortal champion."

But it appears that it was not simply an angel who fought for Queen Elinor, but that the author has intended the relief to come from the "Christchild," the legends of whom were in those days very prevalent among the mediæval Christians. And this supposition is greatly favoured by the last act of the child-champion being to touch the lazar or leper, who is immediately healed of his leprosy.

Our king he kept a false stewàrde,
  Sir Aldingar they him call :
A falser steward than he was one,
  Servde not in bower nor hall.

He wolde have taken our comelye queene,
  Her deere worshippe to betraye :
Our queene she was a good womàn,
  And evermore said him naye.

Sir Aldingar was wrothe in his mind,
  With her hee was never content,
Till traiterous meanes he colde devyse,
  In a fyer to have her *brent.*

There came a *lazar* to the kings gate,
    A lazar both blinde and lame :
He tooke the lazar upon his backe,
    Him on the queenes bed has layne.

" Lye still, lazàr wheras thou lyest,
    Looke thou goe not hence away ;
Ile make thee a whole man and a sound
    In two howers of the day."\*

Then went him forth sir Aldingar,
    And hyed him to our king :
" If I might have grace, as I have space,
    Sad tydings I could bring."

Say on, say on, sir Aldingar,
    Saye on the soothe to mee.
" Our queene hath chosen a new new love,
    And shee will have none of thee.

" If shee had chosen a right good knight,
    The lesse had beene her shame ;
But she hath chose her a lazar man,
    A lazar both blinde and lame,"

If this be true, thou Aldingar,
    The tyding thou tellest to me,
Then will I make thee a rich rich knight,
    Rich both of golde and fee.

But if it be false, sir Aldingar,
    As God nowe grant it bee !
Thy body, I sweare by the holye rood,
    Shall hang on the gallows tree.

He brought our king to the queenes chambèr,
    And opend to him the dore.
A *lodlye* love, king Harry says,
    For our queene dame Elinore !

If thou were a man, as thou art none,
    Here on my sword thoust dye ;
But a payre of new gallowes shall be built,
    And there shalt thou hang on hye.

---

\* He probably insinuates that the king should heal him by his power of touching for the king's evil.

Forth then hyed our king, I wysse,
    And an angry man was hee ;
And soone he found queene Elinore,
    That bride so bright of *blee.*

Now God you save, our queene, madame,
    And Christ you save and see ;
Heere you have chosen a newe newe love,
    And you will have none of mee.

If you had chosen a right good knight,
    The lesse had been your shame :
But you have chose you a lazar man,
    A lazar both blinde and lame.

Therfore a fyer there shall be built,
    And brent all shalt thou bee,—
" Now out alacke ! said our comly queene,
    Sir Aldingar's false to mee.

Now out alacke ! sayd our comlye queene,
    My heart with griefe will *brast.*
I had thought *swevens* had never been true ;
    I had proved them true at last.

I dreamt in my sweven on thursday eve,
    In my bed wheras I laye,
I dreamt a *grype* and a *grimlie* beast
    Had carryed my crowne awaye ;

My *gorgett* and my *kirtle* of golde,
    And all my faire head-geere :
And he wold worrye me with his tush
    And to his nest y-beare :

Saving there came a little 'gray' hawke,
    A merlin him they call,
Which untill the grounde did strike the grype,
    That dead he downe did fall.

*Giffe* I were a man, as now I am none,
    A battell wold I prove,
To fight with that traitor Aldingar;
    Att him I cast my glove.

But seeing Ime able noe battell to make,
    My liege, grant me a knight

"To fight with that traitor Sir Aldingar,
    To maintaine me in my right."

"Now forty dayes I will give thee
    To seeke thee a knight therin :
If thou find not a knight in forty dayes,
    Thy bodye it must brenn."

Then shee sent east, and shee sent west,
    By north and south *bedeene:*
But never a champion colde she find,
    Wolde fight with that knight soe keene.

Now twenty dayes were spent and gone,
    Noe helpe there might be had ;
Many a teare shed our comelye queene,
    And aye her hart was sad.

Then came one of the queenes damsèlles,
    And knelt upon her knee,
"Cheare up, cheare up, my gracious dame,
    I trust yet helpe may be :

And here I will make mine avowe,
    And with the same me binde ;
That never will I return to thee,
    Till I some helpe may finde."

Then forth she rode on a faire palfràye
    Oer hill and dale about :
But never a champion colde she finde,
    Wolde fighte with that knight so stout.

And nowe the daye drewe on a pace,
    When our good queene must dye ;
All woe-begone was that faire damsèlle,
    When she found no helpe was nye.

All woe-begone was that faire damsèlle,
    And the salt teares fell from her eye :
When lo ! as she rode by a rivers side,
    She met with a tinye boye.

A tinye boye she mette, God wot,
    All clad in mantle of golde ;
He seemed noe more in mans likenèsse,
    Then a childe of four yeere olde.

Why grieve you, damselle faire, he sayd,
    And what doth cause you moane ?
The damsell scant wolde deigne a looke,
    But fast she pricked on.

Yet turn againe, thou faire damsèlle,
    And greete thy queene from mee :
When *bale* is att hyest, *boote* is nyest,
    Nowe helpe enoughe may bee.

Bid her remember what she dreamt
    In her bedd, wheras shee laye ;
How when the grype and the grimly beast
    Wolde have carried her crowne awaye,

Even then there came the little gray hawke,
    And saved her from his clawes :
Then bidd the queene be merry at hart,
    For heaven will fende her cause.

Back then rode that faire damsèlle,
    And her hart it lept for glee :
And when she told her gracious dame,
    A gladd woman then was shee.

But when the appointed day was come
    No helpe appeared nye :
Then woeful, woeful was her hart,
    And the teares stood in her eye.

And nowe a fyer was built of wood ;
    And a stake was made of tree ;
And now queene Elinor forth was led,
    A sorrowful sight to see.

Three times the *herault* he waved his hand,
    And three times spake on hye :
Gi*ff* any good knight will fende this dame,
    Come forth, or shee must dye.

No knight stood forth, no knight there came,
    No helpe appeared nye :
And now the fyer was lighted up,
    Queen Elinor she must dye.

And now the fyer was lighted up,
  As hot as hot might bee;
When riding upon a little white steed,
  The tinye boy they see.

'Away with that stake, away with those brands,
  And loose our comelye queene:
I am come to fight with sir Aldingar,
  And prove him a traitor keene."

Forthe then stood sir Aldingar,
  But when he saw the chylde,
He laughed, and scoffed, and turned his backe,
  And weened he had been beguylde.

"Now turne, now turne thee, Aldingar,
  And eyther fighte or flee;
I trust that I shall avenge the wronge,
  Thoughe I am so small to see."

The boye pulld forth a well good sworde
  So gilt it dazzled the *ee;*
The first stroke stricken at Aldingar
  Smote off his leggs by the knee.

"Stand up, stand up, thou false traitòr,
  And fight upon thy feete,
For and thou thrive, as thou begin'st,
  Of height wee shall be meete."

A priest, a priest, sayes Aldingàr,
  While I am a man alive.
A priest, a priest, sayes Aldingàr,
  Me for to *houzle* and shrive.

I wolde have taken our comlie queene,
  Bot shee wolde never consent

Then I thought to betraye her unto our kinge
  In a fyer to have her brent.

There came a lazar to the kings gates,
  A lazar both blind and lame;
I tooke the lazar upon my backe,
  And on her bedd had him layne.

Then ranne I to our comlye king,
  These tidings sore to tell.
But ever alacke! sayes Aldingar,
  *Falsing* never doth well.

Forgive, forgive me, queene, madame,
  The short time I must live.
"Nowe Christ forgive thee, Aldingar,
  As freely I forgive."

Here take thy queene, our king Harryè,
  And love her as thy life,
For never had a king in Christentye
  A truer and fairer wife.

King Henrye ran to claspe his queene,
  And loosed her full sone:
Then turnd to look for the tinye boye;
  The boye was vanisht and gone.

But first he had touchd the lazar man,
  And stroakt him with his hand:
The lazar under the gallowes tree
  All whole and sounde did stand.

The lazar under the gallowes tree
  Was comelye, straight, and tall;
King Henrye made him his head stewàrde,
  To wayte withinn his hall.

### X.—THE GABERLUNZIE MAN.

#### A SCOTTISH SONG.

TRADITION informs us that the author of this song was King James V. of Scotland. This prince (whose character for wit and libertinism bears a great resemblance to that of his gay successor Charles II.) was noted for strolling about his dominions in disguise, and for his frequent gallantries with country girls. Two adventures of this kind he hath celebrated with his own pen, viz. in the ballad of *The Gaberlunzie Man;* and in another, entitled *The Jolly Beggar.*

Sir Walter Scott says of James V. that " he was a monarch whose good and benevolent intentions often rendered his romantic freaks venial if not respectable, since from his anxious attention to the interests of the lower and most oppressed class of his subjects, he was popularly termed the *King of the Commons.* For the purpose of seeing that justice was regularly administered, and frequently from the less justifiable motive of gallantry, he used to traverse the vicinage of his several palaces in various disguises. The two excellent comic songs, entitled *The Gaberlunzie Man,* and *We'll gae nae mair a-roving,* are said to have been founded upon the success of his amorous adventures when travelling in the disguise of a beggar. The latter is perhaps the best comic ballad in any language."

THE *pauky* auld *Carle* came ovir the lee
Wi' mony good-eens and days to mee,
Saying, Goodwife, for zour courtesie,
    Will ze lodge a silly poor man?
The night was cauld, the carle was wat,
And down *azont the ingle* he sat; \*
My dochters shoulders he gan to clap,
    And *cadgily* ranted and sang.

O wow! quo he, were I as free,
As first when I saw this countrie,
How blyth and merry wad I bee!
    And I wad nevir *think lang.*†
He grew *canty,* and she grew *fain;*
But little did her auld minny ken
What thir *slee* twa togither were say'n,
    When wooing they were sa *thrang.*

And O! quo he, ann ze were as black,
As evir the crown of your dadyes hat,
Tis I wad lay thee by my back,
    And awa wi' me thou sould gang.
And O! quoth she, ann I were as white,
As evir the snaw lay on the dike,
Ild clead me braw, and lady-like,
    And awa with thee Ild gang.

Between the twa was made a plot;
They *raise a wee* before the cock,
And wylicly they shot the lock,
    And fast to the *bent* are they gane.
Up the morn the auld wife raise,
And at her leisure put on her claiths,
*Syne* to the servants bed she gaes
    To *speir* for the silly poor man.

She gaed to the bed, whair the beggar lay,
The strae was cauld, he was away,
She clapt her hands, cryd, Dulefu' day!
    For some of our *geir* will be gane.

---

\* Beyond the fire; the fire was in the middle of the room.

† An expression meaning to grieve. "You'll not think long" is constantly used in the north of Ireland for "You won't distress yourself," "You won't grieve."

Some ran to coffer, and some to *kist*,
But nought was stown that could be mist.
She dancid her *lane*, cryd, Praise be blest,
    I have lodgd a leal poor man.

Since naithings awa, as we can learn,
The *kirns* to kirn, and milk to earn,
Gae *butt* the house, lass, and waken my bairn,
    And bid her come quickly *ben*.

The servant gaed where the dochter lay,
The sheets was cauld, she was away,
And fast to her goodwife can say,
    Shes aff with the *gaberlunzie-man*.

O fy *gar ride*, and fy gar rin,
And hast ze, find these traitors agen;
For shees be burnt, and hees be slein,
    The wearyfou gaberlunzie-man.
Some rade upo horse, some ran a fit,
The wife was *wood*, and out o' her wit;
She could na gang, nor yet could she sit,
    But ay did curse and did ban.

Mean time far hind out *owre* the lee,
For snug in a glen, where nane could see,

The twa, with kindlie sport and glee,
    Cut frae a new cheese a *whang*.
The *priving* was gude, it pleas'd them baith,
To lo'e her for ay, he gae her his aith.
Quo she, to leave thee, I will be laith,
    My *winsome* gaberlunzie-man.

O kend my minny I were wi' zou,
*Illfardly* wad she crook her mou,
Sic a poor man sheld nevir *trow*,
    Aftir the gaberlunzie-mon.
My dear, quo he, zee're zet owre zonge;
And hae na learnt the beggars tonge,
To follow me frae toun to toun,
    And carrie the gaberlunzie on.

Wi' *kauk* and *keel*, I'll win zour bread,
And *spindles and whorles* for them wha need,
Whilk is a gentil trade indeed
    The gaberlunzie to carrie—o.
Ill bow my leg and crook my knee,
And draw a black clout owre my ee,
A criple or blind they will cau me:
    While we sall sing and be merrie—o.

---

## XI.—ON THOMAS, LORD CROMWELL.

THE ballad seems to have been composed between the time of Cromwell's commitment to the Tower, June 11, 1540, and that of his being beheaded July 28 following. Notwithstanding our libeller, Cromwell had many excellent qualities: his great fault was too much obsequiousness to the arbitrary will of his master. The original copy, printed at London in 1540, is entitled, "A newe ballade made of Thomas Crumwel, called *Trolle on away.*" To it is prefixed this distich by way of burthen:

    "Trolle on away, trolle on awaye.
      Synge heave and howe rombelowe trolle on away."

BOTH man and chylde is glad to here tell
Of that false traytoure Thomas Crumwell,
Now that he is set to learne to spell.
    Synge trolle on away.

When fortune lokyd the in thy face,
Thou haddyst fayre tyme, but thou lackydyst grace;
Thy cofers with golde thou fyllydst a pace.
    Synge, etc.

Both plate and chalys came to thy fyst,
Thou lockydst them vp where no man wyst,
Tyll in the kynges treasoure suche thinges were myst.
    *Synge, etc.*

Both crust and crumme came thorowe thy handes,
Thy marchaundyse sayled ouer the sandes,
Therfore nowe thou art layde fast in bandes.
    *Synge, etc.*

Fyrste when kynge Henry, God saue his grace!
Perceyud myschefe kyndlyd in thy face,
Then it was tyme to purchase the a place.
    *Synge, etc.*

Hys grace was euer of gentyll nature,
Mouyd with petye, and made the hys *scruyture;*
But thou, as a wretche, suche thinges dyd procure.
    *Synge, etc.*

Thou dyd not remembre, false heretyke,
One God, one fayth, and one kynge catholyke,
For thou hast bene so long a scysmatyke.
    *Synge, etc.*

Thou woldyst not learne to knowe these thre;
But euer was full of iniquite:
Wherfore all this lande hathe ben troubled with the.
    *Synge, etc.*

All they, that were of the new trycke,
Agaynst the churche thou baddest them stycke;
Wherfore nowe thou haste touchyd the quycke,
    *Synge, etc.*

Bothe sacramentes and sacramentalles
Thou woldyst not suffre within thy walles;
Nor let vs praye for all chrysten soules.
    *Synge, etc.*

Of what generacyon thou were no tonge can tell,
Whyther of Chayme, or Syschemell,
Or else sent vs frome the deuyll of hell.
    *Synge, etc.*

Thou woldest neuer to vertue applye,
But couetyd euer to clymme to hye,
And nowe haste thou trodden thy shoo awrye.
    *Synge, etc.*

Who-so-euer dyd winne thou wolde not lose;
Wherfore all Englande doth hate the, as I suppose,
Bycause thou wast false to the redolent rose.
    *Synge, etc.*

Thou myghtest have learned thy cloth to flocke
Upon thy gresy fullers * stocke;
Wherfore lay downe thy heade vpon this blocke.
    *Synge, etc.*

Yet saue that soule, that God hath bought,
And for thy carcas care thou nought,
Let it suffre payne, as it hath wrought.
    *Synge, etc.*

God saue kyng Henry with all his power,
And prynce Edwarde that goodly flowre,
With al hys lordes of great honoure.
  Synge trolle on awaye, syng trolle on away.
  Hevye and how rombelowe trolle on awaye.

The foregoing piece gave rise to a poetic controversy, which was carried on through a succession of seven or eight ballads written for and against Lord Cromwell. These are all preserved in the archives of the Antiquarian Society.

\* Cromwell's father is generally said to have been a blacksmith at Putney; but the author of this ballad would insinuate that either he himself or some of his ancestors were fullers by trade.

## XII.—HARPALUS.

### AN ANCIENT ENGLISH PASTORAL.

THIS beautiful poem, which is perhaps the first attempt at pastoral writing in our language, is preserved among the *Songs and Sonnettes* of the Earl of Surrey, etc., 4to, in that part of the collection which consists of pieces by uncertain auctours. These poems were first published in 1557, ten years after that accomplished nobleman fell a victim to the tyranny of Henry VIII.; but it is presumed most of them were composed before the death of Sir Thomas Wyatt in 1541.

Though written perhaps near half a century before the *Shepherd's Calendar*,\* this will be found far superior to any of those eclogues, in natural unaffected sentiments, in simplicity of style, in easy flow of versification, and all other beauties of pastoral poetry. Spenser ought to have profited more by so excellent a model.

PHYLIDA was a faire mayde,
   As fresh as any flowre;
Whom Harpalus the herdman prayde
   To be his paramour.

Harpalus, and *eke* Corin,
   Were herdmen both *yfere:*
And Phylida could twist and spinne,
   And thereto sing full clere.

But Phylida was all tò coye,
   For Harpalus to winne:
For Corin was her onely joye,
   Who *forst* her not a pinne.

How often would she flowers twine?
   How often garlandes make
Of couslips and of colombine?
   And al for Corin's sake.

But Corin, he had haukes to lure,
   And forced more the field:
Of lovers lawe he toke no cure;
   For once he was *begilde*.

Harpalus prevailed nought,
   His labour all was lost;
For he was fardest from her thought,
   And yet he loved her most.

Therefore waxt he both pale and leane,
   And drye as clot of clay:
His fleshe it was consumed cleane;
   His colour gone away.

His beard it had not long be shave;
   His heare hong all unkempt:
A man most fit even for the grave,
   Whom spitefull love had *spent*.

His eyes were red, and all "forewacht;"
   His face *besprent* with teares:
It semde unhap had him long "hatcht,"
   In mids of his dispaires.

His clothes were blacke, and also bare;
   As one forlorne was he;
Upon his head alwayes he ware
   A wreath of wyllow tree.

His beastes he kept upon the hyll,
   And he sate in the dale;
And thus with sighes and sorrowes shril,
   He gan to tell his tale.

Oh Harpalus! (thus would he say)
   Unhappiest under sunne!
The cause of thine unhappy day,
   By love was first begunne.

---

\* First published in 1579.

For thou wentest first by *sute* to seeke
  A tigre to make tame,
That settes not by thy love a *leeke;*
  But makes thy griefe her game.

As easy it were for to convert
  The frost into "a" flame;
As for to turne a frowarde hert,
  Whom thou so faine wouldst frame.

Corin he liveth carèlesse:
  He leapes among the leaves:
He eates the frutes of thy *redresse:*
  Thou "reapst," he takes the sheaves.

My beastes, a whyle your foode refraine,
  And harke your herdmans sounde;
Whom spitefull love, alas! hath slaine,
  Through-*girt* with many a wounde.

O happy be ye, beastès wilde,
  That here your pasture takes:
I se that ye be not begilde
  Of these your faithfull makes.

The hart he feedeth by the hinde:
  The bucke harde by the do:
The turtle dove is not unkinde
  To him that loves her so.

The ewe she hath by her the ramme:
  The yong cow hath the bull:
The calfe with many a lusty lambe
  Do fede their hunger full.

But, wel-away! that nature wrought
  The, Phylida, so faire:
For I may say that I have bought
  Thy beauty all tò deare.

What reason is that crueltie
  With beautie should have part?
Or els that such great tyranny
  Should dwell in womans hart?

I see therefore to shape my death
  She cruelly is prest;
To th' ende that I may want my breath:
  My dayes been at the best.

O Cupide, graunt this my request,
  And do not stoppe thine eares,
That she may feele within her brest
  The paines of my dispaires:

Of Corin "who" is carèlesse,
  That she may crave her fee:
As I have done in great distresse,
  That loved her faithfully.

But since that I shal die her slave;
  Her slave, and eke her thrall:
Write you, my frendes, upon my grave
  This chaunce that is befall.

"Here lieth unhappy Harpalus
  By cruell love now slaine:
Whom Phylida unjustly thus
  Hath murdred with disdaine."

## XIII.—ROBIN AND MAKYNE.

### AN ANCIENT SCOTTISH PASTORAL.

MR. ROBERT HENRYSON (to whom we are indebted for this poem) appears to so much advantage among the writers of eclogue, that we are sorry we can give little other account of him besides what is contained in the following eloge, written by W. Dunbar, a Scottish poet, who lived about the middle of the 16th century:

> "In Dumferling, he [Death] hath tane Broun,
> With gude Mr. Robert Henryson."

Indeed, some little further insight into the history of this Scottish bard is gained from the title prefixed to some of his poems preserved in the British Museum, viz.: "*The morall Fabillis of Esop*, compylit be Maister Robert Henrisoun, scolmaister of Dunfermling, 1571." Harleian MSS. 3865, § 1.

The poem as it here stands has been revised and amended by Allan Ramsay, from whose *Ever-green* it is chiefly printed.

ROBIN sat on the gude grene hill,
  Keipand a flock of *fie*,
Quhen *mirry* Makyne said him till,
  "O Robin *rew* on me:
I haif thee luivt baith loud and still,
  Thir towmonds twa or thre;
My *dule* in *dern* bot *giff* thou *dill*,
  Doubtless but *dreid* Ill die."

Robin replied, Now by the *rude*,
  Naithing of luve I knaw,
But keip my sheip undir yon wod:
  Lo *quhair* they *raik on raw*.
*Quhat* can have mart thee in thy *mude*,
  Thou Makyne to me schaw;
Or *quhat* is luve, or to be lude?
  Fain wald I *leir* that law.

"The law of luve gin thou wald leir,
  Tak thair an A, B, C;
Be heynd, courtas, and fair of feir,
  Wyse, hardy, kind, and frie,
Sae that nae danger do the *deir*,
  Quhat dule in *dern* thou *drie;*
Press ay to pleis, and blyth appeir,
  Be patient and privie."

Robin, he answert her againe,
  I wat not quhat is luve;
But I haif marvel in certaine
  Quhat makes thee thus *wanrufe*.
The wedder is fair, and I am fain;
  My sheep gais hail abuve;
And sould we pley us on the plain,
  They wald us baith repruve.

"Robin, tak *tent* unto my tale,
  And wirk all as I *reid;*
And thou sall haif my heart all hale,
  Eik and my maiden-heid:
Sen God, he sendis *bute* for *bale*,
  And for murning *remeid*,
*I'dern* with thee bot gif I dale,
  Doubtless I am but deid.'

Makyne, to-morn be this ilk tyde,
  Gif ye will meit me heir,
Maybe my sheip may gang besyde,
  Quhyle we have *liggd* full neir;
But *maugre* haif I, *gif* I byde,
  Frae thay begin to *steir*,
Quhat lyes on heart I will nocht hyd,
  Then Makyne mak gude cheir.

"Robin, thou *reivs* me of my rest;
  I luve bot thee alane."
Makyne, adieu! the sun goes west,
  The day is neir-hand gane.
"Robin, in *dule* I am so drest,
  That luve will be my bane."
Makyn, gae luve *quhair-eir* ye list,
  For leman I luid nane.

"Robin, I stand in sic a style,
  I sich and that full sair."
Makyne, I have bene here this *quyle*;
  At hame I wish I were.
"Robin, my hinny, talk and smyle,
  Gif thou will do nae mair."
Makyne, som other man beguyle,
  For hameward I will fare.

*Syne* Robin on his ways he went,
  As light as leif on tree;
But Makyne murnt and made lament,
  *Scho trow'd* him neir to see.
Robin he *brayd attowre the bent:*
  Then Makyne cried on hie,
"Now may thou sing, for I am *shent!*
  Quhat ailis luve at me?"

Makyne went hame withouten fail,
  And weirylie could weip;
Then Robin in a full fair dale
  Assemblit all his sheip.
Be that some part of Makyne's ail,
  Out-throw his heart could creip;
Hir fast he followt to assail,
  And till her tuke gude *keip.*

Abyd, abyd, thou fair Makyne,
  A word for ony thing;
For all my luve, it sall be thyne,
  Withouten departing.
All *hale* thy heart for *till* have myne,
  Is all my coveting;
My sheip to *morn* quhyle houris nyne,
  Will need of nae keiping.

"Robin, thou hast heard sung and say,
  In gests and storys auld,
The man that will not when he may,
  Sall have nocht when he wald.
I pray to heaven baith nicht and day,
  Be *eiked* their cares sae cauld,
That presses first with thee to play
  Be forrest, firth, or fauld."

Makyne, the nicht is soft and dry,
  The wether warm and fair,
And the grene wod richt neir-hand by,
  To walk *attowre* all where:
There may nae janglers us espy,
  That is in luve contrair;
Therin, Makyne, baith you and I
  Unseen may mak repair.

"Robin, that warld is now away,
  And quyt *brocht* till an end:
And nevir again thereto, *perfay*,
  Sall it be as thou *wend;*
For of my pain thou made but play;
  I words in vain did spend:
As thou hast done, sae sall I say,
  Murn on, I think to mend."

Makyne, the hope of all my *heil,*
  My heart on thee is set;
I'll evermair to thee be leil,
  Quhyle I may live but *lett,*
Never to fail as *uthers* feill,
  Quhat grace so eir I get.
"Robin, with thee I will not *deill;*
  Adieu, for this we met."

Makyne went hameward blyth enough,
  Outowre the *holtis hair;*
Pure Robin murnd, and Makyne leugh;
  Scho sang, and he *sicht* sair:
And so left him bayth wo and *wreuch,*
  In dolor and in care,
Keipand his herd under a *heuch,*
  Amang the rushy *gair.*

## XIV.—GENTLE HERDSMAN, TELL TO ME.

### DIALOGUE BETWEEN A PILGRIM AND HERDSMAN.

THE scene of this beautiful old ballad is laid near Walsingham, in Norfolk, where was anciently an image of the Virgin Mary, famous over all Europe for the numerous pilgrimages made to it, and the great riches it possessed. Erasmus has given a very exact and humorous description of the devotions practised there in his time.

This poem is printed from a copy in the Editor's folio MS. which had greatly suffered by the hand of time; but vestiges of several of the lines remaining, some conjectural supplements have been attempted, which, for greater exactness, are in this one ballad distinguished by italics.

GENTLE heardsman, tell to me,
  Of curtesy I thee pray,
Unto the towne of Walsingham
  Which is the right and ready way.

"Unto the towne of Walsingham
  The way is hard for to be gon;
And verry crooked are those pathes
  For you to find out all alone."

Weere the miles doubled thrise,
  And the way never soe ill,
Itt were not enough for mine offence;
  Itt is soe grievous and soe ill.

"Thy yeeares are young, thy face is faire,
  Thy witts are weake, thy thoughts are greene;
Time hath not given thee leave, as yett,
  For to committ so great a sinne."

Yes, heardsman, yes, soe woldest thou say,
  If thou knewest soe much as I;
My witts, and thoughts, and all the rest,
  Have well deserved for to dye.

I am not what I seeme to bee,
  My clothes and sexe doe differ farr:
I am a woman, woe is me!
  Born to greeffe and irksome care.

*For my beloved, and well-beloved,*
  *My wayward cruelty could kill:*
*And though my teares will nought avail,*
  *Most dearely I bewail him* still.

*He was the flower of* noble wights,
  *None ever more sincere colde* bee;
*Of comely mien and shape* hee was,
  *And tenderlye* hee loved mee.

*When thus I saw he* loved me well,
  *I grewe so proude his* paine to see,
*That I, who did not* know myselfe,
  *Thought scorne of such a youth* as hee.

And grew soe coy and nice to please,
  As women's lookes are often soe,
He might not kisse, nor hand forsooth,
  Unlesse I willed him soe to doe.

Thus being wearyed with delaye
  To see I pittyed not his greeffe,
He gott him to a secrett place,
  And there he dyed without releeffe.

And for his sake these weeds I weare,
  And sacriffice my tender age;
And every day He begg my bread,
  To undergoe this pilgrimage.

Thus every day I fast and pray,
  And ever will doe till I dye;
And gett me to some secrett place,
  For soe did hee, and soe will I.

Now, gentle heardsman, aske no more,
  But keepe my secretts I thee pray;
Unto the towne of Walsingham
  Show me the right and readye way.

"Now goe thy wayes, and God before!
  For he must ever guide thee still:
Turne downe that dale, the right hand path,
  And soe, faire pilgrim, fare thee well!"

## XV.—KING EDWARD IV. AND TANNER OF TAMWORTH

WAS a story of great fame among our ancestors. The author of the *Art of English Poesie*, 1589, 4to, seems to speak of it as a real fact.

The following text is selected (with such other corrections as occurred) from two copies in black letter. The one in the Bodleyan Library, entitled, "*A merrie, pleasant, and delectable historie betweene King Edward the Fourth and a Tanner of Tamworth*, etc., printed at London by John Danter, 1596." This copy, ancient as it now is, appears to have been modernized and altered at the time it was published; and many vestiges of the more ancient readings were recovered from another copy (though more recently printed), in one sheet folio, without date, in the Pepys Collection.

In summer time, when leaves grow greene,
  And blossoms bedecke the tree,
King Edward wolde a hunting ryde,
  Some pastime for to see.

With hawke and hounde he made him bowne,
  With horne, and eke with bowe;
To Drayton Basset he tooke his waye,
  With all his lordes a rowe.

And he had ridden ore dale and downe
  By eight of clocke in the day,
When he was ware of a bold tanner,
  Come ryding along the waye.

A fayre russet coat the tanner had on
  Fast buttoned under his chin,
And under him a good cow-hide,
  And a mare of four shilling.*

Nowe stand you still, my good lordes all,
  Under the grene wood spraye;
And I will wend to yonder fellowe,
  To *weet* what he will saye.

God speede, God speede thee, said our king.
  Thou art welcome, sir, sayd hee.
"The readyest waye to Drayton Basset
  I praye thee to shewe to mee."

"To Drayton Basset woldst thou goe,
  Fro the place where thou dost stand?
The next payre of gallowes thou comest unto,
  Turne in upon thy right hand."

That is an unreadye waye, sayd our king,
  Thou doest but jest I see;
Nowe shewe me out the nearest waye
  And I pray thee wend with mee.

Awaye with a vengeance! quoth the tanner:
  I hold thee out of thy witt:
All daye have I rydden on Brocke my mare,
  And I am fasting yett.

"Go with me downe to Drayton Basset,
  No daynties will we spare;

---

* In the reign of Edward IV., Dame Cecill, lady of Torboke, in her will dated March 7, A.D. 1466, among many other bequests, has this, "Also I will that my sonne Thomas of Torboke have 13s. 4d. to buy him an horse." *Vide* Harleian Catalogue, 2176, 27. Now if 13s. 4d. would purchase a steed fit for a person of quality, a tanner's horse might reasonably be valued at four or five shillings.

All daye shalt thou eate and drinke of the best,
And I will paye thy fare."

Gramercye for nothing, the tanner replyde,
Thou payest no fare of mine:
I trowe I've more nobles in my purse,
Than thou hast pence in thine.

God give thee joy of them, sayd the king,
And send them well to *priefe*.
The tanner wolde faine have beene away,
For he weende he had beene a thiefe.

What art thou, hee sayde, thou fine fellowe,
Of thee I am in great feare,
For the cloathes, thou wearest upon thy backe,
Might beseeme a lord to weare.

I never stole them, quoth our king,
I tell you, sir, by the roode.
"Then thou playest, as many an unthrift doth,
And standest in *midds of thy goode*."*

What tydinges heare you, sayd the kynge,
As you ryde farre and neare?
"I heare no tydinges, sir, by the masse,
But that cowe-hides are deare."

"Cowe-hides! cowe-hides! what things are those?
I marvell what they bee?"
What art thou a foole? the tanner reply'd;
I carry one under mee.

What craftsman art thou, said the king,
I praye thee tell me trowe.
"I am a barker,† sir, by my trade;
Nowe tell me what art thou?"

I am a poore courtier, sir, quoth he,
That am forth of service worne;
And faine I wolde thy prentise bee,
Thy cunninge for to learne.

---

* *i.e.* hast no other wealth but what thou carriest about thee.
† *i.e.* a dealer in bark.

Marrye heaven forfend, the tanner replyde,
That thou my prentise were:
Thou woldst spend more good than I shold winne
By fortye shilling a yere.

Yet one thinge wolde I, sayd our king,
If thou wilt not seeme strange:
Thoughe my horse be better than thy mare,
Yet with thee I faine wold change.

"Why if with me thou faine wilt change,
As change full well maye wee,
By the faith of my bodye, thou proude fellowe,
I will have some *boot* of thee."

That were against reason, sayd the king,
I sweare, so mote I thee:
My horse is better than thy mare,
And that thou well mayst see.

"Yea, sir, but Brocke is gentle and mild,
And softly she will fare:
Thy horse is unrulye and wild, I wiss;
Aye skipping here and theare."

What boote wilt thou have? our king reply'd;
Now tell me in this stound.
"Noe pence, nor half pence, by my faye,
But a noble in gold so round."

"Here's twentye groates of white moneye,
Sith thou will have it of mee."
I would have sworne now, quoth the tanner,
Thou hadst not had one penniè.

But since we two have made a change,
A change we must abide,
Although thou hast got Brocke my mare,
Thou gettest not my cowe-hide.

I will not have it, sayd the kynge,
I sweare, so mought I thee;
Thy foule cowe-hide I wolde not beare,
If thou woldst give it to mee.

The tanner hee tooke his good cowe-hide,
   That of the cow was hilt;
And threwe it upon the king's sadèlle,
   That was soe fayrelye gilte.

"Now help me up, thou fine fellòwe,
   'Tis time that I were gone:
When I come home to Gyllian my wife,
   Sheel say I am a gentilmon."

The king he tooke him up by the legge;
   The tanner a f— lett fall.
Nowe marrye, good fellowe, sayd the kyng,
   Thy courtesye is but small.

When the tanner he was in the kinges sadèlle,
   And his foote in the stirrup was;
He marvelled greatlye in his minde,
   Whether it were golde or brass.

But when his steede saw the cows taile wagge,
   And eke the blacke cowe-horne;
He stamped, and stared, and awaye he ranne,
   As the devill had him borne.

The tanner he pulld, the tanner he sweat,
   And held by the pummil fast:
At length the tanner came tumbling downe;
   His necke he had well-nye *brast*.

Take thy horse again with a vengeance, he sayd,
   With mee he shall not byde.
"My horse wolde have borne thee well enoughe,
   But he knewe not of thy cowe-hide.

Yet if againe thou fainè woldst change,
   As change full well may wee,
By the faith of my bodye, thou jolly tannèr,
   I will have some boote of thee."

What boote wilt thou have, the tanner replyd,
   Nowe tell me in this stounde?
"Noe pence nor halfpence, sir, by my faye,
   But I will have twentye pound."

"Here's twentye groates out of my purse;
   And twentye I have of thine:
And I have one more, which we will spend
   Together at the wine."

The king set a bugle horne to his mouthe,
   And blewe both loude and shrille:
And soone came lords, and soone came knights,
   Fast ryding over the hille.

Nowe, out alas! the tanner he cryde,
   That ever I sawe this daye!
Thou art a strong thiefe, yon come thy fellowes
   Will beare my cowe-hide away.

They are no thieves, the king replyde,
   I sweare, soe mote I thee:
But they are the lords of the north countrèy,
   Here come to hunt with mee.

And soone before our king they came,
   And knelt downe on the grounde:
Then might the tanner have beene awaye,
   He had *lever* than twentye pounde.

A coller, a coller, here: sayd the kyng,
   A coller he loud gan crye:
Then woulde he lever then twentye pound,
   He had not beene so nighe.

A coller, a coller, the tanner he sayd,
   I trowe it will breed sorrowe:
After a coller commeth a halter,
   I trow I shall be hang'd to-morrowe.

Be not afraid tanner, said our king;
  I tell thee, so mought I thee,
Lo here I make thee the best esquire
  That is in the North countrie.*

For Plumpton-parke I will give thee,
  With tenements faire beside:

'Tis worth three hundred markes by the
  yeare,
To maintaine thy good cowe-hide.

Gramercye, my liege, the tanner replyde,
  For the favour thou hast me showne;
If ever thou comest to merry Tamwòrth,
  Neates leather shall clout thy shoen.

## XVI.—AS YE CAME FROM THE HOLY LAND.

### DIALOGUE BETWEEN A PILGRIM AND TRAVELLER.

THE scene of this song is the same as in No. XIV. The pilgrimage to Walsingham suggested the plan of many popular pieces.

The following ballad was once very popular; it is quoted in Fletcher's *Knight of the Burning Pestle*, Act ii. Sc. ult., and in another old play called *Hans Beer-pot, his Invisible Comedy*, etc., 4to, 1618, Act i. The copy below was communicated to the Editor by the late Mr. Shenstone as corrected by him from an ancient copy, and supplied with a concluding stanza.

As ye came from the holy land
  Of blessed Walsingham,
O met you not with my true love
  As by the way ye came?

"How should I know your true love,
  That have met many a one,
As I came from the holy land,
  That have both come, and gone?"

\* This stanza is restored from a quotation of this ballad in Selden's *Titles of Honour*, who produces it as a good authority to prove that one mode of creating esquires at that time was by the imposition of a collar. His words are: "Nor is that old pamphlet of the *Tanner of Tamworth and King Edward the Fourth* so contemptible, but that wee may thence note also an observable passage, wherein the use of making esquires, by giving collars, is expressed." (*sub tit.* Esquire; and *vide* in *Spelmanni Glossar. Armiger.*) This form of creating esquires actually exists at this day among the sergeants-at-arms, who are invested with a collar (which they wear on collar days) by the king himself. This information I owe to Samuel Pegge, Esq., to whom the public is indebted for that curious work the *Curialia*, 4to.

My love is neither white,* nor browne,
  But as the heavens faire;
There is none hath her form divine,
  Either in earth, or ayre.

"Such an one did I meet, good sir,
  With an angelicke face;
Who like a nymphe, a queene appeard
  Both in her gait, her grace."

Yes: she hath cleane forsaken me,
  And left me all alone;
Who some time loved me as her life,
  And called me her owne.

"What is the cause she leaves thee thus,
  And a new way doth take,
That some times loved thee as her life,
  And thee her joy did make?"

I that loved her all my youth,
  Growe old now as you see;
Love liketh not the falling fruite,
  Nor yet the withered tree.

\* *Sc.* pale.

For love is like a carelesse childe,
   Forgetting promise past :
He is blind, or deaf, whenere he list ;
   His faith is never fast.

His fond desire is fickle found,
   And yieldes a trustlesse joye ;
Wonne with a world of toil and care,
   And lost ev'n with a toye.

Such is the love of womankinde,
   Or Loves faire name abusde,
Beneathe which many vaine desires,
   And follyes are excusde.

" But true love is a lasting fire,
   Which viewless vestals * tend,
That burnes for ever in the soule,
   And knowes nor change, nor end."

## XVII.—HARDYKNUTE.

### A SCOTTISH FRAGMENT.

This poem, which for some time passed for ancient, owes its existence to the pen of Mrs. Wardlaw, whose maiden name was Halket. She professed to have discovered it written on shreds of paper ; but a suspicion arose that it was her own. Some able judges pronounced it modern, and the lady in a manner acknowledged it to be so by producing the last two stanzas beginning "There's nae light." This lady was a sister of Sir Peter Halket of Pitferran, who was killed in America with General Bradock in 1755.

The ballad is laid at the time when Haco or Haquin, king of Norway, demanded the delivering up of the Islands of Bute, Arran, and others, in the Frith of Clyde, as belonging to the Western Isles promised to him by the usurper Donald Bain.

Alexander III. would not comply with this demand, and Haco appeared with a fleet of 160 sail, having 20,000 troops on board, who landed and took the castle of Ayr. Haco made himself master of Bute and Arran, and passed over to Cunningham. Great resistance was made on the part of the Scots, and an engagement took place at Largs. Both parties fought with great resolution, and at last the Norwegians were defeated with great slaughter.

### I.

STATELY stept he east the wa',
   And stately stept he west,
Full seventy years he now had seen,
   Wi' scarce seven years of rest.
He liv'd when Britons breach of faith
   Wrought Scotland mickle wae :
And ay his sword tauld to their cost,
   He was their deadlye fae.

### II.

High on a hill his castle stood,
   With ha's and tow'rs a height,
And goodly chambers fair to se,
   Where he lodged mony a knight.
His dame sae peerless anes and fair,
   For chast and beauty deem'd,

Nae *marrow* had in all the land,
   Save Elenor the queen.

### III.

Full thirteen sons to him she bare,
   All men of valour stout :
In bloody fight with sword in hand
   Nine lost their lives *bot* doubt :
Four yet remain, lang may they live
   To stand by liege and land ;
High was their fame, high was their might,
   And high was their command.

### IV.

Great love they bare to Fairly fair,
   Their sister saft and dear,

---

   * *Sc.* angels.

Her girdle shaw'd her middle *gimp*,
  And gowden glist her hair.
What waefu' wae her beauty bred?
  Waefu' to young and auld,
Waefu' I trow to kyth and kin,
  As story ever tauld.

### V.

The king of Norse in summer tyde,
  Puff'd up with pow'r and might,
Landed in fair Scotland the isle
  With mony a hardy knight.
The tydings to our good Scots king
  Came, as he sat at dine,
With noble chiefs in brave aray,
  Drinking the blood-red wine.

### VI.

"To horse, to horse, my royal liege,
  Your faes stand on the strand,
Full twenty thousand glittering spears
  The king of Norse commands."
Bring me my steed Mage dapple gray,
  Our good king rose and cry'd,
A trustier beast in a' the land
  A Scots king nevir try'd.

### VII.

Go, little page, tell Hardyknute,
  That lives on hill sae hie,
To draw his sword, the dread of faes,
  And haste and follow me.
The little page flew swift as dart
  Flung by his master's arm,
"Come down, come down, lord Hardyknute,
  And rid your king frae harm."

### VIII.

Then red red grew his dark-brown cheeks,
  Sae did his dark-brown brow;
His looks grew keen, as they were wont
  In dangers great to do;
He's ta'en a horn as green as glass,
  And gi'en five sounds sae shill,
That trees in green wood shook thereat,
  Sae loud rang ilka hill.

### IX.

His sons in manly sport and glee,
  Had past that summer's morn,
When low down in a grassy dale,
  They heard their father's horn.
That horn, quo' they, ne'er sounds in peace,
  We've other sport to bide.
And soon they hy'd them up the hill,
  And soon were at his side.

### X.

"Late late the yestreen I ween'd in peace
  To end my lengthened life,
My age might well excuse my arm
  Frae manly feats of strife,
But now that Norse do's proudly boast
  Fair Scotland to inthrall,
It's ne'er be said of Hardyknute,
  He fear'd to fight or fall.

### XI.

"Robin of Rothsay, bend thy bow,
  Thy arrows shoot sae leel,
That mony a comely countenance
  They've turned to deadly pale.
*Brade* Thomas take you but your lance,
  You need nae weapons mair,
If you fight wi't as you did anes
  'Gainst Westmoreland's fierce heir.

### XII.

"And Malcolm, light of foot as stag
  That runs in forest wild,
Get me my thousands three of men
  Well bred to sword and shield:
Bring me my horse and *harnisine*,
  My blade of mettal clear.
If faes but ken'd the hand it bare,
  They soon had fled for fear.

### XIII.

"Farewell my dame sae peerless good
  (And took her by the hand),
Fairer to me in age you seem,
  Than maids for beauty fam'd.

My youngest son shall here remain
 To guard these stately towers,
And shut the silver bolt that keeps
 Sae fast your painted bowers."

### XIV.

And first she wet her comely cheiks,
 And then her boddice green,
Her silken cords of twirtle twist,
 Well plett with silver sheen ;
And apron set with mony a dice
 Of needle-wark sae rare,
Wove by nae hand, as ye may guess,
 Save that of Fairly fair.

### XV.

And he has ridden o'er muir and moss,
 O'er hills and mony a glen,
When he came to a wounded knight
 Making a heavy mane ;
"Here maun I lye, here maun I dye,
 By treacherie's false guiles ;
Witless I was that e'er ga faith
 To wicked woman's smiles."

### XVI.

"Sir knight, gin you were in my bower,
 To lean on silken seat,
My lady's kindly care you'd prove,
 Who ne'er knew deadly hate ;
Herself wou'd watch you a' the day,
 Her maids a dead of night ;
And Fairly fair your heart wou'd chear,
 As she stands in your sight.

### XVII.

"Arise, young knight, and mount your stead,
 Full *lowns* the *shynand* day :
Choose frae my menzie whom ye please
 To lead you on the way."
With smileless look, and visage wan,
 The wounded knight reply'd,
"Kind chieftain, your intent pursue,
 For here I maun abyde.

### XVIII.

To me nae after day nor night
 Can e're be sweet or fair,
But soon beneath some draping tree,
 Cauld death shall end my care."
With him nae pleading might prevail ;
 Brave Hardyknute to gain
With fairest words, and reason strong,
 Strave courteously in vain.

### XIX.

Syne he has gane far hynd out o'er
 Lord Chattan's land sae wide ;
That lord a worthy wight was ay,
 When faes his courage sey'd :
Of Pictish race by mother's side,
 When Picts rul'd Caledon,
Lord Chattan claim'd the princely maid,
 When he sav'd Pictish crown.

### XX.

Now with his fierce and stalwart train,
 He reach'd a rising hight,
*Quhair braid* encampit on the dale,
 Norss *menzie* lay in sicht.
"Yonder my valiant sons and feirs
 Our raging *revers* wait
On the unconquert Scottish sward
 To try with us their fate.

### XXI.

Make orisons to him that sav'd
 Our sauls upon the *rude ;*
Syne bravely shaw your veins are fill'd
 With Caledonian blude."
Then furth he drew his trusty glave,
 While thousands all around
Drawn frae their sheaths glanc'd in the sun ;
 And loud the bougles sound.

### XXII.

To joyn his king adoun the hill
 In hast his merch he made,
While, playand *pibrochs*, minstralls *meit*
 Afore him stately strade.

"Thrice welcome valiant *stoup of weir*,
  Thy nations shield and pride;
Thy king nae reason has to fear
  When thou art by his side."

### XXIII.

When bows were bent and darts were
    thrawn;
  For *thrang* scarce could they flee;
The darts clove arrows as they met,
  The arrows dart the tree.
Lang did they rage and fight fu' fierce,
  With little *skaith* to mon,
But bloody bloody was the field,
  Ere that lang day was done.

### XXIV.

The king of Scots, that *sindle* brook'd
  The war that look'd like play,
Drew his braid sword, and brake his bow,
  Sin bows seem'd but delay.
Quoth noble Rothsay, "Mine I'll keep,
  I wat it's bled a score."
Haste up, my merry men, cry'd the king,
  As he rode on before.

### XXV.

The king of Norse he sought to find,
  With him to *mense the faught*,
But on his forehead there did light
  A sharp *unsonsie* shaft;
As he his hand put up to feel
  The wound, an arrow keen,
O waefu' chance! there pinn'd his hand
  In midst between his een.

### XXVI.

"Revenge, revenge, cry'd Rothsay's heir,
  Your mail-coat sha' na bide
The strength and sharpness of my dart:"
  Then sent it through his side.
Another arrow well he mark'd,
  It pierc'd his neck in twa,
His hands then *quat* the silver reins,
  He low as earth did fa'.

### XXVII.

"Sair bleids my liege, sair, sair he bleeds!"
  Again wi' might he drew
And gesture dread his sturdy bow,
  Fast the braid arrow flew:
Wae to the knight he *ettled* at;
  Lament now queen Elgreed;
High dames too wail your darling's fall,
  His youth and comely meed.

### XXVIII.

"Take aff, take aff his costly *jupe*
  (Of gold well was it twin'd,
Knit like the fowler's net, through *quhilk*
  His steelly harness shin'd),
Take, Norse, that gift frae me, and bid
  Him venge the blood it bears;
Say, if he face my bended bow,
  He sure nae weapon fears."

### XXIX.

Proud Norse with giant body tall,
  Braid shoulders and arms strong,
Cry'd, "Where is Hardyknute sae fam'd,
  And fear'd at Britain's throne:
Tho' Britons tremble at his name,
  I soon shall make him wail,
That e'er my sword was made sae sharp,
  Sae saft his coat of mail."

### XXX.

That brag his stout heart cou'd na bide,
  It lent him youthfu' micht:
"I'm Hardyknute; this day, he cry'd,
  To Scotland's king I *heght*
To lay thee low, as horses hoof;
  My word I mean to keep."
Syne with the first stroke e'er he strake,
  He *garr'd* his body bleed.

### XXXI.

Norss' een like gray goshawk's stair'd
    wyld,
  He sigh'd wi' shame and spite;
"Disgrac'd is now my far-fam'd arm
  That left thee power to strike:"

Then ga' his head a blow sae fell,
  It made him doun to stoup,
As *laigh* as he to ladies us'd
  In courtly guise to *lout*.

### XXXII.

Fu' soon he rais'd his bent body,
  His bow he marvell'd sair,
Sin blows till then on him but darr'd
  As touch of Fairly fair:
Norse marvell'd too as sair as he
  To see his stately look;
Sae soon as e'er he strake a fae,
  Sae soon his life he took.

### XXXIII.

Where like a fire to heather set,
  Bauld Thomas did advance,
Ane sturdy fae with look enrag'd
  Up toward him did prance;
He spurr'd his steid through thickest ranks
  The hardy youth to quell,
Wha stood unmov'd at his approach
  His fury to repell.

### XXXIV.

"That short brown shaft sae meanly trimm'd,
  Looks like poor Scotlands gear,
But dreadfull seems the rusty point!"
  And loud he leugh in jear.
"Oft Britons *bood* * has dimm'd its shine;
  This point cut short their vaunt:"
Syne pierc'd the boasters bearded cheek:
  Nae time he took to taunt.

### XXXV.

Short while he in his saddle swang,
  His stirrup was nae stay,
Sae feeble hang his unbent knee
  Sure taiken he was *fey:*
*Swith* on the harden't clay he fell,
  Right far was heard the thud:
But Thomas look't nae as he lay
  All waltering in his blud:

---
\* Blood (?).

### XXXVI.

With careless gesture, mind unmov't,
  On rode he north the plain;
His seem in throng of fiercest strife,
  When winner ay the same:
Not yet his heart dames dimplet check
  Could *mease* soft love to bruik,
Till vengefu' Ann return'd his scorn,
  Then languid grew his luik.

### XXXVII.

In thraws of death, with *walowit* cheik
  All panting on the plain,
The fainting corps of warriours lay,
  Ne're to arise again;
Ne're to return to native land,
  Nae mair with blithsome sounds
To boast the glories of the day,
  And shaw their shining wounds.

### XXXVIII.

On Norways coast the widowit dame
  May wash the rocks with tears,
May lang luik ow'r the shipless seas
  Befor her mate appears.
Cease, Emma, cease to hope in vain;
  Thy lord lyes in the clay;
The valiant Scots nae *revers thole*
  To carry life away.

### XXXIX.

Here on a lee, where stands a cross
  Set up for monument,
Thousands fu' fierce that summer's day
  Fill'd keen war's black intent.
Let Scots, while Scots, praise Hardyknute
  Let Norse the name ay dread,
Ay how he faught, aft how he spar'd,
  Shall latest ages read.

### XL.

Now loud and chill blew th' westlin wind,
  Sair beat the heavy shower,
*Mirk* grew the night ere Hardyknute
  Wan near his stately tower.

His tow'r that us'd wi' torches blaze
  To shine sae far at night,
Seem'd now as black as mourning weed,
  Nae marvel sair he sigh'd.

### XLI.

"There's nae light in my lady's bower,
  There's nae light in my ha';
Nae blink shines round my Fairly fair,
  Nor ward stands on my wa.'
What bodes it? Robert, Thomas,
    say;"—
Nae answer fitts their dread.

"Stand back, my sons, I'le be your
    guide?"
But by they past with speed.

### XLII.

"As fast I've sped owre Scotlands faes,"—
  There ceas'd his brag of weir,
Sair sham'd to mind ought but his dame,
  And maiden Fairly fair.
Black fear he felt, but what to fear
  He wist nae yet; wi' dread
Sair shook his body, sair his limbs,
  And a' the warrior fled.

THE END OF BOOK THE FIRST.

## SERIES THE SECOND.—BOOK II.

### I.—A BALLAD OF LUTHER, THE POPE, A CARDINAL, AND A HUSBANDMAN.

In the former book we brought down this second series of poems as low as about the middle of the sixteenth century. We now find the muses deeply engaged in religious controversy. The sudden revolution wrought in the opinions of mankind by the Reformation, is one of the most striking events in the history of the human mind. It could not but engross the attention of every individual in that age, and therefore no other writings would have any chance to be read, but such as related to this grand topic. The alterations made in the established religion by Henry VIII., the sudden changes it underwent in the three succeeding reigns within so short a space as eleven or twelve years, and the violent struggles between Catholicism and growing Protestantism, could not but interest all mankind. Accordingly every pen was engaged in the dispute. The followers of the old and new profession (as they were called) had their respective ballad-makers; and every day produced some popular sonnet for or against the Reformation. The following ballad, and that entitled *Little John Nobody*, may serve for specimens of the writings of each party. Both were written in the reign of Edward VI., and are not the worst that were composed upon the occasion. Controversial divinity is no friend to poetic flights. Yet this ballad of *Luther and the Pope* is not altogether devoid of spirit; it is of the dramatic kind, and the characters are tolerably well sustained; especially that of Luther, which is made to speak in a manner not unbecoming the spirit and courage of that vigorous reformer. It is printed from the original black-letter copy (in the Pepys Collection, vol. I. folio), to which is prefixed a large wooden cut, designed and executed by some eminent master.

#### THE HUSBANDMAN.

Let us lift up our hartes all,
  And prayse the Lordes magnificence,
Which hath given the wolues a fall,
  And is become our strong defence:
For they thorowe a false pretens
From Christes bloude dyd all us leade,\*
  Gettynge from every man his pence,
As satisfactours for the deade.

For what we with our Flayles coulde get
  To kepe our house, and servauntes;
That did the Freers from us fet,
  And with our soules played the merchauntes:
And thus they with theyr false warrantes
Of our sweate have easelye lyved,
  That for fatnesse theyr belyes pantes,
So greatlye have they thus deceaued.

They spared not the fatherlesse,
  The carefull, nor the pore wydowe;
They wolde have somewhat more or lesse,
  If it above the ground did growe:
But now we Husbandmen do knowe
Al their subteltye, and their false caste;
  For the Lorde hath them overthrowe
With his swete worde now at the laste.

---

\* *i.e.* denied us the cup; see below.

### DOCTOR MARTIN LUTHER.

Thou antichrist, with thy thre crownes,
   Hast usurped kynges powers,
As having power over realmes and townes,
    Whom thou oughtest to serve all
      houres :
Thou thinkest by thy jugglyng colours
Thou maist lykewise Gods word oppresse ;
   As do the deceatful foulers,
When they theyr nettes craftelye dresse.

Thou flatterest every prince, and lord,
   Thretening poore men with swearde and
    fyre ;
All those, that do followe Gods worde,
   To make them cleve to thy desire,
   Theyr bokes thou burnest in flaming
    fire ;
Cursing with boke, bell, and candell,
   Such as to reade them have desyre,
Or with them are wyllynge to meddell.

Thy false power wyl I bryng down,
   Thou shalt not raygne many a yere,
I shall dryve the from citye and towne,
   Even with this pen that thou seyste
    here :
Thou fyghtest with swerd, shylde, and
    speare,
But I wyll fyght with Gods worde ;
   Which is now so open and cleare,
That it shall brynge the under the
   borde.*

### THE POPE.

Though I brought never so many to hel,
   And to utter dampnacion,
Throughe myne ensample, and consel,
   Or thorow any abhominacion,
Yet doth our lawe excuse my fashion.
And thou, Luther, arte accursed ;
   For blamynge me, and my condicion,
The holy decres have the condempned.

Thou stryvest against my purgatory,
   Because thou findest it not in scripture ;
As though I by myne auctorite
   Myght not make one for myne honoure.
Knowest thou not, that I have power
To make, and mar, in heaven and hell,
   In erth, and every creature?
Whatsoever I do it must be well.

As for scripture, I am above it ;
   Am not I Gods hye vicare?
Shulde I be bounde to folowe it,
   As the carpenter his ruler?*
Nay, nay, hereticks ye are,
That will not obey my auctoritie.
   With this sworde I wyll declare,
That ye shal al accursed be.

### THE CARDINAL.

I am a Cardinall of Rome,
   Sent from Christes hye vicary,
To graunt pardon to more, and sume,
   That wil Luther resist strongly :
He is a greate hereticke treuly,
And regardeth to much the scripture ;
   For he thinketh onely thereby
To subdue the popes high honoure :

Receive ye this pardon devoutely,
   And loke that ye agaynst him fight ;
Plucke up youre herts, and be manlye,
   For the pope sayth ye do but ryght :
And this be sure, that at one flyghte,
Allthough ye be overcome by chaunce,
   Ye shall to heaven go with greate
    myghte ;
God can make you no resistaunce.

But these heretikes for their medlynge
   Shall go down to hel every one ;
For they have not the popes blessynge,
   Nor regarde his holy pardon :
They thinke from all destruction
By Christes bloud to be saved,
   Fearynge not our excommunicacion,
Therefore shall they al be dampned.

---

* *i.e.* make thee knock under the table.

* *i.e.* his rule.

## II.—JOHN ANDERSON MY JO.

### A SCOTTISH SONG.

WHILE in England verse was made the vehicle of controversy, and Catholicism was attacked in it by logical argument or stinging satire, we may be sure the zeal of the Scottish Reformers would not suffer their pens to be idle, but many a pasquil was discharged at the priests, and their encroachments on property.

It is a received tradition in Scotland, that at the time of the Reformation, ridiculous and obscene songs were composed to be sung by the rabble to the tunes of the most favourite hymns in the Latin service. *Green Sleeves and Pudding Pies* (designed to ridicule the Catholic clergy) is said to have been one of these metamorphosed hymns; *Maggy Lauder* was another; *John Anderson my Jo* was a third. The original music of all these burlesque sonnets was very fine. To give a specimen of their manner, we have inserted one of the least offensive.

In the present edition this song is much improved by some new readings communicated by a friend, who thinks by the "seven bairns" in the second stanza are meant the seven sacraments, five of which were the spurious offspring of mother Church, as the first stanza contains a satirical allusion to the luxury of the popish clergy.

| WOMAN. | MAN. |
|---|---|
| JOHN ANDERSON my jo, cum in as ze gae bye, | And how doe ze, Cummer? and how hae ze threven? |
| And ze sall get a sheips heid weel baken in a pye; | And how mony bairns hae ze? WOM. Cummer, I hae seven. |
| Weel baken in a pye, and the haggis in a pat; | MAN. Are they to zour awin gude man? WOM. Na, Cummer, na; |
| John Anderson my jo, cum in, and ze's get that. | For five of them were gotten, *quhan* he was awa'. |

## III.—LITTLE JOHN NOBODY.

WE have here a witty libel on the Reformation under King Edward VI., written about the year 1550, and preserved in the Pepys Collection, British Museum, and Strype's *Memoirs of Cranmer*. The author artfully declines entering into the merits of the cause, and wholly reflects on the lives and actions of many of the Reformed.

The reader will remark the fondness of our satirist for alliteration: in this he was guilty of no affectation or singularity; his versification is that of Pierce Plowman's *Visions*, in which a recurrence of similar letters is essential: to this he has only superadded rhyme, which in his time began to be the general practice.

| | |
|---|---|
| IN december, when the dayes draw to be short, | As I past by a place privily at a port, |
| After november, when the nights wax noysome and long: | I saw one sit by himself making a song: |

His last talk of trifles, who told with his tongue
That few were fast i' th' faith. I *freyned*
that *freake,*
Whether he wanted wit, or some had done him wrong.
  He said, he was little John Nobody, that durst not speake.

John Nobody, quoth I, what news? thou soon note and tell
What maner men thou meane, thou are so mad.
He said, These gay gallants, that wil construe the gospel,
As Solomon the sage, with semblance full sad ;
To discusse divinity they nought adread ;
More meet it were for them to milk *kye* at a *fleyke.*
Thou lyest, quoth I, thou *losel*, like a leud lad.
  He said he was little John Nobody, that durst not speake.

Its meet for every man on this matter to talk,
And the glorious gospel ghostly to have in mind ;
It is sothe said, that sect *but* much unseemly *skalk,*
As boyes babble in books, that in scripture are blind :
Yet to their fancy soon a cause will find ;
As to live in lust, in lechery to *leyke :*
Such caitives count to be come of Cains kind ; *
  But that I little John Nobody durst not speake.

For our reverend father hath set forth an order,
Our service to be said in our seignours tongue ;

---

\* So in *Pierce the Plowman's Creed*, the proud friars are said to be
  " Of Caymes kind." *Vide* sig. C *ij.* b.

As Solomon the sage set forth the scripture ;
Our suffrages, and services, with many a sweet song,
With homilies, and godly books us among,
That no stiff, stubborn stomacks we should *freyke :*
But wretches nere worse to do poor men wrong ;
  But that I little John Nobody dare not speake.

For bribery was never so great, since born was our Lord,
And whoredom was never les hated, sith Christ *harrowed hel,*
And poor men are so sore punished commonly through the world,
That it would grieve any one, that good is, to hear tel.
For al the homilies and good books, yet their hearts be so *quel,*
That if a man do amisse, with mischiefe they wil him wreake ;
The fashion of these new fellowes it is so vile and fell :
  But that I little John Nobody dare not speake.

Thus to live after their lust, that life would they have,
And in lechery to leyke al their long life ;
For al the preaching of Paul, yet many a proud knave
Wil move mischiefe in their mind both to maid and wife
To bring them in advoutry, or else they wil strife,
And in brawling about baudery, Gods commandments breake :
But of these frantic il fellowes, few of them do thrife ;
  Though I little John Nobody dare not speake.

If thou company with them, they wil
   currishly *carp*, and not care
According to their foolish fantacy; but
   fast wil they naught:
Prayer with them is but prating; therefore they it forbear:
Both almes deeds, and holiness, they hate
   it in their thought:
Therefore pray we to that prince, that
   with his bloud us bought,
That he wil mend that is amiss: for many
   a manful *freyke*
Is sorry for these sects, though they say
   little or nought;
   And that I little John Nobody dare not
     once speake.

Thus in no place, this Nobody, in no time
   I met,
Where no man, "ne" nought was, nor
   nothing did appear;
Through the sound of a synagogue for
   sorrow I swett,
That "Aeolus" through the eccho did
   cause me to hear.
Then I drew me down into a dale, where-
   as the dumb deer
Did shiver for a shower; but I shunted
   from a freyke:
For I would no wight in this world wist
   who I were,
   But little John Nobody, that dare not
     once speake.

## IV.—QUEEN ELIZABETH'S VERSES, WHILE PRISONER AT WOODSTOCK,

### WRIT WITH CHARCOAL ON A SHUTTER,

ARE preserved by Hentzner, in that part of his *Travels* which has been reprinted in so elegant a manner at Strawberry Hill. The old orthography, and one or two ancient readings of Hentzner's copy, are here restored.

    OH, Fortune! how thy restless wavering state
      Hath fraught with cares my troubled witt!
    Witnes this present prisonn, whither fate
      Could beare me, and the joys I quit.
    Thou causedest the guiltie to be losed
    From bandes, wherein are innocents inclosed:
      Causing the guiltles to be straite reserved,
      And freeing those that death hath well deserved.
    But by her envie can be nothing wroughte,
    So God send to my foes all they have thoughte.

A.D. MDLV.                                               ELIZABETHE, PRISONNER.

## V.—THE HEIR OF LINNE.

THE original of this ballad is found in the Editor's folio MS., the breaches and defects in which rendered the insertion of supplemental stanzas necessary. These it is hoped the reader will pardon, as indeed the completion of the story was suggested by a modern ballad on a similar subject.

From the Scottish phrases here and there discernible in this poem, it should seem to have been originally composed beyond the Tweed.

The Heir of Linne appears not to have been a Lord of Parliament, but a Laird, whose title went along with his estate.

### PART THE FIRST.

LITHE and listen, gentlemen,
  To sing a song I will beginne:
It is of a lord of faire Scotland,
  Which was the unthrifty heire of Linne.

His father was a right good lord,
  His mother a lady of high degree;
But they, alas! were dead, him froe,
  And he lov'd keeping companie.

To spend the daye with merry cheare,
  To drinke and revell every night,
To card and dice from eve to morne,
  It was, I ween, his hearts delighte.

To ride, to runne, to rant, to roare,
  To alwaye spend and never spare,
I wott, an' it were the king himselfe,
  Of gold and fee he *mote* be bare.

Soe fares the unthrifty lord of Linne
  Till all his gold is gone and spent;
And he maun sell his landes so broad,
  His house, and landes, and all his rent.

His father had a keen stewàrde,
  And John o' the Scales was called hee:
But John is become a gentel-man,
  And John has gott both gold and fee.

Sayes, Welcome, welcome, lord of Linne,
  Let nought disturb thy merry cheere;
Iff thou wilt sell thy landes soe broad,
  Good store of gold Ile give thee heere.

My gold is gone, my money is spent;
  My lande nowe take it unto thee:
Give me the golde, good John o' the Scales,
  And thine for aye my lande shall bee.

Then John he did him to record draw,
  And John he cast him a gods-pennie;*
But for every pounde that John agreed,
  The lande, I wis, was well worth three.

He told him the gold upon the borde,
  He was right glad his land to winne;
The gold is thine, the land is mine,
  And now Ile be the lord of Linne.

Thus he hath sold his land soe broad,
  Both hill and holt, and moore and fenne,
All but a poore and lonesome lodge,
  That stood far off in a lonely glenne.

For soe he to his father *hight*.
  My sonne, when I am gonne, sayd hee,
Then thou wilt spend thy lande so broad,
  And thou wilt spend thy gold so free:

But sweare me nowe upon the *roode*,
  That lonesome lodge thou'lt neverspend;
For when all the world doth frown on thee,
  Thou there shalt find a faithful friend.

---

* *i.e.* earnest-money; from the French *Denier à Dieu*. At this day, when application is made to the Dean and Chapter of Carlisle to accept an exchange of the tenant under one of their leases, a piece of silver is presented by the new tenant, which is still called a God's-penny.

The heire of Linne is full of golde:
  And come with me, my friends, sayd
    hee,
Let's drinke, and rant, and merry make,
  And he that spares, ne'er *mote he thee.*

They ranted, drank, and merry made,
  Till all his gold it waxed thinne;
And then his friendes they slunk away;
  They left the unthrifty heire of Linne.

He had never a penny left in his purse,
  Never a penny left but three,
And one was brass, another was lead,
  And another it was white monèy.

Nowe well-aday, sayd the heire of
    Linne,
  Nowe well-aday, and woe is mee,
For when I was the lord of Linne,
  I never wanted gold nor fee.

But many a trustye friend have I,
  And why shold I feel *dole* or care?
Ile borrow of them all by turnes,
  Soe need I not be never bare.

But one, I wis, was not at home;
  Another had payd his gold away;
Another call'd him thriftless loone,
  And bade him sharpely wend his way.

Now well-aday, sayd the heire of Linne,
  Now well-aday, and woe is me;
For when I had my landes so broad,
  On me they liv'd right merrilee.

To beg my bread from door to door
  I wis, it were a *brenning* shame:
To rob and steal it were a sinne:
  To worke my limbs I cannot frame.

Now Ile away to lonesome lodge,
  For there my father bade me wend;
When all the world should frown on
    mee,
  I there should find a trusty friend.

## PART THE SECOND.

AWAY then hyed the heire of Linne
  Oer hill and *holt,* and moore and fenne,
Untill he came to lonesome lodge,
  That stood so lowe in a lonely glenne.

He looked up, he looked downe,
  In hope some comfort for to winne:
But bare and *lothly* were the walles,
  Here's sorry cheare, quo' the heire of
    Linne.

The little windowe dim and darke
  Was hung with ivy, brere, and yewe;
No shimmering sunn here ever shone;
  No halesome breeze here ever blew.

No chair, ne table he mote spye,
  No chearful hearth, ne welcome bed,
Nought save a rope with *renning* noose,
  That dangling hung up o'er his head.

And over it in broad letters,
  These words were written so plain to
    see:
"Ah! gracelesse wretch, hast spent thine
    all,
  And brought thyselfe to penurie?

All this my boding mind misgave,
  I therefore left this trusty friend:
Let it now sheeld thy foule disgrace,
  And all thy shame and sorrows end."

Sorely *shent* wi' this rebuke,
  Sorely shent was the heire of Linne;
His heart, I wis, was near to *brast*
  With guilt and sorrowe, shame and
    sinne.

Never a word spake the heire of Linne,
  Never a word he spake but three:
"This is a trusty friend indeed,
  And is right welcome unto mee."

Then round his necke the corde he drewe,
  And sprang aloft with his bodie:
When lo! the ceiling burst in twaine,
  And to the ground came tumbling hee.

Astonyed lay the heire of Linne,
 Ne knewe if he were live or dead :
At length he looked, and sawe a *bille*,
 And in it a key of gold so redd.

He took the *bill*, and lookt it on,
 Strait good comfort found he there :
Itt told him of a hole in the wall,
 In which there stood three chests infere.*

Two were full of the beaten golde,
 The third was full of white monèy ;
And over them in broad lettèrs
 These words were written so plaine to see :

"Once more, my sonne, I sette thee clere ;
 Amend thy life and follies past ;
For but thou amend thee of thy life,
 That rope must be thy end at last."

And let it bee, sayd the heire of Linne ;
 And let it bee, but if I amend : †
For here I will make mine avow,
 This *reade* ‡ shall guide me to the end.

Away then went with a merry cheare,
 Away then went the heire of Linne ;
I wis, he neither ceas'd ne blanne,
 Till John o' the Scales house he did winne.

And when he came to John o' the Scales,
 Upp at the speere§ then looked hee ;
There sate three lords upon a rowe,
 Were drinking of the wine so free.

And John himself sate at the bord-head,
 Because now lord of Linne was hee.

---

\* *i.e.* together.
† *i.e.* unless I amend.
‡ *i.e.* advice, counsel.
§ Perhaps the hole in the door or window by which it was *speered, i.e.* sparred, fastened, or shut. In Bale's second part of the *Acts of English Votaries,* we have this phrase (fol. 38): " *The dore thereof oft tymes opened and* speared *agayne.*"

I pray thee, he said, good John o' the Scales,
 One forty pence for to lend mee.

Away, away, thou thriftless loone ;
 Away, away, this may not bee :
For Christs curse on my head, he sayd,
 If ever I trust thee one pennie.

Then bespake the heire of Linne,
 To John o' the Scales wife then spake he :
Madame, some almes on me bestowe,
 I pray for sweet saint Charitie.

Away, away, thou thriftless loone,
 I swear thou gettest no almes of mee ;
For if we shold hang any *losel* heere,
 The first we wold begin with thee.

Then bespake a good fellowe,
 Which sat at John o' the Scales his bord ;
Sayd, Turn againe, thou heire of Linne ;
 Some time thou wast a well good lord :

Some time a good fellow thou hast been,
 And sparedst not thy gold and fee ;
Therefore Ile lend thee forty pence,
 And other forty if need bee.

And ever, I praye thee, John o' the Scales,
 To let him sit in thy companie :
For well I wot thou hadst his land,
 And a good bargain it was to thee.

Up then spake him John o' the Scales,
 All *wood* he answer'd him againe :
Now Christs curse on my head, he sayd,
 But I did lose by that bargàine.

And here I proffer thee, heire of Linne,
 Before these lords so faire and free,
Thou shalt have it backe again better cheape,
 By a hundred markes, than I had it of thee.

I drawe you to record, lordes, he said,
 With that he cast him a gods pennie:
Now by my fay, sayd the heire of Linne,
 And here, good John, is thy money.

And he pull'd forth three bagges of gold,
 And layd them down upon the bord:
All woe begone was John o' the Scales,
 Soe *shent* he cold say never a word.

He told him forth the good red gold,
 He told it forth mickle dinne.
The gold is thine, the land is mine,
 And now Ime againe the lord of Linne.

Sayes, Have thou here, thou good fellòwe,
 Forty pence thou didst lend mee:

Now I am againe the lord of Linne,
 And forty pounds I will give thee.
He make the keeper of my forrest,
 Both of the wild deere and the tame;
For but I reward thy bounteous heart,
 I wis, good fellowe, I were to blame.

Now welladay! sayth Joan o' the Scales:
 Now welladay! and woe is my life!
Yesterday I was lady of Linne,
 Now Ime but John o' the Scales his wife.

Now fare thee well, sayd the heire of Linne;
 Farewell now, John o' the Scales, said hee:
Christs curse light on me, if ever again
 I bring my lands in jeopardy.

---

## VI.—GASCOIGNE'S PRAISE OF THE FAIR BRIDGES, AFTERWARDS LADY SANDES,

### ON HER HAVING A SCAR IN HER FOREHEAD.

GEORGE GASCOIGNE was a celebrated poet in the early part of Queen Elizabeth's reign, and appears to great advantage among the miscellaneous writers of that age. He was author of three or four plays, and of many smaller poems, one of the most remarkable of which is a satire in blank verse, called the *Steele-glass*, 1576, 4to.

Mr. Thomas Warton thinks "Gascoigne has much exceeded all the poets of his age, in smoothness and harmony of versification." But the truth is, scarce any of the earlier poets of Queen Elizabeth's time are found deficient in harmony and smoothness, though those qualities appear so rare in the writings of their successors.

In court whoso demaundes
 What dame doth most excell;
For my conceit I must needes say,
 Faire Bridges beares the bel.

Upon whose lively cheeke,
 To prove my judgment true,
The rose and lillie seeme to strive
 For equall change of hewe:

And therewithall so well
 Hir graces all agree;

No frowning cheere dare once presume
 In hir sweet face to bee.

Although some lavishe lippes,
 Which like some other best,
Will say, the blemishe on hir browe
 Disgraceth all the rest.

Thereto I thus replie;
 God wotte, they little knowe
The hidden cause of that mishap,
 Nor how the harm did growe:

For when dame Nature first
    Had framde hir heavenly face,
And thoroughly bedecked it
    With goodly gleames of grace;

It lyked hir so well:
    Lo here, quod she, a peece
For perfect shape, that passeth all
    Appelles' worke in Greece.

This bayt may chaunce to catche
    The greatest God of love,
Or mightie thundring Jove himself,
    That rules the roast above.

But out, alas! those wordes
    Were vaunted all in vayne:
And some unseen wer present there,
    Pore Bridges, to thy pain.

For Cupide, crafty boy,
    Close in a corner stoode,
Not blyndfold then, to gaze on hir:
    I gesse it did him good.

Yet when he felte the flame
    Can kindle in his brest,
And herd dame Nature boast by hir
    To break him of his rest.

His hot newe-chosen love
    He chaunged into hate,
And sodeynly with mightie mace
    Gan rap hir on the pate.

It greeved Nature muche
    To see the cruell deede
Mee seemes I see hir, how she wept
    To see hir dearling bleede.

Wel yet, quod she, this hurt
    Shal have some helpe I trowe:
And quick with skin she coverd it,
    That whiter is than snowe.

Wherwith Dan Cupide fled,
    For feare of further flame,
When angel-like he saw hir shine,
    Whome he had smit with shame.

Lo, thus was Bridges hurt
    In cradel of hir kind.
The coward Cupide brake hir browe
    To wreke his wounded mynd.

The skar still there remains;
    No force, there let it bee:
There is no cloude that can eclipse
    So bright a sunne as she.

\*\*\* The lady here celebrated was Catharine, daughter of Edmond, Second Lord Chandos, wife of William, Lord Sandys. See Collins's *Peerage*, vol. ii. p. 133, ed. 1779.

## VII.—FAIR ROSAMOND.

MOST of the circumstances in this popular story of King Henry II. and the beautiful Rosamond have been taken for fact by our English historians, who, unable to account for the unnatural conduct of Queen Eleanor in stimulating her sons to rebellion, have attributed it to jealousy, and supposed that Henry's amour with Rosamond was the object of that passion.

Our old English annalists seem, most of them, to have followed Higden the monk of Chester, whose account, with some enlargements, is thus given by Stow: "Rosamond the fayre daughter of Walter lord Clifford, concubine to Henry II. (poisoned by queen Elianor, as some thought), dyed at Woodstocke [A.D. 1177], where king Henry had made for her a house of wonderfull working; so that no man or woman might come to her, but he that was instructed by the king, or such as were right secret with him touching the matter. This house after some was named Labyrinthus, or Dedalus worke, which was wrought like unto a knot in a garden, called a Maze; but it was commonly said, that lastly the queene came to her by a clue of thridde, or silke, and so dealt with her, that she lived not long after; but when she was dead, she was buried at Godstow in an house of nunnes, beside Oxford, with these verses upon her tombe:

> "Hic jacet in tumbâ, Rosa mundi, non Rosa munda:
> Non redolet, sed olet, quæ redolere solet."

How the queen gained admittance into Rosamond's bower is differently related. Holinshed speaks of it as "the common report of the people, that the queene ... founde hir out by a silken thread, which the king had drawne after him out of hir chamber with his foot, and dealt with hir in such sharpe and cruell wise, that she lived not long after." Vol. iii. p. 115. On the other hand, in Speede's *History* we are told that the jealous queen found her out "by a clew of silke, fallen from Rosamund's lappe, as shee sate to take ayre, and suddenly fleeing from the sight of the searcher, the end of her silke fastened to her foot, and the clew still unwinding, remained behinde: which the queene followed, till shee had found what she sought, and upon Rosamund so vented her spleene, as the lady lived not long after." 3d ed. p. 509. Our ballad-maker with more ingenuity, and probably as much truth, tells us the clue was gained by surprise from the knight who was left to guard her bower.

It is observable that none of the old writers attribute Rosamond's death to poison (Stowe, above, mentions it merely as a slight conjecture); they only give us to understand that the queen treated her harshly—with furious menaces, we may suppose, and sharp expostulations, which had such effect on her spirits that she did not long survive it. Indeed, on her tombstone, as we learn from a person of credit, among other fine sculptures was engraven the figure of a cup. This, which perhaps at first was an accidental ornament (perhaps only the chalice), might in after-times suggest the notion that she was poisoned; at least this construction was put upon it, when the stone came to be demolished after the nunnery was dissolved. The account is, that "the tombstone of Rosamund Clifford was taken up at Godstow, and broken in pieces, and that upon it were interchangeable weavings drawn out and decked with roses red and green, and the picture of the cup, out of which she drank the poison given her by the queen, carved in stone."

Rosamond's father having been a great benefactor to the nunnery of Godstow, where she had also resided herself in the innocent part of her life, her body was conveyed there, and buried in the middle of the choir; in which place it remained till the year 1191, when Hugh, Bishop of Lincoln, caused it to be removed.

History further informs us that King John repaired Godstow nunnery, and endowed it with yearly revenues, "that these holy virgins might releeve with their prayers, the soules of his father king Henrie, and of lady Rosamund there interred." * ... In what situation her remains were found at the dissolution of the nunnery, we learn from Leland: " Rosamundes tumbe at Godstowe nunnery was taken up [of] late; it is a stone with this inscription, *Tumba Rosamundæ*. Her bones were closid in lede, and withyn that bones were closyd yn lether. When it was opened a very swete

---

* *Vide* Reign of Henry II. in Speed's *History*, written by Dr. Barcham, Dean of Docking.

smell came owt of it." See Hearne's discourse above quoted, written in 1718; at which time he tells us, were still seen by the pool at Woodstock the foundations of a very large building, which were believed to be the remains of Rosamond's labyrinth.

Henry had two sons by Rosamond. These were William Longue-espé (or Longsword), Earl of Salisbury, and Geoffrey, Bishop of Lincolne, afterwards Archbishop of York.

The ballad of *Fair Rosamond* appears to have been first published in *Strange Histories or Songs and Sonnets, of Kinges, Princes, Dukes, Lords, Ladyes, Knights, and Gentlemen*, etc., by Thomas Delone, Lond. 1612, 4to. It is now printed (with conjectural emendations) from four ancient copies in black letter, two of them in the Pepys Library.

WHEN as king Henry rulde this land,
   The second of that name,
Besides the queene, he dearly lovde
   A faire and comely dame.

Most peerlesse was her beautye founde,
   Her favour, and her face ;
A sweeter creature in this worlde
   Could never prince embrace.

Her crisped lockes like threads of golde
   Appeard to each man's sight ;
Her sparkling eyes, like Orient pearles,
   Did cast a heavenlye light.

The blood within her crystal cheekes
   Did such a colour drive,
As though the lillye and the rose
   For mastership did strive.

Yea Rosamonde, fair Rosamonde,
   Her name was called so,
To whom our queene, dame Ellinor,
   Was known a deadlye foe.

The king therefore, for her defence
   Against the furious queene,
At Woodstocke builded such a bower,
   The like was never seene.

Most curiously that bower was built
   Of stone and timber strong,
An hundered and fifty doors
   Did to this bower belong :

And they so cunninglye contriv'd
   With turnings round about,

That none but with a clue of thread,
   Could enter in or out.

And for his love and ladyes sake,
   That was so faire and brighte,
The keeping of this bower he gave
   Unto a valiant knighte.

But fortune, that doth often frowne
   Where she before did smile,
The kinges delighte and ladyes joy
   Full soon shee did beguile :

For why, the kinges ungracious sonne,
   Whom he did high advance,
Against his father raised warres
   Within the realme of France.

But yet before our comelye king
   The English land forsooke,
Of Rosamond, his lady faire,
   His farewelle thus he tooke :

"My Rosamonde, my only Rose,
   That pleasest best mine eye :
The fairest flower in all the worlde
   To feed my fantasye :

The flower of mine affected heart,
   Whose sweetness doth excelle :
My royal Rose, a thousand times
   I bid thee nowe farwelle !

For I must leave my fairest flower,
   My sweetest Rose, a space,
And cross the seas to famous France,
   Proud rebelles to abase.

But yet, my Rose, be sure thou shalt
   My coming shortlye see,
And in my heart, when hence I am,
   Ile beare my Rose with mee."

When Rosamond, that ladye brighte,
   Did heare the king saye soe,
The sorrowe of her grieved heart
   Her outward lookes did showe;

And from her cleare and crystall eyes
   The teares gusht out apace,
Which like the silver-pearled dewe
   Ranne downe her comely face.

Her lippes, erst like the corall redde,
   Did waxe both wan and pale,
And for the sorrow she conceivde
   Her vitall spirits faile;

And falling down all in a swoone
   Before king Henryes face,
Full oft he in his princelye armes
   Her bodye did embrace:

And twentye times, with watery eyes,
   He kist her tender cheeke,
Untill he had revivde againe
   Her senses milde and meeke.

Why grieves my Rose, my sweetest Rose?
   The king did often say.
Because, quoth shee, to bloodye warres
   My lord must part awaye.

But since your grace on forrayne coastes
   Amonge your foes unkinde
Must goe to hazard life and limbe,
   Why should I staye behinde?

Nay rather, let me, like a page,
   Your sworde and target beare;
That on my breast the blowes may lighte,
   Which would offend you there.

Or lett mee, in your royal tent,
   Prepare your bed at nighte,
And with sweete baths refresh your grace,
   At your returne from fighte.

So I your presence may enjoye,
   No toil I will refuse;
But wanting you, my life is death;
   Nay, death Ild rather chuse!

"Content thy self, my dearest love;
   Thy rest at home shall bee
In Englandes sweet and pleasant isle;
   For travell fits not thee.

Faire ladies brooke not bloodye warres;
   Soft peace their sexe delightes;
'Not rugged campes, but courtlye bowers;
   Gay feastes, not cruell fightes.'

My Rose shall safely here abide,
   With musicke passe the daye;
Whilst I, amonge the piercing pikes,
   My foes seeke far awaye.

My Rose shall shine in pearle and golde,
   Whilst I'me in armour dighte;
Gay galliards here my love shall dance,
   Whilst I my foes goe fighte.

And you, sir Thomas, whom I truste
   To bee my loves defence;
Be carefull of my gallant Rose
   When I am parted hence."

And therewithall he fetcht a sigh,
   As though his heart would breake:
And Rosamonde, for very griefe,
   Not one plaine word could speake.

And at their parting well they mighte
   In heart be grieved sore;
After that daye faire Rosamonde
   The king did see no more.

For when his grace had past the seas,
   And into France was gone;
With envious heart, queene Ellinor
   To Woodstocke came anone.

And forth she calls this trustye knighte,
   In an unhappy houre;
Who with his clue of twined thread,
   Came from this famous bower.

And when that they had wounded him,
  The queene this thread did gette,
And went where ladye Rosamonde
  Was like an angell sette.

But when the queene with steadfast eye
  Beheld her beauteous face,
She was amazed in her minde
  At her exceeding grace.

Cast off from thee those robes, she said,
  That riche and costlye bee ;
And drinke thou up this deadlye draught,
  Which I have brought to thee.

Then presentlye upon her knees
  Sweet Rosamonde did falle ;
And pardon of the queene she crav'd
  For her offences all.

"Take pitty on my youthfull yeares,
  Faire Rosamonde did crye ;
And lett mee not with poison stronge
  Enforced bee to dye.

I will renounce my sinfull life,
  And in some cloyster bide ;
Or else be banisht, if you please,
  To range the world soe wide.

And for the fault which I have done,
  Though I was forc'd theretoe,
Preserve my life, and punish mee
  As you thinke meet to doe."

And with these words, her lillie handes
  She wrunge full often there ;
And downe along her lovely face
  Did trickle many a teare.

But nothing could this furious queene
  Therewith appeased bee ;
The cup of deadlye poyson stronge,
  As she knelt on her knee,

Shee gave this comelye dame to drinke ;
  Who tooke it in her hand,
And from her bended knee arose,
  And on her feet did stand :

And casting up her eyes to heaven,
  Shee did for mercye calle ;
And drinking up the poison stronge,
  Her life she lost withalle.

And when that death through everye limbe
  Had showde its greatest spite,
Her chiefest foes did plaine confesse
  Shee was a glorious wight.

Her body then they did entomb,
  When life was fled away,
At Godstowe, neare to Oxford towne,
  As may be seene this day.

---

## VIII.—QUEEN ELEANOR'S CONFESSION.

"ELEANOR, the daughter and heiress of William, Duke of Guienne and Count of Poictou, had been married sixteen years to Louis VII., King of France, and had attended him in a croisade, which that monarch commanded against the infidels : but having lost the affections of her husband, and even fallen under some suspicions of gallantry with a handsome Saracen, Louis, more delicate than politic, procured a divorce from her, and restored her those rich provinces which by her marriage she had annexed to the crown of France. The young Count of Anjou, afterwards Henry II., King of England, though at that time but in his nineteenth year, neither discouraged by the disparity of age, nor by the report of Eleanor's gallantry, made such successful courtship to that princess, that he married her six weeks after her divorce, and got possession of all her dominions as a dowery. A marriage thus founded upon interest was not likely to be very happy : it happened accordingly. Eleanor, who had disgusted her first husband by her gallantries, was no less offensive to her second by her jealousy; thus carrying to extremity, in the different parts of her life, every circumstance of female weakness. She had several sons by Henry, whom she spirited up to rebel against him; and endeavouring to escape to them disguised in man's apparel in 1173, she was discovered and thrown into a confinement which seems to have continued till the death of her husband in 1189. She however survived him many years: dying in 1204, in the sixth year of the reign of her youngest son, John." See Hume's *History*, 4to, vol. i. pp. 260, 307; Speed, Stowe, etc.

It is needless to observe, that the following ballad (given, with some corrections, from an old printed copy) is altogether fabulous; whatever gallantries Eleanor encouraged in the time of her first husband, none are imputed to her in that of her second.

QUEENE ELIANOR was a sicke womàn,
   And afraid that she should dye:
Then she sent for two fryars of France
   To speke with her speedilye.

The king calld downe his nobles all,
   By one, by two, by three;
"Earl marshall, Ile goe shrive the queene,
   And thou shalt wend with mee."

A boone, a boone; quoth earl marshàll,
   And fell on his bended knee;
That whatsoever queene Elianor saye,
   No harme thereof may bee.

Ile pawne my landes, the king then cryd,
   My sceptre, crowne, and all,
That whatsoere queen Elianor sayes
   No harme thereof shall fall.

Do thou put on a fryars coat,
   And Ile put on another;
And we will to queen Elianor goe
   Like fryar and his brother.

Thus both attired then they goe:
   When they came to Whitehall,
The bells did ring, and the quiristers sing,
   And the torches did lighte them all.

When that they came before the queene
   They fell on their bended knee;
A boone, a boone, our gracious queene,
   That you sent so hastilee.

Are you two fryars of France, she sayd,
   As I suppose you bee?

But if you are two Englishe fryars,
   You shall hang on the gallowes tree.

We are two fryars of France, they said,
   As you suppose we bee,
We have not been at any masse
   Sith we came from the sea.

The first vile thing that ever I did
   I will to you unfolde;
Earl marshall had my maidenhed,
   Beneath this cloth of golde.

Thats a vile sinne, then sayd the king;
   May God forgive it thee!
Amen, amen, quoth earl marshall;
   With a heavye heart spake hee.

The next vile thing that ever I did,
   To you Ile not denye,
I made a boxe of poyson strong,
   To poison king Henrye.

Thats a vile sinne, then sayd the king,
   May God forgive it thee!
Amen, amen, quoth earl marshall;
   And I wish it so may bee.

The next vile thing that ever I did,
   To you I will discover;
I poysoned fair Rosamonde,
   All in fair Woodstocke bower.

Thats a vile sinne, then sayd the king;
   May God forgive it thee!
Amen, amen, quoth earl marshall;
   And I wish it so may bee.

Do you see yonders little boye,
  A tossing of the balle?
That is earl marshalls eldest sonne,
  And I love him the best of all.

Do you see yonders little boye,
  A catching of the balle?
That is king Henryes youngest sonne,*
  And I love him the worst of all.

His head is fashyon'd like a bull;
  His nose is like a boare.

No matter for that, king Henrye cryd,
  I love him the better therfore.

The king pulled off his fryars coate,
  And appeared all in redde:
She shrieked, and cryd, and wrung her
  hands,
  And sayd she was betrayde.

The king lookt over his left shoulder,
  And a grimme look looked hee,
Earl marshall, he sayd, but for my oathe,
  Or hanged thou shouldst bee.

## IX.—THE STURDY ROCK.

THIS poem, subscribed M. T. [perhaps invertedly for T. Marshall], is preserved in *The Paradise of Daintie Devises.* The two first stanzas may be found accompanied with musical notes in *An howres recreation in musicke,* etc., by Richard Alison, Lond. 1606, 4to: usually bound up with three or four sets of *Madrigals set to music,* by Tho. Weelkes, Lond. 1597, 1600, 1608, 4to. One of these madrigals is so complete an example of the bathos, that I cannot forbear presenting it to the reader.

> "*Thule,*† the period of cosmographie,
>   Doth vaunt of Hecla, whose sulphureous fire
> Doth melt the frozen clime, and thaw the skie,
>   Trinacrian ‡ Ætna's flames ascend not hier:
> These things seeme wondrous, yet more wondrous I,
> Whose heart with feare doth freeze, with love doth fry.
>
> "The Andalusian merchant, that returnes
>   Laden with cutchinele § and china dishes,
> Reports in Spaine how strangely Fogo ‖ burnes
>   Amidst an ocean full of flying fishes:
> These things seeme wondrous, yet more wondrous I,
> Whose heart with feare doth freeze, with love doth fry."

Mr. Weelkes seems to have been of opinion with many of his brethren of later times, that nonsense was best adapted to display the powers of musical composure.

THE sturdy rock for all his strength
  By raging seas is rent in twaine:
The marble stone is pearst at length,
  With little drops of drizling rain:
The oxe doth yeeld unto the yoke,
The steele obeyeth the hammer stroke.

The stately stagge, that seemes so stout,
  By yalping hounds at bay is set:
The swiftest bird, that flies about,
  Is caught at length in fowlers net:
The greatest fish, in deepest brooke,
Is soon deceived by subtill hooke.

---

\* She means that the eldest of these two was by the earl marshall, the youngest by the king.

† Here meant for Iceland.
‡ Sicilian.  § Cochineal.
‖ Terra del Fuego.

Yea man himselfe, unto whose will
  All things are bounden to obey,
For all his wit and worthie skill,
  Doth fade at length, and fall away.
There is nothing but time doeth waste ;
The heavens, the earth consume at last.

But vertue sits triumphing still
  Upon the throne of glorious fame :
Though spiteful death man's body kill,
  Yet hurts he not his vertuous name :
By life or death what so betides,
The state of vertue never *slides*.\*

## X.—THE BEGGAR'S DAUGHTER OF BEDNALL GREEN.

THIS popular old ballad was written in the reign of Elizabeth, as appears not only from the verse where the arms of England are called the "Queenes armes," but from its tunes being quoted in other old pieces written in her time.

It is chiefly given from the Editor's folio MS. compared with two ancient printed copies : the concluding stanzas, which contain the old beggar's discovery of himself, are not, however, given from any of these, being very different from those of the vulgar ballad, which informs us, that at the battle of Evesham (fought August 4, 1265), when Simon de Montfort, the great Earl of Leicester, was slain at the head of the barons, his eldest son Henry fell by his side, and, in consequence of that defeat, his whole family sunk for ever, the king bestowing their great honours and possessions on his second son Edmund, Earl of Lancaster.

"It was an extremely popular ballad, and no wonder. This very house," writes Pepys in his diary, June 25, 1663, of Sir W. Rider's place at Bethnall Green, "was built by the blind beggar of Bednall Green so much talked of and sung in ballads; but they say it was only some outhouses of it (*apud* Mr. Chappell's *Popular Music of the Olden Time*, where the tune is given")."

"The story is pretty, and is told unaffectedly. Each part has its own surprise : the one revealing the wealth, the other the high birth of the beggar. These *denouements* are not supremely noble ; but they are such as please the crowd. Such reverses are always delightful."

### PART THE FIRST.

ITT was a blind beggar, had long lost his sight,
He had a faire daughter of bewty most bright ;
And many a gallant brave suiter had shee,
For none was soe comelye as pretty Bessee.

And though shee was of favor most faire,
Yett seeing shee was but a poor beggars heyre,
Of ancyent housekeepers despised was shee,
Whose sonnes came as suitors to prettye Bessee.

Wherefore in great sorrow faire Bessy did say,
Good father, and mother, let me goe away
To seeke out my fortune, whatever itt bee.
This suite then they granted to prettye Bessee.

Then Bessy, that was of bewtye soe bright,
All cladd in gray russett, and late in the night,
From father and mother alone parted shee ;
Who sighed and sobbed for prettye Bessee.

\* Passes away, goes by. This expression, which has of late years passed into a slang term, is used also by Shakespeare, "Let the world *slide*."

Shee went till shee came to Stratford-le-Bow;
Then knew shee not whither, nor which way to goe:
With teares shee lamented her hard destinie,
So sadd and soe heavy was pretty Bessee.

Shee kept on her journey untill it was day,
And went unto Rumford along the hye way;
Where at the Queenes armes entertained was shee:
Soe faire and wel favoured was pretty Bessee.

Shee had not beene there a month to an end,
But master and mistres and all was her friend:
And every brave gallant, that once did her see,
Was straight-way enamourd of pretty Bessee.

Great gifts they did send her of silver and gold,
And in their songs daylye her love was extold;
Her beawtye was blazed in every degree;
Soe faire and soe comelye was pretty Bessee.

The young men of Rumford in her had their joy;
Shee shewed herself curteous, and modestlye coye;
And at her commandment still wold they bee;
Soe fayre and soe comlye was pretty Bessee.

Foure suitors att once unto her did goe;
They craved her favor, but still she sayd noe;
I wold not wish gentles to marry with mee.
Yett ever they honored prettye Bessee.

The first of them was a gallant young knight,
And he came unto her disguisde in the night;
The second a gentleman of good degree,
Who wooed and sued for prettye Bessee.

A merchant of London, whose wealth was not small,
He was the third suiter, and proper withall:
Her masters own sonne the fourth man must bee,
Who swore he would dye for pretty Bessee.

And, if thou wilt marry with mee, quoth the knight,
Ile make thee a ladye with joy and delight;
My hart's so inthralled by thy bewtle,
That soone I shall dye for prettye Bessee.

The gentleman sayd, Come, marry with mee,
As fine as a ladye my Bessy shal bee:
My life is distressed: O heare me, quoth hee;
And grant me thy love, my prettye Bessee.

Let me bee thy husband, the merchant cold say,
Thou shalt live in London both gallant and gay;
My shippes shall bring home rych jewells for thee,
And I will for ever love pretty Bessee.

Then Bessy shee sighed, and thus shee did say,
My father and mother I meane to obey;
First gett their good will, and be faithfull to mee,
And you shall enjoye your prettye Bessee.

To every one this answer shee made,
Wherfore unto her they joyfullye sayd,

This thing to fulfill wee all doe agree;
But where dwells thy father, my prettye
    Bessee?

My father, shee said, is soone to be seene:
The *seely* blind beggar of Bednall-greene,
That daylye sits begging for charitle,
He is the good father of pretty Bessee.

His markes and his tokens are knowen
    very well;
He alwayes is led with a dogg and a bell:
A seely olde man, God knoweth, is hee,
Yett hee is the father of pretty Bessee.

Nay then, quoth the merchant, thou art
    not for mee:
Nor, quoth the innholder, my wiffe thou
    shalt bee:
I lothe, sayd the gentle, a beggars degree,
And therefore, adewe, my pretty Bessee!

Why then, quoth the knight, hap better
    or worse,
I waighe not true love by the waight of
    the pursse,
And bewtye is bewtye in every degree;
Then welcome unto me, my pretty Bessee.

With thee to thy father forthwith I will
    goe.
Nay soft, quoth his kinsmen, it must not
    be soe;
A poor beggars daughter noe ladye shal
    bee,
Then take thy adew of pretty Bessee.

But soone after this, by breake of the day
The knight had from Rumford stole
    Bessy away.
The younge men of Rumford, as *thicke*
    might bee,
Rode after to feitch againe pretty Bessee.

As swifte as the winde to ryde they were
    seene,
Untill they came neare unto Bednall-
    greene;

And as the knight lighted most courte-
    ouslie,
They all fought against him for pretty
    Bessee.

But rescew came speedilye over the plaine,
Or else the young knight for his love had
    been slaine.
This fray being ended, then straitway he
    see
His kinsmen come rayling at pretty Bessee.

Then spake the blind beggar, Although I
    bee poore,
Yett rayle not against my child at my
    own doore:
Though shee be not decked in velvett and
    pearle,
Yett will I dropp angells with you for my
    girle.

And then, if my gold may better her
    birthe,
And equall the gold that you lay on the
    earth,
Then neyther rayle nor grudge you to see
The blind beggars daughter a lady to bee.

But first you shall promise, and have itt
    well knowne,
The gold that you drop shall all be your
    owne.
With that they replyed, Contented bee wee.
Then here's, quoth the beggar, for pretty
    Bessee.

With that an angell he cast on the ground,
And dropped in angels full three thousand
    pound;\*
And oftentimes itt was proved most plaine,
For the gentlemens one the beggar droppt
    twayne:

Soe that the place, wherin they did sitt,
With gold it was covered every whitt.

---

\* In the Editor's folio MS. it is £500.

The gentlemen then having dropt all their
  store,
Sayd, Now, beggar, hold, for wee have
  noe more.

Thou hast fulfilled thy promise arright.
Then marry, quoth he, my girle to this
  knight;
And heere, added hee, I will now throwe
  you downe
A hundred pounds more to buy her a
  gowne.

The gentlemen all, that this treasure had
  scene,
Admired the beggar of Bednall-greene:
And all those, that were her suitors before,
Their fleshe for very anger they tore.

Thus was faire Besse matched to the
  knight,
And then made a ladye in others despite:
A fairer ladye there never was seene,
Than the blind beggars daughter of
  Bednall-greene.

But of their sumptuous marriage and feast,
What brave lords and knights thither
  were prest,
The second *fitt* shall set forth to your
  sight
With marveilous pleasure, and wished
  delight.

### PART THE SECOND.

OFF a blind beggars daughter most bright,
That late was betrothed unto a younge
  knight;
All the discourse therof you did see;
But now comes the wedding of pretty
  Bessee.

Within a gorgeous palace most brave,
Adorned with all the cost they cold have,
This wedding was kept most sumptuous-
  lle,
And all for the credit of pretty Bessee.

All kind of dainties, and delicates sweete,
Were bought for the banquet, as it was
  most meete;
Partridge, and plover, and venison most
  free,
Against the brave wedding of pretty
  Bessee.

This marriage through England was
  spread by report,
Soe that a great number therto did
  resort
Of nobles and gentles in every degree;
And all for the fame of prettye Bessee.

To church then went this gallant younge
  knight;
His bride followed after, an angell most
  bright,
With troopes of ladyes, the like nere was
  scene
As went with sweete Bessy of Bednall-
  greene.

This marryage being solempnized then,
With musicke performed by the skilfullest
  men,
The nobles and gentles sate downe at that
  tyde,
Each one admiring the beautifull bryde.

Now, after the sumptuous dinner was
  done,
To talke and to reason a number begunn:
They talkt of the blind beggars daughter
  most bright,
And what with his daughter he gave to
  the knight.

Then spake the nobles, "Much marveil
  have wee,
This jolly blind beggar wee cannot here
  see."
My lords, quoth the bride, my father's so
  base,
He is loth with his presence these states
  to disgrace.

"The prayse of a woman in questyon to
bringe
Before her own face, were a flattering
thinge;
But wee thinke thy father's baseness, quoth
they,
Might by thy bewtye be cleane put
awaye."

They had noe sooner these pleasant
words spoke,
But in comes the beggar cladd in a silke
cloke;
A faire velvet capp, and a fether had hee,
And now a musicyan forsooth he wold bee.

He had a daintye lute under his arme,
He touched the strings, which made such
a charme,
Saies, Please you to heare any musicke of
mee,
Ile sing you a song of pretty Bessee.

With that his lute he twanged straightway,
And thereon begann most sweetlye to
play;
And after that lessons were playd two or
three,
He strayn'd out this song most delicatelle.

"A poore beggars daughter did dwell on
a greene,
Who for her fairenesse might well be a
queene:
A blithe bonny lasse, and a daintye was
shee,
And many one called her pretty Bessee.

"Her father hee had noe goods, nor noe
land,
But beggd for a penny all day with his
hand;
And yett to her marriage hee gave
thousands three,*
And still he hath somewhat for pretty
Bessee.

---

* So the folio MS.

"And if any one here her birth doe
disdaine,
Her father is ready, with might and with
maine,
To proove shee is come of noble degree:
Therfore never flout att prettye Bessee."

With that the lords and the companye
round
With harty laughter were readye to
swound;
Att last said the lords, Full well wee may
see,
The bride and the beggar's behoulden to
thee.

On this the bride all blushing did rise,
The pearlie dropps standing within her
faire eyes,
O pardon my father, grave nobles, quoth
shee,
That throughe blind affection thus dotet
on mee.

If this be thy father, the nobles did say,
Well may he be proud of this happy
day;
Yett by his countenance well may wee
see,
His birth and his fortune did never agree:

And therfore, blind man, we pray thee
bewray
(And looke that the truth thou to us doe
say),
Thy birth and thy parentage, what itt
may bee;
For the love that thou bearest to pretty
Bessee.

"Then give me leave, nobles and gentles,
each one,
One song more to sing, and then I have
done;
And if that itt may not winn good report,
Then doe not give me a groat for my
sport.

"[Sir Simon de Montfort my subject shal
  bee ;
Once chiefe of all the great barons was
  hee,
Yet fortune so cruelle this lorde did abase,
Now loste and forgotten are hee and his
  race.

"When the barons in armes did king
  Henrye oppose,
Sir Simon de Montfort their leader they
  chose ;
A leader of courage undaunted was hee,
And oft-times he made their enemyes
  flee.

"At length in the battle on Eveshame
  plaine
The barons were routed, and Montfort
  was slaine ;
Moste fatall that battel did prove unto
  thee,
Thoughe thou wast not borne then, my
  prettye Bessee !

"Along with the nobles, that fell at that
  tyde,
His eldest son Henrye, who fought by his
  side,
Was fellde by a blowe he receivde in the
  fight !
A blowe that deprivde him for ever of
  sight.

"Among the dead bodyes all lifelesse he
  laye,
Till evening drewe on of the following
  daye,
When by a yong ladye discoverd was
  hee ;
And this was thy mother, my prettye
  Bessee !

"A barons faire daughter stept forthe in
  the nighte
To search for her father, who fell in the
  fight,
And seeing yong Montfort, where gasping
  he laye,
Was moved with pitye, and brought him
  awaye.

"In secrette she nurst him, and swaged
  paine,
While he throughe the realme was beleevd
  to be slaine :
At lengthe his faire bride she consented
  to bee,
And made him glad father of prettye
  Bessee.

"And nowe lest oure foes our lives sholde
  betraye,
We clothed ourselves in beggars arraye ;
Her jewelles shee solde, and hither came
  wee :
All our comfort and care was our prettye
  Bessee.]

"And here have wee lived in fortunes
  despite,
Thoughe poore, yet contented with
  humble delighte :
Full forty winters thus have I beene
A silly blind beggar of Bednall-greene.

"And here, noble lordes, is ended the
  song
Of one, that once to your own ranke did
  belong :
And thus have you learned a secrette
  from mee,
That ne'er had beene knowne, but for
  prettye Bessee."

Now when the faire companye everye
  one,
Had heard the strange tale in the song
  he had showne,
They all were amazed, as well they might
  bee,
Both at the blinde beggar and pretty
  Bessee,

With that the faire bride they all did
    embrace,
Saying, Sure thou art come of an honour-
    able race,
Thy father likewise is of noble degree,
And thou art well worthy a lady to bee.

Thus was the feast ended with joye and
    delighte,
A bridegroome most happy then was the
    young knighte,
In joy and felicitie long lived hee,
All with his faire ladye, the pretty Bessee.

## XI.—FANCY AND DESIRE.

### BY THE EARL OF OXFORD.

EDWARD VERE, Earl of Oxford, was in high fame for his poetical talents in the reign of Elizabeth. We have inserted a sonnet of his, which is quoted with great encomiums for its "excellencie and wit," in Puttenham's *Arte of Eng. Poesie*,[*] and found entire in the *Garland of Goodwill*.

Edward, who was the Seventeenth Earl of Oxford, of the family of Vere, succeeded his father in his title and honours in 1562, and died an aged man in 1604.

COME hither shepherd's swayne:
  "Sir, what do you require?"
I praye thee, shewe to me thy name.
  "My name is Fond Desire."

When wert thou borne, Desire?
  "In pompe and pryme of may."
By whom, sweet boy, wert thou begot?
  "By fond Conceit, men say."

Tell me, who was thy nurse?
  "Fresh Youth in sugred joy."
What was thy meate and dayly foode?
  "Sad sighes with great annoy."

What hadst thou then to drinke?
  "Unsavoury lovers teares."
What cradle wert thou rocked in?
  "In hope devoyde of feares."

What lulld thee then asleepe?
  "Sweete speech, which likes me best."

Tell me, where is thy dwelling place?
  "In gentle hartes I rest."

What thing doth please thee most?
  "To gaze on beautye stille."
Whom dost thou thinke to be thy foe?
  "Disdayn of my good wille."

Doth companye displease?
  "Yes, surelye, many one."
Where doth Desire delighte to live?
  "He loves to live alone."

Doth either tyme or age
  Bringe him into decaye?
"No, no, Desire both lives and dyes
  Ten thousand times a daye."

Then, fond Desire, farewelle,
  Thou art no mate for mee;
I sholde be lothe, methinkes, to dwelle
  With such a one as thee.

---

[*] London 1589, p. 172.

## XII.—SIR ANDREW BARTON.

THE father of Sir Andrew Barton having suffered by sea from the Portuguese, he had obtained letters of marque for his two sons to make reprisals upon the subjects of Portugal. It is extremely probable that the court of Scotland granted these letters with no very honest intention. The council board of England, at which the Earl of Surrey held the chief place, was daily pestered with complaints from the sailors and merchants, that Barton, who was called Sir Andrew Barton, under pretence of searching for Portuguese goods, interrupted the English navigation. Henry's situation at that time rendered him backward from breaking with Scotland, so that their complaints were but coldly received. The Earl of Surrey,* however, could not smother his indignation, but gallantly declared at the council board, that while he had an estate that could furnish out a ship, or a son that was capable of commanding one, the narrow seas should not be infested.

"Sir Andrew Barton, who commanded the two Scotch ships, had the reputation of being one of the ablest sea officers of his time. By his depredations, he had amassed great wealth, and his ships were very richly laden. Henry, notwithstanding his situation, could not refuse the generous offer made by the Earl of Surrey. Two ships were immediately fitted out, and put to sea with letters of marque, under his two sons, Sir Thomas† and Sir Edward Howard. After encountering a great deal of foul weather, Sir Thomas came up with the *Lion*, which was commanded by Sir Andrew Barton in person; and Sir Edward came up with the *Union*, Barton's other ship [called by Hall the *Bark of Scotland*]. The engagement which ensued was extremely obstinate on both sides, but at last the fortune of the Howards prevailed. Sir Andrew was killed fighting bravely, and encouraging his men with his whistle, to hold out to the last; and the two Scotch ships, with their crews, were carried into the river Thames [Aug. 2, 1511].

"This exploit had the more merit, as the two English commanders were in a manner volunteers in the service, by their father's order. But it seems to have laid the foundation of Sir Edward's fortune; for, on the 7th of April 1512, the king constituted him (according to Dugdale) Admiral of England, Wales, etc.

"King James 'insisted' upon satisfaction for the death of Barton, and capture of his ship; 'though' Henry had generously dismissed the crews, and even agreed that the parties accused might appear in his courts of admiralty by their attornies, to vindicate themselves." This affair was in a great measure the cause of the battle of Flodden, in which James IV. lost his life.

In the following ballad will be found perhaps some few deviations from the truth of history, to atone for which it has probably recorded many lesser facts which history hath not condescended to relate. I take many of the little circumstances of the story to be real, because I find one of the most unlikely to be not very remote from the truth. In Part ii. v. 156, it is said that England had before "but two ships

---

\* Thomas Howard, afterwards created Duke of Norfolk.

† Called by old historians Lord Howard, afterwards created Earl of Surrey in his father's lifetime. He was father of the poet Earl of Surrey.

of war." Now the *Great Harry* had been built only seven years before, viz. in 1504, which "was properly speaking the first ship in the English navy. Before this period, when the prince wanted a fleet, he had no other expedient but hiring ships from the merchants."—HUME.

This ballad appears to have been written in the reign of Elizabeth.

### THE FIRST PART.

"WHEN Flora with her fragrant flowers
    Bedeckt the earth so trim and gaye,
And Neptune with his daintye showers
    Came to present the monthe of Maye;"
King Henrye rode to take the ayre,
    Over the river of Thames past hee;
When eighty merchants of London came,
    And downe they knelt upon their knee.

"O yee are welcome, rich merchànts;
    Good saylors, welcome unto mee."
They swore by the rood, they were saylors good,
    But rich merchànts they cold not bee:
"To France nor Flanders dare we pass:
    Nor Bourdeaux voyage dare we fare;
And all for a rover that lyes on the seas,
    Who robbs us of our merchant ware."

King Henrye frownd and turned him rounde,
    And swore by the Lord, that was mickle of might,
"I thought he had not beene in the world,
    Durst have wrought England such unright."
The merchants sighed, and said, alas!
    And thus they did their answer frame,
He is a proud Scott, that robbs on the seas,
    And Sir Andrewe Barton is his name.

The king lookt over his left shouldèr,
    And an angrye look then looked hee:
"Have I never a lorde in all my realme,
    Will feitch yond traytor unto mee?"
Yea, that dare I; lord Howard sayes;
    Yea, that dare I with heart and hand;
If it please your grace to give me leave,
    Myselfe wil be the only man.

Thou art but yong; the kyng replyed:
    Yond Scott hath numbred manye a yeare.
"Trust me, my liege, Ile make him quail,
    Or before my prince I will never appeare."
Then bowemen and gunners thou shalt have,
    And chuse them over my realme so free;
Besides good mariners, and shipp-boyes,
    To guide the great shipp on the sea.

The first man, that lord Howard chose,
    Was the ablest gunner in all the realm,
Thoughe he was threescore yeeres and ten;
    Good Peter Simon was his name.
Peter, sais hee, I must to the sea,
    To bring home a traytor live or **dead**:
Before all others I have chosen thee,
    Of a hundred gunners to be the head.

If you, my lord, have chosen mee
    Of a hundred gunners to be the head,
Then hang me up on your maine-mast tree,
    If I misse my marke one shilling bread.\*
My lord then chose a boweman rare,
    Whose active hands had gained fame.
In Yorkshire was this gentleman borne,
    And William Horseley was his name.

Horseley, sayd he, I must with speede
    Go seeke a traytor on the sea,
And now of a hundred bowemen brave
    To be the head I have chosen thee.
If you, quoth hee, have chosen mee
    Of a hundred bowemen to be the head,
On your main-màst Ile hanged bee,
    If I miss twelvescore one penny bread.

---

\* An old English word for *breadth*.

With pikes and gunnes, and bowemen
   bold,
This noble Howard is gone to the sea ;
With a valyant heart and a pleasant
   cheare,
Out at Thames mouth sayled he.
And days he *scant* had sayled three,
   Upon the "voyage," he tooke in hand,
But there he mett with a noble shipp,
   And stoutely made itt stay and stand.

Thou must tell me, lord Howard said,
   Now who thou art, and what's thy
   name ;
And shewe me where thy dwelling is :
   And whither bound, and whence thou
   came.
My name is Henry Hunt, quoth hee
   With a heavye heart, and a carefull
   mind ;
I and my shipp doe both belong
   To the Newcastle, that stands upon
   Tyne.

Hast thou not heard, nowe, Henrye Hunt,
   As thou hast sayled by daye and by
   night,
Of a Scottish rover on the seas ;
   Men call him sir Andrew Barton, knight?
Then ever he sighed, and sayd alas !
   With a grieved mind, and well away !
But over-well I knowe that wight,
   I was his prisoner yesterday.

As I was sayling uppon the sea,
   A Burdeaux voyage for to fare ;
To his *hach-borde* he clasped me,
   And robd me of all my merchant ware :
And mickle debts, God wot, I owe,
   And every man will have his owne ;
And I am nowe to London bounde,
   Of our gracious king to beg a boone.

That shall not need, lord Howard sais ;
   Lett me but once that robber see,
For every penny tane thee froe
   It shall be doubled shillings three.

Nowe God forefend, the merchant said,
   That you shold seek soe far amisse !
God keepe you out of that traitors hands !
   Full litle ye wott what a man hee is.

Hee is brasse within, and steele without,
   With beames on his topcastle stronge ;
And eighteen pieces of ordinance
   He carries on each side along :
And he hath a pinnace deerlye dight,
   St. Andrewes crosse that is his guide ;
His pinnace beareth ninescore men,
   And fifteen canons on each side.

Were ye twentye shippes, and he but
   one ;
I sweare by kirke, and bower, and hall ;
He wold overcome them everye one,
   If once his beames they doe downe fall.*
This is cold comfort, sais my lord,
   To wellcome a stranger thus to the sea :
Yet Ile bring him and his shipp to shore,
   Or to Scottland hee shall carrye mee.

Then a noble gunner you must have,
   And he must aim well with his ee,
And sinke his pinnace into the sea,
   Or else hee never orecome will bee :
And if you chance his shipp to borde,
   This counsel I must give withall,
Let no man to his topcastle goe
   To strive to let his beams downe fall.

---

\* It should seem from hence, that before our marine artillery was brought to its present perfection, some naval commanders had recourse to instruments or machines, similar in use, though perhaps unlike in construction, to the heavy dolphins made of lead or iron used by the ancient Greeks, which they suspended from beams or yards fastened to the mast, and which they precipitately let fall on the enemy's ships, in order to sink them by beating holes through the bottoms of their undecked Triremes, or otherwise damaging them. These are mentioned by Thucydides, lib. vii. p. 256, ed. 1564, folio, and are more fully explained in *Schefferi de Militia Navali*, lib. ii. cap. 5, p. 136, ed. 1653, 4to.

And seven pieces of ordinance,
  I pray your honour lend to mee,
On each side of my shipp along,
  And I will lead you on the sea.
A glasse Ile sett, that may be seene,
  Whether you sayle by day or night;
And to-morrowe, I sweare, by nine of the clocke
  You shall meet with Sir Andrewe Barton knight.

### THE SECOND PART.

The merchant sett my lorde a glasse
  Soe well apparent in his sight,
And on the morrowe, by nine of the clocke,
  He shewed him Sir Andrewe Barton knight.
His hachebord it was "gilt" with gold,
  Soe deerlye *dight* it dazzled the ee:
Nowe by my faith, lord Howarde sais,
  This is a gallant sight to see.

Take in your *ancyents*, standards eke,
  So close that no man may them see;
And put me forth a white willowe wand,
  As merchants use to sayle the sea.
But they stirred neither top, nor mast;*
  Stoutly they past Sir Andrew by.
What English churles are yonder, he sayd,
  That can soe litle curtesye?

Now by the roode, three yeares and more
  I have beene admirall over the sea;
And never an English nor Portingall
  Without my leave can passe this way.
Then called he forth his stout pinnace;
  "Fetch backe yond pedlars nowe to mee:
I sweare by the masse, yon English churles
  Shall all hang att my maine-mast tree."

With that the pinnace itt shott off,
  Full well lord Howard might it ken;
For itt stroke down my lord's fore mast,
  And killed fourteen of his men.

Come hither, Simon, sayes my lord,
  Looke that thy word be true, thou said;
For at my maine-mast thou shalt hang,
  If thou misse thy marke one shilling bread.

Simon was old, but his heart itt was bold.
  His ordinance he laid right lowe;
He put in chaine full nine yardes long,*
  With other great shott lesse, and moe;
And he lette goe his great gunnes shott:
  Soe well he settled itt with his ee,
The first sight that Sir Andrew sawe,
  He see his pinnace sunke in the sea.

And when he saw his pinnace sunke,
  Lord, how his heart with rage did swell!
"Nowe cutt my ropes, itt is time to be gon;
  Ile fetch yond pedlars backe mysell."
When my Lord sawe Sir Andrewe loose,
  Within his heart hee was full *faine:*
"Nowe spread your ancyents, strike up drummes,
  Sound all your trumpetts out amaine."

Fight on, my men, Sir Andrewe sais,
  Weale howsoever this *geere will sway;*
Itt is my lord admirall of England,
  Is come to seeke mee on the sea.
Simon had a sonne, who shott right well,
  That did Sir Andrewe mickle scare;
In att his decke he gave a shott,
  Killed threescore of his men of warre.

Then Henrye Hunt with rigour hott
  Came bravely on the other side,
Soone he drove downe his fore-mast tree,
  And killed fourscore men beside.
Nowe, out alas! Sir Andrewe cryed,
  What may a man now thinke, or say?
Yonder merchant theefe, that pierceth mee,
  He was my prisoner yesterday.

---

\* *i.e.* did not salute.   \* *i.e.* discharged chain shot.

Come hither to me, thou Gordon good,
  That aye wast readye att my call ;
I will give thee three hundred markes,
  If thou wilt let my beames downe fall.
Lord Howard hee then calld in haste,
  "Horseley, see thou be true in stead ;
For thou shalt at the maine-mast hang,
  If thou misse twelvescore one penny
    bread."

Then Gordon swarved the maine-mast
    tree,
  He swarved it with might and maine ;
But Horseley with a bearing * arrowe,
  Stroke the Gordon through the braine;
And he fell unto the haches again,
  And sore his deadlye wounde did
    bleed :
Then word went through Sir Andrews
    men,
  How that the Gordon hee was dead.

Come hither to mee, James Hambilton,
  Thou art my only sisters sonne,
If thou wilt let my beames down fall,
  Six hundred nobles thou hast wonne.
With that he swarved the maine-mast tree,
  He swarved it with nimble art ;
But Horseley with a broad arrowe
  Pierced the Hambilton through the
    heart :

And downe he fell upon the deck,
  That with his blood did streame amaine :
Then every Scott cryed, Well-away !
  Alas a comelye youth is slaine !
All woe begone was Sir Andrew then,
  With griefe and rage his heart did
    swell :
 'Go fetch me forth my armour of proofe,
  For I will to the topcastle myself."

"Goe fetch me forth my armour of
    proofe ;
  That gilded is with gold soe cleare :

---

    * *Sc.* that carries well, etc.

God be with my brother John of Barton !
  Against the Portingalls hee it ware ;
And when he had on his armour of
    proofe,
He was a gallant sight to see :
Ah ! nere didst thou meet with living
    wight,
  My deere brother, could cope with
    thee."

Come hither Horseley, sayes my lord,
  And looke your shaft that itt goe right,
Shoot a good shoote in time of need,
  And for it thou shalt be made a knight.
Ile shoot my best, quoth Horseley then,
  Your honour shall see, with might and
    maine ;
But if I were hanged at your maine-mast,
  I have now left but arrowes twaine.

Sir Andrew he did swarve the tree,
  With right good will he swarved then :
Upon his breast did Horseley hitt,
  But the arrow bounded back agen.
Then Horseley spyed a privye place
  With a perfect eye in a secrette part ;
Under the spole of his right arme
  He smote Sir Andrew to the heart.

"Fight on, my men, Sir Andrew sayes,
  A little Ime hurt, but yett not slaine ;
Ile but lye downe and bleede a while,
  And then Ile rise and fight againe.
Fight on, my men, Sir Andrew sayes,
  And never flinche before the foe ;
And stand fast by St. Andrewes crosse
  Untill you heare my whistle blowe."

They never heard his whistle blow,—
  Which made their hearts waxe sore
    adread :
Then Horseley sayd, Aboard, my lord,
  For well I wott Sir Andrew's dead.
They boarded then his noble shipp,
  They boarded it with might and maine
Eighteen score Scots alive they found,
  The rest were either maimed or slaine.

Lord Howard tooke a sword in hand,
   And off he smote Sir Andrewes head,
"I must have left England many a daye,
   If thou wert alive as thou art dead."
He caused his body to be cast
   Over the hatchbord into the sea,
And about his middle three hundred crownes:
   "Wherever thou land this will bury thee."

Thus from the warres lord Howard came,
   And backe he sayled ore the maine,
With mickle joy and triumphing
   Into Thames mouth he came againe.
Lord Howard then a letter wrote,
   And sealed it with seale and ring;
"Such a noble prize have I brought to your grace,
   As never did subject to a king:

"Sir Andrewes shipp I bring with mee;
   A braver shipp was never none:
Nowe hath your grace two shipps of warr,
   Before in England was but one."
King Henryes grace with royall cheere
   Welcomed the noble Howard home,
And where, said he, is this rover stout,
   That I myselfe may give the doome?

"The rover, he is safe, my liege,
   Full many a fadom in the sea;
If he were alive as he is dead,
   I must have left England many a day:
And your grace may thank four men i' the ship
   For the victory wee have wonne,

These are William Horseley, Henry Hunt,
   And Peter Simon, and his sonne."
To Henry Hunt, the king then sayd,
   In lieu of what was from thee tane,
A noble a day now thou shalt have,
   Sir Andrewes jewels and his chayne.
And Horseley thou shalt be a knight,
   And lands and livings shalt have store;
Howard shall be erle Surrye hight,
   As Howards erst have been before.

Nowe, Peter Simon, thou art old,
   I will maintaine thee and thy sonne:
And the men shall have five hundred markes
   For the good service they have done.
Then in came the queene with ladyes fair
   To see Sir Andrewe Barton knight:
They weend that hee were brought on shore,
   And thought to have seen a gallant sight.

But when they see his deadlye face,
   And eyes soe hollow in his head,
I wold give, quoth the king, a thousand markes,
   This man were alive as hee is dead:
Yett for the manfull part hee playd,
   Which fought soe well with heart and hand,
His men shall have twelvepence a day,
   Till they come to my brother kings high land.

## XIII.—LADY ANNE BOTHWELL'S LAMENT.

#### A SCOTTISH SONG.

THE subject of this pathetic ballad the Editor once thought might possibly relate to the Earl of Bothwell and his desertion of his wife, Lady Jean Gordon, to make room for his marriage with the Queen of Scots. But this opinion he now believes to be groundless; indeed, Earl Bothwell's age, who was upwards of sixty at the time of that marriage, renders it unlikely that he should be the object of so warm a passion as this elegy supposes. He has been since informed, that it entirely refers to a private story: A young lady of the name of Bothwell, or rather Boswell, having been together with her child deserted by her husband or lover, composed these affecting lines herself, which here are given from a copy in the Editor's folio MS. corrected by another in Allan Ramsay's *Miscellany*.

*Balow*, my babe, lye still and sleipe!
It grieves me sair to see thee weipe:
If thoust be silent, Ise be glad,
Thy maining maks my heart ful sad.
Balow, my boy, thy mothers joy,
Thy father *breides* me great annoy.
  Balow, my babe, ly stil and sleipe,
  It grieves me sair to see thee weepe.

Whan he began to court my luve,
And with his sugred wordes * to muve,
His faynings fals, and flattering cheire
To me that time did not appeire:
But now I see, most cruell hee
Cares neither for my babe nor mee.
    Balow, etc.

Lye still, my darling, sleipe a while,
And when thou wakest, sweitly smile:
But smile not, as thy father did,
To cozen maids: nay God forbid!
Bot yett I feire, thou wilt gae neire
Thy fatheris hart, and face to beire.
    Balow, etc.

I cannae chuse, but ever will
Be luving to thy father still:
Whair-eir he gae, whair-eir he ryde,
My luve with him doth still abyde:
In weil or wae, whair-eir he gae,
Mine hart can neire depart him frae.
    Balow, etc.

But doe not, doe not, prettie mine,
To faynings fals thine hart incline;
Be loyal to thy luver trew,
And nevir change hir for a new:
If gude or faire, of hir have care,
For womens banning's wonderous sair.
    Balow, etc.

Bairne, sin thy cruel father is gane,
Thy winsome smiles maun eise my paine;
My babe and I'll together live,
He'll comfort me when cares doe grieve:
My babe and I right saft will ly,
And quite forgeit man's cruelty.
    Balow, etc.

Fareweil, fareweil, thou falsest youth,
That evir kist a womans mouth!
I wish all maides be warnd by mee
Nevir to trust mans curtesy;
For if we doe bot chance to bow,
They'le use us then they care not how.
  Balow, my babe, ly stil, and sleipe,
  It grives me sair to see thee weipe.

---

* When *sugar* was first imported into Europe, it was a very great dainty; and therefore the epithet *sugred* is used by all our old writers metaphorically to express extreme and delicate sweetness. (See above, No. XI. v. 10.) *Sugar* at present is cheap and common, and therefore suggests now a coarse and vulgar idea.

## XIV.—THE MURDER OF THE KING OF SCOTS.\*

THE catastrophe of Henry Stewart, Lord Darnley, the unfortunate husband of Mary Queen of Scots, is the subject of this ballad. It is here related in that partial imperfect manner, in which such an event would naturally strike the subjects of another kingdom, of which he was a native.

Henry, Lord Darnley, was eldest son of the Earl of Lennox, by the Lady Margaret Douglas, niece of Henry VIII. and daughter of Margaret, Queen of Scotland, by the Earl of Angus, whom that princess married after the death of James IV. Darnley, who had been born and educated in England, was but in his twenty-first year, when he was murdered Feb. 9, 1567-8. This crime was perpetrated by the Earl of Bothwell, not out of respect to the memory of Rizzio, but in order to pave the way for his own marriage with the queen.

This ballad (printed, with a few corrections, from the Editor's folio MS.) seems to have been written soon after Mary's escape into England in 1568, see v. 65.

*Woe worth*, woe worth thee, false Scot-
   lànde !
For thou hast ever wrought by sleight ;
The worthyest prince that ever was borne,
   You hanged under a cloud by night.

The queene of France a letter wrote,
   And sealed itt with harte and ringe ;
And bade him come Scotland within,
   And shee wold marry and crowne him
   kinge.

To be a king is a pleasant thing,
   To bee a prince unto a peere :
But you have heard, and soe have I too,
   A man may well buy gold too deare.

There was an Italyan in that place,
   Was as well beloved as ever was hee,
Lord David was his name,
   Chamberlaine to the queene was hee.

If the king had risen forth of his place,
   He wold have sate him downe in the
   cheare,
And tho itt beseemed him not so well,
   Altho the kinge had beene present there.

Some lords in Scotlande waxed wroth,
   And quarrelled with him for the nonce ;

I shall you tell how it befell,
   Twelve daggers were in him att once.

When the queene saw her chamberlaine
   was slaine,
For him her faire cheeks shee did weete,
And made a vowe for a yeare and a day
   The king and shee wold not come in
   one sheete.

Then some of the lords they waxed
   wrothe,
   And made their vow all vehementlye ;
For the death of the queenes chamber-
   laine,
   The king himselfe, how he shall dye.

With gun-powder they strewed his roome,
   And layd greene rushes in his way :
For the traitors thought that very night
   This worthye king for to betray.

To bedd the king he made him bowne ;
   To take his rest was his desire ;
He was noe sooner caste on sleepe,
   But his chamber was on a blasing fire.

Up he lope, and the window brake,
   And hee had thirtye foote to fall ;

---

\* Given in folio as " Earle Bodwell

Lord Bodwell kept a privy watch,
  Underneath his castle wall.

Who have wee here? lord Bodwell sayd :
  Now answer me, that I may know.
"King Henry the eighth my uncle was ;
  For his sweete sake some pitty show."

Who have we here? lord Bodwell sayd,
  Now answer me when I doe speake.
"Ah, lord Bodwell, I know thee well ;
  Some pitty on me I pray thee take."

Ile pitty thee as much, he sayd,
  And as much favor show to thee,
As thou didst to the queenes chamber-
    laine,
  That day thou deemedst him to die.*

Through halls and towers the king they
    ledd,
Through towers and castles that were
    nye,
Through an arbor into an orchárd,
  There on a peare-tree hanged him hye.

When the governor of Scotland heard
  How that the worthye king was slaine ;
He persued the queen so bitterlye,
  That in Scotland shee dare not remaine.

But she is fledd into merry England,
  And here her residence hath taine ;
And through the queene of Englands
    grace,
  In England now shee doth remaine.

---

## XV.—A SONNET BY QUEEN ELIZABETH.

THE following lines, if they display no rich vein of poetry, are yet so strongly characteristic of their great and spirited authoress, that the insertion of them will be pardoned. They are preserved in Puttenham's *Arte of English Poesie*, a book in which are many sly addresses to the queen's foible of shining as a poetess.

THE doubt of future foes
  Exiles my present joy ;
And wit me warnes to shun such snares,
  As threaten mine annoy.

For falshood now doth flow,
  And subjects faith doth ebbe :
Which would not be, if reason rul'd,
  Or wisdome wove the webbe.

But clowdes of joyes untried
  Do cloake aspiring mindes ;
Which turn to raine of late repent,
  By course of changed windes.

The toppe of hope supposed
  The roote of *ruthe* will be ;
And frutelesse all their graffed guiles,
  As shortly all shall see.

Then dazeld eyes with pride,
  Which great ambition blindes,
Shal be unseeld by worthy wights,
  Whose foresight falshood finds.

The daughter of debate,*
  That discord ay doth sowe,
Shal reape no gaine where former rule
  Hath taught stil peace to growe.

No forreine bannisht wight
  Shall ancre in this port ;
Our realme it brookes no strangers force,
  Let them elsewhere resort.

Our rusty sworde with rest
  Shall first his edge employ,
To poll the toppes, that seeke such change,
  Or gape for such like joy.

---

* Pronounced, after the northern manner, *dee*.

* She evidently means here the Queen of Scots.

## XVI.—KING OF SCOTS AND ANDREW BROWNE.*

THIS ballad is a proof of the little intercourse that subsisted between the Scots and English, before the accession of James I. to the crown of England. The tale which is here so circumstantially related does not appear to have had the least foundation in history, but was probably built upon some confused hearsay report of the tumults in Scotland during the minority of that prince, and of the conspiracies formed by different factions to get possession of his person. It should seem from ver. 97 to have been written during the regency, or at least before the death of the Earl of Morton, who was condemned and executed June 2, 1581, when James was in his fifteenth year.

The author, W. Elderton, who had been originally an attorney in the Sheriffs Courts of London, and afterwards (if we may believe Oldys) a comedian, was a facetious companion, whose tippling and rhymes rendered him famous among his contemporaries. He was author of many popular songs and ballads, and is believed to have fallen a victim to his bottle before the year 1592.

"OUT alas!" what a griefe is this
    That princes subjects cannot be true,
But still the devill hath some of his,
    Will play their parts whatsoever ensue ;
Forgetting what a grievous thing
It is to offend the anointed king ?
      Alas for woe, why should it be so,
      This makes a sorrowful heigh ho.

In Scotland is a bonnie kinge,
    As proper a youth as neede to be,
Well given to every happy thing,
    That can be in a kinge to see :
Yet that unluckie country still,
Hath people given to craftie will.
      Alas for woe, etc.

On Whitsun eve it so befell,
    A posset was made to give the king,
Whereof his ladie nurse hard tell,
    And that it was a poysoned thing :
She cryed, and called piteouslie ;
Now help, or els the king shall die !
      Alas for woe, etc.

One Browne, that was an English man,
    And hard the ladies piteous crye,

Out with his sword, and bestir'd him than,
    Out of the doores in haste to flie ;
But all the doores were made so fast,
Out of a window he got at last.
      Alas for woe, etc.

He met the bishop coming fast,
    Having the posset in his hande :
The sight of Browne made him aghast,
    Who bad him stoutly staie and stand.
With him were two that ranne awa,
For feare that Browne would make a fray.
      Alas for woe, etc.

Bishop, quoth Browne, what hast thou there?
    Nothing at all, my friend, sayde he ;
But a posset to make the king good cheere.
    Is it so? sayd Browne, that will I see,
First I will have thyself begin,
Before thou go any further in ;
      Be it weale or woe, it shall be so,
      This makes a sorrowful heigh ho.

The bishop sayde, Browne I doo know,
    Thou art a young man poore and bare ;

---

* Given in folio as " King James and Browne."

Livings on thee I will bestowe :
  Let me go on, take thou no care.
No, no, quoth Browne, I will not be
A traitour for all Christiantie :
    Happe well or woe, it shall be so,
    Drink now with a sorrowfull, etc.

The bishop dranke, and by and by
  His belly burst and he fell downe :
A just rewarde for his traitery.
  This was a posset indeed, quoth Brown !
He serched the bishop, and found the keyes,
To come to the kinge when he did please.
    Alas for woe, etc.

As soon as the king got word of this,
  He humbly fell uppon his knee,
And praysed God that he did misse
  To tast of that extremity :
For that he did perceive and know,
  His clergie would betray him so :
    Alas for woe, etc.

Alas, he said, unhappie realme,
  My father, and grandfather * slaine :
My mother banished, O extreame !
  Unhappy fate, and bitter bayne !
And now like treason wrought for me,
  What more unhappie realme can be !
    Alas for woe, etc.

The king did call his nurse to his grace,
  And gave her twenty poundes a yeere ;
And trustie Browne too in like case,
  He knighted him with gallant geere :

---

\* His father was Henry, Lord Darnley. His grandfather, the old Earl of Lennox, regent of Scotland, and father of Lord Darnley, was murdered at Stirling, Sept. 5, 1571.

And gave him "lands and livings great,
For dooing such a manly feat,
  As he did showe, to the bishop's woe,
  Which made, etc.

When all this treason done and past,
  Tooke not effect of traytery ;
Another treason at the last,
They sought against his majestie :
How they might make their kinge away,
By a privie banket on a daye.
    Alas for woe, etc.

"Another time" to sell the king
  Beyonde the seas they had decreede :
Three noble Earles heard of this thing,
  And did prevent the same with speede.
For a letter came, with such a charme,
That they should doo their king no harme :
    For further woe, if they did soe,
    Would make a sorrowful heigh hoe.

The Earle Mourton told the Douglas then,
  Take heede you do not offend the king ;
But shew yourselves like honest men
  Obediently in every thing :
For his godmother * will not see
Her noble childe misus'd to be
    With any woe ; for if it be so,
    She will make, etc.

God graunt all subjects may be true,
  In England, Scotland, every where :
That no such daunger may ensue,
  To put the prince or state in feare :
That God the highest king may see
Obedience as it ought to be,
    In wealth or woe, God graunt it be so
    To avoide the sorrowful heigh ho.

---

\* Queen Elizabeth.

## XVII.—THE BONNY EARL OF MURRAY.

### A SCOTTISH SONG.

IN December 1591, Francis Stewart, Earl of Bothwell, had made an attempt to seize on the person of his sovereign James VI., but being disappointed, had retired towards the north. The king unadvisedly gave a commission to George Gordon, Earl of Huntley, to pursue Bothwell and his followers with fire and sword. Huntley, under cover of executing that commission, took occasion to revenge a private quarrel he had against James Stewart, Earl of Murray, a relation of Bothwell's. In the night of Feb. 7, 1592, he beset Murray's house, burnt it to the ground, and slew Murray himself, a young nobleman of the most promising virtues, and the very darling of the people. See Robertson's *History*.

YE highlands, and ye lawlands,
  Oh! *quhair* ha ye been?
They hae slaine the Earl of Murray,
  And hae laid him on the green.

Now wae be to thee, Huntley!
  And *quhairfore* did you sae!
I bade you bring him wi' you,
  But forbade you him to slay.

He was a braw gallant,
  And he rid at the ring;
And the bonny Earl of Murray,
  Oh! he might hae been a king.

He was a braw gallant,
  And he playd at the ba';
And the bonny Earl of Murray
  Was the flower among them a'.

He was a braw gallant,
  And he playd at the gluve;
And the bonny Earl of Murray,
  Oh! he was the Queenes luve.

Oh! lang will his lady
  Luke owre the castle Doune,*
Ere she see the Earl of Murray
  Cum sounding throw the toune.

## XVIII.—YOUNG WATERS.

### A SCOTTISH BALLAD.

IT has been suggested to the Editor, that this ballad covertly alludes to the indiscreet partiality which Queen Anne of Denmark is said to have shown for the bonny Earl of Murray, and which is supposed to have influenced the fate of that unhappy nobleman.

ABOUT *Zule*, quhen the wind blew cule,
  And the round tables began,
A'! there is cum to our kings court
  Mony a well-favour'd man.

The queen luikt owre the castle wa,
  Beheld baith dale and down,
And then she saw zoung Waters
  Cum riding to the town.

His footmen they did rin before,
  His horsemen rade behind,
Ane mantel of the burning *gowd*
  Did keip him frae the wind.

---

\* *Castle Doune* here has been thought to mean the Castle of Doune, a seat belonging to the Earls of Murray or Moray.

*Gowden graith'd* his horse before
  And siller shod behind,
The horse *zong* Waters rade upon
  Was fleeter than the wind.

But than spake a wylie lord,
  Unto the queen said he,
O tell me qhua's the fairest face
  Rides in the company.

I've sene lord, and I've sene laird,
  And knights of high degree;
Bot a fairer face than zoung Watèrs
  Mine eyne did never see.

Out then spack the jealous king
  (And an angry man was he),
O, if he had been twice as fair,
  *Zou* micht have excepted me.

Zou're neither laird nor lord, she says,
  Bot the king that wears the crown;
Ther is not a knight in fair Scotland
  Bot to thee maun bow down.

For a' that she could do or say,
  Appeasd he wad nae bee;

Bot for the words which she had said
  Zoung Waters he maun dee.

They hae taen zoung Waters, and
  Put fetters to his feet;
They hae taen zoung Waters, and
  Thrown him in dungeon deep.

Aft I have ridden thro' Stirling town
  In the wind both and the weit;
Bot I neir rade thro' Stirling town
  Wi fetters at my feet.

Aft have I ridden thro' Stirling town
  In the wind both and the rain;
Bot I neir rade thro' Stirling town
  Neir to return again.

They hae taen to the heiding-hill,*
  His zoung son in his craddle,
And they hae taen to the heiding-hill,
  His horse both and his saddle.

They hae taen to the heiding-hill
  His lady fair to see.
And for the words the Queen had spoke
  Zoung Waters he did dee.

---

### XIX.—MARY AMBREE.

In the year 1584, the Spaniards, under the command of Alexander Farnese, Prince of Parma, began to gain great advantages in Flanders and Brabant, by recovering many strongholds and cities from the Hollanders, as Ghent, Antwerp, Mechlin, etc. Some attempt made with the assistance of English volunteers to retrieve the former of those places probably gave occasion to this ballad. I can find no mention of our heroine in history, but the following rhymes rendered her famous among our poets. Ben Jonson often mentions her, and calls any remarkable virago by her name, and in the *Fortunate Isles* he quotes the words of the ballad itself:

> "Mary Ambree
> (Who marched so free
> To the siege of Gaunt,
> . And death could not daunt,
> As the ballad doth vaunt)
> Were a braver wight," e'з.

---

* *i.e.* heading (beheading) hill. The place of execution was anciently an artificial hillock.

It is likewise evident that she is the virago intended by Butler in *Hudibras:*

"A bold virago, stout and tall
  As *Joan* of France or English *Mall.*"

This ballad is printed from a black-letter copy in the Pepys Collection, improved from the Editor's folio MS. and by conjecture. The full title is: *The valorous acts performed at Gaunt by the brave bonnie lass Mary Ambree, who in revenge of her lovers death did play her part most gallantly.* The tune is "The blind beggar," etc.

WHEN captaines couragious, whom death cold not daunte,
Did march to the siege of the citty of Gaunt,
They mustred their souldiers by two and by three,
And the formost in battle was Mary Ambree.

When brave Sir John Major * was slaine in her sight,
Who was her true lover, her joy, and delight,
Because he was slaine most treacherouslie,
Then vow'd to revenge him Mary Ambree.

Shee clothed herselfe from the top to the toe
In buffe of the bravest, most seemelye to showe;
A faire shirt of male † then slipped on shee;
Was not this a brave bonny lass, Mary Ambree?

A helmett of proofe shee strait did provide,
A strong aringe sword shee girt by her side,
On her hand a goodly faire gauntlett put shee;
Was not this a brave bonny lass, Mary Ambree?

---

\* So MS., sergeant-major in PC.
† A peculiar kind of armour, composed of small rings of iron, and worn under the clothes. It is mentioned by Spencer, who speaks of the Irish gallowglass or foot-soldier as "armed in a long shirt of mayl."—*View of the State of Ireland.*

Then tooke shee her sworde and her targett in hand,
Bidding all such, as wold, bee of her band;
To wayte on her person came thousand and three:
Was not this a brave bonny lass, Mary Ambree?

My soldiers, she saith, soe valiant and bold,
Nowe followe your captaine, whom you doe beholde;
Still formost in battel myselfe will I bee:
Was not this a brave bonny lasse, Mary Ambree?

Then cryed out her souldiers, and loude they did say,
Soe well thou becomest this gallant array,
Thy harte and thy weapons soe well do agree,
There was none ever like Mary Ambree.

Shee cheared her souldiers, that foughten for life,
With *ancyent* and standard, with drum and with fife,
With brave clanging trumpetts, that sounded so free;
Was not this a brave bonny lasse, Mary Ambree?

Before I will see the worst of you all
To come into danger of death, or of thrall,
This hand and this life I will venture so free:
Was not this a brave bonny lasse, Mary Ambree?

Shee led upp her souldiers in battaile
   array,
Gainst three times theyr number by breake
   of the daye;
Seven howers in skirmish continued shee:
Was not this a brave bonny lasse, Mary
   Ambree?

She filled the skyes with the smoke of her
   shott,
And her enemyes bodyes with bullets soe
   hott;
For one of her owne men a score killed
   shee:
Was not this a brave bonny lasse, Mary
   Ambree?

And when her false gunner, to spoyle her
   intent,
Away all her pellets and powder had sent,
Straight with her keen weapon shee slasht
   him in three:
Was not this a brave bonny lasse, Mary
   Ambree?

Being falselye betrayed for lucre of hyre,
At length she was forced to make a retyre;
Then her souldiers into a strong castle
   drew shee:
Was not this a brave bonny lasse, Mary
   Ambree?

Her foes they besett her on everye side,
As thinking close siege shee cold never
   abide;
To beate down the walles they all did
   decree:
But stoutlye deffyd them brave Mary
   Ambree.

Then tooke shee her sword and her targett
   in hand,
And mounting the walles all undaunted
   did stand,
There daring their captaines to match any
   three:
O what a brave captaine was Mary Ambree!

Now saye, English captaine, what woldest
   thou give
To ransome thy selfe, which else must not
   live?
Come yield thy selfe quicklye, or slaine
   thou must bee.
Then smiled sweetlye brave Mary Ambree.

Ye captaines couragious, of valour so bold,
Whom thinke you before you now you
   doe behold?
A knight, sir, of England, and captaine
   soe free,
Who shortelye with us a prisoner must
   bee.

No captaine of England; behold in your
   sight
Two brests in my bosome, and therfore
   no knight:
Noe knight, sirs, of England, nor captaine
   you see,
But a poor simple lass, called Mary
   Ambree.

But art thou a woman, as thou dost declare,
Whose valor hath proved so undaunted
   in warre?
If England doth yield such brave lasses
   as thee,
Full well may they conquer, faire Mary
   Ambree.

The prince of Great Parma heard of her
   renowne
Who long had advanced for Englands
   faire crowne;
Hee wooed her and sued her his mistress
   to bee,
And offerd rich presents to Mary Ambree.

But this virtuous mayden despised them
   all,
Ile nere sell my honour for *purple nor
   pall*:
A mayden of England, sir, never will bee
The fere of a monarcke, quoth Mary
   Ambree.

Then to her owne country shee backe did returne,
Still holding the foes of faire England in scorne:

Therfore English captaines of every degree
Sing forth the brave valours of Mary Ambree.

---

## XX.—BRAVE LORD WILLOUGHBY.

PEREGRINE BERTIE, Lord Willoughby of Eresby, had, in the year 1586, distinguished himself at the siege of Zutphen, in the Low Countries. He was the year after made general of the English forces in the United Provinces, in the room of the Earl of Leicester, who was recalled. This gave him an opportunity for signalizing his courage and military skill in several actions against the Spaniards. One of these, greatly exaggerated by popular report, is probably the subject of this old ballad, which, on account of its flattering encomiums on English valour, hath always been a favourite with the people.

Lord Willoughby died in 1601. Both Norris and Turner were famous among the military men of that age.

THE fifteenth day of July,
  With glistering spear and shield,
A famous fight in Flanders
  Was foughten in the field:
The most couragious officers
  Were English captains three;
But the bravest man in battel
  Was brave lord Willoughbèy.

The next was captain Norris,
  A valiant man was hee:
The other captain Turner,
  From field would never flee.
With fifteen hundred fighting men,
  Alas! there were no more,
They fought with fourteen thousand then,
  Upon the bloody shore.

Stand to it noble pikemen,
  And look you round about:
And shoot you right your bow-men,
  And we will keep them out:
You musquet and *calliver* men,
  Do you prove true to me,
I'le be the formost man in fight,
  Says brave lord Willoughbèy.

And then the bloody enemy
  They fiercely did assail,
And fought it out most furiously,
  Not doubting to prevail:
The wounded men on both sides fell
  Most pitious for to see,
Yet nothing could the courage quell
  Of brave lord Willoughbèy.

For seven hours to all mens view
  This fight endured sore,
Until our men so feeble grew
  That they could fight no more;
And then upon dead horses
  Full savourly they eat,
And drank the puddle water,
  They could no better get.

When they had fed so freely,
  They kneeled on the ground,
And praised God devoutly
  For the favour they had found;
And beating up their colours,
  The fight they did renew,
And turning tow'rds the Spaniard,
  A thousand more they slew.

The sharp steel-pointed arrows,
  And bullets thick did fly;
Then did our valiant soldiers
  Charge on most furiously;
Which made the Spaniards waver,
  They thought it best to flee,
They fear'd the stout behaviour
  Of brave lord Willoughbèy.

Then quoth the Spanish general,
  Come let us march away,
I fear we shall be spoiled all
  If here we longer stay;
For yonder comes lord Willoughbey
  With courage fierce and fell,
He will not give one inch of way
  For all the devils in hell.

And then the fearful enemy
  Was quickly put to flight,
Our men persued couragiously,
  And caught their forces quite;
But at last they gave a shout,
  Which eechoed through the sky,
God, and St. George for England!
  The conquerers did cry.

This news was brought to England
  With all the speed might be,
And soon our gracious queen was told
  Of this same victory.
O this is brave lord Willoughbey,
  My love that ever won,
Of all the lords of honour
  'Tis he great deeds hath done.

To the souldiers that were maimed,
  And wounded in the fray,
The queen allowed a pension
  Of fifteen pence a day;
And from all costs and charges
  She quit and set them free:
And this she did all for the sake
  Of brave lord Willoughbèy.

Then courage, noble Englishmen,
  And never be dismaid;
If that we be but one to ten,
  We will not be afraid
To fight with foraign enemies,
  And set our nation free.
And thus I end the bloody bout
  Of brave lord Willoughbèy.

---

## XXI.—VICTORIOUS MEN OF EARTH

This little moral sonnet hath such a pointed application to the heroes of the foregoing and following ballads, that I cannot help placing it here, though the date of its composition is of a much later period. It is extracted from *Cupid and Death, a masque*, by J. S. [James Shirley], presented March 26, 1653. London, printed 1653, 4to.

VICTORIOUS men of earth, no more
  Proclaim how wide your empires are;
Though you binde in every shore,
  And your triumphs reach as far
    As night or day;
Yet you proud monarchs must obey,
And mingle with forgotten ashes, when
Death calls yee to the croud of common men.

Devouring famine, plague, and war,
  Each able to undo mankind,
Death's servile emissaries are:
  Nor to these alone confin'd,
    He hath at will
More quaint and subtle wayes to kill;
A smile or kiss, as he will use the art,
Shall have the cunning skill to break a heart.

## XXII.—THE WINNING OF CALES.

The subject of this ballad is the taking of the city of *Cadiz* (called by our sailors corruptly *Cales*) on June 21, 1596, in a descent made on the coast of Spain, under the command of the Lord Howard, admiral, and the Earl of Essex, general.

The valour of Essex was not more distinguished on this occasion than his generosity: the town was carried sword in hand, but he stopped the slaughter as soon as possible, and treated his prisoners with the greatest humanity, and even affability and kindness. The English made a rich plunder in the city, but missed of a much richer, by the resolution which the Duke of Medina, the Spanish admiral, took, of setting fire to the ships, in order to prevent their falling into the hands of the enemy. It was computed that the loss which the Spaniards sustained from this enterprise amounted to twenty millions of ducats. See Hume's *History*.

The Earl of Essex knighted on this occasion not fewer than sixty persons, which gave rise to the following sarcasm:

> "A gentleman of Wales, a knight of Cales,
> And a laird of the north country;
> But a yeoman of Kent with his yearly rent
> Will buy them out all three."

The ballad is printed, with some corrections, from the Editor's folio MS., and seems to have been composed by some person who was concerned in the expedition. Most of the circumstances related in it will be found supported by history.

Long the proud Spaniards had vaunted to conquer us,
Threatning our country with fyer and sword;
Often preparing their navy most sumptuous
With as great plenty as Spain could afford.
    Dub a dub, dub a dub, thus strike their drums:
    Tantara, tantara, the Englishman comes.

To the seas presentlye went our lord admiral,
With knights couragious and captains full good;
The brave Earl of Essex, a prosperous general,
With him prepared to pass the salt flood.
    Dub a dub, etc.

At Plymouth speedilye, took they ship valiantlye,
Braver ships never were seen under sayle,
With their fair colours spread, and streamers ore their head,
Now bragging Spaniards, take heed of your tayle,
    Dub a dub, etc.

Unto Cales cunninglye, came we most speedilye,
Where the kinges navy securelye did ryde;
Being upon their backs, piercing their butts of sacks,
Ere any Spaniards our coming descryde.
    Dub a dub, etc.

Great was the crying, the running and ryding,
Which at that season was made in that place;

The beacons were fyred, as need then required;
  To hyde their great treasure they had little space.
    Dub a dub, etc.

There you might see their ships, how they were fyred fast,
  And how their men drowned themselves in the sea;
There might you hear them cry, wayle and weep piteously,
  When they saw no shift to scape thence away.
    Dub a dub, etc.

The great St. Phillip, the pryde of the Spaniards,
  Was burnt to the bottom, and sunk in the sea;
But the St. Andrew, and eke the St. Matthew,
  Wee took in fight manfullye and brought away.
    Dub a dub, etc.

The Earl of Essex most valiant and hardye,
  With horsemen and footmen marched up to the town;
The Spanyards, which saw them, were greatly alarmed,
  Did fly for their savegard, and durst not come down.
    Dub a dub, etc.

Now, quoth the noble Earl, courage my soldiers all,
  Fight and be valiant, the spoil you shall have;
And be well rewarded all from the great to the small;
  But looke that the women and children you save.
    Dub a dub, etc.

The Spaniards at that sight, thinking it vain to fight,
  Hung upp flags of truce and yielded the towne;

Wee marched in presentlye, decking the walls on hye,
  With English colours which purchased renowne.
    Dub a dub, etc.

Entering the houses then, of the most richest men,
  For gold and treasure we searched eche day;
In some places we did find, pyes baking left behind,
  Meate at fire rosting, and folkes run away.
    Dub a dub, etc.

Full of rich merchandize, every shop catched our eyes,
  Damasks and sattens and velvets full fayre;
Which soldiers measur'd out by the length of their swords;
  Of all commodities eche had a share.
    Dub a dub, etc.

Thus Cales was taken, and our brave general
  March'd to the market-place, where he did stand:
There many prisoners fell to our several shares,
  Many crav'd mercye, and mercye they fannd.
    Dub a dub, etc.

When our brave General saw they delayed all,
  And wold not ransome their towne as they said,
With their fair wanscots, their presses and bedsteds,
  Their joint-stools and tables a fire we made;
    And when the town burned all in flame,
  With tara, tantara, away wee all came.

## XXIII.—THE SPANISH LADY'S LOVE.

This beautiful old ballad most probably took its rise from one of those descents made on the Spanish coasts in the time of Queen Elizabeth, and in all likelihood from that which is celebrated in the foregoing ballad.

It was a tradition in the west of England, that the person admired by the Spanish lady was a gentleman of the Popham family, and that her picture, with the pearl necklace mentioned in the ballad, was not many years ago preserved at Littlecot, near Hungerford, Wilts, the seat of that respectable family.

Another tradition hath pointed out Sir Richard Leveson, of Trentham, in Staffordshire, as the subject of this ballad, who married Margaret, daughter of Charles, Earl of Nottingham, and was eminently distinguished as a naval officer and commander in all the expeditions against the Spaniards in the latter end of Queen Elizabeth's reign, particularly in that to Cadiz in 1596, when he was aged 27. He died in 1605, and has a monument, with his effigy in brass, in Wolverhampton church.

It is printed from an ancient black-letter copy, corrected in part by the Editor's folio MS.

Will you hear a Spanish lady,
   How shee wooed an English man?
Garments gay as rich as may be
   Decked with jewels she had on.
Of a comely countenance and grace was she,
And by birth and parentage of high degree.

As his prisoner there he kept her,
   In his hands her life did lye;
Cupid's bands did tye them faster
   By the liking of an eye.
In his courteous company was all her joy,
To favour him in any thing she was not coy.

But at last there came commandment
   For to set the ladies free,
With their jewels still adorned,
   None to do them injury.
Then said this lady mild, Full woe is me;
O let me still sustain this kind captivity!

Gallant captain, shew some pity
   To a ladye in distresse;
Leave me not within this city,
   For to dye in heavinesse:
Thou hast set this present day my body free,
But my heart in prison still remains with thee.

"How should'st thou, fair lady, love me,
   Whom thou knowst thy country's foe?
Thy fair wordes make me suspect thee:
   Serpents lie where flowers grow."
All the harm I wishe to thee, most courteous knight,
God grant the same upon my head may fully light.

Blessed be the time and season,
   That you came on Spanish ground;
If our foes you may be termed,
   Gentle foes we have you found:
With our city, you have won our hearts eche one,
Then to your country bear away, that is your owne.

"Rest you still, most gallant lady;
   Rest you still, and weep no more;
Of fair lovers there is plenty,
   Spain doth yield a wonderous store."

Spaniards fraught with jealousy we often
    find,
But Englishmen through all the world are
    counted kind.

Leave me not unto a Spaniard,
    You alone enjoy my heart ;
I am lovely, young, and tender,
    Love is likewise my desert :
Still to serve thee day and night my mind
    is prest ;
The wife of every Englishman is counted
    blest.

"It wold be a shame, fair lady,
    For to bear a woman hence ;
English soldiers never carry
    Any such without offence."
I'll quickly change myself, if it be so,
And like a page Ile follow thee, where'er
    thou go.

"I have neither gold nor silver
    To maintain thee in this case,
And to travel is great charges,
    As you know in every place."
My chains and jewels every one shal be
    thy own,
And eke five hundred pounds in gold that
    lies unknown.

"On the seas are many dangers,
    Many storms do there arise,
Which wil be to ladies dreadful,
    And force tears from watery eyes."
Well in troth I shall endure extremity,
For I could find in heart to lose my life
    for thee.

"Courteous ladye, leave this fancy,
    Here comes all that breeds the strife ;
I in England have already
    A sweet woman to my wife :
I will not falsify my vow for gold nor
    gain,
Nor yet for all the fairest dames that live
    in Spain."

O how happy is that woman
    That enjoys so true a friend !
Many happy days God send her ;
    Of my suit I make an end :
On my knees I pardon crave for my
    offence,
Which did from love and true affection
    first commence.

Commend me to thy lovely lady,
    Bear to her this chain of gold ;
And these bracelets for a token ;
    Grieving that I was so bold :
All my jewels in like sort take thou with
    thee,
For they are fitting for thy wife, but not
    for me.

I will spend my days in prayer,
    Love and all her laws defye ;
In a nunnery will I shroud mee
    Far from any companye :
But ere my prayers have an end, be sure
    of this,
To pray for thee and for thy love I will
    not miss.

Thus farewell, most gallant captain !
    Farewell too my heart's content !
Count not Spanish ladies wanton,
    Though to thee my love was bent :
Joy and true prosperity goe still with thee !
"The like fall ever to thy share, most
    fair ladie."

## XXIV.—ARGENTILE AND CURAN

Is extracted from an ancient historical poem in thirteen books, entitled, *Albion's England*, by William Warner.

The story of *Argentile and Curan* is, I believe, the poet's own invention; it is not mentioned in any of our chronicles. It was, however, so much admired, that not many years after he published it, came out a larger poem on the same subject in stanzas of six lines, entitled, *The most pleasant and delightful historie of Curan, a prince of Danske, and the fayre princesse Argentile, daughter and heyre to Adelbright, sometime king of Northumberland*, etc., by William Webster, London 1617, in eight sheets 4to. An indifferent paraphrase of the following poem.

Though here subdivided into stanzas, Warner's metre is the old-fashioned Alexandrine of fourteen syllables. The reader therefore must not expect to find the close of the stanzas consulted in the pauses.

THE Bruton's "being" departed hence
  Seaven kingdoms here begonne,
Where diversly in divers broyles
  The Saxons lost and wonne.

King Edel and king Adelbright
  In Diria jointly raigne;
In loyal concorde during life
  These kingly friends remaine.

When Adelbright should leave his life,
  To Edel thus he sayes;
By those same bondes of happie love,
  That held us friends alwaies;

By our *by-parted* crowne, of which
  The moyetie is mine;
By God, to whom my soule must passe,
  And so in time may thine;

I pray thee, nay I cònjure thee,
  To nourish, as thine owne,
Thy niece, my daughter Argentile,
  Till she to age be growne;
And then, as thou receivest it,
  Resigne to her my throne.

A promise had for his bequest,
  The testatòr he dies;
But all that Edel undertooke,
  He afterwards denies.

Yet while he "fosters for" a time
  The damsell that was growne
The fairest lady under heaven;
  Whose beautie being knowne,

A many princes seeke her love;
  But none might her obtaine;
For *grippell* Edel to himselfe
  Her kingdome sought to gaine;
And for that cause from sight of such
  He did his ward restraine.

By chance one Curan, sonne unto
  A prince in Danske, did see
The maid, with whom he fell in love,
  As much as man might bee.

Unhappie youth, what should he doe?
  His saint was *kept in mewe;*
Nor he, nor any nobleman
  Admitted to her vewe.

One while in melancholy fits
  He pines himselfe awaye;
Anon he thought by force of arms
  To win her if he maye:

And still against the kings restraint
  Did secretly invay.
At length the high controller Love,
  Whom none may disobay,

*Imbased* him from lordlines
  Into a kitchen drudge,
That so at least of life or death
  She might become his judge.

Accesse so had to see and speake,
  He did his love bewray,
And tells his birth : her answer was,
  She husbandles would stay.

Meane while the king did beate his
    braines,
  His booty to atchieve,
Nor caring what became of her,
  So he by her might thrive ;
At last his resolution was
  Some pessant should her wive.

And (which was working to his wish)
  He did observe with joye
How Curan, whom he thought a drudge,
  Scapt many an amorous toye.*

The king, perceiving such his veine,
  Promotes his vassal still,
Lest that the basenesse of the man
  Should lett, perhaps, his will.

Assured therefore of his love,
  But not suspecting who
The lover was, the king himselfe
  In his behalf did woe.

The lady resolute from love,
  Unkindly takes that he
Should barre the noble, and unto
  So base a match agree :

And therefore shifting out of doores,
  Departed thence by stealth ;
Preferring povertie before
  A dangerous life in wealth.

When Curan heard of her escape,
  The anguish in his hart

---

\* The construction is, "How that many an amorous toy, or foolery of love, 'scaped Curan," *i.e.* escaped from him, being off his guard.

Was more than much, and after her
  From court he did depart ;

Forgetfull of himselfe, his birth,
  His country, friends, and all,
And only minding (whom he mist)
  The foundresse of his thrall.

Nor meanes he after to frequent
  Or court, or stately townes,
But solitarily to live
  Amongst the country grownes.

A brace of years he lived thus,
  Well pleased so to live,
And shepherd-like to feed a flocke
  Himselfe did wholly give.

So wasting, love, by worke, and want,
  Grew almost to the waine :
But then began a second love,
  The worser of the twaine.

A country wench, a neatherds maid,
  Where Curan kept his sheepe,
Did feed her drove : and now on her
  Was all the shepherds keepe.

He *borrowed* on the working daies
  His holy russets* oft,
And of the bacon's fat, to make
  His *startops* blacke and soft.

And least his tarbox should offend,
  He left it at the folde :
Sweete *growte*, or *whig*, his bottle had,
  As much as it might holde.

A sheeve of bread as browne as nut,
  And cheese as white as snow,
And *wildings*, or the seasons fruit
  He did in scrip bestow.

And whilst his py-bald curre did sleepe,
  And sheep-hooke lay him by,
On hollow quilles of oten straw
  He piped melody.

---

\* *i.e.* holy-day russets.

But when he spyed her his saint,
   He wip'd his greasie shooes,
And clear'd the drivell from his beard,
   And thus the shepheard wooes.

"I have, sweet wench, a peece of cheese,
   As good as tooth may chawe,
And bread and wildings souling well,
   (And therewithall did drawe

"His lardrie) and in 'yeaning' see
   Yon crumpling ewe, quoth he,
Did twinne this fall, and twin shouldst thou,
   If I might tup with thee.

"Thou art too elvish, faith thou art,
   Too elvish and too coy:
Am I, I pray thee, beggarly,
   That such a flocke enjoy?

"I wis I am not: yet that thou
   Doest hold me in disdaine
Is *brimme* abroad, and made a gybe
   To all that keepe this plaine.

"There be as *quaint* (at least that thinke
   Themselves as quaint) that crave
The match, that thou, I wot not why,
   Maist, but mislik'st to have.

"How wouldst thou match? (for well I wot,
   Thou art a female) I,
Her know not here that willingly
   With maiden-head would die.

"The plowmans labour hath no end,
   And he a churle will prove:
The craftsman hath more worke in hand
   Then fitteth unto love:

"The merchant, traffiquing abroad,
   Suspects his wife at home:
A youth will play the wanton; and
   An old man prove a *mome*.

"Then chuse a shepheard: with the sun
   He doth his flocke unfold,
And all the day on hill or plaine
   He merrie chat can hold;

"And with the sun doth folde againe;
   Then jogging home betime,
He turnes a crab,* or turnes a round,
   Or sings some merry ryme.

"Nor lacks he gleefull tales, whilst round
   The nut-brown bowl doth trot;
And sitteth singing care away,
   Till he to bed be got:

"Theare sleepes he soundly all the night,
   Forgetting morrow-cares:
Nor feares he blasting of his corne,
   Nor uttering of his wares;

"Or stormes by seas, or stirres on land,
   Or cracke of credit lost:
Not spending franklier than his flocke
   Shall still defray the cost.

"Well wot I, sooth they say, that say
   More quiet nights and daies
The shepheard sleeps and wakes, than he
   Whose cattel he doth graize.

"Beleeve me, lasse, a king is but
   A man, and so am I:
Content is worth a monarchie,
   And mischiefs hit the hie;

"As late it did a king and his
   Not dwelling far from hence,
Who left a daughter, save thyselfe,
   For faire a matchless wench."—
Here did he pause, as if his tongue
   Had done his heart offence.

The *neatresse*, longing for the rest,
   Did egge him on to tell
How faire she was, and who she was.
   "She bore, quoth he, the bell

---

* *i.e.* roasts a crab or apple.

"For beautie: though I clownish am,
  I know what beautie is;
Or did I not, at seeing thee,
  I senceles were to mis.

 . . . . . . .

"Her stature comely, tall; her gate
  Well graced; and her wit
To marvell at, not meddle with,
  As matchless I omit.

"A globe-like head, a gold-like haire,
  A forehead smooth, and hie,
An even nose; on either side
  Did shine a grayish eie:

"Two rosie cheeks, round ruddy lips,
  White just-set teeth within;
A mouth in meane; and underneathe
  A round and dimpled chin.

"Her snowie necke, with blewish veines,
  Stood bolt upright upon
Her portly shoulders: beating balles
  Her veined breasts, anon

"Adde more to beautie. Wand-like was
  Her middle falling still,
And rising whereas women rise:
  —Imagine nothing ill.

"And more, her long, and limber armes
  Had white and azure wrists;
And slender fingers aunswere to
  Her smooth and lillie fists.

"A legge in print, a pretie foot;
  Conjecture of the rest:
For amorous eies, observing forme,
  Think parts obscured best.

"With these, O raretie! with these
  Her tong of speech was spare;
But speaking, Venus seem'd to speake,
  The balle from Ide to bear.

"With Phœbe, Juno, and with both
  Herselfe contends in face;
Wheare equall mixture did not want
  Of milde and stately grace.

"Her smiles were sober, and her lookes
  Were chearefull unto all:
Even such as neither wanton seeme,
  Nor waiward; mell, nor gall.

"A quiet minde, a patient moode,
  And not disdaining any;
Not gybing, gadding, gawdy: and
  Sweete faculties had many.

"A nimph, no tong, no heart, no eie,
  Might praise, might wish, might see;
For life, for love, for forme; more good,
  More worth, more faire than shee.

"Yea such an one, as such was none,
  Save only she was such:
Of Argentile to say the most,
  Were to be silent much."

I knew the lady very well,
  But worthles of such praise,
The neatresse said: and muse I do,
  A shepheard thus should blaze
The "coate" of beautie.* Credit me,
  Thy latter speech bewraies

Thy clownish shape a coined shew.
  But wherefore dost thou weepe?
The shepheard wept, and she was woe,
  And both doe silence keepe.

"In troth, quoth he, I am not such,
  As seeming I professe;
But then for her, and now for thee,
  I from myselfe digresse.

"Her loved I (wretch that I am
  A recreant to be),
I loved her, that hated love,
  But now I die for thee.

"At Kirkland is my fathers court,
  And Curan is my name,
In Edels court sometimes in pompe,
  Till love countrould the same:

---

* *i.e.* emblazon beauty's coat.

"But now—what now?—deare heart, how now?
 What ailest thou to weepe?"
The damsell wept, and he was woe,
 And both did silence keepe.

I graunt, quoth she, it was too much,
 That you did love so much:
But whom your former could not move,
 Your second love doth touch.

Thy twice-beloved Argentile
 Submitteth her to thee,
And for thy double love presents
 Herself a single fee,
In passion not in person chang'd,
 And I, my lord, am she.

They sweetly surfeiting in joy,
 And silent for a space,
When as the extasie had end,
 Did tenderly imbrace;
And for their wedding, and their wish
 Got fitting time and place.

Not England (for of Hengist then
 Was named so this land)
Then Curan had an hardier knight;
 His force could none withstand:
Whose sheep-hooke laid apart, he then
 Had higher things in hand.

First, making knowne his lawfull claime
 In Argentile her right,
He warr'd in Diria,* and he wonne
 Bernicia* too in fight:

And so from trecherous Edel tooke
 At once his life and crowne,
And of Northumberland was king,
 Long raigning in renowne.

---

## XXV.—CORIN'S FATE.

ONLY the three first stanzas of this song are ancient; these are extracted from a small quarto MS. in the Editor's possession, written in the time of Queen Elizabeth. As they seem to want application, this has been attempted by a modern hand.

CORIN, most unhappie swaine,
 Whither wilt thou drive thy flocke?
Little foode is on the plaine;
 Full of danger is the rocke:

Wolfes and beares doe kepe the woodes;
 Forests tangled are with brakes:
Meadowes subject are to floodes;
 Moores are full of miry lakes.

Yet to shun all plaine, and hill,
 Forest, moore, and meadow-ground,
Hunger will as surely kill:
 How may then reliefe be found?

Such is hapless Corins fate:
 Since my waywarde love begunne,
Equall doubts begett debate
 What to seeke, and what to shunne.

Spare to speke, and spare to speed;
 Yet to speke will move disdaine:
If I see her not I bleed,
 Yet her sight augments my paine.

What may then poor Corin doe?
 Tell me, shepherdes, quicklye tell;
For to linger thus in woe
 Is the lover's sharpest hell.

---

* During the Saxon heptarchy, the kingdom of Northumberland (consisting of six northern counties, besides part of Scotland) was for a long time divided into two lesser sovereignties, viz. Deira (called here Diria), which contained the southern parts, and Bernicia, comprehending those which lay north.

## XXVI.—JANE SHORE,

The wife of one Shore, a goldsmith in Lombard Street, and the beautiful mistress of Edward the Fourth, of whom Sir Thomas More says: "Proper she was and faire, nothing in her body that you would have changed, but if you would have wished her somewhat higher. Yet delighted not men so much in her bewty as in her pleasant behaviour. For a proper wit had she, and could both rede wel and write; mery in company, ready and wick of answer, neither mute nor ful of bable; sometimes taunting without displeasure, and not without disport." The king said of all his favourites "the meriest was the Shore's wife, in whom the king therefore toke special pleasure." "For many," goes on More, "he had, but her he loved whose favour, to sai the trouth (for sinne it were to belie the devil), she never abused to any man's hurt, but to many a man's comfort and relief. Where the king toke displeasure, she would mitigate and appease his mind : where men were out of favour she would bring them in his grace : for many that had highly offended shee obtained pardon."

In fact, though sinful and erring herself, she was of kind and generous spirit, and extended her charity to all who stood in need of it.

All this More wrote thirty years after the death of Edward the Fourth, and long after Jane Shore had done open penance in St. Paul's Churchyard by command of Richard the Third, whose anger against her was not so much aroused by her sins as by the kindness and partiality she and Lord Hastings—to whom she became attached after the death of her royal lover—entertained for the young princes. Hastings was beheaded and Jane did penance, but by her beauty won more compassion than Richard won commendation, though none dared to bestow any charity upon her.

Drayton describes her as meane (short) of stature, "her haire of a dark yellow, her face round and full, her eye gray, delicate harmony being betwixt each parts proportion and each proportion's colour, her body fat, white, and smooth, her countenance cheerfull and like to her condition." But the days of her youth and pleasure passed away, and in the reign of Henry the Eighth, More says she was "lene, withered, and dried up, and nothing left but ryvilde skin and bone"—that "at this daye shee beggeth of many at this daye living."

There is an original picture of Jane Shore at the Provost's Lodgings at Eton, and another is in the Provost's Lodge at King's College, Cambridge, to both of which foundations she is supposed to have done friendly offices with Edward the Fourth.

To every stanza is annexed the following burthen :

"Then maids and wives in time amend,
For love and beauty will have end."

If Rosamonde that was so faire,
Had cause her sorrowes to declare,
Then let Jane Shore with sorrowe sing,
That was beloved of a king.

In maiden yeares my beautye bright
Was loved dear of lord and knight ;

But yet the love that they requir'd,
It was not as my friends desir'd.

My parents they, for thirst of gaine,
A husband for me did obtaine ;
And I, their pleasure to fulfille,
Was forc'd to wedd against my wille.

To Matthew Shore I was a wife,
Till lust brought ruin to my life;
And then my life I lewdlye spent,
Which makes my soul for to lament.

In Lombard-street I once did dwelle,
As London yet can witness welle;
Where many gallants did beholde
My beautye in a shop of golde.

I spred my plumes, as wantons doe,
Some sweet and secret friende to wooe,
Because chast love I did not finde
Agreeing to my wanton minde.

At last my name in court did ring
Into the eares of Englandes king,
Who came and lik'd, and love requir'd,
But I made coye what he desir'd:

Yet Mistress Blague, a neighbour neare,
Whose friendship I esteemed deare,
Did saye, It was a gallant thing
To be beloved of a king.

By her persuasions I was led
For to defile my marriage-bed,
And wronge my wedded husband Shore,
Whom I had married yeares before.

In heart and mind I did rejoyce,
That I had made so sweet a choice;
And therefore did my state resigne,
To be king Edward's concubine.

From city then to court I went,
To reape the pleasures of content;
There had the joyes that love could bring,
And knew the secrets of a king.

When I was thus advanc'd on highe,
Commanding Edward with mine eye,
For Mrs. Blague I in short space
Obtainde a livinge from his grace.

No friende I had but in short time
I made unto a promotion climbe;
But yet for all this costlye pride,
My husbande could not mee abide.

His bed, though wronged by a king,
His heart with deadlye griefe did sting;
From England then he goes away
To end his life beyond the sea.

He could not live to see his name
Impaired by my wanton shame;
Although a prince of peerlesse might
Did reape the pleasure of his right.

Long time I lived in the courte,
With lords and ladies of great sorte;
And when I smil'd all men were glad,
But when I frown'd my prince grewe sad.

But yet a gentle minde I bore
To helplesse people, that were poore;
I still redrest the orphans crye,
And sav'd their lives condemnd to dye.

I still had ruth on widowes tears,
I succour'd babes of tender yeares;
And never look'd for other gaine
But love and thankes for all my paine.

At last my royall king did dye,
And then my dayes of woe grew nighe;
When crook-back Richard got the crowne,
King Edwards friends were soon put downe.

I then was punisht for my sin,
That I so long had lived in;
Yea, every one that was his friend,
This tyrant brought to shamefull end.

Then for my lewd and wanton life,
That made a strumpet of a wife,
I penance did in Lombard-street,
In shamefull manner in a sheet.

Where many thousands did me viewe,
Who late in court my credit knewe;
Which made the teares run down my face,
To thinke upon my foul disgrace.

Not thus content, they took from mee
My goodes, my livings, and my fee,
And charg'd that none should me relieve,
Nor any succour to me give.

Then unto Mrs. Blague I went,
To whom my jewels I had sent,
In hope therebye to ease my want,
When riches fail'd, and love grew scant:

But she denyed to me the same,
When in my need for them I came;
To recompence my former love,
Out of her doores shee did me shove.

So love did vanish with my state,
Which now my soul repents too late;
Therefore example take by mee,
For friendship parts in povertie.

But yet one friend among the rest,
Whom I before had seen distrest,
And sav'd his life, condemn'd to die,
Did give me food to succour me:

For which, by lawe, it was decreed
That he was hanged for that deed;
His death did grieve me so much more,
Than had I dyed myself therefore.

Then those to whom I had done good,
Durst not afford mee any food;
Whereby I begged all the day,
And still in streets by night I lay.

My gowns beset with pearl and gold,
Were turn'd to simple garments old;
My chains and gems and golden rings,
To filthy rags and loathsome things.

Thus was I scorn'd of maid and wife,
For leading such a wicked life;
Both sucking babes and children small,
Did make their pastime at my fall.

I could not get one bit of bread,
Whereby my hunger might be fed:
Nor drink, but such as channels yield,
Or stinking ditches in the field.

Thus, weary of my life, at lengthe
I yielded up my vital strength
Within a ditch of loathsome scent,
Where carrion dogs did much frequent:

The which now since my dying daye,
Is Shoreditch call'd, as writers saye;*
Which is a witness of my sinne,
For being concubine to a king.

You wanton wives, that fall to lust,
Be you assur'd that God is just;
Whoredome shall not escape his hand,
Nor pride unpunish'd in this land.

If God to me such shame did bring,
That yielded only to a king,
How shall they scape that daily run
To practise sin with every one?

You husbands, match not but for love,
Lest some disliking after prove;
Women, be warn'd when you are wives,
What plagues are due to sinful lives:
   Then, maids and wives, in time amend,
   For love and beauty will have end.

---

* But it had this name long before, being so called from its being a common sewer (**vulgarly** *shore*) or drain. See Stow.

## XXVII.—CORYDON'S DOLEFUL KNELL.

This little simple elegy is given, with some corrections, from two copies, one of which is in *The golden garland of princely delights.*

My Phillida, adieu love!
  For evermore farewel!
Ay me! I've lost my true love,
  And thus I ring her knell,
    Ding dong, ding dong, ding dong,
    My Phillida is dead!
  I'll stick a branch of willow
  At my fair Phillis' head.

For my fair Phillida
  Our bridal bed was made:
But 'stead of silkes so gay,
  She in her shroud is laid.
    Ding, etc.

Her corpse shall be attended
  By maides in fair array,
Till the obsequies are ended,
  And she is wrapt in clay.
    Ding, etc.

Her herse it shall be carried
  By youths, that do excell;
And when that she is buried,
  I thus will ring her knell,
    Ding, etc.

A garland shall be framed
  By art and natures skill,
Of sundry-colour'd flowers,
  In token of good-will.*
    Ding, etc.

And sundry-colour'd ribbands
  On it I will bestow;
But chiefly black and yellowe:
  With her to grave shall go.
    Ding, etc.

I'll decke her tomb with flowers,
  The rarest ever seen,
And with my tears, as showers,
  I'll keepe them fresh and green.
    Ding, etc.

Instead of fairest colours,
  Set forth with curious art,*
Her image shall be painted
  On my distressed heart.
    Ding, etc.

And thereon shall be graven
  Her epitaph so faire,
"Here lies the loveliest maiden,
  That e'er gave shepheard care."
    Ding, etc.

In sable will I mourne;
  Blacke shall be all my weede:
Ay me! I am forlorne,
  Now Phillida is dead!
    Ding dong, ding dong, ding dong,
    My Phillida is dead!
  I'll stick a branch of willow
  At my fair Phillis' head.

---

\* It is a custom in many parts of England to carry a flowery garland before the corpse of a woman who dies unmarried.

\* This alludes to the painted effigies of alabaster, anciently erected upon tombs and monuments.

**THE END OF THE SECOND BOOK.**

# SERIES THE SECOND.—BOOK III.

## I.—THE COMPLAINT OF CONSCIENCE.

I SHALL begin this Third Book with an old allegoric satire, entitled *The Complaint of Conscience*—a manner of moralizing which, if it was not first introduced by the author of *Pierce Plowman's Visions*, was at least chiefly brought into repute by that ancient satirist. The kind of verse used in this ballad has a strong affinity with the peculiar metre of that writer.

The following song, entitled *The Complaint of Conscience*, is printed from the Editor's folio manuscript. Some corruptions in the old copy are here corrected; the corrections are placed between inverted "commas."

As I walked of late by "an" wood side,
To God for to meditate was my entent;
Where under a hawthorne I suddenlye
    spyed
A silly poor creature ragged and rent,
With bloody teares his face was *besprent*,
    His fleshe and his color consumed
        away,
    And his garments they were all mire,
        mucke, and clay.

This made me muse, and much "to"
    desire
To know what kind of man hee shold bee;
I stept to him straight, and did him
    require
His name and his secretts to shew unto
    mee.
His head he cast up, and wooful was hee,
    My name, quoth he, is the cause of my
        care,
    And makes me scorned, and left here
        so bare.

Then straightway he turnd him, and
    prayd "me" sit downe,
And I will, saithe he, declare my whole
    greefe;
My name is called Conscience :—wheratt
    he did frowne,

He pined to repeate it, and grinded his
    teethe,
" Thoughe now, silly wretche, I'm denyed
    all releef,"
" Yet" while I was young, and tender
    of yeeres,
    I was entertained with kinges, and with
        peeres.

There was none in the court that lived in
    such fame,
For with the kings councell " I " sate in
    commission;
Dukes, earles, and barrons esteem'd of
    my name;
And how that I liv'd there needs no re-
    petition:
I was ever holden in honest condition,
    For howsoever the lawes went in West-
        minster-hall,
    When sentence was given, for me they
        wold call.

No incomes at all the landlords wold take,
But one pore peny, that was their fine;
And that they acknowledged to be for
    my sake.
The poore wold doe nothing without
    councell mine:
I ruled the world with the right line:

For nothing was passed betweene foe
  and friend,
  But Conscience was called to bee at
  "the" end.

Noe bargaines, nor merchandize mer-
  chants wold make
But I was called a witnesse therto:
No use for noe money, nor forfett wold
  take,
But I wold controule them, if that they
  did soe:
"And" that makes me live now in great
  woe,
  For then came in Pride, Sathan's
    disciple,
  That is now entertained with all kind
    of people.

He brought with him three, whose names
  "thus they call,"
That is Covetousnes, Lecherye, Usury,
  beside:
They never prevail'd, till they had wrought
  my downe-fall;
Soe Pride was entertained, but Conscience
  decried,
And "now ever since" abroad have I
  tryed
  To have had entertainment with some
    one or other;
  But I am rejected, and scorned of my
    brother.

Then went I to the Court the gallants to
  winn,
But the porter kept me out of the gate:
To Bartlemew Spittle to pray for my
  sinne,
They bade me goe packe, it was fitt for
  my state;
Goe, goe, threed-bare Conscience, and
  seeke thee a mate.
  Good Lord, long preserve my king,
    prince, and queene,
  With whom evermore I esteemed have
    been.

Then went I to London, where once I did
  "dwell:"
But they bade away with me, when they
  knew my name;
For he will undoe us to bye and to sell!
They bade me goe packe me, and hye
  me for shame:
They lought at my raggs, and there had
  good game;
  This is old threed-bare Conscience,
    that dwelt with saint Peter:
  But they wold not admitt me to be a
    chimney-sweeper.

Not one wold receive me, the Lord "he"
  doth know;
I having but one poor pennye in my
  purse,
On an awle and some patches I did it
  bestow;
"For" I thought better cobble shooes
  than doe worse.
Straight then all the coblers began for to
  curse,
  And by statute wold prove me a rogue,
    and forlorne,
  And whipp me out of towne to
    "seeke" where I was borne.

Then did I remember, and call to my
  minde,
The Court of Conscience where once I
  did sit:
Not doubting but there I some favor
  shold find,
For my name and the place agreed soe
  fit;
But there of my purpose I fayled a whit,
  For "thoughe" the judge us'd my
    name in everye "commission,"
  The lawyers with their quillets wold
    get "my" dismission.

Then Westminster-hall was noe place for
  me;
Good Lord! how the lawyers began to
  assemble,

And fearfull they were, lest there I shold bee!
The silly poore clarkes began for to tremble;
I showed them my cause, and did not dissemble;
  Soe they gave me some money my charges to beare,
  But swore me on a booke I must never come there.

Next the Merchants said, Counterfeite get thee away,
Dost thou remember how wee thee fond?
We banisht thee the country beyond the salt sea,
And sett thee on shore in the New-found land;
And there thou and wee most friendly shook hand,
  And we were right glad when thou didst refuse us;
  For when we wold reape profitt here thou woldst accuse us.

Then had I noe way, but for to goe on
To Gentlemens houses of an ancyent name;
Declaring my greeffes, and there I made moane,
"Telling" how their forefathers held me in fame:
And at letting their farmes "how always I came."
  They sayd, Fye upon thee! we may thee curse:
  "Theire" leases continue, and we fare the worse.

And then I was forced a begging to goe
To husbandmens houses who greeved right sore,
And sware that their landlords had plagued them so,
That they were not able to keepe open doore,
Nor nothing had left to give to the poore:
Therefore to this wood I doe me repayre,
Where hepps and hawes, that is my best fare.

Yet within this same desert some comfort I have
Of Mercy, of Pittye, and of Almes-deeds;
Who have vowed to company me to my grave.
Wee are "all" put to silence, and live upon weeds,
"And hence such cold house-keeping proceeds;"
  Our banishment is its utter decay,
  The which the riche glutton will answer one day.

Why then, I said to him, methinks it were best
To goe to the Clergie; for dailye they preach
Eche man to love you above all the rest;
Of Mercye, and Pittie, and Almes-"deeds," they teach.
O, said he, noe matter of a pin what they preach,
  For their wives and their children soe hange them upon,
  That whosoever gives almes they will* give none.

Then laid he him down, and turned him away,
And prayd me to goe, and leave him to rest.
I told him, I haplie might yet see the day
For him and his fellowes to live with the best.
First, said he, banish Pride, then all England were blest;
  For then those wold love us, that now sell their land,
  And then good "house-keeping wold revive" out of hand.

---

* We ought in justice and truth to read *can*.

## II.—PLAIN TRUTH AND BLIND IGNORANCE.

This excellent old ballad is preserved in the little ancient miscellany, entitled *The Garland of Goodwill*. Ignorance is here made to speak in the broad Somersetshire dialect. The scene we may suppose to be Glastonbury Abbey.

### TRUTH.

God speed you, ancient father,
   And give you a good daye;
What is the cause, I praye you,
   So sadly here you staye?
And that you keep such gazing
   On this decayed place,
The which, for superstition,
   Good princes down did raze?

### IGNORANCE.

*Chill* tell thee, by my *vazen*,*
   That zometimes che have knowne
A vair and goodly abbey
   Stand here of bricke and stone;
And many a holy vrier,
   As ich may say to thee,
Within these goodly cloysters
   Che did full often zee.

### TRUTH.

Then I must tell thee, father,
   In truthe and veritiè,
A sorte of greater hypocrites
   Thou couldst not likely see;
Deceiving of the simple
   With false and feigned lies:
But such an order truly
   Christ never did devise.

### IGNORANCE.

Ah! ah! *che* zmell thee now, man;
   Che know well what thou art;
A vellow of mean learning,
   Thee was not worth a vart:

---

\* *i.e.* faithen; as in the Midland counties they say *housen*, *closen*, for houses, closes.

Vor when we had the old lawe,
   A merry world was then;
And every thing was plenty
   Among all zorts of men.

### TRUTH.

Thou givest me an answer,
   As did the Jewes sometimes
Unto the prophet Jeremye,
   When he accused their crimes:
'Twas merry, sayd the people,
   And joyfull in our realme,
When we did offer spice-cakes
   Unto the queen of heav'n.

### IGNORANCE.

Chill tell thee what, good vellowe,
   Before the vriers went hence,
A bushell of the best wheate
   Was zold vor vourteen pence;
And vorty egges a penny,
   That were both good and newe;
And this che zay my zelf have zeene,
   And yet ich am no Jewe.

### TRUTH.

Within the sacred bible
   We find it written plain,
The latter days should troublesome
   And dangerous be, certaine;
That we should be self-lovers,
   And charity wax colde;
Then 'tis not true religion
   That makes thee grief to holde.

### IGNORANCE.

Chill tell thee my opinion plaine,
   And chould that well ye knewe,

Ich care not for the bible booke;
 Tis too big to be true.
Our blessed ladyes psalter
 Zhall for my money goe;
Zuch pretty prayers, as there bee,*
 The bible cannot zhowe.

### TRUTH.

Nowe hast thou spoken trulye,
 For in that book indeede
No mention of our lady
 Or Romish saint we read:
For by the blessed Spirit
 That book indited was,
And not by simple persons,
 As was the foolish masse.

### IGNORANCE.

*Cham* zure they were not voolishe
 That made the masse, che trowe;
Why, man, 'tis all in Latine,
 And vools no Latine knowe.
Were not our fathers wise men,
 And they did like it well;
Who very much rejoyced
 To heare the *zacring* bell?

### TRUTH.

But many kinges and prophets,
 As I may say to thee,
Have wisht the light that you have,
 And could it never see:
For what art thou the better
 A Latin song to heare,
And understandest nothing,
 That they sing in the quiere?

### IGNORANCE.

O hold thy peace, che praye thee,
 The noise was passing trim
To heare the vriers zinging,
 As we did enter in:

And then to zee the rood-loft
 Zo bravely zet with zaints;—
But now to zee them wandring
 My heart with zorrow vaints.

### TRUTH.

The Lord did give commandment,
 No image thou shouldst make,
Nor that unto idolatry
 You should your self betake:
The golden calf of Israel
 Moses did therefore spoile;
And Baal's priests and temple
 Were brought to utter foile.

### IGNORANCE.

But our lady of Walsinghame
 Was a pure and holy zaint,
And many men in pilgrimage
 Did shew to her complaint.
Yea with zweet Thomas Becket,
 And many other moe:
The holy maid of Kent * likewise
 Did many wonders zhowe.

### TRUTH.

Such saints are well agreeing
 To your profession sure;
And to the men that made them
 So precious and so pure;
The one for being a traytoure,
 Met an untimely death;
The other eke for treason
 Did end her hateful breath.

### IGNORANCE.

Yea, yea, it is no matter,
 Dispraise them how you wille:
But zure they did much goodnesse;
 Would they were with us stille!
We had our holy water,
 And holy bread likewise,
And many holy reliques
 We zaw before our eyes.

---

* Probably alluding to the illuminated psalters, missals, etc.

* By name Eliz. Barton, executed April 21, 1534. Stow, p. 570.

| TRUTH. | IGNORANCE. |
|---|---|
| And all this while they fed you<br>  With vain and empty showe,<br>Which never Christ commanded,<br>  As learned doctors knowe:<br>Search then the holy Scriptures,<br>  And thou shalt plainly see<br>That headlong to damnation<br>  They alway trained thee. | If it be true, good vellowe,<br>  As thou dost zay to mee,<br>Unto my heavenly fader<br>  Alone then will I flee:<br>Believing in the Gospel,<br>  And passion of his Zon,<br>And with the zubtil papistes<br>  Ich have for ever done. |

### III.—THE WANDERING JEW.

The story of the Wandering Jew is of considerable antiquity; it had obtained full credit in this part of the world before the year 1228, as we learn from Matthew Paris. For in that year, it seems, there came an Armenian archbishop into England, to visit the shrines and reliques preserved in our churches; who, being entertained at the monastery of St. Albans, was asked several questions relating to his country, etc. Among the rest a monk, who sat near him, inquired "if he had ever seen or heard of the famous person named Joseph, that was so much talked of; who was present at our Lord's crucifixion and conversed with Him, and who was still alive in confirmation of the Christian faith." The archbishop answered, that the fact was true. And afterwards one of his train, who was well known to a servant of the abbot's, interpreting his master's words, told them in French, "that his lord knew the person they spoke of very well; that he had dined at his table but a little time before he left the East; that he had been Pontius Pilate's porter, by name Cartaphilus; who, when they were dragging Jesus out of the door of the judgment-hall, struck him with his fist on the back, saying, 'Go faster, Jesus, go faster; why dost Thou linger?' Upon which Jesus looked at him with a frown, and said, 'I indeed am going, but thou shalt tarry till I come.' Soon after he was converted, and baptized by the name of Joseph. He lives for ever, but at the end of every hundred years falls into an incurable illness, and at length into a fit or ecstasy, out of which when he recovers, he returns to the same state of youth he was in when Jesus suffered, being then about thirty years of age. He remembers all the circumstances of the death and resurrection of Christ, the saints that arose with him, the composing of the apostles' creed, their preaching, and dispersion; and is himself a very grave and holy person." This is the substance of Matthew Paris's account, who was himself a monk of St. Albans, and was living at the time when this Armenian archbishop made the above relation.

Since his time several impostors have appeared at intervals under the name and character of the Wandering Jew, whose several histories may be seen in Calmet's *Dictionary of the Bible*. See also the *Turkish Spy*, vol. ii. Book iii. Let. 1. The story that is copied in the following ballad is of one who appeared at Hamburgh in 1547, and pretended he had been a Jewish shoemaker at the time of Christ's crucifixion.—The ballad, however, seems to be of later date. It is preserved in black letter in the Pepys Collection.

WHEN as in faire Jerusalem
　　Our Saviour Christ did live,
And for the sins of all the worlde
　　His own deare life did give;
The wicked Jewes with scoffes and scornes
　　Did dailye him molest,
That never till he left his life,
　　Our Saviour could not rest.

When they had crown'd his head with thornes,
　　And scourg'd him to disgrace,
In scornfull sort they led him forthe
　　Unto his dying place,
Where thousand thousands in the streete
　　Beheld him passe along,
Yet not one gentle heart was there,
　　That pityed this his wrong.

Both old and young reviled him,
　　As in the streete he wente,
And nought he found but churlish tauntes,
　　By every ones consente :
His owne deare crosse he bore himselfe,
　　A burthen far too great,
Which made him in the street to fainte,
　　With blood and water sweat.

Being weary thus, he sought for rest,
　　To ease his burthened soule,
Upon a stone; the which a wretch
　　Did churlishly controule ;
And sayd, Awaye, thou king of Jewes,
　　Thou shalt not rest thee here;
Pass on; thy execution place
　　Thou seest nowe draweth neare.

And thereupon he thrust him thence ;
　　At which our Saviour sayd,
I sure will rest, but thou shalt walke,
　　And have no journey stayed.
With that this cursed shoemaker,
　　For offering Christ this wrong,
Left wife and children, house and all,
　　And went from thence along.

Where after he had scene the bloude
　　Of Jesus Christ thus shed,
And to the crosse his bodye nail'd,
　　Awaye with speed he fled,
Without returning backe againe
　　Unto his dwelling place,
And wandred up and downe the worlde,
　　A runnagate most base.

No resting could he finde at all,
　　No ease, nor hearts content ;
No house, nor home, nor biding place :
　　But wandring forth he went
From towne to towne in foreigne landes,
　　With grieved conscience still,
Repenting for the heinous guilt
　　Of his fore-passed ill.

Thus after some fewe ages past
　　In wandring up and downe ;
He much again desired to see
　　Jerusalems renowne,
But finding it all quite destroyd,
　　He wandred thence with woe,
Our Saviours wordes, which he had spoke,
　　To verifie and showe.

"I'll rest, sayd hee, but thou shalt walke,"
　　So doth this wandring Jew
From place to place, but cannot rest
　　For seeing countries newe ;
Declaring still the power of him,
　　Whereas he comes or goes,
And of all things done in the east,
　　Since Christ his death, he showes.

The world he hath still compast round
　　And seene those nations strange,
That hearing of the name of Christ,
　　Their idol gods doe change :
To whom he hath told wondrous thinges
　　Of time forepast, and gone,
And to the princes of the worlde
　　Declares his cause of moane :

Desiring still to be dissolv'd,
　　And yeild his mortal breath ;
But, if the Lord hath thus decreed,
　　He shall not yet see death.

For neither lookes he old nor young,
  But as he did those times,
When Christ did suffer on the crosse
  For mortall sinners crimes.

He hath past through many a foreigne place,
  Arabia, Egypt, Africa,
Grecia, Syria, and great Thrace,
  And throughout all Hungaria.
Where Paul and Peter preached Christ,
  Those blest apostles deare;
There he hath told our Saviours wordes,
  In countries far and neare.

And lately in Bohemia,
  With many a German towne;
And now in Flanders, as tis thought,
  He wandreth up and downe:
Where learned men with him conferre
  Of those his lingering dayes,
And wonder much to heare him tell
  His journeyes, and his wayes.

If people give this Jew an almes,
  The most that he will take
Is not above a groat a time:
  Which he, for Jesus' sake,
Will kindlye give unto the poore,
  And thereof make no spare,
Affirming still that Jesus Christ
  Of him hath dailye care.

He ne'er was seene to laugh nor smile,
  But weepe and make great moane;
Lamenting still his miseries,
  And dayes forepast and gone:
If he heare any one blaspheme,
  Or take God's name in vaine,
He telles them that they crucifie
  Their Saviour Christe againe.

If you had seene his death, saith he,
  As these mine eyes have done,
Ten thousand thousand times would yee
  His torments think upon;
And suffer for his sake all paine
  Of torments, and all woes.
These are his wordes and eke his life
  Whereas he comes or goes.

---

## IV.—THE LYE,

### BY SIR WALTER RALEIGH,

Is found in a very scarce miscellany, entitled "*Davidson's Poems, or a poetical rhapsodie divided into sixe books.* . . . . The 4th impression newly corrected and augmented, and put into a forme more pleasing to the reader. Lond. 1621, 12mo." This poem is reported to have been written by its celebrated author the night before his execution, Oct. 29, 1618. But this must be a mistake, for there were at least two editions of Davidson's poems before that time, one in 1608, the other in 1611. So that unless this poem was an after-insertion in the fourth edition, it must have been written long before the death of Sir Walter: perhaps it was composed soon after his condemnation in 1603. See Oldys' *Life of Sir Walter Raleigh*, p. 173, folio.

Goe, soule, the bodies guest,
  Upon a thankelesse arrant;
Feare not to touche the best,
  The truth shall be thy warrant:
    Goe, since I needs must dye,
    And give the world the lye.

Goe tell the court, it glowes
  And shines like rotten wood;
Goe tell the church it showes
  What's good, and doth no good:
    If church and court reply,
    Then give them both the lye.

# THE LYE.

Tell potentates they live
  Acting by others actions ;
Not lov'd unlesse they give,
  Not strong but by their factions ;
    If potentates reply,
    Give potentates the lye.

Tell men of high condition,
  That rule affairs of state,
Their purpose is ambition,
  Their practise onely hate ;
    And if they once reply,
    Then give them all the lye.

Tell them that brave it most,
  They beg for more by spending,
Who in their greatest cost
  Seek nothing but commending ;
    And if they make reply,
    Spare not to give the lye.

Tell zeale, it lacks devotion ;
  Tell love, it is but lust ;
Tell time, it is but motion ;
  Tell flesh, it is but dust ;
    And wish them not reply,
    For thou must give the lye.

Tell age, it daily wasteth ;
  Tell honour, how it alters ;
Tell beauty, how she blasteth ;
  Tell favour, how she falters ;
    And as they shall reply,
    Give each of them the lye.

Tell wit, how much it wrangles
  In tickle points of nicenesse ;

Tell wisedome, she entangles
  Herselfe in over-wisenesse ;
    And if they do reply,
    Straight give them both the lye.

Tell physicke of her boldnesse ;
  Tell skill, it is pretension ;
Tell charity of coldness ;
  Tell law, it is contention ;
    And as they yield reply,
    So give them still the lye.

Tell fortune of her blindnesse ;
  Tell nature of decay ;
Tell friendship of unkindnesse ;
  Tell justice of delay :
    And if they dare reply,
    Then give them all the lye.

Tell arts, they have no soundnesse,
  But vary by esteeming ;
Tell schooles, they want profoundnesse,
  And stand too much on seeming :
    If arts and schooles reply,
    Give arts and schooles the lye.

Tell faith, it's fled the citie ;
  Tell how the countrey erreth ;
Tell, manhood shakes off pitie ;
  Tell, vertue least preferreth :
    And, if they doe reply,
    Spare not to give the lye.

So, when thou hast, as I
  Commanded thee, done blabbing,
Although to give the lye
  Deserves no less than stabbing,
    Yet stab at thee who will,
    No stab the soule can kill.

## V.—VERSES BY KING JAMES I.

JAMES was a great versifier, and therefore out of the multitude of his poems we have here selected two, which (to show our impartiality) are written in his best and his worst manner. The first would not dishonour any writer of that time; the second is a most complete example of the bathos.

### A SONNET ADDRESSED BY KING JAMES TO HIS SON PRINCE HENRY.

God gives not kings the stile of Gods in vaine,
  For on his throne his scepter do they swey:
    And as their subjects ought them to obey,
So kings should feare and serve their God againe.

If then ye would enjoy a happie reigne,
  Observe the statutes of our heavenly King;
  And from his law make all your laws to spring;
Since his lieutenant here ye should remaine.

Rewarde the just, be stedfast, true and plaine;
  Represse the proud, maintayning aye the right;
  Walke always so, as ever in His sight,
Who guardes the godly, plaguing the prophane.
  And so ye shall in princely vertues shine,
  Resembling right your mightie King divine.

### A SONNET OCCASIONED BY THE BAD WEATHER WHICH HINDERED THE SPORTS AT NEWMARKET IN JANUARY 1616.

This is printed from Drummond of Hawthornden's works, folio.

How cruelly these catives do conspire?
  What loathsome love breeds such a baleful band
  Betwixt the cankred king of Creta land,*
That melancholy old and angry sire,

And him, who wont to quench debate and ire
  Among the Romans, when his ports were clos'd? †
  But now his double face is still dispos'd,
With Saturn's help, to freeze us at the fire.

The earth ore-covered with a sheet of snow,
  Refuses food to fowl, to bird, and beast:
  The chilling cold lets every thing to grow,
And surfeits cattle with a starving feast.
  Curs'd be that love and mought continue short,
  Which kills all creatures, and doth spoil our sport.

\* Saturn.      † Janus.

## VI.—KING JOHN AND THE ABBOT OF CANTERBURY.

THE common popular ballad of *King John and the Abbot* seems to have been abridged and modernized about the time of James I. from one much older, entitled *King John and the Bishop of Canterbury*. The Editor's folio MS. contains a copy of this last, but in too corrupt a state to be reprinted; it however afforded many lines worth reviving, which will be found inserted in the ensuing stanzas, which are chiefly printed from an ancient black-letter copy to the tune of "Derrydown." Both the *King and the Abbot* and the *King and the Bishop* are in the catalogue of ballads printed by Thackeray in the reign of Charles II. "The story upon which these ballads are founded can be traced back to the fifteenth century," so says Mr. Chappell. It was known in the lower Saxon dialect in 1483, and in Spanish literature in 1576. The German poet Bürger in 1784 gave an excellent version of it.

AN ancient story Ile tell you anon
Of a notable prince, that was called King John;
And he ruled England with maine and with might,
For he did great wrong, and mainteiu'd little right.

And Ile tell you a story, a story so merrye,
Concerning the Abbot of Canterburye;
How for his house-keeping, and high renowne,
They rode poste for him to fair London towne.

An hundred men, the king did heare say,
The abbot kept in his house every day;
And fifty golde chaynes, without any doubt,
In velvet coates waited the abbot about.

How now, father abbot, I heare it of thee,
Thou keepest a farre better house than mee,
And for thy house-keeping and high renowne,
I feare thou work'st treason against my crowne.

My liege, quo' the abbot, I would it were knowne,
I never spend nothing, but what is my owne;
And I trust your grace will doe me no deere,
For spending of my owne true-gotten geere.

Yes, yes, father abbot, thy fault it is highe,
And now for the same thou needest must dye;
For except thou canst answer me questions three,
Thy head shall be smitten from thy bodie.

And first, quo' the king, when I'm in this stead,
With my crowne of golde so faire on my head,
Among all my liege-men so noble of birthe,
Thou must tell me to one penny what I am worthe.

Secondlye, tell me, without any doubt,
How soone I may ride the whole world about.
And at the third question thou must not shrink,
But tell me here truly what I do think.

O, these are hard questions for my shallow witt,
Nor I cannot answer your grace as yet:
But if you will give me but three weekes space,
Ile do my endeavour to answer your grace.

Now three weeks space to thee will I give,
And that is the longest time thou hast to live;
For if thou dost not answer my questions three,
Thy lands and thy livings are forfeit to mee.

Away rode the abbot all sad at that word,
And he rode to Cambridge, and Oxenford;
But never a doctor there was so wise,
That could with his learning an answer devise.

Then home rode the abbot of comfort so cold,
And he mett his shepheard a going to fold:
How now, my lord abbot, you are welcome home;
What newes do you bring us from good king John?

"Sad newes, sad newes, shepheard, I must give;
That I have but three days more to live:
For if I do not answer him questions three,
My head will be smitten from my bodie.

"The first is to tell him there in that stead,
With his crowne of golde so fair on his head,
Among all his liege men so noble of birth,
To within one penny of what he is worth.

"The seconde, to tell him, without any doubt,
How soone he may ride this whole world about:
And at the third question I must not shrinke,
But tell him there truly what he does thinke."

Now cheare up, sire abbot, did you never hear yet,
That a fool he may learn a wise man witt?
Lend me horse, and serving men, and your apparel,
And I'll ride to London to answere your quarrel.

Nay frowne not, if it hath bin told unto mee,
I am like your lordship, as ever may bee:
And if you will but lend me your gowne,
There is none shall knowe us at fair London towne.

Now horses, and serving-men thou shalt have,
With sumptuous array most gallant and brave;
With crozier, and miter, and rochet, and cope,
Fit to appeare 'fore our fader the pope.

Now welcome, sire abbot, the king he did say,
Tis well thou'rt come back to keepe thy day
For and if thou canst answer my questions three,
Thy life and thy living both saved shall bee.

And first, when thou seest me here in this stead,
With my crown of golde so fair on my head,
Among all my liege-men so noble of birthe,
Tell me to one penny what I am worth.

"For thirty pence our Saivour was sold
Amonge the false Jewes, as I have bin told;
And twenty nine is the worth of thee,
For I thinke, thou art one penny worser than hee."

The king he laughed, and swore by St.
    Bittel,*
I did not think I had been worth so
    littel!
—Now secondly tell me, without any doubt,
How soone I may ride this whole world
    about.

"You must rise with the sun, and ride
    with the same,
Until the next morning he riseth againe ;
And then your grace need not make any
    doubt,
But in twenty-four hours you'll ride it
    about."

The king he laughed, and swore by St.
    Jone,
I did not think, it could be gone so soone !
—Now from the third question thou must
    not shrinke,
But tell me here truly what I do thinke.

"Yea, that shall I do, and make your
    grace merry :
You thinke I'm the abbot of Canterbúry ;
But I'm his poor shepheard, as plain you
    may see,
That am come to beg pardon for him and
    for mee."

The king he laughed, and swore by the
    masse,
He make thee lord abbot this day in his
    place !
"Now naye, my liege, be not in such speede,
For alacke I can neither write ne reade."

Four nobles a weeke, then I will give thee,
For this merry jest thou hast showne unto
    mee ;
And tell the old abbot when thou comest
    home,
Thou hast brought him a pardon from
    good king John.

---

## VII.—YOU MEANER BEAUTIES.

This little sonnet was written by Sir Henry Wotton, Knight, on that amiable princess, Elizabeth, daughter of James I. and wife of the Elector Palatine, who was chosen King of Bohemia, Sept. 5, 1619. The consequences of this fatal election are well known: Sir Henry Wotton, who in that and the following year was employed in several embassies in Germany on behalf of this unfortunate lady, seems to have had an uncommon attachment to her merit and fortunes, for he gave away a jewel worth a thousand pounds, that was presented to him by the emperor, "because it came from an enemy to his royal mistress the Queen of Bohemia." See *Biog. Britain.*

This song is printed from the *Reliquiæ Wottonianæ*, 1651, with some corrections from an old MS. copy.

You meaner beauties of the night,
    That poorly satisfie our eies
More by your number than your light ;
    You common people of the skies,
    What are you when the Moon shall rise?

Ye violets that first appeare,
    By your pure purple mantles known,
Like the proud virgins of the yeare,
    As if the Spring were all your own ;
    What are you when the Rose is blown?

Ye curious chaunters of the wood,
    That warble forth dame Nature's layes,
Thinking your passions understood
    By your weak accents : what's your
        praise,
    When Philomell her voyce shall raise?

So when my mistris shal be seene
    In sweetnesse of her looks and minde ;
By virtue first, then choyce a queen ;
    Tell me, if she was not design'd
    Th' eclypse and glory of her kind?

---

\* Meaning probably St. Botolph.

## VIII.—THE OLD AND YOUNG COURTIER.

THIS excellent old song, the subject of which is a comparison between the manners of the old gentry, as still subsisting in the times of Elizabeth, and the modern refinements affected by their sons in the reigns of her successors, is given, with corrections, from an ancient black-letter copy in the Pepys Collection, compared with another printed among some miscellaneous "poems and songs" in a book entitled, *Le Prince d'Amour*, 1660, 8vo.

AN old song made by an aged old pate,
Of an old worshipful gentleman, who had a greate estate,
That kept a brave old house at a bountiful rate,
And an old porter to relieve the poor at his gate;
   Like an old courtier of the queen's,
   And the queen's old courtier.

With an old lady, whose anger one word asswages;
They every quarter paid their old servants their wages,
And never knew what belong'd to coachmen, footmen, nor pages,
But kept twenty old fellows with blue coats and badges;
   Like an old courtier, etc.

With an old study fill'd full of learned old books,
With an old reverend chaplain, you might know him by his looks.
With an old buttery hatch worn quite off the hooks,
And an old kitchen, that maintain'd half a dozen old cooks;
   Like an old courtier, etc.

With an old hall, hung about with pikes, guns, and bows,
With old swords, and bucklers, that had borne many shrewde blows,
And an old frize coat, to cover his worship's trunk hose,
And a cup of old sherry, to comfort his copper nose;
   Like an old courtier, etc.

With a good old fashion, when Christmasse was come,
To call in all his old neighbours with bag-pipe and drum,
With good chear enough to furnish every old room,
And old liquor able to make a cat speak, and man dumb;
   Like an old courtier, etc.

With an old falconer, huntsman, and a kennel of hounds,
That never hawked, nor hunted, but in his own grounds,
Who, like a wise man, kept himself within his own bounds,
And when he dyed gave every child a thousand good pounds;
   Like an old courtier, etc.

But to his eldest son his house and land he assign'd,
Charging him in his will to keep the old bountifull mind,
To be good to his old tenants, and to his neighbours be kind:
But in the ensuing ditty you shall hear how he was inclin'd;
   Like a young courtier of the king's,
   And the king's young courtier.

Like a flourishing young gallant, newly
    come to his land,
Who keeps a brace of painted madams at
    his command,
And takes up a thousand pound upon his
    father's land,
And gets drunk in a tavern, till he can
    neither go nor stand ;
        Like a young courtier, etc.

With a new-fangled lady, that is dainty,
    nice, and spare,
Who never knew what belong'd to good
    house-keeping, or care,
Who buyes gaudy-color'd fans to play
    with wanton air,
And seven or eight different dressings of
    other womens hair ;
        Like a young courtier, etc.

With a new-fashion'd hall, built where the
    old one stood,
Hung round with new pictures, that do
    the poor no good,
With a fine marble chimney, wherein
    burns neither coal nor wood,
And a new smooth shovelboard, whereon
    no victuals ne'er stood ;
        Like a young courtier, etc.

With a new study, stuft full of pamphlets
    and plays,
And a new chaplain, that swears faster
    than he prays,

With a new buttery hatch, that opens
    once in four or five days,
And a new French cook, to devise fine
    kickshaws, and toys ;
        Like a young courtier, etc.

With a new fashion, when Christmas is
    drawing on,
On a new journey to London straight we
    all must begone,
And leave none to keep house, but our
    new porter John,
Who relieves the poor with a thump on
    the back with a stone ;
        Like a young courtier, etc.

With a new gentleman-usher, whose
    carriage is compleat,
With a new coachman, footmen, and
    pages to carry up the meat,
With a waiting-gentlewoman, whose
    dressing is very neat,
Who when her lady has din'd, lets the
    servants not eat ;
        Like a young courtier, etc.

With new titles of honour bought with
    his father's old gold,
For which sundry of his ancestors old
    manors are sold ;
And this is the course most of our new
    gallants hold,
Which makes that good house-keeping
    is now grown so cold,
        Among the young courtiers of the
            king,
        Or the king's young courtiers.

## IX.—SIR JOHN SUCKLING'S CAMPAIGNE.

WHEN the Scottish covenanters rose up in arms, and advanced to the English borders in 1639, many of the courtiers complimented the king by raising forces at their own expense. Among these none were more distinguished than the gallant Sir John Suckling, who raised a troop of horse, so richly accoutred that it cost him £12,000. The like expensive equipment of other parts of the army made the king remark, that "the Scots would fight stoutly, if it were but for the Englishmen's fine cloaths."—Lloyd's *Memoirs.* When they came to action, the rugged Scots proved more than a match for the fine showy English, many of whom behaved remarkably ill, and among the rest this splendid troop of Sir John Suckling's.

This humorous pasquil has been generally supposed to have been written by Sir John as a banter upon himself, though some of his contemporaries, however, attributed it to Sir John Mennis, a wit of those times.

SIR JOHN he got him an ambling nag,
   To Scotland for to ride-a,
With a hundred horse more, all his own
   he swore,
   To guard him on every side-a.

No Errant-knight ever went to fight
   With halfe so gay a bravada,
Had you seen but his look, you'ld have
   sworn on a book,
   Hee'ld have conquer'd a whole armada.

The ladies ran all to the windows to see
   So gallant and warlike a sight-a,
And as he pass'd by, they said with a sigh,
   Sir John, why will you go fight-a?

But he, like a cruel knight, spurr'd on;
   His heart would not relent-a,
For, till he came there, what had he to
   fear?
   Or why should he repent-a?

The king (God bless him!) had singular
   hopes
   Of him and all his troop-a:
The borderers they, as they met him on
   the way,
   For joy did hollow, and whoop-a.

None lik'd him so well, as his own colonell,
   Who took him for John de Wert-a;[*]
But when there were shows of gunning
   and blows,
   My gallant was nothing so pert-a.

For when the Scots army came within
   sight,
   And all prepared to fight-a,
He ran to his tent, they ask'd what he
   meant,
   He swore he must needs goe sh'te-a.

The colonell sent for him back agen,
   To quarter him in the van-a;
But Sir John did swear, he would not
   come there,
   To be kill'd the very first man-a.

To cure his fear, he was sent to the reare,
   Some ten miles back, and more-a;
Where Sir John did play at trip and away,
   And ne'er saw the enemy more-a.

---

[*] John de Wert was a German general of great reputation, and the terror of the French in the reign of Louis XIII. Hence his name became proverbial in France, where he was called De Vert. See Bayle's *Dictionary.*

## X.—TO ALTHEA FROM PRISON.

THIS excellent sonnet, which possessed a high degree of fame among the old cavaliers, was written by Colonel Richard Lovelace during his confinement in the gate-house, Westminster, to which he was committed by the House of Commons in April 1642, for presenting a petition from the county of Kent, requesting them to restore the king to his rights, and to settle the government.

This song is printed from a scarce volume of his poems, entitled *Lucasta*, 1649, 12mo, collated with a copy in the Editor's folio MS.

WHEN love with unconfined wings
  Hovers within my gates,
And my divine Althea brings
  To whisper at my grates ;
When I lye tangled in her haire,
  And fetter'd with her eye,
The birds that wanton in the aire,
  Know no such libertye.

When flowing cups run swiftly round
  With no allaying Thames,*
Our carelesse heads with roses crown'd,
  Our hearts with loyal flames ;
When thirsty griefe in wine we steepe,
  When healths and draughts goe free,
Fishes, that tipple in the deepe,
  Know no such libertie.

When, linnet-like, confined I
  With shriller note shall sing
The mercye, sweetness, majestye,
  And glories of my king ;
When I shall voyce aloud how good
  He is, how great should be,
Th' enlarged windes, that curle the flood,
  Know no such libertie.

Stone walls doe not a prison make,
  Nor iron barres a cage,
Mindes, innocent, and quiet, take
  That for an hermitage :
If I have freedom in my love,
  And in my soule am free,
Angels alone, that soare above,
  Enjoy such libertie.

---

## XI.—THE DOWNFALL OF CHARING CROSS.

CHARING CROSS, as it stood before the civil wars, was one of those beautiful Gothic obelisks erected to conjugal affection by Edward I., who built such a one wherever the hearse of his beloved Eleanor rested on its way from Lincolnshire to Westminster. But neither its ornamental situation, the beauty of its structure, nor the noble design of its erection (which did honour to humanity), could preserve it from the merciless zeal of the times : for, in 1647, it was demolished by order of the House of Commons as popish and superstitious. This occasioned the following not unhumorous sarcasm, which has been often printed among the popular sonnets of those times.

The plot referred to in ver. 17 was that entered into by Mr. Waller the poet, and others, with a view to reduce the city and tower to the service of the king ; for which two of them, Nathaniel Tomkins and Richard Chaloner, suffered death, July 5, 1643. *Vid. Athen. Ox.* II. 24.

UNDONE, undone the lawyers are,
  They wander about the towne,

Nor can find the way to Westminster,
  Now Charing Cross is downe :
At the end of the Strand they make a stand,
  Swearing they are at a loss,

---

\* Thames is here used for water in general.

And chafing say, that's not the way,
  They must go by Charing Cross.

The parliament to vote it down
  Conceived it very fitting,
For fear it should fall, and kill them all,
  In the house, as they were sitting.
They were told, god-wot, it had a plot,
  Which made them so hard-hearted,
To give command, it should not stand,
  But be taken down and carted.

Men talk of plots, this might have been
    worse
  For any thing I know,
Than that Tomkins, and Chaloner,
  Were hang'd for long agoe.
Our parliament did that prevent,
  And wisely them defended,
For plots they will discover still,
  Before they were intended.

But neither man, woman, nor child,
  Will say, I'm confident,
They ever heard it speak one word
  Against the parliament.
An informer swore, it letters bore,
  Or else it had been freed;
I'll take, in troth, my Bible oath,
  It could neither write nor read.

The committee said, that verily
  To popery it was bent;
For ought I know, it might be so,
  For to church it never went.
What with excise, and such device,
  The kingdom doth begin
To think you'll leave them ne'er a cross,
  Without doors nor within.

Methinks the common-council shou'd
  Of it have taken pity,
'Cause, good old cross, it always stood
  So firmly to the city.
Since crosses you so much disdain,
  Faith, if I were as you,
For fear the king should rule again,
  I'd pull down Tiburn too.

## XII.—LOYALTY CONFINED.

This excellent old song is preserved in David Lloyd's *Memoires of those that suffered in the cause of Charles I.*, London 1668. The author's name he has not mentioned, but, if tradition may be credited, this song was written by Sir Roger L'Estrange.

BEAT on, proud billows; Boreas blow;
  Swell, curled waves, high as Jove's roof;
Your incivility doth show,
  That innocence is tempest proof;
Though surly Nereus frown, my thoughts
    are calm;
Then strike, Affliction, for thy wounds
    are balm.

That which the world miscalls a jail,
  A private closet is to me:
Whilst a good conscience is my bail,
  And innocence my liberty:
Locks, bars, and solitude, together met,
Make me no prisoner, but an anchoret.

I, whilst I wisht to be retir'd,
  Into this private room was turn'd;
As if their wisdoms had conspir'd
  The salamander should be burn'd;
Or like those sophists, that would drown
    a fish,
I am constrain'd to suffer what I wish.

The cynick loves his poverty;
  The pelican her wilderness;
And 'tis the Indian's pride to be
  Naked on frozen Caucasus:
Contentment cannot smart, Stoicks we
    see
Make torments easie to their apathy.

These manacles upon my arm
 I, as my mistress' favours, wear;
And for to keep my ancles warm,
 I have some iron shackles there:
These walls are but my garrison; this cell,
Which men call jail, doth prove my citadel.

I'm in the cabinet lockt up,
 Like some high-prized margarite,
Or, like the great mogul or pope,
 Am cloyster'd up from publick sight:
Retiredness is a piece of majesty,
And thus, proud sultan, I'm as great as thee.

Here sin for want of food must starve,
 Where tempting objects are not seen;
And these strong walls do only serve
 To keep vice out, and keep me in:
Malice of late's grown charitable sure,
I'm not committed, but am kept secure.

So he that struck at Jason's life,*
 Thinking t' have made his purpose sure,
By a malicious friendly knife
 Did only wound him to a cure:
Malice, I see, wants wit; for what is meant
Mischief, oft-times proves favour by th' event.

---

* See this remarkable story in *Cicero, de Nat. Deorum,* Lib. iii. c. 28; *Cic. de Offic.* Lib. i. c. 30. See also *Val. Max.* i. 8.

When once my prince affliction hath,
 Prosperity doth treason seem;
And to make smooth so rough a path,
 I can learn patience from him:
Now not to suffer shews no loyal heart,
When kings want ease subjects must bear a part.

What though I cannot see my king
 Neither in person or in coin;
Yet contemplation is a thing
 That renders what I have not, mine:
My king from me what adamant can part,
Whom I do wear engraven on my heart?

Have you not seen the nightingale,
 A prisoner like, coopt in a cage,
How doth she chaunt her wonted tale
 In that her narrow hermitage?
Even then her charming melody doth prove,
That all her bars are trees, her cage a grove.

I am that bird, whom they combine
 Thus to deprive of liberty;
But though they do my corps confine,
 Yet maugre hate, my soul is free:
And though immur'd, yet can I chirp, and sing
Disgrace to rebels, glory to my king.

My soul is free, as ambient air,
 Although my baser part's immew'd,
Whilst loyal thoughts do still repair
 T' accompany my solitude:
Although rebellion do my body binde,
My king alone can captivate my minde.

## XIII.—VERSES BY KING CHARLES I.

"This prince, like his father, did not confine himself to prose. Bishop Burnett has given us a pathetic elegy, said to be written by Charles in Carisbrook Castle [in 1648]. The poetry is most uncouth and unharmonious, but there are strong thoughts in it, some good sense, and a strain of majestic piety."—Mr. Walpole's *Royal and Noble Authors*, vol. i. And Hume hath remarked of these stanzas, "that the truth of the sentiment, rather than the elegance of the expression, renders them very pathetic."

GREAT monarch of the world, from whose power springs
The potency and power of kings,
Record the royal woe my suffering sings;

And teach my tongue, that ever did confine
Its faculties in truth's seraphick line,
To track the treasons of thy foes and mine.

Nature and law, by thy divine decree
(The only root of righteous royaltie),
With this dim diadem invested me:

With it, the sacred scepter, purple robe,
The holy unction, and the royal globe:
Yet am I levell'd with the life of Job.

The fiercest furies, that do daily tread
Upon my grief, my grey discrowned head,
Are those that owe my bounty for their bread.

They raise a war, and christen it The Cause,
While sacrilegious hands have best applause,
Plunder and murder are the kingdom's laws;

Tyranny bears the title of taxation,
Revenge and robbery are reformation,
Oppression gains the name of sequestration.

My loyal subjects, who in this bad season
Attend me (by the law of God and reason),
They dare impeach, and punish for high treason.

Next at the clergy do their furies frown,
Pious episcopacy must go down,
They will destroy the crosier and the crown.

Churchmen are chain'd, and schismaticks are freed,
Mechanicks preach, and holy fathers bleed,
The crown is crucified with the creed.

The church of England doth all factions foster,
The pulpit is usurpt by each impostor,
*Extempore* excludes the *Paternoster*.

The Presbyter, and Independent seed
Springs with broad blades. To make religion bleed,
Herod and Pontius Pilate are agreed.

The corner stone's misplac'd by every pavier:
With such a bloody method and behaviour
Their ancestors did crucifie our Saviour.

My royal consort, from whose fruitful womb
So many princes legally have come,
Is forc'd in pilgrimage to seek a tomb.

Great Britain's heir is forced into France,
Whilst on his father's head his foes advance:
Poor child! he weeps out his inheritance.

With my own power my majesty they wound,
In the king's name the king himself's uncrown'd:
So doth the dust destroy the diamond.

With propositions daily they enchant
My people's ears, such as do reason daunt,
And the Almighty will not let me grant.

They promise to erect my royal stem,
To make me great, t' advance my diadem,
If I will first fall down, and worship them!

But for refusal they devour my thrones,
Distress my children, and destroy my bones;
I fear they'll force me to make bread of stones.

My life they prize at such a slender rate,
That in my absence they draw bills of hate,
To prove the king a traytor to the state.

Felons obtain more privilege than I,
They are allow'd to answer ere they die;
'Tis death for me to ask the reason, why.

But, sacred Saviour, with thy words I woo
Thee to forgive, and not be bitter to
Such, as thou know'st do not know what they do.

For since they from their lord are so disjointed,
As to contemn those edicts he appointed,
How can they prize the power of his anointed?

Augment my patience, nullifie my hate,
Preserve my issue, and inspire my mate;
Yet, though we perish, bless this Church and State.

---

## XIV.—THE SALE OF REBELLIOUS HOUSEHOLD STUFF.

THIS sarcastic exultation of triumphant loyalty is printed from an old black-letter copy in the Pepys Collection, corrected by two others, one of which is preserved in *A choice collection of one hundred and twenty loyal songs*, etc., 1684, 12mo.—To the tune of "Old Simon the king."

REBELLION hath broken up house,
   And hath left me old lumber to sell;
Come hither, and take your choice,
   I'll promise to use you well:
Will you buy the old speaker's chair?
   Which was warm and easie to sit in,
And oft hath been clean'd I declare,
   When as it was fouler than fitting.
      Says old Simon the king, etc.

Will you buy any bacon-flitches,
   The fattest, that ever were spent?
They're the sides of the old committees,
   Fed up in the long parliament.
Here's a pair of bellows, and tongs,
   And for a small matter I'll sell ye 'um;
They are made of the presbyters lungs,
   To blow up the coals of rebellion.
      Says old Simon, etc.

I had thought to have given them once
   To some black-smith for his forge;
But now I have considered on't,
   They are consecrate to the church:
So I'll give them unto some quire,
   They will make the big organs roar,
And the little pipes to squeeke higher
   Than ever they could before.
      Says old Simon, etc.

Here's a couple of stools for sale,
   One's square, and t'other is round;
Betwixt them both the tail
   Of the Rump fell down to the ground.
Will you buy the states council-table,
   Which was made of the good wain Scot?
The frame was a tottering Babel
   To uphold the Independent plot.
      Says old Simon, etc.

Here's the beesom of Reformation,
  Which should have made clean the floor,
But it swept the wealth out of the nation,
  And left us dirt good store.
Will you buy the states spinning-wheel,
  Which spun for the roper's trade?
But better it had stood still,
  For now it has spun a fair thread.
    Says old Simon, etc.

Here's a glyster-pipe well try'd,
  Which was made of a butcher's stump,*
And has been safely apply'd,
  To cure the colds of the Rump.
Here's a lump of Pilgrims-Salve,
  Which once was a justice of peace,
Who Noll and the Devil did serve;
  But now it is come to this.
    Says old Simon, etc.

Here's a roll of the states tobacco,
  If any good fellow will take it;
No Virginia had e'er such a smack-o,
  And I'll tell you how they did make it:
'Tis th' Engagement, and Covenant cookt
  Up with the Abjuration oath;
And many of them, that have took't,
  Complain it was foul in the mouth.
    Says old Simon, etc.

Yet the ashes may happily serve
  To cure the scab of the nation,
Whene'er 't has an itch to swerve
  To Rebellion by innovation.
A Lanthorn here is to be bought,
  The like was scarce ever gotten,
For many plots it has found out
  Before they ever were thought on.
    Says old Simon, etc.

Will you buy the Rump's great saddle,
  With which it jocky'd the nation?

And here is the bitt, and the bridle,
  And curb of Dissimulation:
And here's the trunk-hose of the Rump,
  And their fair dissembling cloak,
And a Presbyterian jump,
  With an Independent smock.
    Says old Simon, etc.

Will you buy a Conscience oft turn'd,
  Which serv'd the high-court of justice,
And stretch'd until England it mourn'd:
  But Hell will buy that if the worst is.
Here's Joan Cromwell's* kitching-stuff tub,
  Wherein is the fat of the Rumpers,
With which old Noll's horns she did rub,
  When he was got drunk with false bumpers.
    Says old Simon, etc.

Here's the purse of the public faith;
  Here's the model of the Sequestration,
When the old wives upon their good troth,
  Lent thimbles to ruine the nation.
Here's Dick Cromwell's Protectorship,
  And here are Lambert's commissions,
And here is Hugh Peters his scrip
  Cramm'd with the tumultuous Petitions.
    Says old Simon, etc.

And here are old Noll's brewing vessels,†
  And here are his dray, and his slings;
Here are Hewson's awl, and his bristles;‡
  With diverse other odd things:
And what is the price doth belong
  To all these matters before ye?
I'll sell them all for an old song,
  And so I do end my story.
    Says old Simon, etc.

---

\* Alluding probably to Major-General Harrison, a butcher's son, who assisted Cromwell in turning out the Long Parliament, April 20, 1653.

\* This was a cant name given to Cromwell's wife by the Royalists, though her name was Elizabeth. She was taxed with exchanging the kitchen stuff for the candles used in the Protector's household, etc. See *Gentleman's Magazine* for March 1788, p. 242.

† Cromwell had in his younger years followed the brewing trade at Huntingdon.

‡ Colonel Hewson is said to have been originally a cobbler.

## XV.—THE BAFFLED KNIGHT, OR LADY'S POLICY,

GIVEN (with some corrections) from a MS. copy, and collated with two printed ones in Roman character in the Pepys Collection.

THERE was a knight was drunk with wine,
   A riding along the way, sir;
And there he met with a lady fine,
   Among the cocks of hay, sir.

Shall you and I, O lady faire,
   Among the grass sit down-a?
And I will have a special care
   Of rumpling of your gowne-a.

Upon the grass there is a dewe,
   Will spoil my damask gowne, sir:
My gowne and kirtle they are newe,
   And cost me many a crowne, sir.

I have a cloak of scarlet red,
   Upon the ground I'll throwe it;
Then, lady faire, come lay thy head;
   We'll play, and none shall knowe it.

O yonder stands my steed so free
   Among the cocks of hay, sir;
And if the pinner should chance to see,
   He'll take my steed away, sir.

Upon my finger I have a ring,
   It's made of finest gold-a,
And, lady, it thy steed shall bring
   Out of the pinner's fold-a.

O go with me to my father's hall;
   Fair chambers there are three, sir:
And you shall have the best of all,
   And I'll your chamberlaine bee, sir.

He mounted himself on his steed so tall,
   And her on her dapple gray, sir:
And there they rode to her father's hall,
   Fast pricking along the way, sir.

To her father's hall they arrived strait;
   'Twas moated round about-a;
She slipped herself within the gate,
   And lockt the knight without-a.

Here is a silver penny to spend,
   And take it for your pain, sir;
And two of my father's men I'll send
   To wait on you back again, sir.

He from his scabbard drew his brand,
   And wiped it upon his sleeve-a:
And cursed, he said, be every man,
   That will a maid believe-a!

She drew a bodkin from her haire,
   And whip'd it upon her gown-a;
And curs'd be every maiden faire,
   That will with men lye down-a!

A herb there is, that lowly grows,
   And some do call it rue, sir:
The smallest dunghill cock that crows,
   Would make a capon of you, sir.

A flower there is, that shineth bright,
   Some call it mary-gold-a:
He that wold not when he might,
   He shall not when he wold-a.

The knight was riding another day,
   With cloak and hat and feather:
He met again with that lady gay,
   Who was angling in the river.

Now, lady faire, I've met with you,
   You shall no more escape me;
Remember, how not long agoe
   You falsely did intrap me.

The lady blushed scarlet red,
   And trembled at the stranger:
How shall I guard my maidenhead
   From this approaching danger?

He from his saddle down did light,
   In all his riche attyer;
And cryed, As I am a noble knight,
   I do thy charms admyer.

He took the lady by the hand,
   Who seemingly consented;
And would no more disputing stand:
   She had a plot invented.

Looke yonder, good sir knight, I pray,
   Methinks I now discover
A riding upon his dapple gray,
   My former constant lover.

On tip-toe peering stood the knight,
   Fast by the rivers brink-a;
The lady pusht with all her might:
   Sir knight, now swim or sink-a.

O'er head and ears he plunged in,
   The bottom faire he sounded;
Then rising up, he cried amain,
   Help, helpe, or else I'm drownded!

Now, fare-you-well, sir knight, adieu!
   You see what comes of fooling:
That is the fittest place for you;
   Your courage wanted cooling.

Ere many days, in her fathers park,
   Just at the close of eve-a,
Again she met with her angry sparke;
   Which made this lady grieve-a.

False lady, here thou'rt in my powre,
   And no one now can hear thee:
And thou shalt sorely rue the hour,
   That e'er thou dar'dst to jeer me.

I pray, sir knight, be not so warm
   With a young silly maid-a:

I vow and swear I thought no harm,
   'Twas a gentle jest I played-a.

A gentle jest, in soothe, he cry'd,
   To tumble me in and leave me!
What if I had in the river dy'd?—
   That fetch will not deceive me.

Once more I'll pardon thee this day,
   Tho' injur'd out of measure;
But then prepare without delay
   To yield thee to my pleasure.

Well then, if I must grant your suit,
   Yet think of your boots and spurs, sir:
Let me pull off both spur and boot,
   Or else you cannot stir, sir.

He set him down upon the grass,
   And begg'd her kind assistance;
Now, smiling thought this lovely lass,
   I'll make you keep your distance.

Then pulling off his boots half-way;
   Sir knight, now I'm your betters;
You shall not make of me your prey;
   Sit there like a knave in fetters.

The knight when she had served soe,
   He fretted, fum'd, and grumbled:
For he could neither stand nor goe,
   But like a cripple tumbled.

Farewell, sir knight, the clock strikes ten,
   Yet do not move nor stir, sir:
I'll send you my father's serving men,
   To pull off your boots and spurs, sir.

This merry jest you must excuse,
   You are but a stingless nettle:
You'd never have stood for boots or shoes,
   Had you been a man of mettle.

All night in grievous rage he lay,
   Rolling upon the plain-a;
Next morning a shepherd past that way,
   Who set him right again-a.

Then mounting upon his steed so tall,
  By hill and dale he swore-a:
I'll ride at once to her father's hall;
  She shall escape no more-a.

I'll take her father by the beard,
  I'll challenge all her kindred;
Each dastard soul shall stand affeard;
  My wrath shall no more be hindred.

He rode unto her father's house,
  Which every side was moated:
The lady heard his furious vows,
  And all his vengeance noted.

Thought shee, sir knight, to quench your rage,
  Once more I will endeavour:
This water shall your fury 'swage,
  Or else it shall burn for ever.

Then faining penitence and feare,
  She did invite a parley:
Sir knight, if you'll forgive me heare,
  Henceforth I'll love you dearly.

My father he is now from home,
  And I am all alone, sir:
Therefore a-cross the water come;
  And I am all your own, sir.

False maid, thou canst no more deceive;
  I scorn the treacherous bait-a:
If thou would'st have me thee believe,
  Now open me the gate-a.

The bridge is drawn, the gate is barr'd,
  My father he has the keys, sir;
But I have for my love prepar'd
  A shorter way and easier.

Over the moate I've laid a plank
  Full seventeen feet in measure:
Then step a-cross to the other bank,
  And there we'll take our pleasure.

These words she had no sooner spoke,
  But strait he came tripping over:
The plank was saw'd, it snapping broke;
  And sous'd the unhappy lover.

## XVI.—WHY SO PALE?

FROM Sir John Suckling's *Poems*. This sprightly knight was born in 1613, and cut off by a fever about the twenty-ninth year of his age. See above, Song IX. of this book.

Why so pale and wan, fond lover?
  Prethee, why so pale?
Will, when looking well can't move her,
  Looking ill prevail?
  Prethee why so pale?

Why so dull and mute, young sinner?
  Prethee why so mute?
Will, when speaking well can't win her,
  Saying nothing doe't?
  Prethee why so mute?

Quit, quit for shame; this will not move,
  This cannot take her;
If of herself she will not love,
  Nothing can make her.
  The devil take her!

## XVII.—OLD TOM OF BEDLAM.

#### MAD SONG THE FIRST.

It is worth attention, that the English have more songs and ballads on the subject of madness than any of their neighbours. Whether there be any truth in the insinuation, that we are more liable to this calamity than other nations, or that our native gloominess hath peculiarly recommended subjects of this cast to our writers, we certainly do not find the same in the printed collections of French, Italian songs, etc.

This is given from the Editor's folio MS. compared with two or three old printed copies. With regard to the author of this old rhapsody, in Walton's *Complete Angler*, cap. 3, is a song in praise of angling, which the author says was made at his request "by Mr. William Basse, one that has made the choice songs of the *Hunter in his Career* and of *Tom of Bedlam*, and many others of note," p. 84. See Sir John Hawkins' curious edition, 8vo, of that excellent old book.

Forth from my sad and darksome cell,
Or from the deepe abysse of hell,
Mad Tom is come into the world againe
To see if he can cure his distempered braine.

Feares and cares oppresse my soule;
Harke, howe the angrye Furcys houle!
Pluto laughes, and Proserpine is gladd
To see poore naked Tom of Bedlam madd.

Through the world I wander night and day
To seeke my straggling senses,
In an angrye moode I mett old Time,
With his pentarchye of tenses:

When me he spyed,
Away he hyed,
For time will stay for no man:
In vaine with cryes
I rent the skyes,
For pity is not common.

Cold and comfortless I lye:
Helpe, oh helpe! or else I dye!
Harke! I heare Apollo's teame,
The carman 'gins to whistle;
Chast Diana bends her bowe,
The boare begins to bristle.

Come, Vulcan, with tools and with tackles,
To knocke off my troublesome shackles;
Bid Charles make ready his waine
To fetch me my senses againe.

Last night I heard the dog-star bark;
Mars met Venus in the darke;
Limping Vulcan het an iron barr,
And furiouslye made at the god of war:

Mars with his weapon laid about,
But Vulcan's temples had the gout,
For his broad horns did so hang in his light,
He could not see to aim his blowes aright:

Mercurye, the nimble post of heaven,
Stood still to see the quarrell;
Gorrel-bellyed Bacchus, gyant-like,
Bestryd a strong-beere barrell.

To mee he dranke,
I did him thanke,
But I could get no cyder;
He dranke whole butts
Till he burst his gutts,
But mine were ne'er the wyder.

Poore naked Tom is very drye;
A little drinke for charitye!

Harke, I hear Acteon's horne!
  The huntsmen whoop and hallowe:
Ringwood, Royster, Bowman, Jowler,
  All the chase do followe.

The man in the moone drinkes clarret,
Eates powder'd beef, turnip, and carret,
  But a cup of old Malaga sack
Will fire the bushe at his backe.

## XVIII.—THE DISTRACTED PURITAN,

### MAD SONG THE SECOND,

WAS written about the beginning of the seventeenth century by the witty Bishop Corbet, and is printed from his *Poems*, 12mo, 1672, compared with a more ancient copy in the Editor's folio MS.

AM I mad, O noble Festus,
When zeal and godly knowledge
  Have put me in hope
  To deal with the pope,
As well as the best in the college?
  Boldly I preach, hate a cross, hate a
    surplice,
  Mitres, copes, and rochets;
  Come hear me pray nine times a
    day,
  And fill your heads with crotchets.

In the house of pure Emanuel *
I had my education,
  Where my friends surmise
  I dazel'd my eyes
With the sight of revelation.
  Boldly I preach, etc.

They bound me like a bedlam,
They lash'd my four poor quarters;
  Whilst this I endure,
  Faith makes me sure
To be one of Foxes martyrs.
  Boldly I preach, etc.

These injuries I suffer
Through antichrist's perswasion:

---

* Emmanuel College, Cambridge, was originally a seminary of Puritans.

Take off this chain,
  Neither Rome nor Spain
Can resist my strong invasion.
  Boldly I preach, etc.

Of the beast's ten horns (God bless us!)
I have knock'd off three already;
  If they let me alone,
  I'll leave him none:
But they say I am too heady.
  Boldly I preach, etc.

When I sack'd the seven-hill'd city,
I met the great red dragon;
  I kept him aloof
  With the armour of proof,
Though here I have never a rag on.
  Boldly I preach, etc.

With a fiery sword and target,
There fought I with this monster:
  But the sons of pride
  My zeal deride,
And all my deeds misconster.
  Boldly I preach, etc.

I un-hors'd the Whore of Babel,
With the lance of Inspiration;
  I made her stink,
  And spill the drink
In her cup of abomination.
  Boldly I preach, etc.

I have seen two in a vision
With a flying book * between them.
  I have been in despair
  Five times in a year,
And been cur'd by reading Greenham.†
  Boldly I preach, etc.

I observ'd in Perkin's tables ‡
The black line of damnation ;
  Those crooked veins
  So stuck in my brains,
That I fear'd my reprobation.
  Boldly I preach, etc.

In the holy tongue of Canaan
I plac'd my chiefest pleasure :
Till I prick'd my foot
With an Hebrew root,
That I bled beyond all measure.
  Boldly I preach, etc.

I appear'd before the Archbishop *
And all the high commission ;
  I gave him no grace,
  But told him to his face,
That he favour'd superstition.
  Boldly I preach, hate a cross, hate a
    surplice,
  Mitres, copes, and rochets :
  Come hear me pray nine times a
    day,
  And fill your heads with crotchets.

## XIX.—THE LUNATIC LOVER,

### MAD SONG THE THIRD,

Is given from an old printed copy in the British Museum, compared with another in the Pepys Collection, both in black letter.

GRIM king of the ghosts, make haste,
  And bring hither all your train ;
See how the pale moon does waste,
  And just now is in the wane.

---

* Alluding to some visionary exposition of Zech. v. 1 ; or, if the date of this song would permit, one might suppose it aimed at one *Coppe*, a strange enthusiast, author of a book entitled *The Fiery Flying Roll*. He afterwards published a recantation, part of whose title is, *The Fiery Flying Roll's Wings clipt*, etc.

† See Greenham's *Works*, fol. 1605, particularly the tract entitled, *A sweet Comfort for an Afflicted Conscience*.

‡ See Perkin's *Works*, fol. 1616, vol. i. p. 11, where is a large half sheet folded, containing "A survey or table declaring the order of the causes of salvation and damnation," etc., the pedigree of damnation being distinguished by a broad black zig-zag line.

Come, you night-hags, with all your
    charms,
  And revelling witches away,
And hug me close in your arms ;
  To you my respects I'll pay.

I ll court you, and think you fair,
  Since love does distract my brain :'
I'll go, I'll wed the night-mare,
  And kiss her, and kiss her again :
But if she prove peevish and proud,
  Then, a pise on her love ! let her go ;
I'll seek me a winding shroud,
  And down to the shades below.

A lunacy sad I endure,
  Since reason departs away ;
I call to those hags for a cure,
  As knowing not what I say.

---

* Archbishop Laud.

The beauty, whom I do adore,
  Now slights me with scorn and disdain;
I never shall see her more:
  Ah! how shall I bear my pain!

I ramble, and range about
  To find out my charming saint;
While she at my grief does flout,
  And smiles at my loud complaint.
Distraction I see is my doom,
  Of this I am now too sure;
A rival is got in my room,
  While torments I do endure.

Strange fancies do fill my head,
  While wandering in despair,
I am to the desarts lead,
  Expecting to find her there.
Methinks in a spangled cloud
  I see her enthroned on high;
Then to her I crie aloud,
  And labour to reach the sky.

When thus I have raved awhile,
  And wearyed myself in vain,
I lye on the barren soil,
  And bitterly do complain.
Till slumber hath quieted me,
  In sorrow I sigh and weep;
The clouds are my canopy
  To cover me while I sleep.

I dream that my charming fair
  Is then in my rival's bed,
Whose tresses of golden hair
  Are on the fair pillow bespread.
Then this doth my passion inflame,
  I start, and no longer can lie:
Ah! Sylvia, art thou not to blame
  To ruin a lover? I cry.

Grim king of the ghosts, be true,
  And hurry me hence away,
My languishing life to you
  A tribute I freely pay.
To the Elysian shades I post
  In hopes to be freed from care,
Where many a bleeding ghost
  Is hovering in the air.

---

## XX.—THE LADY DISTRACTED WITH LOVE,

### MAD SONG THE FOURTH,

WAS originally sung in one of Tom D'Urfey's comedies of Don Quixote, acted in 1694 and 1696, and probably composed by himself.

FROM rosie bowers, where sleeps the god of love,
  Hither ye little wanton cupids fly;
Teach me in soft melodious strains to move
  With tender passion my heart's darling joy:
Ah! let the soul of musick tune my voice,
To win dear Strephon, who my soul enjoys.

  Or, if more influencing
    Is to be brisk and airy,
With a step and a bound,
With a frisk from the ground,
  I'll trip like any fairy.

As once on Ida dancing
  Were three celestial bodies:
With an air, and a face,
And a shape, and a grace,
  I'll charm, like beauty's goddess.

Ah! 'tis in vain! 'tis all, 'tis all in vain!
Death and despair must end the fatal pain:
Cold, cold despair, disguis'd like snow and rain,

Falls on my breast; bleak winds in
    tempests blow;
My veins all shiver, and my fingers glow:
My pulse beats a dead march for lost
    repose,
And to a solid lump of ice my poor fond
    heart is froze.

Or say, ye powers, my peace to crown,
Shall I thaw myself and drown
    Among the foaming billows?
Increasing all with tears I shed,

On beds of ooze, and crystal pillows,
Lay down, lay down my love-sick head?

No, no, I'll strait run mad, mad, mad;
    That soon my heart will warm;
When once the sense is fled, is fled,
    Love has no power to charm.
Wild thro' the woods I'll fly, I'll fly,
    Robes, locks—shall thus—be tore!
A thousand, thousand times I'll dye
Ere thus, thus, in vain,—ere thus in
    vain adore.

---

## XXI.—THE DISTRACTED LOVER,

#### MAD SONG THE FIFTH,

WAS written by Henry Carey, a celebrated composer of music at the beginning of the eighteenth century, and author of several little theatrical entertainments, which the reader may find enumerated in the *Companion to the Play-house*, etc. The sprightliness of this songster's fancy could not preserve him from a very melancholy catastrophe, which was effected by his own hand.

I GO to the Elysian shade,
    Where sorrow ne'er shall wound me;
Where nothing shall my rest invade,
    But joy shall still surround me.

I fly from Celia's cold disdain,
    From her disdain I fly;
She is the cause of all my pain,
    For her alone I die.

Her eyes are brighter than the mid-day
    sun,
When he but half his radiant course has
    run,
When his meridian glories gaily shine,
And gild all nature with a warmth
    divine.

See yonder river's flowing tide,
    Which now so full appears;
Those streams, that do so swiftly glide,
    Are nothing but my tears.

There I have wept till I could weep no
    more,
And curst mine eyes, when they have
    wept their store:
Then, like the clouds, that rob the azure
    main,
I've drain'd the flood to weep it back
    again.

    Pity my pains,
    Ye gentle swains!
Cover me with ice and snow,
I scorch, I burn, I flame, I glow!

    Furies, tear me,
    Quickly bear me
To the dismal shades below!
    Where yelling, and howling,
    And grumbling, and growling,
Strike the ear with horrid woe.

    Hissing snakes,
    Fiery lakes

Would be a pleasure, and a cure :
Not all the hells,
Where Pluto dwells,
Can give such pain as I endure.

To some peaceful plain convey me,
On a mossey carpet lay me,
Fan me with ambrosial breeze,
Let me die, and so have ease!

## XXII.—THE FRANTIC LADY.

### MAD SONG THE SIXTH.

This, like No. XX., was originally sung in one of D'Urfey's comedies of Don Quixote (first acted about the year 1694), and was probably composed by that popular songster, who died Feb. 26, 1723.

I BURN, my brain consumes to ashes!
Each eye-ball too like lightning flashes!
Within my breast there glows a solid fire,
Which in a thousand ages can't expire!

 Blow, blow, the winds' great ruler!
 Bring the Po, and the Ganges hither,
 'Tis sultry weather ;
 Pour them all on my soul,
 It will hiss like a coal,
 But be never the cooler.

'Twas pride hot as hell,
That first made me rebell,

From love's awful throne a curst angel I fell ;
And mourn now my fate,
Which myself did create :
Fool, fool, that consider'd not when I was well!

Adieu! ye vain transporting joys!
Off, ye vain fantastic toys!
That dress this face—this body—to allure!
Bring me daggers, poison, fire!
Since scorn is turn'd into desire.
All hell feels not the rage, which I, poor I, endure.

## XXIII.—LILLI BURLERO.

The following rhymes, slight and insignificant as they may now seem, had once a most powerful effect, and contributed not a little towards the great revolution in 1688.

Burnet says : "A foolish ballad was made at that time, treating the Papists, and chiefly the Irish, in a very ridiculous manner, which had a burden said to be Irish words, 'Lero, lero, lilliburlero,' that made an impression on the [king's] army that cannot be imagined by those that saw it not. The whole army, and at last the people, both in city and country, were singing it perpetually. And perhaps never had so slight a thing so great an effect."

It was written, or at least republished, on the Earl of Tyrconnel's going a second time to Ireland, in October 1688. Perhaps it is unnecessary to mention that General Richard Talbot, newly created Earl of Tyrconnel, had been nominated by King James II. to the lieutenancy of Ireland in 1686, on account of his being a furious Papist, who had recommended himself to his bigoted master by his arbitrary treatmes of the Protestants in the preceding year, when only lieutenant-general, and whose subsequent conduct fully justified his expectations and their fears.

*Lilliburlero* and *Bullen-a-lah* are said to have been the words of distinction used among the Irish Papists in their massacre of the Protestants in 1641.

The song is attributed by some to Lord Wharton; by others, to Lord Dorset.

Ho! broder Teague, dost hear de decree?
    Lilli burlero, bullen a-la.
Dat we shall have a new deputie,
    Lilli burlero, bullen a-la.
        Lero lero, lilli burlero, lero lero,
            bullen a-la,
        Lero lero, lilli burlero, lero lero,
            bullen a-la.

Ho! by shaint Tyburn,\* it is de Talbote:
    Lilli, etc.
And he will cut de Englishmen's troate.
    Lilli, etc.

Dough by my shoul de English do praat,
    Lilli, etc.
De law's on dare side, and Creish knows what.
    Lilli, etc.

But if dispence do come from de pope,
    Lilli, etc.
We'll hang Magna Charta and dem in a rope.
    Lilli, etc.

For de good Talbot is made a lord,
    Lilli, etc.
And with brave lads is coming aboard:
    Lilli, etc.

Who all in France have taken a sware,
    Lilli, etc.

---

\* "Ho, by my shoul," another ed.

Dat dey will have no protestant heir.
    Lilli, etc.

Ara! but why does he stay behind?
    Lilli, etc.
Ho! by my shoul 'tis a protestant wind.
    Lilli, etc.

But see de Tyrconnel is now come ashore,
    Lilli, etc.
And we shall have commissions gillore.
    Lilli, etc.

And he dat will not go to de mass,
    Lilli, etc.
Shall be turn out, and look like an ass.
    Lilli, etc.

Now, now de hereticks all go down,
    Lilli, etc.
By Chrish and shaint Patrick, de nation's our own.
    Lilli, etc.

Dare was an old prophesy found in a bog,
    Lilli, etc.
"Ireland shall be rul'd by an ass and a dog."
    Lilli, etc.

And now dis prophesy is come to pass,
    Lilli, etc.
For Talbot's de dog, and JA—S is de ass.
    Lilli, etc.

## XXIV.—THE BRAES OF YARROW,

### IN IMITATION OF THE ANCIENT SCOTS MANNER.

WAS written by William Hamilton of Bangour, Esq., who died March 25, 1754, aged fifty. It is printed from an elegant edition of his poems, published at Edinburgh, 1760, 12mo. This song was written in imitation of an old Scottish ballad on a similar subject, with the same burden to each stanza.

*A.* Busk ye, busk ye, my bonny bonny bride,
 Busk ye, busk ye, my winsome marrow,
 Busk ye, busk ye, my bonny bonny bride,
 And think nae mair on the Braes of Yarrow.

*B.* Where gat ye that bonny bonny bride?
 Where gat ye that winsome marrow?
*A.* I gat her where I dare na weil be seen,
 Puing the birks on the Braes of Yarrow.

 Weep not, weep not, my bonny bonny bride,
 Weep not, weep not, my winsome marrow;
 Nor let thy heart lament to leive
 Puing the birks on the Braes of Yarrow.

*B.* Why does she weep, thy bonny bonny bride?
 Why does she weep, thy winsome marrow?
 And why dare ye nae mair weil be seen
 Puing the birks on the Braes of Yarrow?

*A.* Lang maun she weep, lang maun she, maun she weep,
 Lang maun she weep with dule and sorrow;
 And lang maun I nae mair weil be seen
 Puing the birks on the Braes of Yarrow.

For she has tint her luver, luver dear,
 Her luver dear, the cause of sorrow;
And I hae slain the comliest swain
 That eir pu'd birks on the Braes of Yarrow.

Why rins thy stream, O Yarrow, Yarrow, reid?
 Why on thy braes heard the voice of sorrow?
And why yon melancholious weids
 Hung on the bonny birks of Yarrow?

What's yonder floats on the rueful rueful flude?
 What's yonder floats? O dule and sorrow!
O 'tis he the comely swain I slew
 Upon the duleful Braes of Yarrow.

Wash, O wash his wounds, his wounds in tears,
 His wounds in tears with dule and sorrow;
And wrap his limbs in mourning weids,
 And lay him on the Braes of Yarrow.

Then build, then build, ye sisters, sisters sad,
 Ye sisters sad, his tomb with sorrow;
And weep around in waeful wise
 His hapless fate on the Braes of Yarrow.

Curse ye, curse ye, his useless, useless shield,
 My arm that wrought the deed of sorrow;

The fatal spear that pierc'd his breast,
   His comely breast on the Braes of
   Yarrow.

Did I not warn thee, not to, not to luve?
   And warn from fight? but to my
   sorrow
Too rashly bauld a stronger arm
   Thou mett'st and fell'st on the Braes
   of Yarrow.

Sweet smells the birk, green grows,
   green grows the grass,
Yellow on Yarrow's banks the gowan,
Fair hangs the apple frae the rock,
   Sweet the wave of Yarrow flowan.

Flows Yarrow sweet? as sweet, as
   sweet flows Tweed,
As green its grass, its gowan as yel-
   low,
As sweet smells on its braes the birk,
   The apple frae its rock as mellow.

Fair was thy luve, fair fair indeed thy
   luve,
In flow'ry bands thou didst him fetter;
Tho' he was fair, and weil beluv'd again,
   Than me he never luv'd thee better.

Busk ye, then busk, my bonny bonny
   bride,
Busk ye, busk ye, my winsome mar-
   row,
Busk ye, and luve me on the banks of
   Tweed,
   And think nae mair on the Braes of
   Yarrow.

C. How can I busk a bonny bonny bride?
   How can I busk a winsome marrow?
How luve him upon the banks of Tweed,
   That slew my luve on the Braes of
   Yarrow?

O Yarrow fields, may never never rain
   Nor dew thy tender blossoms cover,
For there was basely slain my luve,
   My luve, as he had not been a lover.

The boy put on his robes, his robes of
   green,
   His purple vest, 'twas my awn sew-
   ing:
Ah! wretched me! I little, little kenn'd
   He was in these to meet his ruin.

The boy took out his milk-white, milk-
   white steed,
   Unheedful of my dule and sorrow:
But ere the toofall of the night
   He lay a corps on the Braes of Yar-
   row.

Much I rejoyc'd that waeful waeful day;
   I sang, my voice the woods returning:
But lang ere night the spear was flown,
   That slew my luve, and left me
   mourning.

What can my barbarous barbarous
   father do,
But with his cruel rage pursue me?
My luver's blood is on thy spear,
   How canst thou, barbarous man,
   then wooe me?

My happy sisters may be, may be
   proud
   With cruel and ungentle scoffin',
May bid me seek on Yarrow's Braes
   My luver nailed in his coffin.

My brother Douglas may upbraid,
   upbraid,
   And strive with threatning words to
   muve me:
My luver's blood is on thy spear,
   How canst thou ever bid me luve
   thee?

Yes, yes, prepare the bed, the bed of
   luve,
   With bridal sheets my body cover,

Unbar, ye bridal maids, the door,
   Let in the expected husband lover.

But who the expected husband husband is?
   His hands, methinks, are bath'd in slaughter:
Ah me! what ghastly spectre's yon
Comes in his pale shroud, bleeding after?

Pale as he is, here lay him, lay him down,
   O lay his cold head on my pillow;
Take aff, take aff these bridal weids,
And crown my careful head with willow.

Pale tho' thou art, yet best, yet best beluv'd,
   O could my warmth to life restore thee!
Yet lye all night between my breists,
   No youth lay ever there before thee.

Pale, pale indeed, O luvely luvely youth!
Forgive, forgive so foul a slaughter:
And lye all night between my breists;
   No youth shall ever lye there after.

*A.* Return, return, O mournful, mournful bride,
Return, and dry thy useless sorrow:
Thy luver heeds none of thy sighs,
   He lyes a corps in the Braes of Yarrow.

## XXV.—ADMIRAL HOSIER'S GHOST

WAS a party song written by the ingenious author of *Leonidas*, on the taking of Porto Bello from the Spaniards by Admiral Vernon, Nov. 22, 1739. The case of Hosier, which is here so pathetically represented, was briefly this:—In April 1726, that commander was sent with a strong fleet into the Spanish West Indies, to block up the galleons in the ports of that country, or, should they presume to come out, to seize and carry them into England; he accordingly arrived at the Bastimentos near Porto Bello, but being employed rather to overawe than to attack the Spaniards, with whom it was probably not our interest to go to war, he continued long inactive on that station, to his own great regret. He afterwards removed to Carthagena, and remained cruising in these seas, till far the greater part of his men perished deplorably by the diseases of that unhealthy climate. This brave man, seeing his best officers and men thus daily swept away, his ships exposed to inevitable destruction, and himself made the sport of the enemy, is said to have died of a broken heart. Such is the account of Smollett, compared with that of other less partial writers.

As near Porto-Bello lying
   On the gently swelling flood,
At midnight with streamers flying
   Our triumphant navy rode;
There while Vernon sate all-glorious
   From the Spaniards' late defeat:
And his crews, with shouts victorious,
   Drank success to England's fleet:

On a sudden shrilly sounding,
   Hideous yells and shrieks were heard;
Then each heart with fear confounding,
   A sad troop of ghosts appear'd.
All in dreary hammocks shrouded,
   Which for winding-sheets they wore,
And with looks by sorrow clouded
   Frowning on that hostile shore.

On them gleam'd the moon's wan lustre,
  When the shade of Hosier brave
His pale bands were seen to muster
  Rising from their watry grave.
O'er the glimmering wave he hy'd him,
  Where the Burford* rear'd her sail,
With three thousand ghosts beside him,
  And in groans did Vernon hail.

Heed, oh heed our fatal story,
  I am Hosier's injur'd ghost,
You who now have purchas'd glory
  At this place where I was lost!
Tho' in Porto-Bello's ruin
  You now triumph free from fears,
When you think on our undoing,
  You will mix your joy with tears.

See these mournful spectres sweeping
  Ghastly o'er this hated wave,
Whose wan cheeks are stain'd with weeping;
  These were English captains brave.
Mark those numbers pale and horrid,
  Those were once my sailors bold:
Lo, each hangs his drooping forehead,
  While his dismal tale is told.

I, by twenty sail attended,
  Did this Spanish town affright;
Nothing then its wealth defended
  But my orders not to fight.
Oh! that in this rolling ocean
  I had cast them with disdain,
And obey'd my heart's warm motion
  To have quell'd the pride of Spain!

For resistance I could fear none,
  But with twenty ships had done

---

\* Admiral Vernon's ship.

What thou, brave and happy Vernon,
  Hast achiev'd with six alone.
Then the bastimentos never
  Had our foul dishonour seen,
Nor the sea the sad receiver
  Of this gallant train had been.

Thus, like thee, proud Spain dismaying,
  And her galleons leading home,
Though condemn'd for disobeying,
  I had met a traitor's doom,
To have fallen, my country crying
  He has play'd an English part,
Had been better far than dying
  Of a griev'd and broken heart.

Unrepining at thy glory,
  Thy successful arms we hail;
But remember our sad story,
  And let Hosier's wrongs prevail.
Sent in this foul clime to languish,
  Think what thousands fell in vain,
Wasted with disease and anguish,
  Not in glorious battle slain.

Hence with all my train attending
  From their oozy tombs below,
Thro' the hoary foam ascending,
  Here I feed my constant woe:
Here the bastimentos viewing,
  We recal our shameful doom,
And our plaintive cries renewing,
  Wander thro' the midnight gloom.

O'er these waves for ever mourning
  Shall we roam depriv'd of rest,
If to Britain's shores returning
  You neglect my just request;
After this proud foe subduing,
  When your patriot friends you see,
Think on vengeance for my ruin,
  And for England sham'd in me.

## XXVI.—JEMMY DAWSON.

JAMES DAWSON was one of the Manchester rebels, who was hanged, drawn, and quartered, on Kennington Common, in the county of Surrey, July 30, 1746. This ballad is founded on a remarkable fact which was reported to have happened at his execution. It was written by the late William Shenstone, Esq., soon after the event, and has been printed amongst his posthumous works, 2 vols. 8vo. It is here given from a MS. which contained some small variations from that printed copy.

COME listen to my mournful tale,
  Ye tender hearts, and lovers dear;
Nor will you scorn to heave a sigh,
  Nor will you blush to shed a tear.

And thou, dear Kitty, peerless maid,
  Do thou a pensive ear incline;
For thou canst weep at every woe,
  And pity every plaint, but mine.

Young Dawson was a gallant youth,
  A brighter never trod the plain;
And well he lov'd one charming maid,
  And dearly was he lov'd again.

One tender maid she lov'd him dear,
  Of gentle blood the damsel came,
And faultless was her beauteous form,
  And spotless was her virgin fame.

But curse on party's hateful strife,
  That led the faithful youth astray
The day the rebel clans appear'd:
  O had he never seen that day!

Their colours and their sash he wore,
  And in the fatal dress was found;
And now he must that death endure,
  Which gives the brave the keenest wound.

How pale was then his true love's cheek,
  When Jemmy's sentence reach'd her ear!
For never yet did Alpine snows
  So pale, nor yet so chill appear.

With faltering voice she weeping said,
  Oh, Dawson, monarch of my heart,
Think not thy death shall end our loves,
  For thou and I will never part.

Yet might sweet mercy find a place,
  And bring relief to Jemmy's woes,
O George, without a prayer for thee
  My orisons should never close.

The gracious prince that gives him life
  Would crown a never-dying flame,
And every tender babe I bore
  Should learn to lisp the giver's name.

But though, dear youth, thou should'st be dragg'd
  To yonder ignominious tree,
Thou shalt not want a faithful friend
  To share thy bitter fate with thee.

O then her mourning-coach was call'd,
  The sledge mov'd slowly on before;
Tho' borne in a triumphal car,
  She had not lov'd her favourite more.

She followed him, prepar'd to view
  The terrible behests of law;
And the last scene of Jemmy's woes
  With calm and stedfast eye she saw.

Distorted was that blooming face,
  Which she had fondly lov'd so long;
And stifled was that tuneful breath,
  Which in her praise had sweetly sung:

And sever'd was that beauteous neck,
　Round which her arms had fondly clos'd:
And mangled was that beauteous breast,
　On which her love-sick head repos'd:

And ravish'd was that constant heart,
　She did to every heart prefer;
For though it could his king forget,
　'Twas true and loyal still to her.

Amid those unrelenting flames
　She bore this constant heart to see;
But when 'twas moulder'd into dust,
　Now, now, she cried, I'll follow thee.

My death, my death alone can show
　The pure and lasting love I bore:
Accept, O heaven, of woes like ours,
　And let us, let us weep no more.

The dismal scene was o'er and past,
　The lover's mournful hearse retir'd;
The maid drew back her languid head,
　And sighing forth his name expir'd.

Tho' justice ever must prevail,
　The tear my Kitty sheds is due;
For seldom shall she hear a tale
　So sad, so tender, and so true.

**THE END OF THE THIRD BOOK.**

## SERIES THE THIRD.—BOOK I.

### I.—POEMS ON KING ARTHUR, ETC.

THE third volume being chiefly devoted to romantic subjects, may not be improperly introduced with a few slight strictures on the old Metrical Romances: a subject the more worthy attention, as it seems not to have been known to such as have written on the nature and origin of books of chivalry, that the first compositions of this kind were in verse, and usually sung to the harp.

#### ON THE ANCIENT METRICAL ROMANCES, ETC.

I. THE first attempts at composition among all barbarous nations are ever found to be poetry and song. The praises of their gods, and the achievements of their heroes, are usually chanted at their festival meetings. These are the first rudiments of history. It is in this manner that the savages of North America preserve the memory of past events, and the same method is known to have prevailed among our Saxon ancestors, before they quitted their German forests. The ancient Britons had their bards, and the Gothic nations their scalds or popular poets, whose business it was to record the victories of their warriors, and the genealogies of their princes, in a kind of narrative songs, which were committed to memory, and delivered down from one reciter to another. So long as poetry continued a distinct profession, and while the bard, or scald, was a regular and stated officer in the prince's court, these men are thought to have performed the functions of the historian pretty faithfully; for though their narrations would be apt to receive a good deal of embellishment, they are supposed to have had at the bottom so much of truth as to serve for the basis of more regular annals. At least succeeding historians have taken up with the relations of these rude men, and, for want of more authentic records, have agreed to allow them the credit of true history.

After letters began to prevail, and history assumed a more stable form, by being committed to plain simple prose, these songs of the scalds or bards began to be more amusing than useful; and in proportion as it became their business chiefly to entertain and delight, they gave more and more into embellishment, and set off their recitals with such marvellous fictions as were calculated to captivate gross and ignorant minds. Thus began stories of adventures with giants and dragons, and witches and enchanters, and all the monstrous extravagances of wild imagination, unguided by judgment and uncorrected by art.

This seems to be the true origin of that species of romance which so long celebrated feats of chivalry, and which, at first in metre and afterwards in prose, was the entertainment of our ancestors, in common with their contemporaries on the Continent, till the satire of Cervantes, or rather the increase of knowledge and classical literature, drove them off the stage, to make room for a more refined species of fiction, under the name of French Romances, copied from the Greek.

That our old romances of chivalry may be derived in a lineal descent from the ancient historical songs of the Gothic bards and scalds, will be shown below, and indeed appears the more evident, as many of those songs are still preserved in the north, which exhibit all the seeds of chivalry before it became a solemn institution. "Chivalry, as a distinct military order, conferred in the way of investiture, and accompanied with the solemnity of an oath, and other ceremonies," was of later date, and sprung out of the feudal constitution. But the ideas of chivalry prevailed long before in all the Gothic nations, and may be discovered a sin embryo in the customs, manners, and opinions of every branch of that people. That fondness of going in quest of adventures, that spirit of challenging to single combat, and that respectful complaisance shown to the fair sex (so different from the manners of the Greeks and Romans), all are of Gothic origin, and may be traced up to the earliest times among all the northern nations. These existed long before the feudal ages, though they were called forth and strengthened in a peculiar manner under that constitution, and at length arrived to their full maturity in the times of the Crusades, so replete with romantic adventures.*

Even the common arbitrary fictions of romance were (as is hinted above) most of them familiar to the ancient scalds of the north long before the time of the Crusades. They believed the existence of giants and dwarfs; they entertained opinions not unlike the more modern notion of fairies; they were strongly possessed with the belief of spells and enchantment; and were fond of inventing combats with dragons and monsters.

The opinion therefore seems very untenable, which some learned and ingenious men have entertained, that the turn for chivalry, and the taste for that species of romantic fiction were caught by the Spaniards from the Arabians or Moors after their invasion of Spain, and from the Spaniards transmitted to the bards of Armorica, and thus diffused through Britain, France, Italy, Germany, and the north. For it seems utterly incredible that one rude people should adopt a peculiar taste and manner of writing or thinking from another, without borrowing at the same time any of their particular stories and fables, without appearing to know anything of their heroes, history, laws, and religion. When the Romans began to adopt and imitate the

---

* The seeds of chivalry sprung up so naturally out of the original manners and opinions of the northern nations, that it is not credible they arose so late as after the establishment of the feudal system, much less the Crusades; nor, again, that the romances of chivalry were transmitted to other nations through the Spaniards from the Moors and Arabians. Had this been the case, the first French romances of chivalry would have been on Moorish or at least Spanish subjects; whereas the most ancient stories of this kind, whether in prose or verse, whether in Italian, French, English, etc., are chiefly on the subjects of Charlemagne and the Paladins, or of our British Arthur and his Knights of the Round Table, etc., being evidently borrowed from the fabulous chronicles of the supposed Archbishop Turpin, and of Jeffery of Monmouth. Not but some of the oldest and most popular French romances are also on Norman subjects, as *Richard Sans-peur, Robert le Diable*, etc.; whereas I do not recollect so much as one in which the scene is laid in Spain, much less among the Moors, or descriptive of Mahometan manners. Even in *Amadis de Gaul*, said to have been the first romance printed in Spain, the scene is laid in Gaul and Britain; and the manners are French, which plainly shows from what school this species of fabling was learnt and transmitted to the southern nations of Europe.

Grecian literature, they immediately naturalized all the Grecian fables, histories, and religious stories, which became as familiar to the poets of Rome as of Greece itself; whereas all the old writers of chivalry, and of that species of romance, whether in prose or verse, whether of the northern nations or of Britain, France, and Italy, not excepting Spain itself,* appear utterly unacquainted with whatever relates to the Mahometan nations. Thus with regard to their religion, they constantly represent them as worshipping idols, as paying adoration to a golden image of Mahomet, or else they confound them with the ancient pagans. And indeed in all other respects they are so grossly ignorant of the customs, manners, and opinions of every branch of that people, especially of their heroes, champions, and local stories, as almost amounts to a demonstration that they did not imitate them in their songs or romances: for as to dragons, serpents, necromancies, why should these be thought only derived from the Moors in Spain so late as after the eighth century, since notions of this kind appear too familiar to the northern scalds, and enter too deeply into all the northern mythology, to have been transmitted to the unlettered Scandinavians, from so distant a country, at so late a period? If they may not be allowed to have brought these opinions with them in their original migrations from the north of Asia, they will be far more likely to have borrowed them from the Latin poets after the Roman conquests in Gaul, Britain, Germany, etc. For I believe one may challenge the maintainers of this opinion to produce any Arabian poem or history that could possibly have been then known in Spain, which resembles the old Gothic romances of chivalry half so much as the *Metamorphoses* of Ovid.

But we well know that the Scythian nations, situate in the countries about Pontus, Colchis, and the Euxine Sea, were in all times infamous for their magic arts: and as Odin and his followers are said to have come precisely from those parts of Asia, we can readily account for the prevalence of fictions of this sort among the Gothic nations of the north, without fetching them from the Moors in Spain, who for many centuries after their irruption lived in a state of such constant hostility with the unsubdued Spanish Christians, whom they chiefly pent up in the mountains, as gave them no chance of learning their music, poetry, or stories; and this, together with the religious hatred of the latter for their cruel invaders, will account for the utter ignorance of the old Spanish romancers in whatever relates to the Mahometan nations, although so nearly their own neighbours.

On the other hand, from the local customs and situations, from the known manners and opinions of the Gothic nations in the north, we can easily account for all the ideas of chivalry and its peculiar fictions. For, not to mention their distinguished respect for the fair sex, so different from the manners of the Mahometan nations, their national and domestic history so naturally assumes all the wonders of this species of fabling, that almost all their historical narratives appear regular romances. One

---

* The little narrative songs on Morisco subjects, which the Spaniards have in great abundance, and which they call peculiarly Romances, have nothing in common with their proper romances (or histories) of chivalry, which they call *Historias de Cavallerias*. These are evidently imitations of the French, and show a great ignorance of Moorish manners; and with regard to the Morisco or song romances, they do not seem to be of very great antiquity; few of them appear, from their subjects, much earlier than the reduction of Granada, in the fifteenth century; from which period, I believe, may be plainly traced among the Spanish writers a more perfect knowledge of Moorish customs, etc.

might refer, in proof of this, to the old northern sagas in general; but to give a particular instance, it will be sufficient to produce the *History of King Regner Lodbrog*, a celebrated warrior and pirate, who reigned in Denmark about the year 800. This hero signalized his youth by an exploit of gallantry. A Swedish prince had a beautiful daughter, whom he intrusted (probably during some expedition) to the care of one of his officers, assigning a strong castle for their defence. The officer fell in love with his ward, and detained her in his castle, spite of all the efforts of her father. Upon this he published a proclamation through all the neighbouring countries, that whoever would conquer the ravisher and rescue the lady should have her in marriage. Of all that undertook the adventure, Regner alone was so happy as to achieve it: he delivered the fair captive, and obtained her for his prize. It happened that the name of this discourteous officer was Orme, which in the Icelandic language means serpent: wherefore the scalds, to give the more poetical turn to the adventure, represent the lady as detained from her father by a dreadful dragon, and that Regner slew the monster to set her at liberty. This fabulous account of the exploit is given in a poem still extant, which is even ascribed to Regner himself, who was a celebrated poet, and which records all the valiant achievements of his life.

With marvellous embellishments of this kind the scalds early began to decorate their narratives; and they were the more lavish of these in proportion as they departed from their original institution; but it was a long time before they thought of delivering a set of personages and adventures wholly feigned. Of the great multitude of romantic tales still preserved in the libraries of the north, most of them are supposed to have had some foundation in truth; and the more ancient they are, the more they are believed to be connected with true history.

It was not, probably, till after the historian and the bard had been long disunited, that the latter ventured at pure fiction. At length, when their business was no longer to instruct or inform, but merely to amuse, it was no longer needful for them to adhere to truth. Then succeeded fabulous songs and romances in verse, which for a long time prevailed in France and England, before they had books of chivalry in prose. Yet in both these countries the minstrels still retained so much of their original institution as frequently to make true events the subject of their songs; and indeed, as during the barbarous ages the regular histories were almost all written in Latin by the monks, the memory of events was preserved and propagated among the ignorant laity by scarce any other means than the popular songs of the minstrels.

II. The inhabitants of Sweden, Denmark, and Norway, being the latest converts to Christianity, retained their original manners and opinions longer than the other nations of Gothic race; and therefore they have preserved more of the genuine compositions of their ancient poets than their southern neighbours. Hence the progress, among them, from poetical history to poetical fiction is very discernible; they have some old pieces, that are in effect complete romances of chivalry. They have also (as hath been observed) a multitude of sagas or histories on romantic subjects, containing a mixture of prose and verse, of various dates, some of them written since the times of the Crusades, others long before; but their narratives in verse only are esteemed the more ancient.

Now, as the irruption of the Normans or Northmen into France under Rollo did not take place till towards the beginning of the tenth century, at which time the scaldic art was arrived at the highest perfection in Rollo's native country, we can easily trace the descent of the French and English romances of chivalry from the northern sagas. That conqueror doubtless carried many scalds with him from the north, who transmitted their skill to their children and successors. These, adopting the religion, opinions, and language of the new country, substituted the heroes of Christendom instead of those of their pagan ancestors, and began to celebrate the feats of Charlemagne, Roland, and Oliver, whose true history they set off and embellished with the scaldic figments of dwarfs, giants, dragons, and enchantments. The first mention we have in song of those heroes of chivalry is in the mouth of a Norman warrior at the conquest of England; and this circumstance alone would sufficiently account for the propagation of this kind of romantic poems among the French and English.

But this is not all; it is very certain that both the Anglo-Saxons and the Franks had brought with them, at their first emigrations into Britain and Gaul, the same fondness for the ancient songs of their ancestors which prevailed among the other Gothic tribes, and that all their first annals were transmitted in these popular oral poems. This fondness they even retained long after their conversion to Christianity, as we learn from the examples of Charlemagne and Alfred. Now poetry, being thus the transmitter of facts, would as easily learn to blend them with fictions in France and England as she is known to have done in the north, and that much sooner, for the reasons before assigned. This, together with the example and influence of the Normans, will easily account to us why the first romances of chivalry that appeared both in England and France were composed in metre as a rude kind of epic songs. In both kingdoms, tales in verse were usually sung by minstrels to the harp on festival occasions; and doubtless both nations derived their relish for this sort of entertainment from their Teutonic ancestors, without either of them borrowing it from the other. Among both peoples, narrative songs on true or fictitious subjects had evidently obtained from the earliest times. But the professed romances of chivalry seem to have been first composed in France, where also they had their name.

The Latin tongue ceased to be spoken in France about the ninth century, and was succeeded by what was called the Romance tongue, a mixture of the language of the Franks and bad Latin. As the songs of chivalry became the most popular compositions in that language, they were emphatically called Romans or Romants, though this name was at first given to any piece of poetry. The romances of chivalry can be traced as early as the eleventh century. I know not if the *Roman de Brut*, written in 1155, was such. But if it was, it was by no means the first poem of the kind; others more ancient are still extant. And we have already seen that, in the preceding century, when the Normans marched down to the battle of Hastings, they animated themselves by singing (in some popular romance or ballad) the exploits of Roland and the other heroes of chivalry.

So early as this I cannot trace the songs of chivalry in English. The most ancient I have seen is that of Hornechild, described below, which seems not older than the twelfth century. However, as this rather resembles the Saxon poetry than the French, it is not certain that the first English romances were translated from that language. We have seen above, that a propensity to this kind of fiction prevailed among all the Gothic nations; and though, after the Norman Conquest, this country abounded with French romances, or with translations from the French, there is good reason to believe that the English had original pieces of their own.

The stories of King Arthur and his Round Table may be reasonably supposed of the growth of this island; both the French and the Armoricans probably had them from Britain. The stories of Guy, and Bevis, with some others, were probably the invention of English minstrels.* On the other hand, the English procured translations of such romances as were most current in France; and in the list given at the conclusion of these remarks many are doubtless of French original.

The first prose books of chivalry that appeared in our language were those printed by Caxton;† at least, these are the first I have been able to discover, and these are all translations from the French. Whereas romances of this kind had been long current in metre, and were so generally admired in the time of Chaucer that his *Rhyme of Sir Thopas* was evidently written to ridicule and burlesque them.

He expressly mentions several of them by name in a stanza, which I shall have occasion to quote more than once in this volume:

> "Men speken of Romaunces of pris,
> Of Horn-Child, and of Ipotis,
> Of Bevis, and Sire Guy,
> Of Sire Libeux, and Pleindamour,
> But Sire Thopas, he bereth the flour
> Of real chevalrie."‡

Most if not all of these are still extant in MS. in some or other of our libraries. As many of these contain a considerable portion of poetic merit, and throw great light on the manners and opinions of former times, it were to be wished that some of the best of them were rescued from oblivion. A judicious collection of them accurately published, with proper illustrations, would be an important accession to our stock of ancient English literature. Many of them exhibit no mean attempts at epic poetry, and though full of the exploded fictions of chivalry, frequently display great descriptive and inventive powers in the bards who composed them. They are at least generally equal to any other poetry of the same age. They cannot indeed be put in competition with the nervous productions of so universal and commanding a genius as Chaucer; but they have a simplicity that makes them be read with less interruption, and be more easily understood; and they are far more

---

* It is most credible that these stories were originally of English invention, even if the only pieces now extant should be found to be translations from the French. What now pass for the French originals were probably only amplifications or enlargements of the old English story. That the French romancers borrowed some things from the English, appears from the word Termagant, which they took up from our minstrels, and corrupted into Tervagaunte. See vol i. p. 77, and Gloss. "Termagant."

† *Recuyel of the Hystoryes of Troy,* 1471; *Godfroye of Boloyne,* 1481; *Le Morte de Arthur,* 1485; *The Life of Charlemagne,* 1485, etc. As the old minstrelsy wore out, prose books of chivalry became more admired, especially after the Spanish romances began to be translated into English towards the end of Queen Elizabeth's reign; then the most popular metrical romances began to be reduced into prose, as Sir Guy, Bevis, etc.

‡ *Canterbury Tales* (Tyrwhitt's edition), vol. ii. p. 238. In all the former editions which I have seen, the name at the end of the fourth line is Blandamoure.

spirited and entertaining than the tedious allegories of Gower, or the dull and prolix legends of Lydgate. Yet, while so much stress was laid upon the writings of these last, by such as treat of English poetry, the old metrical romances, though far more popular in their time, were hardly known to exist. But it has happened, unluckily, that the antiquaries, who have revived the works of our ancient writers, have been, for the most part, men void of taste and genius, and therefore have always fastidiously rejected the old poetical romances, because founded on fictitious or popular subjects, while they have been careful to grub up every petty fragment of the most dull and insipid rhymist, whose merit it was to deform morality or obscure true history. Should the public encourage the revival of some of those ancient epic songs of chivalry, they would frequently see the rich ore of an Ariosto or a Tasso, though buried it may be among the rubbish and dross of barbarous times.

Such a publication would answer many important uses: It would throw new light on the rise and progress of English poetry, the history of which can be but imperfectly understood if these are neglected: It would also serve to illustrate innumerable passages in our ancient classic poets, which, without their help, must be for ever obscure. For, not to mention Chaucer and Spenser, who abound with perpetual allusions to them, I shall give an instance or two from Shakespeare, by way of specimen of their use.

In his play of *King John* our great dramatic poet alludes to an exploit of Richard I. which the reader will in vain look for in any true history. Faulconbridge says to his mother, Act i. Sc. i.:

> "Needs must you lay your heart at his dispose . . .
> Against whose furie and unmatched force,
> The awlesse lion could not wage the fight,
> Nor keepe his princely heart from Richard's hand:
> He that perforce robs Lions of their hearts
> May easily winne a woman's."

The fact here referred to is to be traced to its source only in the old romance of *Richard Ceur De Lyon*, in which his encounter with a lion makes a very shining figure. I shall give a large extract from this poem, as a specimen of the manner of these old rhapsodists, and to show that they did not in their fictions neglect the proper means to produce the ends, as was afterwards so childishly done in the prose books of chivalry.

The poet tells us that Richard, in his return from the Holy Land, having been discovered in the habit of "a palmer in Almayne," and apprehended as a spy, was by the king thrown into prison. Wardrewe, the king's son, hearing of Richard's great strength, desires the jailor to let him have a sight of his prisoners. Richard being the foremost, Wardrewe asks him "if he dare stand a buffet from his hand," and that on the morrow he shall return him another. Richard consents, and receives a blow that staggers him. On the morrow, having previously waxed his hands, he waits his antagonist's arrival. Wardrewe accordingly, proceeds the story, "held forth as a trewe man," and Richard gave him such a blow on the cheek, as broke his jaw-bone, and killed him on the spot. The king, to revenge the death of his son, orders, by the advice of one Eldrede, that a lion, kept purposely from food, shall be turned loose upon Richard. But the king's daughter, having fallen in love with him, tells him of her father's resolution, and at his request procures him forty ells of white silk "kerchers;" and here the description of the combat begins:

> \* The kever-chiefs \* he toke on honde,
> And aboute his arme he wonde ;
> And thought in that ylke while,
> To slee the lyon with some gyle.
> And syngle in a kyrtyll he stode,
> And abode the lyon fyers and wode,
> With that came the jaylere,
> And other men that wyth him were,
> And the lyon them amonge ;
> His pawes were stiffe and stronge.
> The chambre dore they undone,
> And the lyon to them is gone.
> Rycharde sayd, Helpe, lorde Jesu!
> The lyon made to hym venu,
> And wolde hym have all to rente:
> Kynge Rycharde besyde hym glente,†
> The lyon on the breste hym spurned,
> That aboute he tourned.
> The lyon was hongry and megre,
> And bette his tayle to be egre ;
> He loked aboute as he were madde;
> Abrode he all his pawes spradde.
> He cryed lowde, and yaned ‡ wide,
> Kynge Rycharde bethought hym that tyde
> What hym was beste, and to hym sterte,
> In at the throte his honde he gerte,
> And hente out the herte with his honde,
> Lounge and all that he there fonde.
> The lyon fell deed to the grounde :
> Rycharde felte no wem,§ ne wounde.
> He fell on his knees on that place,
> And thanked Jesu of his grace."
>
> . . . . . . .

What follows is not so well, and therefore I shall extract no more of this poem. For the above feat, the author tells us, the king was deservedly called

"Stronge Rycharde Cure de Lyowne."

That distich which Shakespeare puts in the mouth of his madman in *King Lear*, Act. iii. Sc. iv.,

"Mice and rats and such small deere
Have been Tom's food for seven long yeare,"

has excited the attention of the critics. Instead of *deere*, one of them, Dr. Warburton, would subsitute *geer;* and another, Dr. Grey, *cheer*. But the ancient reading is established by the old romance of Sir Bevis, which Shakespeare had doubtless often

---

\* *i.e.* handkerchiefs. Here we have the etymology of the word, viz. *couvre le chef.*
† *i.e.* slipped aside.      ‡ *i.e.* yawned.      § *i.e.* hurt

heard sung to the harp. This distich is part of a description there given of the hardships suffered by Bevis, when confined for seven years in a dungeon:

> "Rattes and myse and such small dere
> Was his meate that seven yere."

III. In different parts of this work, the reader will find various extracts from these old poetical legends, to which I refer him for further examples of their style and metre. To complete this subject, it will be proper at least to give one specimen of their skill in distributing and conducting their fable, by which it will be seen that nature and common sense had supplied to these old simple bards the want of critical art, and taught them some of the most essential rules of epic poetry.—I shall select the romances of *Libius Disconius*,\* as being one of those mentioned by Chaucer, and either shorter or more intelligible than the others he has quoted.

My copy is divided into nine parts or cantos, the several arguments of which are as follows.

### PART I.

Opens with a short exordium to bespeak attention: the hero is described; a natural son of Sir Gawain, a celebrated knight of King Arthur's court, who being brought up in a forest by his mother, is kept ignorant of his name and descent. He early exhibits marks of his courage, by killing a knight in single combat, who encountered him as he was hunting. This inspires him with a desire of seeking adventures: therefore cloathing himself in his enemy's armour, he goes to King Arthur's court, to request the order of knighthood. His request granted, he obtains a promise of having the first adventure assigned him that shall offer.—A damsel named Ellen, attended by a dwarf, comes to implore King Arthur's assistance, to rescue a young princess, "the Lady of Sinadone" their mistress, who is detained from her rights, and confined in prison. The adventure is claimed by the young knight Sir Lybius: the king assents; the messengers are dissatisfied, and object to his youth; but are forced to acquiesce. And here the first book closes with a description of the ceremony of equipping him forth.

### PART II.

Sir Lybius sets out on the adventure: he is derided by the dwarf and the damsel on account of his youth: they come to the bridge of Perill, which none can pass without encountering a knight called William de la Braunch. Sir Lybius is challenged: they just with their spears: De la Braunch is dismounted: the battle is renewed on foot: Sir William's sword breaks: he yields. Sir Lybius makes him swear to go and present himself to King Arthur, as the first-fruits of his valour. The conquered knight sets out for King Arthur's court: is met by three knights, his kinsmen; who, informed of his disgrace, vow revenge, and pursue the conqueror. The next day they overtake him: the eldest of the three attacks Sir Lybius; but is overthrown to the ground. The two other brothers assault him: Sir Lybius is wounded; yet cuts off

---

\* So it is entitled in the Editor's MS. But the true title is, *Les beaux disconnus*, or The fair unknown. See a note on the *Canterbury Tales*, vol. iv. p. 333.

the second brother's arm : the third yields ; Sir Lybius sends them all to King Arthur. In the third evening he is awaked by the dwarf, who has discovered a fire in the wood.

### PART III.

Sir Lybius arms himself, and leaps on horseback : he finds two giants roasting a wild boar, who have a fair lady their captive. Sir Lybius, by favour of the night, runs one of them through with his spear : is assaulted by the other : a fierce battle ensues : he cuts off the giant's arm, and at length his head. The rescued lady (an earl's daughter) tells him her story ; and leads him to her father's castle ; who entertains him with a great feast ; and presents him at parting with a suit of armour and a steed. He sends the giant's head to King Arthur.

### PART IV.

Sir Lybius, maid Ellen, and the dwarf, renew their journey : they see a castle stuck round with human heads ; and are informed it belongs to a knight called Sir Gefferon, who, in honour of his lemman or mistress, challenges all comers : he that can produce a fairer lady, is to be rewarded with a milk-white faulcon, but if overcome, to lose his head. Sir Lybius spends the night in the adjoining town : in the morning goes to challenge the faulcon. The knights exchange their gloves : they agree to just in the market place : the lady and maid Ellen are placed aloft in chairs : their dresses : the superior beauty of Sir Gefferon's mistress described : the ceremonies previous to the combat. They engage : the combat described at large : Sir Gefferon is incurably hurt ; and carried home on his shield. Sir Lybius sends the faulcon to King Arthur ; and receives back a large present in florins. He stays forty days to be cured of his wounds, which he spends in feasting with the neighbouring lords.

### PART V.

Sir Lybius proceeds for Sinadone : in a forest he meets a knight hunting, called Sir Otes de Lisle : maid Ellen charmed with a very beautiful dog, begs Sir Lybius to bestow him upon her : Sir Otes meets them, and claims his dog : is refused : being unarmed he rides to his castle, and summons his followers : they go in quest of Sir Lybius : a battle ensues : he is still victorious, and forces Sir Otes to follow the other conquered knights to King Arthur.

### PART VI.

Sir Lybius comes to a fair city and castle by a riverside, beset round with pavilions or tents: he is informed, in the castle is a beautiful lady besieged by a giant named Maugys, who keeps the bridge, and will let none pass without doing him homage : this Lybius refuses : a battle ensues : the giant described : the several incidents of the battle ; which lasts a whole summer's day : the giant is wounded ; put to flight ; slain. The citizens come out in procession to meet their deliverer : the lady invites him into her castle : falls in love with him ; and seduces him to her embraces. He forgets the princess of Sinadone, and stays with this bewitching lady a twelvemonth.

This fair sorceress, like another Alcina, intoxicates him with all kinds of sensual pleasure; and detains him from the pursuit of honour.

### PART VII.

Maid Ellen by chance gets an opportunity of speaking to him; and upbraids him with his vice and folly: he is filled with remorse, and escapes the same evening. At length he arrives at the city and castle of Sinadone: is given to understand that he must challenge the constable of the castle to single combat, before he can be received as a guest. They just: the constable is worsted: Sir Lybius is feasted in the castle: he declares his intention of delivering their lady; and inquires the particulars of her history. "Two Necromancers have built a fine palace by sorcery, and there keep her inchanted, till she will surrender her duchy to them, and yield to such base conditions as they would impose."

### PART VIII.

Early on the morning Sir Lybius sets out for the inchanted palace. He alights in the court: enters the hall: the wonders of which are described in strong Gothic painting. He sits down at the high table: on a sudden all the lights are quenched: it thunders, and lightens; the palace shakes; the walls fall in pieces about his ears. He is dismayed and confounded: but presently hears horses neigh, and is challenged to single combat by the sorcerers. He gets to his steed: a battle ensues, with various turns of fortune: he loses his weapon; but gets a sword from one of the Necromancers, and wounds the other with it: the edge of the sword being secretly poisoned, the wound proves mortal.

### PART IX.

He goes up to the surviving sorcerer, who is carried away from him by inchantment: at length he finds him, and cuts off his head: he returns to the palace to deliver the lady; but cannot find her: as he is lamenting, a window opens, through which enters a horrible serpent with wings and a woman's face: it coils round his neck and kisses him; then is suddenly converted into a very beautiful lady. She tells him she is the lady of Sinadone, and was so enchanted, till she might kiss her Sir Gawain, or some one of his blood: that he has dissolved the charm, and that herself and her dominions may be his reward. The knight (whose descent is by this means discovered) joyfully accepts the offer; makes her his bride, and then sets out with her for King Arthur's court.

Such is the fable of this ancient piece: which, the reader may observe, is as regular in its conduct as any of the finest poems of classical antiquity. If the execution, particularly as to the diction and sentiments, were but equal to the plan, it would be a capital performance; but this is such as might be expected in rude and ignorant times, and in a barbarous unpolished language.

## I.—THE BOY AND THE MANTLE.

TESTS of the purity of wives or ladye-loves have ever been a favourite subject with old romance writers. The mantle is not so common a test as others; indeed, there are few ancient productions in which it is given. The *Fablian du Mantel Mantaille*, which is supposed to have appeared late in the thirteenth century, is one. But the horn is a more common ordeal; and flowers, magic mirrors, a cup of tears, crowns, a girdle, as the famous girdle of Florinel in the *Faerie Queene*, have all played their part. In the *Morte d'Arthur*, a horn is received by King Mark, who with it tries the faith of La Beale Isoud. This horn was intended for King Arthur, and was sent to him by Morgan le Fay, a sorceress, who, though sister of Arthur, had attempted to destroy him through the means of a magic mantle. However, he was saved from it by the Lady of the Lake.

Then we have the sword that was sent to Arthur's court, that none but a "passing good man" could draw from its sheath; which sword was unsheathed by Balin, and was after his death re-won by Sir Galahad, the knight who was holy enough to achieve the Sangreal. Setting aside excalibar, which was the test of royalty, we have the mantle, the horn, and the sword, which will stand for the knife.

And though Bishop Percy says that "we have just reason to suppose that the ballad was written before the romance was translated into English," yet there seems some grounds for suggesting that the ballad may have been compiled from fragments of the romance, as the author is acquainted with the personages of King Arthur's court. "The ballad is printed *verbatim* from the folio MS."

IN the third day of May,
To Carleile did come
A kind curteous child,
That cold much of wisdome.

A kirtle and a mantle
This child had uppon,
With "brouches" and ringes
Full richelye bedone.

He had a sute of silke
About his middle drawne;
Without he cold of curtesye
He thought itt much shame.

God speed thee, king Arthur,
Sitting at thy meate:
And the goodly queene Guénever,
I cannott her forgett.

I tell you, lords, in this hall;
I hett you all to "heede;"

Except you be the more surer
Is you for to dread.

He plucked out of his "*poterner*,"
And longer wold not dwell,
He pulled forth a pretty mantle,
Betweene two nut-shells.

Have thou here, king Arthur;
Have thou heere of mee:
Give itt to thy comely queene
Shapen as itt is alreadye.

Itt shall never become that wiffe,
That hath once done amisse.
Then every knight in the kings court
Began to care for "his."

Forth came dame Guénever;
To the mantle shee her "hied;"
The ladye shee was newfangle,
But yett shee was affrayd,

When shee had taken the mantle,
She stoode as shee had beene madd:
It was from the top to the toe
As sheeres had itt shread.

One while it was "*gule;*"
Another while was itt greene;
Another while was it wadded:
Ill itt did her beseeme.

Another while was it blacke
And bore the worst hue:
By my troth, quoth king Arthur,
I thinke thou be not true.

Shee threw downe the mantle,
That bright was of blee;
Fast with a rudd redd,
To her chamber can shee flee.

She curst the weaver, and the *walker*,
That clothe that had wrought;
And bade a vengeance on his crowne,
That hither hath itt brought.

I had rather be in a wood,
Under a greene tree;
Then in king Arthurs court
Shamed for to bee.

Kay called forth his ladye,
And bade her come neere;
Saies, Madam, and thou be guiltye,
I pray thee hold thee there.

Forth came his ladye
Shortlye and anon;
Boldlye to the mantle
Then is shee gone.

When she had tane the mantle,
And cast it her about;
Then was shee bare
"Before all the rout."

Then every knight,
That was in the kings court,
Talked, laughed, and showted
Full oft att that sport,

Shee threw downe the mantle,
That bright was of blee;
Fast, with a red rudd,
To her chamber can shee flee.

Forth came an old knight
Pattering ore a creede,
And he proferred to this litle boy
Twenty markes to his meede;

And all the time of the Christmasse
Willinglye to ffeede;
For why this mantle might
Doe his wiffe some need.

When she had tane the mantle,
Of cloth that was made,
Shee had no more left on her,
But a tassell and a threed:
Then every knight in the kings court
Bade evill might shee speed.

Shee threw downe the mantle,
That bright was of blee;
And fast, with a redd rudd,
To her chamber can shee flee.

Craddocke called forth his ladye,
And bade her come in;
Saith, Winne this mantle, ladye,
With a litle *dinne.*

Winne this mantle, ladye,
And it shal be thine,
If thou never did amisse
Since thou wast mine.

Forth came Craddockes ladye
Shortlye and anon;
But boldlye to the mantle
Then is shee gone.

When she had tane the mantle,
And cast it her about,
Upp att her great toe
It began to crinkle and crowt:
Shee said, bowe downe, mantle,
And shame me not for nought

Once I did amisse,
I tell you certainlye,
When I kist Craddockes mouth
Under a greene tree ;
When I kist Craddockes mouth
Before he marryed mee.

When shee had her shreeven,
And her sines shee had tolde ;
The mantle stoode about her
Right as shee wold :

Seemelye of coulour
Glittering like gold :
Then every knight in Arthurs court
Did her behold.

Then spake dame Guénever
To Arthur our king ;
She hath tane yonder mantle
Not with right, but with wronge.

See you not yonder woman,
That maketh her self soe "cleane"?
I have seene tane out of her bedd
Of men fiveteene ;

Priests, clarkes, and wedded men
From her bedeene :
Yett shee taketh the mantle,
And maketh her self cleane.

Then spake the litle boy,
That kept the mantle in hold ;
Sayes, king, chasten thy wiffe,
Of her words shee is to bold :

Shee is a bitch and a witch,
And a whore bold :
King, in thine owne hall
Thou art a cuckold.

The litle boy stoode
Looking out a dore ;
"And there as he was lookinge
He was ware of a wyld bore."

He was ware of a wyld bore,
Wold have werryed a man :
He pulld forth a wood kniffe,
Fast thither that he ran :
He brought in the bores head,
And quitted him like a man.

He brought in the bores head,
And was wonderous bold :
He said there was never a cuckolds kniffe
Carve itt that cold.

Some rubbed their knives
Uppon a whetstone :
Some threw them under the table,
And said they had none.

King Arthur and the child
Stood looking upon them ;
All their knives edges
Turned backe againe.

Craddocke had a litle knive
Of iron and of steele ;
He *britled* the bores head
Wonderous weele ;
That every knight in the kings court
Had a morssell.

The litle boy had a horne,
Of red gold that ronge :
He said, there was noe cuckolde
Shall drinke of my horne ;
But he shold it sheede
Either behind or beforne.

Some shedd on their shoulder,
And some on their knee ;
He that cold not hitt his mouthe,
Put it in his eye :
And he that was a cuckold
Every man might him see.

Craddocke wan the horne,
And the bores head :
His ladie wan the mantle
Unto her meede.
Everye such a lovely ladye
God send her well to speede.

## II.—THE MARRIAGE OF SIR GAWAINE

Is chiefly taken from the fragment of an old ballad in the Editor's MS. which he has reason to believe more ancient than the time of Chaucer, and which furnished that bard with his *Wife of Bath's Tale*. The original was so extremely mutilated, half of every leaf being torn away, that without large supplements, etc., it was deemed improper for this collection: these it has therefore received, such as they are. They are not here particularly pointed out, because the fragment itself will now be found printed at the end of this volume.

### PART THE FIRST.

KING ARTHUR lives in merry Carleile,
    And seemely is to see;
And there with him queene Guenever,
    That bride soe bright of blee.

And there with him queene Guenever,
    That bride so bright in bowre:
And all his barons about him stoode,
    That were both *stiffe* and *stowre*.

The king a royale Christmasse kept,
    With mirth and princelye cheare;
To him repaired many a knighte,
    That came both farre and neare.

And when they were to dinner sette,
    And cups went freely round:
Before them came a faire damsèlle,
    And knelt upon the ground.

A boone, a boone, O kinge Arthure,
    I beg a boone of thee;
Avenge me of a carlish knighte,
    Who hath *shent* my love and mee.

At Tearne-Wadling* his castle stands,
    Near to that lake so fair,
And proudlye rise the battlements,
    And streamers deck the air.

Noe gentle knighte, nor ladye gay,
    May pass that castle-walle:
But from that foule discurteous knighte,
    Mishappe will them befalle.

Hee's twyce the size of common men,
    Wi' thewes, and sinewes stronge,
And on his backe he bears a clubbe,
    That is both thicke and longe.

This grimme barône 'twas our harde happe,
    But yester morne to see;
When to his bowre he bare my love,
    And sore misused mee.

And when I told him, king Arthure
    As lyttle shold him spare;
Goe tell, sayd hee, that cuckold kinge,
    To meete mee if he dare.

Upp then *sterted* king Arthure,
    And sware by hille and dale,
He ne'er wolde quitt that grimme barône,
    Till he had made him quail.

---

* Tearne-Wadling is the name of a small lake near Hesketh in Cumberland, on the road from Penrith to Carlisle. There is a tradition that an old castle once stood near the lake, the remains of which were, not long since, visible. Tearn, in the dialect of that country, signifies a small lake, and is still in use.

Goe fetch my sword Excalibar:
  Goe saddle mee my steede;
Nowe, by my faye, that grimme baròne
  Shall rue this ruthfulle deede.

And when he came to Tearne Wadlinge
  Benethe the castle walle:
"Come forth; come forth; thou proude baròne,
  Or yielde thyself my thralle."

On magicke grounde that castle stoode,
  And fenc'd with many a spelle:
Noe valiant knighte could tread thereon,
  But straite his courage felle.

Forth then rush'd that carlish knight,
  King Arthur felte the charme:
His sturdy sinewes lost their strengthe,
  Downe sunke his feeble arme.

Nowe yield thee, yield thee, kinge Arthure,
  Now yield thee unto mee:
Or fighte with mee, or lose thy lande,
  Noe better termes maye bee,

Unlesse thou sweare upon the rood,
  And promise on thy faye,
Here to returne to Tearne-Wadling,
  Upon the new-yeare's daye:

And bringe me worde what thing it is
  All women moste desyre:
This is thy ransome, Arthur, he sayes,
  Ile have noe other hyre.

King Arthur then helde up his hande,
  And sware upon his faye,
Then tooke his leave of the grimme baròne,
  And faste hee rode awaye.

And he rode east, and he rode west,
  And did of all inquyre,
What thing it is all women crave,
  And what they most desyre.

Some told him riches, pompe, or state;
  Some rayment fine and brighte;
Some told him mirthe; some flatterye,
  And some a jollye knighte.

In letters all king Arthur wrote,
  And seal'd them with his ringe:
But still his minde was helde in doubte,
  Each tolde a different thinge.

As ruthfulle he rode over a more,
  He saw a ladye sette
Betweene an oke, and a greene hollèye,
  All clad in red * scarlette.

Her nose was crookt and turnd outwàrde,
  Her chin stoode all awrye;
And where as sholde have been her mouthe,
  Lo! there was set her eye:

Her haires, like serpents, clung aboute
  Her cheekes of deadlye hewe:
A worse-form'd ladye than she was,
  No man mote ever viewe.

To hail the king in seemelye sorte
  This ladye was fulle faine:
But king Arthure, all sore amaz'd,
  No aunswere made againe.

What wight art thou, the ladye sayd,
  That wilt not speake to mee;
Sir, I may chance to ease thy paine,
  Though I bee foule to see.

If thou wilt ease my paine, he sayd,
  And helpe me in my neede;
Ask what thou wilt, thou grimme ladyè,
  And it shall bee thy meede.

O sweare mee this upon the roode,
  And promise on thy faye;

---

\* This was a common phrase in our old writers; so Chaucer, in his Prologue to the *Canterbury Tales,* says of the wife of Bath:
  "Her hosen were of fyne scarlet red."

And here the secrette I will telle,
  That shall thy ransome paye.

King Arthur promis'd on his faye,
  And sware upon the roode;
The secrette then the ladye told,
  As lightlye well shee cou'de.

Now this shall be my paye, sir king,
  And this my guerdon bee,
That some yong fair and courtlye knight,
  Thou bringe to marrye mee.

Fast then pricked king Arthure
  Ore hille, and dale, and downe:
And soone he founde the barone's bowre:
  And soone the grimme baroune.

He bare his clubbe upon his backe,
  Hee stoode bothe stiffe and stronge;
And, when he had the letters reade,
  Awaye the lettres flunge.

Nowe yielde thee, Arthur, and thy lands,
  All forfeit unto mee;
For this is not thy paye, sir king,
  Nor may thy ransome bee.

Yet hold thy hand, thou proud baròne,
  I praye thee hold thy hand;
And give mee leave to speake once more
  In reskewe of my land.

This morne, as I came over a more,
  I saw a ladye sette
Betwene an oke and a greene hollèye,
  All clad in red scarlètte.

Shee sayes, all women will have their wille,
  This is their chief desyre;
Now yield, as thou art a barone true,
  That I have payd mine hyre.

An earlye vengeaunce light on her!
  The carlish baron swore:
Shee was my sister tolde thee this,
  And shee's a mishapen whore.

But here I will make mine avowe,
  To do her as ill a turne:
For an ever I may that foule theefe gette,
  In a fyre I will her burne.

### PART THE SECONDE.

HOMEWARDE *pricked* king Arthure,
  And a wearye man was hee;
And soone he mette queene Guenever,
  That bride so bright of blee.

What newes! what newes! thou noble king,
  Howe, Arthur, hast thou sped?
Where hast thou hung the carlish knighte?
  And where bestow'd his head?

The carlish knight is safe for mee,
  And free fro mortal harme:
On magicke grounde his castle stands,
  And fenc'd with many a charme.

To bowe to him I was fulle faine,
  And yielde mee to his hand:
And, but for a lothly ladye, there
  I sholde have lost my land.

And nowe this fills my hearte with woe,
  And sorrowe of my life;
I swore a yonge and courtlye knight,
  Sholde marry her to his wife.

Then bespake him sir Gawàine,
  That was ever a gentle knighte:
That lothly ladye I will wed;
  Therefore be merrye and lighte.

Nowe naye, nowe naye, good sir Gawàine;
  My sister's sonne yee bee;
This lothlye ladye's all too grimme,
  And all too foule for yee.

Her nose is crookt and turn'd outwàrde;
  Her chin stands all awrye;
A worse form'd ladye than shee is
  Was never seen with eye.

What though her chin stand all awrye,
　And shee be foule to see:
I'll marry her, unkle, for thy sake,
　And I'll thy ransome bee.

Nowe thankes, nowe thankes, good sir
　Gawàine;
And a blessing thee betyde!
To-morrow wee'll have knights and squires,
　And wee'll goe fetch thy bride.

And wee'll have hawkes and wee'll have
　houndes,
　To cover our intent;
And wee'll away to the greene forèst,
　As wee a hunting went.

Sir Lancelot, sir Stephen bolde,
　They rode with them that daye;
And foremoste of the companye
　There rode the stewarde Kaye:

Soe did sir Banier and sir Bore,
　And eke Sir Garratte keene;
Sir Tristram too, that gentle knight,
　To the forest freshe and greene.

And when they came to the greene
　forrèst,
　Beneathe a faire holley tree
There sate that ladye in red scarlètte
　That unseemelye was to see.

Sir Kay beheld that lady's face,
　And looked upon her *sweere;*
Whoever kisses that ladye, he sayes,
　Of his kisse he stands in feare.

Sir Kay beheld that ladye againe,
　And looked upon her snout;
Whoever kisses that ladye, he sayes,
　Of his kisse he stands in doubt.

Peace, brother Kay, sayde sir Gawàine,
　And amend thee of thy life:
For there is a knight amongst us all,
　Must marry her to his wife.

What marry this foule queane, quoth Kay,
　I' the devil's name anone;
Gett mee a wife wherever I maye,
　In sooth shee shall be none.

Then some tooke up their hawkes in haste,
　And some took up their houndes;
And sayd they wolde not marry her,
　For cities, nor for townes.

Then bespake him king Arthùre,
　And sware there by this daye;
For a little foule sighte and mislikinge,
　Yee shall not say her naye.

Peace, lordings, peace; sir Gawaine sayd;
　Nor make debate and strife;
This lothlye ladye I will take,
　And marry her to my wife.

Nowe thankes, nowe thankes, good sir
　Gawaine,
And a blessinge be thy meede!
For as I am thine owne ladyè,
　Thou never shalt rue this deede.

Then up they took that lothly dame,
　And home anone they bringe:
And there sir Gawaine he her wed,
　And married her with a ringe.

And when they were in wed-bed laid,
　And all were done awaye:
"Come turne to mee, mine owne wed-lord,
　Come turne to mee I praye."

Sir Gawaine scant could lift his head,
　For sorrowe and for care;
When, lo! instead of that lothelye dame,
　Hee sawe a young ladye faire.

Sweet blushes stayn'd her rud-red cheeke,
　Her eyen were blacke as sloe:
The ripening cherrye swellde her lippe,
　And all her necke was snowe.

Sir Gawaine kiss'd that lady faire,
　Lying upon the sheete:

And swore, as he was a true knighte,
 The spice was never soe sweete.

Sir Gawaine kiss'd that lady brighte,
 Lying there by his side:
"The fairest flower is not soe faire:
 Thou never can'st bee my bride."

I am thy bride, mine owne deare lorde,
 The same whiche thou didst knowe,
That was soe lothlye, and was wont
 Upon the wild more to goe.

"Nowe, gentle Gawaine, chuse, quoth shee,
 And make thy choice with care;
Whether by night, or else by daye,
 Shall I be foule or faire?

"To have thee foule still in the night,
 When I with thee should playe!
I had rather farre, my lady deare,
 To have thee foule by daye."

What when gaye ladyes goe with their lordes
 To drinke the ale and wine;
Alas! then I must hide myself,
 I must not goe with mine?

"My faire ladyè, sir Gawaine sayd,
 I yield me to thy skille;
Because thou art mine owne ladyè,
 Thou shalt have all thy wille."

Nowe blessed be thou, sweete Gawàine,
 And the daye that I thee see;
For as thou seest mee at this time,
 Soe shall I ever bee.

My father was an aged knighte,
 And yet it chanced soe,
He tooke to wife a false ladyè,
 Whiche broughte me to this woe.

Shee witch'd mee, being a faire yonge maide,
 In the greene forèst to dwelle;
And there to abide in lothlye shape,
 Most like a fiend of helle.

Midst mores and mosses, woods and wilds,
 To lead a lonesome life:
Till some yong faire and courtlye knighte
 Wolde marrye me to his wife:

Nor fully to gaine mine owne trewe shape,
 Such was her devilish skille;
Until he wolde yielde to be rul'd by mee,
 And let mee have all my wille.

She witch'd my brother to a carlish boore,
 And made him *stiffe* and stronge;
And built him a bowre on magicke grounde,
 To live by rapine and wronge.

But now the spelle is broken throughe,
 And wronge is turnde to righte;
Henceforth I shall bee a faire ladyè,
 And hee be a gentle knighte.

## III.—KING RYENCE'S CHALLENGE.

THIS song is more modern than many of those which follow it, but is placed here for the sake of the subject. It was sung before Queen Elizabeth at the grand entertainment at Kenilworth Castle in 1575, and was probably composed for that occasion.

The story in *Morte Arthur*, whence it is taken, runs as follows: " Came a messenger hastely from king Ryence of North Wales,—saying, that king Ryence had discomfited and overcomen eleaven kings, and everiche of them did him homage, and that was this: they give him their beards cleane flayne off,—wherefore the messenger came for king Arthur's beard, for king Ryence had purfeled a mantell with kings beards, and there lacked for one a place of the mantell, wherefore he sent for his beard, or else he would enter into his lands, and brenn and slay, and never leave till he have thy head and thy beard. Well, said king Arthur, thou hast said thy message, which is the most villainous and lewdest message that ever man heard sent to a king. Also thou mayest see my beard is full young yet for to make a *purfell* of, but tell thou the king that—or it be long he shall do to me homage on both his knees, or else he shall leese his head." [B. i. c. 24.]

Stow tells us, that King Arthur kept his round table at "diverse places, but especially at Carlion, Winchester, and Camalet in Somersetshire." This Camalet, "sometimes a famous towne or castle, is situate on a very high tor or hill," etc. [See an exact description in Stow's *Annals*, ed. 1631, p. 55.]

As it fell out on a Pentecost day,
  King Arthur at Camelot kept his court
    royall,
With his faire queene dame Guenever the
    gay;
And many bold barons sitting in hall;
  With ladies attired in *purple and pall;*
And heraults in hewkes, hooting on high,
Cryed, *Largesse, Largesse, Chevaliers tres-
    hardie.*\*

A doughty dwarfe to the uppermost deas
  Right pertlye gan prickle, kneeling on
    knee;
With *steven* fulle stoute amids all the preas,
  Sayd, Nowe sir king Arthur, God save
    thee, and see!
Sir Ryence of North-gales greeteth well
    thee,

And bids thee thy beard anon to him
    send,
Or else from thy jaws he will it off rend.

For his robe of state is a rich scarlet
    mantle,
  With eleven kings beards bordered\*
    about,
And there is room lefte yet in a kantle,
  For thine to stande, to make the twelfth
    out:
  This must be done, be thou never so
    stout;
This must be done, I tell thee no fable,
*Maugre* the teethe of all thy round table.

When this mortal message from his
    mouthe past,
  Great was the noyse bothe in hall and in
    bower:
The king fum'd; the queene screecht;
    ladies were aghast;

---

\* The heralds resounded these words as oft as they received of the bounty of the knights. See *Memoires de la Chevalerie*, tom. 1, p. 99. The expression is still used in the form of installing Knights of the Garter.

\* *i.e.* set round the border, as furs are now round the gowns of magistrates.

Princes puff'd; barons blustred; lords began lower;
Knights stormed; squires startled, like steeds in a *stower:*
Pages and yeomen yell'd out in the hall,
Then in came sir Kay, the "king's" seneschal.

Silence, my soveraignes, quoth this courteous knight,
And in that *stound* the *stowre* began still:
"Then" the dwarfe's dinnerfull *decrely* was *dight;*
Of wine and wassel he had his wille:
And, when he had eaten and drunken his fill,

An hundred pieces of fine coyned gold
Were given this dwarf for his message bold.

But say to sir Ryence, thou dwarf, quoth the king,
That for his bold message I do him defye;
And shortlye with basins and pans will him ring
Out of North-gales; where he and I
With swords, and not razors, quickly shall trye,
Whether he or king Arthur will prove the best barbor;
And therewith he shook his good sword Escalàbor.

## IV.—KING ARTHUR'S DEATH.

### A FRAGMENT.

THE subject of this ballad is evidently taken from the old romance *Morte Arthur*, but with some variations, especially in the concluding stanzas, in which the author seems rather to follow the traditions of the old Welsh bards, who "believed that King Arthur was not dead, but conveied awaie by the Fairies into some pleasant place, where he should remaine for a time, and then returne againe and reign in as great authority as ever." The same tradition was popular amongst the Germans with regard to their emperor, Frederic Barbarossa, who, attended by a dwarfish boy, nods in the depths of Kyffhaveer until at some great crisis he shall awake up and come forth to reign again over his loving subjects.

This fragment, being very incorrect and imperfect in the original MS., hath received some conjectural emendations, and even a supplement of three or four stanzas composed from the romance of *Morte Arthur*.

* * * * * * * * *

ON Trinitye Mondaye in the morne,
This sore battayle was doom'd to bee;
Where manye a knighte cry'd *Wellawaye!*
Alacke, it was the more pittle.

Ere the first crowinge of the cocke,
When as the kinge in his bed laye,

He thoughte sir Gawaine to him came,[*]
And there to him these wordes did saye.

---

[*] Sir Gawaine had been killed at Arthur's landing on his return from abroad. The romance says that his ghost appeared to the king, warning him not to fight.

Nowe, as you are mine unkle deare,
  And as you prize your life, this daye
O meet not with your foe in fighte;
  Putt off the battayle, if yee maye.

For sir Launcelot is nowe in Fraunce,
  And with him many an hardye knighte:
Who will within this moneth be backe,
  And will assiste ye in the fighte.

The kynge then call'd his nobles all,
  Before the breakinge of the daye;
And tolde them howe sir Gawaine came,
  And there to him these wordes did saye.

His nobles all this counsayle gave,
  That earlye in the morning, hee
Shold send awaye an herauld at armes,
  To aske a parley faire and free.

Then twelve good knightes king Arthure chose,
  The best of all that with him were:
To parley with the foe in field,
  And make with him agreement faire.

The king he charged all his hoste,
  In readinesse there for to bee:
But noe man sholde noe weapon sturre,
  Unlesse a sword drawne they shold see.

And Mordred on the other parte,
  Twelve of his knights did likewise bringe;
The beste of all his companye,
  To hold the parley with the kinge.

Sir Mordred alsoe charged his hoste,
  In readinesse there for to bee;
But noe man sholde noe weapon sturre,
  But if a sworde drawne they shold see.

For he durste not his unkle truste,
  Nor he his nephewe, sothe to tell:
Alacke! it was a woefulle case,
  As ere in Christentye befelle.

But when they were together mette,
  And both to faire accordance broughte;
And a month's league betweene them sette,
  Before the battayle sholde be foughte;

An addere crept forth of a bushe,
  Stunge one o' th' king's knightes on the knee:
Alacke! it was a woefulle chance,
  As ever was in Christentie.

When the knighte found him wounded sore,
  And sawe the wild-worme hanginge there;
His sworde he from his scabberde drewe:
  A piteous case, as ye shall heare.

For when the two hostes sawe the sworde,
  They joyned battayle instantlye;
Till of soe manye noble knightes,
  On one side there were left but three.

For all were slain that durst abide,
  And but some fewe that fled awaye:
Ay mee! it was a bloodye fielde,
  As ere was foughte on summer's daye.

Upon king Arthur's partyè,
  Onlye himselfe escaped there,
And Lukyn duke of Gloster free,
  And the king's butler Bedevere.\*

And when the king beheld his knightes,
  All dead and scattered on the molde;
The teares fast trickled downe his face;
  That manlye face in fight so bolde.

Nowe reste yee all, brave knights, he said,
  Soe true and faithful to your trust:
And must yee then, ye valiant hearts,
  Be lefte to moulder into dust!

---

\* In the *Morte d'Arthur* we read, "Sir Lucan de butlere and his brother Sir Bedivere."

Most loyal have yee been to mee,
  Most true and faithful unto deathe :
And, oh ! to rayse yee up againe,
  How freelye could I yield my breathe !

But see the traitor's yet alive,
  Lo where hee stalkes among the deade !
Nowe bitterlye he shall abye :
  And vengeance fall upon his head.

O staye, my liege, then sayd the duke ;
  O staye for love and charitie ;
Remember what the vision spake,
  Nor meete your foe, if it may bee.

O, staye mee not, thou worthye wight,
  This debt my loyal knights I owe :
Betide me life, betide me death,
  I will avenge them of their foe.

Then straite he grasp'd his trustye speare,
  And on his horse then mounted hee :
As his butler holpe him to his horse,
  His bowels gushed to his knee.

Alas ! then sayd the noble king,
  That I should live this sight to see !
To see this good knight here be slaine,
  All for his love in helping mee !

He put his speare into his reste,
  And to sir Mordred loud gan crye ;
Nowe sette thyself upon thy guarde,
  For, traitor, nowe thy death is nye.

Sir Mordred lifted up his sworde,
  And fierce to meet the king ran hee :
The king his speare he through him thrust ;
  A fathom thorow his bodie.

When Mordered felt the stroke of death,
  And found that he was wounded soe ;
He thruste himselfe upon the speare,
  And strucke the king a deadlye blowe.

Then grimmlye dyed sir Mordered,
  Presentlye upon that tree :

And bloody streames ranne from the kinge
  Ere to the duke returned hee.

Sir Lukyn then he thus bespake,
  Sir knighte, thou hast beene faithfulle tryde,
Nowe take my sword Excalibar,
  That hangs so freelye by my syde :

O take my sword Excalibar,
  And there into the river throwe :
For here, henceforth, benethe this tree,
  All use of weapons I foregoe.

And fare thee well, thou trustye sword,
  A better neer had valiant knighte,
With thee full ofte, and manye a daye,
  Have I withstood my foe in fighte.

With this good fauchion in my hande,
  Oft have I reapd the bloody feelde :
But nowe the fatalle houre is come,
  That never more I may thee weelde.

The duke to the river side he went,*
  And there his owne sword in threwe he :
But he kept back Excalibar,
  He kept it back in privitie.

For all of *coleyne* was the blade ;
  And all the hilte of precious stone :
And ever alacke ! then sayd the knighte,
  Must such a sword awaye be throwne ?

Then backe he came unto the kinge,
  Who sayd, Sir Lukyn, what did yee see ?
Nothing, my liege, save that the winde
  Blewe oer the waters faire and free.

O goe againe, then said the kinge,
  O good sir Lukyn, goe againe :

---

* In the *Morte d'Arthur*, Sir Lucan, who has been wounded, is overcome with the exertion of lifting the king, and dies. It is Bedivere who is commanded to throw Excalibar into the water.

Into the rivere throwe my sword,
  Nor keepe me lingering here in paine.

The duke then to the river went,
  And the kings scabberd in threwe hee;
But hee kept backe Excalibar,
  And hid it underneathe a tree.

Then backe he came to tell the kinge,
  Who sayde, Sir Lukyn, sawe ye oughte?
Nothinge, my liege, save that the winde
  Nowe with the angrye waters fought.

O Lukyn, Lukyn, said the kinge,
  Twice hast thou dealt deceytfullye:
Alacke, whom may we ever truste,
  When suche a knighte soe false can bee?

Saye, wouldst thou have thy master dead;
  All for a sword, that wins thine eye:
Nowe goe againe, and throwe it in,
  Or here the one of us shall dye.

The duke, all *shent* with this rebuke,
  No aunswere made unto the kinge:
But to the rivere tooke the sworde,
  And threwe it far as he coulde flinge.

A hande and an arme did meete the sworde,
  And flourishd three times in the air;
Then sunke benethe the renninge streme,
  And of the duke was seene noe mair.

All sore astonied stood the duke;
  He stood as still, as still mote bee:
Then hastend backe to telle the kinge;
  But he was gone from under the tree.

But to what place he cold not tell,
  For never after hee did him spye:
But hee sawe a barge goe from the land,
  And hee heard ladyes howle and crye.*

And whether the kinge were there, or not,
  Hee never knewe, nor ever colde:
For from that sad and direfulle daye,
  Hee never more was seene on molde.

---

## V.—THE LEGEND OF KING ARTHUR.

WE have here a short summary of King Arthur's history as given by Jeff. of Monmouth and the old chronicles, with the addition of a few circumstances from the romance *Morte Arthur.*

Printed from the Editor's ancient folio manuscript.

OF Brutus' blood, in Brittaine borne,
  King Arthur I am to name;
Through Christendome, and Heathynesse,
  Well knowne is my worthy fame.

In Jesus Christ I doe beleeve;
  I am a christyan bore:
The Father, Sone, and Holy Gost,
  One God, I doe adore.

In the four hundred ninetieth yeere,*
  Over Brittaine I did rayne,
After my savior Christ his byrth:
  What time I did maintaine

The fellowshipp of the table round,
  Soe famous in those dayes;
Whereatt a hundred noble knights,
  And thirty sat alwayes:

Who for their deeds and martiall feates,
  As bookes done yett record,
Amongst all other nations
  Wer feared throwgh the world.

---

* He began his reign A.D. 515, according to the chronicles.

* Ladies was the word which our old English writers used for nymphs.

And in the castle off Tyntagill
  King Uther mee begate
Of Agyana,* a bewtyous ladye,
  And come of "hie" estate.

And when I was fifteen yeere old,
  Then was I crowned kinge :
All Brittaine that was att an uprore,
  I did to quiett bringe.

And drove the Saxons from the realme,
  Who had opprest this land ;
All Scotland then throughe manly feats
  I conquered with my hand.

Ireland, Denmarke, Norway,
  These countryes wan I all ;
Iseland, Gotheland, and Swethland ;
  And made their kings my thrall

I conquered all Gallya,
  That now is called France ;
And slew the hardye Froll† in feild,
  My honor to advance.

And the ugly gyant Dynabus‡
  Soe terrible to vewe,
That in Saint Barnards mount did lye,
  By force of armes I slew :

And Lucyus the emperour of Rome
  I brought to deadly wracke ;
And a thousand more of noble knightes
  For feare did turne their backe :

Five kinges of "paynims" I did kill
  Amidst that bloody strife ;
Besides the Grecian emperour
  Who alsoe lost his liffe.

Whose carcasse I did send to Rome
  Cladd poorlye on a beere ;

---

\* She is named Igerna or Igraine in the old chronicles.
† Froll, according to the chronicles, was a Roman knight governor of Gaul.
‡ Danibus, MS.

And afterward I past Mount-Joye
  The next approaching yeere.

Then I came to Rome, where I was mett
  Right as a conquerour,
And by all the cardinalls solempnelye
  I was crowned an emperour.

One winter there I made abode :
  Then word to mee was brought
Howe Mordred had oppressd the crowne :
  What treason he had wrought

Att home in Brittaine with my queene ;
  Therfore I came with speede
To Brittaine backe, with all my power,
  To quitt that traiterous deede :

And soone at Sandwiche I arrivde,
  Where Mordred me withstoode :
But yett at last I landed there,
  With effusion of much blood.

For there my nephew sir Gawaine dyed,
  Being wounded in that sore,
The whiche sir Lancelot in fight
  Had given him before.

Thence chased I Mordered away,
  Who fledd to London right,
From London to Winchester, and
  To Cornewalle tooke his flyght.

And still I him pursued with speed
  Till at the last wee mett :
Wherby an appointed day of fight
  Was there agreed and sett.

Where we did fight, of mortal life
  Eche other to deprive,
Till of a hundred thousand men
  Scarce one was left alive.

There all the noble chivalrye
  Of Brittaine tooke their end.
O see how fickle is their state
  That doe on feates* depend !

---

\* Feats of arms, fighting.

There all the traiterous men were slaine,
   Not one escapte away ;
And there dyed all my vallyant knightes.
   Alas! that woefull day!

Two and twenty yeere I ware the crowne
   In honor and great fame ;
And thus by death was suddenlye
   Deprived of the same.

## VI.—A DYTTIE TO HEY DOWNE.

COPIED from an old MS. in the Cotton Library [Vesp. A. 25], entitled "Divers things of Hen. viij's time."

WHO sekes to tame the blustering winde,
   Or causse the floods bend to his wyll,
Or els against dame nature's *kinde*
   To "change" things frame by cunning skyll :
That man I thinke bestoweth paine,
Thoughe that his laboure be in vaine.

Who strives to breake the sturdye steele,
   Or goeth about to staye the sunne ;
Who thinks to causse an oke to reele,
   Which never can by force be done :
That man likewise bestoweth paine,
Thoughe that his laboure be in vaine.

Who thinks to stryve against the streame,
   And for to sayle without a maste ;

Unlesse he thinks perhapps to faine,
   His travell ys forelorne and waste ;
And so in cure of all his paine,
   His travell ys his cheffest gaine.

So he lykewise, that goes about
   To please eche eye and every eare,
Had nede to have withouten doubt
   A golden gyft with hym to beare ;
For evyll report shall be his gaine,
Though he bestowe both toyle and paine.

God grant eche man one to amend ;
   God send us all a happy place ;
And let us pray unto the end,
   That we may have our prince's grace :
Amen, amen! so shall we gaine
A dewe reward for all our paine.

## VII.—GLASGERION.

GLASGERION is probably "the gret Glascurion," whom Chaucer elevates to a position beside Orpheus and Arion. The Scotch version of the ballad gives him qualities akin to those of the lover of Eurydice, since he was so excellent a harper that "he'd harpit a fish out o' saut water, or water out o' a stane."

   Gawain Douglas follows Chaucer's example, and places him with Orpheus in his *Palace of Honour*. The poem is printed from the folio MS.

GLASGERION was a kings owne sonne,
   And a harper he was goode :
He harped in the kinges chambere,
   Where cuppe and caudle stoode.

And soe did hee in the queens chamber,
   Till ladies waxed "glad."

And then bespake the kinges daughter ;
   And these wordes thus shee sayd.

Strike on, strike on, Glasgèrion,
   Of thy striking doe not *blinne:*
Theres never a stroke comes oer thy harpe,
   But it glads my hart withinne.

Faire might he fall, ladye, quoth hee,
  Who taught you nowe to speake!
I have loved you, ladye, seven longe yeere
  My minde I neere durst breake.

But come to my bower, my Glasgeriòn,
  When all men are att rest :
As I am a ladie true of my promise,
  Thou shalt bee a welcome guest.

Home then came Glasgèrion,
  A glad man, lord! was hee.
And, come thou hither, Jacke my boy ;
  Come hither unto mee.

For the kinge's daughter of Normandye
  Hath granted mee my boone :
And att her chambere must I bee
  Beffore the cocke have crowen.

O master, master, then quoth hee,
  Lay your head downe on this stone :
For I will waken you, master deere,
  Afore it be time to gone.

But up then rose that *lither* ladd,
  And hose and shoone did on :
A coller he cast upon his necke,
  Hee seemed a gentleman.

And when he came to the ladye's chamber,
  He *thrild* upon a pinn.\*
The lady was true of her promise,
  Rose up and lett him in.

He did not take the lady gaye
  To boulster nor to bed :
"Nor thoughe hee had his wicked wille,
  A single word he sed."

He did not kisse that ladye's mouthe,
  Nor when he came, nor *youd :*

---

\* This is elsewhere expressed "twirled the pin" or "tirled at the pin" (see B. ii. s. vi. v. 3 ), and seems to refer to the turning round the button on the outside of a door, by which the latch rises, still used in cottages.

And sore mistrusted that ladye gay,
  He was of some churls bloud.

But home then came that lither ladd,
  And did off his hose and shoone ;
And cast the coller from off his necke :
  He was but a churlès sonne.

Awake, awake, my deere master,
  The cock hath well-nigh crowen.
Awake, awake, my master deere,
  I hold it time to be gone.

For I have saddled your horsse, mastèr,
  Well bridled I have your steede :
And I have served you a good breakfast :
  For thereof ye have need.

Up then rose good Glasgeriòn,
  And did on hose and shoone ;
And cast a coller about his necke :
  For he was a kinge his sonne.

And when he came to the ladye's chamber,
  He thrild upon the pinne :
The ladye was more than true of promise,
  And rose and let him inn.

Saies, whether have you left with me
  Your bracelett or your glove?
Or are you returned backe againe
  To know more of my love?

Glasgèrion swore a full great othe,
  By oake, and ashe, and thorne ;
Lady, I was never in your chambèr,
  Sith the time that I was borne.

O then it was your lither foot-page,
  He hath beguiled mee.
Then shee pulled forth a litle pen-knlffe,
  That hanged by her knee :

Sayes, there shall noe churlès blood
  Within my bodye spring :
No churlès blood shall ever defile
  The daughter of a kinge.

Home then went Glasgèrion,
   And woe, good lord, was hee.
Sayes, come thou hither, Jacke my boy,
   Come hither unto mee.

If I had killed a man to night,
   Jacke, I would tell it thee :
But if I have not killed a man to night,
   Jacke, thou hast killed three.

And he puld out his bright browne sword,
   And dryed it on his sleeve,
And he smote off that lither ladd's head,
   Who did his ladye grieve.

He sett the swords poynt till his brest,
   The pummil untill a stone :
Throw the falsenesse of that lither ladd,
   These three lives werne all gone.

## VIII.—OLD ROBIN OF PORTINGALE.

FROM an ancient copy in the Editor's folio MS., which was judged to require considerable corrections. In the former edition the hero of this piece had been called Sir Robin, but that title not being in the MS. is now omitted.

LET never again soe old a man
   Marrye soe young a wife,
As did old Robin of Portingale ;
   Who may rue all the dayes of his life.

For the mayors daughter of Lin, god wott,
   He chose her to his wife,
And thought with her to have lived in love,
   But they fell to hate and strife.

They scarce were in their wed-bed laid,
   And scarce was hee asleepe,
But upp shee rose, and forth shee goes,
   To the steward, and gan to weepe.

Sleepe you, wake you, faire sir Gyles?
   Or be you not within?
Sleepe you, wake you, faire Sir Gyles,
   Arise and let me inn.

O, I am waking, sweete, he said,
   Sweete ladye, what is your will?
I have *unbethought* me of a wile
   How my wed-lord weell *spill*.

Twenty-four good knights, shee sayes,
   That dwell about this towne,
Even twenty-four of my next cozèns,
   Will helpe to *dinge* him downe.

All that beheard his little footepage,
   As he watered his masters steed ;
And for his masters sad perllle
   His verry heart did bleed.

He mourned still, and wept full sore ;
   I sweare by the holy roode
The teares he for his master wept
   Were blent water and bloude.

And that beheard his deare mastèr
   As he stood at his garden pale :
Sayes, Ever alacke, my litle foot-page,
   What causes thee to wail?

Hath any one done to thee wronge
   Any of thy fellowes here?
Or is any of thy good friends dead,
   That thou shedst manye a teare?

Or, if it be my head bookes-man,
   Aggrieved he shal bee :
For no man here within my howse,
   Shall doe wrong unto thee.

O, it is not your head bookes-man,
   Nor none of his degree :
But, on to-morrow ere it be noone
   All deemed to die are yee.

And of that bethank your head stewàrd,
  And thank your gay ladie.
If this be true, my litle foot-page,
  The heyre of my land thoust bee.

If it be not true, my dear mastèr,
  No good death let me die.
If it be not true, thou litle foot-page,
  A dead corse shalt thou lie.

O call now downe my faire ladye,
  O call her downe to mee :
And tell my ladye gay how sicke
  And like to die I bee.

Downe then came his ladye faire,
  All clad in *purple and pall:*
The rings that were on her fingèrs,
  Cast light thorrow the hall.

What is your will, my owne wed-lord?
  What is your will with mee?
O see, my ladye deere, how sicke,
  And like to die I bee.

And thou be sicke, my own wed-lord,
  Soe sore it grieveth me :
But my five maydens and myselfe
  Will "watch thy" bedde for thee.

And at the waking of your first sleepe,
  We will a hott drinke make :
And at the waking of your "next" sleepe,
  Your sorrowes we will slake.

He put a silk cote on his backe,
  And mail of manye a fold :
And hee putt a steele cap on his head,
  Was gilt with good red gold.

He layd a bright browne sword by his side,
  And another att his feete :
"And twentye good knights he placed at hand,
  To watch him in his sleepe."

And about the middle time of the night,
  Came twentye-four traitours inn :
Sir Giles he was the foremost man,
  The leader of that *ginn.*

Old Robin with his bright browne sword,
  Sir Gyles head soon did winn :
And scant of all those twenty-four,
  Went out one quick agenn.

None save only a litle foot page,
  Crept forth at a window of stone :
And he had two armes when he came in,
  And he went back with one.

Upp then came that ladie gaye
  With torches burning bright :
She thought to have brought sir Gyles a drinke,
  Butt she found her owne wedd knight.

The first thinge that she stumbled on
  It was sir Gyles his foote :
Sayes, Ever alacke, and woe is mee !
  Here lyes my sweete hart-roote.

The next thinge that she stumbled on
  It was sir Gyles his heade :
Sayes, Ever, alacke, and woe is me !
  Heere lyes my true love deade.

Hee cutt the pappes beside her brest,
  And did her body spille ;
He cutt the eares beside her heade,
  And bade her love her fille.

He called then up his little foot-page,
  And made him there his heyre ;
And sayd, henceforth my worldlye goodes
  And countrye I forsweare.

He shope the crosse on his right shouldèr,
  Of the white "clothe" and the redde,*
And went him into the holy land,
  Wheras Christ was quicke and dead.

In the foregoing piece, *Giles,* steward to a rich old merchant trading to *Portugal,* is qualified with the title of *Sir,* not as being a knight, but rather, I conceive, as having received an inferior order of priesthood.

---

\* Every person who went on a crusade to the Holy Land usually wore a cross on his

## IX.—CHILD WATERS.

CHILD is frequently used by our old writers as a title. It is repeatedly given to Prince Arthur in the *Faerie Queene*, and the son of a king is in the same poem called "Child Tristram." Mr. Theobald supposes this use of the word was received along with their romances from the Spaniards, with whom *Infante* signifies a "Prince." A more eminent critic tells us, that "in the old times of chivalry, the noble youth, who were candidates for knighthood, during the time of their probation were called *Infans, Varlets, Damoysels, Bacheliers.* The most noble of the youth were particularly called *Infans.*" A late commentator on Spenser observes, that the Saxon word *cnihz*, knight, signifies also a "child."

This is one of the most beautiful of the old ballads, showing most pathetically the strength of a woman's devotion. It is given by Jamieson as *Burd Ellen*, which seems the better title, as Ellen, not Child Waters, is the centre of attraction. Burger's version of this ballad, which he gives as *Graf Walter*, is very fine, and written with much artistic skill. There are slight alterations in it, but on the whole it keeps close to the copy before us. One verse we subjoin on account of its extreme beauty. It is Ellen's answer to the offer of a heritage for her child :—

> "Ein Liebeskuss von deinem Mund,
> So purpurroth und süss
> Gilt mir für Land und Lent' und Burg
> Und war' sein Paradiess."

The ballad following is taken from the Editor's folio.

CHILDE WATERS in his stable stoode
 And stroakt his milke white steede :
To him a fayre yonge ladye came
 As ever ware womans weede.

Sayes, Christ you save, good Childe Waters ;
 Sayes, Christ you save, and see :
My girdle of gold that was too longe,
 Is now too short for mee.

And all is with one chyld of yours,
 I feele sturre att my side :
My gowne of greene it is too straighte ;
 Before, it was too wide.

---

upper garment, on the right shoulder, as a badge of his profession. Different nations were distinguished by crosses of different colours. The English wore white, the French red, etc. This circumstance seems to be confounded in the ballad.

If the child be mine, faire Ellen, he sayd,
 Be mine as you tell mee ;
Then take you Cheshire and Lancashire both,
 Take them your owne to bee.

If the childe be mine, faire Ellen, he sayd,
 Be mine, as you doe sweare :
Then take you Cheshire and Lancashire both,
 And make that child your heyre.

Shee saies, I had rather have one kisse,
 Child Waters, of thy mouth ;
Than I wolde have Cheshire and Lancashire both,
 That lye by north and south.

And I had rather have one twinkling,
 Childe Waters, of thine ee ;

Then I wolde have Cheshire and Lan-
    cashire both,
  To take them mine owne to bee.

To morrow, Ellen, I must forth ryde
  Farr into the north countrie ;
The fairest lady that I can find,
  Ellen, must goe with mee.

"Thoughe I am not that lady fayre,
  Yet let me go with thee :"
And ever I pray you, Child Watèrs,
  Your foot-page let me bee.

If you will my foot-page be, Ellèn,
  As you doe tell to mee ;
Then you must cut your gowne of greene,
  An inch above your knee :

Soe must you doe your yellowe lockes,
  An inch above your ee :
You must tell no man what is my name ;
  My foot-page then you shall bee.

Shee, all the long day Child Waters rode,
  Ran barefoote by his side ;
Yett was he never soe courteous a knighte,
  To say, Ellen, will you ryde ?

Shee, all the long day Child Waters rode,
  Ran barefoote thorow the broome ;
Yett hee was never soe curteous a knighte,
  To say, put on your shoone.

Ride softlye, shee sayd, O Childe Waters,
  Why doe you ryde soe fast ?
The childe, which is no man's but thine,
  My bodye itt will *brast*.

Hee sayth, seest thou yonder water, Ellen,
  That flows from banke to brimme.—
I trust to God, O Child Waters,
  You never will see mee swimme.

But when shee came to the waters side,
  Shee sayled to the chinne :
Except the Lord of heaven be my speed,
  Now must I learne to swimme.

The salt waters bare up her clothes ;
  Our Ladye bare upp her chinne :
Childe Waters was a woe man, good Lord,
  To see faire Ellen swimme.

And when shee over the water was,
  Shee then came to his knee :
He said, Come hither, thou faire Ellèn,
  Loe yonder what I see.

Seest thou not yonder hall, Ellèn ?
  Of redd gold shines the yate :
Of twenty foure faire ladyes there,
  The fairest is my mate.

Seest thou not yonder hall, Ellèn ?
  Of redd gold shines the towre :
There are twenty four faire ladyes there,
  The fairest is my paramoure.

I see the hall now, Child Waters,
  Of redd golde shines the yate :
God give you good now of yourselfe,
  And of your worthye mate.

I see the hall now, Child Waters,
  Of redd golde shines the towre :
God give you good now of yourselfe,
  And of your paramoure.

There twenty four fayre ladyes were
  A playing att the ball :
And Ellen the fairest ladye there,
  Must bring his steed to the stall.

There twenty four fayre ladyes were
  A playinge at the chesse ;
And Ellen the fayrest ladye there,
  Must bring his horse to gresse.

And then bespake Childe Waters sister,
  These were the wordes said shee :
You have the prettyest foot-page, brother,
  That ever I saw with mine ee.

But that his bellye it is soe bigg,
  His girdle goes wonderous hie :

And let him, I pray you, Childe Watèrs,
  Goe into the chamber with mee.

It is not fit for a little foot-page,
  That has run throughe mosse and myre,
To go into the chamber with any ladye,
  That weares soe riche attyre.

It is more meete for a little foot-page,
  That has run throughe mosse and myre,
To take his supper upon his knee,
  And sitt downe by the kitchen fyer.

But when they had supped every one,
  To bedd they tooke theyr waye:
He sayd, come hither, my little foot-page,
  And hearken what I saye.

Goe thee downe into yonder towne,
  And low into the street;
The fayrest ladye that thou can finde,
  Hyer her in mine armes to sleepe,
And take her up in thine armes twaine,
  For filinge * of her feete.

Ellen is gone into the towne,
  And low into the streete:
The fairest ladye that shee cold find,
  Shee hyred in his armes to sleepe;
And tooke her up in her armes twayne,
  For filing of her feete.

I praye you nowe, good Childe Watèrs,
  Let mee lye at your bedd's feete:
For there is noe place about this house,
  Where I may 'saye † a sleepe.

"He gave her leave, and fair Ellèn
  Down at his bed's feet laye:"
This done the nighte drove on apace,
  And when it was neare the daye,

---
\* *i.e.* defiling.
† *i.e.* essay, attempt.

---

Hee sayd, Rise up, my little foot-page,
  Give my steede corne and haye;
And soe doe thou the good black oats,
  To carry mee better awaye.

Up then rose the faire Ellèn,
  And gave his steede corne and hay:
And soe shee did the good blacke oates,
  To carry him the better away.

Shee leaned her backe to the manger side,
  And grievouslye did groane:
Shee leaned her back to the manger side,
  And there shee made her moane.

And that beheard his mother deere,
  Shee heard her there *monànd*.\*
Shee sayd, Rise up, thou Childe Watèrs,
  I think thee a cursed man.

For in thy stable is a ghost,
  That grievouslye doth grone:
Or else some woman laboures of childe,
  She is soe woe-begone.

Up then rose Childe Waters soon,
  And did on his shirte of silke;
And then he put on his other clothes,
  On his body as white as milke.

And when he came to the stable dore,
  Full still there hee did stand,
That hee mighte heare his fayre Ellèn,
  Howe shee made her *monànd*. \*

She sayd, Lullabye, mine owne deere child,
  Lullabye, dere child, dere;
I wold thy father were a king,
  Thy mother layd on a biere.

Peace now, hee said, good faire Ellèn,
  Be of good cheere, I praye;
And the bridal and the churching both
  Shall bee upon one day.

---
\* *i.e.* moaning, bemoaning, etc.

## X.—PHILLIDA AND CORYDON.

This sonnet is given from a small quarto MS. in the Editor's possession, written in the time of Queen Elizabeth; the author was Nicholas Breton.

*Phillida and Corydon* is one of the songs in "The Honourable Entertainment gieven to the Queene's Majestic in Progresse at Elvetham in Hampshire, by the R. H. the Earle of Hertford, 1591."

"On Wednesday morning about 9 o'clock, as her Majestie opened a casement of her gallerie window, ther were 3 excellent musitians, who being disguised in auncient country attire, did greet her with a pleasant song of *Corydon and Phillida*, made in 3 parts of purpose. The song, as well for the worth of the dittie, as the aptnesse of the note thereto applied, it pleased her Highnesse after it had been once sung to command it againe, and highly to grace it with her cheerefull acceptance and commendation."

In the merrie moneth of Maye,
In a morne by break of daye,
With a troope of damselles playing
Forthe "I yode" forsooth a maying:

When anon by a wood side,
Where as Maye was in his pride,
I espièd all alone
Phillida and Corydon.

Much adoe there was, god wot;
He wold love, and she wold not.
She sayde, never man was trewe;
He sayes, none was false to you.

He sayde, hee had lovde her longe:
She sayes, love should have no wronge.

Corydon wold kisse her then:
She sayes, maydes must kisse no men,

Tyll they doe for good and all.
When she made the shepperde call
All the heavens to wytnes truthe,
Never loved a truer youthe.

Then with manie a prettie othe,
Yea and nay, and faith and trothe;
Suche as *seelie* shepperdes use
When they will not love abuse;

Love, that had bene long deluded,
Was with kisses sweete concluded;
And Phillida with garlands gaye
Was made the lady of the Maye.

## XI.—LITTLE MUSGRAVE AND LADY BARNARD.*

This ballad is ancient, and has been popular; we find it quoted in many old plays. It is given from an old printed copy in the British Museum, with corrections, some of which are from a fragment in the Editor's folio MS.

As it fell out on a highe holye daye,
  As many bee in the yeare,
When yong men and maides together do goe,
  Their masses and mattins to heare,

Little Musgrave came to the church door,
  The priest was at the mass;
But he had more mind of the fine women,
  Then he had of our Ladyes grace.

---

* In folio, Lord Barnard and Little Musgrave.

And some of them were clad in greene,
    And others were clad in pall;
And then came in my lord Barnarde's wife,
    The fairest among them all.

Shee cast an eye on little Musgrave
    As bright as the summer sunne:
O then bethought him little Musgrave,
    This ladye's heart I have wonne.

Quoth she, I have loved thee, little Musgrave,
    Fulle long and manye a daye.
So have I loved you, ladye faire,
    Yet word I never durst saye.

I have a bower at Bucklesford-Bury,*
    Full daintilye bedight,
If thoult wend thither, my little Musgrave,
    Thoust *lig* in mine armes all night.

Quoth hee, I thanke yee, ladye faire,
    This kindness yee shew to mee;
And whether it be to my weale or woe,
    This night will I lig with thee.

All this beheard a little foot-page,
    By his ladye's coach as he ranne:
Quoth he, thoughe I am my ladye's page,
    Yet Ime my lord Barnarde's manne.

My lord Barnard shall knowe of this,
    Although I lose a limbe.
And ever whereas the bridges were broke,
    He layd him downe to swimme.

Asleep or awake, thou lord Barnard,
    As thou art a man of life,
Lo! this same night at Bucklesford-Bury
    Litle Musgrave's in bed with thy wife.

If it be trew, thou litle foot-page,
    This tale thou hast told to mee,
Then all my lands in Bucklesford-Bury
    I freelye will give to thee.

But and it be a lye, thou litle foot-page,
    This tale thou hast told to mee,

---

\* Bucklefield-berry, fol. MS.

On the highest tree in Bucklesford-Bury
    All hanged shalt thou bee.

Rise up, rise up, my merry men all,
    And saddle me my good steede;
This night must I to Bucklesford-bury;
    God wott, I had never more neede.

Then some they whistled, and some they sang,
    And some did loudlye saye,
Whenever lord Barnarde's horne it blewe,
    Awaye, Musgrave, away.

Methinkes I heare the throstle cocke,
    Methinkes I heare the jay,
Methinkes I heare lord Barnard's horne;
    I would I were awaye.

Lye still, lye still, thou little Musgrave,
    And huggle me from the cold;
For it is but some shepharde's boye
    A whistling his sheepe to the fold.

Is not thy hawke upon the pearche,
    Thy horse eating corne and haye?
And thou a gay lady within thine armes:
    And wouldst thou be awaye?

By this lord Barnard was come to the dore,
    And lighted upon a stone:
And he pulled out three silver keyes,
    And opened the dores eche one.

He lifted up the coverlett,
    He lifted up the sheete.;
How now, how now, thou little Musgrave,
    Dost find my gaye ladye sweete?

I find her sweete, quoth little Musgrave,
    The more is my griefe and paine;
Ide gladlye give three hundred poundes
    That I were on yonder plaine.

Arise, arise, thou little Musgrave,
    And put thy cloathes nowe on,
It shall never be said in my countree,
    That I killed a naked man.

I have two swordes in one scabbarde,
    Full deare they cost my purse;

And thou shalt have the best of them,
    And I will have the worse.

The first stroke that little Musgrave
    strucke,
He hurt lord Barnard sore ;
The next stroke that lord Barnard strucke,
    Little Musgrave never strucke more.

With that bespake the ladye faire,
    In bed whereas she laye,
Althoughe thou art dead, my little
    Musgrave,
Yet for thee I will praye :

And wishe well to thy soule will I,
    So long as I have life ;
So will I not do for thee, Barnàrd,
    Thoughe I am thy wedded wife.

He cut her pappes from off her brest ;
    Great pitye it was to see
The drops of this fair ladye's bloode
    Run trickling downe her knee.

Wo worth, wo worth ye, my merrye men
    all,
You never were borne for my goode :
Why did you not offer to stay my hande,
    When you sawe me wax so woode ?

For I have slaine the fairest sir knighte,
    That ever rode on a steede ;
So have I done the fairest lady,
    That ever ware womans weede.

A grave, a grave, lord Barnard cryde,
    To putt these lovers in ;
But laye my ladye o' the upper hande,
    For shee comes o' the better kin.

## XII.—THE EW-BUGHTS, MARION.

### A SCOTTISH SONG.

THIS sonnet appears to be ancient : that and its simplicity of sentiment have recommended it to a place here.

WILL ze gae to the *ew-bughts*, Marion,
    And wear in the sheip wi' mee?
The sun shines *sweit*, my Marion,
    But nae half sae sweit as thee.
O Marion's a bonnie lass ;
    And the blyth blinks in her ee :
And fain wad I marrie Marion,
    Gin Marion wad marrie mee.

Theire's gowd in zour garters, Marion ;
    And siller on zour white hauss-bane : *
Fou faine wad I kisse my Marion
    At eene *quhan* I cum hame.
Theire's braw lads in Earnslaw, Marion,
    Quha gape and glowr wi their ee
At kirk, quhan they see my Marion ;
    Bot nane of them lues like mee.

Ive nine milk-ews, my Marion,
    A cow and a brawney *quay ;*
Ise gie tham au to my Marion,
    Just on her bridal day.
And zees get a grein *sey* apron,
    And waistcote o' London broun ;
And wow bot ze will be vaporing
    Quhaneir ze gang to the toun.

Ime yong and stout, my Marion,
    None dance lik mee on the greine ;
And gin ze forsak me, Marion,
    Ise een gae draw up wi' Jeane.
Sae put on zour *pearlins*, Marion,
    And kirtle oth' *cramasie*,
And sune as my chin has nae haire on,
    I sall cum west, and see zee.

---

\* *i.e.* the neck-bone. Marion had probably a silver locket on, tied close to her neck with a ribband, an usual ornament in Scotland, where a sore throat is called "a sair hause," propeily halse; or probably necklace, the Ger. *Helsband*, necklace, following the same derivation (?).

## XIII.—THE KNIGHT, AND SHEPHERD'S DAUGHTER.

This ballad (given from an old black-letter copy, with some corrections) was popular in the time of Queen Elizabeth.

There was a shepherds daughter
  Came tripping on the waye;
And there by chance a knighte shee mett,
  Which caused her to staye.

Good morrowe to you, beauteous maide,
  These words pronounced hee:
O I shall dye this daye, he sayd,
  If Ive not my wille of thee.

The Lord forbid, the maide replyde,
  That you shold waxe so wode!
" But for all that shee could do or saye,
  He wold not be withstood."

Sith you have had your wille of mee,
  And put me to open shame,
Now, if you are a courteous knighte,
  Tell me what is your name?

Some do call mee Jacke, sweet heart,
  And some do call mee Jille;
But when I come to the king's faire courte
  They call me Wilfulle Wille.

He sett his foot into the stirrup,
  And awaye then he did ride;
She tuckt her girdle about her middle,
  And ranne close by his side.

But when she came to the brode watèr,
  She sett her brest and swamme;
And when she was got out againe,
  She tooke to her heels and ranne.

He never was the courteous knighte,
  To saye, faire maide, will ye ride?
And she was ever too loving a maide
  To saye, sir knighte, abide.

When she came to the king's faire courte,
  She knocked at the ring;
So readye was the king himself
  To let this faire maide in.

Now Christ you save, my gracious liege.
  Now Christ you save and see,
You have a knighte within your courte
  This daye hath robbed mee.

What hath he robbed thee of, sweet heart?
  Of *purple or of pall?*
Or hath he took thy gaye gold ring
  From off thy finger small?

He hath not robbed mee, my liege,
  Of purple nor of pall:
But he hath gotten my maiden head,
  Which grieves mee worst of all.

Now if he be a batchelor,
  His bodye Ile give to thee;
But if he be a married man,
  High hanged he shall bee.

He called downe his merrye men all,
  By one, by two, by three;
Sir William used to bee the first,
  But nowe the last came hee.

He brought her downe full fortye pounde,
  Tyed up withinne a glove:
Faire maid, Ile give the same to thee;
  Go, secke thee another love.

O Ile have none of your gold, she sayde,
  Nor Ile have none of your fee;
But your faire bodye I must have,
  The king hath granted mee.

Sir William ranne and fetchd her then
  Five hundred pound in golde,
Saying, faire maide, take this to thee,
  Thy fault will never be tolde.

T'is not the gold that shall mee tempt,
  These words then answered shee,
But your own bodye I must have,
  The king hath granted mee.

Would I had dranke the water cleare,
  When I did drinke the wine,
Rather than any shepherds brat
  Shold bee a ladye of mine!

Would I had drank the puddle foule,
  When I did drink the ale,
Rather than ever a shepherds brat
  Shold tell me such a tale!

A shepherds brat even as I was,
  You mote have let me bee,
I never had come to the kings faire courte,
  To crave any love of thee.

He sett her on a milk-white steede,
  And himself upon a graye;
He hung a bugle about his necke,
  And soe they rode awaye.

But when they came unto the place,
  Where marriage-rites were done,
She proved herself a dukes daughtèr,
  And he but a squires sonne.

Now marrye me, or not, sir knight,
  Your pleasure shall be free:
If you make me ladye of one good towne,
  Ile make you lord of three.

Ah! cursed bee the gold, he sayd,
  If thou hadst not been trewe,
I shold have forsaken my sweet love,
  And have changed her for a newe.

And now their hearts being linked fast,
  They joyned hand in hande:
Thus he had both purse, and person too,
  And all at his commande.

## XIV.—THE SHEPHERD'S ADDRESS TO HIS MUSE.

THIS poem, originally printed from the small MS. volume mentioned above in No. X., has been improved by a more perfect copy in *England's Helicon*, where the author is discovered to be N. Breton.

GOOD Muse, rocke me aslepe
  With some sweete harmony:
This wearie eyes is not to kepe
  Thy wary company.

Sweete Love, begon a while,
  Thou seest my heavines:
Beautie is borne but to beguyle
  My harte of happines.

See howe my little flocke,
  That lovde to feede on highe,
Doe headlonge tumble downe the rocke,
  And in the valley dye.

The bushes and the trees,
  That were so freshe and greene,
Doe all their deintie colors leese,
  And not a leafe is seene.

The blacke birde and the thrushe,
  That made the woodes to ringe,
With all the rest, are now at hushe,
  And not a note they singe.

Swete Philomele, the birde
  That hath the heavenly throte,
Doth nowe, alas! not once afforde
  Recordinge of a note.

The flowers have had a frost,
  The herbs have loste their savoure;
And Phillida the faire hath lost
  "For me her wonted" favour.

Thus all these careful sights
  So kill me in conceit:
That now to hope upon delights,
  It is but meere deceite.

And therefore, my sweete Muse,
  That knowest what helpe is best,
Doe nowe thy heavenlie conninge use
  To sett my harte at rest:

And in a dreame bewraie
  What fate shal be my *frende;*
Whether my life shall still decaye,
  Or when my sorrowes ende.

## XV.—LORD THOMAS AND FAIR ELLINOR

Is given (with corrections) from an ancient copy in black letter in the Pepys Collection, entitled, *A Tragical Ballad on the Unfortunate Love of Lord Thomas and Fair Ellinor, together with the Downfall of the Browne Girl.* In the same collection may be seen an attempt to modernize this old song, and reduce it to a different measure, a proof of its popularity.

LORD THOMAS he was a bold forrestèr,
   And a chaser of the kings deere;
Faire Ellinor was a fine womàn,
   And lord Thomas he loved her deare.

Come riddle my riddle, dear mother, he sayd,
   And riddle us both as one;
Whether I shall marrye with faire Ellinòr,
   And let the browne girl alone?

The browne girl she has got houses and lands,
   Faire Ellinor she has got none,
And therefore I charge thee on my blessing,
   To bring me the browne girl home.

And as it befelle on a high holidaye,
   As many there are beside,
Lord Thomas he went to faire Ellinòr,
   That should have been his bride.

And when he came to faire Ellinors bower,
   He knocked there at the ring,
And who was so readye as faire Ellinòr,
   To lett lord Thomas withinn.

What newes, what newes, lord Thomas, she sayd?
   What newes dost thou bring to mee?
I am come to bid thee to my wedding,
   And that is bad newes for thee.

O God forbid, lord Thomas, she sayd,
   That such a thing should be done;
I thought to have been the bride my selfe,
   And thou to have been the bridegrome.

Come riddle my riddle, dear mother, she sayd,
   And riddle it all in one;
Whether I shall goe to lord Thomas his wedding,
   Or whether shall tarry at home?

There are manye that are your friendes, daughtèr,
   And manye a one your foe,
Therefore I charge you on my blessing,
   To lord Thomas his wedding don't goe.

There are manye that are my friendes, mothèr;
   But were every one my foe,
Betide me life, betide me death,
   To lord Thomas his wedding I'ld goe.

She cloathed herself in gallant attire,
   And her merrye men all in greene;
And as they rid through every towne,
   They took her to be some queene.

But when she came to lord Thomas his gate,
   She knocked there at the ring;
And who was so readye as lord Thomàs,
   To lett faire Ellinor in.

Is this your bride, fair Ellinor sayd?
   Methinks she looks wonderous browne;
Thou mightest have had as faire a womàn,
   As ever trod on the grounde.

Despise her not, fair Ellin, he sayd,
   Despise her not unto mee;
For better I love thy little fingèr,
   Than all her whole bodèe.

This browne bride had a little penknife,
  That was both long and sharpe,
And betwixt the short ribs and the long,
  She prick'd faire Ellinor's harte.

O Christ thee save, lord Thomas, hee sayd,
  Methinks thou lookst wonderous wan;
Thou usedst to look with as fresh a colour,
  As ever the sun shone on.

Oh, art thou blind, lord Thomas? she sayd,
  Or canst thou not very well see?

Oh! dost thou not see my owne hearts bloode
  Run trickling down my knee.

Lord Thomas he had a sword by his side;
  As he walked about the halle,
He cut off his brides head from his shoulders,
  And threw it against the walle.

He set the hilte against the grounde,
  And the point against his harte.
There never three lovers together did meete,
  That sooner againe did parte.

## XVI.—CUPID AND CAMPASPE.

This elegant little sonnet is found in the third act of an old play, entitled *Alexander and Campaspe*, written by John Lilye, a celebrated writer in the time of Queen Elizabeth. That play was first printed in 1591; but this copy is given from a later edition.

CUPID and my Campaspe playd
At cardes for kisses; Cupid payd:
He stakes his quiver, bow and arrows,
His mothers doves, and teame of sparrows;
Loses them too; then down he throws
The coral of his lippe, the rose
Growing on's cheek (but none knows how),
With these, the crystal of his browe,
And then the dimple of his chinne;
All these did my Campaspe winne.
At last he set her both his eyes,
She won, and Cupid blind did rise.
  O Love! has she done this to thee?
  What shall, alas! become of mee?

## XVII.—THE LADY TURNED SERVING-MAN

Is given from a written copy containing some improvements (perhaps modern ones) upon the popular ballad entitled, *The Famous Flower of Serving-men; or the Lady turned Serving-man.*

You beauteous ladyes, great and small,
  I write unto you one and all,
Whereby that you may understand
  What I have suffered in the land.

I was by birth a lady faire,
  An ancient barons only heire,
And when my good old father dyed,
  Then I became a young knighte's bride.

And there my love built me a bower,
Bedeck'd with many a fragrant flower;
A braver bower you ne'er did see
Then my true-love did build for mee.

And there I livde a ladye gay,
Till fortune wrought our loves decay:
For there came foes so fierce a band,
That soon they over-run the land.

They came upon us in the night,
And *brent* my bower, and slew my knight;
And trembling hid in man's array,
I scant with life escap'd away.

In the midst of this extremitie,
My servants all did from me flee:
Thus was I left myself alone,
With heart more cold than any stone.

Yet though my heart was full of care,
Heaven would not suffer me to dispaire,
Wherefore in haste I chang'd my name
From faire Elise to sweet Williame:

And therewithall I cut my haire,
Resolv'd my man's attire to weare;
And in my beaver, hose and band,
I travell'd far through many a land.

At length all wearied with my toil,
I sate me downe to rest awhile;
My heart it was so fill'd with woe,
That downe my cheeke the teares did flow.

It chanc'd the king of that same place
With all his lords a hunting was,
And seeing me weepe, upon the same
Askt who I was, and whence I came.

Then to his grace I did replye,
I am a poore and friendlesse boye,
Though nobly borne, nowe forc'd to bee
A serving-man of lowe degree.

Stand up, faire youth, the king reply'd,
For thee a service I'll provyde:

But tell me first what thou canst do;
Thou shalt be fitted thereunto.

Wilt thou be usher of my hall,
To wait upon my nobles all?
Or wilt be taster of my wine,
To 'tend on me when I shall dine?

Or wilt thou be my chamberlaine,
About my person to remaine?
Or wilt thou be one of my guard,
And I will give thee great reward?

Chuse, gentle youth, said he, thy place.
Then I reply'd, If it please your grace
To shew such favour unto mee,
Your chamberlaine I faine would bee.

The king then smiling gave consent,
And straitwaye to his court I went;
Where I behavde so faithfullie,
That hee great favour showd to mee.

Now marke what fortune did provide;
The king he would a hunting ride
With all his lords and noble traine,
Sweet William must at home remaine.

Thus being left alone behind,
My former state came in my mind:
I wept to see my man's array;
No longer now a ladye gay.

And meeting with a ladyes vest,
Within the same myself I drest;
With silken robes, and jewels rare,
I deckt me, as a ladye faire:

And taking up a lute straitwaye,
Upon the same I strove to play;
And sweetly to the same did sing,
As made both hall and chamber ring.

" My father was as brave a lord,
As ever Europe might afford;
My mother was a lady bright;
My husband was a valiant knight;

"And I myself a ladye gay,
Bedeckt with gorgeous rich array;
The happiest lady in the land
Had not more pleasure at command.

"I had my musicke every day,
Harmonious lessons for to play;
I had my virgins fair and free
Continually to wait on mee.

"But now, alas! my husband's dead,
And all my friends are from me fled,
My former days are past and gone,
And I am now a serving-man."

And fetching many a tender sigh,
As thinking no one then was nigh,
In pensive mood I laid me lowe,
My heart was full, the tears did flowe.

The king, who had a huntinge gone,
Grewe weary of his sport anone,
And leaving all his gallant traine,
Turn'd on the sudden home againe:

And when he reach'd his statelye tower,
Hearing one sing within his bower,
He stopt to listen, and to see
Who sung there so melodiouslie.

Thus heard he everye word I sed,
And saw the pearlye teares I shed,
And found to his amazement there,
Sweete William was a ladye faire.

Then stepping in, Faire ladye, rise,
And dry, said he, those lovelye eyes,
For I have heard thy mournful tale,
The which shall turne to thy availe.

A crimson dye my face orespred,
I blusht for shame, and hung my head,
To find my sex and story knowne,
When as I thought I was alone.

But to be briefe, his royall grace
Grewe so enamour'd of my face,
The richest gifts he proffered mee,
His mistress if that I would bee.

Ah! no, my liege, I firmlye sayd,
I'll rather in my grave be layd,
And though your grace hath won my heart,
I ne'er will act soe base a part.

Faire ladye, pardon me, sayd hee,
Thy virtue shall rewarded bee;
And since it is soe fairly tryde,
Thou shalt become my royal bride.

Then strait to end his amorous strife,
He tooke sweet William to his wife,
The like before was never seene,
A serving-man became a queene.

## XVIII.—GIL MORRICE.

### A SCOTTISH BALLAD.

ONE of the most popular of the olden ballads, of which there have been several editions.

The one in the Editor's folio edition, under title of *Child Maurice*, which gives "John Stewart" for Lord Barnard and "Child Maurice" for Gil Morice, is one of the most forcible.

The copy here brought before the reader having passed through "refining" hands, loses much of its early strength. The "greenwood" is said by Mr. Motherwell to be .. 'o. .-t of Dundaff in Stirlingshire. This pathetic story suggested the tragedy of *Dougla.*

GIL MORRICE was an erlès son,
    His name it waxed wide;
It was nae for his great richès,
    Nor *zet* his mickle pride;
Bot it was for a lady gay,
    That livd on Carron side.

*Quhair* sall I get a bonny boy,
    That will win hose and shoen;
That will gae to lord Barnards ha',
    And bid his lady cum?
And ze maun rin my errand, Willie;*
    And ze may rin wi' pride;
*Quhen* other boys gae on their foot,
    On horse-back ze zall ride.

O no! Oh no! my master dear!
    I dare nae for my life;
I'll no gae to the bauld baròns,
    For to triest furth his wife.
My bird Willie, my boy Willie;
    My dear Willie, he sayd:
How can ze strive against the stream?
    For I sall be obeyd.

Bot, O my master dear! he cryd,
    In grene wod ze're zour lain;
Gi owre sic thochts, I walde ze rede,
    For fear ze should be tain.
Haste, haste, I say, gae to the ha',
    Bid hir cum here wi speid:

If ze refuse my heigh command,
    Ill gar zour body bleid.

Gae bid hir take this gay mantèl,
    'Tis a' gowd bot the hem;*
Bid hir cum to the gude grene wode,
    And bring nane bot hir lain:
And there it is, a silken sarke,
    Hir ain hand sewd the sleive;
And bid hir cum to Gill Morice,
    *Speir* nae bauld barons leave.

Yes, I will gae zour black errand,
    Though it be to zour cost;
Sen ze by me will nae be warn'd,
    In it ze sall find frost.
The baron he is a man of might,
    He neir could bide to taunt,
As ze will see before its nicht,
    How sma' ze hae to vaunt.

And sen I maun zour errand rin
    Sae sair against my will,
I'se mak a vow and keip it trow,
    It sall be done for ill.
And quhen he came to broken *brigue*,
    He bent his bow and swam;
And quhen he came to grass growing,
    Set down his feet and ran.

And quhen he came to Barnards ha',
    Would neither *chap* nor ca':

---

\* Something seems wanting here.

\* Perhaps "bout the hem."

Bot set his bent bow to his breist,
  And lichtly lap the wa'.\*
He wauld nae tell the man his errand,
  Though he stude at the gait ;
Bot straiht into the ha' he cam,
  Quhair they were set at meit.

Hail! hail! my gentle sire and dame!
  My message winna waite ;
Dame, ze maun to the gude grene wod
  Before that it be late.
Ze're bidden tak this gay mantèl,
  Tis a' gowd bot the hem :
Zou maun gae to the gude grene wode,
  Ev'n by your sel alane.

And there it is, a silken *sarke*,
  Your ain hand sewd the sleive ;
Ze maun gae speik to Gill Morice ;
  Speir nae bauld barons leave.
The lady stamped wi' hir foot,
  And winked wi' hir ee ;
Bot a' that she coud say or do,
  Forbidden he wad nae bee.

Its surely to my bow'r-woman ;
  It neir could be to me.
I brocht it to lord Barnards lady ;
  I trow that ze be she.
Then up and spack the wylie nurse
  (The bairn upon hir knee),
If it be cum frae Gill Morice,
  It's deir welcum to mee.

Ze leid, ze leid, ze filthy nurse,
  Sae loud I heird ze lee ;
I brocht it to lord Barnards lady ;
  I trow ze be nae shee.
Then up and spack the bauld baròn,
  An angry man was hee ;
He's tain the table wi' his foot,
  Sae has he wi' his knee ;
Till siller cup and "mazer" † dish
  In flinders he gard flee.

\* Could this be the wall of the castle?
† *i.e.* a drinking cup of maple ; other edit.
read "ezar."

Gae bring a robe of zour *clidlng*,
  That hings upon the pin ;
And I'll gae to the gude grene wode,
  And speik wi' zour lemmàn.
O bide at hame, now lord Barnàrd,
  I *warde* ze bide at hame ;
Neir *wyte* a man for violence,
  That neir *wate* ze wi' nane.

Gil Morice sate in gude grene wode,
  He whistled and he sang :
O what mean a' the folk coming,
  My mother tarries lang.
His hair was like the threeds of gold,
  Drawne frae Minerva's loome :
His lipps like roses drapping dew,
  His breath was a' perfume.

His brow was like the mountain snae
  Gilt by the morning beam :
His cheeks like living roses glow :
  His een like azure stream.
The boy was clad in robes of grene,
  Sweete as the infant spring :
And like the mavis on the bush,
  He gart the vallies ring.

The baron came to the grene wode,
  Wi' mickle dule and care,
And there he first spied Gill Morice
  Kameing his zellow hair :
That sweetly wavd around his face,
  That face beyond compare :
He sang sae sweet it might dispel
  A' rage but fell despair.

Nae wonder, nae wonder, Gill Morice,
  My lady loed thee weel,
The fairest part of my bodie
  Is blacker than thy heel.
Zet neir the less now, Gill Morice,
  For a' thy great beautiè,
Ze's *rew* the day ze eir was born ;
  That head sall gae wi' me.

Now he has drawn his trusty brand,
  And *slaited* on the strae ;

And thro' Gill Morice' fair body
  He's gar cauld iron gae.
And he has tain Gill Morice' head
  And set it on a speir;
The meanest man in a' his train
  Has gotten that head to bear.

And he has tain Gill Morice up,
  Laid him across his steid,
And brocht him to his painted bowr,
  And laid him on a bed.
The lady sat on castil wa',
  Beheld baith dale and doun;
And there she saw Gill Morice' head
  Cum trailing to the toun.

Far better I loe that bluidy head,
  Both and that zellow hair,
Than lord Barnard, and a' his lands,
  As they *lig* here and thair.
And she has tain her Gill Morice,
  And kissed baith mouth and chin:
I was once as fow of Gill Morice,
  As the *hip* is o' the *stean*.

I got ze in my father's house,
  Wi' mickle sin and shame;
I brocht thee up in gude grene wode,
  Under the heavy rain.
Oft have I by thy cradle sitten,
  And fondly seen thee sleip;
But now I gae about thy grave,
  The saut tears for to weip.

And syne she kissd his bluidy cheik,
  And syne his bluidy chin:
O better I loe my Gill Morice
  Than a' my kith and kin!
Away, away, ze ill womàn,
  And an il deith mait ze dee:
Gin I had kend he'd bin zour son,
  He'd neir bin slain for mee.

*Obraid* me not, my lord Barnard!
  Obraid me not for shame!
Wi' that saim speir O pierce my heart!
  And put me out o' pain.
Since nothing bot Gill Morice head
  Thy jelous rage could quell,
Let that saim hand now tak hir life,
  That neir to thee did ill.

To me nae after days nor nichts
  Will eir be saft or kind;
I'll fill the air with heavy sighs,
  And greet till I am blind.
Enouch of blood by me's bin spilt,
  Seek not zour death frae mee;
I rather *lourd* it had been my sel
  Than eather him or thee.

With waefò wae I hear zour plaint:
  Sair, sair I rew the deid,
That eir this cursed hand of mine
  Had gard his body bleid.
Dry up zour tears, my winsome dame,
  Ze neir can heal the wound;
Ze see his head upon the speir,
  His heart's blude on the ground.

I curse the hand that did the deid,
  The heart that thocht the ill;
The feet that bore me wi' silk speid,
  The comely zouth to kill.
I'll ay lament for Gill Morice,
  As gin he were mine ain;
I'll neir forget the dreiry day
  On which the *zouth* was slain.

\*\*\* Since it was first printed, the Editor has been assured that the foregoing ballad is still current in many parts of Scotland, where the hero is universally known by the name of Child Maurice, pronounced by the common people Cheild or Cheeld, which occasioned the mistake.

**THE END OF THE FIRST BOOK.**

# SERIES THE THIRD.—BOOK II.

## I.—THE LEGEND OF SIR GUY.

THE oldest known form of *Guy of Warwick* is an Anglo-Norman one of the thirteenth century, composed doubtless from fragments that had floated hither and thither for some time previous.

The legend of Guy given here is published from an ancient MS. copy in the Editor's old folio volume, under the title of *Guy and Phillis*, collated with two printed ones, one of which is in black letter in the Pepys Collection.

"*The Legend of Sir Guy*," says Percy, "contains a short summary of the exploits of this famous champion as recorded in the old story-books, and is commonly entitled, 'A Pleasant Song of the Valiant Deeds of Chivalry atchieved by that Noble Knight, Sir Guy of Warwick, who, for the Love of Fair Phelis, became a Hermit, and dyed in a cave of craggy rockes, a mile distant from Warwick.'"

Rous, a priest of Guy's Cliff, in the fifteenth century, writes with regard to fair Phillis: "Dame Felys daughter and heire to Erle Rohand, for her beauty called Felyle Belle, or Felys the Faire, by true inheritance Countess of Warwick and ladye and wyfe to the most victorious Sir Guy; to whom, in his woinge time, she made great straungenes, and caused him for her sake to put himself in meny greate distresse, dangers, and perills; but when they wer wedded, and wer but a little season togither, he departed from her to her greate hevynes, and never was conversant with her after to her understandinge."

So he left the countess, and took upon himself pilgrim's weeds, which he wore to his life's end. His last battle was his victory over Colbrand, the Danish giant. He returned to Warwick, unknown to any but the king. "And two days before his deathe," says Rous, "an angell informed him of his passage oute of this world, and of his ladyes the day fourtnight after him."

So popular had the history of Guy of Warwick become, and so widely had it spread, that we are told by Dugdale, that in the year 1410, Lord Beauchamp, travelling in the East, was at Jerusalem invited to the palace by the Soldan's lieutenant, who had heard he was a descendant of Sir Guy of Warwick, of whom they had read in their own books; and who, after "royally feasting him, presented him with three precious stones of great value, besides divers cloaths of silk and gold given to his servants."

WAS ever knight for ladyes sake
    Soe tost in love, as I sir Guy
For Phelis fayre, that lady bright
    As ever man beheld with eye?

She gave me leave myself to try,
    The valiant knight with sheeld and speare,
Ere that her love shee wold grant me;
    Which made mee venture far and neare.

Then proved I a baron bold,
    In deeds of armes the doughtyest knight
That in those dayes in England was,
    With sworde and speare in feild to fight.

An English man I was by birthe:
    In faith of Christ a christyan true:
The wicked lawes of infidells
    I sought by prowesse to subdue.

"Nine" hundred twenty yeere and odde
  After our Saviour Christ his birth,
When king Athelstone wore the crowne,
  I lived heere upon the earth.

Sometime I was of Warwicke erle,
  And, as I sayd, of very truth
A ladyes love did me constraine
  To seeke strange ventures in my youth.

To win me fame by feates of armes
  In strange and sundry heathen lands;
Where I atchieved for her sake
  Right dangerous conquests with my hands.

For first I sayled to Normandye,
  And there I stoutlye wan in fight
The emperours daughter of *Almaine*,
  From manye a vallyant worthye knight.

Then passed I the seas to Greece
  To helpe the emperour in his right;
Against the mightye souldans hoaste
  Of puissant Persians for to fight.

Where I did slay of Sarazens,
  And heathen pagans, manye a man;
And slew the souldans cozen deere,
  Who had to name doughtye Coldrân.

Eskeldered a famous knight
  To death likewise I did pursue:
And Elmayne king of Tyre alsoe,
  Most terrible in fight to viewe.

I went into the souldans hoast,
  Being thither on embassage sent,
And brought his head awaye with mee;
  I having slaine him in his tent.

There was a dragon in that land
  Most fiercelye mett me by the waye
As hee a lyon did pursue,
  Which I myself did alsoe slay.

Then soon I past the seas from Greece,
  And came to Pavye land aright:
Where I the duke of Pavye killed,
  His hainous treason to requite.

To England then I came with speede,
  To wedd faire Phelis lady bright:
For love of whome I travelled farr
  To try my manhood and my might.

But when I had espoused her,
  I stayd with her but fortye dayes,
Ere that I left this ladye faire,
  And went from her beyond the seas.

All cladd in gray, in pilgrim sort,
  My voyage from her I did take
Unto the blessed Holy-land,
  For Jesus Christ my Saviours sake.

Where I erle Jonas did redeeme,
  And all his sonnes, which were fifteene,
Who with the cruell Sarazens
  In prison for long time had beene.

I slew the gyant Amarant
  In battell fiercelye hand to hand:
And doughty Barknard killed I,
  A treacherous knight of Pavye land.

Then I to England came againe,
  And here with Colbronde fell I fought:
An ugly gyant, which the Danes
  Had for their champion hither brought.

I overcame him in the feild,
  And slewe him soone right valliantlye;
Wherebye this land I did redeeme
  From Danish tribute utterlye.

And afterwards I offered upp
  The use of weapons solemnlye
At Winchester, whereas I fought,
  In sight of manye farr and nye.

"But first," neare Winsor, I did slaye
  A bore of passing might and strength;
Whose like in England never was
  For hugenesse both in bredth and length.

Some of his bones in Warwicke yett*
   Within the castle there doe lye:
One of his sheeld-bones to this day
   Hangs in the citye of Coventrye.

On Dunsmore heath I alsoe slewe
   A monstrous wyld and cruell beast,
Calld the Dun-cow of Dunsmore heath;
   Which manye people had opprest.

Some of her bones in Warwicke yett*
   Still for a monument doe lye;
And there exposed to lookers viewe
   As wonderous strange, they may espye.

A dragon in Northumberland
   I alsoe did in fight destroye,
Which did bothe man and beast oppresse,
   And all the countrye sore annoye.

At length to Warwicke I did come,
   Like pilgrim poore, and was not knowne;
And there I lived a hermitts life
   A mile and more out of the towne.

Where with my hands I hewed a house
   Out of a craggy rocke of stone;†

And lived like a palmer poore
   Within that cave myself alone:

And daylye came to begg my bread
   Of Phelis att my castle gate;
Not knowne unto my loved wiffe,
   Who dailye mourned for her mate.

Till att the last I fell sore sicke,
   Yea sicke soe sore that I must dye;
I sent to her a ring of golde,
   By which shee knew me presentlye.

Then shee repairing to the cave
   Before that I gave up the ghost;
Herself closd up my dying eyes:
   My Phelis faire, whom I lovd most.

Thus dreadful death did me arrest,
   To bring my corpes unto the grave;
And like a palmer dyed I,
   Wherby I sought my soule to save.

My body that endured this toyle,
   Though now it be consumed to mold;
My statue faire engraven in stone,
   In Warwicke still you may behold.

---

## II.—GUY AND AMARANT.

THE Editor found this poem in his ancient folio manuscript among the old ballads; its author is Samuel Rowlands, one of the minor poets of the reigns of Elizabeth and James, perhaps later. An edition was published in 1649.

GUY journeyes towards that sanctifyed ground,
   Whereas the Jewes fayre citye sometime stood,
Wherin our Saviours sacred head was crownd,
   And where for sinfull man he shed his blood:

To see the sepulcher was his intent,
   The tombe that Joseph unto Jesus lent.

With tedious miles he tyred his wearye feet,
   And passed desart places full of danger,
At last with a most woefull wight* did meet,
   A man that unto sorrow was noe stranger:

---

\* These relics, together with Guy's porridge-pot, staff, spear, thumb-ring, etc., are still to be seen at Warwick Castle.
† Guy's Cliff, near Warwick.

\* Erle Jonas, mentioned in the foregoing ballad.

For he had fifteen sonnes, made captives all
To slavish bondage, in extremest thrall.

A gyant called Amarant detained them,
  Whom noe man durst encounter for his strength:
Who in a castle, which he held, had chaind them:
  Guy questions, where? and understands at length
The place not farr.—Lend me thy sword, quoth hee,
Ile lend my manhood all thy sonnes to free.

With that he goes, and lays upon the dore,
  Like one that sayes, I must, and will come in:
The gyant never was soe rowz'd before:
  For noe such knocking at his gate had bin:
Soe takes his keyes, and clubb, and cometh out
Staring with ireful countenance about.

Sirra, quoth hee, what business hast thou heere?
  Art come to feast the crowes about my walls?
Didst never heare, noe ransome can him cleere,
  That in the compasse of my furye falls:
For making me to take a porters paines,
With this same clubb I will dash out thy braines.

Gyant, quoth Guy, y'are quarrelsome I see,
  Choller and you seem very neere of kin:
Most dangerous at the clubb belike you bee;
  I have bin better armd, though nowe goe thin;
But shew thy utmost hate, enlarge thy spight,
Keene is my weapon, and shall doe me right.

Soe draws his sword, salutes him with the same
  About the head, the shoulders, and the side:
Whilst his erected clubb doth death proclaime,
  Standinge with huge Colossus' spacious stride,
Putting such vigour to his knotty beame,
That like a furnace he did smoke extreame.

But on the ground he spent his strokes in vaine,
  For Guy was nimble to avoyde them still,
And ever ere he heav'd his clubb againe,
  Did brush his plated coat against his will:
Att such advantage Guy wold never fayle,
To bang him soundlye in his coate of mayle.

Att last through thirst the gyant feeble grewe,
  And sayd to Guy, As thou'rt of humane race,
Shew itt in this, give natures wants their dewe,
  Let me but goe, and drinke in yonder place:
Thou canst not yeeld to "me" a smaller thing,
Than to graunt life, thats given by the spring.

I graunt thee leave, quoth Guye, goe drink thy last,
  Go pledge the dragon, and the salvage bore:*
Succeed the tragedyes that they have past,
  But never thinke to taste cold water more:

---

\* Which Guy had slain before.

Drinke deepe to Death and unto him
　carouse:
Bid him receive thee in his earthen house.

Soe to the spring he goes, and slakes his
　thirst ;
Takeing the water in extremely like
Some wracked shipp that on a rocke is
　burst,
　Whose forced hulke against the stones
　　does stryke ;
Scooping it in soe fast with both his
　hands,
That Guy admiring to behold it stands.

Come on, quoth Guy, let us to worke
　againe,
　Thou stayest about thy liquor over-
　　long ;
The fish, which in the river doe remaine,
　Will want thereby ; thy drinking doth
　　them wrong :
But I will see their satisfaction made,
With gyants blood they must and shall
　be payd.

Villaine, quoth Amarant, Ile crush thee
　streight ;
　Thy life shall pay thy daring toungs
　　offence :
This clubb, which is about some hundred
　weight,
Is deathes commission to dispatch thee
　hence :
Dresse thee for ravens dyett I must
　needes ;
And breake thy bones, as they were made
　of reedes.

Incensed much by these bold pagan
　bostes,
　Which worthye Guy cold ill endure to
　　heare,
Ile hewes upon those bigg supporting
　postes,
　Which like two pillars did his bodye
　　beare :

Amarant for those wounds in choller
　growes,
And desperatelye att Guy his clubb he
　throwes :

Which did directly on his body light,
　Soe violent, and weighty there-withall,
That downe to ground on sudden came
　the knight ;
And, ere he cold recover from the fall,
The gyant gott his clubb againe in fist,
And aimd a stroke that wonderfullye mist.

Traytor, quoth Guy, thy falshood Ile
　repay,
This coward act to intercept my bloode.
Sayes Amarant, Ile murther any way,
　With enemyes all vantages are good :
O could I poyson in thy nostrils blowe,
Be sure of it I wold dispatch thee soe.

Its well, said Guy, thy honest thoughts
　appeare,
　Within that beastlye bulke where
　　devills dwell ;
Which are thy tenants while thou livest
　heare,
　But will be landlords when thou comest
　　in hell :
Vile miscreant, prepare thee for their den,
Inhumane monster, hatefull unto men.

But breathe thy selfe a time, while I goe
　drinke,
　For flameing Phœbus with his fyerye
　　eye
Torments me soe with burning heat, I
　thinke
　My thirst wold serve to drinke an
　　ocean drye :
Forebar a litle, as I delt with thee.
Quoth Amarant, Thou hast noe foole of
　mee.

Noe, sillye wretch, my father taught more
　witt,
　How I shold use such enemyes as thou ;

By all my gods I doe rejoice at itt,
 To understand that thirst constraines
  thee now ;
For all the treasure, that the world
  containes,
One drop of water shall not coole thy
 . vaines.

Releeve my foe ! why, 'twere a madmans
  part :
Refresh an adversarye to my wrong !
If thou imagine this, a child thou art :
 Noe, fellow, I have known the world
  too long
To be soe simple : now I know thy want,
A minutes space of breathing I'll not
  grant,

And with these words heaving aloft his
  clubb
 Into the ayre, he swings the same
  about :
Then shakes his lockes, and doth his
  temples rubb,
 And, like the Cyclops, in his pride doth
  strout :
Sirra, sayes hee, I have you at a lift,
Now you are come unto your latest shift.

Perish forever : with this stroke I send
  thee
 A medicine, that will doe thy thirst
  much good ;
Take noe more care for drinke before I
  end thee,
 And then we'll have carouses of thy
  blood :
Here's at thee with a butcher's downright
  blow,
To please my furye with thine overthrow.

Infernall, false, obdurate feend, said Guy,
 That seemst a lumpe of crueltye from
  hell ;
Ungratefull monster, since thou dost deny
 The thing to mee wherin I used thee
  well :

With more revenge, than ere my sword
  did make,
On thy accursed head revenge Ile take.

Thy gyants longitude shall shorter shrinke
 Except thy sun-scorcht skin be weapon
  proof ;
Farewell my thirst ; I doe disdaine to
  drinke ;
 Streames keepe your waters to your
  owne behoof ;
Or let wild beasts be welcome thereunto ;
With those pearle drops I will not have
  to do.

Here, tyrant, take a taste of my good-will,
 For thus I doe begin my bloodye bout :
You cannot chuse but like the greeting
  ill ;
 It is not that same clubb will beare
  you out ;
And take this payment on thy shaggye
  crowne—
A blowe that brought him with a ven-
  geance downe.

Then Guy sett foot upon the monsters
  brest,
 And from his shoulders did his head
  divide ;
Which with a yawninge mouth did gape,
  unblest ;
 Noe dragons jawes were ever seene soe
  wide
To open and to shut, till life was spent.
Then Guy tooke keyes, and to the castle
  went.

Where manye woefull captives he did
  find,
 Which had beene tyred with extremityes ;
Whom he in friendly manner did unbind,
 And reasoned with them of their
  miseryes :
Eche told a tale with teares, and sighes,
  and cryes,
All weeping to him with complaining
  eyes.

There tender ladyes in darke dungeons
    lay,
  That were surprised in the desart wood,
And had noe other dyett everye day,
  But flesh of humane creatures for their
    food :
Some with their lovers bodyes had beene
    fed,
And in their wombes their husbands
    buryed.

Now he bethinkes him of his being there,
  To enlarge the wronged brethren from
    their woes :
And, as he searcheth, doth great clamours
    heare,
  By which sad sound's direction on he
    goes,
Untill he findes a darksome obscure gate,
Arm'd strongly ouer all with iron plate.

That he unlockes, and enters, where
    appeares
  The strangest object that he ever saw ;
Men that with famishment of many yeares,
  Were like deathes picture, which the
    painters draw ;
Divers of them were hanged by eche
    thombe ;
Others head-downward : by the middle
    some.

With diligence he takes them from the
    walle,
  With lybertye their thraldome to
    acquaint :
Then the perplexed knight their father
    calls,
  And sayes, Receive thy sonnes though
    poore and faint :
I promisd you their lives, accept of that ;
But did not warrant you they shold be fat.

The castle I doe give thee, heere's the
    keyes,
  Where tyranye for many yeeres did
    dwell :
Procure the gentle tender ladyes ease,
  For pittyes sake, use wronged women
    well :
Men easilye revenge the wrongs men do ;
But poore weake women have not strength
    thereto.

The good old man, even overjoyed with
    this,
  Fell on the ground, and wold have kist
    Guys feete :
Father, quoth he, refraine soe base a
    kiss,
  For age to honor youth I hold unmeete :
Ambitious pryde hath hurt me all it can,
I goe to mortifie a sinfull man.

---

### III.—THE AULD GOOD-MAN.

#### A SCOTTISH SONG.

I HAVE not been able to meet with a more ancient copy of this humorous old song than that printed in the *Tea-Table Miscellany*, etc., which seems to have admitted some corruptions.

LATE in an evening forth I went
  A little before the sun gade down,
And there I chanc'd by accident,
  To light on a battle new begun :
A man and his wife wer fawn in a strife,
  I canna weel tell ye how it began ;

But aye she wail'd her wretched life,
  Cryeng, Evir alake, mine auld goodman!

#### HE.

Thy auld goodman, that thou tells of,
  The country kens where he was born,

Was but a silly poor vagabond,
   And *ilka* ane leugh him to scorn :
For he did spend and make an end
   Of gear " his fathers nevir " wan ;
He *gart* the poor stand frae the door ;
   Sae tell nae mair of thy auld goodman.

### SHE.

My heart, alake ! is liken to break,
   Whan I think on my winsome John,
His blinkan ee, and gait sae free,
   Was naithing like thee, thou *dosend* drone ;
Wi' his rosie face, and flaxen hair,
   And skin as white as ony swan,
He was large and tall, and comely withall ;
   Thou'lt nevir be like mine auld goodman.

### HE.

Why dost thou *plein ?* I thee maintein ;
   For meal and *mawt* thou disna want :
But thy wild bees I canna please,
   Now whan our gear gins to grow scant :

Of houshold stuff thou hast enough ;
   Thou wants for neither pot nor pan ;
Of sicklike ware he left thee bare ;
   Sae tell nae mair of thy auld goodman.

### SHE.

Yes I may tell, and fret my sell,
   To think on those blyth days I had,
Whan I and he together ley
   In armes into a well-made bed :
But now I sigh and may be sad,
   Thy courage is cauld, thy colour wan,
Thou falds thy feet, and fa's asleep ;
   Thou'lt nevir be like mine auld goodman.

Then coming was the night sae dark,
   And gane was a' the light of day :
The *carle* was fear'd to miss his mark,
   And therefore wad nae longer stay :
Then up he gat, and ran his way,
   I trowe, the wife the day she wan ;
And aye the owreword of the fray
   Was, Evir alake ! mine auld goodman.

---

## IV.—FAIR MARGARET AND SWEET WILLIAM.

THIS seems to be the old song quoted in Fletcher's *Knight of the Burning Pestle,* Acts ii. and iii., although the six lines there preserved are somewhat different from those in the ballad as it stands at present. The reader will not wonder at this, when he is informed that this is only given from a modern printed copy picked up on a stall. Its full title is, *Fair Margaret's Misfortunes ; or Sweet William's frightful dreams on his wedding night, with the sudden death and burial of those noble lovers.*

The lines preserved in the play are this distich :

    "You are no love for me, Margaret,
    I am no love for you ;"

and the following stanza :

    "When it was grown to dark midnight,
      And all were fast asleep,
    In came Margaret's grimly ghost
      And stood at William's feet."

These lines have acquired an importance by giving birth to one of the most beautiful ballads in our own or any language. See the song entitled *Margaret's Ghost* at the end of this volume.

As it fell out on a long summer's day,
  Two lovers they sat on a hill;
They sat together that long summer's day,
  And could not talk their fill.

I see no harm by you, Margarèt,
  And you see none by mee;
Before to-morrow at eight o' the clock
  A rich wedding you shall see.

Fair Margaret sat in her bower-window,
  Combing her yellow hair;
There she spyed sweet William and his
    bride,
  As they were a riding near.

Then down she layd her ivory combe,
  And braided her hair in twain:
She went alive out of her bower,
  But ne'er came alive in't again.

When day was gone, and night was come,
  And all men fast asleep,
Then came the spirit of fair Marg'ret,
  And stood at Williams feet.

Are you awake, sweet William? shee said;
  Or, sweet William, are you asleep?
God give you joy of your gay bride-bed,
  And me of my winding sheet.

When day was come, and night was gone,
  And all men wak'd from sleep,
Sweet William to his lady sayd,
  My dear, I have cause to weep.

I dreamt a dream, my dear ladyè,
  Such dreames are never good:
I dreamt my bower was full of red "wine,"
  And my bride-bed full of blood.

Such dreams, such dreams, my honoured
    Sir,
  They never do prove good;
To dream thy bower was full of red
    "wine,"
  And thy bride-bed full of blood.

He called up his merry men all,
  By one, by two, and by three;
Saying, I'll away to fair Marg'ret's bower,
  By the leave of my ladiè.

And when he came to fair Marg'ret's
    bower,
  He knocked at the ring;
And who so ready as her seven brethrèn
  To let sweet William in.

Then he turned up the covering-sheet,
  Pray let me see the dead;
Methinks she looks all pale and wan,
  She hath lost her cherry red.

I'll do more for thee, Margarèt,
  Than any of thy kin;
For I will kiss thy pale wan lips,
  Though a smile I cannot win.

With that bespake the seven brethrèn,
  Making most piteous mone:
You may go kiss your jolly brown bride,
  And let our sister alone.

If I do kiss my jolly brown bride,
  I do but what is right;
I neer made a vow to yonder poor corpse
  By day, nor yet by night.

Deal on, deal on, my merry men all,
  Deal on your cake and your wine: *
For whatever is dealt at her funeral to-day,
  Shall be dealt to-morrow at mine.

Fair Margaret dyed to-day, to-day,
  Sweet William dyed the morrow:
Fair Margaret dyed for pure true love,
  Sweet William dyed for sorrow.

Margaret was buryed in the lower chancèl,
  And William in the higher:
Out of her brest there sprang a rose,
  And out of his a briar.

---

* Alluding to the dole anciently given at funerals.

They grew till they grew unto the church top,
   And then they could grow no higher;
And there they tyed in a true lovers knot,
   Which made all the people admire.

Then came the clerk of the parish,
   As you the truth shall hear,
And by misfortune cut them down,
   Or they had now been there.

---

### V.—BARBARA ALLEN'S CRUELTY.

GIVEN, with some corrections, from an old black-letter copy, entitled *Barbara Allen's Cruelty, or the Young Man's Tragedy.*

IN Scarlet towne, where I was borne,
   There was a faire maid dwellin,
Made every youth crye, Wel-awaye!
   Her name was Barbara Allen.

All in the merrye month of May,
   When greene buds they were swellin,
Yong Jemmye Grove on his death-bed lay,
   For love of Barbara Allen.

He sent his man unto her then,
   To the town where shee was dwellin;
You must come to my master deare,
   Giff your name be Barbara Allen.

For death is printed on his face,
   And ore his hart is stealin:
Then haste away to comfort him,
   O lovelye Barbara Allen.

Though death be printed on his face,
   And ore his harte is stealin,
Yet little better shall he bee
   For bonny Barbara Allen.

So slowly, slowly, she came up,
   And slowly she came nye him;
And all she sayd, when there she came,
   Yong man, I think y'are dying.

He turnd his face unto her strait,
   With deadlye sorrow sighing;
O lovely maid, come pity mee,
   Ime on my deth-bed lying.

If on your death-bed you doe lye,
   What needs the tale you are tellin;
I cannot keep you from your death;
   Farewell, sayd Barbara Allen.

He turnd his face unto the wall,
   As deadlye pangs he fell in:
Adieu! adieu! adieu to you all,
   Adieu to Barbara Allen.

As she was walking ore the fields,
   She heard the bell a knellin;
And every stroke did seem to saye,
   Unworthy Barbara Allen.

She turnd her bodye round about,
   And spied the corps a coming:
Laye down, laye down the corps, she sayd,
   That I may look upon him.

With scornful eye she looked downe,
   Her cheeke with laughter swellin;
Whilst all her friends cryd out amaine;
   Unworthye Barbara Allen.

When he was dead, and laid in grave,
   Her harte was struck with sorrowe,
O mother, mother, make my bed,
   For I shall dye to-morrowe.

Hard-harted creature him to slight,
   Who loved me so dearlye:
O that I had beene more kind to him,
   When he was alive and neare me!

She, on her death-bed as she laye,
  Beg'd to be buried by him;
And sore repented of the daye,
  That she did ere denye him.

Farewell, she sayd, ye virgins all,
  And shun the fault I fell in:
Henceforth take warning by the fall
  Of cruel Barbara Allen.

## VI.—SWEET WILLIAM'S GHOST.

### A SCOTTISH BALLAD.

From Allan Ramsay's *Tea-Table Miscellany*, but claimed by, and often ascribed to, Mallet. Mr. W. Chappell, in the *Antiquary*, vol. i., shows reasons for disputing this claim.

There came a ghost to Margaret's door,
  With many a grievous grone,
And ay he *tirled* at the pin;
  But answer made she none.

Is this my father Philip?
  Or is't my brother John?
Or is't my true love Willie,
  From Scotland new come home?

'Tis not thy father Philip;
  Nor yet thy brother John:
But tis thy true love Willie,
  From Scotland new come home.

O sweet Margret! O dear Margret!
  I pray thee speak to mee:
Give me my faith and troth, Margret,
  As I gave it to thee.

Thy faith and troth thou'se nevir get,
  "Of me shalt nevir win,"
Till that thou come within my bower,
  And kiss my cheek and chin.

If I should come within thy bower,
  I am no earthly man:
And should I kiss thy rosy lipp,
  Thy days will not be lang.

O sweet Margret, O dear Margret,
  I pray thee speak to mee:
Give me my faith and troth, Margret,
  As I gave it to thee.

Thy faith and troth thou'se nevir get,
  "Of me shalt nevir win,"
Till thou take me to yon kirk yard,
  And wed me with a ring.

My bones are buried in a kirk yard
  Afar beyond the sea,
And it is but my sprite, Margret
  That's speaking now to thee.

She stretched out her lily-white hand,
  As for to do her best:
Hae there your faith and troth, Willie,
  God send your soul good rest.

Now she has kilted her robes of green,
  A piece below her knee:
And a' the live-lang winter night
  The dead corps followed shee.

Is there any room at your head, Willie?
  Or any room at your feet?
Or any room at your side, Willie,
  Wherein that I may creep?

There's nae room at my head, Margret,
  There's nae room at my feet,
There's no room at my side, Margret,
  My coffin is made so meet.

Then up and crew the red red cock,
  And up then crew the gray:
Tis time, tis time, my dear Margret,
  That "I" were gane away.

No more the ghost to Margret said,
   But, with a grievous grone,
Evanish'd in a cloud of mist,
   And left her all alone.

O stay, my only true love, stay,
   The constant Margret cried :
Wan grew her cheeks, she clos'd her een,
   Stretch'd her saft limbs, and died.

## VII.—SIR JOHN GREHME AND BARBARA ALLAN.

### A SCOTTISH BALLAD.

PRINTED, with a few conjectural emendations, from a written copy.

It was in and about the Martinmas time,
   When the greene leaves wer a fallan ;
That Sir John Grehme o' the west countrye,
   Fell in luve wi' Barbara Allan.

He sent his man down throw the towne,
   To the plaice wher she was dwellan :
O haste and cum to my maister deare,
   Gin ye bin Barbara Allan.

O *hooly*, hooly raise she up,
   To the plaice wher he was lyan ;
And whan she drew the curtain by,
   Young man, I think ye're dyan.\*

O its I'm sick, and very very sick,
   And its a' for Barbara Allan.
O the better for me ye'se never be,
   Though your harts blude wer spillan.

Remember ye nat in the tavern, sir,
   Whan ye the cups wer fillan ;
How ye made the healths gae round and round,
   And slighted Barbara Allan?

He turn'd his face unto the wa',
   And death was with him dealan ;
Adiew ! adiew ! my dear friends a',
   Be kind to Barbara Allan.

Then hooly, hooly raise she up,
   And hooly, hooly left him ;
And sighan said, she could not stay,
   Since death of life had reft him.

She had not gane a mile but twa,
   Whan she heard the deid-bell knellan ;
And everye jow the deid-bell geid,
   Cried, Wae to Barbara Allan !

O mither, mither, mak my bed,
   O mak it saft and narrow :
Since my love died for me to day,
   Ise die for him to morrowe.

---

\* An ingenious friend thinks the rhymes "dyan" and "lyan" ought to be transposed, as the taunt, "Young man, I think ye're lyan," would be very characteristical.

## VIII.—THE BAILIFF'S DAUGHTER OF ISLINGTON.

FROM an ancient black-letter copy in the Pepys Collection, with some improvements. Islington in Norfolk is probably the place here meant.

THERE was a youthe, and a well-beloved youthe,
    And he was a squire's son:
He loved the bayliffe's daughter deare,
    That lived in Islington.

Yet she was coye, and would not believe
    That he did love her soe,
Noe nor at any time would she
    Any countenance to him showe.

But when his friendes did understand
    His fond and foolish minde,
They sent him up to faire London,
    An apprentice for to binde.

And when he had been seven long yeares,
    And never his love could see:
Many a teare have I shed for her sake,
    When she little thought of mee.

Then all the maids of Islington
    Went forth to sport and playe,
All but the bayliffe's daughter deare;
    She secretly stole awaye.

She pulled off her gowne of greene,
    And put on ragged attire,
And to faire London she would go
    Her true love to enquire.

And as she went along the high road,
    The weather being hot and drye,
She sat her downe upon a green bank,
    And her true love came riding bye.

She started up, with a colour soe redd,
    Catching hold of his bridle-reine;
One penny, one penny, kind sir, she sayd,
    Will ease me of much paine.

Before I give you one penny, sweet-heart,
    Praye tell me where you were borne.
At Islington, kind sir, sayd shee,
    Where I have had many a scorne.

I prythee, sweet-heart, then tell to mee,
    O tell me, whether you knowe
The bayliffe's daughter of Islington.
    She is dead, sir, long agoe.

If she be dead, then take my horse,
    My saddle and bridle also;
For I will into some farr countrye,
    Where noe man shall me knowe.

O staye, O staye, thou goodlye youthe,
    She standeth by thy side;
She is here alive, she is not dead,
    And readye to be thy bride.

O farewell griefe, and welcome joye,
    Ten thousand times therefore;
For nowe I have founde mine owne true love,
    Whom I thought I should never see more.

## IX.—THE WILLOW TREE.

### A PASTORAL DIALOGUE.

FROM the small black-letter collection, entitled *The Golden Garland of princely Delights*, collated with two other copies, and corrected by conjecture.

#### WILLY.

How now, shepherde, what meanes that?
Why that willowe in thy hat?
Why thy scarffes of red and yellowe
Turn'd to branches of greene willowe?

#### CUDDY.

They are chang'd, and so am I;
Sorrowes live, but pleasures die:
Phillis hath forsaken mee,
Which makes me weare the willowe-tree.

#### WILLY.

Phillis! shee that lov'd thee long?
Is shee the lass hath done thee wrong?
Shee that lov'd thee long and best,
Is her love turned to a jest?

#### CUDDY.

Shee that long true love profest,
She hath robb'd my heart of rest:
For she a new love loves, not mee;
Which makes me wear the willowe-tree.

#### WILLY.

Come then, shepherde, let us joine,
Since thy happ is like to mine:
For the maid I thought most true
Mee hath also bid adieu.

#### CUDDY.

Thy hard happ doth mine appease,
Companye doth sorrowe ease:
Yet, Phillis, still I pine for thee,
And still must weare the willowe-tree.

#### WILLY.

Shepherde, be advis'd by mee,
Cast off grief and willowe-tree:
For thy grief brings her content,
She is pleas'd if thou lament.

#### CUDDY.

Herdsman, I'll be rul'd by thee,
There lyes grief and willowe-tree:
Henceforth I will do as they,
And love a new love every day.

---

## X.—THE LADY'S FALL

Is given (with corrections) from the Editor's ancient folio MS., collated with two printed copies in black letter; one in the British Museum, the other in the Pepys Collection.

MARKE well my heavy dolefull tale,
   You loyall lovers all,
And heedfully beare in your brest
   A gallant ladyes fall.
Long was she wooed, ere shee was wonne,
   To lead a wedded life,
But folly wrought her overthrowe
   Before shee was a wife.

Too soone, alas! shee gave consent
   And yeelded to his will,
Though he protested to be true,
   And faithfull to her still.
Shee felt her body altered quite,
   Her bright hue waxed pale,
Her lovelye cheeks chang'd color white,
   Her strength began to fayle.

Soe that with many a sorrowful sigh,
  This beauteous ladye milde,
With greeved hart, perceived herselfe
  To have conceived with childe.
Shee kept it from her parents sight
  As close as close might bee,
And soe put on her silken gowne
  None might her swelling see.

Unto her lover secretly
  Her greefe shee did bewray,
And, walking with him hand in hand,
  These words to him did say ;
Behold, quoth shee, a maids distresse
  By love brought to thy bowe,
Behold I goe with childe by thee,
  Tho none thereof doth knowe.

The litle babe springs in my wombe
  To heare its fathers voyce,
Lett it not be a bastard called,
  Sith I made thee my choyce :
Come, come, my love, perform thy vowe
  And wed me out of hand ;
O leave me not in this extreme
  Of griefe, alas ! to stand.

Think on thy former promises,
  Thy oathes and vowes eche one ;
Remember with what bitter teares
  To mee thou madest thy moane.
Convay me to some secrett place,
  And marry me with speede ;
Or with thy rapyer end my life,
  Ere further shame proceede.

Alacke ! my beauteous love, quoth hee,
  My joye, and only dear ;
Which way can I convay thee hence,
  When dangers are so near ?
Thy friends are all of hye degree,
  And I of meane estate ;
Full hard it is to gett thee forthe
  Out of thy fathers gate.

Dread not thy life to save my fame,
  For, if thou taken bee,

My selfe will step betweene the swords,
  And take the harme on mee :
Soe shall I scape dishonor quite ;
  And if I should be slaine,
What could they say, but that true love
  Had wrought a ladyes bane.

But feare not any further harme ;
  My selfe will soe devise,
That I will ryde away with thee
  Unknowen of mortall eyes :
Disguised like some pretty page
  Ile meete thee in the darke,
And all alone Ile come to thee
  Hard by my fathers parke.

And there, quoth hee, Ile meete my deare
  If God soe lend me life,
On this day month without all fayle
  I will make thee my wife.
Then with a sweet and loving kisse,
  They parted presentlye,
And att their partinge brinish teares
  Stoode in eache others eye.

Att length the wished day was come,
  On which this beauteous mayd,
With longing eyes, and strange attire,
  For her true lover stayd.
When any person shee espyed
  Come ryding ore the plaine,
She hop'd it was her owne true love :
  But all her hopes were vaine.

Then did shee weepe and sore bewayle
  Her most unhappy fate ;
Then did shee speake these woefull words,
  As succourless she sate ;
O false, forsworne, and faithlesse man,
  Disloyall in thy love,
Hast thou forgott thy promise past,
  And wilt thou perjured prove ?

And hast thou now forsaken mee
  In this my great distresse,
To end my dayes in open shame,
  Which thou mightst well redresse ?

Woe worth the time I eer believ'd
  That flattering tongue of thine;
Wold God that I had never seene
  The teares of thy false eyne.

And thus with many a sorrowful sigh,
  Homewards shee went againe;
Noe rest came in her waterye eyes,
  Shee felt such privye paine.
In travail strong shee fell that night,
  With many a bitter throwe;
What woefull paines shee then did feel,
  Doth eche good woman knowe.

Shee called up her waiting mayd,
  That lay at her bedds feete,
Who musing at her mistress woe,
  Began full fast to weepe.
Weepe not, said shee, but shutt the dores,
  And windowes round about,
Let none bewray my wretched state,
  But keepe all persons out.

O mistress, call your mother deare
  Of women you have neede,
And of some skilfull midwifes helpe,
  That better may you speed.
Call not my mother for thy life,
  Nor fetch no woman here;

The midwifes helpe comes all too late,
  My death I doe not feare.

With that the babe sprang from her wombe,
  No creature being nye,
And with one sighe, which brake her hart,
  This gentle dame did dye.
The lovely litle infant younge,
  The mother being dead,
Resigned its new received breath
  To him that had it made.

Next morning came her own true love,
  Affrighted at the newes,
And he for sorrow slew himselfe,
  Whom eche one did accuse.
The mother with her new borne babe,
  Were laide both in one grave:
Their parents overworne with woe,
  No joy thenceforth cold have.

Take heed, you dayntye damsells all,
  Of flattering words beware,
And to the honour of your name
  Have an especial care.
Too true, alas! this story is,
  As many one can tell:
By others harmes learne to be wise,
  And you shall do full well.

## XI.—WALY WALY, LOVE BE BONNY.

### A SCOTTISH SONG.

THIS is a very ancient song, but we could only give it from a modern copy. Some editions instead of the four last lines in the second stanza have these, which have too much merit to be wholly suppressed:

  "Whan cockle shells turn siller bells,
    And muscles grow on every tree,
  When frost and snaw sall warm us aw',
    Than sall my love prove true to me."
        See the *Orpheus Caledonius*, etc.

Arthur's Seat, mentioned in ver. 17, is a hill near Edinburgh, at the bottom of which is St. Anthony's well.

O *waly* waly up the bank,
  And waly waly down the brae,
And waly waly yon burn side,
  Where I and my love wer wont to gae.

I leant my back unto an aik,
  I thought it was a trusty tree;
But first it bow'd, and syne it brak,
  Sae my true love did *lichtly* me.

O waly waly, gin love be bonny,
  A little time while it is new;
But when its auld, it waxeth cauld,
  And fades awa' like morning dew.
O wherfore shuld I *busk* my head?
  Or wherfore shuld I kame my hair?
For my true love has me forsook,
  And says he'll never loe me mair.

Now Arthur-seat sall be my bed,
  The sheets shall neir be *fyl'd* by me:
Saint Anton's well sall be my drink,
  Since my true love has forsaken me.
Marti'mas wind, when wilt thou blaw,
  And shake the green leaves aff the tree?
O gentle death, whan wilt thou cum?
  For of my life I am wearie.

'Tis not the frost, that freezes fell,
  Nor blawing snaws inclemencie;
'Tis not sic cauld that makes me cry,
  But my loves heart grown cauld to me.
Whan we came in by Glasgowe town,
  We were a comely sight to see,
My love was cled in black velvet,
  And I my sell in cramasie.

But had I wist, before I kisst,
  That love had been sae ill to win;
I had lockt my heart in a case of gowd,
  And pinnd it with a siller pin.
And, oh! if my young babe were born,
  And set upon the nurses knee,
And I my sell were dead and gane!
  For a maid again Ise never be.

## XII.—THE BRIDE'S BURIAL.

FROM two ancient copies in black letter, one in the Pepys Collection, the other in the British Museum. To the tune of "The Lady's Fall."

COME mourne, come mourne with mee,
  You loyall lovers all;
Lament my loss in weeds of woe,
  Whom griping grief doth thrall.

Like to the drooping vine,
  Cut by the gardener's knife,
Even so my heart, with sorrow slaine,
  Doth bleed for my sweet wife.

By death, that grislye ghost,
  My turtle dove is slaine,
And I am left, unhappy man,
  To spend my days in paine.

Her beauty late so bright,
  Like roses in their prime,
Is wasted like the mountain snowe,
  Before warme Phebus' shine.

Her faire red colour'd cheeks
  Now pale and wan; her eyes,
That late did shine like crystal stars,
  Alas, their light it dies:

Her prettye lilly hands,
  With fingers long and small,
In colour like the earthly claye,
  Yea, cold and stiff withall.

When as the morning-star
  Her golden gates had spred
And that the glittering sun arose
  Forth from fair Thetis' bed.

Then did my love awake,
  Most like a lilly-flower,
And as the lovely queene of heaven,
  So shone shee in her bower.

Attired was shee then;
  Like Flora in her pride,
Like one of bright Diana's nymphs,
  So look'd my loving bride.

And as fair Helens face
  Did Grecian dames besmirche,
So did my dear exceed in sight
  All virgins in the church.

When we had knitt the knott
  Of holy wedlock-band,
Like alabaster joyn'd to jett,
  So stood we hand in hand;

Then lo! a chilling cold
  Strucke every vital part,
And griping grief, like pangs of death,
  Seiz'd on my true love's heart.

Down in a swoon she fell,
  As cold as any stone;
Like Venus picture lacking life,
  So was my love brought home.

At length her rosye red,
  Throughout her comely face,
As Phœbus beames with watry cloudes
  Was cover'd for a space.

When with a grievous groane,
  And voice both hoarse and drye,
Farewell, quoth she, my loving friend,
  For I this daye must dye; .

The messenger of God
  With golden trumpe I see,
With manye other angels more,
  Which sound and call for mee.

Instead of musicke sweet,
  Go toll my passing-bell;
And with sweet flowers strow my grave,
  That in my chamber smell.

Strip off my bride's arraye,
  My cork shoes from my feet;
And, gentle mother, be not coye
  To bring my winding-sheet.

My wedding dinner drest,
  Bestowe upon the poor,
And on the hungry, needy, maimde,
  Now craving at the door.

Instead of virgins yong,
  My bride-bed for to see,
Go cause some cunning carpenter,
  To make a chest for mee.

My bride laces of silk
  Bestowd, for maidens meet,
May fitly serve, when I am dead,
  To tye my hands and feet.

And thou, my lover true,
  My husband and my friend,
Let me intreat thee here to staye,
  Until my life doth end.

Now leave to talk of love,
  And humblye on your knee,
Direct your prayers unto God:
  But mourn no more for mee.

In love as we have livde,
  In love let us depart;
And I, in token of my love,
  Do kiss thee with my heart.

O staunch those bootless teares,
  Thy weeping tis in vaine;
I am not lost, for wee in heaven
  Shall one daye meet againe.

With that shee turn'd aside,
  As one dispos'd to sleep,
And like a lamb departed life:
  Whose friends did sorely weep.

Her true love seeing this,
  Did fetch a grievous groane,
As tho' his heart would burst in twaine,
  And thus he made his moane.

O darke and dismal daye,
  A daye of grief and care,
That hath bereft the sun so bright,
  Whose beams refresht the air.

Now woe unto the world,
  And all that therein dwell,
O that I were with thee in heaven,
  For here I live in hell.

And now this lover lives
  A discontented life,
Whose bride was brought unto the grave
  A maiden and a wife.

A garland fresh and faire
  Of lillies there was made,
In sign of her virginitye,
  And on her coffin laid.

Six maidens all in white,
  Did beare her to the ground:
The bells did ring in solemn sort,
  And made a dolefull sound.

In earth they laid her then,
  For hungry wormes a preye;
So shall the fairest face alive
  At length be brought to claye.

## XIII.—DULCINA.

GIVEN from two ancient copies, one in black print, in the Pepys Collection, the other in the Editor's folio MS.

As at noone Dulcina rested
  In her sweete and shady bower,
Came a shepherd, and requested
  In her lapp to sleepe an hour.
    But from her looke
    A wounde he tooke
Soe deepe, that for a further boone
    The nymph he prayes.
    Whereto shee sayes,
  Forgoe me now, come to me soone.

But in vayne shee did conjure him
  To depart her presence soe;
Having a thousand tongues to allure him,
  And but one to bid him goe:
    Where lipps invite,
    And eyes delight,
And cheekes, as fresh as rose in june,
    Persuade delay;
    What boots, she say,
  Forgoe me now, come to me soone?

He demands what time for pleasure
  Can there be more fit than now:
She sayes, night gives love that leysure,
  Which the day can not allow.
    He sayes, the sight
    Improves delight.
Which she denies: Nights mirkie noone
    In Venus' playes
    Makes bold, shee sayes;
  Forgoe me now, come to mee soone.

But what promise or profession
  From his hands could purchase scope?
Who would sell the sweet possession
  Of suche beautye for a hope?
    Or for the sight
    Of lingering night
Foregoe the present joyes of noone?
    Though ne'er soe faire
    Her speeches were,
  Forgoe me now, come to mee soone.

How, at last, agreed these lovers?
  Shee was fayre, and he was young:
The tongue may tell what th'eye discovers;
  Joyes unseene are never sung.
    Did shee consent,
    Or he relent;
Accepts he night, or grants shee noone;
    Left he her a mayd,
    Or not; she sayd
  Forgoe me now, come to me soone.

## XIV.—THE LADY ISABELLA'S TRAGEDY.

THIS ballad is given from an old black-letter copy in the Pepys Collection, collated with another in the British Museum, H. 263, folio. It is there entitled *The Lady Isabella's Tragedy, or the Step-Mother's Cruelty.*

THERE was a lord of worthy fame,
    And a hunting he would ride,
Attended by a noble traine
    Of gentrye by his side.

And while he did in chase remaine,
    To see both sport and playe ;
His ladye went, as she did feigne,
    Unto the church to praye.

This lord he had a daughter deare,
    Whose beauty shone so bright,
She was belov'd, both far and neare,
    Of many a lord and knight.

Fair Isabella was she call'd,
    A creature faire was shee ;
She was her fathers only joye ;
    As you shall after see.

Therefore her cruel step-mother
    Did envye her so much,
That daye by daye she sought her life,
    Her malice it was such.

She bargain'd with the master-cook
    To take her life awaye :
And taking of her daughters book,
    She thus to her did saye.

Go home, sweet daughter, I thee praye,
    Go hasten presentlie ;
And tell unto the master-cook
    These wordes that I tell thee.

And bid him dresse to dinner streight
    That faire and milk-white doe,
That in the parke doth shine so bright,
    There's none so faire to showe.

This ladye fearing of no harme,
    Obey'd her mother's will ;
And presentlye she hasted home,
    Her pleasure to fulfill.

She streight into the kitchen went,
    Her message for to tell ;
And there she spied the master-cook,
    Who did with malice swell.

Nowe, master-cook, it must be soe,
    Do that which I thee tell :
You needes must dresse the milk-white doe,
    Which you do knowe full well.

Then streight his cruell bloodye hands,
    He on the ladye layd ;
Who quivering and shaking stands,
    While thus to her he sayd :

Thou art the doe that I must dresse ;
    See here, behold my knife ;
For it is pointed presently
    To ridd thee of thy life.

O then, cried out the scullion-boye,
    As loud as loud might bee ;
O save her life, good master-cook,
    And make your pyes of mee !

For pityes sake do not destroye
    My ladye with your knife ;
You know shee is her father's joye,
    For Christes sake save her life.

I will not save her life, he sayd,
    Nor make my pyes of thee ;
Yet if thou dost this deed bewraye,
    Thy butcher I will bee.

Now when this lord he did come home
  For to sit downe and eat ;
He called for his daughter deare,
  To come and carve his meat.

Now sit you downe, his ladye sayd,
  O sit you downe to meat :
Into some nunnery she is gone ;
  Your daughter deare forget.

Then solemnlye he made a vowe,
  Before the companie :
That he would neither eat nor drinke,
  Until he did her see.

O then bespake the scullion-boye,
  With a loud voice so hye :
If now you will your daughter see,
  My lord, cut up that pye :

Wherein her fleshe is minced small,
  And parched with the fire ;
All caused by her step-mothèr,
  Who did her death desire.

And cursed bee the master-cook,
  O cursed may he bee !
I proffered him my own heart's blood,
  From death to set her free.

Then all in blacke this lord did mourne ;
  And for his daughters sake,
He judged her cruell step-mothèr
  To be burnt at a stake.

Likewise he judg'd the master-cook
  In boiling lead to stand ;
And made the simple scullion-boye
  The heire of all his land.

## XV.—A HUE AND CRY AFTER CUPID.

THIS song is a kind of translation of a pretty poem of Tasso's, called *Amore fuggitivo*, generally printed with his *Aminta*, and originally imitated from the first *Idyllium* of Moschus.

It is extracted from Ben Jonson's masque at the marriage of Lord Viscount Hadington, on Shrove-Tuesday 1608.

BEAUTIES, have yee seen a toy,
Called Love, a little boy,
Almost naked, wanton, blinde ;
Cruel now, and then as kinde?
If he be amongst yee, say ;
He is Venus' run-away.

Shee, that will but now discover
Where the winged wag doth hover,
Shall to-night receive a kisse,
How and where herselfe would wish :
But who brings him to his mother
Shall have that kisse, and another.

Markes he hath about him plentie ;
You may know him among twentie :
All his body is a fire,
And his breath a flame entire ;

Which, being shot, like lightning, in,
Wounds the heart, but not the skin.

Wings he hath, which though yee clip,
He will leape from lip to lip,
Over liver, lights, and heart ;
Yet not stay in any part.
And, if chance his arrow misses,
He will shoot himselfe in kisses.

He doth beare a golden bow,
And a quiver hanging low,
Full of arrowes, which outbrave
Dian's shafts ; where, if he have
Any head more sharpe than other,
With that first he strikes his mother.

Still the fairest are his fuell,
When his daies are to be cruell;
Lovers hearts are all his food,
And his baths their warmest bloud:
Nought but wounds his hand doth season,
And he hates none like to Reason.

Trust him not: his words, though sweet,
Seldome with his heart doe meet:
All his practice is deceit;
Everie gift is but a bait:
Not a kisse but poyson beares;
And most treason's in his teares.

Idle minutes are his raigne;
Then the straggler makes his gaine,
By presenting maids with toyes
And would have yee thinke hem joyes;
'Tis the ambition of the elfe
To have all childish as himselfe.

If by these yee please to know him,
Beauties, be not nice, but show him.
Though yee had a will to hide him,
Now, we hope, yee'le not abide him,
Since yee heare this falser's play,
And that he is Venus' run-away.

## XVI.—THE KING OF FRANCE'S DAUGHTER.*

"THE story of this ballad seems to be taken from an incident in the domestic history of Charles the Bald, King of France. His daughter Judith was betrothed to Ethelwulph, King of England; but before the marriage was consummated, Ethelwulph died, and she returned to France, whence she was carried off by Baldwyn, Forester of Flanders, who, after many crosses and difficulties, at length obtained the king's consent to their marriage, and was made Earl of Flanders. This happened about A.D. 863.—See Rapin, Henault, and the French historians." So writes the bishop; but this account is not true to history, as Judith married Ethelwulph with her father's consent and went to England with him. He died two years afterwards, and Judith married his son Ethelbert, which caused great public disapprobation, and a separation was effected. After this, Judith returned to her father's court and eloped with Baldwin, Grand Forester of France. Eventually the king became reconciled to this marriage, Baldwin was made Count of Flanders, and their daughter Matilda married William the Conqueror.

The following copy is given from the Editor's ancient folio MS., collated with another in black letter in the Pepys Collection, entitled *An excellent Ballad of a prince of England's courtship to the king of France's daughter*, etc. To the tune of 'Crimson Velvet.'

IN the dayes of old,
    When faire France did flourish,
Storyes plaine have told,
    Lovers felt annoye.
The queene a daughter bare,
    Whom beautye's queene did nourish:
She was lovelye faire,
    She was her fathers joye.
A prince of England came,
Whose deeds did merit fame,

But he was exil'd, and outcast:
Love his soul did fire,
Shee granted his desire,
    Their hearts in one were linked fast.
Which when her father proved,
Sorelye he was moved,
    And tormented in his minde.
He sought for to prevent them;
And, to discontent them,
    Fortune cross'd these lovers kinde.

---

* Given in folio as *In the Days of Old*.

When these princes twaine
  Were thus barr'd of pleasure,
Through the kinges disdaine,
  Which their joyes withstoode:
The lady soone prepar'd
  Her jewells and her treasure:
Having no regard
  For state and royall bloode;
In homelye poore array
She went from court away,
  To meet her joye and hearts delight;
Who in a forrest great
Had taken up his seat,
  To wayt her coming in the night.
But, lo! what sudden danger
To this princely stranger
  Chanced, as he sate alone!
By outlawes he was robbed,
And with ponyards stabbed,
  Uttering many a dying grone.

The princesse, arm'd by love,
  And by chaste desire,
All the night did rove
  Without dread at all:
Still unknowne she past
  In her strange attire;
Coming at the last
  Within echoes call,—
You faire woods, quoth shee,
Honoured may you bee,
  Harbouring my hearts delight;
Which encompass here
My joye and only deare,
  My trustye friend, and comelye knight.
Sweete, I come unto thee,
Sweete, I come to woo thee;
  That thou mayst not angry bee
For my long delaying;
For thy curteous staying
  Soone amendes Ile make to thee.

Passing thus alone
  Through the silent forest,
Many a grievous grone
  Sounded in her eares:

She heard one complayne
  And lament the sorest,
Seeming all in payne,
  Shedding deadly teares.
Farewell, my deare, quoth hee,
Whom I must never see;
  For why my life is att an end,
Through villaines crueltye:
For thy sweet sake I dye,
  To show I am a faithfull friend.
Here I lye a bleeding,
While my thoughts are feeding
  On the rarest beautye found.
O hard happ, that may be!
Little knowes my ladye
  My heartes blood lyes on the ground.

With that a grone he sends
  Which did burst in sunder
All the tender bands
  Of his gentle heart.
She, who knewe his voice,
  At his wordes did wonder;
All her former joyes
  Did to griefe convert.
Strait she ran to see,
Who this man shold bee,
  That soe like her love did seeme:
Her lovely lord she found
Lye slaine upon the ground,
  Smear'd with gore a ghastlye streame.
Which his lady spying,
Shrieking, fainting, crying,
  Her sorrows could not uttered bee:
Fate, she cryed, too cruell:
For thee—my dearest jewell,
  Would God! that I had dyed for thee.

His pale lippes, alas!
  Twentye times she kissed,
And his face did wash
  With her trickling teares:
Every gaping wound
  Tenderlye she pressed,

And did wipe it round
　With her golden haires.
Speake, faire love, quoth shee,
Speake, faire prince, to mee,
　One sweete word of comfort give:
Lift up thy deare eyes,
Listen to my cryes,
　Thinke in what sad griefe I live.
All in vaine she sued,
All in vaine she wooed,
　The prince's life was fled and gone.
There stood she still mourning,
Till the suns retourning,
　And bright day was coming on.

In this great distresse
　Weeping, wayling ever,
Oft shee cryed, alas!
　What will become of mee?
To my fathers court
　I returne will never:
But in lowlye sort
　I will a servant bee.
While thus she made her mone,
Weeping all alone,
　In this deepe and deadlye feare:
A for'ster all in greene,
Most comelye to be seene,
　Ranging the woods did find her there.
Moved with her sorrowe,
Maid, quoth hee, good morrowe,
　What hard happ has brought thee here?
Harder happ did never
Two kinde hearts dissever:
　Here lyes slaine my brother deare.

Where may I remaine,
　Gentle for'ster, shew me,
'Till I can obtaine
　A service in my neede?
Paines I will not spare:
　This kinde favour doe mee,
It will ease my care;
　Heaven shall be thy meede.

The for'ster all amazed,
On her beautye gazed,
　Till his heart was set on fire.
If, faire maid, quoth hee,
You will goe with mee,
　You shall have your hearts desire.
He brought her to his mother,
And above all other
　He sett forth his maidens praise.
Long was his heart inflamed,
At length her love he gained,
　And fortune crown'd his future dayes.

Thus unknowne he wedde
　With a kings faire daughter:
Children seven they had,
　Ere she told her birth.
Which when once he knew,
　Humblye he besought her,
He to the world might shew
　Her rank and princelye worth.
He cloath'd his children then
(Not like other men),
　In partye-colours strange to see:
The right side cloth of gold,
The left side to behold,
　Of woollen cloth still framed hee.\*
Men thereatt did wonder;
Golden fame did thunder
　This strange deede in every place:
The king of France came thither,
It being pleasant weather,
　In those woods the hart to chase.

---

\* This will remind the reader of the livery and device of Charles Brandon, a private gentleman, who married the Queen-dowager of France, sister of Henry VIII. At a tournament which he held at his wedding, the trappings of his horse were half cloth of gold, and half frieze, with the following motto:

" Cloth of gold, do not despise,
　Tho' thou art matcht with cloth of frize;
Cloth of frize, be not too bold,
　Tho' thou art matcht with cloth of gold."

See Sir W. Temple's *Miscellany*, vol. iii. p. 356.

The children then they bring,
  So their mother will'd it,
Where the royall king
  Must of force come bye:
Their mothers riche array,
  Was of crimson velvet:
Their fathers all of gray,
  Seemelye to the eye.
Then this famous king,
  Noting every thing,
Askt how he durst be so bold
To let his wife soe weare,
And decke his children there
  In costly robes of pearl and gold.
The forrester replying,
And the cause descrying,
  To the king these words did say,
Well may they, by their mother,
Weare rich clothes with other,
  Being by birth a princesse gay.

The king aroused thus,
  More heedfullye beheld them,
Till a crimson blush
  His remembrance crost.
The more I fix my mind
  On thy wife and children,
The more methinks I find
  'The daughter which I lost.
Falling on her knee,
' I am that child,' quoth shee ;
  ' Pardon mee, my soveraine liege.'
The king perceiving this,
  His daughter deare did kiss,
While joyfull teares did stopp his speeche.
With his traine he tourned,
And with them sojourned.
  Strait he dubb'd her husband knight ;
Then made him erle of Flanders,
And chiefe of his commanders :
  Thus were their sorrowes put to flight.

---

### XVII.—THE SWEET NEGLECT.

THIS little madrigal (extracted from Ben Jonson's *Silent Woman*) is in imitation of a Latin poem beginning *Semper munditias, semper Basilissa, decoras*, etc.

STILL to be neat, still to be drest,
As you were going to a feast :
Still to be poud'red, still perfum'd :
Lady, it is to be presum'd,
Though art's hid causes are not found,
All is not sweet, all is not sound.

Give me a looke, give me a face,
That makes simplicitie a grace ;
Robes loosely flowing, haire as free :
Such sweet neglect more taketh me,
Than all th' adulteries of art,
That strike mine eyes, but not my heart.

---

### XVIII.—THE CHILDREN IN THE WOOD.

THE subject of this very popular ballad (which has been set in so favourable a light by the *Spectator*, No. 85) seems to be taken from an old play, entitled, *Two lamentable Tragedies ; the one of the murder of Maister Beech, a chandler in Thames-streete, etc. The other of a young child murthered in a wood by two ruffians, with the consent of his unkle.* By Rob. Yarrington, 1601, 4to. Our ballad-maker has strictly followed the play in the description of the father and mother's dying charge : in the uncle's promise to take care of their issue : his hiring two ruffians to destroy his ward, under pretence of sending him to school : their choosing a wood to perpetrate the murder in : one of the ruffians relenting, and a battle ensuing, etc. In other respects he has departed from the play. In the latter the scene is laid in Padua: there is but one child: which is murdered by a sudden stab of the unrelenting ruffian: he is slain himself by his less bloody companion; but ere he dies gives the other a mortal wound: the latter living just long enough to impeach the uncle; who, in consequence of this impeachment, is arraigned and executed by the hand of justice, etc. Whoever compares the play with the ballad, will have no doubt but the former is the original: the language is far more obsolete, and such a vein of simplicity runs through the whole performance, that, had the ballad been written first, there is no doubt but every circumstance of it would have been received into the drama: whereas this was probably built on some Italian novel.

Printed from two ancient copies, one of them in black letter in the Pepys Collection. Its title at large is, *The Children in the Wood; or, The Norfolk Gentleman's Last Will and Testament.* To the tune of " Rogero," etc.

Now ponder well, you parents deare,
   These wordes, which I shall write;
A doleful story you shall heare,
   In time brought forth to light.
A gentleman of good account
   In Norfolke dwelt of late,
Who did in honour far surmount
   Most men of his estate.

Sore sicke he was, and like to dye,
   No helpe his life could save;
His wife by him as sicke did lye,
   And both possest one grave.
No love between these two was lost,
   Each was to other kinde,
In love they liv'd, in love they dyed,
   And left two babes behinde:

The one a fine and pretty boy,
   Not passing three yeares olde;
The other a girl more young than he,
   And fram'd in beautyes molde.
The father left his little son,
   As plainlye doth appeare,
When he to perfect age should come,
   Three hundred poundes a yeare.

And to his little daughter Jane
   Five hundred poundes in gold,
To be paid downe on marriage-day,
   Which might not be controll'd:
But if the children chance to dye,
   Ere they to age should come,

Their uncle should possesse their wealth;
   For so the wille did run.

Now, brother, said the dying man,
   Look to my children deare;
Be good unto my boy and girl,
   No friendes else have they here:
To God and you I recommend
   My children deare this daye;
But little while be sure we have
   Within this world to staye.

You must be father and mother both,
   And uncle all in one;
God knowes what will become of them,
   When I am dead and gone.
With that bespake their mother deare,
   O brother kinde, quoth shee,
You are the man must bring our babes
   To wealth or miserie:

And if you keep them carefully,
   Then God will you reward;
But if you otherwise should deal,
   God will your deedes regard.
With lippes as cold as any stone,
   They kist their children small:
God bless you both, my children deare;
   With that the teares did fall.

These speeches then their brother spake
   To this sicke couple there,
The keeping of your little ones
   Sweet sister, do not feare:

God never prosper me nor mine,
  Nor aught else that I have,
If I do wrong your children deare,
  When you are layd in grave.

The parents being dead and gone,
  The children home he takes,
And bringes them straite into his house,
  Where much of them he makes.
He had not kept these pretty babes
  A twelvemonth and a daye,
But, for their wealth, he did devise
  To make them both awaye.

He bargain'd with two ruffians strong,
  Which were of furious mood,
That they should take these children young,
  And slaye them in a wood.
He told his wife an artful tale,
  He would the children send
To be brought up in faire London,
  With one that was his friend.

Away then went those pretty babes,
  Rejoycing at that tide,
Rejoycing with a merry minde,
  They should on cock-horse ride.
They prate and prattle pleasantly,
  As they rode on the waye,
To those that should their butchers be,
  And work their lives decaye:

So that the pretty speeche they had,
  Made Murder's heart relent;
And they that undertooke the deed,
  Full sore did now repent.
Yet one of them more hard of heart,
  Did vowe to do his charge,
Because the wretch, that hired him,
  Had paid him very large.

The other won't agree thereto,
  So here they fall to strife;
With one another they did fight,
  About the childrens life:
And he that was of mildest mood,
  Did slaye the other there,

Within an unfrequented wood;
  The babes did quake for feare!
He took the children by the hand,
  Teares standing in their eye,
And bad them straitwaye follow him,
  And look they did not crye:
And two long miles he ledd them on,
  While they for food complaine:
Staye here, quoth he, I'll bring you bread,
  When I come back againe.

These pretty babes, with hand in hand,
  Went wandering up and downe;
But never more could see the man
  Approaching from the town:
Their prettye lippes with black-berries,
  Were all besmear'd and dyed,
And when they sawe the darksome night,
  They sat them downe and cryed.

Thus wandered these poor innocents,
  Till deathe did end their grief,
In one anothers armes they dyed,
  As wanting due relief:
No burial "this" pretty "pair"
  Of any man receives,
Till Robin-red-breast piously
  Did cover them with leaves.

And now the heavy wrathe of God
  Upon their uncle fell;
Yea, fearfull fiends did haunt his house,
  His conscience felt an hell:
His barnes were fir'd, his goodes consum'd,
  His landes were barren made,
His cattle dyed within the field,
  And nothing with him stayd.

And in a voyage to Portugal
  Two of his sonnes did dye;
And to conclude, himselfe was brought
  To want and miserye:
He pawn'd and mortgaged all his land
  Ere seven yeares came about.
And now at length this wicked act
  Did by this meanes come out:

The fellowe, that did take in hand
  These children for to kill,
Was for a robbery judg'd to dye,
  Such was God's blessed will:
Who did confess the very truth,
  As here hath been display'd:
Their uncle having dyed in gaol,
  Where he for debt was layd.

You that executors be made,
  And overseers eke
Of children that be fatherless,
  And infants mild and meek;
Take you example by this thing,
  And yield to each his right,
Lest God with such like miserye
  Your wicked minds requite.

## XIX.—A LOVER OF LATE.

PRINTED, with a few slight corrections, from the Editor's folio MS.

A LOVER of late was I,
  For Cupid would have it soe,
The boy that hath never an eye,
  As every man doth know:
I sighed and sobbed, and cryed, alas!
For her that laught, and called me ass.

Then knew not I what to doe,
  When I saw itt was in vaine
A lady soe coy to wooe,
  Who gave me the asse soe plaine:
Yet would I her asse freelye bee,
Soe shee would helpe, and beare with mee.

An' I were as faire as shee,
  Or shee were as kind as I,
What payre cold have made, as wee,
  Soe prettye a sympathye:
I was as kind as shee was faire,
But for all this wee cold not paire.

Paire with her that will for mee,
  With her I will never paire;
That cunningly can be coy,
  For being a little faire.
The asse Ile leave to her disdaine;
And now I am myselfe againe.

## XX.—THE KING AND MILLER OF MANSFIELD.

IT has been a favourite subject with our English ballad-makers to represent our kings conversing, either by accident or design, with the meanest of their subjects. Of the former kind, besides this song of *The King and the Miller*, we have *King Henry and the Soldier; King James I. and the Tinker; King William III. and the Forester*, etc. Of the latter sort, are *King Alfred and the Shepherd; King Edward IV. and the Tanner; King Henry VIII. and the Cobbler*, etc. A few of the best of these are admitted into this collection. Both the author of the following ballad, and others who have written on the same plan, seem to have copied a very ancient poem, entitled *John the Reeve*, which is built on an adventure of the same kind, that happened between King Edward Longshanks and one of his reeves or bailiffs. This is a piece of great antiquity, being written before the time of Edward IV., and for its genuine humour, diverting incidents, and faithful picture of rustic manners, is infinitely superior to all that have been since written in imitation of it. The Editor has a copy in his ancient folio MS., but its length rendered it improper for this volume, it consisting of more than 900 lines. It contains also some corruptions, and the Editor chooses to defer its publication, in hopes that some time or other he shall be able to remove them.

The following is printed, with corrections, from the Editor's folio MS., collated with an old black-letter copy in the Pepys Collection, entitled, *A pleasant ballad of King Henry II. and the Miller of Mansfield*, etc.

PART THE FIRST.

HENRY, our royall king, would ride a hunting
  To the greene forest so pleasant and faire;
To see the harts skipping, and dainty does tripping:
  Unto merry Sherwood his nobles repaire:
Hawke and hound were unbound, all things prepar'd
  For the game, in the same, with good regard.

All a long summers day rode the king pleasantlye,
  With all his princes and nobles eche one;
Chasing the hart and hind, and the bucke gallantlye,
  Till the dark evening forc'd all to turne home.
Then at last, riding fast, he had lost quite
All his lords in the wood, late in the night.

Wandering thus wearilye, all alone, up and downe,
  With a rude miller he mett at the last:
Asking the ready way unto faire Nottingham;
  Sir, quoth the miller, I meane not to jest,
Yet I thinke, what I thinke, sooth for to say,
You doe not lightlye ride out of your way.

Why, what dost thou think of me, quoth our king merrily,
  Passing thy judgment upon me so briefe?
Good faith, sayd the miller, I meane no to flatter thee;
  I guess thee to bee but some gentleman thiefe;
Stand thee backe, in the darke; light not adowne,
Lest that I presentlye crack thy knaves crowne.

Thou dost abuse me much, quoth the king, saying thus;
  I am a gentleman; lodging I lacke.
Thou hast not, quoth th' miller, one groat in thy purse;
  All thy inheritance hanges on thy backe.
I have gold to discharge all that I call;
If it be forty pence, I will pay all.\*

If thou beest a true man, then quoth the miller,
  I sweare by my toll-dish, I'll lodge thee all night.
Here's my hand, quoth the king, that was I ever.
  Nay, soft, quoth the miller, thou may'st be a sprite.
Better I'll know thee, ere hands we will shake;
With none but honest men hands will I take.

Thus they went all along unto the millers house:
  Where they were seething of puddings and souse:
The miller first enter'd in, after him went the king;
  Never came hee in soe smokye a house.

---

\* The king says this.

Now, quoth hee, let me see here what you are,
Quoth our king, looke your fill, and doe not spare.

I like well thy countenance, thou hast an honest face;
With my son Richard this night thou shalt lye.
Quoth his wife, by my troth, it is a handsome youth,
Yet it's best, husband, to deal warilye.
Art thou no run away, prythee, youth, tell?
Shew me thy passport, and all shal be well.

Then our king presentlye, making lowe courtesye,
With his hatt in his hand, thus he did say:
I have no passport, nor never was servitor,
But a poor courtyer, rode out of my way;
And for your kindness here offered to mee,
I will requite you in everye degree.

Then to the miller his wife whisper'd secretlye,
Saying, It seemeth, this youth's of good kin,
Both by his apparel, and eke by his manners;
To turne him out, certainlye, were a great sin.
Yea, quoth hee, you may see, he hath some grace
When he doth speake to his betters in place.

Well, quo' the millers wife, young man, ye're welcome here;
And, though I say it, well lodged shall be:
Fresh straw will I have, laid on thy bed so brave,
And good brown hempen sheets likewise, quoth shee.

Aye, quoth the good man; and when that is done,
Thou shalt lye with no worse than our own sonne.

Nay, first, quoth Richard, good-fellowe, tell me true,
Hast thou noe creepers within thy gay hose?
Or art thou not troubled with the scabbado?
I pray, quoth the king, what creatures are those?
Art thou not lowsy, nor scabby? quoth he:
If thou beest, surely thou lyest not with mee.

This caus'd the king, suddenlye, to laugh most heartilye,
Till the teares trickled fast downe from his eyes.
Then to their supper were they set orderlye,
With hot bag-puddings, and good apple-pyes;
Nappy ale, good and stale, in a browne bowle,
Which did about the board merrilye trowle.

Here, quoth the miller, good fellowe, I drinke to thee,
And to all "cuckholds, wherever they bee."
I pledge thee, quoth our king, and thanke thee heartilye
For my good welcome in everye degree:
And here, in like manner, I drinke to thy sonne.
Do then, quoth Richard, and quicke let it come.

Wife, quoth the miller, fetch me forth lightfoote,
And of his sweetnesse a little we'll taste.

A fair ven'son pastye brought she out
    presentlye.
  Eate, quoth the miller, but, sir, make
    no waste.
Here's dainty lightfoote! In faith, sayd
    the king,
I never before eat so daintye a thing.

I wis, quoth Richard, no daintye at all it
    is,
For we doe eate of it everye day.
In what place, sayd our king, may be
    bought like to this?
We never pay pennye for itt, by my fay:
From merry Sherwood we fetch it home
    here;
Now and then we make bold with our
    kings deer.

Then I thinke, sayd our king, that it is
    venison.
  Eche foole, quoth Richard, full well
    may know that:
Never are wee without two or three in the
    roof,
Very well fleshed, and excellent fat:
But, prythee, say nothing wherever thou
    goe;
We would not, for two pence, the king
    should it knowe.

Doubt not, then sayd the king, my
    promist secresye;
  The king shall never know more on't
    for mee.
A cupp of lambs-wool they dranke unto
    him then,
And to their bedds they past presentlie.
The nobles, next morning, went all up
    and down,
For to seeke out the king in everye
    towne.

At last, at the millers "cott," soone they
    espy'd him out,
  As he was mounting upon his faire
    steede;

To whom they came presently, falling
    down on their knee;
  Which made the millers heart wofully
    bleede;
Shaking and quaking, before him he stood,
Thinking he should have been hang'd, by
    the rood.

The king perceiving him fearfully
    trembling,
  Drew forth his sword, but nothing he
    sed:
The miller downe did fall, crying before
    them all,
Doubting the king would have cut off
    his head.
But he his kind courtesye for to requite,
Gave him great living, and dubb'd him a
    knight.

## PART THE SECOND.

When as our royall king came home
    from Nottingham,
  And with his nobles at Westminster
    lay;
Recounting the sports and pastimes they
    had taken,
In this late progress along on the
    way;
Of them all, great and small, he did
    protest,
The miller of Mansfield's sport liked him
    best.

And now, my lords, quoth the king, I am
    determined
  Against St. George's next sumptuous
    feast,
That this old miller, our new confirm'd
    knight,
  With his son Richard, shall here be my
    guest:
For, in this merryment, 'tis my desire
To talke with the jolly knight, and the
    young squire.

When as the noble lords saw the kinges
    pleasantness,
  They were right joyfull and glad in
    their hearts :
A pursuivant there was sent straighte on
    the business,
  The which had often-times been in
    those parts.
When he came to the place, where they
    did dwell,
  His message orderlye then gan he tell.

God save your worshippe, then said the
    messenger,
  And grant your ladye her own hearts
    desire ;
And to your sonne Richard good fortune
    and happiness ;
  That sweet, gentle, and gallant young
    squire.
Our king greets you well, and thus he doth
    say,
  You must come to the court on St.
    George's day ;

Therfore, in any case, faile not to be in
    place.
  I wis, quoth the miller, this is an odd
    jest :
What should we doe there? faith, I am
    halfe afraid.
  I doubt, quoth Richard, to be hang'd
    at the least.
Nay, quoth the messenger, you doe mis-
    take ;
  Our king he provides a great feast for
    your sake.

Then sayd the miller, By my troth,
    messenger,
  Thou hast contented my worshippe full
    well.
Hold here are three farthings, to quite
    thy gentleness,
  For these happy tydings, which thou
    dost tell.

Let me see, hear thou mee ; tell to our
    king,
  We'll wayt on his mastershipp in everye
    thing.

The pursuivant smiled at their simplicitye,
  And, making many leggs, tooke their
    reward ;
And his leave taking with great humilitye,
  To the kings court againe he repair'd ;
Shewing unto his grace, merry and free,
  The knightes most liberall gift and
    bountie.

When he was gone away, thus gan the
    miller say,
  Here come expences and charges in-
    deed ;
Now must we needs be brave, tho' we
    spend all we have ;
  For of new garments we have great
    need :
Of horses and serving-men we must have
    store,
  With bridles and saddles, and twentye
    things more.

Tushe, sir John, quoth his wife, why
    should you frett or frowne?
  You shall ne'er be att no charges for
    mee ;
For I will turne and trim up my old
    russet gowne,
  With everye thing else as fine as may bee ;
And on our mill-horses swift we will ride,
  With pillowes and pannells, as we shall
    provide.

In this most statelye sort, rode they unto
    the court,
  Their jolly sonne Richard rode fore-
    most of all ;
Who set up, for good hap,* a cocks
    feather in his cap,
  And so they jetted downe to the kings
    hall ;

---

* *i.e.* for good luck ; they were going on a hazardous expedition.

The merry old miller with hands on his side ;
His wife, like maid Marian, did mince at that tide.*

The king and his nobles that heard of their coming,
Meeting this gallant knight with his brave traine ;
Welcome, sir knight, quoth he, with your gay lady :
Good sir John Cockle, once welcome againe :
And so is the squire of courage soe free.
Quoth Dicke, A bots on you! do you know mee ?

Quoth our king gentlye, how should I forget thee ?
That wast my owne bed-fellowe, well it I wot.
Yea, sir, quoth Richard, and by the same token,
Thou with thy lying didst make the bed hot.
Thou whore-son unhappy knave, then quoth the knight,
Speake cleanly to our king, or else go sh—.

The king and his courtiers laugh at this heartily,
While the king taketh them both by the hand ;
With the court-dames, and maids, like to the queen of spades
The miller's wife did soe orderly stand.
A milk-maid's courtesye at every word ;
And downe all the folkes were set to the board.

---

\* Maid Marian in the Morris dance, was represented by a man in woman's clothes, who was to take short steps in order to sustain the female character.

There the king royally, in princelye majestye,
Sate at his dinner with joy and delight ;
When they had eaten well, then he to jesting fell,
And in a bowle of wine dranke to the knight :
Here's to you both, in wine, ale, and beer ;
Thanking you heartilye for my good cheer.

Quoth sir John Cockle, I'll pledge you a pottle,
Were it the best ale in Nottinghamshire :
But then said our king, now I think of a thing ;
Some of your lightfoote I would we had here.
Ho ! ho ! quoth Richard, full well I may say it,
'Tis knavery to eate it, and then to betray it.

Why art thou angry? quoth our king merrilye ;
In faith, I take it now very unkind :
I thought thou wouldst pledge me in ale and wine heartily.
Quoth Dicke, You are like to stay till I have din'd :
You feed us with twatling dishes soe small ;
Zounds, a blacke-pudding is better than all.

Aye, marry, quoth our king, that were a daintye thing,
Could a man get but one here for to eate.
With that Dicke straite arose, and pluckt one from his hose,
Which with heat of his breech gan to sweate.

The king made a proffer to snatch it away:—
'Tis meat for your master: good sir, you must stay.

Thus in great merriment was the time wholly spent;
And then the ladyes prepared to dance.
Old Sir John Cockle, and Richard, incontinent
  Unto their places the king did advance.
Here with the ladyes such sport they did make,
The nobles with laughing did make their sides ake.

Many thankes for their paines did the king give them,
  Asking young Richard then, if he would wed;
Among these ladyes free, tell me which liketh thee?
Quoth he, Jugg Grumball, Sir, with the red head:
She's my love, she's my life, her will I wed;
She hath sworn I shall have her maidenhead.

Then sir John Cockle the king call'd unto him,
And of merry Sherwood made him o'er seer;
And gave him out of hand three hundred pound yearlye:
Take heed now you steale no more of my deer:
And once a quarter let's here have your view;
And now, sir John Cockle, I bid you adieu.

## XXI.—THE SHEPHERD'S RESOLUTION.

This beautiful old song was written by George Wither, who was born June 11, 1588, and in his younger years distinguished himself by some pastoral pieces. Afterwards becoming involved in the political and religious disputes in the times of James I. and Charles I., he employed his poetical vein in severe pasquils on the court and clergy, and was occasionally a sufferer for the freedom of his pen.

Shall I, wasting in dispaire,
Dye because a woman's faire?
Or make pale my cheeks with care
'Cause another's rosie are?
Be shee fairer then the day,
Or the flowry meads in may;
  If she be not so to me,
  What care I how faire shee be?

Shall my foolish heart be pin'd
'Cause I see a woman kind?
Or a well-disposed nature
Joyned with a lovely feature?
Be shee meeker, kinder, than
The turtle-dove or pelican:
  If shee be not so to me,
  What care I how kind shee be?

Shall a woman's virtues move
Me to perish for her love?
Or, her well-deservings knowne,
Make me quite forget mine owne?
Be shee with that goodnesse blest,
Which may merit name of Best;
  If she be not such to me,
  What care I how good she be?

Cause her fortune seems too high,
Shall I play the foole and dye?
Those that beare a noble minde,
Where they want of riches find,
Thinke what with them they would doe,
That without them dare to woe;
  And, unlesse that minde I see,
  What care I how great she be?

Great or good, or kind or faire,
I will ne'er the more dispaire:
If she love me, this beleeve;
I will die ere she shall grieve.

If she slight me when I wooe,
I can scorne and let her goe:
If shee be not fit for me,
What care I for whom she be?

---

## XXII.—QUEEN DIDO.

SUCH is the title given in the Editor's folio MS. to this excellent old ballad, which, in the common printed copies, is inscribed *Eneas, Wandering Prince of Troy*. It is here given from that MS., collated with two different printed copies, both in black letter, in the Pepys Collection.

WHEN Troy towne had, for ten yeeres
  "past,"
    Withstood the Greekes in manfull
      wise,
Then did their foes encrease soe fast,
  That to resist none could suffice:
Wast lye those walls, that were soe good,
And corne now growes where Troy towne
  stoode.

Æneas, wandering prince of Troy,
  When he for land long time had
    sought,
  At length arriving with great joy,
    To mighty Carthage walls was
      brought;
Where Dido queene, with sumptuous
  feast,
Did entertaine that wandering guest.

And, as in hall at meate they sate,
  The queene, desirous newes to heare,
"Says, of thy Troys unhappy fate"
  Declare to me, thou Trojan deare:
The heavy hap and chance soe bad,
That thou, poore wandering prince, hast
  had.

And then anon this comelye knight,
  With words demure, as he cold well,
Of his unhappy ten yeares "fight,"
  Soe true a tale began to tell,
With words soe sweete, and sighes soe
  deepe,
That oft he made them all to weepe.

And then a thousand sighs he *fet*,
  And every sigh brought tearesamaine;
That where he sate the place was wett,
  As though he had seene those warrs
    againe:
Soe that the queene, with *ruth* therfore,
Said, Worthy prince, enough, no more.*

And then the darksome night drew on,
  And twinkling starres the skye be-
    spred;
When he his dolefull tale had done,
  And every one was layd in bedd:
Where they full sweetly tooke their rest,
Save only Dido's boyling brest.

This silly woman never slept,
  But in her chamber, all alone,
As one unhappye, alwayes wept,
  And to the walls shee made her mone;
That she shold still desire in vaine
The thing, she never must obtaine.

And thus in grieffe she spent the night,
  Till twinkling starres the skye were
    fled,
And Phœbus, with his glistering light,
  Through misty cloudes appeared red;
Then tidings came to her anon,
That all the Trojan shipps were gone.

And then the queene with bloody knife
  Did arme her hart as hard as stone,
Yet, something loth to loose her life,
  In woefull wise she made her mone;

And, rowling on her carefull bed,
With sighes and sobbs, these words shee
   sayd :

  O wretched Dido queene! quoth shee,
    I see thy end approacheth neare ;
  For hee is fled away from thee,
    Whom thou didst love and hold so
     deare :
What is he gone, and passed by?
O hart, prepare thyselfe to dye.

  Though reason says, thou shouldst
    forbeare,
  And stay thy hand from bloudy stroke;
  Yet fancy bids thee not to fear,
    Which fetter'd thee in Cupids yoke.
Come death, quoth shee, resolve my
   smart !—
And with those words shee peerced her
   hart.

  When death had pierced the tender
    hart
    Of Dido, Carthaginian queene ;
  Whose bloudy knife did end the smart,
    Which shee sustain'd in mournfull
     teene ;
Æneas being shipt and gone,
Whose flattery caused all her mone ;

  Her funerall most costly made,
    And all things finisht mournfullye ;
  Her body fine in mold was laid,
    Where itt consumed speedilye :
Her sisters teares her tombe bestrewde ;
Her subjects griefe their kindnesse shewed.

  Then was Æneas in an ile
    In Grecya, where he stayd long space,
  Wheras her sister in short while
    Writt to him to his vile disgrace ;
In speeches bitter to his mind
Shee told him plaine he was unkind.

  False-harted wretch, quoth shee, thou
    art ;
    And traiterouslye thou hast betraid

Unto thy lure a gentle hart,
    Which unto thee much welcome
     made ;
My sister deare, and Carthage' joy,
  Whose folly bred her deere annoy.

  Yett on her death-bed when shee lay,
    Shee prayd for thy prosperitye,
  Beseeching god, that every day
    Might breed thy great felicitye :
Thus by thy meanes I lost a friend ;
Heavens send thee such untimely end.

  When he these lines, full fraught with
    gall,
    Perused had, and wayed them right,
  His lofty courage then did fall ;
    And straight appeared in his sight
Queene Dido's ghost, both grim and pale :
Which made this valliant souldier quaile.

  Æneas, quoth this ghastly ghost,
    My whole delight when I did live,
  Thee of all men I loved most ;
    My fancy and my will did give ;
For entertainment I thee gave,
Unthankefully thou didst me grave.

  Therfore prepare thy flitting soule
    To wander with me in the aire :
  Where deadlye griefe shall make it
    howle,
Because of me thou tookst no care :
Delay not time, thy glasse is run,
Thy date is past, thy life is done.

  O stay a while, thou lovely sprite,
    Be not soe hasty to convay
  My soule into eternall night,
    Where itt shall ne're behold bright
     day.
O doe not frowne ; thy angry looke
Hath "all my soule with horror shooke."*

  But, woe is me! all is in vaine,
    And bootless is my dismall crye ;

---

\* MS.: *Hath* made my breath my life forsooke.

Time will not be recalled againe,
  Nor thou surcease before I dye.
O lett me live, and make amends
To some of thy most dearest friends.

But seeing thou obdurate art,
  And wilt no pittye on me show,
Because from thee I did depart,
  And left unpaid what I did owe:

I must content myselfe to take
What lott to me thou wilt partake.

And thus, as one being in a trance,
  A multitude of uglye feinds
About this woffull prince did dance;
  He had no helpe of any friends:
His body then they tooke away,
And no man knew his dying day.

## XXIII.—THE WITCHES' SONG.

FROM Ben Jonson's *Masque of Queens*, presented at Whitehall, Feb. 2, 1609.

#### 1 WITCH.

I HAVE been all day looking after
A raven feeding upon a quarter:
And, soone as she turn'd her beak to the south,
I snatch'd this morsell out of her mouth.

#### 2 WITCH.

I have beene gathering wolves' haires,
The madd dogges foames, and adders eares;
The spurging of a deadmans eyes:
And all since the evening starre did rise.

#### 3 WITCH.

I last night lay all alone
O' the ground, to heare the mandrake grone;
And pluckt him up, though he grew full low:
And, as I had done, the cocke did crow.

#### 4 WITCH.

And I ha' beene chusing out this scull
From charnell houses that were full;
From private grots, and publike pits;
And frighted a sexton out of his wits.

#### 5 WITCH.

Under a cradle I did crepe
By day; and, when the childe was a-sleepe

At night, I suck'd the breath; and rose,
And pluck'd the nodding nurse by the nose.

#### 6 WITCH.

I had a dagger: what I did with that?
Killed an infant to have his fat.
A piper it got at a church-ale.
I bade him again blow wind i' the taile.

#### 7 WITCH.

A murderer, yonder, was hung in chaines;
The sunne and the wind had shrunke his veines:
I bit off a sinew; I clipp'd his haire;
I brought off his ragges, that danc'd i' the ayre.

#### 8 WITCH.

The scrich-owles egges and the feathers blacke,
The bloud of the frogge, and the bone in his backe
I have been getting; and made of his skin
A purset, to keepe sir Cranion in.

#### 9 WITCH.

And I ha' beene plucking (plants among)
Hemlock, henbane, adders-tongue,
Night-shade, moone-wort, libbards-bane;
And twise by the dogges was like to be tane.

10 WITCH.

I from the jawes of a gardiner's bitch
Did snatch these bones, and then leap'd
  the ditch:
Yet went I back to the house againe,
Kill'd the blacke cat, and here is the
  braine.

11 WITCH.

I went to the toad, breedes under the wall,
I charmed him out, and he came at my
  call;

I scratch'd out the eyes of the owle before;
I tore the batts wing: what would you
  have more?

DAME.

Yes: I have brought, to helpe your vows,
Horned poppie, cypresse boughes,
  The fig-tree wild, that growes on tombes,
And juice, that from the larch-tree comes,
  The basiliskes bloud, and the vipers
    skin:
  And now our orgies let's begin.

---

## XXIV.—ROBIN GOOD-FELLOW,

*Alias* Pucke, *alias* Hobgoblin, in the creed of ancient superstition. This song, which Peck attributes to Ben Jonson (though it is not found among his works), is chiefly printed from an ancient black-letter copy in the British Museum. It seems to have been originally intended for some masque.

This ballad is entitled, in the old black-letter copies, *The Merry Pranks of Robin Goodfellow.* To the tune of "Dulcina," etc.

FROM Oberon, in fairye land,
  The king of ghosts and shadowes there,
Mad Robin I, at his command,
  Am sent to viewe the night-sports here.
    What revell rout
    Is kept about,
  In every corner where I go,
    I will o'ersee,
    And merry bee,
  And make good sport, with ho, ho, ho!

More swift than lightening can I flye
  About this aery welkin soone,
And, in a minutes space, descrye
  Each thing that's done belowe the
    moone,
    There's not a hag
    Or ghost shall wag,
  Or cry, ware Goblins! where I go;
    But Robin I
    Their feates will spy,
  And send them home, with ho, ho, ho!

Whene'er such wanderers I meete,
  As from their night-sports they trudge
    home;
With counterfeiting voice I greete
  And call them on, with me to roame
    Thro' woods, thro' lakes,
    Thro' bogs, thro' brakes;
  Or else, unseene, with them I go,
    All in the nicke
    To play some tricke
  And frolicke it, with ho, ho, ho!

Sometimes I meete them like a man;
Sometimes, an ox, sometimes, a hound;
And to a horse I turn me can;
  To trip and trot about them round.
    But if, to ride,
    My backe they stride,
  More swift than wind away I go,
    Ore hedge and lands,
    Thro' pools and ponds
  I whirry, laughing, ho, ho, ho!

When lads and lasses merry be,
  With possets and with juncates fine ;
Unseene of all the company,
  I eat their cakes and sip their wine ;
    And, to make sport,
    I fart and snort ;
And out the candles I do blow :
    The maids I kiss ;
    They shrieke—Who's this?
I answer nought, but ho, ho, ho !

Yet now and then, the maids to please,
  At midnight I card up their wooll ;
And while they sleepe, and take their ease,
  With wheel to threads their flax I pull.
    I grind at mill
    Their malt up still ;
I dress their hemp, I spin their tow.
    If any 'wake,
    And would me take,
I wend me, laughing, ho, ho, ho !

When house or harth doth sluttish lye,
  I pinch the maidens black and blue ;
The bed-clothes from the bedd pull I,
  And lay them naked all to view.
    'Twixt sleepe and wake,
    I do them take,
And on the key-cold floor them throw.
    If out they cry,
    Then forth I fly,
And loudly laugh out, ho, ho, ho !

When any need to borrowe ought,
  We lend them what they do require :
And for the use demand we nought ;
  Our owne is all we do desire.
    If to repay
    They do delay,
Abroad amongst them then I go,
    And night by night,
    I them affright
With pinchings, dreames, and ho, ho, ho !

When lazy queans have nought to do,
  But study how to cog and lye ;
To make debate and mischief too,
  'Twixt one another secretlye :
    I marke their gloze,
    And it disclose,
To them whom they have wronged so ;
    When I have done,
    I get me gone,
And leave them scolding, ho, ho, ho !

When men do traps and engines set
  In loop holes, where the vermine creepe,
Who from their foldes and houses, get
  Their duckes and geese, and lambes and sheepe :
    I spy the gin,
    And enter in,
And seeme a vermine taken so ;
    But when they there
    Approach me neare,
I leap out laughing, ho, ho, ho !

By wells and rills, in meadowes greene,
  We nightly dance our hey-day guise ;
And to our fairye king and queene
  We chant our moon-light minstrelsies.
    When larks 'gin sing,
    Away we fling ;
And babes new borne steal as we go,
    And elfe in bed
    We leave instead,
And wend us laughing, ho, ho, ho !

From hag-bred Merlin's time have I
  Thus nightly revell'd to and fro :
And for my pranks men call me by
  The name of Robin Good-fellow.
    Fiends, ghosts, and sprites,
    Who haunt the nightes,
The hags and goblins do me know ;
    And beldames old
    My feates have told ;
So *Vale, Vale ;* ho, ho, ho !

## XXV.—THE FAIRY QUEEN.

We have here a short display of the popular belief concerning Fairies. Our Saxon ancestors believed in the existence of a kind of diminutive demons, or middle species between men and spirits, whom they called Duergar or Dwarfs, and to whom they attributed many wonderful performances, far exceeding human art.

This song is given (with some corrections by another copy) from a book entitled *The Mysteries of Love and Eloquence*, etc. Lond. 1658, 8vo.

Come, follow, follow me,
You, fairy elves that be:
Which circle on the greene,
Come follow Mab your queene.
Hand in hand let's dance around,
For this place is fairye ground.

When mortals are at rest,
And snoring in their nest;
Unheard, and unespy'd,
Through key-holes we do glide;
Over tables, stools, and shelves,
We trip it with our fairy elves.

And, if the house be foul
With platter, dish, or bowl,
Up stairs we nimbly creep,
And find the sluts asleep:
There we pinch their armes and thighes;
None escapes, nor none espies.

But if the house be swept,
And from uncleanness kept,
We praise the household maid,
And duely she is paid:
For we use before we goe
To drop a tester in her shoe.

Upon a mushroome's head
Our table-cloth we spread;
A grain of rye, or wheat,
Is manchet, which we eat;
Pearly drops of dew we drink
In acorn cups fill'd to the brink.

The brains of nightingales,
With unctuous fat of snailes,
Between two cockles stew'd,
Is meat that's easily chew'd;
Tailes of wormes, and marrow of mice,
Do make a dish that's wonderous nice.

The grashopper, gnat, and fly,
Serve for our minstrelsie;
Grace said, we dance a while,
And so the time beguile:
And if the moon doth hide her head,
The gloe-worm lights us home to bed.

On tops of dewie grasse
So nimbly do we passe,
The young and tender stalk
Ne'er bends when we do walk:
Yet in the morning may be seen
Where we the night before have been.

## XXVI.—THE FAIRIES FAREWELL.

This humorous old song fell from the hand of the witty Dr. Corbet (afterwards Bishop of Norwich, etc.), and is printed from his *Poetica Stromata*, 1648, 12mo, compared with the third edition of his poems, 1672.

The departure of fairies is here attributed to the abolition of monachism. Dr. Richard Corbet, Bishop of Oxford, and afterwards Bishop of Norwich, died in 1635, œtat. 52.

Farewell rewards and Fairies!
  Good housewives now may say;
For now foule sluts in dairies,
  Doe fare as well as they:
And though they sweepe their hearths no less
  Than mayds were wont to doe,
Yet who of late for cleanliness
  Finds sixe-pence in her shoe?

Lament, lament old Abbies,
  The fairies lost command;
They did but change priests babies,
  But some have chang'd your land:
And all your children stoln from thence
  Are now growne Puritanes,
Who live as changelings ever since,
  For love of your demaines.

At morning and at evening both
  You merry were and glad,
So little care of sleepe and sloth,
  These prettie ladies had.
When Tom came home from labour,
  Or Ciss to milking rose,
Then merrily went their tabour,
  And nimbly went their toes.

Witness those rings and roundelayes
  Of theirs, which yet remaine;
Were footed in queene Maries dayes
  On many a grassy playne.
But since of late Elizabeth
  And later James came in;
They never danc'd on any heath,
  As when the time hath bin.

By which wee note the fairies
  Were of the old profession:
Their songs were *Ave Maries*,
  Their dances were procession.
But now, alas! they all are dead,
  Or gone beyond the seas,
Or farther for religion fled,
  Or else they take their ease.

A tell-tale in their company
  They never could endure;
And whoso kept not secretly
  Their mirth, was punish'd sure:
It was a just and christian deed
  To pinch such blacke and blue:
O how the common-welth doth need
  Such justices as you!

Now they have left our quarters;
  A Register they have,
Who can preserve their charters;
  A man both wise and grave.
An hundred of their merry pranks
  By one that I could name
Are kept in store; con twenty thanks
  To William for the same.

To William Churne of Staffordshire
  Give laud and praises due,
Who every meale can mend your cheare
  With tales both old and true:
To William all give audience,
  And pray yee for his noddle:
For all the fairies' evidence
  Were lost, if it were addle.

**THE END OF BOOK THE SECOND.**

## SERIES THE THIRD.—BOOK III.

### I.—THE BIRTH OF ST. GEORGE.

THE incidents in this and the other ballad of *St. George and the Dragon*, are chiefly taken from the old story-book of the *Seven Champions of Christendome*, which Bishop Hall says was among the most popular stories of his time. And Warton even thinks that Spenser took hints from it for his *Faery Queene*.

Richard Johnson, author of the *Seven Champions*, lived in the reign of Elizabeth and James, and his work is probably the bringing together of the metrical romances of former ages. It seems to us that scarce justice enough has been done to him for the service he has rendered romantic literature. He has brought the whole of the series of traditions, fragments, and ballads together, making the patron saint of England the centre round which the whole revolves, in the same manner that Sir Thomas Mallony re-animated the Arthurian legends.

St. George, according to Butler, was born in Cappadocia; thus he became a soldier under Diocletian, but resigned his commissions and posts when that Emperor waged war against the Christian religion. He became the patron saint of soldiers, because he had been a military man himself.

The Greeks are said to have given him the title of "the Great Martyr," and he is the patron saint of several Eastern nations. The English are held to have chosen him as their tutelar saint under the first Norman kings; thus the council at Oxford in 1222 commanded his feast to be kept a holiday of the lesser rank, and Edward III. under his name and ensign instituted the most noble order of knighthood in England.

However, there is not much to be learned of him with certainty; but having been made the patron saint, and "St. George for England" being the national war-cry, it was naturally not long before poets began to celebrate his praises, and to clothe their hero with all the valiant deeds and romantic adventures possible. And from this beginning we have a series of metrical romances which add to our collection of ancient reliques.

It cannot be denied but that the following ballad is for the most part modern; yet it embodies the account given by older writers.

LISTEN, lords, in bower and hall,
  I sing the wonderous birth
Of brave St. George, whose valourous arm
  Rid monsters from the earth:

Distressèd ladies to relieve
  He travell'd many a day;
In honour of the Christian faith,
  Which shall endure for aye.

In Coventry sometime did dwell
  A knight of worthy fame,
High steward of this noble realme;
  Lord Albert was his name.

He had to wife a princely dame,
  Whose beauty did excell.
This virtuous lady, being with child,
  In sudden sadness fell:

For thirty nights no sooner sleep
  Had clos'd her wakeful eyes,
But, lo! a foul and fearful dream
  Her fancy would surprize:

She dreamt a dragon fierce and fell
  Conceiv'd within her womb;
Whose mortal fangs her body rent
  Ere he to life could come.

All woe-begone and sad was she;
  She nourisht constant woe:
Yet strove to hide it from her lord,
  Lest he should sorrow know.

In vain she strove; her tender lord,
  Who watch'd her slightest look,
Discover'd soon her secret pain,
  And soon that pain partook.

And when to him the fearful cause
  She weeping did impart,
With kindest speech he strove to heal
  The anguish of her heart.

Be comforted, my lady dear,
  Those pearly drops refrain;
Betide me weal, betide me woe,
  I'll try to ease thy pain.

And for this foul and fearful dream,
  That causeth all thy woe,
Trust me I'll travel far away
  But I'll the meaning knowe.

Then giving many a fond embrace,
  And shedding many a teare,
To the weïrd lady of the woods
  He purpos'd to repaire.

To the weïrd lady of the woods,
  Full long and many a day,
Thro' lonely shades and thickets rough
  He winds his weary way.

At length he reach'd a dreary dell
  With dismal yews o'erhung;
Where cypress spred its mournful boughs,
  And pois'nous nightshade sprung.

No chearful gleams here pierc'd the gloom,
  He hears no chearful sound;
But shrill night-ravens' yelling scream,
  And serpents hissing round.

The shriek of fiends and damnèd ghosts
  Ran howling thro' his ear:

A chilling horror froze his heart,
  Tho' all unus'd to fear.

Three times he strives to win his way,
  And pierce those sickly dews:
Three times to bear his trembling corse
  His knocking knees refuse.

At length upon his beating breast
  He signs the holy crosse;
And, rousing up his wonted might,
  He treads th' unhallow'd mosse.

Beneath a pendant craggy cliff,
  All vaulted like a grave,
And opening in the solid rock,
  He found the inchanted cave.

An iron gate clos'd up the mouth,
  All hideous and forlorne;
And, fasten'd by a silver chain,
  Near hung a brazed horne.

Then offering up a secret prayer,
  Three times he blowes amaine:
Three times a deepe and hollow sound
  Did answer him againe.

"Sir knight, thy lady beares a son,
  Who, like a dragon bright,
Shall prove most dreadful to his foes,
  And terrible in fight.

"His name advanc'd in future times
  On banners shall be worn:
But lo! thy lady's life must passe
  Before he can be born."

All sore opprest with fear and doubt,
  Long time lord Albert stood;
At length he winds his doubtful way
  Back thro' the dreary wood.

Eager to clasp his lovely dame,
  Then fast he travels back:
But when he reach'd his castle gate,
  His gate was hung with black.

In every court and hall he found
  A sullen silence reigne ;
Save where, amid the lonely towers,
  He heard her maidens 'plaine ;

And bitterly lament and weep,
  With many a grievous grone :
Then sore his bleeding heart misgave,
  His lady's life was gone.

With faultering step he enters in,
  Yet half affraid to goe ;
With trembling voice asks why they grieve,
  Yet fears the cause to knowe.

"Three times the sun hath rose and set ;"
  They said, then stopt to weep :
"Since heaven hath laid thy lady deare
  In death's eternal sleep.

"For, ah ! in travel sore she fell,
  So sore that she must dye ;
Unless some shrewd and cunning leech
  Could ease her presentlye.

"But when a cunning leech was fet,
  Too soon declared he,
She or her babe must lose its life ;
  Both saved could not be.

"Now take my life, thy lady said,
  My little infant save :
And O commend me to my lord,
  When I am laid in grave.

"O tell him how that precious babe
  Cost him a tender wife :
And teach my son to lisp her name,
  Who died to save his life.

"Then calling still upon thy name,
  And praying still for thee ;
Without repining or complaint,
  Her gentle soul did flee."

What tongue can paint lord Albert's woe,
  The bitter tears he shed,
The bitter pangs that wrung his heart,
  To find his lady dead?

He beat his breast : he tore his hair ;
  And shedding many a tear,
At length he askt to see his son ;
  The son that cost so dear.

New sorrowe seiz'd the damsells all :
  At length they faultering say ;
"Alas ! my lord, how shall we tell ?
  Thy son is stoln away.

"Fair as the sweetest flower of spring,
  Such was his infant mien :
And on his little body stampt
  Three wonderous marks were seen :

"A blood-red cross was on his arm ;
  A dragon on his breast :
A little garter all of gold
  Was round his leg exprest.

"Three carefull nurses we provide
  Our little lord to keep :
One gave him sucke, one gave him food,
  And one did lull to sleep.

"But lo ! all in the dead of night,
  We heard a fearful sound :
Loud thunder clapt ; the castle shook ;
  And lightning flasht around.

"Dead with affright at first we lay ;
  But rousing up anon,
We ran to see our little lord :
  Our little lord was gone !

"But how or where we could not tell ;
  For lying on the ground,
In deep and magic slumbers laid,
  The nurses there we found."

O grief on grief ! lord Albert said :
  No more his tongue cou'd say,
When falling in a deadly swoone,
  Long time he lifeless lay.

At length restor'd to life and sense
  He nourisht endless woe,
No future joy his heart could taste,
  No future comfort know.

So withers on the mountain top
  A fair and stately oake,
Whose vigorous arms are torne away
  By some rude thunder-stroke.

At length his castle irksome grew,
  He loathes his wonted home;
His native country he forsakes,
  In foreign lands to roame.

There up and downe he wandered far,
  Clad in a palmer's gown:
Till his brown locks grew white as wool,
  His beard as thistle down.

At length, all wearied, down in death
  He laid his reverend head.
Meantime amid the lonely wilds
  His little son was bred.

There the weïrd lady of the woods
  Had borne him far away,
And train'd him up in feates of armes,
  And every martial play.

## II.—ST. GEORGE AND THE DRAGON.

THE following ballad is given (with some corrections) from two ancient black-letter copies in the Pepys Collection, one of which is in 12mo, the other in folio.

OF Hector's deeds did Homer sing;
  And of the sack of stately Troy,
What griefs fair Helena did bring,
  Which was sir Paris' only joy:
And by my pen I will recite
St. George's deeds, an English knight.

Against the Sarazens so rude
  Fought he full long and many a day;
Where many gyants he subdu'd,
  In honour of the Christian way:
And after many adventures past
To Egypt land he came at last.

Now, as the story plain doth tell,
  Within that countrey there did rest
A dreadful dragon fierce and fell,
  Whereby they were full sore opprest:
Who by his poisonous breath each day,
Did many of the city slay.

The grief whereof did grow so great
  Throughout the limits of the land,
That they their wise-men did intreat
  To shew their cunning out of hand;

What way they might this fiend destroy,
That did the countrey thus annoy.

The wise-men all before the king
  This answer fram'd incontinent;
The dragon none to death might bring
  By any means they could invent:
His skin more hard than brass was found,
That sword nor spear could pierce nor wound.

When this the people understood,
  They cryed out most piteouslye,
The dragon's breath infects their blood,
  That every day in heaps they dye:
Among them such a plague it bred,
The living scarce could bury the dead.

No means there were, as they could hear,
  For to appease the dragon's rage,
But to present some virgin clear,
  Whose blood his fury might asswage;
Each day he would a maiden eat,
For to allay his hunger great.

This thing by art the wise-men found,
  Which truly must observed be;
Wherefore throughout the city round
  A virgin pure of good degree
Was by the king's commission still
Taken up to serve the dragon's will.

Thus did the dragon every day
  Untimely crop some virgin flowr,
Till all the maids were worn away,
  And none were left him to devour:
Saving the king's fair daughter bright,
Her father's only heart's delight.

Then came the officers to the king
  That heavy message to declare,
Which did his heart with sorrow sting;
  She is, quoth he, my kingdom's heir:
O let us all be poisoned here,
Ere she should die, that is my dear.

Then rose the people presently,
  And to the king in rage they went;
They said his daughter dear should dye,
  The dragon's fury to prevent:
Our daughters all are dead, quoth they,
And have been made the dragon's prey:

And by their blood we rescued were,
  And thou hast sav'd thy life thereby;
And now in sooth it is but faire,
  For us thy daughter so should die.
O save my daughter, said the king;
And let ME feel the dragon's sting.

Then fell fair Sabra on her knee,
  And to her father dear did say,
O father, strive not thus for me,
  But let me be the dragon's prey;
It may be, for my sake alone
This plague upon the land was thrown.

'Tis better I should dye, she said,
  Than all your subjects perish quite;
Perhaps the dragon here was laid,
  For my offence to work his spite:
And after he hath suckt my gore,
Your land shall feel the grief no more.

What hast thou done, my daughter dear,
  For to deserve this heavy scourge?
It is my fault, as may appear,
  Which makes the gods our state to purge;
Then ought I die, to stint the strife,
And to preserve thy happy life.

Like mad-men, all the people cried,
  Thy death to us can do no good;
Our safety only doth abide
  In making her the dragon's food.
Lo! here I am, I come, quoth she,
Therefore do what you will with me.

Nay stay, dear daughter, quoth the queen,
  And as thou art a virgin bright,
That hast for vertue famous been,
  So let me cloath thee all in white;
And crown thy head with flowers sweet,
An ornament for virgins meet.

And when she was attired so,
  According to her mother's mind,
Unto the stake then did she go;
  To which her tender limbs they bind:
And being bound to stake a thrall,
She bade farewell unto them all.

Farewell, my father dear, quoth she,
  And my sweet mother meek and mild;
Take you no thought nor weep for me,
  For you may have another child;
Since for my country's good I dye,
Death I receive most willinglye.

The king and queen and all their train
  With weeping eyes went then their way,
And let their daughter there remain,
  To be the hungry dragon's prey:
But as she did there weeping lye,
Behold St. George came riding by.

And seeing there a lady bright
  So rudely tyed unto a stake,
As well became a valiant knight,
  He straight to her his way did take:

'Tell me, sweet maiden, then quoth he,
What caitif thus abuseth thee?

And, lo! by Christ his cross I vow,
  Which here is figured on my breast,
I will revenge it on his brow,
  And break my lance upon his chest:
And speaking thus whereas he stood,
The dragon issued from the wood.

The lady that did first espy
  The dreadful dragon coming so,
Unto St. George aloud did cry,
  And willed him away to go;
Here comes that cursed fiend, quoth she,
That soon will make an end of me.

St. George then looking round about,
  The fiery dragon soon espy'd,
And like a knight of courage stout,
  Against him did most fiercely ride;
And with such blows he did him greet,
He fell beneath his horse's feet.

For with his launce that was so strong,
  As he came gaping in his face,
In at his mouth he thrust along;
  For he could pierce no other place:
And thus within the lady's view
This mighty dragon straight he slew.

The savour of his poisoned breath
  Could do this holy knight no harm.
Thus he the lady sav'd from death,
  And home he led her by the arm;
Which when king Ptolemy did see,
There was great mirth and melody.

When as that valiant champion there
  Had slain the dragon in the field,
To court he brought the lady fair,
  Which to their hearts much joy did yield.
He in the court of Egypt staid
Till he most falsely was betray'd.

That lady dearly loved the knight,
  He counted her his only joy;

But when their love was brought to light,
  It turn'd unto their great annoy:
Th' Morocco king was in the court,
Who to the orchard did resort,

Dayly to take the pleasant air,
  For pleasure sake he us'd to walk,
Under a wall he oft did hear
  St. George with lady Sabra talk:
Their love he shew'd unto the king,
Which to St. George great woe did bring.

Those kings together did devise
  To make the Christian knight away,
With letters him in curteous wise
  They straightway sent to Persia:
But wrote to the sophy him to kill,
And treacherously his blood to spill.

Thus they for good did him reward
  With evil, and most subtilly
By such vile meanes they had regard
  To work his death most cruelly;
Who, as through Persia land he rode,
With zeal destroy'd each idol god.

For which offence he straight was thrown
  Into a dungeon dark and deep;
Where, when he thought his wrongs upon,
  He bitterly did wail and weep:
Yet like a knight of courage stout,
At length his way he digged out.

Three grooms of the king of Persia
  By night this valiant champion slew,
Though he had fasted many a day;
  And then away from thence he flew
On the best steed the sophy had;
Which when he knew he was full mad.

Towards Christendom he made his flight,
  But met a gyant by the way,
With whom in combat he did fight
  Most valiantly a summer's day:
Who yet, for all his bats of steel,
Was forc'd the sting of death to feel.

Back o'er the seas with many bands
  Of warlike souldiers soon he past,
Vowing upon those heathen lands
  To work revenge; which at the last,
Ere thrice three years were gone and spent,
He wrought upon his heart's content.

Save onely Egypt land he spar'd
  For Sabra bright her only sake,
And, ere for her he had regard,
  He meant a tryal kind to make:
Mean while the king, o'ercome in field,
Unto saint George did quickly yield.

Then straight Morocco's king he slew,
  And took fair Sabra to his wife,
But meant to try if she were true
  Ere with her he would lead his life:
And, tho' he had her in his train,
She did a virgin pure remain.

Toward England then that lovely dame
  The brave St. George conducted strait,
An eunuch also with them came,
  Who did upon the lady wait;
These three from Egypt went alone.
Now mark St. George's valour shown.

When as they in a forest were,
  The lady did desire to rest;
Mean while St. George to kill a deer,
  For their repast did think it best:
Leaving her with the eunuch there,
Whilst he did go to kill the deer.

But lo! all in his absence came
  Two hungry lyons fierce and fell,
And tore the eunuch on the same
  In pieces small, the truth to tell;
Down by the lady then they laid,
Whereby they shew'd she was a maid.

But when he came from hunting back,
  And did behold this heavy chance,
Then for his lovely virgin's sake
  His courage strait he did advance,
And came into the lions sight,
Who ran at him with all their might.

Their rage did him no whit dismay,
  Who, like a stout and valiant knight,
Did both the hungry lyons slay
  Within the lady Sabra's sight:
Who all this while sad and demure,
There stood most like a virgin pure.

Now when St. George did surely know
  This lady was a virgin true,
His heart was glad, that erst was woe,
  And all his love did soon renew:
He set her on a palfrey steed,
And towards England came with speed.

Where being in short space arriv'd
  Unto his native dwelling place;
Therein with his dear love he liv'd,
  And fortune did his nuptials grace:
They many years of joy did see,
And led their lives at Coventry.

## III.—LOVE WILL FIND OUT THE WAY.

This excellent song is ancient, but we could only give it from a modern copy.

Over the mountains,
   And over the waves;
Under the fountains,
   And under the graves;
Under floods that are deepest,
   Which Neptune obey;
Over rocks that are steepest,
   Love will find out the way.

Where there is no place
   For the glow-worm to lye;
Where there is no space
   For receipt of a fly;
Where the midge dares not venture,
   Lest herself fast she lay;
If love come, he will enter,
   And soon find out his way.

You may esteem him
   A child for his might;
Or you may deem him
   A coward from his flight:
But if she, whom love doth honour,
   Be conceal'd from the day,
Set a thousand guards upon her,
   Love will find out the way.

Some think to lose him,
   By having him confin'd;
And some do suppose him,
   Poor thing, to be blind:
But if ne'er so close ye wall him,
   Do the best that you may,
Blind love, if so ye call him,
   Will find out his way.

You may train the eagle
   To stoop to your fist;
Or you may inveigle
   The phenix of the east;
The lioness, ye may move her
   To give o'er her prey;
But you'll ne'er stop a lover:
   He will find out his way.

---

## IV.—LORD THOMAS AND FAIR ANNET,

### A SCOTTISH BALLAD,

Seems to be composed (not without improvements) out of two ancient English ones, printed in the former part of this volume.* If this had been the original, the authors of those two ballads would hardly have adopted two such different stories; besides, this contains enlargements not to be found in either of the others. It is given, with some corrections, from a MS. copy transmitted from Scotland.

Lord Thomas and fair Annet
   Sate a' day on a hill;
Whan night was cum, and sun was sett,
   They had not talkt their fill.

Lord Thomas said a word in jest,
   Fair Annet took it ill:
A'! I will nevir wed a wife
   Against my ain friends will.

---

\* *Lord Thomas and Fair Ellinor,* and *Fair Margaret and Sweet William.*

Gif ye wull nevir wed a wife,
   A wife wull neir wed yee.
Sae he is hame to tell his mither,
   And knelt upon his knee:

O *rede*, O rede, mither, he says,
   A gude rede gie to mee:
O sall I tak the nut-browne bride,
   And let faire Annet bee?

The nut-browne bride haes gowd and gear,
   Fair Annet she has gat nane;
And the little beauty fair Annet has,
   O it wull soon be gane!

And he has till his brother gane:
   Now, brother, rede ye mee;
A' sall I marrie the nut-browne bride,
   And let fair Annet bee?

The nut-browne bride has oxen, brother,
   The nut-browne bride has *kye;*
I wad hae ye marrie the nut-browne bride,
   And cast fair Annet bye.

Her oxen may dye i' the house, Billie,
   And her kye into the *byre;*
And I sall hae nothing to my sell,
   Bot a fat *fadge* by the fyre.

And he has till his sister gane:
   Now, sister, rede ye mee;
O sall I marrie the nut-browne bride,
   And set fair Annet free?

Ise rede ye tak fair Annet, Thomas,
   And let the browne bride alane;
Lest you sould sigh and say, Alace!
   What is this we brought hame?

No, I will tak my mithers counsel,
   And marrie me owt o' hand;
And I will tak the nut-browne bride;
   Fair Annet may leive the land.

Up then rose fair Annets father
   Twa hours or it wer day,

And he is gane into the bower,
   Wherein fair Annet lay.

Rise up, rise up, fair Annet, he says,
   Put on your silken *sheene;*
Let us gae to St. Maries kirke,
   And see that rich weddeen.

My maides, gae to my dressing-roome,
   And dress to me my hair;
Whair-eir yee laid a plait before,
   See yee lay ten times mair.

My maids, gae to my dressing-room,
   And dress to me my smock;
The one half is o' the holland fine,
   The other o' needle-work.

The horse fair Annet rade upon,
   He amblit like the wind,
Wi' siller he was shod before,
   Wi' burning gowd behind.

Four and twenty siller bells
   Wer a' tyed till his mane,
And yae *tift* o' the norland wind,
   They tinkled ane by ane.

Four and twenty gay gude knichts
   Rade by fair Annets side,
And four and twanty fair ladies,
   As gin she had bin a bride.

And whan she cam to Maries kirk,
   She sat on Maries stean:
The *cleading* that fair Annet had on
   It *skinkled* in their een.

And whan she cam into the kirk,
   She shimmer'd like the sun;
The belt that was about her waist,
   Was a' wi' pearles bedone.

She sat her by the nut-browne bride,
   And her een they wer sae clear,
Lord Thomas he clean forgat the bride,
   Whan fair Annet she drew near.

He had a rose into his hand,
  And he gave it kisses three,
And reaching by the nut-browne bride,
  Laid it on fair Annets knee.

Up then spak the nut-browne bride.
  She spak wi' meikle spite ;
And whair gat ye that rose-water,
  That does mak yee sae white ?

O I did get the rose-water
  Whair ye wull neir get nane,
For I did get that very rose-water
  Into my mithers wame.

The bride she drew a long bodkin,
  Frae out her gay head-gear,
And strake fair Annet into the heart,
  That word she nevir spak mair.

Lord Thomas he saw fair Annet wex pale,
  And marvelit what *mote* bee :

But whan he saw her dear hearts blude,
  A' *wood*-wroth wexed hee.

He drew his dagger, that was sae sharp,
  That was sae sharp and meet,
And drave into the nut-browne bride,
  That fell deid at his feit.

Now stay for me, dear Annet, he sed,
  Now stay, my dear, he cry'd ;
Then strake the dagger untill his heart,
  And fell deid by her side.

Lord Thomas was buried without kirk-wa',
  Fair Annet within the quiere ;
And o' the tane thair grew a birk,
  The other a bonny briere.

And ay they grew, and ay they threw,
  As they wad faine be neare ;
And by this ye may ken right weil,
  They were twa luvers deare.

---

## V.—UNFADING BEAUTY.

This little beautiful sonnet is reprinted from a small volume of *Poems*, by Thomas Carew, Esq., one of the gentlemen of the privie-chamber, and sewer in ordinary to his Majesty (Charles I.). Lond. 1640.

Hee, that loves a rosie cheeke,
  Or a corall lip admires,
Or from star-like eyes doth seeke
  Fuell to maintaine his fires,
As old time makes these decay,
So his flames must waste away.

But a smooth and stedfast mind,
  Gentle thoughts, and calme desires,
Hearts with equal love combin'd,
  Kindle never-dying fires :
Where these are not, I despise
Lovely cheekes, or lips, or eyes.

· · · · · ·

## VI.—GEORGE BARNWELL.

The subject of this ballad is sufficiently popular from the modern play which is founded upon it. This was written by George Lillo, a jeweller of London, and first acted about 1730. As for the ballad, it was printed at least as early as the middle of the seventeenth century.

### THE FIRST PART.

ALL youths of fair England
   That dwell both far and near,
Regard my story that I tell,
   And to my song give ear.

A London lad I was,
   A merchant's prentice bound;
My name George Barnwell; that did spend
   My master many a pound.

Take heed of harlots then,
   And their enticing trains;
For by that means I have been brought
   To hang alive in chains.

As I, upon a day,
   Was walking through the street
About my master's business,
   A wanton I did meet.

A gallant dainty dame,
   And sumptuous in attire;
With smiling look she greeted me,
   And did my name require.

Which when I had declar'd,
   She gave me then a kiss,
And said, if I would come to her,
   I should have more than this.

Fair mistress, then quoth I,
   If I the place may know,
This evening I will be with you,
   For I abroad must go

To gather monies in,
   That are my master's due:
And ere that I do home return,
   I'll come and visit you.

Good Barnwell, then quoth she,
   Do thou to Shoreditch come,
And ask for Mrs. Millwood's house,
   Next door unto the Gun.

And trust me on my truth,
   If thou keep touch with me,
My dearest friend, as my own heart
   Thou shalt right welcome be.

Thus parted we in peace,
   And home I passed right;
Then went abroad, and gathered in,
   By six o'clock at night,

An hundred pound and one:
   With bag under my arm
I went to Mrs. Millwood's house,
   And thought on little harm;

And knocking at the door,
   Straightway herself came down;
Rustling in most brave attire,
   With hood and silken gown.

Who, through her beauty bright,
   So gloriously did shine,
That she amaz'd my dazzling eyes,
   She seemed so divine.

She took me by the hand,
   And with a modest grace,

Welcome, sweet Barnwell, then quoth she,
  Unto this homely place.

And since I have thee found
  As good as thy word to be:
A homely supper, ere we part,
  Thou shalt take here with me.

O pardon me, quoth I,
  Fair mistress, I you pray;
For why, out of my master's house,
  So long I dare not stay.

Alas, good sir, she said,
  Are you so strictly ty'd,
You may not with your dearest friend
  One hour or two abide?

Faith, then the case is hard:
  If it be so, quoth she,
I would I were a prentice bound,
  To live along with thee:

Therefore, my dearest George,
  List well what I shall say,
And do not blame a woman much,
  Her fancy to bewray.

Let not affection's force
  Be counted lewd desire;
Nor think it not immodesty,
  I should thy love require.

With that she turn'd aside,
  And with a blushing red,
A mournful motion she bewray'd
  By hanging down her head.

A handkerchief she had
  All wrought with silk and gold:
Which she to stay her trickling tears
  Before her eyes did hold.

This thing unto my sight
  Was wondrous rare and strange;
And in my soul and inward thought
  It wrought a sudden change:

That I so hardy grew,
  To take her by the hand:
Saying, Sweet mistress, why do you
  So dull and pensive stand?

Call me no mistress now,
  But Sarah, thy true friend,
Thy servant, Millwood, honouring thee,
  Until her life hath end.

If thou wouldst here alledge,
  Thou art in years a boy;
So was Adonis, yet was he
  Fair Venus' only joy.

Thus I, who ne'er before
  Of woman found such grace,
But seeing now so fair a dame
  Give me a kind embrace,

I supt with her that night,
  With joys that did abound;
And for the same paid presently,
  In money twice three pound.

An hundred kisses then,
  For my farewel she gave;
Crying, Sweet Barnwell, when shall I
  Again thy company have?

O stay not hence too long,
  Sweet George, have me in mind.
Her words bewicht my childishness,
  She uttered them so kind:

So that I made a vow,
  Next Sunday without fail,
With my sweet Sarah once again
  To tell some pleasant tale.

When she heard me say so,
  The tears fell from her eye;
O George, quoth she, if thou dost fail,
  Thy Sarah sure will dye.

Though long, yet loe! at last,
  The appointed day was come,

That I must with my Sarah meet;
  Having a mighty sum

Of money in my hand,*
  Unto her house went I,
Whereas my love upon her bed
  In saddest sort did lye.

What ails my heart's delight,
  My Sarah dear? quoth I;
Let not my love lament and grieve,
  Nor sighing pine, and die.

But tell me, dearest friend,
  What may thy woes amend,
And thou shalt lack no means of help,
  Though forty pound I spend.

With that she turn'd her head,
  And sickly thus did say,
Oh me, sweet George, my grief is great,
  Ten pound I have to pay

Unto a cruel wretch;
  And God he knows, quoth she,
I have it not. Tush, rise, I said,
  And take it here of me.

Ten pounds, nor ten times ten,
  Shall make my love decay.
Then from my bag into her lap,
  I cast ten pounds straightway.

All blithe and pleasant then,
  To banqueting we go;
She proffered me to lye with her,
  And said it should be so.

And after that same time,
  I gave her store of coyn,
Yea, sometimes fifty pound at once;
  All which I did purloyn.

---

\* The having a sum of money with him on Sunday, etc., shows this narrative to have been penned before the civil wars; the strict observance of the Sabbath was owing to the change of manners at that period.

And thus I did pass on;
  Until my master then
Did call to have his reckoning in
  Cast up among his men.

The which when as I heard,
  I knew not what to say:
For well I knew that I was out
  Two hundred pound that day.

Then from my master straight
  I ran in secret sort;
And unto Sarah Millwood there
  My case I did report.

"But how she us'd this youth,
  In this his care and woe,
And all a strumpet's wiley ways,
  The Second Part may showe."

### THE SECOND PART.

YOUNG BARNWELL comes to thee,
  Sweet Sarah, my delight;
I am undone unless thou stand
  My faithful friend this night.

Our master to accompts
  Hath just occasion found;
And I am caught behind the hand
  Above two hundred pound:

And now his wrath to 'scape,
  My love, I fly to thee,
Hoping some time I may remaine
  In safety here with thee.

With that she knit her brows,
  And looking all aquoy,
Quoth she, What should I have to do
  With any prentice boy?

And seeing you have purloyn'd
  Your master's goods away,
The case is bad, and therefore here
  You shall no longer stay.

Why, dear, thou know'st, I said,
  How all which I could get,
I gave it, and did spend it all
  Upon thee every whit.

Quoth she, Thou art a knave,
  To charge me in this sort,
Being a woman of credit fair,
  And known of good report:

Therefore I tell thee flat,
  Be packing with good speed;
I do defie thee from my heart,
  And scorn thy filthy deed.

Is this the friendship, that
  You did to me protest?
Is this the great affection, which
  You so to me exprest?

Now fie on subtle shrews!
  The best is, I may speed
To get a lodging any where
  For money in my need.

False woman, now farewell,
  Whilst twenty pound doth last,
My anchor in some other haven
  With freedom I will cast.

When she perceiv'd by this,
  I had store of money there:
Stay, George, quoth she, thou art too quick;
  Why, man, I did but jeer:

Dost think for all my speech,
  That I would let thee go?
Faith no, said she, my love to thee
  I wiss is more than so.

You scorne a prentice boy,
  I heard you just now swear,
Wherefore I will not trouble you—
  Nay, George, hark in thine ear;

Thou shalt not go to-night,
  What chance soe're befall:

But man we'll have a bed for thee,
  O else the devil take all.

So I by wiles bewitcht,
  And snar'd with fancy still,
Had then no power to "get" away,
  Or to withstand her will.

For wine on wine I call'd,
  And cheer upon good cheer;
And nothing in the world I thought
  For Sarah's love too dear.

Whilst in her company,
  I had such merriment;
All, all too little I did think,
  That I upon her spent.

A fig for care and thought!
  When all my gold is gone,
In faith, my girl, we will have more,
  Whoever I light upon.

My father's rich, why then
  Should I want store of gold?
Nay with a father sure, quoth she,
  A son may well make bold.

I've a sister richly wed,
  I'll rob her ere I'll want.
Nay then, quoth Sarah, they may well
  Consider of your scant.

Nay, I an uncle have;
  At Ludlow he doth dwell:
He is a grazier, which in wealth
  Doth all the rest excell.

Ere I will live in lack,
  And have no coyn for thee:
I'll rob his house, and murder him,
  Why should you not? quoth she:

Was I a man, ere I
  Would live in poor estate;
On father, friends, and all my kin,
  I would my talons grate.

For without money, George,
  A man is but a beast :
But bringing money, thou shalt be
  Always my welcome guest.

For shouldst thou be pursued
  With twenty hues and cryes,
And with a warrant searched for
  With Argus' hundred eyes,

Yet here thou shalt be safe ;
  Such privy ways there be,
That if they sought an hundred years,
  They could not find out thee.

And so carousing both
  Their pleasures to content :
George Barnwell had in little space
  His money wholly spent.

Which done, to Ludlow straight
  He did provide to go,
To rob his wealthy uncle there ;
  His minion would it so.

And once he thought to take
  His father by the way,
But that he fear'd his master had
  Took order for his stay.\*

Unto his uncle then
  He rode with might and main,
Who with a welcome and good cheer
  Did Barnwell entertain.

One fortnight's space he stayed,
  Until it chanced so,
His uncle with his cattle did
  Unto a market go.

His kinsmen rode with him,
  Where he did see right plain,
Great store of money he had took :
  When coming home again,

---

\* *i.e.* for stopping and apprehending him at his father's.

Sudden within a wood,
  He struck his uncle down,
And beat his brains out of his head ;
  So sore he crackt his crown.

Then seizing fourscore pound,
  To London straight he hyed,
And unto Sarah Millwood all
  The cruell fact descryed.

'Tush, 'tis no matter, George,
  So we the money have
To have good cheer in jolly sort,
  And deck us fine and brave.

Thus lived in filthy sort,
  Until their store was gone:
When means to get them any more,
  I wis, poor George had none.

Therefore in railing sort,
  She thrust him out of door:
Which is the just reward of those
  Who spend upon a whore.

O ! do me not disgrace
  In this my need, quoth he.
She call'd him thief and murderer,
  With all the spight might be :

To the constable she sent,
  To have him apprehended ;
And shewed how far, in each degree,
  He had the laws offended.

When Barnwell saw her drift,
  To sea he got straightway ;
Where fear and sting of conscience
  Continually on him lay.

Unto the lord mayor then,
  He did a letter write ;
In which his own and Sarah's fault
  He did at large recite.

Whereby she seized was
  And then to Ludlow sent :
Where she was judg'd, condemn'd, and hang'd,
  For murder incontinent.

There dyed this gallant quean,
  Such was her greatest gains:
For murder in Polonia,
  Was Barnwell hanged in chains.

Lo! here's the end of youth,
  That after harlots haunt;
Who in the spoil of other men,
  About the streets do flaunt.

## VII.—THE STEDFAST SHEPHERD.
### GEORGE WITHER.

HENCE away, thou Syren, leave me,
  Pish! unclaspe these wanton armes;
Sugred words can ne'er deceive me,
  Though thou prove a thousand charmes.
    Fie, fie, forbeare;
    No common snare
Can ever my affection chaine:
    Thy painted baits,
    And poore deceits,
Are all bestowed on me in vaine.

I'me no slave to such, as you be;
  Neither shall that snowy brest,
Rowling eye, and lip of ruby
  Ever robb me of my rest:
    Goe, goe, display
    Thy beautie's ray
To some more-soone enamour'd swaine:
    Those common wiles
    Of sighs and smiles
Are all bestowed on me in vaine.

I have elsewhere vowed a dutie;
  Turne away thy tempting eye:
Shew not me a painted beautie;
  These impostures I defie:
    My spirit lothes
    Where gaudy clothes
And fained othes may love obtaine:
    I love her so,
    Whose looke sweares No;
That all your labours will be vaine.

Can he prize the tainted posies,
  Which on every brest are worne;
That may plucke the virgin roses
  From their never-touched thorne?

I can goe rest
  On her sweet brest,
That is the pride of Cynthia's traine:
    Then stay thy tongue;
    Thy mermaid song
Is all bestowed on me in vaine.

Hee's a foole, that basely dallies,
  Where each peasant mates with him:
Shall I haunt the thronged vallies,
  Whilst ther's noble hils to climbe?
    No, no, though clownes
    Are scar'd with frownes
I know the best can but disdaine
    And those Ile prove:
    So will thy love
Be all bestowed on me in vaine.

I doe scorne to vow a dutie,
  Where each lustfull lad may wooe:
Give me her, whose sun-like beautie
  Buzzards dare not soare unto:
    Shee, shee it is
    Affoords that blisse
For which I would refuse no paine:
    But such as you,
    Fond fooles, adieu;
You seeke to captive me in vaine.

Leave me then, you Syrens, leave me;
  Seeke no more to worke my harmes:
Craftie wiles cannot deceive me,
  Who am proofe against your charmes:
    You labour may
    To lead astray
The heart, that constant shall remaine:
    And I the while
    Will sit and smile
To see you spend your time in vaine.

## VIII.—THE SPANISH VIRGIN, OR EFFECTS OF JEALOUSY.

The subject of this ballad is taken from a folio collection of tragical stories, entitled *The theatre of God's judgments*, by Dr. Beard and Dr. Taylor, 1642, Part ii. p. 89. The text is given (with corrections) from two copies, one of them in black letter in the Pepys Collection. In this every stanza is accompanied with the following distich by way of burden:

"Oh jealousie! thou art nurst in hell:
Depart from hence, and therein dwell."

All tender hearts, that ake to hear
   Of those that suffer wrong;
All you, that never shed a tear,
   Give heed unto my song.

Fair Isabella's tragedy
   My tale doth far exceed:
Alas, that so much cruelty
   In female hearts should breed!

In Spain a lady liv'd of late,
   Who was of high degree;
Whose wayward temper did create
   Much woe and misery.

Strange jealousies so filled her head
   With many a vain surmize,
She thought her lord had wrong'd her bed,
   And did her love despise.

A gentlewoman passing fair
   Did on this lady wait;
With bravest dames she might compare;
   Her beauty was compleat.

Her lady cast a jealous eye
   Upon this gentle maid;
And taxt her with disloyaltye;
   And did her oft upbraid.

In silence still this maiden meek
   Her bitter taunts would bear,
While oft adown her lovely cheek
   Would steal the falling tear.

In vain in humble sort she strove
   Her fury to disarm;
As well the meekness of the dove
   The bloody hawke might charm.

Her lord, of humour light and gay,
   And innocent the while,
As oft as she came in his way,
   Would on the damsell smile.

And oft before his lady's face,
   As thinking her her friend,
He would the maiden's modest grace
   And comeliness commend.

All which incens'd his lady so,
   She burnt with wrath extreame;
At length the fire that long did glow,
   Burst forth into a flame.

For on a day it so befell,
   When he was gone from home,
The lady all with rage did swell,
   And to the damsell come.

And charging her with great offence,
   And many a grievous fault;
She bade her servants drag her thence,
   Into a dismal vault,

That lay beneath the common-shore:
   A dungeon dark and deep:
Where they were wont, in days of yore,
   Offenders great to keep,

There never light of chearful day
　Dispers'd the hideous gloom;
But dank and noisome vapours play
　Around the wretched room:

And adders, snakes, and toads therein,
　As afterwards was known,
Long in this loathsome vault had bin,
　And were to monsters grown.

Into this foul and fearful place,
　The fair one innocent
Was cast, before her lady's face;
　Her malice to content.

This maid no sooner enter'd is,
　But strait, alas! she hears
The toads to croak, and snakes to hiss:
　Then grievously she fears.

Soon from their holes the vipers creep,
　And fiercely her assail:
Which makes the damsel sorely weep,
　And her sad fate bewail.

With her fair hands she strives in vain
　Her body to defend:
With shrieks and cries she doth complain,
　But all is to no end.

A servant listning near the door,
　Struck with her doleful noise,
Strait ran his lady to implore;
　But she'll not hear his voice.

With bleeding heart he goes agen
　To mark the maiden's groans;
And plainly hears, within the den,
　How she herself bemoans.

Again he to his lady hies
　With all the haste he may:
She into furious passion flies,
　And orders him away.

Still back again does he return
　To hear her tender cries;
The virgin now had ceas'd to mourn;
　Which fill'd him with surprize.

In grief, and horror, and affright,
　He listens at the walls;
But finding all was silent quite,
　He to his lady calls.

Too sure, O lady, now quoth he,
　Your cruelty hath sped;
Make hast, for shame, and come and see;
　I fear the virgin's dead.

She starts to hear her sudden fate,
　And does with torches run:
But all her haste was now too late,
　For death his worst had done.

The door being open'd, strait they found
　The virgin stretch'd along:
Two dreadful snakes had wrapt her round,
　Which her to death had stung.

One round her legs, her thighs, her wast,
　Had twin'd his fatal wreath:
The other close her neck embrac'd,
　And stopt her gentle breath.

The snakes, being from her body thrust,
　Their bellies were so fill'd,
That with excess of blood they burst,
　Thus with their prey were kill'd.

The wicked lady, at this sight,
　With horror strait ran mad;
So raving dy'd, as was most right,
　'Cause she no pity had.

Let me advise you, ladies all,
　Of jealousy beware:
It causeth many a one to fall,
　And is the devil's snare.

## IX.—JEALOUSY, TYRANT OF THE MIND.

This song is by Dryden, being inserted in his tragi-comedy of *Love Triumphant*, etc. On account of the subject, it is inserted here.

What state of life can be so blest,
As love that warms the gentle brest;
'Two souls in one; the same desire
To grant the bliss, and to require?
   If in this heaven a hell we find,
     Tis all from thee,
     O Jealousie!
   Thou tyrant, tyrant of the mind.

All other ills, though sharp they prove,
Serve to refine and perfect love:
In absence, or unkind disdaine,
Sweet hope relieves the lovers paine;
But, oh, no cure but death we find
     To sett us free
     From Jealousie,
   Thou tyrant, tyrant of the mind.

False in thy glass all objects are,
Some sett too near, and some too far:
Thou art the fire of endless night,
The fire that burns, and gives no light.
All torments of the damn'd we find
     In only thee,
     O Jealousie!
   Thou tyrant, tyrant of the mind.

---

## X.—CONSTANT PENELOPE.

The ladies are indebted for the following notable documents to the Pepys Collection, where the original is preserved in black letter, and is entitled, *A Looking-glass for Ladies, or A Mirrour for Married Women.* Tune, "Queen Dido, or Troy town."

When Greeks and Trojans fell at strife,
   And lords in armour bright were seen;
When many a gallant lost his life
   About fair Hellen, beauty's queen;
Ulysses, general so free,
Did leave his dear Penelope.

When she this wofull news did hear,
   That he would to the warrs of Troy;
For grief she shed full many a tear,
   At parting from her only joy:
Her ladies all about her came,
To comfort up this Grecian dame.

Ulysses, with a heavy heart,
   Unto her then did mildly say,
The time is come that we must part;
   My honour calls me hence away;
Yet in my absence, dearest, be
My constant wife, Penelope.

Let me no longer live, she say'd,
   Then to my lord I true remain;
My honour shall not be betray'd
   Until I see my love again;
For I will ever constant prove,
As is the loyal turtle-dove.

Thus did they part with heavy chear,
   And to the ships his way he took;
Her tender eyes dropt many a tear;
   Still casting many a longing look:
She saw him on the surges glide,
And unto Neptune thus she cry'd:

Thou god, whose power is in the deep,
   And rulest in the ocean main,
My loving lord in safety keep
   Till he return to me again:
That I his person may behold,
To me more precious far than gold.

Then straight the ships with nimble sails
  Were all convey'd out of her sight :
Her cruel fate she then bewails,
  Since she had lost her hearts delight.
Now shall my practice be, quoth she,
True vertue and humility.

My patience I will put in ure,
  My charity I will extend ;
Since for my woe there is no cure,
  The helpless now I will befriend :
The widow and the fatherless
I will relieve, when in distress.

Thus she continued year by year
  In doing good to every one ;
Her fame was noised every where,
  To young and old the same was known,
That she no company would mind,
Who were to vanity inclin'd.

Mean while Ulysses fought for fame,
  'Mongst Trojans hazarding his life :
Young gallants, hearing of her name,
  Came flocking for to tempt his wife :
For she was lovely, young, and fair,
No lady might with her compare.

With costly gifts and jewels fine,
  They did endeavour her to win ;
With banquets and the choicest wine,
  For to allure her unto sin :
Most persons were of high degree,
Who courted fair Penelope.

With modesty and comely grace
  Their wanton suits she did denye :
No tempting charms could e'er deface
  Her dearest husband's memorye ;
But constant she would still remain,
Hopeing to see him once again.

Her book her dayly comfort was,
  And that she often did peruse ;
She seldom looked in her glass ;
  Powder and paint she ne'er would use.
I wish all ladies were as free
From pride, as was Penelope.

She in her needle took delight,
  And likewise in her spinning-wheel ;
Her maids about her every night
  Did use the distaff and the reel :
The spiders, that on rafters twine,
Scarce spin a thread more soft and fine.

Sometimes she would bewail the loss
  And absence of her dearest love :
Sometimes she thought the seas to cross,
  Her fortune on the waves to prove.
I fear my lord is slaine, quoth she,
He stays so from Penelope.

At length the ten years siege of Troy
  Did end ; in flames the city burn'd ;
And to the Grecians was great joy,
  To see the towers to ashes turn'd :
Then came Ulysses home to see
His constant, dear Penelope.

O blame her not if she was glad,
  When she her lord again had seen.
Thrice-welcome home, my dear, she said,
  A long time absent thou hast been :
The wars shall never more deprive
Me of my lord whilst I'm alive.

Fair ladies all, example take ;
  And hence a worthy lesson learn,
All youthful follies to forsake,
  And vice from virtue to discern :
And let all women strive to be
As constant as Penelope.

## XI.—TO LUCASTA, ON GOING TO THE WARS.

By Colonel Richard Lovelace, from the volume of his poems, entitled *Lucasta*, Lond. 1649, 12mo.

TELL me not, sweet, I am unkinde,
   That from the nunnerie
Of thy chaste breast and quiet minde,
   To warre and armes I flie.

True, a new mistresse now I chase,
   The first foe in the field ;
And with a stronger faith imbrace
   A sword, a horse, a shield.

Yet this inconstancy is such,
   As you too shall adore ;
I could not love thee, deare, so much,
   Lov'd I not honour more.

## XII.—VALENTINE AND URSINE.

THE old story-book of Valentine and Orson (which suggested the plan of this tale, but it is not strictly followed in it) was originally a translation from the French, being one of their earliest attempts at romance. See *Le Bibliothèque de Romans*, etc.

The circumstance of the bridge of bells is taken from the old metrical legend of *Sir Bevis*, and has also been copied in the *Seven Champions*. The original lines are,

> "Over the dyke a bridge there lay,
> That man and beest might passe away :
> Under the brydge were sixty belles ;
> Right as the Romans telles ;
> That there might no man passe in,
> But all they rang with a gyn."

In the Editor's folio MS. was an old poem on this subject, in a wretched corrupt state, unworthy the press, from which were taken such particulars as could be adopted.*

### PART THE FIRST.

WHEN Flora 'gins to decke the fields
   With colours fresh and fine,
Then holy clerkes their mattins sing
   To good Saint Valentine !

The king of France that morning fair
   He would a hunting ride :
To Artois forest prancing forth
   In all his princelye pride.

To grace his sports a courtly train
   Of gallant peers attend ;
And with their loud and cheerful cryes
   The hills and valleys rend.

Through the deep forest swift they pass,
   Through woods and thickets wild ;
When down within a lonely dell
   They found a new-born child ;

All in a scarlet kercher lay'd
   Of silk so fine and thin ;

---

\* The title given to it there is, *The Emperour and Childe*.

A golden mantle wrapt him round,
  Pinn'd with a silver pin.

The sudden sight surpriz'd them all;
  The courtiers gather'd round;
They look, they call, the mother seek;
  No mother could be found.

At length the king himself drew near,
  And as he gazing stands,
The pretty babe look'd up and smil'd,
  And stretch'd his little hands.

Now, by the rood, king Pepin says,
  This child is passing fair:
I wot he is of gentle blood;
  Perhaps some prince's heir.

Goe bear him home unto my court
  With all the care ye may:
Let him be christen'd Valentine,
  In honour of this day:

And look me out some cunning nurse;
  Well nurtur'd let him bee;
Nor ought be wanting that becomes
  A bairn of high degree.

They look'd him out a cunning nurse;
  And nurtur'd well was hee;
Nor ought was wanting that became
  A bairn of high degree.

Thus grewe the little Valentine,
  Belov'd of king and peers;
And shew'd in all he spake or did
  A wit beyond his years.

But chief in gallant feates of arms
  He did himself advance,
That ere he grewe to man's estate
  He had no peere in France.

And now the early downe began
  To shade his youthful chin;
When Valentine was dubb'd a knight,
  That he might glory win.

A boon, a boon, my gracious liege,
  I beg a boon of thee!
The first adventure that befalls,
  May be reserv'd for mee.

The first adventure shall be thine;
  The king did smiling say.
Nor many days, when lo! there came
  Three palmers clad in graye.

Help, gracious lord, they weeping say'd;
  And knelt, as it was meet:
From Artoys forest we be come,
  With weak and wearye feet.

Within those deep and drearye woods
  There wends a savage boy;
Whose fierce and mortal rage doth yield
  Thy subjects dire annoy.

'Mong ruthless beares he sure was bred;
  He lurks within their den:
With beares he lives; with beares he feeds,
  And drinks the blood of men.

To more than savage strength he joins
  A more than human skill:
For arms, ne cunning may suffice
  His cruel rage to still:

Up then rose sir Valentine,
  And claim'd that arduous deed.
Go forth and conquer, say'd the king,
  And great shall be thy meed.

Well mounted on a milk-white steed,
  His armour white as snow;
As well beseem'd a virgin knight,
  Who ne'er had fought a foe:

To Artoys forest he repairs
  With all the haste he may;
And soon he spies the savage youth
  A rending of his prey.

His unkempt hair all matted hung
  His shaggy shoulders round;

His eager eye all fiery glow'd:
 His face with fury frown'd.

Like eagles' talons grew his nails:
 His limbs were thick and strong;
And dreadful was the knotted oak
 He bare with him along.

Soon as sir Valentine approach'd,
 He starts with sudden spring;
And yelling forth a hideous howl,
 He made the forests ring.

As when a tyger fierce and fell
 Hath spyed a passing roe,
And leaps at once upon his throat;
 So sprung the savage foe;

So lightly leap'd with furious force
 The gentle knight to seize:
But met his tall uplifted spear,
 Which sunk him on his knees.

A second stroke so stiff and stern
 Had laid the savage low;
But springing up, he rais'd his club,
 And aim'd a dreadful blow.

The watchful warrior bent his head,
 And shun'd the coming stroke;
Upon his taper spear it fell,
 And all to shivers broke.

Then lighting nimbly from his steed,
 He drew his burnisht brand:
The savage quick as lightning flew
 To wrest it from his hand.

Three times he grasp'd the silver hilt;
 Three times he felt the blade;
Three times it fell with furious force;
 Three ghastly wounds it made.

Now with redoubled rage he roar'd;
 His eye-ball flash'd with fire;
Each hairy limb with fury shook;
 And all his heart was ire.

Then closing fast with furious gripe,
 He clasp'd the champion round,
And with a strong and sudden twist
 He laid him on the ground.

But soon the knight, with active spring,
 O'erturned his hairy foe:
And now between their sturdy fists
 Past many a bruising blow.

They roll'd and grappled on the ground,
 And there they struggled long:
Skilful and active was the knight;
 The savage he was strong.

But brutal force and savage strength
 To art and skill must yield:
Sir Valentine at length prevail'd,
 And won the well-fought field.

Then binding straight his conquer'd foe
 Fast with an iron chain,
He tyes him to his horse's tail,
 And leads him o'er the plain.

To court his hairy captive soon
 Sir Valentine doth bring;
And kneeling downe upon his knee,
 Presents him to the king.

With loss of blood and loss of strength
 The savage tamer grew;
And to Sir Valentine became
 A servant try'd and true.

And 'cause with beares he erst was bred,
 Ursine they call his name;
A name which unto future times
 The Muses shall proclame.


### PART THE SECOND.

In high renown with prince and peere
 Now liv'd Sir Valentine:
His high renown with prince and peere
 Made envious hearts repine.

It chanc'd the king upon a day
  I'repar'd a sumptuous feast :
And there came lords, and dainty dames,
  And many a noble guest.

Amid their cups, that freely flow'd,
  Their revelry and mirth,
A youthful knight tax'd Valentine
  Of base and doubtful birth.

The foul reproach, so grossly urg'd,
  His generous heart did wound :
And strait he vow'd he ne'er would rest
  Till he his parents found.

Then bidding king and peers adieu,
  Early one summer's day,
With faithful Ursine by his side,
  From court he took his way.

O'er hill and valley, moss and moor,
  For many a day they pass ;
At length, upon a moated lake,\*
  They found a bridge of brass.

Beyond it rose a castle fair,
  Y-built of marble stone :
The battlements were gilt with gold,
  And glittred in the sun.

Beneath the bridge, with strange device,
  A hundred bells were hung ;
That man, nor beast, might pass thereon,
  But strait their larum rung.

This quickly found the youthful pair,
  Who boldly crossing o'er,
The jangling sounds bedeaft their ears,
  And rung from shore to shore.

Quick at the sound the castle gates
  Unlock'd and opened wide,
And strait a gyant huge and grim
  Stalk'd forth with stately pride.

---

\* *i.e.* a lake that served for a moat to a castle.

Now yield you, caytiffs, to my will ;
  He cried with hideous roar ;
Or else the wolves shall eat your flesh,
  And ravens drink your gore.

Vain boaster, said the youthful knight,
  I scorn thy threats and thee :
I trust to force thy brazen gates,
  And set thy captives free.

Then putting spurs unto his steed,
  He aim'd a dreadful thrust ;
The spear against the gyant glanc'd,
  And caus'd the blood to burst.

Mad and outrageous with the pain,
  He whirl'd his mace of steel :
The very wind of such a blow
  Had made the champion reel.

It haply mist ; and now the knight
  His glittering sword display'd,
And riding round with whirlwind speed
  Oft made him feel the blade.

As when a large and monstrous oak
  Unceasing axes hew :
So fast around the gyant's limbs
  The blows quick-darting flew.

As when the boughs with hideous fall
  Some hapless woodman crush :
With such a force the enormous foe
  Did on the champion rush.

A fearful blow, alas! there came,
  Both horse and knight it took,
And laid them senseless in the dust ;
  So fatal was the stroke.

Then smiling forth a hideous grin,
  The gyant strides in haste,
And, stooping, aims a second stroke :
  "Now caytiff breathe thy last !"

But ere it fell, two thundering blows
  Upon his scull descend ;

From Ursine's knotty club they came,
  Who ran to save his friend.

Down sunk the gyant gaping wide,
  And rolling his grim eyes:
The hairy youth repeats his blows:
  He gasps, he groans, he dies.

Quickly sir Valentine reviv'd
  With Ursine's timely care:
And now to search the castle walls
  The venturous youths repair.

The blood and bones of murder'd knights
  They found where'er they came:
At length within a lonely cell
  They saw a mournful dame.

Her gentle eyes were dim'd with tears;
  Her cheeks were pale with woe:
And long sir Valentine besought
  Her doleful tale to know.

"Alas! young knight," she weeping said,
  "Condole my wretched fate;
A childless mother here you see;
  A wife without a mate.

"These twenty winters here forlorn
  I've drawn my hated breath;
Sole witness of a monster's crimes,
  And wishing aye for death.

"Know, I am sister of a king,
  And in my early years
Was married to a mighty prince,
  The fairest of his peers.

"With him I sweetly liv'd in love
  A twelvemonth and a day:
When, lo! a foul and treacherous priest
  Y-wrought our loves' decay.

"His seeming goodness wan him pow'r;
  He had his master's ear:
And long to me and all the world
  He did a saint appear.

"One day, when we were all alone,
  He proffer'd odious love:
The wretch with horrour I repuls'd,
  And from my presence drove.

"He feign'd remorse, and piteous beg'd
  His crime I'd not reveal:
Which, for his seeming penitence,
  I promis'd to conceal.

"With treason, villainy, and wrong,
  My goodness he repay'd:
With jealous doubts he fill'd my lord,
  And me to woe betray'd.

"He hid a slave within my bed,
  Then rais'd a bitter cry.
My lord, possest with rage, condemn'd
  Me, all unheard, to dye.

"But, 'cause I then was great with child,
  At length my life he spar'd:
But bade me instant quit the realme,
  One trusty knight my guard.

"Forth on my journey I depart,
  Opprest with grief and woe;
And tow'rds my brother's distant court,
  With breaking heart, I goe.

"Long time thro' sundry foreign lands
  We slowly pace along:
At length, within a forest wild,
  I fell in labour strong:

"And while the knight for succour sought,
  And left me there forlorn,
My childbed pains so fast increast
  Two lovely boys were born.

"The eldest fair, and smooth, as snow
  That tips the mountain hoar:
The younger's little body rough
  With hairs was cover'd o'er.

"But here afresh begin my woes;
  While tender care I took

To shield my eldest from the cold,
   And wrap him in my cloak;

"A prowling bear burst from the wood,
   And seiz'd my younger son:
Affection lent my weakness wings,
   And after them I run.

"But all forewearied, weak and spent,
   I quickly swooned away;
And there beneath the greenwood shade
   Long time I lifeless lay.

"At length the knight brought me relief,
   And rais'd me from the ground:
But neither of my pretty babes
   Could ever more be found.

"And, while in search we wander'd far,
   We met that gyant grim;
Who ruthless slew my trusty knight,
   And bare me off with him.

"But charm'd by heav'n, or else my griefs,
   He offer'd me no wrong;
Save that within these lonely walls
   I've been immur'd so long."

Now, surely, said the youthful knight,
   You are lady Bellisance,
Wife to the Grecian emperor:
   Your brother's king of France.

For in your royal brother's court
   Myself my breeding had;
Where oft the story of your woes
   Hath made my bosom sad.

If so, know your accuser's dead,
   And dying own'd his crime;
And long your lord hath sought you out
   Thro' every foreign clime.

And when no tidings he could learn
   Of his much-wronged wife,
He vow'd thenceforth within his court
   To lead a hermit's life.

Now heaven is kind! the lady said;
   And dropt a joyful tear:
Shall I once more behold my lord?
   That lord I love so dear?

But, madam, said sir Valentine,
   And knelt upon his knee;
Know you the cloak that wrapt your babe,
   If you the same should see.

And pulling forth the cloth of gold,
   In which himself was found;
The lady gave a sudden shriek,
   And fainted on the ground.

But by his pious care reviv'd,
   His tale she heard anon:
And soon by other tokens found,
   He was indeed her son.

But who's this hairy youth? she said;
   He much resembles thee:
The bear devour'd my younger son,
   Or sure that son were he.

Madam, this youth with bears was bred,
   And rear'd within their den.
But recollect ye any mark
   To know your son agen?

Upon his little side, quoth she,
   Was stampt a bloody rose.
Here, lady, see the crimson mark
   Upon his body grows!

Then clasping both her new-found sons,
   She bath'd their cheeks with tears;
And soon towards her brother's court
   Her joyful course she steers.

What pen can paint king Pepin's joy,
   His sister thus restor'd!
And soon a messenger was sent
   To chear her drooping lord:

Who came in haste with all his peers,
  To fetch her home to Greece;
Where many happy years they reign'd
  In perfect love and peace.

To them Sir Ursine did succeed,
  And long the scepter bare,
Sir Valentine he stay'd in France,
  And was his uncle's heir.

---

## XIII.—THE DRAGON OF WANTLEY.

This humorous song (as a former Editor\* has well observed) is to old metrical romances and ballads of chivalry, what Don Quixote is to prose narratives of that kind—a lively satire on their extravagant fictions. Mr. Bosville of Thorp, in Yorkshire, gave the following explanation of it:—

Wharncliffe Lodge, and Wharncliffe Wood (vulgarly pronounced Wantley), are in the parish of Penniston, in Yorkshire. The rectory of Penniston was part of the dissolved monastery of St. Stephen's, Westminster, and was granted to the Duke of Norfolk's family, who therewith endowed an hospital, which he built at Sheffield, for women. The trustees let the impropriation of the great tithes of Penniston to the Wortley family, who got a great deal by it, and wanted to get still more; for Mr. Nicholas Wortley attempted to take the tithes in kind, but Mr. Francis Bosville opposed him, and there was a decree in favour of the modus in 37th Eliz. The vicarage of Penniston did not go along with the rectory, but with the copyhold rents, and was part of a large purchase made by Ralph Bosville, Esq., from Queen Elizabeth, in the second year of her reign: and that part he sold in 12th Eliz. to his elder brother Godfrey, the father of Francis; who left it, with the rest of his estate, to his wife, for her life, and then to Ralph, third son of his uncle Ralph. The widow married Lyonel Rowlestone, lived eighteen years, and survived Ralph.

This premised, the ballad apparently relates to the lawsuit carried on concerning this claim of tithes made by the Wortley family. "Houses and churches were to him geese and turkeys:" which are titheable things, the dragon chose to live on. Sir Francis Wortley, the son of Nicholas, attempted again to take the tithes in kind: but the parishioners subscribed an agreement to defend their modus. And at the head of the agreement was Lyonel Rowlestone, who is supposed to be one of "the stones, dear Jack, which the dragon could not crack." The agreement is still preserved in a large sheet of parchment, dated 1st of James I., and is full of names and seats, which might be meant by the coat of armour, "with spikes all about, both within and without." More of More-hall was either the attorney or counsellor, who conducted the suit. He is not distinctly remembered, but More-hall is still extant at the very bottom of Wantley [Wharncliffe] Wood, and lies so low that it might be said to be in a well: as the Dragon's den [Wharncliffe Lodge] was at the top of the wood, "with Matthew's house hard by it." The keepers belonging to the Wortley family were named, for many generations,

---

\* *Collection of Historical Ballads*, in 3 vols., 1727.

Matthew Northall: the last of them left this lodge, within memory, to be keeper to the Duke of Norfolk.

*N.B.*—The "two days and a night," mentioned in ver. 125, as the duration of the combat, was probably that of the trial at law.

OLD stories tell, how Hercules
  A dragon slew at Lerna,
With seven heads, and fourteen eyes,
  To see and well discern-a :
But he had a club, this dragon to drub,
  Or he had ne'er done it, I warrant ye :
But More of More-hall, with nothing at all,
  He slew the dragon of Wantley.

This dragon had two furious wings,
  Each one upon each shoulder ;
With a sting in his tayl, as long as a flayl,
  Which made him bolder and bolder.
He had long claws, and in his jaws
  Four and forty teeth of iron ;
With a hide as tough as any buff,
  Which did him round environ.

Have you not heard how the Trojan horse
  Held seventy men in his belly?
This dragon was not quite so big,
  But very near, I'll tell ye.
Devoured he poor children three,
  That could not with him grapple ;
And at one sup he eat them up,
  As one would eat an apple.

All sorts of cattle this dragon did eat,
  Some say he ate up trees,
And that the forests sure he would
  Devour up by degrees :
For houses and churches were to him geese and turkies ;
  He ate all, and left none behind,
But some stones, dear Jack, that he could not crack,
  Which on the hills you will find.

In Yorkshire, near fair Rotherham,
  The place I know it well ;
Some two or three miles, or thereabouts,
  I vow I cannot tell ;
But there is a hedge, just on the hill edge,
  And Matthew's house hard by it ;
O there and then was this dragon's den,
  You could not chuse but spy it.

Some say, this dragon was a witch ;
  Some say, he was a devil,
For from his nose a smoke arose,
  And with it burning snivel ;
Which he cast off, when he did cough,
  In a well that he did stand by ;
Which made it look, just like a brook
  Running with burning brandy.

Hard by a furious knight there dwelt,
  Of whom all towns did ring,
For he could wrestle, play at quarter-staff, kick, cuff and huff,
  Call son of a whore, do any kind of thing :
By the tail and the main, with his hands twain
  He swung a horse till he was dead ;
And that which is stranger, he for very anger
  Eat him all up but his head.

These children, as I told, being eat ;
  Men, women, girls, and boys,
Sighing and sobbing, came to his lodging,
  And made a hideous noise :
O save us all, More of More-hall,
  Thou peerless knight of these woods ;
Do but slay this dragon, who won't leave us a rag on,
  We'll give thee all our goods.

Tut, tut, quoth he, no goods I want ;
  But I want, I want, in sooth,

A fair maid of sixteen, that's brisk and
    keen,
  With smiles about the mouth ;
Hair black as sloe, skin white as snow,
  With blushes her cheeks adorning ;
To anoynt me o'er night, ere I go to fight,
  And to dress me in the morning.

This being done, he did engage
  To hew the dragon down ;
But first he went, new armour to
  Bespeak at Sheffield town ;
With spikes all about, not within but
    without,
  Of steel so sharp and strong ;
Both behind and before, arms, legs, and
    all o'er,
  Some five or six inches long.

Had you but seen him in this dress,
  How fierce he look'd and how big,
You would have thought him for to be
  Some Egyptian porcupig :
He frighted all, cats, dogs, and all,
  Each cow, each horse, and each hog :
For fear they did flee, for they took him
    to be
  Some strange outlandish hedge-hog.

To see this fight, all people then
  Got up on trees and houses,
On churches some, and chimneys too ;
  But these put on their trowses,
Not to spoil their hose. As soon as he
    rose,
  To make him strong and mighty,
He drank by the tale, six pots of ale,
  And a quart of aqua-vitæ.

It is not strength that always wins,
  For wit doth strength excell ;
Which made our cunning champion
  Creep down into a well ;
Where he did think, this dragon would
    drink,
  And so he did in truth ;
And as he stoop'd low, he rose up and
    cry'd, boh !
  And hit him in the mouth.

Oh, quoth the dragon, pox take thee,
    come out,
  Thou disturb'st me in my drink :
And then he turn'd, and s— at him ;
  Good lack how he did stink :
Beshrew thy soul, thy body's foul,
  Thy dung smells not like balsam ;
Thou son of a whore, thou stink'st so
    sore,
  Sure thy diet is unwholsome.

Our politick knight, on the other side,
  Crept out upon the brink,
And gave the dragon such a douse,
  He knew not what to think :
By cock, quoth he, say you so, do you
    see?
  And then at him he let fly
With hand and with foot, and so they
    went to't ;
  And the word it was, Hey boys, hey !

Your words, quoth the dragon, I don't
    understand ;
  Then to it they fell at all,
Like two wild boars so fierce, if I
    may
  Compare great things with small.
Two days and a night, with this dragon
    did fight
  Our champion on the ground ;
Tho' their strength it was great, their skill
    it was neat,
  They never had one wound.

At length the hard earth began to quake,
  The dragon gave him a knock,
Which made him to reel, and straitway
    he thought,
  To lift him as high as a rock,
And thence let him fall. But More of
    More-hall,
  Like a valiant son of Mars,
As he came like a lout, so he turn'd him
    about,
  And hit him a kick on the a—

Oh, quoth the dragon, with a deep sigh,
  And turn'd six times together,
Sobbing and tearing, cursing and swear-
  ing
Out of his throat of leather ;
More of More-hall ! O thou rascal !
Would I had seen thee never ;
With the thing at thy foot, thou hast
  prick'd my tail,
And I'm quite undone for ever.

Murder, murder, the dragon cry'd,
  Alack, alack, for grief ;
Had you but mist that place, you could
  Have done me no mischief.
Then his head he shaked, trembled and
  quaked,
And down he laid and cry'd ;
First on one knee, then on back tumbled
  he,
So groan'd, and kickt, and dy'd.

---

## XIV.—ST. GEORGE FOR ENGLAND.

### THE FIRST PART.

As the former song is in ridicule of the extravagant incidents in old ballads and metrical romances ; so this is a burlesque of their style, particularly of the rambling transitions and wild accumulation of unconnected parts, so frequent in many of them.

This ballad is given from an old black-letter copy in the Pepys Collection, "imprinted at London, 1612." It is more ancient than many of the preceding ; but we place it here for the sake of connecting it with the second part.

WHY doe you boast of Arthur and his
  knightes,
Knowing " well " how many men have
  endured fightes?
For besides king Arthur, and Lancelot
  du lake,
Or sir Tristram de Lionel, that fought
  for ladies sake ;
Read in old histories, and there you
  shall see
How St. George, St. George the dragon
  made to flee.
St. George he was for England ; St.
  Dennis was for France ;
Sing, *Honi soit qui mal y pense.*

Mark our father Abraham, when first
  he resckued Lot
Onely with his household, what conquest there he got :

David was elected a prophet and a
  king,
He slew the great Goliah, with a stone
  within a sling :
Yet these were not knightes of the
  table round ;
Nor St. George, St. George, who the
  dragon did confound.
St. George he was for England ; St.
  Dennis was for France ;
Sing, *Honi soit qui mal y pense.*

Jephthah and Gideon did lead their
  men to fight,
They conquered the Amorites, and put
  them all to flight :
Hercules his labours "were" on the
  plaines of Basse ;
And Sampson slew a thousand with
  the jawbone of an asse,

And eke he threw a temple downe, and
  did a mighty spoyle :
But St. George, St. George he did the
  dragon foyle.
St. George he was for England ; St.
  Dennis was for France ;
Sing, *Honi soit qui mal y pense.*

The warres of ancient monarchs it were
  too long to tell,
And likewise of the Romans, how farre
  they did excell ;
Hannyball and Scipio in many a fielde
  did fighte :
Orlando Furioso he was a worthy
  knighte :
Remus and Romulus, were they that
  Rome did builde :
But St. George, St. George the dragon
  made to yielde.
St. George he was for England ; St.
  Dennis was for France ;
Sing, *Honi soit qui mal y pense.*

The noble Alphonso, that was the
  Spanish king,
The order of the red scarffes and
  bandrolles in did bring :\*
He had a troope of mighty knightes,
  when first he did begin,
Which sought adventures farre and
  neare, that conquest they might win ;
The ranks of the Pagans he often put
  to flight :
But St. George, St. George did with
  the dragon fight.
St. George he was for England ; St.
  Dennis was for France ;
Sing, *Honi soit qui mal y pense.*

Many "knights" have fought with
  proud Tamberlaine :
Cutlax the Dane, great warres he did
  maintaine :
Rowland of Beame, and good "sir"
  Olivere
In the forest of Acon slew both woolfe
  and beare :
Besides that noble Hollander, "sir"
  Goward with the bill :
But St. George, St. George the dragon's
  blood did spill.
St. George he was for England ; St.
  Dennis was for France ;
Sing, *Honi soit qui mal y pense.*

Valentine and Orson were of King
  Pepin's blood :
Alfride and Henry they were brave
  knightes and good :
The four sons of Aymon, that follow'd
  Charlemaine :
Sir Hughon of Burdeaux, and Godfrey
  of Bullaine :
These were all French knightes that
  lived in that age :
But St. George, St. George the dragon
  did assuage.
St. George he was for England ; St.
  Dennis was for France ;
Sing, *Honi soit qui mal y pense.*

Bevis conquered Ascapart, and after
  slew the boare,
And then he crost beyond the seas to
  combat with the moore :
Sir Isenbras and Eglamore, they were
  knightes most bold ;
And good Sir John Mandeville of travel
  much hath told :
There were many English knightes
  that Pagans did convert :
But St. George, St. George pluckt out
  the dragon's heart.
St. George he was for England ; St.
  Dennis was for France,
Sing, *Honi soit qui mal y pense.*

---

\* This probably alludes to "An ancient order of knighthood, called the Order of the Band, instituted by Don Alphonsus, King of Spain. . . . To wear a red riband of three fingers' breadth," etc. See Ames, *Typog.* p. 327.

The noble earl of Warwick, that was call'd sir Guy,
The infidels and pagans stoutlie did defie;
He slew the giant Brandimore, and after was the death
Of that most ghastly dun cowe, the divell of Dunsmore heath;
Besides his noble deeds all done beyond the seas:
But St. George, St. George the dragon did appease.
St. George he was for England; St. Dennis was for France;
Sing, *Honi soit qui mal y pense.*

Richard Cœur-de-lion, erst king of this land,
He the lion gored with his naked hand:[*]
The false duke of Austria nothing did he feare;
But his son he killed with a boxe on the eare;
Besides his famous actes done in the holy lande:
But St. George, St. George the dragon did withstande.

[*] Alluding to the fabulous exploits attributed to this king in the old romances. See the dissertation prefixed to this volume.

St. George he was for England; St. Dennis was for France;
Sing, *Honi soit qui mal y pense.*

Henry the fifth he conquered all France,
And quartered their arms, his honour to advance:
He their cities razed, and threw their castles downe,
And his head he honoured with a double crowne:
He thumped the French-men, and after home he came:
But St. George, St. George he did the dragon tame.
St. George he was for England; St. Dennis was for France;
Sing, *Honi soit qui mal y pense.*

St. David of Wales the Welsh-men much advance:
St. Jaques of Spaine, that never yet broke lance:
St. Patricke of Ireland, which was St. Georges boy,
Seven yeares he kept his horse, and then stole him away:
For which knavish act, as slaves they doe remaine:
But St. George, St. George the dragon he hath slaine.
St. George he was for England; St. Dennis was for France;
Sing, *Honi soit qui mal y pense.*

## XV.—ST. GEORGE FOR ENGLAND.

#### THE SECOND PART

WAS written by John Grubb, M.A., of Christ Church, Oxford. The occasion of its being composed is said to have been as follows:—A set of gentlemen of the University had formed themselves into a club, all the members of which were to be of the name of George; their anniversary feast was to be held on St. George's day. Our author solicited strongly to be admitted; but his name being unfortunately John, this disqualification was dispensed with only upon this condition, that he would compose a song in honour of their patron saint, and would every year produce one or more new stanzas, to be sung on their annual festival. This gave birth to the following humorous performance, the several stanzas of which were the produce of many successive anniversaries.

THE story of king Arthur old
  Is very memorable,
The number of his valiant knights,
  And roundness of his table:
The knights around his table in
  A circle sate, d'ye see:
And altogether made up one
  Large hoop of chivalry.
He had a sword, both broad and sharp,
  Y-*cleped* Caliburn,
Would cut a flint more easily
  Than pen-knife cuts a corn;
As case-knife does a capon carve,
  So would it carve a rock,
And split a man at single slash,
  From noddle down to nock.
As Roman Augur's steel of yore
  Dissected Tarquin's riddle,
So this would cut both conjurer
  And whetstone thro' the middle.
He was the cream of Brecknock,
  And flower of all the Welsh:
But George he did the dragon fell,
  And gave him a plaguy squelsh.
St. George he was for England; St. Dennis was for France;
Sing, *Honi soit qui mal y pense.*

Pendragon, like his father Jove,
  Was fed with milk of goat;
And like him made a noble shield
  Of she-goat's shaggy coat:
On top of burnisht helmet he
  Did wear a crest of leeks;
And onions' heads, whose dreadful nod
  Drew tears down hostile cheeks.
Itch and Welsh blood did make him hot,
  And very prone to ire;
H' was ting'd with brimstone, like a match,
  And would as soon take fire.
As brimstone he took inwardly
  When scurf gave him occasion,
His postern puff of wind was a
  Sulphureous exhalation.
The Briton never tergivers'd,
  But was for adverse drubbing,
And never turn'd his back to aught,
  But to a post for scrubbing.
His sword would serve for battle, or
  For dinner, if you please;
When it had slain a Cheshire man,
  'Twould toast a Cheshire cheese.
He wounded, and, in their own blood,
  Did anabaptize Pagans:
But George he made the dragon an
  Example to all dragons.
St. George he was for England; St. Dennis was for France;
Sing, *Honi soit qui mal y pense.*

Brave Warwick Guy, at dinner time,
  Challeng'd a gyant savage ;
And streight came out the unweildy lout
  Brim-full of wrath and cabbage :
He had a phiz of latitude,
  And was full thick i' th' middle ;
The cheeks of puffed trumpeter,
  And paunch of squire Beadle.*
But the knight fell'd him, like an oak,
  And did upon his back tread ;
The valiant knight his weazon cut,
  And Atropos his packthread.
Besides he fought with a dun cow,
  As say the poets witty,
A dreadful dun, and horned too,
  Like dun of Oxford city :
The fervent dog-days made her mad,
  By causing heat of weather,
Syrius and Procyon baited her,
  As bull-dogs did her father :
Grasiers, nor butchers this fell beast,
  E'er of her frolick hindred ;
John Dosset † she'd knock down as flat,
  As John knocks down her kindred :
Her heels would lay ye all along,
  And kick into a swoon ;
Frewin's ‡ cow-heels keep up your corpse,
  But hers would beat you down.
She vanquisht many a sturdy wight,
  And proud was of the honour ;
Was pufft by mauling butchers so,
  As if themselves had blown her.
At once she kickt, and pusht at Guy,
  But all that would not fright him ;
Who wav'd his winyard o'er sir-loyn,
  As if he'd gone to knight him.
He let her blood, frenzy to cure,
  And eke he did her gall rip ;
His trenchant blade, like cook's long spit,
  Ran thro' the monster's bald-rib :

---

\* Men of bulk answerable to their places, as is well known at Oxford.
† A butcher that then served the college.
‡ A cook, who on fast nights was famous for selling cow-heel and tripe.

He rear'd up the vast crooked rib,
  Instead of arch triumphal :
But George hit th' dragon such a pelt,
  As made him on his bum fall.
St. George he was for England ; St. Dennis was for France ;
Sing, *Honi soit qui mal y pense.*

Tamerlain, with Tartarian bow,
  The Turkish squadrons slew ;
And fetch'd the pagan crescent down,
  With half-moon made of yew :
His trusty bow proud Turks did gall
  With showers of arrows thick,
And bow-strings, without strangling, sent
  Grand-Visiers to old Nick :
Much turbants, and much Pagan pates
  He made to humble in dust ;
And heads of Saracens he fixt
  On spear, as on a sign-post :
He coop'd in cage Bajazet the prop
  Of Mahomet's religion,
As if 't had been the whispering bird,
  That prompted him, the pigeon.
In Turkey-leather scabbard, he
  Did sheath his blade so trenchant
But George he swing'd the dragon's a.
  And cut off every inch on't.
St. George he was for England ;
  Dennis was for France ;
Sing, *Honi soit qui mal y pense.*

The amazon Thalestris was
  Both beautiful and bold ;
She sear'd her breasts with iron hot,
  And bang'd her foes with cold.
Her hand was like the tool, wherewith
  Jove keeps proud mortals under :
It shone just like his lightning,
  And batter'd like his thunder.
Her eye darts lightning, that would blast
  The proudest he that swagger'd,
And melt the rapier of his soul,
  In its corporeal scabbard.
Her beauty, and her drum to foes
  Did cause amazement double ;

As timorous larks amazed are
  With light, and with a low-bell:
With beauty, and that lapland-charm,\*
  Poor men she did bewitch all;
Still a blind whining lover had,
  As Pallas had her scrich-owl.
She kept the chastness of a nun
  In armour, as in cloyster:
But George undid the dragon just
  As you'd undo an oister.
St. George he was for England; St.
  Dennis was for France;
Sing, *Honi soit qui mal y pense.*

Stout Hercules was offspring of
  Great Jove and fair Alcmene:
One part of him celestial was,
  One part of him terrene.
To scale the hero's cradle-walls
  Two fiery snakes combin'd,
And, curling into swaddling cloaths,
  About the infant twin'd:
But he put out these dragons' fires,
  And did their hissing stop;
As red-hot iron with hissing noise
  Is quencht in blacksmith's shop.
He cleans'd a stable, and rubb'd down
  The horses of new-comers;
And out of horse-dung he rais'd fame,
  As Tom Wrench† does cucumbers.
He made a river help him through;
  Alpheus was under-groom;
The stream, disgust at office mean,
  Ran murmuring thro' the room:
This liquid ostler to prevent
  Being tired with that long work,
His father Neptune's trident took,
  Instead of three-tooth'd dung-fork.
This Hercules, as soldier, and
  As spinster, could take pains;
His club would sometimes spin ye flax,
  And sometimes knock out brains:
H' was forc'd to spin his miss a shift
  By Juno's wrath and her-spite;

---

\* The drum.
† Who kept **Paradise Gardens at Oxford.**

Fair Omphale whipt him to his wheel,
  As cook whips barking turn-spit.
From man, or churn, he well knew how
  To get him lasting fame:
He'd pound a giant, till the blood,
  And milk till butter came.
Often he fought with huge battoon,
  And oftentimes he boxed;
Tapt a fresh monster once a month,
  As Hervey\* doth fresh hogshead.
He gave Anteus such a hug,
  As wrestlers give in Cornwall:
But George he did the dragon kill,
  As dead as any door-nail.
St. George he was for England; St.
  Dennis was for France;
Sing, *Honi soit qui mal y pense.*

The Gemini, sprung from an egg,
  Were put into a cradle:
Their brains with knocks and bottled-
    ale,
  Were often-times full addle:
And, scarcely hatch'd, these sons of
    him,
  That hurls the bolt trisulcate,
With helmet-shell on tender head,
  Did tustle with red-ey'd pole-cat.
Castor a horseman, Pollux tho'
  A boxer was, I wist:
The one was fam'd for iron heel;
  Th' other for leaden fist.
Pollux to shew he was a god,
  When he was in a passion
With fist made noses fall down flat
  By way of adoration:
This fist, as sure as French disease,
  Demolish'd noses' ridges:
He like a certain lord† was fam'd
  For breaking down of bridges.

---

\* A noted drawer at the Mermaid tavern in Oxford.
† Lord Lovelace broke down the bridges about Oxford at the beginning of the Revolution. See on this subject a ballad in Smith's *Poems*, p. 102. London, 1713.

Castor the flame of fiery steed,
  With well-spur'd boots took down;
As men, with leathern buckets, quench
  A fire in country town.
His famous horse, that liv'd on oats,
  Is sung on oaten quill;
By bards' immortal provender
  The nag surviveth still.
This shelly brood on none but knaves
  Employ'd their brisk artillery:
And flew as naturally at rogues,
  As eggs at thief in pillory.\*
Much sweat they spent in furious fight,
  Much blood they did effund:
Their whites they vented thro' the pores;
  Their yolks thro' gaping wound:
Then both were cleans'd from blood and dust
  To make a heavenly sign;
The lads were, like their armour, scowr'd,
  And then hung up to shine;
Such were the heavenly double-Dicks,
  The sons of Jove and Tyndar:
But George he cut the dragon up,
  As he had bin duck or windar.
St. George he was for England; St.
  Dennis was for France;
Sing, *Honi soit qui mal y pense.*

Gorgon a twisted adder wore
  For knot upon her shoulder:
She kemb'd her hissing periwig,
  And curling snakes did powder.
These snakes they made stiff changelings
  Of all the folks they hist on;
They turned barbars into hones,
  And masons into free-stone:
Sworded magnetic Amazon
  Her shield to load-stone changes;

---

\* It has been suggested by an ingenious correspondent that this was a popular subject at that time:

  "Not carted Bawd, or Dan de Foe,
  In wooden Ruff ere bluster'd so."

          Smith's *Poems*, p. 117.

Then amorous sword by magic belt
  Clung fast unto her haunches.
This shield long village did protect,
  And kept the army from-town,
And chang'd the bullies into rocks,
  That came t' invade Long-Compton.\*
She post-diluvian stores unmans,
  And Pyrrha's work unravels;
And stares Deucalion's hardy boys
  Into their primitive pebbles.
Red noses she to rubies turns,
  And noddles into bricks:
But George made dragon laxative;
  And gave him a bloody flix.
St. George he was for England; St.
  Dennis was for France;
Sing, *Honi soit qui mal y pense.*

By boar-spear Meleager got
  An everlasting name,
And out of haunch of basted swine,
  He hew'd eternal fame.
This beast each hero's trouzers ript,
  And rudely shew'd his bare-breech,
Prickt but the wem, and out there came
  Heroic guts and garbadge.
Legs were secur'd by iron boots
  No more than peas by peascods:
Brass helmets, with inclosed sculls,
  Wou'd crackle in's mouth like chesnuts.
His tawny hairs erected were
  By rage, that was resistless;
And wrath, instead of cobler's wax,
  Did stiffen his rising bristles.
His tusk lay'd dogs so dead asleep,
  Nor horn, nor whip cou'd wake 'um:
It made them vent both their last blood,
  And their last album-græcum.
But the knight gor'd him with his spear,
  To make of him a tame one,
And arrows thick, instead of cloves,
  He stuck in monster's gammon.

---

\* See the account of Rolricht Stones, in Dr. Plott's *History of Oxfordshire*

For monumental pillar, that
  His victory might be known,
He rais'd up in cylindric form,
  A collar of the brawn.
He sent his shade to shades below,
  In Stygian mud to wallow ;
And eke the stout St. George eftsoon,
  He made the dragon follow.
St. George he was for England ; St.
  Dennis was for France ;
Sing, *Honi soit qui mal y pense.*

Achilles of old Chiron learnt
  The great horse for to ride ;
H' was taught by th' Centaur's rational part,
  The hinnible to bestride.
Bright silver feet, and shining face
  Had that stout hero's mother ;
As rapier's silver'd at one end,
  And wounds you at the other.
Her feet were bright, his feet were swift,
  As hawk pursuing sparrow :
Her's had the metal, his the speed
  Of Braburn's * silver arrow.
Thetis to double pedagogue
  Commits her dearest boy ;
Who bred him from a slender twig
  To be the scourge of Troy :
But ere he lasht the Trojans, h' was
  In Stygian waters steept ;
As birch is soaked first in piss,
  When boys are to be whipt.
With skin exceeding hard, he rose
  From lake, so black and muddy,
As lobsters from the ocean rise,
  With shell about their body :
And, as from lobster's broken claw,
  Pick out the fish you might :
So might you from one unshell'd heel
  Dig pieces of the knight.
His myrmidons robb'd Priam's barns
  And hen-roosts, says the song ;

Carried away both corn and eggs,
  Like ants from whence they sprung.
Himself tore Hector's pantaloons,
  And sent him down bare-breech'd
To pedant Radamanthus, in
  A posture to be switch'd.
But George he made the dragon look,
  As if he had been bewitch'd.
St. George he was for England ; St.
  Dennis was for France ;
Sing, *Honi soit qui mal y pense.*

Full fatal to the Romans was
  The Carthaginian Hannibal ;
him I mean, who gave them such
  A devilish thump at Cannæ :
Moors thick, as goats on Penmenmure,
  Stood on the Alpes's front :
Their one-eyed guide,* like blinking mole,
  Bor'd thro' the hind'ring mount :
Who, baffled by the massy rock,
  Took vinegar for relief ;
Like plowmen, when they hew their way
  Thro' stubborn rump of beef.
As dancing louts from humid toes
  Cast atoms of ill savour
To blinking Hyatt,† when on vile crowd
  He merriment does endeavour,
And saws from suffering timber out
  Some wretched tune to quiver :
So Romans stunk and squeak'd at sight
  Of Affrican carnivor.
The tawny surface of his phiz
  Did serve instead of vizzard :
But George he made the dragon have
  A grumbling in his gizzard.
St. George he was for England ; St.
  Dennis was for France ;
Sing, *Honi soit qui mal y pense.*

---

\* Braburn, a gentleman commoner of Lincoln College, gave a silver arrow to be shot for by the archers of the University of Oxford.

\* Hannibal had but one eye.
† A one-eyed fellow, who pretended to make fiddles as well as play on them, well known at that time in Oxford.

The valour of Domitian,
  It must not be forgotten;
Who from the jaws of worm-blowing
    flies,
  Protected veal and mutton.
A squadron of flies errant,
  Against the foe appears;
With regiments of buzzing knights,
  And swarms of volunteers:
The warlike wasp encourag'd 'em
  With animating hum;
And the loud brazen hornet next,
  He was their kettle-drum:
The Spanish don Cantharido
  Did him most sorely pester,
And rais'd on skin of vent'rous knight
  Full many a plaguy blister.
A bee whipt thro' his button-hole,
  As thro' key-hole a witch,
And stabb'd him with her little tuck
  Drawn out of scabbard breech:
But the undaunted knight lifts up
  An arm both big and brawny,
And slasht her so, that here lay head,
  And there lay bag and honey:
Then 'mongst the rout he flew as swift,
  As weapon made by Cyclops,
And bravely quell'd seditious buz,
  By dint of massy fly-flops.
Surviving flies do curses breathe,
  And maggots too at Cæsar:
But George he shav'd the dragon's
    beard,
  And Askelon * was his razor.
St. George he was for England; St. Dennis
    was for France;
Sing, *Honi soit qui mal y pense.*

John Grubb, the facetious writer of the foregoing song, makes a distinguished figure among the Oxford wits so humorously enumerated in the following distich:

"Alma novem genuit celebres Rhedycina
    poetas
  Bub, Stubb, Grubb, Crabb, Trap, Young,
    Carey, Tickel, Evans."

These were Bub Dodington (the late lord Melcombe), Dr. Stubbes, our poet Grubb, Mr. Crabb, Dr. Trapp the poetry-professor, Dr. Edw. Young the author of *Night-Thoughts*, Walter Carey, Thomas Tickle, Esq., and Dr. Evans the epigrammatist.

## XVI.—MARGARET'S GHOST.

THIS ballad, which appeared in some of the public newspapers in or before the year 1724, came from the pen of David Mallet, Esq., who informs us that the plan was suggested by the four verses quoted in the introductory remarks to *Fair Margaret and Sweet William*, which he supposed to be the beginning of some ballad now lost.

"These lines," says he, "naked of ornament and simple as they are, struck my fancy, and bringing fresh into my mind an unhappy adventure much talked of formerly, gave birth to the following poem, which was written many years ago."

'TWAS at the silent solemn hour,
  When night and morning meet;
In glided Margaret's grimly ghost,
  And stood at William's feet.

Her face was like an April morn,
  Clad in a wintry cloud:
And clay-cold was her lily hand,
  That held her sable shroud.

So shall the fairest face appear,
  When youth and years are flown:
Such is the robe that kings must wear,
  When death has reft their crown.

Her bloom was like the springing flower,
  That sips the silver dew;

---

* The name of St. George's sword.

The rose was budded in her cheek,
  Just opening to the view.

But love had, like the canker-worm,
  Consum'd her early prime:
The rose grew pale, and left her cheek;
  She dy'd before her time.

"Awake!" she cry'd, "thy true love calls,
  Come from her midnight grave;
Now let thy pity hear the maid
  Thy love refus'd to save.

"This is the dark and dreary hour
  When injur'd ghosts complain;
Now yawning graves give up their dead,
  To haunt the faithless swain.

"Bethink thee, William, of thy fault,
  Thy pledge and broken oath:
And give me back my maiden vow,
  And give me back my troth.

"Why did you promise love to me,
  And not that promise keep?
Why did you swear mine eyes were bright,
  Yet leave those eyes to weep?

"How could you say my face was fair,
  And yet that face forsake?
How could you win that virgin heart,
  Yet leave that heart to break?

"Why did you say my lip was sweet,
  And made the scarlet pale?
And why did I, young witless maid,
  Believe the flattering tale?

"That face, alas! no more is fair;
  These lips no longer red:
Dark are my eyes, now clos'd in death,
  And every charm is fled.

"The hungry worm my sister is;
  This winding-sheet I wear:
And cold and weary lasts our night,
  Till that last morn appear.

"But hark! the cock has warn'd me hence!
  A long and last adieu!
Come see, false man, how low she lies,
  Who dy'd for love of you."

The lark sung loud; the morning smil'd
  With beams of rosy red:
Pale William shook in ev'ry limb,
  And raving left his bed.

He hyed him to the fatal place
  Where Margaret's body lay:
And stretch'd him on the grass-green turf,
  That wrapt her breathless clay:

And thrice he call'd on Margaret's name,
  And thrice he wept full sore:
Then laid his cheek to her cold grave,
  And word spake never more.

## XVII.—LUCY AND COLIN

WAS written by Thomas Tickell, Esq., the celebrated friend of Mr. Addison, and editor of his works.

It is a tradition in Ireland, that this song was written at Castletown, in the county of Kildare, at the request of the then Mrs. Conolly—probably on some event recent in that neighbourhood.

OF Leinster, fam'd for maidens fair,
   Bright Lucy was the grace ;
Nor e'er did Liffy's limped stream
   Reflect so fair a face.

Till luckless love and pining care
   Impair'd her rosy hue,
Her coral lip, and damask cheek,
   And eyes of glossy blue.

Oh! have you seen a lily pale,
   When beating rains descend?
So droop'd the slow-consuming maid ;
   Her life now near its end.

By Lucy warn'd, of flattering swains
   Take heed, ye easy fair :
Of vengeance due to broken vows,
   Ye perjured swains, beware.

Three times, all in the dead of night,
   A bell was heard to ring ;
And at her window, shrieking thrice,
   The raven flap'd his wing.

Too well the love-lorn maiden knew
   That solemn boding sound ;
And thus, in dying words, bespoke
   The virgins weeping round.

"I hear a voice you cannot hear,
   Which says, I must not stay :
I see a hand you cannot see,
   Which beckons me away.

"By a false heart, and broken vows,
   In early youth I die.
Am I to blame, because his bride
   Is thrice as rich as I?

"Ah, Colin! give her not thy vows;
   Vows due to me alone :
Nor thou, fond maid, receive his kiss,
   Nor think him all thy own.

"To-morrow in the church to wed,
   Impatient, both prepare ;
But know, fond maid, and know, false man,
   That Lucy will be there.

"Then, bear my corse, ye comrades, bear,
   The bridegroom blithe to meet ;
He in his wedding-trim so gay,
   I in my winding-sheet."

She spoke, she died ;—her corse was borne,
   The bridegroom blithe to meet ;
He in his wedding trim so gay,
   She in her winding-sheet.

Then what were perjur'd Colin's thoughts?
   How were those nuptials kept ?
The bride-men flock'd round Lucy dead,
   And all the village wept.

Confusion, shame, remorse, despaire,
   At once his bosom swell :
The damps of death bedew'd his brow,
   He shook, he groan'd, he fell.

From the vain bride (ah, bride no more !)
   The varying crimson fled,
When, stretch'd before her rival's corse,
   She saw her husband dead.

Then to his Lucy's new-made grave,
   Convey'd by trembling swains,
One mould with her, beneath one sod,
   For ever now remains.

Oft at their grave the constant hind
   And plighted maid are seen;
With garlands gay, and true-love knots,
   They deck the sacred green.

But, swain forsworn, whoe'er thou art,
   This hallow'd spot forbear:
Remember Colin's dreadful fate,
   And fear to meet him there.

---

## XVIII.—THE BOY AND THE MANTLE,

### AS REVISED AND ALTERED BY A MODERN HAND.

In the *Fabliaux ou Contes*, 1781, 5 tom. 12mo, of M. Le Grand (tom. I. p. 54), is printed a modern version of the old tale *Le Court Mantel*, under a new title, *Le Manteau maltaillé*, which contains the story of this ballad much enlarged, so far as regards the mantle, but without any mention of the knife or the horn.

In Carleile dwelt king Arthur,
   A prince of passing might;
And there maintain'd his table round,
   Beset with many a knight.

And there he kept his Christmas
   With mirth and princely cheare,
When, lo! a straunge and cunning boy
   Before him did appeare.

A kirtle and a mantle
   This boy had him upon,
With brooches, rings, and *ouches*,
   Full daintily bedone.

He had a *sarke* of silk
   About his middle meet;
And thus, with seemely curtesy,
   He did king Arthur greet.

" God speed thee, brave king Arthur,
   Thus feasting in thy bowre;
And Guenever thy goodly queen,
   That fair and peerlesse flowre.

" Ye gallant lords, and lordings,
   I wish you all take heed,
Lest, what ye deem a blooming rose
   Should prove a cankred weed."

Then straitway from his bosome
   A little wand he drew;
And with it eke a mantle
   Of wondrous shape and hew.

" Now have thou here, king Arthur,
   Have this here of mee,
And give unto thy comely queen,
   All-shapen as you see.

" No wife it shall become,
   That once hath been to blame."
Then every knight in Arthur's court
   Slye glaunced at his dame.

And first came lady Guenever,
   The mantle she must trye.
This dame, she was new-fangled,
   And of a roving eye.

When she had tane the mantle,
   And all was with it cladde,
From top to toe it shiver'd down,
   As tho' with sheers *beshradde*.

One while it was too long,
   Another while too short,
And wrinkled on her shoulders
   In most unseemly sort,

Now green, now red it seemed,
  Then all of sable hue.
"Beshrew me, quoth king Arthur,
  I think thou beest not true."

Down she threw the mantle,
  Ne longer would not stay;
But, storming like a fury,
  To her chamber flung away.

She curst the whoreson weaver,
  That had the mantle wrought:
And doubly curst the froward impe,
  Who thither had it brought.

"I had rather live in desarts
  Beneath the green-wood tree:
Than here, base king, among thy groomes,
  The sport of them and thee."

Sir Kay call'd forth his lady,
  And bade her to come near:
"Yet dame, if thou be guilty,
  I pray thee now forbear."

This lady, pertly gigling,
  With forward step came on,
And boldly to the little boy
  With fearless face is gone.

When she had tane the mantle,
  With purpose for to wear:
It shrunk up to her shoulder,
  And left her b—side bare.

Then every merry knight,
  That was in Arthur's court,
Gib'd, and laugh, and flouted,
  To see that pleasant sport.

Downe she threw the mantle,
  No longer bold or gay,
But with a face all pale and wan,
  To her chamber slunk away.

Then forth came an old knight,
  A pattering o'er his creed;
And proffer'd to the little boy
  Five nobles to his meed;

"And all the time of Christmass
  Plumb-porridge shall be thine,
If thou wilt let my lady fair
  Within the mantle shine."

A saint his lady seemed,
  With step demure and slow,
And gravely to the mantle
  With mincing pace doth goe.

When she the same had taken,
  That was so fine and thin,
It shrivell'd all about her,
  And show'd her dainty skin.

Ah! little did her mincing,
  Or his long prayers bestead;
She had no more hung on her,
  Than a tassel and a thread.

Down she threwe the mantle,
  With terror and dismay,
And, with a face of scarlet,
  To her chamber hyed away.

Sir Cradock call'd his lady,
  And bade her to come neare:
"Come win this mantle, lady,
  And do me credit here.

"Come win this mantle, lady,
  For now it shall be thine,
If thou hast never done amiss,
  Sith first I made thee mine."

The lady gently blushing,
  With modest grace came on,
And now to trye the wondrous charm
  Courageously is gone.

When she had tane the mantle,
  And put it on her backe,
About the hem it seemed
  To wrinkle and to cracke.

"Lye still," shee cryed, "O mantle!
  And shame me not for nought,
I'll freely own whate'er amiss,
  Or blameful I have wrought.

"Once I kist Sir Cradocke,
  Beneathe the green wood tree:
Once I kist Sir Cradocke's mouth
  Before he married mee."

When thus she had her shriven,
  And her worst fault had told,
The mantle soon became her
  Right comely as it shold.

Most rich and fair of colour,
  Like gold it glittering shone:
And much the knights in Arthur's court
  Admired her every one.

Then towards king Arthur's table
  The boy he turned his eye:
Where stood a boar's head garnished
  With bayes and rosemarye.

When thrice he o'er the boar's head
  His little wand had drawne,
Quoth he, "There's never a cuckold's knife
  Can carve this head of brawne."

Then some their whittles rubbed
  On whetstone, and on hone:
Some threwe them under the table,
  And swore that they had none.

Sir Cradock had a little knife,
  Of steel and iron made;
And in an instant thro' the skull
  He thrust the shining blade.

He thrust the shining blade
  Full easily and fast;
And every knight in Arthurs court
  A morsel had to taste.

The boy brought forth a horne,
  All golden was the rim;

Said he, "No cuckolde ever can
  Set mouth unto the brim.

No cuckold can this little horne
  Lift fairly to his head;
But or on this, or that side,
  He shall the liquor shed."

Some shed it on their shoulder,
  Some shed it on their thigh;
And hee that could not hit his mouth,
  Was sure to hit his eye.

Thus he, that was a cuckold,
  Was known of every man:
But Cradock lifted easily,
  And wan the golden can.

Thus boar's head, horn and mantle,
  Were this fair couple's meed:
And all such constant lovers,
  God send them well to speed.

Then down in rage came Guenever,
  And thus could spightful say,
"Sir Cradock's wife most wrongfully
  Hath borne the prize away.

"See yonder shameless woman,
  That makes herselfe so clean:
Yet from her pillow taken
  Thrice five gallants have been.

"Priests, clarkes, and wedded men,
  Have her lewd pillow prest:
Yet she the wonderous prize forsooth
  Must beare from all the rest."

Then bespake the little boy,
  Who had the same in hold:
"Chastize thy wife, king Arthur,
  Of speech she is too bold:

"Of speech she is too bold,
  Of carriage all too free;

Sir king, she hath within thy hall
A cuckold made of thee.

"All frolick light and wanton
She hath her carriage borne:
And given thee for a kingly crown
To wear a cuckold's horne."

The Rev. Evan Evans, editor of the *Specimens of Welsh Poetry*, 4to, affirmed that the story of the *Boy and the Mantle* is taken from what is related in some of the old Welsh MSS. of Tegan Earfron, one of King Arthur's mistresses. She is said to have possessed a mantle that would not fit any immodest or incontinent woman; this (which, the old writers say, was reckoned among the curiosities of Britain) is frequently alluded to by the old Welsh bards.

---

## XIX.—THE ANCIENT FRAGMENT OF THE MARRIAGE OF SIR GAWAINE.

Another poem in this volume, entitled *The Marriage of Sir Gawaine*, having been offered to the reader with large conjectural supplements and corrections, the old fragment itself is here literally and exactly printed from the Editor's folio MS. with all its defects, inaccuracies, and errata.

This ballad had most unfortunately suffered by having half of every leaf in this part of the MS. torn away; and, as about nine stanzas generally occur in the half-page now remaining, it is concluded that the other half contained nearly the same number of stanzas.

KINGE ARTHUR liues in merry Carleile *
and seemely is to see
and there he hath w$^{th}$ him Queene Genev$^r$
y$^t$ bride soe bright of *blee*.

And there he hath w$^{th}$ him Queene Genever
y$^t$ bride soe bright in bower
& all his barons about him stoode
y$^t$ were both *stiffe* and *stowre*.

The K. kept a royall Christmasse
of mirth & great honor
. . . when . . . . .
[*About nine stanzas wanting.*]

And bring me word what thing it is
y$^e$ a woman most desire
this shalbe thy ransome Arthur he sayes
for Ile haue noe other hier.

K. Arthur then held vp his hand
according thene as was the law

---

* Carleile, so often mentioned in the ballads of King Arthur, the Editor once thought might probably be a corruption of Caer-leon, an ancient British city on the river Uske, in Monmouthshire, which was one of the places of King Arthur's chief residence; but he is now convinced that it is no other than Carlisle, in Cumberland; the old English minstrels, being most of them northern men, naturally represented the hero of romance as residing in the north; and many of the places mentioned in the old ballads are still to be found there, as Tearne-Wadling, etc. Near Penrith is still seen a large circle, surrounded by a mound of earth, which retains the name of Arthur's Round Table.

he tooke his leaue of the baron there
and homword can he draw

And when he came to Merry Carlile
to his chamber he is gone
and ther came to him his Cozen S$^r$
Gawaine
as he did make his mone

And there came to him his Cozen S$^r$
Gawaine
y$^t$ was a curteous knight
why sigh yo$^u$ soe sore vnckle Arthur he
said
or who hath done thee vnright

O peace o peace thou gentle Gawaine
y$^t$ faire may thee be ffall
for if thou knew my sighing soe deepe
thou wold not *meruaile* att all

Ffor when I came to tearne wadling
a bold barron there I fand
w$^{th}$ a great club vpon his backe
standing stiffe & strong

And he asked me wether I wold fight
or from him I shold be gone
o else I must him a ransome pay
& soe dep't him from

To fight w$^{th}$ him I saw noe cause
me thought it was not meet
for he was *stiffe* & strong w$^{th}$ all
his strokes were nothing sweete

Therfor this is my ransome Gawaine
I ought to him to pay
I must come againe as I am sworne
vpon the Newyeers day

And I must bring him word what thing
it is

[*About nine stanzas wanting.*]

Then king Arthur drest him for to ryde
in one soe rich array
toward the foresaid Tearne wadling
y$^t$ he might keepe his day

And as he rode over a more
hee see a lady where shee sate
betwixt an oke and a greene hollen
she was cladd in red scarlett

Then there as shold have stood her
mouth
then there was sett her eye
the other was in her forhead fast
the way that she might see

Her nose was crooked & turnd outward
her mouth stood foule a wry
a worse formed lady then shee was
neuerman saw w$^{th}$ his eye

To *halch* vpon him k. Arthur
this lady was full faine
but k. Arthur had forgott his lesson
what he shold say againe

What knight art thou the lady sayd
that wilt not speake tome
of me thou nothing dismayd
tho I be vgly to see

for I haue halched yo$^u$ curteouslye
& yo$^u$ will not me againe
yett I may happen S$^r$ knight shee said
to ease thee of thy paine

Giue thou ease me lady he said
or helpe me any thing
thou shalt haue gentle Gawaine my cozen
and marry him w^th a ring

Why if I helpe thee not thou noble k. Arthur
of thy owne hearts desiringe
of gentle Gawaine . . .
  [*About nine stanzas wanting.*]

And when he came to the tearne wadling
the baron there cold he srinde
w^th a great weapon on his backe
standing stiffe & stronge

And then he tooke k. Arthurs letters in his hands
& away he cold them fling
& then he puld out a good browne sword
& cryd himselfe a k.

And he sayd I haue thee & thy land Arthur
to doe as it pleaseth me
for this is not thy ransome sure
therfore yeeld thee to me.

And then bespoke him noble Arthur
& bad him hold his hands
& give me leave to speake my mind
in defence of all my land

the said as I came over a More
I see a lady where shee sate
betweene an oke & a green hollen
shee was clad in red scarlette

And she says a woman will haue her will
& this is all her cheef desire
doe me right as thou art a baron of sckill
this is thy ransome & all thy hyer

He sayes an early vengeance light on her
she walkes on yonder more
it was my sister that told thee this
she is a misshapen hore

But heer Ile make mine avow to god
to do her an euill turne
For an euer I may thate fowle theefe get
in a fyer I will her burne

  [*About nine stanzas wanting.*]

## THE SECOND PART.

Sir Lancelott & s^r Steven bold
they rode w^th them that day
and the formost of the company
there rode the steward Kay

Soe did S^r Banier & S^r Bore
S^r Garrett w^th them soe gay
soe did S^r Tristeram y^t gentle k^t
to the forrest fresh and gay

And when he came to the greene forrest
vnderneath a greene holly tree
their sate that lady in red scarlet
y^t vnseemly was to see

S^r Kay beheld this Ladys face
& looked vppon her suire
whosoeuer kisses this lady he sayes
of his kisse he stands in feare

Sʳ Kay beheld the lady againe
& looked vpon her snout
whosoeuer kisses this lady he saies
of his kisse he stands in doubt

———

Peace coz. Kay then said Sʳ Gawaine
amend thee of thy life
for there is a knight amongst us all
yᵗ must marry her to his wife

———

What wedd her to wiffe then said Sʳ Kay
in the diuells name anon
gett me a wiffe where ere I may
for I had rather be slaine

———

Then soome tooke vp their hawkes in hast
& some tooke vp their hounds
& some sware they wold not marry her
for City nor for towne

———

And then be spake him noble k. Arthur
& sware there by this day
for a little foule sight & misliking
           [*About nine stanzas wanting.*]

———

Then shee said choose thee gentle Gawaine
truth as I doe say
wether thou wilt haue me in this likenesse
in the night or else in the day

———

And then bespake him Gentle Gawaine
wᵗʰ one soe mild of moode
sayes well I know what I wold say
god grant it may be good

———

To haue thee fowle in the night
when I wᵗʰ thee shold play
yet I had rather if I might
haue thee fowle in the day

———

What when Lords goe wᵗʰ ther seires shee said
both to the Ale and wine
alas then I must hyde my selfe
I must not goe withinne

———

And then bespake him gentle gawaine
said Lady thats but a skill
And because thou art my owne lady
thou shalt haue all thy will

———

Then she said blesed be thou gentle Gawaine
this day yᵗ I thee see
for as thou see me att this time
from henceforth I wilbe

———

My father was an old knight
& yett it chanced soe
that he marryed a younge lady
yᵗ brought me to this woe

———

Shee witched me being a faire young Lady
to the greene forrest to dwell
& there I must walke in womans likenesse
most like a feeind of hell

———

She witched my brother to a Carlist B....
           [*About nine stanzas wanting.*]
that looked soe foule & that was wont
on the wild more to goe

———

Come kisse her Brother Kay then said Sʳ Gawaine
& amend thee of thy liffe
I sweare this is the same lady
yᵗ I marryed to my wiffe.

Sʳ Kay kissed that lady bright
standing vpon his ffeete
he swore as he was trew knight
the spice was neuer soe sweete

Well Coz. Gawaine sayes Sʳ Kay
thy chance is fallen arright
for thou hast gotten one of the fairest
    maids
I euer saw wᵗʰ my sight

It is my fortune said Sʳ Gawaine
for my Vnckle Arthurs sake
I am glad as grasse wold be of raine
great Joy that I may take

Sʳ Gawaine tooke the lady by the one
    arme
Sʳ Kay tooke her by the tother
they led her straight to k. Arthur
as they were brother & brother

K. Arthur welcomed them there all
& soe did lady Geneuer his queene
wᵗʰ all the knights of the round table
most seemly to be seene.

K. Arthur beheld that lady faire
that was soe faire & bright
he thanked christ in trinity
for Sʳ Gawaine that gentle knight

Soe did the knights both more and
    lesse
reioyced all that day
for the good chance yᵗ hapened was
to Sʳ Gawaine & his lady gay.   Ffinis.

In the facsimile copies, after all the care which has been taken, it is very possible that a redundant *e*, etc., may have been added or omitted.

**THE END OF THE THIRD BOOK.**

# GLOSSARY.

## A

*A*, of.
*A', au*, S., all.
*Abacke*, back.
*Aboue, aboon*, S., above.
*Aboven ous*, above us.
*Abowght*, about.
*Abraide*, abroad.
*Abye*, suffer, pay for.
*Acton*, armour made of taffeta or leather quilted, etc., worn under the habergeon.
*Adeid of nicht*, S., in dead of night.
*Advoutry, advouterous*, adultery, adulterous.
*Aff*, S., off.
*Aft*, S., oft.
*Ahte*, ought.
*Aik*, S., oak.
*Ain, awin*, S., own.
*Aith*, S., oath.
*Al, albeit*, although.
*Al gife, all gyf*, although.
*Alate*, of late.
*Alemaigne*, F., Germany.
*Alyes*, probably corrupted for *algates*, always.
*Ancient*, a flag, banner.
*Ancyent*, standard.
*Ane*, S., one, an, a.
*Angel*, a coin worth 10s.
*Ann*, if.
*Ant*, and.

*Apliht, al aplyht*, quite complete.
*Aquoy*, coy, shy.
*Aras, arros*, arrows.
*Arcir*, archer.
*Argabushe*, harquebusse, an old-fashioned kind of musket.
*Arhyt*, aright.
*Ase*, as.
*Assinde*, assigned.
*Assoyled*, absolved.
*Astate*, estate, also a great person.
*Ath, athe*, o' th', of the.
*Attowre*, S., out over, over and above.
*Auld*, S., old.
*Aule*, awl.
*Aureat*, golden.
*Austerne*, stern, austere.
*Avaunce*, boast.
*Avowe*, vow.
*Avoyd*, p. 54, col. 2, void, vacate.
*Axed*, asked.
*Ayauce*, p. 73, col. 1, against.
*Aye*, ever, also, ah, alas!
*Azein*, against.
*Azont*, S., beyond.
*Azont the ingle*, S., beyond the fire. The fire was in the middle of the room,

## B

*Ba'*, S., ball.
*Bacheleere*, knight,

# GLOSSARY.

*Baile*, evil, mischief.
*Bairded*, S., bearded.
*Bairne, bairn*, child.
*Baith, baithe*, both.
*Bale*, evil, mischief.
*Balow*, S., a nursery term, hush, lullaby, etc.
*Balysbete*, p. 5, col. 2, better our bales, *i.e.* remedy our evils.
*Ban*, curse; *banning*, cursing.
*Baud*, bond, covenant.
*Banderolles*, streamers, little flags.
*Bane*, bone.
*Bar*, bare.
*Bar-hed*, bare-headed, or perhaps bared.
*Barne, berne*, man, person.
*Base court*, the lower court of a castle.
*Basnete, basnite, basnyte, basonet, basonette*, helmet.
*Battes*, heavy sticks, clubs.
*Baud*, bold.
*Bauzen skinne*, p. 80, col. 1, perhaps sheep's leather dressed and coloured red; F. *barane*, sheep's leather.
*Bayard*, a noted blind horse in the old romances.
*Be*, S., by.
*Be that*, by that time.
*Bearing arrow*, an arrow that carries well; or perhaps *bearing* or *birring*, *i.e.* whirling or whirring.
*Bearn*, S., child, human creature.
*Bed*, bade.
*Bede*, offer, engage.
*Bedeene*, immediately.
*Bedight*, bedecked.
*Bedone*, wrought, made up.
*Bedyls*, beadles.
*Beete*, did beat.
*Begylde*, beguiled.
*Beheard*, heard.
*Belive, belyfe, belive*, immediately, by and by, shortly.
*Ben*, in; *ben o house*, inner room.
*Ben*, be, are.
*Ben, bene*, been.

*Ben*, within doors.
*Bende-bow*, a bent bow (?).
*Bene, bean*, an expression of contempt; also *bane*.
*Bene*, fremitus.
*Bent*, S., long grass, also wild fields where bents, etc., grow.
*Beoth*, be, are.
*Ber the prys*, bare the prize.
*Bereth*, bareth.
*Berne*. See Bearn.
*Bernes*, barns.
*Berys*, beareth.
*Beseeme*, become.
*Besette*, beset, attacked.
*Beshradde*, cut into shreds.
*Beshrewme*, a lesser form of imprecation.
*Besmirche*, to soil, discolour.
*Besprent*, besprinkled.
*Beste, beest*, art.
*Bested*, abode.
*Bestis*, beasts.
*Bestrawghted*, distracted.
*Bet*, better; *bett*, did beat.
*Beth*, be, are.
*Bewraies*, discovers, betrays.
*Bi mi leauté*, by my loyalty, honesty.
*Bickarte*, bicker'd, skirmished.
*Bille, bill*, note letter.
*Birk*, S., birch tree.
*Blan, blane, blanne, did blin, i.e.* linger, stop.
*Blare*, to emblazon, display.
*Blaw*, S., blow.
*Blee*, colour, complexion.
*Bleid*, S., *blede*, bleed.
*Blent*, ceased.
*Blink*, a glimpse of light.
*Blinkan, blinkand*, S., twinkling.
*Blinking*, squinting.
*Blinne*, cease, give over.
*Blist*, blessed.
*Blive*, immediately.
*Bluid*, blood.
*Blyth*, joyful, sprightly.
*Blyve*, S., instantly.
*Boare*, bare.

# GLOSSARY. 421

*Boist, boisteris*, S., boast, boasters.
*Bollys*, bowls.
*Boltez*, shafts, arrows.
*Bomen*, bowmen.
*Bood*, (prob.) blood.
*Bookesman*, clerk, secretary.
*Boote, bute*, good, advantage, help.
*Borde*, board, table; *brynge thee under the borde*, bring thee to the ground.
*Bore*, born.
*Borowe*, to redeem by a pledge.
*Borrowe, borowe*, pledge, surety.
*Borrowed*, warranted, pledged, changed.
*Bot*, both, besides.
*Bot*, without.
*Bot and*, and also.
*Bote, boot, boote*, advantage, help, assistance.
*Bougill*, S., bugle-horn, hunting-horn.
*Bougills*, S., bugle-horns.
*Bounde, bowynd, bowned*, prepared, got ready.
*Bowan*, to dwell.
*Bowndyn*, bounden.
*Bowne*, going.
*Bowne*, ready; *bowned*, prepared.
*Bowne*, to dine.
*Bowre, bower*, any bowed or arched room, a parlour, chamber.
*Brade, braid*, S., broad.
*Brae*, the brow or side of a hill.
*Brakes*, tufts of fern.
*Brand, brande*, sword.
*Brast*, burst.
*Braw*, brave; *braifly*, S., bravely.
*Brayd*, arose, hastened.
*Brayd attowre the bent*, hasted over the field.
*Brayde*, drew out, unsheathed.
*Bred*, broad.
*Brede*, breadth.
*Breech*, breeches.
*Breeden*, to breed, to cause.
*Brenand-drake*, fiery serpent, a meteor of firework so called, burning embers or firebrands; Ger. *brennend*, burning. *Drache*, dragon—fiery dragon (?).

*Breng, bryng*, bring.
*Brenn*, S., burn; Ger. *brennen*, to burn.
*Brere*, briar.
*Brether*, brethren.
*Bridal* (properly *bride-al*), feast.
*Brigue, brigg*, bridge.
*Brimme*, public, universally known.
*Britled*, carved.
*Brocht*, S., brought.
*Brodinge*, pricking.
*Broht*, brought.
*Brooche, brouche*, a spit, a bodkin, any ornamental trinket.
*Brooke*, bear, endure, enjoy.
*Brouk her with winne*, enjoy her with pleasure.
*Browd*, broad.
*Brozt*, brought.
*Bryttlynge, brytlyng*, cutting up, quartering, carving.
*Buen, bueth*, been, be, are.
*Buik*, S., book.
*Burgens buds*, young shoots.
*Burn, bourn*, brook.
*Bushment*, ambush, a snare.
*Busk*, dress.
*Busk and boun*, make yourselves ready and go.
*Busket, buskt*, dressed.
*But*, S., without, out of doors.
*But if*, unless.
*But without, but let*, without hindrance.
*Bute*, S., boot, advantage.
*Butt*, the outer room.
*By thre*, of three.
*Bydys, bides*, abides.
*Byears, beeres*, biers.
*Byll, bill*, halbert or battle-axe.
*By-parted*, divided into two parts.
*Byre*, S., a cow-house.
*Byste, beest*, art.

## C

*Cadgily*, S., merrily, cheerfully.
*Calde*, called.

*Calluer*, a kind of musket.
*Camscho*, S., stern, grim.
*Can, cane*, began.
*Can*, know, understand.
*Canne*, S., cannot.
*Cannes*, wooden cups, bowls.
*Cantabanqui*, ballad singers, singers on benches.
*Cantles, Cantells*, pieces, corners.
*Canty*, S., cheerful, chatty.
*Capul*, a poor horse.
*Capull hyde*, horse hide.
*Carle*, churl, clown, used in the north for a strong, hale old man.
*Carline*, S., the feminine of carle.
*Carlish*, churlish, discourteous.
*Carpe*, to speak, censure, complain.
*Cast*, mean, intend.
*Cau*, call.
*Cauld*, cold.
*Cawte*. *Vide* Kawte.
*Caytiffe*, caitiff, slave.
*Certes*, certainly.
*Cetywall* or *Setiwall*, the herb Valerian, also mountain spikenard.
*Cham* (Somerset), I am.
*Chap*, knock.
*Che* (Somerset dialect), I.
*Check*, to rate at.
*Cheefe*, the upper part of the scutcheon in heraldry.
*Cheild*, fellow.
*Cheis*, S., choose.
*Chevaliers*, F., knights.
*Child*, knight.
*Chill* (Somerset dialect), I will.
*Chould*, I would.
*Christentie, Chrystentye, Chrystiante*, Christendom.
*Church-ale*, a wake, a feast in commemoration of the dedication of a church.
*Churl*, clown, villain.
*Chyf, chyfe*, chief.
*Chylded*, brought forth, was delivered.
*Chylder*, children.
*Claiths*, S., clothes.
*Clawde*, clawed, tore, scratched.

*Clead*, S., clothed.
*Cleading*, clothing.
*Cled*, S., clad.
*Clenking*, clinking, jingling.
*Clepe, cleaped*, call, called.
*Clerke*, scholar.
*Cliding*, clothing.
*Clim*, short for Clement.
*Clough*, a broken cliff.
*Clowch*, clutch, grasp.
*Coate*, cot, cottage.
*Cockers*, a sort of buskins or short boots.
*Codiwin, cordwayne*, properly, Spanish or Cordovan leather.
*Cohorted*, incited, exhorted.
*Cokeney*, diminutive for cook.
*Cold*, could, knew.
*Cold rost* (a phrase), nothing to the purpose.
*Collayne, Coleyne*, Cologne.
*Com*, came.
*Comen, commyn*, come.
*Con, can, gan*, began.
*Con thanks*, give thanks.
*Confare*, went, passed.
*Confectered, confetered*, confederated.
*Conspringe* (a phrase), sprung.
*Coote*, coat.
*Cophead*, the top of anything, Sax.
*Cors*, body.
*Corsiare*, courser, steed.
*Cost*, coast side.
*Cote*, cottage or coat.
*Cotydyallye*, daily, every day.
*Could dye*, died (a phrase).
*Could his good*, knew what was good for him.
*Coulde, cold*, could.
*Countie*, count, earl.
*Couth*, could.
*Couthen*, knew.
*Coyntrie*, Coventry.
*Cramasie*, S., crimson.
*Crancky, crancke*, merry, sprightly.
*Cranion*, skull.
*Crech*, crutch.
*Crepyls*, cripples.

*Cricke*, ant, small insect.
*Crinkle*, wrinkle.
*Cristes cors*, Christ's curse.
*Croft*, inclosure.
*Croiz*, cross.
*Cronykle*, chronicle.
*Crook*, twist, distort, make lame.
*Crouneth*, crown ye.
*Crowch*, crutch.
*Crowt*, to pucker up.
*Crumpling*, crooked.
*Cryance*, belief.
*Cule*, S., cool.
*Cum*, S., come, came.
*Cummer*, gossip, friend.
*Cure*, care, heed, regard.

## D

*Dale*, deal; *botgive idale*, unless ideal.
*Dampned*, damned, condemned.
*Dan*, title of respect, from Dominus.
*Danske*, Denmark.
*Darh* (perhaps from thar), there.
*Darred*, S., hit.
*Daukin*, dimunitive of David.
*Daunger-hault*, coyness holdeth.
*Dawes* (Intro.), days.
*Dealare, deland*, S., dealing.
*Deare-day, dere-day*, charming, pleasant day.
*Deas, dais*, the high table in a hall.
*Dee, de, dey, dy*, die.
*Deed* (Intro.), dead.
*Deed is do*, deed is done.
*Deelye dight, deereley dight*, richly fitted out
*Deemed*, doomed, judged.
*Deepe-fette*, deep-fetched.
*Deere*, hurt, mischief.
*Deerly*, preciously, richly.
*Deid*, S. *dede*, deed, item dead.
*Deid-bell*, passing bell.
*Deimt*, S., deem'd, esteem'd.
*Deip*, S. *depe*, deep.
*Deir, deere, dere*, dear, item hurt, trouble, disturb.

*Dele, deill*, deal.
*Dell, deal*, part; every dell, every part.
*Demains*, demesnes, estate in lands.
*Deme*, judge, deemed, doomed.
*Dent*, a dint, blow.
*Deol, dole*, grief.
*Depured*, purified, run clear.
*Dere, deye*, die.
*Dere, deere*, dear, also hurt.
*Derked*, darkened.
*Dern*, S., secret.
*Descreeve*, describe.
*Descrye, descrive*, describe.
*Dewys*, devise.
*Deze*, die.
*Dight-dicht*, decked, dressed.
*Diht, dyht*, dispose, order.
*Dill*, still, calm, mitigate.
*Dill, dole*, grief, pain; *dill I drye*, pain I suffer.
*Dill was dight*, grief was upon him.
*Ding*, knock, beat.
*Dint*, stroke, blow.
*Dis*, this.
*Distrayne*, distract.
*Distrere*, the horse rode by a knight in the tournament.
*Dochter*, daughter.
*Dois*, S. *doys*, does.
*Dol.* See Deol, Dule.
*Dolefuldumps*, sorrowful gloom, heaviness of heart.
*Dosend*, dosing, drowsy, torpid, benumbed, etc.
*Doth, dothe*, doeth, do.
*Doubteous*, doubtful.
*Doughte, doughetie, doughete, doughtye*, doughty, formidable.
*Doughtiness of dent*, sturdiness of blows.
*Dounae*, am not able.
*Doup*, down.
*Doute*, doubt, item fear.
*Douzty*, doughty.
*Dozter*, daughter.
*Doz-trogh*, a dough-trough, a kneading-trough.
*Drake.* See Brenand-drake.

*Dre, drie*, suffer.
*Dreid, dreede, drede*, dread.
*Drie*, S., suffer.
*Dring*, drink.
*Drouyers*, drovers.
*Drowe*, drew.
*Drynge*, drink.
*Dryvars, drovyers*, drovers.
*Duble-dyse*, double (false) dice.
*Dude*, did, *dudert*, didst.
*Dughtie*, doughty.
*Dule*, S. *duel, dol, dole*, grief.
*Dyan, dyand*, S., dying.
*Dyce*, S., dice, chequer-work.
*Dyd, dyde*, did.
*Dyght, dight*, dressed, put on.
*Dyht*, to dispose, order.
*Dynte*, dint, blow, stroke.
*Dyrt.* *Vid.* Dight.
*Dysgysynge*, disguising, masking.

E

*E*, S. *eie*, eye; *een, eyne*, eyes.
*E*, even, evening.
*Eame, eme*, uncle.
*Eard*, earth.
*Earn*, S., to curdle, to make cheese.
*Eathe*, easy.
*Eather*, either.
*Ech, eche, eiche, elke*, each.
*Effund*, pour forth.
*Eftsoon*, in a short time.
*Eiked*, S., added, enlarged.
*Ein*, even.
*Eir, evir*, S., e'er, ever.
*Eke*, also *eike*, each.
*Eldridge, elriche, elritch, elriche*, wild, hideous, ghostly.
*Elke*, each.
*Ellumynge*, embellishing.
*Ellyconys*, S., Helicons.
*Elvish*, peevish, fantastical.
*Eme*, kinsman, uncle.
*Endyed*, dyed.
*Ene*, S. *eyn*, eyes; *ene*, S., even.

*Enharpid*, hooked or edged with mortal dread.
*Enkankered*, cankered.
*Entendement*, F., understanding.
*Ententifly*, to the intent, purposely.
*Er, ere*, before; *ere*, ear.
*Erst*, S., heretofore; Ger. *erst*, formerly.
*Etermynable*, interminable.
*Ettled*, aimed.
*Everychone*, every one.
*Ewbughts* or *Ewe-boughts*, small inclosures or pens.
*Ezar*, azure.

F

*Fa*, fall.
*Fach, fech*, fetch.
*Fader, fatheris*, S., father, fathers.
*Fadge*, S., thick loaf of bread, any coarse heap of stuff.
*Fain, faine, fayne*, glad, fond.
*Faine, fayne*, feign.
*Fair of feir*, of a fair look.
*Falds*, S., thou foldest.
*Fallan, falland*, S., falling.
*Fals*, false or falleth.
*Falser*, a deceiver, a hypocrite.
*Falsing*, deceiving, being untruthful.
*Fang*, seize, carry off.
*Fannes*, instruments for winnowing corn.
*Farden*, fared, flashed.
*Fare*, go, pass, travel.
*Farley*, wonder.
*Fauzt, faucht, fought*, It., fight.
*Fawn*, fallen.
*Fay*, S., faith.
*Fayere*, fair.
*Fayne*, glad, fond.
*Fayson, foyson, fuyson*, plenty, substance.
*Faytors*, deceivers.
*Fe*, fee, reward.
*Fe, fee*, reward, also bribe.
*Feare, fere, feire*, mate.
*Feat*, nice, neat.
*Featously*, neatly, dexterously.
*Feil*, S. *fele*, many.

*Feir*, S. *fere*, fear.
*Felay, Feloy*, fellow.
*Fele*, furious ; *fell*, skin.
*Feltleled*, prepared, got ready.
*Fend*, defend.
*Fendys*, fiends ; *fendys pray*, prey of the fiend.
*Fere*, fear, companion, wife.
*Ferlict-o*, wondered.
*Ferly*, wonder, wonderful.
*Fersly*, fiercely.
*Fesante*, pheasant.
*Fet, fette*, fetched.
*Feys, predestinated* to death or some misfortune, under a fatality.
*Feztyng*, fighting.
*Fil*, S., beasts, cattle.
*Filde*, field.
*Fillan, filland*, filling.
*Finaunce*, fine, forfeiture.
*Find frost*, find mischance or disaster.
*Firth, frith*, a wood, an arm of the sea.
*Fit*, S., foot, feet.
*Fitt*, division, part.
*Flayne*, flayed.
*Flearing*, fleering, mocking.
*Fles*, S., fleece.
*Fleyke*, a large hurdle.
*Flindars*, S., pieces, splinters.
*Flyte*, to contend, to scold.
*Fond*, contrive, endeavour, fly.
*Fonde*, found, contrive, endeavour.
*Foo*, foes.
*Forbode*, commandment.
*Force*, no force, no matter.
*Forced*, regarded, heeded.
*For-fought*, over-fought.
*Formare*, former.
*Fors, I dono fors*, I don't care.
*Forsede, forst*, heeded, regarded.
*Forsters of the fe*, foresters of the king's demesne.
*Fort*, drunk.
*Forthy*, therefore.
*Forthynketh*, repenteth, vexeth, troubleth.
*Forwatch, forewacht*, overwatched, kept awake.

*Forwearied*, much wearied.
*Fou, fow*, S., full, fuddled.
*Fowkin*, a cant word for a fart.
*Frae*, S., fro, from.
*Freake, freke, freyke*, person, human creature.
*Freere, frere*, mate, companion.
*Freers*, friars.
*Freits*, ill omens, ill luck.
*Freyke*, freak, humour indulged.
*Freyned*, asked.
*Frie*, S., *fre*, free.
*Fyers*, fierce.
*Fykkill*, fickle.
*Fyled, fyling*, defiled, defiling.
*Fyll*, fell.
*Fyr*, fire.

## G

*Ga, gais*, go, goes.
*Gaberlunzie, gaberlunye*, a wallet.
*Gadlings, gadelyngys*, gadders, idle fellows.
*Gadryng*, gathering.
*Gae*, S., gave.
*Gae, gaes*, S., go, goes.
*Gair, geer*, dress.
*Galliard*, a sprightly kind of dance.
*Gamon*, to make game, to sport ; hence backgammon.
*Gane, gan*, began.
*Gane*, S., gone.
*Gang*, S., go.
*Ganyde*, gained.
*Garde, garred*, made.
*Gare, gar*, make, force, compel.
*Gargeyld*, the spout of a gutter, gargoyled.
*Garland*, the ring with which the mark was set to be shot at.
*Gart, garred*, made.
*Gate*, way ; "*gang your gate*," go your way.
*Gayed*, made gay.
*Gear, geire, geir, gair*, S., goods, effects, stuff.

*Gederede ye host*, gathered together the army.
*Geere will sway*, the matter will turn out.
*Gef, geve*, gave.
*Geid*, S., gave.
*Gerte*, pierced.
*Geste*, act, feat, story.
*Getinge*, what he had got, plunder, booty.
*Geve, geuen, gevend*, give, given.
*Giff, gife*, if.
*Gillore*, plenty.
*Gimp*, jimp, neat, slender.
*Gin*, S., an, if.
*Gin, ginn*, engine, contrivance, plan.
*Gins*, begins.
*Gip*, an interjection of contempt.
*Girt*, pierced; *thorough-girt*, pierced through.
*Give owre*, S., to surrender.
*Glaive*, F., sword.
*Glede*, a red-hot coal.
*Glente*, glanced, slipt.
*Glist*, glistened.
*Glose*, set a false gloss or colour.
*Glowr*, S., stare or frown.
*Gloze*, canting, fair outside.
*God before*, i.e. God be thy guide.
*Gode*, good; *godness*, goodness.
*Gone*, go.
*Good-e'ens*, good e'ening.
*Gorgett*, necklace or band.
*Gowan*, crow-foot or gold-cup.
*Gowd*, S. *gould*, gold.
*Graine*, scarlet.
*Graithed gowan*, caparisoned with gold.
*Gramercye*, I thank you (grand-mercie).
*Graunge*, granary, also country-house.
*Graythed*, S., decked, put on.
*Gre, gree*, prize, victory.
*Grea-hondes*, grey-hounds.
*Grece*, a step.
*Greece*, fat.
*Greet*, weep.
*Grennyng*, grinning.
*Gret*, great, grieved, swoln.
*Greves*, groves, bushes.
*Grippel*, griping, miserly.

*Groundwa*, ground-wall.
*Growende, growynd*, ground.
*Grownes*, grounds.
*Growte*, small beer.
*Grype*, a griffin.
*Grysely*, dreadfully.
*Gule*, red.
*Gyn*, engine, contrivance.
*Gyrd*, girded, lashed.
*Gyse*, S., guise, form, fashion.

## H

*Ha*, S., hall.
*Ha*, have.
*Habbe ase he brew*, have as he brews.
*Habergeon*, F., lesser coat of mail.
*Hable*, able.
*Hach-borde*, probably upper deck; Ger. *Hochbordschiff*, ship lying high out of water.
*Haggis*, a country dish.
*Hail, hall*, S., whole, altogether.
*Halched, halsed*, embraced, fell on his neck.
*Halt*, holdeth.
*Handbow*, the long-bow.
*Hare*, their.
*Haried, harried, haryed, harowed*, robbed, plundered.
*Harlocke*, charlocke, or wild rape.
*Harnisine*, harness, armour.
*Harrowed*, disturbed.
*Hartly-lust*, hearty desire.
*Harwos*, harrows.
*Hastanddis*, hasty, rash fellows, upstarts.
*Hatcht*, fondled.
*Hau*, have (plural).
*Hauke*, hawk.
*Hauld*, to hold, also hold, stronghold.
*Hauss-bane*, the neck bone (halse-bone).
*Haves*, effects, riches.
*Hawberk*, a coat of mail.
*Hawkin* or *Halkin*, dimin. of Harry.
*Hayll*, advantage, profit.
*Haysell*, hazel.
*He, hee, hye*, high.

*He, hie hye,* hasten.
*Heal,* hail.
*Heare, hear,* here, hair.
*Hech,* hatch, small door.
*Hede, hed, hede, hied, he'ed,* he would, heed, head.
*Heere,* hear.
*Heght.* See Heicht.
*Heicht,* S., height.
*Heiding-hill,* the beheading hill.
*Heil, hele,* S. *hell,* health (?), or welfare, happiness, salvation; Ger. *heil* (?).
*Heir,* here, hear.
*Helen,* heal.
*Hench,* rock, steep hill.
*Hend,* kind, gentle.
*Henne,* hence.
*Hent, hente,* held, laid hold of, received.
*Hente,* held, pulled.
*Heo,* they.
*Her,* hare, their.
*Herault,* herald.
*Here,* their, hear, hair.
*Herkneth,* hearken ye.
*Hert, hertis,* heart, hearts.
*Hes,* S., has.
*Hest,* hast.
*Het,* hot.
*Hett, hight,* bid, call, command.
*Heuch,* S., a rock or steep hill.
*Hevede, hevedest,* had, hadst.
*Heveriche, hevenrich,* heavenly.
*Hewkes,* heralds' coats.
*Hewying, hewinge,* hewing, hacking.
*Hewyne,* in to, hewn in two.
*Heyd,* S., hied.
*Hey-day guise,* frolick, manner.
*Heynd, hend,* gentle, obliging.
*Heyze,* high.
*Hi, hie,* he.
*Hicht; a-hicht,* on height.
*Hie,* haste.
*Hie, hye, he, hee,* high.
*Hight,* engaged, promised, named.
*Hilt,* taken off, flayed.
*Hinch-boys,* pages of honour.
*Hinde, hend,* gentle.

*Hings,* S., hangs.
*Hinney,* S., honey.
*Hip,* a trailing berry.
*Hit,* it.
*Hode,* hood, cap.
*Hole, holl,* whole.
*Hollen,* probably a corruption for holly.
*Holtes,* woods, groves.
*Holtes,* hair, hoar hills.
*Holy,* wholly, or perhaps hole, whole.
*Hom, hem,* them.
*Honden,* hands.
*Hone,* hand.
*Houge,* hang, hung.
*Hoo, ho,* an interjection, stop.
*Hooly,* S., slowly.
*Hop-hall,* limping, halting.
*Houzle,* give the sacrament.
*Hoved,* heaved, hovered.
*Huerte,* heart.
*Huggle,* hug, clasp.
*Hye,* high.
*Hyghte,* on high, aloud.
*Hyndattowre,* behind, over, or about.
*Hynde,* behind, about.
*Hyp-halt,* lame in the hip.
*Hystoriall,* historical.
*Hyznes,* highness.
*Hyzt,* promised.

I

*I lore, I lost,* I strike, stricken.
*I wisse,* I wot (I know), verily.
*Ich,* I.
*Icha,* each.
*Iclipped,* yclept, named.
*Ifere,* together.
*Ilfardly, ill-favoured,* uglily.
*Ilka, ilke, ilk, ilk-on,* S., each, every one.
*Imbated,* debased, lowered.
*Impe,* a little demon or child.
*Inough,* enough.
*Intres,* entrance, admittance.
*Ise,* I shall.
*I-tuned,* tuned.
*Iye,* eye.

## GLOSSARY.

## J

*Jenkin*, diminutive of John.
*Jimp*, S., slender.
*Jo*, sweetheart, friend (contraction of joy).
*Jow*, S., joll or jowl.

## K

*Kame*, comb.
*Kantle-piece*, corner.
*Karlis of kynde*, churls by nature.
*Karls, carls*, churls.
*Kauk*, S., chalk.
*Kawte*, cautious.
*Keel*, S., raddle.
*Keipand*, keeping.
*Kem*, comb.
*Kemperye man*, fighting man.
*Kempes*, soldiers, warriors.
*Kempt*, combed.
*Kepers*, watchers.
*Kept in mew*, kept in solitude or confinement.
*Kever chefes*, handkerchiefs.
*Kexis*, sticks used for candles.
*Kilted*, S., tucked up.
*Kind, kinde*, nature.
*Kirm*, S., churn.
*Kists*, S., chests.
*Kit*, cut.
*Knave*, servant.
*Knellan, knelland*, S., knelling, ringing the knell.
*Knyled*, knelt.
*Krene*, active.
*Kurteis*, courteous.
*Kyd, kid, kithe*, made known, shown.
*Kye*, cattle.
*Kyrtell, kirtle*, sometimes a man's undergarment.
*Kythe*, appear, declare.

## L

*Lacke*, want.
*Laide unto her*, imputed to her.
*Laigh*, low.
*Laith*, S., loth.
*Laithly*, S., loathsome, hideous.
*Lambs-wool*, a cant phrase for ale and roasted apples, P.
*Lane, lain*, lone; *her lane*, alone by her self.
*Langsome*, long, tedious.
*Lap*, leaped.
*Lass*, less.
*Lauch, lauched*, S., laugh, laughed.
*Launde*, lawn.
*Layden*, laid.
*Laye*, law.
*Lay-land*, land not ploughed, greensward.
*Layne*, lien.
*Lazar*, leper.
*Leal, leil*, loyal, honest, true.
*Leane*, conceal, hide.
*Leantè*, loyalty.
*Leanyde*, leaned.
*Lease, leasunge*, lying, falsehood.
*Lee, lea*, field.
*Lee*, lie.
*Leck*, phrase of contempt.
*Leer, lere*, look.
*Leese*, S., lose.
*Leeve*, dear.
*Lefe, leeve*, dear.
*Leid*, S., lyed.
*Leir*, S. *lere*, learn.
*Leman, leaman, leiman*, lover, mistress.
*Lengeth in*, resideth in.
*Let, lett, latte*, hinder, slacken.
*Lettyng*, hindrance.
*Leuch, leugh*, S., laughed.
*Lever, liefer*, rather.
*Lewd*, ignorant, scandalous.
*Leyke, like*, play.
*Leyre, lere*, learning, lore.
*Libbard*, leopard.
*Libbards-bane*, a herb so called.
*Lichtly*, easily.
*Lie*, S., *lee*, field, plain.
*Lig*, S., lie.
*Limitacioune*, a certain precinct allowed to the limitour.

# GLOSSARY.

*Limitours*, friars, licensed to beg.
*Lingell*, a thread of hemp rubbed with rosin, etc., used by rustics for mending their shoes.
*Lire*, flesh complexion.
*Lith, lithe, lythe*, attend, hearken, listen.
*Lither*, idle, worthless, naughty, froward.
*Liver*, deliver.
*Liverance*, deliverance.
*Lodlye*, loathsome. *Vide* Lothly.
*Lo'e, loed*, S., love, loved.
*Loht* . . . (Ballad i. ver. 45), query, pleasure, desire, Ger. *Lust*, or reward, Ger. *Lohnen*.
*Loke*, lock of wool.
*Longes*, lungs.
*Loo*, halloo.
*Lope*, leaped.
*Lore*, lost.
*Lorrel, losel*, a sorry, worthless person.
*Lothly* (*vide* Lodlye), loathsome.
*Loud and still*, at all times.
*Lought, lowe, lugh*, laughed.
*Loun, lown, loon, lowne*, rascal.
*Lounge*, lung.
*Lourd, lour*, S. *lever*, had rather.
*Louted, lowtede, lowttede*, bowed, did obeisance.
*Lowe*, a little hill.
*Lowns*, blazes.
*Lowte, lout*, bow, stoop.
*Lude, luid, luvit*, S., loved.
*Luef, lues, luve*, S., loves, love.
*Lugh*, laughed.
*Lurden, lurdeyne*, sluggard, drone.
*Lust*, desire, pleasure.
*Lyard*, grey steed, as *Bayard*, bay horse.
*Lynde, lyne*, lime tree.
*Lys*, lies.
*Lyvar*, liver.
*Lyzt*, light.

## M

*Maden*, made.
*Mahounde, Mahowne*, Mahomet.

*Maiste*, mayest.
*Makys*, makes, mates.
*Mane*, man, moan.
*Mangonel*, an engine used for discharging stones, arrows, etc.
*Maniveere, meniveere, meninver*, a species of fur.
*March perti*, in the parts lying upon the marshes.
*March-pine*, march-pane, a kind of biscuit.
*Marrow*, S., equal.
*Mart*, S., marred, hurt, damaged.
*Masterye, mayestry*, trial of skill, high proof of skill.
*Maugre*, in spite of, ill-will.
*Maun*, S., must.
*Mavis*, S., a thrush.
*Mawt*, S., malt.
*Maye*, maid.
*Me, men, me con* (men 'gan).
*Mean*, moderate, middle-sized.
*Meany*, train, company.
*Meate*. See Meite.
*Meaten*, meted, measured.
*Meede*, reward.
*Meid*, S., mood.
*Meise*, S., soften, reduce, mitigate.
*Meit*, S., *meet*, fit, proper.
*Mell*, honey, meddle, mingle.
*Mense the faught*, S. P., measure the battle.
*Menzie*, S. *meaney*, retinue, company
*Mervayle*, wonder, marvel.
*Me-thuncheth*, methinks.
*Meyné*. See Meany.
*Mickle*, much, great.
*Minged*, mentioned.
*Minny*, mother.
*Mirke, mirkie*, dark, black.
*Miscreants*, unbelievers.
*Misken*, mistake.
*Mister*, S., to need.
*Mo, moe*, more.
*Moiening*, by means of.
*Monte*, a dull, stupid person.
*Monand*, moaning, grieving.

## GLOSSARY.

*Mone*, moon.
*Mone-lizt*, moonlight.
*Monynday*, Monday.
*More*, originally a hill, but (the hills of the north being generally full of bogs) signifies marshy ground.
*Morn*, morrow.
*Mort*, death of the deer.
*Mot, mote, mowe, may, mou*, S., a mouth.
*Mou*, S., mouth.
*Mought I thee, mote I thee*, may I thrive.
*Muchele bost*, great boast.
*Mulne*, mill.
*Mun, maun*, S., must.
*Mure, mures*, wild downs.
*Murnt*, mourned.
*Myllan, milan*, steel.
*Myne-ye-ple*, many plies, or folds.
*Myrry*, merry.
*Mysuryd*, misused.

### N

*Ne*, not.
*Near, ner, nere*, ne'er, never.
*Neat*, oxen.
*Neatheerd*, a keeper of cattle.
*Neatresse*, a female keeper of cattle.
*Neigh*, approach; *neigh him neare*, come near him.
*Neir*, S.; *nere, ne'er*, never.
*Neist, nyest*, next, nearest.
*Nere ne were*, were it not for.
*Nicht*, S., night.
*Nicked*, notched, cut.
*Nicked him of naye*, nicked him (or cut him?) with a refusal; or Ger. *nicken*, to nod, *nodded* or "shook her head in sign of no." Folio, *nicked*, refused.
*Noble*, gold coin, value 6s. 8d.
*Nobles*, nobleness.
*Nodlys*, noddles, heads.
*Nom*, took *nome*, name.
*Nonce*, purpose.
*None*, took.
*None*, noon.

*Nonys*, nonce.
*Norse*, S., Norway.
*North-gales*, North-Wales.
*Nou*, now.
*Nourice*, S., nurse.
*Nowls*, noddles, heads.
*Nozt*, nought, not.
*Nyzt*, night.

### O

*Obraid*, S., upbraid.
*Ocht*, S., ought.
*Oferling*, superior, opposed to underling.
*On-foughten*, unfoughten, unfought.
*On-loft*, aloft.
*Onys*, once.
*Or, ere*, before.
*Ost, oste, oost*, host.
*Ou, oure*, you, your.
*Out ower*, S., quite over.
*Out-brayde*, drew out, unsheathed.
*Out-horn*, the summoning to arms by the sound of a horn.
*Outrake*, an out-ride or expedition.
*Oware of none*, hour of noon.
*Owches bosses*, or buttons of gold.
*Owene, awen, ain*, S., own.
*Owre word*, S., the last word, the burthen of a song.

### P

*Pa*, S., the river Po.
*Palle*, a robe of state; *purple and pall*, i.e. a purple robe or cloak, a phrase.
*Palmer*, a pilgrim who, having been to the Holy Land, carried a palm branch.
*Pardé, perdie*, verily.
*Paregall*, equal.
*Parfight*, perfect.
*Pattering*, murmuring, mumbling.
*Pauky*, S., shrewd, saucy.
*Paves*, a pavice, a shield that covered the whole body.

# GLOSSARY.

*Pay*, liking, satisfaction.
*Paynim*, pagan.
*Peakish*, p. 97, col. 7.
*Pearlins*, a coarse sort of bone-lace.
*Pece, piece, sc.* of cannon.
*Peere, pere, peer*, equal.
*Pees*, peace.
*Pees, pese*, peace.
*Pele*, a baker's peel.
*Pentarchy of tenses*, five tenses.
*Per fay*, verily.
*Perchmune*, F., parchment.
*Perelous, parlous*, perilous, dangerous.
*Perkin*, diminutive of Peter.
*Persit*, pierced.
*Perte*, part.
*Pertyd*, parted.
*Pertye*, pity.
*Philomene, Philomel*, the nightingale.
*Pibrochs*, Highland war tunes.
*Piece*, S., a little.
*Pight, pyght*, pitched.
*Pil'd*, peeled, bald.
*Plaine, plein*, complaint.
*Playferes*, playfellows.
*Plein, pleyne*, complain.
*Plett*, S., platted.
*Plowmell*, a small wooden hammer fixed to the plough.
*Pollys, Polls*, head.
*Pompal*, p. 61, col. 2, pompous.
*Popingay*, a parrot.
*Porcupig*, porcupine.
*Poterner, porterner*, pocket or pouch.
*Poudered*, a term in Heraldry for sprinkled.
*Pow, pou, powed*, S., pull, pulled.
*Powlls*, heads.
*Pownnes*, pounds.
*Preas, prece, prese*, press.
*Preced*, pressed.
*Prest*, F., ready.
*Prestly, prestlye*, readily, quickly.
*Pricke, pricked*, spurred forward, hurried forward.
*Pricke*, a mark to shoot at.
*Pricke-wande*, a wand set up for a mark.

*Priefe*, prove.
*Priving*, S., proving, tasting.
*Prude*, pride, proud.
*Pryke*, the mark.
*Pryme*, daybreak.
*Prys*, prize.
*Puing*, S., pulling.
*Purfel*, an ornament of embroidery.
*Purfelled*, embroidered.
*Purvayed*, provided.
*Pyp'd a good*, piped so well.

## Q

*Quadrant*, four-square.
*Quaint*, cunning.
*Quarry*, slaughtered game, etc.
*Quat*, S., quitted.
*Quay, quhey*, a young heifer.
*Quean*, sorry, base woman.
*Quel*, cruel.
*Quelch*, a blow, or bang.
*Quere*, quire, choir.
*Quest*, inquest.
*Quha*, S., who.
*Quhair, quhar*, S., where, where'er.
*Quhairfore*, wherefore.
*Quhan, whan*, S., when.
*Quhaneer*, S., whene'er.
*Quhat*, S., what.
*Quhatben*, S., what.
*Quhen*, S., when.
*Quhilk*, which.
*Quhy*, S., why.
*Quillets*, quibbles.
*Quitt*, require.
*Quo*, quoth.
*Quyle*, while.
*Quyrry*, quarry.
*Quyte*, requited.
*Quyknit*, S., quickened.

## R

*Rade*, S., rode.
*Rae*, a roe.

*Raik*, S., to go apace; *raik on row*, go fast in a row.
*Raise*, S., rose.
*Ranted*, S., were merry.
*Rashing*, the stroke by a wild boar with his fangs.
*Raught*, reached.
*Rayne*, *reane*, rain.
*Raysse*, race.
*Razt*, raught, self-bereft.
*Reachles*, careless, reckless, heedless.
*Reade*, read, rede, advice, advise, speak, speech; Ger. *reden*, to speak, to discourse.
*Reas*, raise.
*Reave*, bereave.
*Reckt*, regarded.
*Redresse*, care, labour.
*Reek*, smoke.
*Refe*, bereave.
*Refe*, *reve*, *reeve*, bailiff.
*Reid*, S., advise.
*Reid*, S., reed; *rede*, red.
*Reid roan*, S., red roan.
*Remeid*, S., remedy.
*Renish*, *renisht*, shining, cleansed, purified; Ger. *reinigen*, to clean, to purify, easily corrupted to *reniged*, *renisht* (?).
*Renn*, run, p. 57, col. 2; Ger. *rennen*, to run.
*Renyed*, refused.
*Reve*, *reiv*, bereave.
*Revers*, S., robbers, pirates.
*Rew*, S., take pity; *rewe*, pity, repent; Ger. *reuen*, to repent; *rene*, repentance.
*Rewth*, ruth, repentance.
*Richt*, right.
*Riddle*, a corruption of reade, advise.
*Ride*, make an inroad.
*Rin*, S., run.
*Rise*, shoot, bush, shrub.
*Rive*, rife, abounding.
*Roche*, rock.
*Rood*, *roode*, cross, crucifix.
*Rood-loft*, the place in the church where the images were set up.
*Roode-cross*, crucifix.

*Roune*, *roone*, run.
*Route*, go about, travel.
*Routhe*, ruth, pity.
*Row*, *rowd*, S., roll, rolled.
*Rowght*, rout.
*Rowned*, *rownyd*, whispered.
*Rowyned*, round.
*Rudd*, ruddiness, complexion.
*Rude*, S., *rood*, cross.
*Ruell-bones*, bones diversely coloured, from the F. *rouelle*, a small ring or hoop.
*Rues*, *rwethe*, pitieth.
*Rugged*, pulled with violence.
*Rushy*, or *rashy gair*, rushy stuff, ground.
*Ruth*, *ruthe*, pity, woe.
*Ruthful*, rueful, woeful.
*Ryde*, make an inroad.
*Rydere*, ranger.
*Rynde*, rent.
*Ryschys*, rushes.
*Rywe*, rue.
*Ryzt*, right.

## S

*Safer*, sapphire.
*Saft*, S., soft.
*Saif*, S., safe; *savely*, **safely**.
*Saim*, S., same.
*Sark*, shirt, shift.
*Sat*, *sete*, set.
*Saut*, S., salt.
*Saw*, *say*, speech, discourse.
*Say* (*assay*), attempt.
*Say*, saw.
*Sayne*, say.
*Schall*, shall.
*Schapped*, perhaps *swapped*.
*Schattered*, scattered.
*Schaw*, S., show.
*Schene*, *sheen*, shining, fine; Ger. *schön*, fine.
*Schip*, S., a ship.
*Schiples*, S., shipless.
*Scho*, she.
*Schoone*, shoes.

# GLOSSARY. 433

*Schoote*, shot, let go.
*Schowte, schowtte*, shout.
*Schrill*, S., shrill.
*Schuke*, S., shook.
*Sclat*, slate, table book of slates.
*Scomfit*, discomfit.
*Scot*, tax, revenue, reckoning.
*Se, sees*, S., sea, seas.
*Se, sene, seying*, see, seen, seeing.
*Seetywall.   See* Cetywall.
*Seik*, S. *seke*, seek.
*Seile, sele*, bliss.
*Sek*, sack.
*Sely*, simple.
*Sen*, S., since.
*Seneschall*, steward.
*Senvy*, mustard-seed, F. *senvie*.
*Seve*, seven.
*Sevenyzt*, (probably) sennight.
*Sey, say*, a kind of woollen stuff.
*Seyd*, S., saw.
*Shaws*, little woods.
*Shear*, entirely.
*Shee*, S., she shall.
*Sheene, shene*, shining, glitter; Ger. *schön*, fine.
*Sheeve, shive*, a great slice of bread.
*Sheits, shetes*, S., sheets.
*Shent*, shamed, disgraced.
*Shepenes*, sheep pens.
*Shield bone*, the blade bone.
*Sho, scho*, S., she.
*Shoke*, p. 25, col. 2, shookest.
*Shope*, shaped.
*Shorte*, S., shorten.
*Shradds*, twigs (Folio).
*Shreeven, shriven*, absolved.
*Shrew*, a bad, ill-tempered person.
*Shreward*, a male shrew.
*Shrift*, confession.
*Shrive*, confess, hear confession.
*Shroggs*, shrubs, thorns.
*Shullen*, shall.
*Shunted*, shunned.
*Shurting*, recreation, pastime.
*Shyars*, shires.
*Shynand*, S., shining.

*Sib*, akin, related.
*Side*, S., long.
*Sied*, S., saw.
*Sighan, sighand*, S., sighing.
*Sigh-clout, sythe-clout*, a straining cloth, a cloth to strain milk.
*Sik, sike*, such.
*Siker*, surely, certainly, safely(?); Ger. *sicher*.
*Sindle*, S., seldom.
*Skaith, scath*, harm, mischief.
*Skalk*, malicious, perverse, (or perhaps) knavery, roguery, from Ger. *Schalk*.
*Skinker*, one who serves drink.
*Skinkled*, S., glittered.
*Skomfit*, discomfit.
*Slade*, a breadth of greensward.
*Slated, slaited*, S., whetted or wiped.
*Slattered*, slit, broke into splinters.
*Sle, slee, sley, slo*, slay; *sleest*, slayest.
*Slean, slone*, slain.
*Slee*, sly.
*Slo, sloe*, slay.
*Slode*, slit, split.
*Slone*, slain.
*Sloughe*, slew.
*Sna', snaw*, S., snow.
*Soldain, soldan*, sultan.
*Soll, saulle, sowle*, soul.
*Sond*, a present, a sending.
*Sonne*, S. *son*, sun.
*Sort*, company.
*Soth, sothe, south, southe, soath, sute*, truth.
*Soth Ynglonde*, South England.
*Soudan, soudain, souldan, soldan, sowdan*, sultan.
*Sould*, S. *suld*, should.
*Souling*, victualling.
*Sowne*, sound (rhyth. gr.).
*Sowre, soare*, sore.
*Sowter*, shoemaker.
*Soy*, silk.
*Speered, sparred*, fastened, shut.
*Speir*, S., *spere, speare, speere, spire*, ask, inquire.
*Spendyd*, spent; *spanned*, grasped, strained.
*Spens, spence*, expense.

2 E

## GLOSSARY.

*Spill, spille,* spoil.
*Spillan, spilland,* S., spilling.
*Spindles and whorles,* instruments used for spinning in Scotland.
*Spole,* shoulder, F. *espaule.*
*Sporeles, spurless,* without spurs.
*Sprente,* spurted, sprung out.
*Spurging,* froth that purges out.
*Spurn, spurne,* a kick.
*Spyll,* spoiled, destroyed.
*Squelsh,* a blow or bang.
*Stabille,* stablish.
*Stane,* S. *stean,* stone.
*Stark,* stiff, strong; Ger. *starke,* strong, Folio gives strong.
*Start, sterte,* started.
*Startopes,* buskins, half boots.
*Stead, stede,* place.
*Stean,* stone.
*Steid,* steed.
*Steir,* S., stir.
*Stel, stele,* steel; *steilly,* S., steely.
*Sterne,* stares.
*Sterris,* stars.
*Stert, sterte, sterted,* started.
*Steven,* time, voice.
*Stint,* stop, stopped.
*Stirande,* stage, a stirring travelling journey.
*Stoand,* time; *a-stound,* a-while.
*Stonderes,* standers-by.
*Stound, stonde, stunde,* space, moment, hour, time.
*Stoup of weir,* pillar of war.
*Stour, stower, stoure,* fight, disturbance.
*Stown,* stolen.
*Stowre,* strong, robust, fierce.
*Stra, strae,* S., straw.
*Strekene, stricken,* struck.
*Strick,* strict.
*Styntyde,* stinted, stayed, stopped.
*Styrande,* starting.
*Styrt,* start.
*Suar,* sure.
*Summere,* a sumpter horse.
*Sumpters,* horses that carry clothes, furniture, etc.

*Suore by ys chin,* sworn by his chin.
*Suore by ys cop,* by his head.
*Suthe, suth, surth,* soon, quickly.
*Swa,* so.
*Swaird,* the grassy surface.
*Swapte, swappea, swopede,* struck violently.
*Sware,* oath.
*Swarvde, swarved,* climbed.
*Swat, swatte, swotte,* did swear.
*Swearde, swerd,* sword.
*Sweare,* swearing, oath.
*Sweaven,* a dream.
*Sweere, swire,* neck.
*Sweit,* sweet.
*Swepyl,* the staff of the flail.
*Swinkers, swynkers,* labourers.
*Swith,* quickly, instantly.
*Swyke,* sigh.
*Swyoing,* whoring.
*Swypyng,* striking fast.
*Sych,* such.
*Syd,* side.
*Syde-shear, sydis-shear,* on all sides.
*Syne,* S., then, afterward.
*Syshemell,* Ishmael.
*Syzt,* sight.


### T

*Taine,* S. *tane,* token.
*Take, taiken,* taken.
*Talents,* golden ornaments, hung.
*Targe,* target shield.
*Te,* to.
*Te he!* interjection of laughing.
*Teene, tene,* sorrow, wrath.
*Teenfu,* wrathful, furious.
*Tent,* S., heed.
*Termagaunt,* the god of the Saracens, or perhaps the Teutonic Mars.
*Terry,* diminutive of Terence.
*Tha,* them; *thah,* though.
*Thame,* S., them.
*Than,* S., then.

*Thar, theire, ther, thore*, there.
*The*, they.
*The, thee*, thrive.
*The, thee, thend*, the end.
*The wear*, they were.
*Thear, ther*, there.
*Thewes*, manners.
*Thie*, thy.
*Thii*, they.
*Thilke*, this.
*Thir-towmonds*, S., these two months.
*Tho*, then, those, the.
*Thocht*, thought.
*Thole, tholed*, suffer, suffered.
*Thouse*, S., thou art.
*Thoust*, thou shalt or shouldest.
*Thraldom*, captivity.
*Thrall*, captive.
*Thrang*, close together, also throng.
*Thrawis*, S., throes.
*Thre, thrie*, S., three.
*Threape*, to argue.
*Thrif*, thrive.
*Thrilled*, twirled, turned round.
*Thritte*, thirty.
*Throng*, hastened.
*Thropes*, villages.
*Throw*, S., through.
*Thruch, throuch*, S., through.
*Thud*, noise of a fall.
*Tibbe*, diminutive of Isabel.
*Tift*, S., puff of wind.
*Tild down*, pitched at.
*Till*, entice; *till* also means to.
*Timkin*, diminutive of Timothy.
*Tine*, lose.
*Tint*, S., lost.
*Tirled*, twirled.
*To, too*, item two.
*Tone, t'one*, the one.
*Too-fall*, S., twilight.
*Tor*, a tower, high rock, or hill.
*Tow, towe*, two; *twa*, S., two.
*Tow*, to let down with a rope, etc.
*Towirs*, towers.
*Towyn*, town.
*Traiterye*, treason.

*Trauaile*, travel.
*Tres-hardie*, very hardy or bold (?).
*Trichard*, F., treacherous.
*Tricthen*, trick, deceive.
*Trie*, S., *tre*, tree.
*Triest furth*, draw forth to an assignation.
*Trifulcate*, three-forked.
*Trough, trouth*, troth.
*Trow*, think, know.
*Trowthe, troth, tru*, true.
*Troyde*, broad.
*Trumpe*, lie.
*Trumps*, musical instruments fit for a mock tournament.
*Tuke gude keip*, S., kept a close eye.
*Tul*, S. *till*, to.
*Turn*, occasion.
*Tush*, an interjection of contempt or impatience.
*Twin'd*, parted, separated.
*Twirtle*, twist.
*Tyr-magan*, the mighty Tyr, the god of war.

## U

*Uch*, each.
*Ugsome*, shocking, horrible.
*Unbethought*, bethought.
*Undermerles*, afternoons.
*Unmacklye*, misshapen.
*Unmufit*, S., undisturbed.
*Unseeled*, opened.
*Unsett steven*, unappointed time, unexpectedly.
*Unsonsie*, S., unlucky.
*Untill*, unto, till signifying *to*, as *intill*, into.
*Ure*, use.
*Uthers*, others.

## V

*Vair* (Somerset dialect), **fair**.
*Valzient*, S., valiant.

*Vazen* (Som.), for *faithen*, faiths.
*Venn*, approach, coming.
*Vices*, contracted for devices.
*Vilane*, rascally.
*Vive* (Som.), five.
*Voyded*, quitted.
*Vriers* (Som.), friars.

## W

*Wa*, S., way, wall.
*Wad*, S. *wold*, *wolde*, would.
*Wadded*, from *woad*, of a light-blue colour.
*Wae*, *waefo'*, woe, woful.
*Waeworth*, S., woe betide.
*Waine*, waggon.
*Walker*, a fuller of cloth.
*Wallowit*, S., faded, withered.
*Waltered*, *weltered*, rolled along; also *wallowed*.
*Waly*, an interjection of grief.
*Wame*, *wem*, womb.
*Wan neir*, S., draw near.
*Wane*, the same as ane one.
*Wanrufe*, S., uneasy.
*War*, aware; *war ant wys*, way and wise.
*Ward*, toward.
*Warde*, S., advise, forewarn.
*Warke*, S., work.
*Waryd*, S., accursed.
*Waryson*, reward.
*Wat*, am aware.
*Wat*, S., wet.
*Wate*, S., *weete*, *wete*, *witte*, *wot*, *wote*, *wotte*, know.
*Wate*, S., blamed, from *wyte*, to blame.
*Wayde*, waxed.
*Weal*, wail.
*Weare in*, S., drive in gently.
*Wee*, little.
*Weede*, clothing, dress.
*Weel*, well, also we'll.
*Weet*, wet.
*Weid*, S. *wede*, *weed*, clothes, clothing.

*Weil*, S. *weepe*, weep.
*Weinde*, S. *wende*, went; *weende*, *weened*, thought.
*Weir*, war.
*Weird*, wizard, witch.
*Weldynge*, ruling.
*Welkin*, the sky.
*Well away*, exclamation of pity.
*Wem*, hurt.
*Weme*, womb.
*Wend*, *wends*, go, goes, also to turn about.
*Wende*, *weened*, thought.
*Wene*, *weenest*, ween, weenest.
*Wereth*, defendeth.
*Werre*, *weir*, S., war; *warris*, S., wars.
*Werryed*, worried.
*Wes*, was.
*Westlin*, S., western.
*Whang*, S., a large slice.
*Wheder*, whither.
*Wheleying*, *whelying*, wheeling, turning round.
*Whig*, sour whey.
*Whittles*, knives.
*Whoard*, hoard.
*Whorles*. *Vide* Spindles.
*Whos*, whoso.
*Whyllys*, whilst.
*Wighty*, strong.
*Wild*, worm, serpent.
*Wildings*, wild apples.
*Wilfull*, wandering, perverse, erring.
*Will*, shall.
*Win*, S., get, gain.
*Windar*, contraction of *windhover*, a kind of hawk.
*Windling*, S., winding.
*Winnae*, will not.
*Wirke wisher*, work more wisely.
*Wiss*, know; *wist*, knew; Ger. *wissen*, to know.
*Wisse*, direct, govern; Ger. *weisen*, to advise.
*Wit*, *weet*, know, understand.
*Wo*, woo, woe.
*Wobster*, S. *webster*, weaver.

# GLOSSARY. 437

*Wode, wod,* wood, also mad, wild.
*Wode-ward,* toward the wood.
*Woe-man,* a sorrowful man.
*Woe-worth,* woe be to you.
*Won, wont,* usage.
*Won'd, wonn'd,* dwelt.
*Wonde,* wound, winded.
*Wonders,* wondrous.
*Wone,* one.
*Wonne,* dwell.
*Woodweele, wodewale,* the golden owl, a bird of the thrush kind.
*Wood-wroth,* S., furiously enraged.
*Worshipfully friended,* of worshipful friends.
*Wot, wote,* know; *I wote,* verily.
*Wouche,* mischief.
*Wow,* an exclamation of wonder, also vow, London dialect.
*Wrang,* S., wrung.
*Wreake,* pursue revengefully.
*Wrench,* wretchedness.
*Wringe,* contended with violence.
*Writhe,* twisted; *wrotyn,* wrought.
*Wroken,* revenged.
*Wull,* S., will.
*Wyght, wyghtye,* strong, lusty.
*Wyld,* wild deer.
*Wynde, wende,* go.
*Wynne, win,* joy.
*Wynnen,* win, gain.
*Wysse, wisse,* govern.
*Wyste,* knew.
*Wyt, wit, weet,* know.
*Wytch wyselyer,* work more wisely.
*Wyte,* blame.

## Y

*Y,* I.
*Yae,* S., each.
*Yate,* gate.
*Yaued,* yawned.
*Yave,* gave.
*Y-beare, y-boren,* bear, borne.
*Y-built,* built.

*Ych, yche,* each.
*Ycha, ilka,* each, every.
*Y-cholde-yef,* I should if.
*Y-chone, y-chon,* each one.
*Y-chulle,* I shall.
*Y-chyseled,* cut with the chisel.
*Y-cleped,* named, called.
*Y-con,* chosen.
*Y-con'd,* taught, instructed.
*Ydle,* idle.
*Yearded,* buried.
*Ye-bent, y-bent,* bent.
*Yede, yode,* went.
*Yee,* eye.
*Yenoughe, ynoughe,* enough.
*Yerle, yerlle,* earl.
*Yerly,* early.
*Yerrarchy,* hierarchy.
*Yese,* ye shall.
*Ye-seth, y-seth,* in faith.
*Y-fere,* together.
*Y-founde,* found.
*Ylke, ilk,* same; *that ylk,* that same.
*Ylythe,* listen.
*Yn,* house, home.
*Yngglishe, Ynglysshe,* English.
*Ynglonde,* England.
*Yode, yond,* went.
*Y-picking,* picking, culling, gathering.
*Y's,* is, his, in his.
*Y-slain,* slain.
*Ystonge,* stung.
*Y'th,* in the.
*Y-were,* were.
*Y-wis,* verily.
*Y-wrought,* wrought.
*Y-wys,* truly, verily.
*Y-yote,* molten, melted.

## Z

*Zacring-bell,* sacring-bell.
*Ze,* S., ye; *zee're,* ye are.
*Zede, yede,* went.
*Zee, zeene* (Som.), see, seen.
*Zees,* ye shall.

*Zef, yef*, if.
*Zeirs*, S., years.
*Zellow*, S., yellow.
*Zeme*, take care of, *seman*.
*Zent*, through.
*Zestrene*, yestere'en.
*Zit*, S. *zet*, yet.
*Zonder*, S., yonder.

*Zong*, S., young.
*Zou*, S., you; *zour*, S., your.
*Zoud*, S., you'd, you would.
*Zour-lane, your-lane*, alone, by yourself.
*Zouth*, S., youth.
*Zule*, S., Yule, Christmas.
*Zung*, S., young.

FREDERICK WARNE & CO., Publishers,

## HANDY INFORMATION BOOKS.

In crown 8vo, cloth gilt, price 2s. 6d. each.

*BY A MEMBER OF THE ARISTOCRACY.*

**THE MANNERS AND RULES OF GOOD SOCIETY.** Fourteenth and thoroughly Revised Edition. (New Tpye.)

**SOCIETY SMALL TALK**; or, What to Say, and When to Say it. Eighth Edition.

**THE MANAGEMENT OF SERVANTS**: A Practical Guide to the Routine of Domestic Service. Third Edition.

**PARTY GIVING ON EVERY SCALE**; or, The Cost of Entertainments. Second Edition.

**THE LETTER WRITER OF MODERN SOCIETY.** Second Edition.

**FOOD AND FEEDING.** By Sir HENRY THOMPSON, F.R.C.S. Fifth Revised Edition.

**MENUS MADE EASY**; or, How to Order Dinner, and give the Dishes their French names. By NANCY LAKE. Third Edition.

**THE HOME**, as it Should be: Its Duties and Amenities. By L. VALENTINE. Second Edition.

**OUR SONS**: How to Start Them in Life. By ARTHUR KING. Second Edition.

**HOW WE ARE GOVERNED**; or, The Crown, the Senate, and the Bench. By FONBLANQUE. Fifteenth Edition, thoroughly revised by SMALMAN SMITH.

**HINTS ON BUSINESS**: Financial and Legal. By R. DENNY URLIN, F.S.S. A very useful book about Investments, Income, and other matters.

**HEALTH, BEAUTY, AND THE TOILET**: Letters to Ladies from a Lady Doctor. By ANNA KINGSFORD, M.D., Paris. Second Edition.

In crown 8vo, price 2s. 6d., cloth gilt.

**THE ELECTRIC LIGHT IN OUR HOMES.** By ROBERT HAMMOND (The Hammond Electric Light and Power Supply Company, Limited). With Original Illustrations and Photographs.

## HANDY MANUALS.

In crown 8vo, price 2s. 6d., cloth gilt; or picture boards, 2s.

**THE DOMESTIC EDUCATOR** (formerly entitled THE YOUNG WOMAN'S BOOK): A Gathering of Useful Information in Household Matters, Taste, Duties, Study, &c. With Practical Illustrations.

In large crown 8vo, price 2s. 6d., cloth gilt; or picture boards, 2s.

**BEST OF EVERYTHING.** By the Author of "Enquire Within." Containing 1,800 Useful Articles on how to obtain "The Best of Everything," with a Special Calendar for the Cook and Gardener for each Month.

Bedford Street, Strand.

FREDERICK WARNE & CO., Publishers,

## USEFUL BOOKS for the COUNTRY or the HOME.

Fcap. and crown 8vo, cloth or picture boards, 1s. each, fully Illustrated.

COMMON SHELLS OF THE SEA SHORE.
COMMON SEA WEEDS OF THE BRITISH COAST.
FLOWERS AND THE FLOWER GARDEN.
VEGETABLES: How to Grow Them.
MODERN GYMNAST (THE).
POULTRY: Breeding, Rearing, &c.
ANGLING: A Practical Guide to Fishing, &c.
THE ORCHARD AND FRUIT GARDEN
A FERN BOOK FOR EVERYBODY.
BIRD KEEPING. By C. E. DYSON.
ENGLISH WILD FLOWERS. By J. T. BURGESS.
HARDY PLANTS FOR LITTLE FRONT GARDENS.
THE DOG: Its Varieties and Management.
THE BRITISH BIRD PRESERVER.
LOUDON'S AMATEUR GARDENER.
COMPANION LETTER WRITER (THE).
THE MODERN FENCER. By Captain GRIFFITHS.
ONE THOUSAND OBJECTS FOR THE MICROSCOPE.
LADIES' AND GENTLEMEN'S LETTER WRITER.
THE MONEY MARKET: What it Is, What it Does, and How it is Managed.
THE ART OF VENTRILOQUISM.
CARPENTRY AND JOINERY. Or 1s. 6d., cloth.
THE MAGIC LANTERN MANUAL. Or 2s., cloth.
ADVICE TO SINGERS. By a Singer.
MODERN ETIQUETTE. (Entirely re-written.)
WASHING AND CLEANING.
MAGIC AND ITS MYSTERIES.
WATER: Its Composition, Collection, and Distribution. By J. PARRY. Or 1s. 6d., cloth.
THE MODERN COUNTY COURT GUIDE. By SMALMAN SMITH. Or 1s. 6d., cloth.
HOW TO SEND A BOY TO SEA. By FRANKLIN FOX, formerly Surveyor to Lloyd's Agency at Kurrachi, and Captain P. and O. Service.

*Uniform with the above, 1s. 6d. each.*

THE SHEEP. } New Editions, by G. ARMATAGE.
CATTLE.
THE HORSE: Its Varieties and Management in Health and Disease.
OUT-DOOR COMMON BIRDS: Their Habits, &c. 80 Illusts.

Bedford Street, Strand.

FREDERICK WARNE & CO., Publishers,

## DICTIONARIES.

In large crown 8vo, price 3s. 6d., cloth gilt; or half-bound, 5s. Ditto, half-bound, with Patent Index, 6s.; or half-calf, 7s. 6d.
**NUTTALL'S STANDARD DICTIONARY OF THE ENGLISH LANGUAGE.** New Edition, thoroughly Revised and Extended throughout by the Rev. JAMES WOOD. Containing all the Newest Words, 100,000 References, with full Pronunciation, Etymology, Definition, Technical Terms, Illustrations, &c.

Large demy 18mo, 288 pp., price 1s., cloth gilt, Illustrated.
**WALKER'S PEARL DICTIONARY.** Edited throughout from the most recent approved Authorities, by P. A. NUTTALL, LL.D.

In crown 8vo, price 1s., cloth gilt, Illustrated.
**JOHNSON'S SHILLING DICTIONARY MODERNIZED.** Edited from the most approved Authorities.

In crown 48mo, price 1s., cloth limp, 640 pp.; roan 2s.
**WARNE'S BIJOU DICTIONARY.** Pearl type, with Portrait of Dr. JOHNSON. Edited from the Authorities of JOHNSON, WALKER, WEBSTER, RICHARDSON, WORCESTER, SHERIDAN, &c.

In demy 18mo, cloth boards, price 6d., 290 pp.,
WARNE'S POPULAR EDITION OF
**WALKER'S PRONOUNCING DICTIONARY,** with WEBSTER'S Definitions and WORCESTER'S Improvements.

In 24mo, price 1s., cloth; or 1s. 6d., French morocco, gilt edges.
**WORCESTER'S POCKET DICTIONARY.** Illustrated.

In imperial 4to, price 31s. 6d., cloth; or half russia, cloth sides, 42s.
**WORCESTER'S DICTIONARY OF THE ENGLISH LANGUAGE.** With New Supplement to 1881.

In square 16mo, cloth boards, 2s. 6d. each.
**FRENCH. NUGENT'S PRONOUNCING.** By BROWN and MARTIN.
**GERMAN. WILLIAMS' PRONOUNCING.**

## BIJOU TREASURIES.

In 48mo, price 1s. 6d., cloth gilt; or roan, pocket-book style, 2s. 6d.
**THE BIJOU CALCULATOR AND MERCANTILE TREASURY.** Containing Ready Reckoner, Interest Tables, Trade and Commercial Tables, and all Forms, &c., used in Business, 640 pp.

In 48mo, price 1s. 6d., cloth gilt; or roan, pocket-book style, 2s. 6d.
**THE BIJOU GAZETTEER OF THE WORLD.** New and Revised Edition. Briefly describing, as regards Position, Area, and Population, every Country and State; their Sub-divisions, Provinces, Counties, Principal Towns, Villages, Mountains, Rivers, Lakes, Capes, &c. 30,000 References. By W. R. ROSSER and W. J. GORDON.

In 48mo, price 1s. 6d., cloth gilt; or roan, pocket-book style, 2s. 6d.
**BIJOU BIOGRAPHY OF THE WORLD:** A Reference Book of the Names, Dates, and Vocations of the Distinguished Men and Women of Every Age and Nation. By WILLIAM JOHN GORDON.

FREDERICK WARNE & CO., Publishers,

## GARDENING, BOTANICAL BOOKS, &c.

In medium 8vo, price £2 2s., cloth gilt and gilt top.
### The FLOWERING PLANTS of GREAT BRITAIN.
By ANNE PRATT. Fine Edition. In Three Volumes. Containing upwards of Two Hundred and Forty Coloured Plates.

In medium 8vo, price 12s. 6d., cloth gilt and gilt edges.
### THE FERNS OF GREAT BRITAIN, AND THEIR ALLIES, THE CLUB-MOSSES, PEPPERWORTS, AND HORSETAILS.
By ANNE PRATT. Containing 41 Coloured Plates.

In crown 8vo, price 3s. 6d., cloth gilt.
### ENGLISH WILD FLOWERS. By J. T. BURGESS.
Fine Edition. With numerous Illustrations and Coloured Plates.

NEW EDITION OF LOUDON'S TREES AND SHRUBS.
In half green Persian, price £1 5s., gilt top.
### LOUDON'S TREES AND SHRUBS.
Containing the Hardy Trees and Shrubs of Great Britain, Native and Foreign, and nearly Three Thousand Illustrations.

ALSO IN
### WARNE'S USEFUL BOOKS.
In boards or cloth, Illustrated, price 1s. each.

**A FERN BOOK FOR EVERYBODY.** By M. C. COOKE.
**ENGLISH WILD FLOWERS.** By J. T. BURGESS.
**FLOWERS AND THE FLOWER GARDEN.** By E. WATTS.
**LOUDON'S AMATEUR GARDENER'S CALENDAR.** Revised by W. ROBINSON.
**ORCHARD AND FRUIT GARDEN.** By E. WATTS.
**VEGETABLES, AND HOW TO GROW THEM.** By E. WATTS.

Bedford Street, Strand.

FREDERICK WARNE & CO., Publishers,

# READY RECKONERS.

In demy 18mo, price 1s., cloth.
**THE MODEL READY RECKONER.** With Interest and Commission Tables. Also the Value of Foreign Gold and Silver Coins.

And, price 6d. each, cloth.
**WARNE'S BIJOU READY RECKONER.** Royal 32mo.
**WARNE'S LARGE-TYPE READY RECKONER.** Demy 18mo.

In royal 64mo, price 1d., sewed; or cloth, 2d.
**WARNE'S TABLE BOOK.** Edited by NUTTALL. With very complete Information. 400th Thousand.

In oblong 18mo, price 1s., cloth.
**WARNE'S DISCOUNT AND COMMISSION TABLES.** Containing Seven Thousand Calculations, at from ⅛ to 95 per cent. on amounts from 1d. to £1,000. By W. J. GORDON, Chartered Accountant.

In 48mo, price 1s., cloth gilt.
**MY MARKET TABLE.** Showing the Value of any Article at per Pound and Ounce, from 6d. to 1s. 6d.

In 48mo, price 1s. 6d., cloth gilt; or in pocket book style, price 2s. 6d., roan, gilt edges.
**THE BIJOU CALCULATOR AND MERCANTILE TREASURY.** With Ready Reckoner, Interest, Trade and Commercial Tables, and all Forms, &c., used in Business. 640 pp.

In oblong 8vo, price 2s., patent morocco.
**HOPPUS'S MEASURER.** Enlarged and Revised; the Contents being given in Feet, Inches, and Twelfth-parts of an Inch. Edited by WM. RICHARDSON.

In crown 8vo, price 2s. 6d., cloth.
**THE AVOIRDUPOIS WEIGHT CALCULATOR AND READY RECKONER.** With Interest and Discount Tables. By ARTHUR E. KING.

---

A COUNTING-HOUSE NECESSITY.
 large crown 8vo, price 5s., cloth gilt.
**STANDARD COMMERCIAL HANDBOOK.** Comprising a ... ary of the English Language, with 30,000 References; a Gazetteer of the World, with 30,000 References and a complete Mercantile Calculator of Interest Tables, Trade Tables, and all known Information necessary for Commercial Transactions.
"Invaluable as a desk companion."—*Bankers' Journal.*

---

Bedford Street, Strand.

FREDERICK WARNE & CO., Publishers,

## THE CHANDOS LIBRARY.

*Series of Standard Works in all Classes of Literature.*

In crown 8vo, price 3s. 6d. each, new style, cloth gilt, marbled sides.

**THE PERCY ANECDOTES.** By REUBEN and SHOLTO PERCY. Verbatim Reprint of Original Edition. Introduction by JOHN TIMBS. Original Steel Portraits, and Index. Four Vols., each Complete in itself.

**PEPYS'S DIARY AND CORRESPONDENCE.** With Seven Steel Portraits arranged as a Frontispiece, Memoir, and full Index.

**JOHNSON'S LIVES OF THE POETS.** With Critical Observations, and a Sketch of the Author's Life by Sir WALTER SCOTT.

**EVELYN'S DIARY AND CORRESPONDENCE.** Edited by BRAY. With Frontispiece and full Index.

**POPE'S HOMER'S ILIAD AND ODYSSEY.** FLAXMAN's Illustrations.

**THE KORAN.** A Verbatim Reprint. With Maps, Plans, &c.

**THE TALMUD (SELECTIONS FROM).** By H. POLANO. With Maps, Plans, &c.

**GIL BLAS (THE ADVENTURES OF).** By LE SAGE.

**ROSCOE'S ITALIAN NOVELISTS.**
**ROSCOE'S GERMAN NOVELISTS.** } Complete Editions.
**ROSCOE'S SPANISH NOVELISTS.**

**MEMOIRS OF THE LIFE OF SIR WALTER SCOTT.** By J. G. LOCKHART. Condensed and Revised. With Portrait.

**LORD BACON'S ESSAYS AND HISTORICAL WORKS.**

---

## THE ALBION POETS.

*Complete Editions, in large type, with Explanatory Notes.*

In large crown 8vo, cloth gilt, 3s. 6d.; cloth, gilt top, leather label, gilt lettered, hand-trimmed to give large margin, 5s.; half-calf, marbled edges, 8s.; full-calf, marbled edges, 9s.; full-calf, red under gold edges, 10s. 6d.

1. SHAKSPEARE—THE PLAYS AND POEMS. 1,136 pp.
2. BYRON'S POETICAL WORKS. 736 pp.
3. LONGFELLOW'S POETICAL WORKS. 638 pp.
4. SCOTT'S POETICAL WORKS. 766 pp.
5. MILTON'S POETICAL WORKS.
6. WORDSWORTH'S POETICAL WORKS.

---

Bedford Street, Strand.

FREDERICK WARNE & CO., Publishers,

## THE CAVENDISH LIBRARY.

Printed on superfine paper. A Series of Standard Works, uniformly bound, in large crown 8vo, gilt, uncut, price 3s. 6d. per volume.

### HALF-HOURS WITH THE BEST AUTHORS.
Edited by CHARLES KNIGHT. In Four Volumes, with Steel Frontispieces. Each Volume contains Extracts from our Great Standard Authors, including MACAULAY, THACKERAY, SMOLLETT, ADDISON, DICKENS, CHARLES KINGSLEY, DE QUINCEY, MILTON, CHARLOTTE BRONTË, GEORGE ELIOT, ISAAC D'ISRAELI, and others.

### HALF-HOURS OF ENGLISH HISTORY.
In Four Volumes, with Steel Frontispieces.

Edited by CHARLES KNIGHT.
Vol. I. *From the Roman Period to the Death of Henry III.*
Vol. II. *From Edward I. to the Death of Elizabeth.*

Edited by L. VALENTINE.
Vol. III. *From James I. to William and Mary.*
Vol. IV. *From Anne to Victoria.*

### THE RISE OF THE DUTCH REPUBLIC.
By JOHN LOTHROP MOTLEY. Complete Edition, in Three Volumes, with Notes, Index, &c.

### HISTORY OF THE WAR IN THE PENINSULA,
and in the South of France, from the Year 1807 to the Year 1814. By Major-General W. F. P. NAPIER, C.B. Six Volumes, with Notes, Steel Portrait, and 55 Maps and Plans.

### HALF-HOURS WITH THE BEST AMERICAN AUTHORS.
Selected and Edited by CHARLES MORRIS. In Four Volumes, containing Extracts from the following Authors: L. M. ALCOTT, JOHN BURROUGHS, MARK TWAIN, OLIVER WENDELL HOLMES, WASHINGTON IRVING, J. R. LOWELL, LONGFELLOW, MOTLEY, POE, PRESCOTT, BAYARD TAYLOR, WHITTIER, and others.

---

THIRD LARGE EDITION.

In fcap. 4to, price 10s. 6d., cloth gilt, gilt edges; or morocco, £1 1s.

### OTHER MEN'S MINDS:
Seven Thousand Choice Extracts on History, Science, Philosophy, Religion, &c. From Standard Authors. Classed in Alphabetical Order. Edited and Selected by E. DAVIES, D.D.

---

Bedford Street, Strand.

**FREDERICK WARNE & CO., Publishers,**

## COMPENDIUMS OF ENGLISH LITERATURE.

In Four Vols., with a complete Index and Steel Illustrations, crown 8vo, price 20s., cloth gilt; or half-calf extra, 35s.

# HALF-HOURS WITH THE BEST AUTHORS

Remodelled by its Original Editor, CHARLES KNIGHT, with Selections from Authors, added, whose works have placed them amongst the "Best Authors" since the publication of the First Edition.

\*\*\* This book contains 320 Extracts of the best efforts of our great Standard Authors, whether they be Poets or Historians, Essayists or Divines, Travellers or Philosophers, arranged so as to form half an hour's reading for every day of the year. The student finds a taste of every quality, and a specimen of every style. Should he grow weary of one author, he can turn to another; and if inclined to be critical, he can weigh the merits of one writer against those of his fellow. It gives us a glimpse of the celebrities assembled within its portals. At a glance the student can obtain some idea of the subject. Such books are the true foundations of that knowledge which renders men celebrated and famous.

In Two Vols., demy 8vo, price 10s., cloth; 12s. with gilt edges; or half-calf extra, 17s.

**PEOPLE'S EDITION OF HALF-HOURS WITH THE BEST AUTHORS**
Selected and Edited by CHARLES KNIGHT. With 16 Steel Portraits.

In this Edition the Biographies are revised, the Pagination of the Volumes completed, and the Serial nature of the Original Work entirely done away with; it now forms a Handsome Library Book.

In Four Vols., crown 8vo, price 20s., cloth gilt; or half-calf extra, 35s.

# HALF-HOURS OF ENGLISH HISTORY

(LIBRARY EDITION), with Steel Portraits, new style of binding.

Volumes 1 and 2, from the Roman Period to the Death of Elizabeth, Selected and Edited, with Notes, by CHARLES KNIGHT. Volumes 3 and 4, continuing the History from James to Victoria, by L. VALENTINE.

Contains the Choicest Historical Extracts from upwards of Fifty Standard Authors, including BURKE, PALGRAVE, GUIZOT, SHERIDAN KNOWLES, THIERRY, H. TAYLOR, Rev. JAMES WHITE, CHARLES KNIGHT, G. L. CRAIK, LANDOR, HUME, KEATS, HALLAM, SOUTHEY, SHAKSPEARE, FROISSART, Sir WALTER SCOTT, HALL, BARANTE, Lord BACON, CAVENDISH, Bishop BURNET, Rev. H. H. MILMAN, WORDSWORTH, Lord MACAULAY; with a General Index.

The articles are chiefly selected so as to afford a succession of graphic parts of English History, chronologically arranged, from the consideration that the portions of history upon which general readers delight to dwell are those which tell some story which is complete in itself, or furnish some illustration which has a separate as well as a general interest.

In Two Vols., demy 8vo, price 10s., cloth; 12s. with gilt edges; or half-calf extra, 17s.

**PEOPLE'S EDITION OF HALF-HOURS OF ENGLISH HISTORY.**
From the Roman Period to Victoria. With Steel Portraits, new style of binding.

Volume I., from the Roman Period to the Death of Elizabeth, Selected and Edited, with Notes, by CHARLES KNIGHT. Volume II., containing the History from James to Victoria, by L. VALENTINE.

**Bedford Street, Strand.**

www.ingramcontent.com/pod-product-compliance
Lightning Source LLC
Chambersburg PA
CBHW022144300426
44115CB00006B/337